Violence and Represen........ .... Uprisings

Providing a *longue durée* perspective on the Arab uprisings of 2011, Benoît Challand narrates the transformation of citizenship in the Arab Middle East, from a condition of latent citizenship in the colonial and post-independence era to the revolutionary dynamics that stimulated democratic participation. Considering the parallel histories of citizenship in Yemen and Tunisia, Challand develops innovative theories of violence and representation that view cultural representations as calls for a decentralized political order and democratic accountability over the security forces. He argues that a new collective imaginary emerged in 2011 when the people represented itself as the only legitimate power able to decide when violence ought to be used to protect all citizens from corrupt power. Shedding light upon uprisings in Yemen and Tunisia, but also elsewhere in the Middle East, this book offers deeper insights into conceptions of violence, representation, and democracy.

BENOÎT CHALLAND is Associate Professor at the New School for Social Research in New York. He has published widely on civil society in the Middle East, including *Palestinian Civil Society: Foreign Donors and the Power to Promote and Exclude* (2009), *The Arab Uprisings and Foreign Assistance* (co-edited with F. Bicchi and S. Heydemann, 2016), and *Imagining Europe: Myth, Memory and Identity* (co-authored with Chiara Bottici, 2013).

The Global Middle East

General Editors

Arshin Adib-Moghaddam, *SOAS, University of London*
Ali Mirsepassi, *New York University*

Editorial Advisory Board

Faisal Devji, *University of Oxford*
John Hobson, *University of Sheffield*
Firoozeh Kashani-Sabet, *University of Pennsylvania*
Madawi Al-Rasheed, *London School of Economics and Political Science*
David Ryan, *University College Cork, Ireland*

The Global Middle East series seeks to broaden and deconstruct the geographical boundaries of the "Middle East" as a concept to include North Africa, Central and South Asia, and diaspora communities in Western Europe and North America. The series features fresh scholarship that employs theoretically rigorous and innovative methodological frameworks resonating across relevant disciplines in the humanities and the social sciences. In particular, the general editors welcome approaches that focus on mobility, the erosion of nation-state structures, travelling ideas and theories, transcendental techno-politics, the decentralization of grand narratives, and the dislocation of ideologies inspired by popular movements. The series will also consider translations of works by authors in these regions whose ideas are salient to global scholarly trends but have yet to be introduced to the Anglophone academy.

Other books in the series:

1. *Transnationalism in Iranian Political Thought: The Life and Times of Ahmad Fardid*, Ali Mirsepassi
2. *Psycho-nationalism: Global Thought, Iranian Imaginations*, Arshin Adib-Moghaddam
3. *Iranian Cosmopolitanism: A Cinematic History*, Golbarg Rekabtalaei
4. *Money, Markets and Monarchies: The Gulf Cooperation Council and the Political Economy of the Contemporary Middle East*, Adam Hanieh

Violence and Representation in the Arab Uprisings

BENOÎT CHALLAND
The New School, New York

CAMBRIDGE
UNIVERSITY PRESS

CAMBRIDGE
UNIVERSITY PRESS

University Printing House, Cambridge CB2 8BS, United Kingdom

One Liberty Plaza, 20th Floor, New York, NY 10006, USA

477 Williamstown Road, Port Melbourne, VIC 3207, Australia

314–321, 3rd Floor, Plot 3, Splendor Forum, Jasola District Centre, New Delhi – 110025, India

103 Penang Road, #05–06/07, Visioncrest Commercial, Singapore 238467

Cambridge University Press is part of the University of Cambridge.

It furthers the University's mission by disseminating knowledge in the pursuit of education, learning, and research at the highest international levels of excellence.

www.cambridge.org
Information on this title: www.cambridge.org/9781108490184
DOI: 10.1017/9781108780421

First published 2023

A catalogue record for this publication is available from the British Library.

Library of Congress Cataloging-in-Publication Data
Names: Challand, Benoît, 1972– author.
Title: Violence and representation in the Arab uprisings / Benoît Challand.
Description: Cambridge, United Kingdom ; New York, NY : Cambridge University Press, 2023. | Series: The global Middle East ; 21 | Includes bibliographical references and index.
Identifiers: LCCN 2022024527 (print) | LCCN 2022024528 (ebook) | ISBN 9781108490184 (hardback) | ISBN 9781108748261 (paperback) | ISBN 9781108780421 (ebook)
Subjects: LCSH: Political participation – Arab countries. | Citizenship – Arab countries. | Political violence – Arab countries. | Arab Spring, 2010– | Arab countries – Politics and government.
Classification: LCC JQ1850.A91 C43 2023 (print) | LCC JQ1850.A91 (ebook) | DDC 909/.097492708312–dc23/eng/20220805
LC record available at https://lccn.loc.gov/2022024527
LC ebook record available at https://lccn.loc.gov/2022024528

ISBN 978-1-108-49018-4 Hardback
ISBN 978-1-108-74826-1 Paperback

To all Arab citizens who continue redrawing the graffitis that their government erases.

Contents

Maps

Figures

Tables

Acknowledgments

Without all the interviews I carried out with Tunisian and Yemeni activists and intellectuals, I would have never been able to bring this new manuscript to fruition. They are too many contributors to be listed here, and their names can be found in the following pages and in the appendix section. Their taking the time to discuss made me discover what it means "to engage" with democracy in the Arab Middle East. The dedication below is for all of those who have taken an active, creative role during and after 2011. But because of the harsh repressive conditions that exist throughout the region, and in particular in Yemen, destroyed by an endless civil war, the dedication is also to all contributing anonymously to this project of a more egalitarian society in the Arab worlds.

I could have never reached the people interviewed without the introduction and recommendations that a few colleagues gave me at the beginning of my fieldwork in two new countries. For Yemen, I am particularly grateful to Nadia Al-Sakkaf, Rafat Al-Akhali, Celine Morgan, Zaid bin Ali Alwazir, Laurent Bonnefoy and Joshua S. Rogers for sharing ideas and thoughts about the post-2011 episodes. Sheila Carapico, who read a section on the National Dialogue, was essential in identifying gaps in my arguments and I want to express my gratitude to her. François Burgat, for his invitation to join a group of French students for Arabic courses in Sanaa, deserves also a special word of appreciation, even if this was a long time ago. In Tunisia, Moncef Kartas, Hela Yousfi, Michaël Ayari, Nadia Marzouki, and Souhail Belhadj-Klaz put me in touch with people from different parts of the country. Their rich experience allowed me to go well beyond the capital city of Tunis. I want to thank finally, in this rubric, Mohamed Mahmoud Ould-Mohamedou and Riccardo Bocco for their leadership in organizing conferences in Amman and Cairo in 2012 and 2013, which planted the seeds for this project.

The book project was realized when I held faculty positions at the University of Fribourg (Switzerland), the Scuola Normale Superiore in Florence, and at the New School for Social Research in New York. I am grateful for the institutional, financial, and intellectual support I have received in all three universities. May the colleagues of these departments be thanked for engaging with me on the issues of "Arab revolutions," even when the topic ceased to be as pressing as it was in 2011.

Many of my students were exposed to ideas that have eventually found ways into this book, and I want to thank them all for their questions and comments. A few students from New York University, Kevorkian Center, have also left a mark on this project. I am grateful to Brooke Reynolds, Soleiman Moustafa, Anna Reumert, and more recently Cyrus Roedel and Ella Wind, for discussion on the themes of this book. The group of PhD students involved in the reading group "Theoria. Global Sociology" at the New School for Social Research also deserves a special place in these acknowledgments. They engaged with an earlier version of this text, during the early COVID-19 restrictions. Antti Tarvainen, Francisco Gonzalez Camelo and Zach Leamy sent me extremely detailed comments, but all the inputs and questions from Arya Vaghyenegar, Aryana Ghazi Hessami, Aura Hernandez Cardenas, Can Akin, Emmanuel Guerisoli, Julian Gomez Delgado, Ihor Andriichuk, Kirti Varma, Maya Herman, Sidra Kamran, Udeepta Chakravarty, and Ye Liu have been deeply appreciated.

Rossana Tuffaro, Nathanael Mannone, Ester Sigillò, Laurent Bonnefoy, Moncef Kartas, Michaël Ayari, and Chiara Bottici, who provided feedback on the entire manuscript, deserve all my gratitude. Other colleagues sent me invaluable feedback on portions of the text, in particular Salma Bakr, Alaa Tartir, Elvire Corboz, Aaron Jakes, Souhail Belhadj, Carole Villiger, Michael Ferguson, Mondher Kilani, and Manal Jamal. A distinct group of post-doc fellows at the European University Institute, in particular George Fahmi and Matteo Albanese, as well as two doctoral students from Palazzo Strozzi, Federica Stagni and Rosa Bur, must be thanked for debates on the Middle East.

My colleagues at the New School for Social Research, in particular Carlos Forment, Miriam Ticktin, Andrew Arato, Emma Park, Dmitri Nikulin, Anne McNevin, Andreas Kalyvas, and the Visiting Professor Mark Ayyash deserve recognition for discussion not so much on this text specifically, but on stimulating debates dealing with questions of equality and democratic theory.

All the research assistants, Ella Wind, Francisco Gonzalez Camelo, Lebogang Mokwena, Lucas Ballestin, Wilhelmina Agbemakplido, Ye Liu, and Zach Leamy have done a fantastic job in identifying material for this book, and polishing the manuscript.

I am most grateful to the entire editorial team at Cambridge University Press, in particular the Series Editors, and Commissioning Editor Maria Marsh, and the anonymous reviewers. Stephanie Taylor and Rachel Inmrie helped bring the production to fruition through the difficult circumstances created by COVID-19. Finally, I want to extend a word of gratitude to Joshua Hey, the copy-editor. Not only did he show immense patience and precision, but he also learned intricate details of Arabic transliteration in no time! To all of them, many thanks!

As the formula goes: all remaining errors remain mine.

Finally, I am grateful to my family, and their indefectible patience in seeing this book project coming to an end. It has been enriched by all the travels we have done together and by the numerous discussions around the themes of these books. I know "Yemen" and "Tunisia" now resonate in a particular way in the life of Alissa, Leo and Chiara. In the same manner: traveling to these two countries has also changed my own perspective on the Arab Middle East.

Prolegomenon: A Two-Layered Book

The book unfolds at two tempos, and resonates at two levels. Metaphorically this double take on the question of violence and representation can be approached like the famous Italian song of the partisans, *O Bella Ciao*. This song celebrating resistance against the Nazi occupation of Italy toward the end of WW2 was based on an older song, a plea from female rice-weeders working under extremely exploitative conditions. That original tune had a much slower pace, evoking the torments of brutal bosses and the sting of mosquitoes while working endless days in the wet rice fields of the Po River plain. The pace of the partisans' reinterpretation is twice this speed and evokes the expectations of struggles by Italians-turned-partisans against the Nazi invaders. In its most famous rendering, the two songs were interwoven in the eponymous 1962 spectacle of *Bella Ciao*, which made its singer Giovanna Daffini and her slightly nasal voice famous. Since then the song has become a widely known hymn for the fight for freedom, and recognized as the main chant of the Italian partisan movement.[1] It is no wonder that the song became an international icon for the fight against oppression, as we saw in the 2019 popular protests in Iraq, Lebanon, Kurdistan and Palestine, where it was re-adapted and played in the streets to express rage against corruption and the high cost of living.[2]

This book can be read with reference to two different measures, or paces: one, historical, dealing with the long-term problem and slow transformation of citizenship in the Middle East; and one with a faster pace of the revolutionary moments of 2011, which originally breathed enthusiasm for democratic collective action in the region

---

[1] The texts of these two songs are reproduced at the end of this overview. For a history of the song, see Bermani (2003: 223–263), Toscano (2010), and Pestelli (2016). I introduced the reference to *Bella Ciao* when writing this book well before it became popular in the Middle East in 2019.

[2] On the Arab re-adaptation of the Italian song, see Bouattia (2019).

and now fades back into the longer historical *durée* of latent citizenship. For that matter, the slow-paced interpretation of Arab citizenship constitutes Part I and Part III of the book, while Part II is about the disruptive, creative, and also dramatic flows of events and processes generated by the 2011 Uprisings. Like the partisan version of *Bella Ciao*, the expectations are high and the end dramatically bitter. Yet a legacy remains for those able to admire, in Italy, the freedom flower mentioned in the last verse, and in the Middle East, the micro-practices of radical democracy.

The book can also be read on two levels: as a historical sociology of the Middle East, and as an exercise in applied social and political theory. Indeed, *Violence and Representation in the Arab Uprisings* combines historical and empirical research on the meaning of citizenship and collective mobilization in the Arab Middle East through a study of the 2011 Uprisings. It explains, historically, the existence in most Arab polities of a suppressed form of citizenship, a situation that emerged in relation to a peculiar European history. This history has been sanitized of its colonial past, allowing for a "normal" or "virtuous" form of citizenship in Europe, giving rise to theories of the civilizing and disciplining processes, or the liberal fiction of equality of chances in democratic regimes. The flip side of the coin resulted, in the Middle East, in a skewed state–society relationship characterized by brutal repression and a lack of citizens' freedom. After having established this relational perspective on bifurcated citizenships, the book proceeds to an empirical analysis of the 2011 Uprisings ("the Arab Spring") and suggests that despite serious setbacks, an important legacy remains perceptible in everyday life in certain Arab countries, namely the will to assert the force of collective mobilization to resist the ruthless and unjust use of the means of coercion by Arab states. The focus proposed in this book on the 2011 protests builds around the new collective imaginary, or the collective force of the people (what is termed in the book as *vis populi*) as a force representing itself as the sovereign power with the ability to decide how violence ought to be used in each polity of the region. This original message represents a profound change for Arab people who have since been able to re-energize their own democratic projects. This analysis also forms the basis for a new theory of representation, for Middle Easterners and Europeans alike, in a new effort to rethink key themes of democratic participation, informal and formal political change, and the conundrum of violence–civility–citizenship. Despite talks of "failures" in the Arab Uprisings, the book describes how positive citizenship still remains enshrined in everyday or informal political practices in some of the Arab countries that witnessed mass protests in 2011.

The aim of this book extends beyond what could be labeled "Middle Eastern studies." It is also a contribution to the long endeavor of social theory: How do social groups *know* that they act as such and that they have generated an ability to influence the contours of publics, and of a collectivity? The book investigates the crossroads of social and democratic theory: How do groups that have emerged to disrupt the given, normal flow of political action know that they are generating or sustaining new democratic expectations? How do new norms arise from the practice of protests, caravans, or sit-ins demanding the inclusion of the marginalized? How do democratic rules coalesce, or gel in everyday practice? How does informal collective action produce, or not, new formal political, legal, or constitutional orders? And, to return to the metaphor of the partisan song *Bella Ciao* that fades back into the original and slow version of the rice-weeders' melodic complaint: how do formal representations, for example political parties, national parliaments, or hegemonic discourses about international order of security and stability, undermine the fast-paced informal demands and practices for more participatory and egalitarian politics?

Rendered visually, the theme of the book is captured in a caricature by Tunisian political scientist and artist Sadri Khiari,[3] in a drawing added to an article on the Jemna protests in 2016 (Figure 0.1).[4] Jemna is a small date-cultivating oasis in the rural center of Tunisia. At the start of 2011, its inhabitants occupied what used to be collective land, claiming that in the 1960s the state had unduly leased the land to corrupt private actors. After the revolution, an association was created for the defense of the oasis, but the state refused to recognize the cooperative, now in charge of production, as a legitimate body. The struggle lingers on to this day, with national debates about whether

---

[3] Drawing and text by Sadri Khiari. Reproduced with author's authorization.

[4] Khiari's cartoon captures one of the many episodes of the still ongoing Jemna occupation. He also makes a larger point about the centrality of land to many of the issues that Tunisia has been facing (dignity, migration, jihadism, etc.). More on Jemna in Section 6.3.

Figure 0.1 "What are your values?" Tunisia 2016.

such a participative planning and self-governance model could or should be expanded to other state-owned agricultural lands as a way to generate local participatory actions. A paraphrased title of this caricature, drawn five years after the spontaneous occupation of the oasis on January 11, 2011, could be "radical representation as collective or individual struggle?" In the first of three sketches, a standing person asks a group of six persons crawling on the ground, each under the weight of a stone presumably symbolizing their oppression, "What are your values? What do you fight for?" In the second, one person on the ground replies "[We fight] for ourselves!" Finally, the standing person turns her back on the crawling people and leaves with a disappointed "Pfff!," which could be translated as "What the heck!" to express disappointment with the self-centered response as opposed to an expression of shared oppression.

Interpreted on the theoretical level, this vignette is about how collectives can emerge through protests or public actions. How do people account for their engagements? How do people express commitments to new norms? In relation to democratic theory, how does one group move from a situation of segmented demands or localized protests to aggregative, principled, and/or national demands for change? If we take democratization to be the "transfer of power coupled with modification of the mutual rights and obligations between the state and its citizens" (Giugni, McAdam, and Tilly 1998: xv), how does the sense of *mutual* rights as opposed to isolated demands emerge and crystalize? How, in the cartoon's spirit, do we move from atomized individuals to a collective with articulated demands? How did the historically marginalized regions of Tunisia and Yemen manage to imagine and enact a unified polity? In this book's language, how does informal action create significance and impact the existence of a formal political order, moving from a condition of latent citizenship to one of active citizenship?

Violence and Representation in the Arab Uprisings proposes historical and diachronic answers to these questions. It suggests a dialectical relation between state and society that pivots around issues of coercion and violence. The restlessness that emerges from informality in 2011 fits the geography of fractured territories and to a large extent overlaps with earlier zones of civic exclusion at the early stages of state-formation discussed in Part I. Part II analyzes the production of a new collective imaginary that grows from demands for better economic redistribution and for democratic participation. This informality has partly remained through the force of symbolic representation, but it does not limit itself to mere acts of representational politics. It also proposes new formal channels for representations (recursive civic movements, demands for decentralization or federalism, investing in a new generation of activists and politicians, literary and artistic creativity to tackle political problems, etc.) and, overall, contributes to a new form and content of citizenship. More than formal citizenship, the book argues that the legacy of 2011 resides in a new social life of citizenship[5] that might

---

[5] Isin and Nielsen (2008) speak of "citizen act," while James Tully (as quoted in Bijl & Van Klinken 2019: 195) focused on the spontaneous, bottom up and non-deliberative form of citizenship that he calls "civic citizenship."

not be visible at the macro-level of "politics" but may re-emerge in remote parts of Arab countries, perhaps even years after the actual 2011 protests.

Part III explains the mechanisms that ushered the return of a slower pace of latent citizenship (and of the original version of *Bella Ciao*). A comparative analysis of social spaces, decentralization and federalism, cultural creativity, and civic participation in times of increased securitization illustrates the return of "strong men" and of security institutions in politics. Not all is lost, however, as the last sections of the book show how the faster pace of the revolutionary period, which had assembled or synchronized different temporalities and spaces of participation, remains engrained in micro-practices of collective action.[6] To a certain extent, the individual people crawling on the ground in Figure 0.1 have indeed managed to keep a collective form of resistance.

The Conclusions of the book try to apply some insights about the power of radical representation to countries that were not rocked by the same scale of protest as seen in Tunisia, Egypt, Yemen, or Libya, but did experience popular uprisings, for example the protests that emerged in 2019 in Sudan and Algeria. For those fighting for recognition of their rights, there is something emboldening in seeing two gerontocrats forced out of power, Omar Al-Bashir in Khartoum and Abdelaziz Bouteflika in Algiers in April 2019. The determination of popular protests, only marginally supported by parties and associations, was in full display in demanding the departure of these ageing leaders but also in refusing the permanent custodianship that military groups have had for decades in most Arab republics (Sayigh 2015).

The form and content of the Sudanese protests converge with what I have elsewhere called the counter-power of civil society (Challand 2011; 2013), and with this book's focus on informal politics that stubbornly refuse to be outfoxed by the security establishment. Unquestionably, each radical protest in Arab countries after 2011[7] has had local needs and specificities in moving people to demand more participation, but in all of this dissent

---

[6] Hmed (2016a: 74, 91) speaks of synchronization of temporalities and of social times in his analysis of the Qasba protests in Tunis. I borrow from him, but add the spatial and imaginary dimensions.

[7] Similar protests occurred in the Kurdish provinces of Iraq and Syria.

there was a common rejection of the illegitimate use of physical force by local authorities against their own citizens and a demand for democratic accountability over the means of coercion, what I call *vis populi*.

One central point on the iconoclastic take on violence developed here: In this book I will claim that violence can be democratic. By that, I don't mean that informal politics, or people in general, can or should directly manage the means of coercion. Neither do I call to undo police, military, and other security apparatuses. I take violence from its original Latin root *vis*, which means "force," "power," "energy," and ultimately "violence." The term is clearly distinct from *"violentia*," meaning violence as destruction. I argue that Arab demonstrators in 2011 have been claiming *vis populi*, that is "the force," "might," or the "will" of the people, to indicate that the state's violence had been misplaced and turned unjustly against each country's citizens. Instead, 2011 was the time chosen by the masses to reconsider how physical force might look in the context of a more just, socially equitable, and pacified social contract. The argument made by protestors, and the process through which this was articulated, i.e. through the power of informal politics that combined cultural and political representation, expressed a profoundly democratic demand.

Thus, force in this book has two components: one crushing, the other foundational. Violence can lead to the condition of latent or negative citizenship, but in the *vis populi* form, it can also, constitute the basis for a new and more democratic political order. In the very foundations of citizenship, be it in Europe or in the Middle East, there is as much violence as there is civility. Moving away from the common view of violence as solely a destructive force, as well as from the view that violence breeds counter-violence, violence is here seen as an aggregative *theme*, not a practice. To paraphrase Mark Ayyash (2020: 14) about the multiple semantics of violence, I contend that new imaginaries around violence have created or forced "a space in which the interaction between the protagonists forms, continues, and transforms," here democratically, via radical representation.

* * *

For those not familiar with the famous Italian song, the texts of the two versions are reproduced here. The slow and original version is that of the rice-weeders (*Le Mondine*), or rice-workers, an all-female work force enduring hard working conditions bent over rice plants in mud or malaria-infested waters the whole day while paid miserable wages. Two stories, two paces, and two spaces. The pedestrian harshness of going to work in a given rice field and the boredom of repetition of the opening words: "*alla mattina . . . in risaia mi tocca andar,*" "every morning, I have to go to work." This contrasts with the unique occurrence of "*una mattina,*" one specific morning, in an exceptional moment that starts the partisan song. The pace is faster, there is a community of fighters, partisans, united in a much larger space of resistance, a country, and a more metaphorical predicament. Here, it is fast paced, enthralling, but there are also tortuous and dangerous revolutionary moments. To use again Khiari's rhetorical question of the vignette, "What are your values? What do you fight for?," in the slow version, the rice-weeders long for their own freedom and ability to decide how to work ("*lavoreremo in libertà,*" we will work with freedom). In the fast-paced version, it is the partisans that summon the listeners to carry on the fight and struggle in much more extraordinary wartime conditions, risking even death.

Lyrics of O *Bella Ciao* in two versions: *Le Mondine* (slow)
and O *Partigiano* (fast)

O *Bella Ciao*
(Original version: *Le Mondine*)[8]

Alla mattina, appena alzata,
O Bella ciao, bella ciao, bella ciao, ciao, ciao,
Alla mattina, appena alzata,
In risaia mi tocca andar.

E tra gli insetti e le zanzare,
O Bella ciao, bella ciao, bella ciao, ciao, ciao,
E tra gli insetti e le zanzare,
Duro lavoro mi tocca far.

O *Bella Ciao*
(Original, witd slower rhytdm)

Every morning, barely woken up,
Bye, bye, o beautiful woman! (O *bella ciao!*)
Every morning, barely woken up
I have to go into the rice fields.

And amidst the insects and the mosquitoes,
Bella ciao!
And amidst the insects and the mosquitoes,
A grueling labor awaits me.

The boss stands, hands on his staff,

---

[8] *Le Mondine* is the Italian name given to the female rice-weeders. Text and translation (with a few personal changes) from https://lyricstranslate.com/en/all a-mattina-appena-alzata-early-morning-barely-woken.html.

Il Capo in piedi col suo bastone,
O Bella ciao, bella ciao, bella ciao, ciao,
ciao,
Il Capo in piedi col suo bastone,
E noi curve a lavorar.

O mamma mia, o che tormento,
O Bella ciao, bella ciao, bella ciao, ciao,
ciao,
O mamma mia, o che tormento,
Io t'invoco ogni doman.

Ma verra' un giorno che tutte quante
O Bella ciao, bella ciao, bella ciao, ciao,
ciao,
Ma verra' un giorno che tutte quante
lavoreremo in libertà

Bella ciao!
The boss stands, hands on his staff,
While we bend to work.

Oh mother, what a torment,
Bella ciao!
Oh mother, what a torment,
I call out your name every day.

But there will be a day when all together,
Bella ciao!
But there will be a day when all together,
we will work in freedom.

O Bella Ciao
Canto del partigiano, faster rhythm[9]

O Bella Ciao, Partisan version
Faster rhythm

Una mattina mi sono alzato
o bella ciao bella ciao bella ciao ciao ciao
una mattina mi sono alzato
e ci ho trovato l'invasor.

One morning I awakened,
Bye, bye, o beautiful woman! (*O bella ciao!*)
One morning I awakened
And I found the invader.

O partigiano portami via,
o bella ciao...
o partigiano portami via
che mi sento di morir.

Oh partisan carry me away,
Bella ciao!
oh partisan carry me away
Because I feel death approaching

E se io muoio da partigiano,
o bella ciao, ...
e se io muoio da partigiano
tu mi devi seppellir.

And if I die as a partisan,
Bella ciao!
and if I die as a partisan
then you must bury me.

Seppellire lassù in montagna,
o bella ciao, ...
seppellire lassù in montagna
sotto l'ombra di un bel fior.

Bury me up in the mountain,
Bella ciao!
bury me up in the mountain
under the shade of a beautiful flower

---

[9] Text from www.ildeposito.org/canti/bella-ciao and personal translation.

Tutte le genti che passeranno,	And all those who shall pass,
o bella ciao, ...	*Bella ciao!*
e le genti che passeranno	and all those who shall pass
mi diranno «che bel fior.»	will tell me "what a beautiful flower."
E' questo il fiore del partigiano	This is the flower of the partisan,
o bella ciao, ...	*Bella ciao!*
questo è il fiore del partigiano	this is the flower of the partisan
morto per la libertà	who died for freedom

Introduction

0.1 Why Connect State Violence with Representation?

Studies of the 2011 Arab Uprisings have generated a flurry of comments and analyses based on a series of dichotomies: Success or failure? A civil or an Islamic state? An Arab spring or an Arab winter? A reformist path or a revolutionary *tabula rasa*? These are only some of the most influential. Other analysts consider the episodes that shook the entire Arab world in 2011 as a mere detour with no real impact, and highlight continuities in Arab politics. Such views not only populate the layperson's ideas or the media's coverage about the Arab world, but also abound in many scholarly works. One should instead propose a more historical and complex circuit of analysis. *Violence and Representation in the Arab Uprisings* is located at the crossroads of historical and sociological studies and offers counter-narratives about issues of representation and the place that violence occupied in the pivotal months of the 2011 Uprisings. In particular, it sheds comparative light on the attempt by the collective forces to offer an alternative, more democratic management of "legitimate violence." This book tackles *three inter-related sets of arguments that build on a central question: what is the relation between the informal politics of popular participation, the struggle for a more democratic polity, and the management of, or the publicly sanctioned use of, violence?*

Firstly, the book argues that, even if each of the national uprisings had distinct origins and trajectories, a common kernel existed in all the Arab upheavals that went beyond fighting against corruption and social inequalities: protests and revolutions were an attempt to remodel the link between *political representation* and *violence*. Far from the sanitized and idealized interpretation of the Arab Uprisings as non-violent movements, I describe both how the masses used the theme of violence in the 2011 Uprisings, and how they projected an alternative path to the management of "legitimate violence."[1]

Vis populi, the Latin phrase I coined for this book, has multiple connotations and is meant to illustrate the complexity of the processes behind the revolutionary moments of 2011. *Vis populi* can be translated variously as "the force of the people," "collective might," or "the will of an assembled multitude." The focus of this book is on how the two terms, *vis* and *populus* are articulated together. On its own, *vis* can mean "violence," but it is only a tertiary meaning of the term.[2] I prefer translating by force, will, or might because it is associated with the term *populi*, people as multitude, or an assemblage of different civic groups coming together and rejecting the violence of the state and of its official leadership. Combining the two dimensions, *vis populi* is read as the "collective force of the people to decide how violence ought to be used by the state." The involvement of the Arab masses in different acts of more or less symbolic "violence" as well as the different facets of violence can be articulated in one word: representation. The Arab masses in 2011 reinvented *political representation* by gathering and occupying public squares. In and around these spaces, they also invented a new imaginary, what is more aptly called *cultural representation*, in which the people (in Arabic, *al-sha'ab*) imagined for themselves a new role in punishing past tyrants and in defining a new, more democratic, and *less violent* system by projecting images of an alternative form of politics in which they can act and be treated as rights-bearing citizens. The assembled people functioned as a homology to the previously fractured social and political spaces that became united by the presence and demands of a unified people in 2011.

---

[1] I am not arguing that reconnecting representations and violence was the motive that led to a chain of uprisings in 2011. Instead, I am arguing that this specific nexus can be identified in all Arab protests, and it is this commonality that made me propose an alternative theory of democratic participation. The phrase "legitimate violence" comes from Max Weber's famous definition of the modern state. See Part II.

[2] The Latin term *vis* (fem.) is the nominative of the defective Latin word meaning "force, power, energy, violence." The meaning of *vis* is thus broader than *violentia* (*-ae*, fem.), which is limited in its meaning to violence as destruction (Castiglioni 1996: 1408). The noun *vis* derives from the verb *volo, velle, volui*, i.e. "to want." *Vis populi* is an inchoate project, a habitus, or a process, which needs constant reaffirmation and approval by a multitude of actors and which aims at giving greater voice to the people in political processes.

The most famous Arabic slogans of 2011 captured this idea of the collective will: *al-sha'ab yurid isqat an-nizam*, "the people want the fall of the regime." The protesters insisted on human dignity (*karama insaniyya*) and the end of unjust violence by corrupt and autocratic regimes. The sociological puzzle that this book addresses is how *informal* and *formal* political engagements are interconnected in phases of large popular mobilizations calling for revolutionary change and for *democratic forms of accountability* over the *means of coercion*. These uprisings force us to rethink the intermediary space that exists between the informal and formal realms of politics, for example the inchoate or contradictory citizenship actions that demanded political reforms, the occupation of former police or military sites, Tunisian solidarity caravans meant to prefigure new policies for better redistribution, or Yemeni encampments in squares (*sahat*) demanding a new constitution.

Secondly, this book builds a *historical account of popular mobilizations* that runs against pervasive interpretations of the Arab Uprisings as incidents that emerged out of nowhere. The Arab Uprisings, in those interpretations, literally were an "Arab Spring," a moment of sudden progress, an unstoppable burst, and a flow of shiny novelty that replaced decaying models. The phrases "Arab Uprisings" and "2011 Uprisings," used throughout this book, are a more faithful rendering of the diversity of trajectories and evolutions of distinct national protests. The term "uprising" is also a reminder that these protests were at times messy and conflictual, with unclear projects, with riots and rage coexisting next to democratic demands. By and large, even if they had some of the trappings, these historical events were not revolutions (a contested issue that will be discussed in Part II). Historically, these uprisings were the result of an open dialectical, rather than linear, relationship between society and state. For this reason, Part I will elaborate on the historical roots that made state force and violence illegitimate and pushed the Arab masses to the margins of politics (Chalcraft 2016). The next four chapters explain how we moved in the first two or three years of the Uprisings from a period where revolutionary practices and symbols abounded (Part II), to another period, discussed in Part III, with only limited revolutionary outcomes.

Thirdly, I argue that *theory* and *practice* must *be brought together* to redefine the relationship between popular participation and the publicly sanctioned use of violence. Theories of political representation must be gauged with a view to the practices of self-representation and should serve to bring Arab and Western political theory closer: Euro-American, or Western, social theory can learn immensely from these episodes of mass mobilization. For this reason, we will see how ideas of citizenry (*muwatin*), "social contract" ('*aqd ijtima'i*) or "civil society" (*mujtama' madani*) are the object of contentious interpretations and sources of collective action in the Arab worlds, and are not just corner-stones of modern Euro-American political theory. Connecting theory and practice therefore also entails focusing on the link between formal and informal dimensions of citizenship: New laws or constitutions were passed after the 2011 Uprisings, but the question, an empirical one, is to assess whether Arab citizens' course of action on a daily basis was improved or hindered by such changes. In a nutshell, if the mass protests of 2011 are considered, as I substantiate below (Chapter 3), an achievement of spontaneity, in the etymological sense of the word, namely that the people were the *source* of their own action, how can informality generate formal political change? And once the machine of formal changes (mostly a reformist dynamic, often termed "transition")[3] is set, what happens to mundane, day-to-day acts of citizenship? What spaces are left for a more democratic (again, in the etymological sense of the word, i.e. *the power of the people*) and accountable form of management of "legitimate violence"? How did the cultural representations of past violence and of unified protesters that emerged everywhere in Arab streets and squares re-shape political representation and democratic control over the use of the means of coercion?

In all three arguments, the book *relocates* violence in relation to various forms of (popular) representation before, during, and after the Arab Uprisings of 2011. Violence has a multiplicity of locations, or meanings including negative aspects (unwanted destruction, killing), neutral components (the management of physical coercion by state or official institutions, such as the police or armed forces, whose potential

---

[3] The concept of transition has been criticized numerous times, some inviting us to refer to "transformation" instead (Heydemann 2015). Carothers (2002) warned that "transition" implied an automatic democratic telos. Since then, authors have pointed to the fact that there can be a transition from one type of autocracy to another. In Tunisia, the term has been criticized for assuming a Western example as the end point towards which the process of transition is often envisaged. For a critique applied to Tunisia, see Dakhlia (2016) and Chouikha and Gobe (2015: 6).

exercise of mandated violence is necessary to establish peaceful relations inside and on the borders of a given polity), but also more constructive components (de-escalation measures undertaken by collective action, enacting of alternative force to resist the use of physical force by an oppressive regime, or demands for transitional justice). *Vis populi* refers to the neutral and positive components of violence (the next lines will explain why "positive").

Part I identifies the historical circumstances that turned state or "legitimate" violence into illegitimate violence and limited the significance of citizenship. Chapters 1 and 2 show how colonial and post-independence patterns have led to a condition of *negative citizenship*. This phrase, borrowed from French political scientist Michel Camau,[4] describes the situation in which ruthless state apparatuses barred any critical civic engagement or participatory forms of representation. In Arab countries, this component of repressive statehood was clustered around security forces (Ayubi 1995), favored political clienteles and the neopatriarchy (Sharabi 1988), and prevented the emergence of mechanisms of accountability over core functions of the state (taxation, use of legitimate means). It is the existence and resilience of deeply corrupt and militarized governments, rather than alleged cultural factors, that best explains the historical lack of democratic life in Arab countries. Part I discusses the international *and* domestic roots of this situation of latent, or curtailed, citizenship and identifies the limited spaces where citizenship (or aspiration for it) has existed. One can therefore consider that it is a *latent*, or even at times negative, form of citizenship that emerged historically, and which explains the sudden burst of civic activism in 2011.

Part II deals with the new habitus of *vis populi* described as the interface between active citizenship battling for, and structuring, new spaces of participation and the old model of latent or negative citizenship. Historical territorial and social fragmentations, in particular what I will call the uneven distribution of violence in Tunisia and Yemen, explain the coming together of geographical and political peripheries in the 2011 Uprisings. The protests turned the illegitimate use of state coercion on its head and indicated, sometimes with destructions of buildings (negative violence), sometimes with non-violent

---

[4] Quoted in Chouikha and Gobe (2015: 5).

protests (neutral violence), what would be a more democratic way to organize and redeploy coercive means (positive violence).

Chapter 3 places a focal lens on the eventful mobilizations of 2011 (Della Porta 2014) and investigates how self-representation of the people constitutes an instance where informal political gestures spur a call for formal political change, based on a new political imaginary in which the people projects itself as the legitimate owner of the means of coercion. The chants calling for more social justice and human dignity throughout 2011 have often been set in relation to economic grievances and labor injustice (Beinin 2015; Alexander & Bassiouny 2014), or as a consequence of neoliberal devastation (Armbrust 2019; Akcali 2016). This is certainly true, but seen from a different perspective, they were also expressing the hope that these revolutions would usher in a new political order, an order able to recognize the power of informal, popular, cross-class mobilizations and demands for an accountable management of security apparatuses, as well as the fair exercise of punitive justice.

Chapter 4 discusses the crossroads that these popular mobilizations faced, and the many constraints and institutions that forced actors to choose reformist over revolutionary paths to political change. Efforts to redraw the space of political participation (a new constitution, national dialogues, decentralization reforms) and security reforms were thwarted by formal institutions and regrouping elites, and it was these that were challenged in 2011.

Chapter 5 offers two tales of decentralization: In Yemen, the project of a federalist constitution, with a contentious map cutting the country into six regions without grassroots approval, precipitated a three-way civil war. Yet, federalism remained a popular project in Yemen, as the study of associational, artistic, and literary life suggests. In Tunisia, the project of decentralization moved forward, with municipal elections covering the entirety of the territory held for the first time in May 2018. But despite high expectations and a myriad of small civic actions anticipating the formal implementation of decentralization, calculated delays by the central authority hollowed out the process. Chapter 6 describes the dangers of securitization and of the return of "strong men" to politics. I analyze these two trends in relation to various issues: transitional justice, the memorialization of the 2011 Uprisings, and the attempt by President Kais Saied to monopolize power in Tunisia since the summer of 2021; hegemonic international actors using the language of the global war on terror to derail the democratic process in Yemen (Al-Eriani 2020: 1142); and formal politics sapping the revolutionary energies. I show that, as a result of these interactions, the actors involved in Part II (namely, the marginalized, women, the youth of all walks of life) who sustained the Uprisings have been gradually silenced by an older, male, generation and by the recomposition of the security apparatus in Tunisia and the multiplication of armed forces in Yemen.

Part III also illustrates that not everything is lost from the initial revolutionary moments and expectations: In Tunisia, a myriad of everyday practices mirror the methods that people developed during the months of December 2010 until March 2011; new social roles are enacted outside of the parliament and municipalities, for instance, with everyday campaigns dealing with access to sidewalks or civic education; in Yemen, a cascade of civic campaigns, cultural events, and artistic creativity were meant to empower a new generation of political actors. These were disrupted by the tragic reality of a regional war that broke out in 2015, and reinforced the sense that only localized dialogues and de facto decentralization can retain a modicum of civic life in the midst of quasi total destruction.

Before discussing the link between violence and political and cultural representation, let me give a few examples of this new political imaginary ushered in during the early months of protests in 2011. The first example can be seen in four drawings from the early months of 2011. Two are from Egypt and two from Tunisia. Figures 0.2 and 0.3 portray Khaled Sa'id, a young Alexandrian who was beaten to death by policemen in June 2010 for posting proof of the local police's corruption on the internet. The shocking images of his disfigured body suddenly became a symbol for Egyptian youth taking revenge on President Mubarak and his cronies. In Figure 0.2, Sa'id is brought back to life with the ultimate power of holding a weakened Mubarak in his hand. His role behind the revolution was evoked through the metonymy of the hashtag #Jan25, a reference to the starting date of the protests in Egypt, on January 25, 2011.[5] Figure 0.3 invokes the same young Alexandrian but with a different message: this time the graffiti mixes a trail of (older) blood dripping and mixing with the text stating: "the

---

[5] It is well documented that the name of Khaled Sa'id and the Facebook page *kullunā khāled sa'īd*, "We are all Khaled Sa'id," were a rallying cry that led to the initial protests and the encampment on Tahrir Square in Cairo.

Figure 0.2 #Jan25. Khaled Saʿid holding former Egyptian President Mubarak. 2011.

police in the service of the people" (*al-shurta fi khidmat al-shaʿab*). This was an old regime slogan used in the early years of Mubarak's tenure claiming that police were there to serve the people (Soliman 2011: 65). The image, with blood dripping from above to symbolize the recurrent violent abuses by state security forces, now pouring over the face of Khaled Saʿid, suggests the falsity of the former official message. Saʿid's smile *might* suggest that his sacrifice could ignite the people against the regime.[6] At any rate, the regime and its police could not continue governing by sheer force the way they had done for decades and in full impunity.

---

[6] It could also be that the smiling martyr simply comes from a photo given by
   a family, with the smile unconnected to the actual graffiti, as an Egyptian scholar
   reminded me.

Figure 0.3 "The police in the service of the people" (*"al-shurṭa fī khidmat al-shaʿab"*). Egypt 2011.

The Tunisian drawings (Figures 0.4[7] and 0.5[8]) show the efforts of the people to topple the tyrannical power of President Ben Ali and his political party, the RCD,[9] also called *Tajammuʿ* in Arabic, the ruling faction since Ben Ali assumed power in 1987. In Figure 0.4, the country, in green, is depicted as asphyxiated by a two-headed snake, one being the RCD and the other Ben Ali. The only way to stop the bleeding of the country is to use violence, here a knife held by "the people" (*al-shaʿab*), to get rid of the monstrous animal. Like the next image, the poster suggests that the job is only half done: Ben Ali's head has been severed, but the head of the RCD still needs to be cut off. In Figure 0.5,

---

[7] Source: *Dégage!* (2011: 138). This picture was probably taken in Tunis, at an unknown date, but probably on or after January 14, 2011.

[8] Source: *Dégage!* (2011: 127). This poster was probably used in protests in the days after the departure of Ben Ali, but no later than the end of the first Qasba sit-in. See Chapter 3 for more information on these crucial weeks of the Tunisian Uprising.

[9] Acronyms are listed in the pages introducing the three parts of the book.

Figure 0.4 The people, Ben Ali and the RCD. Tunisia 2011.

the people, here symbolized by a bleeding and suffering hand, have freed a dove carrying the Tunisian flag. The bird has been let out of the cage built by the RCD and the former government (in Arabic red letters). Yet, the dove risks being shot by the gun controlled by "the new government," a reference to one of the transition governments appointed after the departure of Ben Ali, either on January 15, 2011 (the so-called provisory government of Mohammed Ghannouchi) (see Chouikha and Gobe 2015: 81; Yousfi 2015: 111, fn. 20) or the government established following the first Qasba protests on January 27, 2011 (the government nicknamed Ghannouchi II – readers can find a chronology of key episodes in the Arab worlds at the start of each Part of the book) (see, e.g., Krichen 2016: 87–89; Gobe 2012). The drawing shows that this governmental reshuffle was only a cosmetic change, with freedom and peace still in peril.

Figure 0.5 A dove and two governments. Tunisia 2011.

The next chapters will explain in detail why, how, and when these actors and symbols were used in mass demonstrations, but note the similarities here. All four pictures depict violence, with blood present in three of them. The message of a brutal past that still threatens the present or the future (a green, more prosperous Tunisia, or a dove flying freely) is common to all. These drawings, in particular Figure 0.2, are not just carnivalesque or a temporary reversal of authority. The superposition of Khaled Sa'id with past spilled blood in Figure 0.2 could signify a moment where the former guardians are now guarded by the people, a theme at play in Figure 0.3. Thus, rather than the classical aporia of *quis custodes ispos custodiet?* (who will guard the guardians?), these visual messages have an answer to the "guardian paradox": The guardians will be guarded by the people. That is, the people are the only possible guardians to guarantee justice in the future. This is precisely the message of Figures 0.2 and 0.3, where Khalid Sa'id's gaze is not focusing on Mubarak (the tyrant whose violence must be reduced in Figure 0.2), but on the onlookers, the revolutionary people, reminding them that his death should not have been in vain. The people, either the masses carrying these posters, or "*al-sha'ab*" as marked in text or stencils, are the actors that indicate what is legitimate violence in a display marked by dramatic oppositions of colors (red opposed to the green of the country or the white dove) or size (a large Khaled holding a tiny Mubarak). Thus, a discourse analysis of the protests allows us to assess the multiple qualities of violence and evade the risk of subjective assessments. *Vis populi* is not just able to end illegitimate coercion, but also charts a path for a democratic project.

Other texts written in 2011 conjure a more explicit and direct association between the past sacrifices or fear encountered by the people and a new basis for a future political order. Poetry and music, analyzed in many works on the 2011 events,[10] and political tracts speak of the hope to turn shared past fear into a new, more democratic, collective future. Two sets of examples, one dealing with Tunisian music and the other with more academic or political interventions in the public sphere in Lebanon, Yemen, and Palestine can illustrate the point.

Amel Mathouthi, born in 1982, is a young Tunisian poet and singer who was present in the streets of Tunis at the time of the revolution. Capturing the spirit of the ongoing protests, her songs, written in a Tunisian dialect, became famous in the weeks of protest in 2011. One of these is entitled *Kalamti Hurra*, "My Word Is Free." Some of the lyrics encapsulate the point of a transformation of past fear and oppression into a constructive political alternative:

> I am among the free people who are not afraid
> I am the secrets that will never die
> I am with those whose voice refuses to comply [or surrender]
> [...]

---

[10] See, e.g., Caton, Al-Eryani, & Aryani (2014) on Yemeni popular art in the Uprising; Gröndahl (2012), Shalakany (2014), and Ramsay (2017) for Egypt; Lacquaniti (2015) for Tunisia.

I am the right of the oppressed
[...]
I am free and my word is free
[...]
I am the voice of those who are not dying
We build out of iron some fragile clay
Which becomes birds
Which becomes our homes [...][11]

The theme of fear (*khawf*, here in the first verse "the free people who are not afraid") is a trope in all Arab revolts. The individual singer must articulate injustice and oppression, with words that express human dignity and hope for a better future. The shift from the solitary or individual "I" (*ana* repeated multiple times in the first verse) to the plural "we" (expressed in the verb *nasna'*, "we build" or "we will build") is an eloquent turn expressing the collective ability, or hope, to construct a new future, one with wings (the earthly and fragile clay that turns into birds), and which is a place of shelters (our homes, our places of dwelling).

The violence of the state, in particular of formal institutions, was confronted explicitly in many slogans or testimonies. In Tunisia, in the first national protests organized by lawyers in Tunis on December 28, 2010, halfway between the self-immolation of Mohammed Bouazizi on December 17, 2010 and the toppling of Ben Ali on January 14, 2011, one of the slogans was *wizarat al-dakhliyya idarat irhabiyya*, "The Ministry of the Interior is the Administration of Terrorism" – "administration" thus being the real source of terrorism. A day later, in Sousse, another short slogan *tunis sha'ab, la hukuma* ("Tunisia is a people, not a government") reminded the regime that power resides not in some distant, formal institution acting on behalf of the state (an illegitimate government), but in the people

---

[11] My translation. The original Arabic lyrics are reproduced in *Dégage!* (2011: 158):

Anā aḥrār mā yukhāfūsh	/ *Anā asrār mā yumūtūsh*	/ *Anā ṣawt il[a] mā*
Anā ḥaqq al-mathlūmīn	/ [...] *Anā ḥurr wa kalamtī ḥurra* [...]	*raḍakhūsh* [...]
Anā ṣawt il[a] mā mātūsh	/ *naṣna' mal ḥadīd ṣalṣal*	/ *wa nabnī bīhu 'ishqa jadīda*
Tawlī aṭyār	/ *Tawlī dyār* [...]	

themselves.[12] In all this material, the people are the sovereign and the ultimate actor deciding when to apply physical force – *vis populi*. Pictoral representations carried by the various segments of the population synthesize and express a similar desire for justice and active political participation.

Legitimacy in and of violence was thus a burning question in the moments of 2011 when the tables were turned on decades-old autocratic regimes. During and after the processes that led to the ousting of four dictators (Tunisian President Ben Ali on January 14, 2011, the Egyptian *ra'is* Mubarak on February 11, 2011, Yemeni President Ali Abdallah Saleh in November 2011, and the killing of Libyan leader Muammar Gaddafi on October 20, 2011), Arab intellectuals called for a new social contract. This was true not only in countries where the Uprisings managed to force their presidents out of power, but also in neighboring countries. On March 27, 2011, Lebanese political scientist and former minister of culture Ghassan Salamé penned an opinion piece in the daily *Al-Nahar* requesting a move "toward a new contract between the state and society" (*nahw 'aqd jadid bayn al-dawla wal-mujtama'*) (quoted in Sha'ban 2012). In Palestine, a few months before his death in 2013, Eyad El-Sarraj, a famous Palestinian psychologist from Gaza, made a similar plea on his Facebook page. With the process of reconciliation between Fatah and Hamas, the feuding ruling Palestinian parties, going nowhere, he expressed the hope that law in general and a "social contract" (*'aqd ijtima'i*) in particular would put an end to the tyranny and the use of torture in Palestine.[13] Palestine is often left out of accounts of the Arab Uprisings or of social theory at large,[14] but the mode of self-expression and the call for a more democratic leadership witnessed there were identical to those experienced in other countries, such as the anticipations generated in Yemen with the creation of a National Dialogue Conference in 2013, which will be analyzed in greater detail in Chapters 4 and 5.

---

[12] As quoted in *Dégage!* (2011: 128 and 129).

[13] www.facebook.com/eyad.sarraj.3/posts/290704124362794 (post dated October 17, 2012).

[14] For an illustration, for example, of how the texts of Deleuze on Palestine are overlooked by political theorists, see Medien (2019b). I want to thank Salma Shamel for pointing at Lebanese writer Elias Khoury making a similar observation on the marginalization of Palestine in relation to the Arab Uprisings and Arab politics. See www.facebook.com/khoury.elias.9/posts/26818446185 71307 (post dated December 10, 2019).

To be sure, these poetic texts and political commentaries show an awareness of the fragility of the process launched in 2011. Nonetheless, they project a new type of representation of the people as an assembled body and as the ultimate source of – because of its collective and articulated set of demands – the monopoly on legitimate violence. For this reason, I want to explore how representation and violence are central not only in our understanding of the Arab Uprisings, but also for more general theories of democracy. Democracy, the power of the people, is a modern political system that should offer broad mechanisms for inclusion in formal institutions of representation *and* equality in front of death and before the apparatuses of coercion.[15] Democracy is thus more than a procedural mechanism to choose elected bodies and representatives; it also involves a plurality of practices of contestation. The Uprisings of 2011 were calling for radical politics, or radical representation, understood as the declared objective of generating a substantial shift towards more democratic enfranchisement, facilitating full participation in public life, and enhancing full equality for all segments of a given polity, with particular regard to the means of coercion.

More will be said in Part I about violence, its forms, its origins, and its multiple institutional nestings in Arab polities, as well as the relationship between the state and violence. But throughout this work, I define violence not simply as a destructive force but as a mechanism involving the deliberate use of force (physical, symbolic, or systemic), and serving to enact domination and/or coercion.[16] Such deliberate use of voluntary force,[17] when applied for legitimate uses, is entailed in the *vis populi* described in this book, and constitutes a crucially different approach than Hannah Arendt's deliberate use of force. Arendt (1977a) paved the ground for the dominant apprehension of violence as instrumental, e.g. violence as destruction, or violence exerted to obtain political recognition ("resistance" or "terrorism"). For her, violence can never be legitimate. Only power, understood as the ability to act in concert, can be legitimate (Arendt

---

[15] For some similar observations, see Balibar (2015).

[16] I believe that my definition captures not only the acts, the phenomena of violence as destruction, but also the condition that flows from the systemic condition of oppression. The definition also covers "symbolic violence" and the *attempt* by the masses, or the people, to re-domesticate the means of coercion.

[17] On the voluntary dimension of violence, see Bobbio & Matteucci (1983: 1240).

1977a: 46–52). Here, and in opposition to Arendt, *vis populi* is also foundational and creative, because it establishes new parameters, some discursive, that enable mass popular protest to come together, and it sets a path towards the democratic accountability of institutions of coercion.[18] Mark Ayyash (2020) also addresses pointed criticism to the reduction of violence to mere destruction, the first understanding of violence in the literature, or corrective counterviolence, the second widespread understanding of the concept. Ayyash proposes a third and fourth path to grasp the multi-dimensionality of violence: the semantic and hermeneutic paths. I will leave aside the fourth path, too post-structural and Derridian for my purposes, but concentrate on the third one. In Ayyash's (2020: 14) terms, the third path or type of study of "violence forces a space in which the interaction between the protagonists forms, continues, and transforms." He calls this dimension mimetic, because the dialogue about violence "allows the analyst to become a voice of a different order in the conversation over violence by exploring what is said 'over and above' those who proclaim and employ violence" (Ayyash 2020: 13). As I will show in the coming chapters, the symbolism of violence in the 2011 Uprisings very often constitutes a mirror of past geography of the uneven distribution of violence and of the long winding processes and differentiated spaces that have generated latent citizenship, from the (pre-)colonial to the post-independence era, and following that, from the last decades into the protests of 2011.

Chapter 3 substantiates how such a symbolic space around the theme of violence emerged and crystalized around a variety of discourses and images proposed by "the people," the "many," or the "masses." This space of convergence, rendered potentially democratic by the demand for direct civic participation, is where informal propositions articulate a rearrangement of political representation with a unifying and reconnecting political project. This space is fundamentally democratic and fragile because it requires a constant reiteration of coming together and of expressing what is legitimacy. *Vis populi* generally does not entail *doing* acts of violence (though there were some instances of this) but

---

[18] *Vis populi* is thus different from populist violence, the violence done in the name of a mythically unified people. *Vis populi* is the force of an always re-assembled multitude that represents and retains internal diversity. Because it is engaged with the present moment (see Chapter 3), its legitimacy cannot be usurped or taken away by populist leaders claiming to speak for the whole.

making it visible. It discloses the unequal past deployment of coercion and induces a scopic form of violence in politics (scopic, for "seeing" in Greek like in tele-scope). This new semantic space around violence, the *vis populi*, was a re-founding moment for citizenship in the Middle East. It was both a strength and a weakness. The informality and fluidity of seeing and being seen as a group and of denunciatory scopic practices like those in Figures 0.2–0.5 are very vulnerable and amenable to repressive measures targeting precisely these dimensions. It is not surprising that counter-revolutionary forces in Cairo, Manama, or Sanaa exercised such great effort to forbid physical access to Tahrir, Lulu' and Taghayyir squares, to erase the graffiti in Tahrir Square or Mohammed Mahmoud Street in Cairo, or at the end of Bourguiba Avenue in Tunis, in the streets of Yemen, or even to blind protestors.

0.2 Rethinking Democratic Theory Based on the Arab Uprisings

In the following pages, I want to show how the violence–representation connection matters for democratic theory, possibly also for our general understanding of revolutions. After all, this book is not only a reconstruction of the dynamics that traversed a selection of Arab countries,[19] but also a contribution to social theory, and to a lesser extent political theory.[20] Social theory explains the passage from informal to formal collective action, for example, in the line of John Chalcraft's (2016) distinction between transgressive and contained mobilizations, Asef Bayat's (2008; 2017) work on unrecognized street politics and leaderless revolutions, or Stacey Philbrick Yadav's (2011; 2015) invitation to attend to neighborly relations generated in sit-ins and their broader political meaning for solidarity and justice. Social

---

[19] There are many excellent comparative accounts of the Arab Uprisings; I am thinking of the essential work of Khosrokhavar (2012), Amar & Prashad (2013), Achcar (2013), Brownlee, Masoud, & Reynolds (2015), Akcali (2016), Bellin & Lane (2016), Ould Mohamedou & Sisk (2016), Ottaway (2017), and Hartshorn (2019) just to name a few. In this book, I concentrate on Arab republics, since monarchies have a larger array of tools to repress democratic participation.

[20] Political theory deals with arguments of civil society and deliberative democracy and is mainly based on abstract theorizing. The approach chosen here is much more "hands on" and based on local projects and the directions suggested by local actors themselves.

movement theory thus seeks to explain why the structuration of initial protests varies across time and space (e.g. Della Porta 2014) and has identified classical hurdles inhibiting spontaneity from transitioning into more structured organizations (Abdelrahman 2015; Leach 2005; 2009). New material, based on historical, comparative, and ethnographic methods, is needed to substantiate the plurality of citizenship practices and to explore some of the new dimensions of citizenship.

The 2011 Uprisings force us to rethink the intermediary space that exists between the informal and formal realms of politics, for example the inchoate and/or contradictory citizenship actions and artistic efforts to draw new maps for a sense of territorial belonging, or caravans of solidarity prefiguring multi-directional redistribution. The passage that I propose to explore between informal and formal spheres of political engagement is that of the social imaginary, a concept that I draw from the work of philosopher Cornelius Castoriadis. In what follows, the social imaginary is the connecting collective imagination that allows for a critique of the political conditions at the time of the Uprisings, and which signifies the necessity to profoundly alter mechanisms of political representation. Radical politics starts with an abundance of movements, ideas, and representational practices that are successful only insofar as these projects affect political society, understood as "... that arena in which the polity specifically arranges itself to contest the legitimate right to exercise control over public power and the state apparatus" (Linz & Stepan 1996: 8). This step can only take place once political representation makes the official means of coercion accountable to its citizens. But let me clarify the meaning of "representation."

Representation can mean both cultural depiction (a country asphyxiated by a snake that represents certain political actors) and delegation (sending a representative to parliament).[21] While other languages use different terms to make the distinction between these two significations clear, English does not. In Arabic, the dominant regional language, various terms are used: *taswir* or *ta'bir* for the former, and *tamthil* (or

---

[21] For a detailed theory and definitions of the different components of political representation, see Pitkin (1967) or the forum around Nadia Urbinati's work in *Contemporary Political Theory* (CPT 2014). These works are important, but they consider representation in a *constituted* polity or in an *existing* democratic system. This book deals with *constituting* efforts and non-democratic political systems.

tamthil siyasi "political representation" or *niyaba*, for "deputation") for the latter.[22]

The etymological roots of these words might help "visualize" or grasp the fundamental differences at play: *Tamthil* comes from the Arabic root *ma-tha-la*, which stands for "to appear, to resemble," and in the second form *maththala* as "to represent, to act, to exemplify" (or as a noun, the root means "example, actor"), while *taswir* comes from the root *sa-wa-ra*, the verb "to draw, to depict" (as in the word *sura*, the Arabic noun for "picture"). The alternative term, *ta'bir*, can be translated as assertion, utterance, or expression, from the verb *'a-ba-ra*, which in the second form means "to interpret," "to state clearly, declare, assert," or "to give expression" (see Wehr (1976), p. 498).

Often, in particular after the cultural turn in the social sciences, as I will show below, there has been a tendency to focus on one of these two dimensions of representation in separation from one another, or at the expense of the other: generally cultural or discursive representation eclipses the political dimension. Similar to the effort to glue Arab history and theory together with the European ones, I propose to reconnect *political* and *cultural* representations. Only in this way can we see the common aspiration towards democracy.[23]

The examples above and in the following chapters suggest that a capacity for both self-representation and political representation is essential for democratic aspirations. It is essential to acknowledge that both representations in the sense of *taswir*, as representational practices,[24] and *tamthil*, as delegation, are key ingredients for democratic or

---

[22] I am grateful to Salma Shamel for pointing to the debates around these Arabic terms in early twentieth century. For example, in Cairo, the cultural capital of the Arab world, new terms were introduced, for example, in the influential texts of reformist Mohammed Abduh (1849–1905) to distinguish painting (*taṣwīr*) from sculptures (*tamāthīl*). Dina Ramadan (2013: 42–50, here 47, fn. 119) states "there is no entry for *al-tamāthīl* in Lane's nineteenth-century Arabic–English Lexicon (collected in the first half of the nineteenth century) which suggests that "Abduh might have been using a fairly new or recent term." See also sources on theorizations on "images," or *ṣuwar*, in Seggerman (2019: 62).

[23] The fact that cultural representation, the by-product of the social imaginary, can enable a different route to political representation should make it clear that cultural representation and the ability for self-representation are *political* acts. At first sight paired as the dichotomy of cultural–political representations, they are in reality deeply connected, and in this book, by the embodied and often visual presence of *vis populi*. Similarly, praxes and representations are interconnected.

[24] A phrase I take from Khalid (2015: 162).

emancipatory politics, especially when these new forms of representation (visual and political) are made and reinvented by local actors themselves.[25] This reconnection was what produced a new social imaginary nourished by the first weeks of protests in 2011, awash with symbolic representations of the massive occupations, the use of national flags, and "caravans of freedom" (in Tunisia), which emboldened the protestors to call for an overhaul of their political system. The first component, *taswir*, can be defined, in a metaphorical way, as a screen on which images of one's own identity are projected and circulated. As such, it includes the images a society has produced (expressing what it is and what it wants to be), as well as images the masses have inherited and received (how others perceive these images as well as how they perceive the way others perceive them). The collective imaginary and images of a society are not fixed, nor do they share a given essence. Rather, they are relational, that is they rely on constantly evolving, complex, and mutual perceptions between selves and others, governed and governing, or between putative center(s) and imagined peripheries. For example, in Figure 0.4, the two-headed snake preys upon the whole of Tunisia, but it seems that the southern half of the country encounters the most suffering. Yet if Tunisia were to sever the two heads of the snake, the country *imagined as a whole* would be on a better, more prosperous course. It would re-flourish entirely.

Representation as depiction both re-shapes and expresses a political imaginary, which can produce slogans and common political discourses that spur political action and the definition of new social roles that contribute to a revolutionary trend. Note that I am not arguing that *taswir(at)* as (visual or symbolic) representation(s) is given, but that, as philosopher Castoriadis would put it, they are both constituted and constituting, or, to take an Arab intellectual's formulation (Al-Jabri 1998: 8), reason (or the rationality of these images) is both constituting and constituted.[26] As applied to the Arab revolts,

---

[25] Despite the heaviness that the choice carries, I will keep the Arabic terms to distinguish politics from cultural representation, and occasionally also the German dyad discussed in the next pages on Edward Said. This is justified by my choice in establishing a connection between theory and practice and between "Arab" and "European" theory.

[26] This means that imaginaries are both new sources *constituting* a basis for new courses of action, or old ones, *constituted* of pre-defined ideas and concepts (e.g. a national flag, a long-used symbol, potentially also used in a less emancipatory way) (Challand 2011). Al-Jabri (1998) speaks of constituting reason (*al- 'aql al-*

taswir is only a first step, or a preliminary method of bringing, synchronizing the presence of the many; it does not construct a new form
of democratic order in itself, but generates the conditions for future
actions. It is at this point that *tamthil*, as the actual action to delegate
authority to a representative, comes in. Only when a certain form of
taswir, capturing the novelty of these revolts, remained possible, open-
ended, and skeptical of the past uses of violence could the principle of
political representation (*tamthil*) be re-thought and experienced along
new lines and take new, more democratic, forms. This has been the
core, in my view, of the Arab revolutionary intentions, a principle
which has survived the initial phase of mass protests in 2011 and
which will also be termed "radical representation" in this
monograph.[27] Radical representation here resonates with an old
method of Ibn Khaldun's, who has demonstrated the role that poetics
(*shi'ir*), the imaginary (*khiyyal*), and revelation can play "in inspiring
and encouraging people" politically: The sociologist Syed Farid Alatas
has shown how fruitful the application of this approach can be for
deciphering contemporary sociological puzzles.[28]

I insist on connecting the three components together because much in
the literature dealing with the Middle East of the last 20 or 30 years has
concentrated on *cultural* components of representation. One fundamental example comes from the groundbreaking work of Edward Said
(1978) in confronting the Orientalist bias in the depiction of the Middle
East. It was certainly important, back in the 1970s, to show, in
a Foucauldian vein, how literature, opera, painting, or even "scientific"

---

mukawwin) and constituted reason (*al-ʿaql al-mukawwan*), less in the sense that
reason is given, and more in the sense that it evolves on specific (cultural)
traditions, Greek, Arab and modern forms of rationality.

[27] To paraphrase Arendt on revolutions, self-representation was a form of
liberation, but it was not freedom. "Liberation may be the condition of freedom
but by no means leads automatically to it" (Arendt 1977b: 19).

After years of dictatorships, censorship, and crack downs on dissidence, the
sheer fact of being able to depict and confront the violence of the police against
its own people (*vide* Figure 0.2 with Khaled Saʿid) or against the whole country
(Figures 0.4 and 0.5 for Tunisia) was in itself a revolutionary break from the
past. Such representational practices – constituting – were an empowering
moment that facilitated further mobilization, and new constituted bodies. But in
themselves they did not create a new political order.

[28] Alatas (2014: 13–14) and Al-Jabri (1998: 30, 153) discuss different aspects of
the relation between surface and hidden meanings (*zahir* and *batin*), as well as
demonstrative proof (*burhan*), elements that are essential for Arab critique. On
imagination and historical reasoning in Ibn Khaldun, see also Ghazoul (1986).

work on the Middle East, or the Orient at large, served European and Western control over the East through the production of discourses insisting on cultural differences. But Edward Said, and many of his epigones, mistakenly confused the two different components of representation and focused only on *cultural* representation.

This confusion is best encapsulated in the initial exergue of Marx's *Eighteenth Brumaire* describing the problem of French peasants, with which Said opens his *opus*: "[Peasants] cannot represent themselves; they must be represented" (Said 1978: 2). Especially after the so-called cultural turn, for a reader unaware of the original meaning and context of Marx's quote, the term "representation" could easily be understood as a question of the depiction of peasants. The latter, like the Easterners or Orientals in Said's deconstruction, would derive their representation only through another reference group, albeit turned upside down (as in the case of Orientalist oppositions such as modern/traditional, rational/irrational, etc.). As a result, peasants were denied here the capacity to decide their own fate, to represent themselves in discourses or images.

In reality Marx was not talking about the problem of representation-as-depiction, but about the incapacity, deriving from their intractable divisions, to gather and speak as one group and thus to actively engage in politics for themselves; and it is precisely the fact that other social groups managed to represent them that leads, according to Marx, to Bonapartism.[29] Thus, as suggested by the German term chosen by Marx, the above quotation does not refer to the problem of representation as depiction (*taswir*, in Marx's chosen term in German: *Darstellung*) but to that of political representation (in German: *Vertretung*, the correspondence for the Arabic term *tamthil*).[30]

---

[29] "Incapable of enforcing their class interest in their own name, whether through a parliament or through a convention. They cannot represent themselves, they must be represented. Their representative must at the same time appear as their master" (Marx & Engels 1950: 303). Spivak (1988) famously engages with similar questions of representation in social theory. While she also distinguishes the two meanings of representation, she likens *Vertretung* to "rhetoric-as-persuasion" and *Darstellung* to "rhetoric-as-trope" (Spivak 1988: 277). Thus, both terms are events, and entail a post-structuralist preference for representation as enunciations, not as political practices.

[30] The original German version is unequivocally about *Vertretung*: "*Sie [Bauern] können sich nicht vertreten, sie müssen vertreten werden*" (ch. 7 of *Eighteenth Brumaire*). One Arabic translation (Said s.d., translated by Kamāl Abu Dīb) uses the correct term, *tamthil*, to mirror the original German phrase: *innahum 'ājizūn*

Like in Arabic, the two meanings are clearly distinct and easily recognizable in German: representation as depiction is termed *Darstellung* while political representation is translated as *Vertretung*. Similarly, the etymological roots in German disambiguate the two meanings of representation: the verb *vertreten*, or the noun *Vertretung*, which can also mean replacing (*eine Stellvertreterin*, a substitute), is built on the German prefix *ver-*, which often indicates movement (as in *verlegen*, to move), and *treten*, to walk. "To step up" rings somewhat similar to the German meaning of *vertreten* since it also evokes the action of moving up to fulfill a (political) function. *Darstellen*, in opposition, is the action of presenting, or making stand (*stellen*), in front, or publicly (*dar-*), and can be translated as "to disclose."

This "mistake" of Said of confusing the two dimensions of "representation" has also had consequences, in my view, for our comprehension of the Arab Uprisings. Many analyses of the Arab events that have arisen since the first weeks of 2011 have given too much attention to the *depiction* of their unfolding, at the expense of trying to decipher the dynamics at play in the question of *political representation*. But however important this critique is, I would like to argue that, like the misquote of Said,[31] concentrating only on the Orientalist depiction of the "Arab Spring" risks obfuscating another aspect of representation that these revolts have unearthed: the 2011 Uprisings disclosed the people's sovereign power, their capacity to engage in politics in and for themselves, be it as organized groups hitherto repressed or marginalized (e.g. trade unions), as informal coalitions (e.g. self-proclaimed revolutionary bodies), or as the multitude[32] reclaiming the ultimate and legitimate control of physical violence.

'an tamthīli anfusihim; yanbaghī ān yumththalū (see Said s.d.: 28). Like the original sentence in Marx's *Eighteenth Brumaire*, the subject "they" is unspecified, while the version chosen by Edward Said in the original replaces "they" with the actual object of the discussions of who can or cannot represent themselves *politically*, in Marx's analysis in terms of party politics, namely peasants. The other Arabic version, translated by Dr. Mohammed 'Anāni (1995, published by Maktabat Baghdad, and its 2006 revised and augmented version) does not quote the Marx epigram (Said 1995: 42) and starts the introduction directly with the reference of a French journalist visiting Beirut during the Civil War.

[31] On this "error" of Said, see Richardson (1990) and I. Habib (2005).
[32] On the link between the "multitude" and the Arab uprisings, see Hardt & Negri (2013) and Kilani (2014) for Tunisia.

In other words, these revolts have also disclosed a new form of the self-representation *of* and *by* the people. Yet, the ensuing events, in particular the return to a full military dictatorship in Egypt or the tragedy of the Yemeni and Syrian wars, are a cruel reminder that these attempts at renegotiating representation are also problematically connected to the organization and the control of violence. It is through the recourse to violence that the people were blinded, at times literally, in order to deny them their recovered capacity of self-representation.

The aim of this monograph is to reconnect critically these two strands of representation, and through this reconnection reflect on why the deepening of the democratic transition took place only in certain countries. In the wake of Said's *Orientalism* and Timothy Mitchell's *Colonizing Egypt*, studies of the Middle East have been focusing predominantly on *cultural* features, *discursive* domination, centrality of the *gaze*, etc. A major piece of scholarship in itself, Mitchell's work ultimately generates a sense of sharp separations and of the fixity of the European gaze, a criticism that has been equally levelled against Said's generalization about "the West." Mitchell (1988: 12–13) offers a revealing definition of representation as a "system of signification(s)."[33] Are modernity, freedoms, citizenship only *discursive representation* or restless *projects* or *praxes* that allow for the emergence of some form of emancipation, call it democracy, radical democracy, republicanism, that a variety of social groups have fought to attain throughout the world? Chapter 2 in particular will discuss this democratic ferment in the history of the Middle East and argues that in looking only at the *concepts*, such as modernity, citizenship, or concentrate, the European or Western gaze yet again misses out *actions* on the ground by Arab citizens or obfuscates the social life of citizenship there.

0.3 Definitions, Sources, and Methods

The following chapters present in greater detail the dialectic of state–society relations in Arab countries, before and after the 2011 Uprisings. Chapter 1 deals with the history of repression

---

[33] In her work with peasant's consciousness in Egypt, Clément (2012: 9–10) makes a similar critique on the overemphasis on cultural and textual representation in Mitchell's work. For a criticism of the unwilling cultural separations that a certain type of post-modern or post-colonial studies produces, see Watson & Wilder (2018: Introduction).

there and with the reasons state violence has been mostly, if not uniquely, illegitimate. The origins of such problems are traceable to colonial and post-independence times, with an incomplete process of state-building, a locus of political sociology that needs revisiting in light of the *vis populi* argument (Chapter 2). Chapter 3 documents the power of the combined cultural and political representations in the first months of the Uprisings and its relation to the question of violence. It argues that the revolutionary moment resided in the ability of the masses to converge in powerful, temporary alliances (what I call informal coalitions, namely mixed classes, social and age groups, political factions, denizens with citizens of different geographical origins, etc.) and to articulate radical demands for change through physical presence and the intimation to act in the immediate present (what I call presentism). Chapter 4 identifies the forking paths that revolutionary actors and the multitude faced in Tunisia and Yemen: some attempts to propose a new revolutionary legitimacy based on the direct popular representation; a reformist agenda in part steered by external or conservative domestic actors; and the regrouping of (security) elites to hijack the "revolutionary" process. Chapters 5 and 6 illustrate the lasting impact of informal campaigns to maintain spaces of participation around issues of decentralization, transitional justice, and demands for accountability of the security apparatuses.

The detailed analyses in the last two chapters disprove the arguments made by many that the 2011 events have been unsuccessful in redrawing the map of democratic participation. Old recipes by governments in Arab countries cast a shadow over Tunisian and Yemeni citizens. Despite the Saudi bombing in March 2015 and the outbreak of a three-way civil war in recent years, Yemeni laypeople and artists, and not just elites, still strive to recompose a unified and more democratic polity via concrete proposals for decentralization and the implementation of federalism. In a bittersweet manner, Chapter 6 analyzes how, after 2018, the movement towards a southern secession, with the proposed creation of a new country that does not even carry the name "Yemen" (Arabian South, *al-junub al-arabi*), has been itself a paradoxical outcome of the mixed representational assemblies and sit-ins that were everywhere to be seen in the northern parts of Yemen in 2011, but which often cleaved on generational lines. Attention to the ensuing security fragmentation in the entire country will alas send the reader back to the situation during colonial times in Yemen, where central authority, in the south and in the north, were challenged by a myriad of armed forces benefiting from external, neo-imperial(ist) support.[34]

For Tunisia, I will concentrate on ambiguous yet encouraging signs of democratic participation in everyday life, including in remote southern towns. I will indicate how the models of 2011 are still the basis for new forms of political participation and alternatives for political representation for Tunisians of all walks of life. But it would be a mistake to see these daily protests and small-scale campaigns as an automatically *democratic* mode of civic engagement: The panorama drawn in the Chapter 6 is a mix of positive steps forward and ambiguous returns to the past. The idea of a half-full glass conveys the current reality in Tunisia, where formal political representation, around parties or trade unions, constitutes paradoxical barriers to the spread of informal coalitions and acts of citizenship.

The ensuing arc of chapters deals with the dialectical, rather than linear, relations between society and the state, violence and civility, and between informal and formal politics. The constituting or positive enactment of popular sovereignty in 2011 generates new dynamics, collective movement, and inchoate political action. Overall, this is an active refusal of the conditions of latent citizenship, a process that combines old geographies disregarding certain groups with new circuits of political creativity. Subjects who have been silenced for decades become actors of new projects, and joined forces in a way that will change state–society relations in the future.

Since this is not an account of the actual techniques of mobilization (say, about resource mobilization), or about sectoral reforms (say a study of the Ministry of the Interior, or of legal change), the methodological challenges are many and need to be set in relation to broader theoretical arguments. Trying to document spontaneous acts is hard and requires multiple lenses of analysis. Indeed, there is no way one can plan fieldwork in advance to record these new political imaginaries; it leaves very few traces, except in accounts by actors present on that occasion, but in the age of easy technology (smart phones), it is easy to find visual evidence. The task of the social scientist is then to propose

---

[34] We used capitalized "South" and "North" to refer to formal entities that existed in Yemen between 1967 and 1990 (or "Southerners" to describe the citizens of South Yemen), while the terms south(ern) and north(ern), without capital, make reference to loose or relational descriptions of regions in Tunisia and Yemen.

new methods of comparison (between advanced capitalist societies and [post]colonial polities, across the Arab Middle East, and within two countries with distinctive histories of marginalization), assemble these different (re-)sources, and patiently combine them with historical material (to understand the pre-history and origins of these events), and confront them with interviews and detailed observations on a selection of cases.

This book is therefore based on a multiplicity of methods: discourse analysis (of texts, posters, slogans, pictures, maps, etc.), interviews, ethnographic immersion in Tunisia, a compilation of datasets (on associations, new laws), interviews with Yemeni actors in the diaspora who were involved in drafting a new constitution and debating "federalism" there, videos posted by Yemenis on social media to capture the mood on the ground, and finally, historical analysis. These methods are pointed towards two clear objects of study: the historically influenced processes of democratic mobilization that generated a connecting and articulating imaginary in the revolutionary moments of 2011 on the one hand, and the transformation, more or less successful, of a negative or latent form to an active form of citizenship on the other. This permutation, complex and at times contradictory, as we will see in Chapters 5 and 6, is generally studied at the level of formal politics (a new constitution, the formation of political parties, redistribution of official state resources, etc.). My focus will mostly be on the informal realm and everyday practices. Working exclusively at one or the other scale (micro or macro) would go against the earlier stated commitment to reconcile, rather than oppose in binary pairs, theory and practice, "West" and "East." I chose to study informal politics through four thematic clusters: everyday practice, civil society, state, and revolution. This selection, and its subsequent methodological preference, is meant to add to a new vein of social research on the Middle East, and to contribute to ongoing theoretical studies on democratic life, both in the particular context of the Middle East (e.g. Chalcraft 2016; Wedeen 1999; 2008; Kurzman 2005) and in more general terms (Balibar 2015; Rancière 2006; 2012; Wedeen 2019). But let me first explain and briefly define these four clusters.

The study of *everyday practices* (democratic, activist, citizen, or otherwise) needs to be set in relation to structures of domination. It only makes sense to focus on practice, defined as the "actual performance or application, or as a repeated or customary action" (Merriam Webster Dictionary) if it is connected to hegemony. For example, the anodyne fact of sipping a coffee in a café can become a political act if it reclaims a space on the sidewalk usually forbidden to clients, or if women, usually excluded from this type of establishment in the Middle East (women mostly go to tea-houses), start to occupy, collectively, a male space. By underlining everyday practice, I want to avoid the "activist fallacy," or what is described in the social movement literature as the "fallacy of upper nodes" (Johnston 1995: 240). Johnston describes the risk of taking the point of view of members of the upper echelons in social movement organizations as the only entry point into the study of frames. But his work shows that the cognition of low-ranking participants differs greatly from that of leaders within a movement. Similarly, there is a tendency by social scientists to look for people formally engaged "in politics," as if there was a clear barrier between everyday life and political engagement conceived only if a person is *active*, i.e. enrolled in a party or a union, or working for an association. Let us note that most everyday practices discussed in the following chapters are related to the use of (social) spaces, a link that will beg questions about the emancipatory or democratizing dimension behind the occupation of public spaces.

Practice comes with theory and vice versa. For that reason, when I speak of a "theory of radical representation," I don't claim it to be a theoretical postulate that can, based on the hypothetico-deductive model, be tested. Theory here is not "prediction."[35] Theory means observing, watching, and generating lessons based on detailed observation (Wolin 1968: 319). Theory is what I do, as a scholar, but it is also, as I will try to show over the pages of this book, what the multitude in Tunisia or Yemen have been doing and continue to do in their restless attempt at generating a more just social order. This is done through scopic politics – watching, but also showing that the authorities are being watched – the last resort of democratic demands when formal channels are impossible.

Civil society is the source of collective autonomy (Challand 2009: 34–36). It can function as a counter-power to state power and/or to undemocratic forces, with or without a state.[36] As such, it is often

---

[35] See Ayyash (2018: 25) for a similar claim and attempt at "generating a novel perspective."

[36] Palestine is a case where civil society has played an important historical role for democratic life, notwithstanding the absence of a sovereign Palestinian state. Even if civil society has historically been thought of in relation to the state (the two terms were coterminous in early modern philosophy), the former can exist without the latter. See Challand (2009: 25–58).

considered in the realm of informal exchanges and opposed to political society, the realm of formality (Linz & Stepan 1996: 7–8). This opposition is widespread but not without risks. It can be helpful to actually draw a clear line for the study of political process, but it might give the impression that, on the ground, the distinction is clear with no overlap possible. It also obfuscates the fact that civil society, increasingly taken as a set of (pre-)formalized institutions (clubs, charities, NGOs, etc.), also gathers informal spaces of debate. For this reason, I insist on proposing a method to substantiate and analyze social imaginaries. The dividing line between belonging to civil society and being excluded from it is an expressed commitment to the common good (religious or secular), an ability to engage in debates, and a de facto respect for pluralism. In this book, civil society creates a link between citizenship and democracy whenever civility comes into play.[37] Rather than a process characteristic of individuals who learn new techniques, etiquette, and manners (Balibar 2015: chapter 2), I prefer to follow Eiko Ikegami's understanding of civility, namely "a ritual technology of interpersonal exchanges that shapes a kind of intermediate zone of social relationship between the intimate and the hostile" (Ikegami 2005: 28). This description, more historical and sociological, bypasses the expectation that a state or state actors (as with the royal court discussed by Norbert Elias 1939/2000) are the guarantors or uphold the standards of civility. Civility therefore involves informal exchanges, such as cultural practices, civil society activities, and interactions in the public sphere.

The *state* in this book is not capitalized precisely to remind us that it is not an idealized, supra-individual, or supra-societal entity. All too often people associate the state with a formal institution, various organizations coordinated by a governing body in charge of the "legitimate use of physical force." This seems in line with the famous definition given by Max Weber in *Politics as a Vocation*. Instead, I want to put the stress on the first two words of this definition. Max Weber (1919/1958: 8) says that the state is "the *human community* that successfully claims the monopoly of the legitimate use of physical

---

[37] On civility and the civilizing process, see Elias (1939/2000). See also Balibar (2015) on violence and politics. For a rich discussion of the early Islamic tradition of civility, see Salvatore (2016).

force within a given territory."[38] It is the people, the action and practice of citizens or individuals kept on the threshold of citizenship (women, workers, people of different ethnic or geographic origins, etc.), that gives life to this state. The state is thus a constant and everyday practice, one that mitigates the risks of unjust violence, one that is based on informal debates of civil society, and the result of historical negotiations to find a solution to blunt unjust authority.

I use Weber as an entry point because his definition is the most accurate, and certainly the most quoted, definition of the state. It is also the most *misquoted* definition for the omission of the "human community." But from that, I depart from Weber who had a conservative vision of politics and placed little trust in the *demos*, or in this human community. After all Weber was not invested, except maybe outside of the lecture halls and the occasional "political" lecture (*Politik als Beruf*), in changing the social order.[39] Weber never really questioned who qualified as "humans" in the context of empires and colonies.[40] He was interested in pointing at what *holds* politics and society stable. In connecting state *with* society, I am much more in line with Antonio Gramsci (1891–1937), who saw the two as deeply interconnected.[41] This Italian intellectual developed a view of civil society as a site for struggle and emancipation that I fully adhere to. Civil society is the space for collective autonomy (Challand 2009: 34–36, 92). Like Gramsci, I believe that bottom up participation, re-conscientization, here via *representational politics*, can help the many, the masses, or the people to re-shape what is the "state" and what it should do, in particular with regards to the means of coercion and the

---

[38] In the original version, the state is defined as follows: "*Staat ist diejenige menschliche Gesellschaft, welche innerhalb eines bestimmten Gebietes – dies: das 'Gebiet', gehört zum Merkmal – das Monopol legitimer physischer Gewaltsamkeit für sich (mit Erfolg) beansprucht*" (M. Weber 1919/1958: 8).

[39] For Weber, the demos are a shapeless mass that will never govern actively; on the contrary it is governed and separate from the bureaucracy, which plays a much more important role as it roots power in a legal-rational authority. For a criticism of Weber, see, e.g., Kalyvas (2008: 71).

[40] Recent studies indicate that he did not have a very generous view of colonial subjects, drawing possible parallels between African Americans in the USA and Polish peasant workers in Prussia. See Zimmerman (2012: 206–215).

[41] For new Gramscian perspectives on the Middle East, see the rich special issues of *Middle East Critique* 30(1) (2021), edited by John Chalcraft and Alessandra Marchi, and of *Journal of North African Studies* (2020), edited by Gennaro Gervasio and Patrizia Manduchi.

use of physical force. It should be "legitimate" from the view of society, its diversity, pluralism, and embodied practice of civility and autonomy.

Because of the relational approach favored, I will also argue that the international (or supranational) influences on state–society relations need to be considered. Theories of "state-making" are too often theories of European state-making that ignore inequalities and asymmetries in the international environment that exist at the times of the various state-making experiences. Weber and many scholars of state-making assume a supranational environment made of like-minded state actors, namely ones that accept the premises of the Westphalian Order, with states recognizing each other's sovereignty, or turning a blind eye on the colonial/imperial violence done on peripheral (quasi-)states in the name of civility or civilization. In the contemporary setting, discourses of civility or white men's burden are often replaced by discourses of technical expertise, where top-down engineered democratization or paternalistic assessment of "state-failure" completely ignores citizens' self-representation. Part I demonstrates the influences of imperial and colonial formations on state–society relations (the generation of latent citizenship), while Part III will suggest that a new dimension, that of neo-imperialism, curtails the ability of robust civic participation to emerge in the Middle East today.

Finally, and in the same vein, *revolution* is summed up in a Castoriadisian formula: Revolution occurs when people can be their own source of inspiration; revolution is about spontaneity, namely "the excess of the result over the causes" (Castoriadis 1976: 11). Revolution is about the excess of movement, inchoate, informal politics, converging and connecting social imaginaries. It is a process in which new social roles, new spaces (or connective movements in spaces), and new vocabularies are invested in allowing for the "auto-institution of society," able to create its own, new, radical imaginary that helps undo former regimes of power. Methodologically, this definition invites social scientists to find more granular evidence and expression than a Skocpolian definition of revolution, which would draw on the structural analysis of, say, administrative and military collapses or class structures.[42]

---

[42] Skocpol (1979: 155). For Theda Skocpol, social revolutions are rapid, basic transformations of a society's state and class structures (with bottom up class revolts and the coincidence of political with social transformations). See Skocpol (1979: 5).

Concentrating on Castoriadis does not mean that classical studies of revolutions are not helpful. Indeed, throughout the book I will follow Charles Tilly's seminal work (1978: 189–194), which distinguishes between the revolutionary *intentions* (opposing past injustices and territorial fragmentations; Chapter 3), revolutionary *movements* (reconnecting these peripheries for a common mobilization; Chapter 4), and revolutionary *outcomes* (the renewed forms of limited representation; Chapters 4–6). Since many studies already exist about whether it is apt to call the Uprisings revolutions or not (Ayari 2011; Khosrokhavar 2012; Hanieh 2013; Ottaway 2017), I decided to focus on those gray, under-studied areas of informal citizen actions, and on how these can be contributors to the type of (symbolic) revolutions that Castoriadis describes, for example in his text "The Hungarian Source" (Castoriadis 1976).

By and large, scholars agree that, whatever the standards or definitions applied, the Arab Uprisings were not revolutions.[43] That does not prevent people from thinking of these events as revolutions given the significance of their symbolic achievements, albeit partial and/or temporary. In the interviews I gathered over the last years, many Tunisians (the same is true for Egyptians and Yemenis), use the term "revolution," but mainly to refer to the first months of the mass mobilization. Very few still believed they were, as of 2016 and 2017, in a revolutionary process, while many are inconsistent in the use of the terms. For example, some of my interlocutors sustain that the events of winter 2010/2011 in Tunisia were not a revolution, yet, when assessing the opposite political faction (typically one of the two main parties now in power, namely Nidaa Tounes ["The Call of Tunis"], a loose secular coalition, or the Islamist party Ennahda) they refer to them as "counter-revolutionary forces." How can there be a counter-revolution if no revolution ever took place? Since the vast majority of my respondents used the term "revolution," I will relay this term in the text, even if the analysis I offer, in particular in Chapter 4, establishes that, *stricto sensu*, no social or economic revolutions occurred. As in the previous sentence, the quotation marks will express my distance from the claim that the uprisings were "revolutions," but in the interviews I will leave the term unmarked to express the respondent's inclination.

---

[43] For a discussion of the failed promises of four generations of theories of revolution, see Lawson (2016).

This book is in line with earlier comparative writings on cultural and popular resistance in the contemporary Middle East, in particular the works of Charles Tripp and John Chalcraft. Common forms of resistance, and the importance of the social imaginary, in particular the arts (Tripp 2013) and popular politics, distinguished between contained and transgressive mobilizations (Chalcraft 2016), have been indispensable elements in the making of the modern Middle East. Like these two authors, I share the view that Arab peoples are not passive societies. They exist not only in reaction to the West or to imperialism, but are their own source of inspiration, and have their own agency. While for Tripp (2013) contestation is situated firmly in structures of domination – not just economic, but also coercive, administrative, gendered, and discursive power – Chalcraft (2016: 9) invites us not only to look at these structures of domination, but also to identify contention as rooted in hegemonic (re-)articulations. Hegemony (how to build blocks of consent without physical imposition) is a larger concept that allows us to avoid the trap of formal or top-down politics. A popular re-articulation of hegemony, for Chalcraft, means that there is a possibility for previously unorganized or apolitical actors to erupt as new, innovative, and self-identified actors. These sporadic emergences are what Chalcraft terms "transgressive mobilization" (p. 25), and stand in opposition to "contained mobilization," i.e. more institutionalized and pre-constituted actors.[44]

Chalcraft thus opens the door to informalism with care: we should not fetishize it (Chalcraft 2016: 27), but by building a historical and cultural sociology of the Middle East, one should avoid a top-down reading of Arab politics.[45] One should also avoid the mechanical expectations that underpin a lot of the social movement literature, for example about the necessary pre-existence of mobilizing structures or of clear political opportunities. Dangerous shortcuts and bad surprises follow if civil society is reduced to its organized components, associations, and NGOs, or if it is a-critically described as an agent of

---

[44] Wary of too stark a dichotomy, Chalcraft notes that these two categories are not mutually exclusive and that there are points of contact, for example when the charismatic component of transgressive mobilization turns into contained mobilization, citing the evolution of Hezbollah in the 2000s (Chalcraft 2016: 25). Part I elaborates further on Chalcraft's concepts.

[45] Much of the literature on the Middle East focuses on elites (Hourani), diplomatic history (Yapp), or political economy (Owen, Richards and Waterbury) (Chalcraft 2016: 10–14).

democracy. Civil society might also be a place for polarization, exclusion, and even destructive political projects (Marchetti & Tocci 2011). Even *vis populi* is not exempt of slippage towards partisan coercion and localized vengeance, as we will see in Tunisia with the transformation of the Leagues for the Protection of the Revolution or in the dynamics facilitating the spreading of the civil war in Yemen, with the multiplication of popular committees and new security forces.

* * *

The present text is as much an essay in historical and political sociology as it is an attempt to suture theory with practice and to suggest how Arab *demoi* have been sources of inspiration for theory-making. I encourage a dialogue between the two (northern and southern) shores of the Mediterranean, one that ceases to reify regions around cultural identities and that proposes, instead, a relational and transversal perspective about citizenship, collective actions, and the constitutive role of violence in politics.

Transversal, for me, adds to all these components of relational sociology by insisting on the transformative potential of these relations. Relations traverse entities: "Arab politics" is thus nothing but the sum of "local" Arab forces and power, combined with the influence of external forces, European in the past, now mostly American, Chinese, or Gulf-based. Transversal sociology also allows for combining the larger politics of comparison (beyond the usual units of analysis – and thus adding a transnational or translocal dimension) but adds an element of transformative force (a view that does not exist in the metaphor of the "mechanical interaction," where the billiard balls hit each other but remain identical in terms of shape, color, and content).

Recent sociological theory has warned Euro-American scholarship of the lack of awareness of historical processes outside of these geographical realms. Gurminder Bhambra (2014) has called for "connected sociology," while Go & Lawson (2017) invite scholars to construct more diverse research projects of historical global sociology, piecing together various historical experiences to generate new typologies or ideal-types that are not always based on the history of the usual suspects such as France, Germany, or Russia. In his focus on armed forces, for example, Tarak Barkawi (2017: 72) suggests that "the organization of violence is seen as socially productive, as generative of certain political orders, at home, abroad, and internationally. ...

The imperial and the peripheral are in part constitutive of the metropolitan."[46]

"Transversal" will be rendered below with the analogy of the Moebius strip,[47] that long piece of paper twisted in the middle and glued together at its extremities. It seems that the two sides are clearly different and unconnected, but one just needs to follow the surface of the strip with a pencil, or a finger, to realize that the surface is one continuous side. Similarly, the ensuing narrative about violence, citizenship and the constitution of modern states across the Mediterranean will function as a Moebius strip: Even if we have very compelling accounts in historical sociology about the gradual monopolization and reduction of violence by modern states in Europe (M. Weber 1919/1958; Elias 1939/2000; Foucault 1977; Tilly 1990), these accounts function as if the "surface" of the history of legitimate violence had only one side, the European experience, when in reality this story is *relationally, transversally, and cumulatively* connected to the experience and processes that unfolded in the southern Mediterranean. Equally, a history of state-making in the Arab worlds can only make sense if we consider the origins, forms, and reasons for policing and exacting physical coercion in Europe. In other words, a transversal history of the phenomenon of violence in state-making should compel the readers to realize that the "erasure" of violence "here" (in northern Mediterranean, or in core capitalist countries that have adopted a rapid path towards political modernity) was actually connected to the exaction of brute and perverse violence "there" (in the peripheries or in the regions engulfed by colonialism and/or imperialism, in short south of the Mediterranean). Similarly, theories of civilization, progress, and modernization in advanced capitalist societies may have reinforced certain culturalist interpretations about the resilience of violence (as destruction) in the Middle East.

[46] This idea of co-constitution was already at the heart of Cooper and Stoler's *Tensions of Empire* (1997). Some have followed the call to assemble metropole and colony in the same analytic frame, but very little study has been done about a relational and transversal study of citizenship in Europe and in the Middle East. Even a recent, important contribution by social theorists Joas & Knöbl (2013), who tackled the links between war and social thoughts, fails to really study the distorted political processes that undermined in the colonies the emergence of a pacified or civilized social contract.

[47] The idea of the Moebius strip came from reading Balibar's *Violence and Civility*, but he uses the image in a totally different, non-colonial context (2015: 12). I am grateful to Agnes Czajka for pointing to the use made of the same image in Agamben (1995). See also Bigo (2001).

The term "transversal" is preferable because it evokes the transformative power of traversing relations or phenomena, thus creating
a dialectic, or movement, that connects a universal to a particular, or
a co-constitutive, relation, rather than imagining only one territorial
origin for a concept or practice. We will see how "modes of encroachment" is a phrase that captures some of these ambiguous forces connecting various parts of the world beyond the simple dyad of European
and American imperialisms (Chapter 1). "Transversal" adds to the
growing research agenda of relational sociology.[48]

If I use the term "postcolonial" in this book, I don't take the concept to
point at or describe a different place (Algeria is postcolonial) or a different
time (what has happened since the end of colonialism and effective
independence). Postcolonial is, for me, the relational characteristic that
connects, for example, Algeria to France in a complex circle of mutual
influence and of mirroring effects of past imbrications and current situations or patterns that have some origins in the colonial period (see in
particular Mbembe 2006; Shepard 2008: 269–273). The more or less
explicit racialized understanding of Frenchness cannot be said to be the
direct result of colonialism, but can be explained by the gradual transformation of asymmetries and the exclusion of (French) Algerian Muslims
at the time of the colonies. This morphed into new cultural expressions of
marginalization and exclusion towards Maghrebans in the twenty-first
century.[49] Postcolonial concern seeks "to overcome its epistemic confines" (that is, how certain concepts or biases were solidified in colonial
times). "It refers to a relational position against and beyond colonialism,
including colonialism's very culture" (Go 2016: 9).

While informed by some scholarship labeled "postcolonial" or "postcolonial," the perspective adopted here is that of a *critical-colonial*

---

[48] Relational sociology has the objective of avoiding the fallacy of substantialism
(Emirbayer 1997), namely advancing problematic statements such as "power is
this" or "power does that." Power should not be hypostatized: Power is only an
abstraction; it cannot be located. Instead, one needs to consider how a situation
of power affects the interactions between various social groups, and *as
a consequence of this mutual influence*, social relations are changed or
influenced. For an overview of the advances of relational sociology, see
Dépelteau (2018).

[49] On the morphing and relexification of past racist justifications for French or
white superiority into contemporary cultural statements, see Balibar (1991) and
his discussion of neo-racism. See also Shepard (2008) for a very detailed
description of the emergence of a racialized legal practice against Muslims in
French Algeria.

approach. With this expression, I mean an approach that unifies the contributions coming from different fields of critical colonial studies, including post- and de-colonial studies and critical race studies. I prefer to use the expression "critical-colonial," to point to the ensemble of critical investigations into the colonial conditions whose legacies, or conceptual tools, remain alive in present, lived spaces. While the term "post-colonial" may surreptitiously suggest a movement beyond that colonial past, a question that I would like to leave open, the term "de-colonial theory" performatively reinstates the speaking subject who is authorized to decide how to undo the colonial past, and thus, when used by theorists of European descent, like me, can equally be interpreted as a gesture imbued with colonial hubris that thus reproduces the same coloniality of power it aims to undo (Bottici & Challand 2019).

I will close this conceptual section by reflecting on my positionality (how my location and position in the academic field might influence and/ or introduce some bias or a prioris in the current study). As a Swiss scholar, having worked previously in Palestine, and located professionally in the USA and at the time of the research in Switzerland and Italy, doing research in the region comes with advantages and disadvantages. The two countries studied in greater detail here, Tunisia and Yemen, differed greatly in terms of access. Being Swiss made it easier to move around there, as a citizen of a country with no heavy colonial involvement in the region. I was not able to conduct fieldwork in Yemen in recent years because of the ongoing civil war. However, a previous period of study in Yemen in the early 2000s allowed me to travel extensively in Sanaa and around the country, north to Mahwit and Hajja, west to Hodeida and Kamran, south to Ibb and east to Marib and the Hadhramawt, all the way to Seyun. Thanks to the support of François Burgat, who took some liberties to organize off-limits visits (it was already difficult to head north of Sanaa), I interacted with Yemenis from all walks of life for the six weeks I was there, and got to know French PhD students who would soon become leading scholars of Yemeni and/or Saudi politics (Laurent Bonnefoy, Pascal Ménoret, Stéphane Lacroix). Testimonials about the 2011 dynamics come from Yemenis I interviewed during international conferences in Amman and Cairo in 2012 and 2013, and over Skype and emails in recent years. Zaid bin Ali Alwazir, Rafat Al-Akhali, Joshua Rogers, and Laurent Bonnefoy were helpful in identifying new Yemeni respondents in the last months (April 2019–January 2021), but I acknowledge here a great debt to all 12 Yemenis who accepted, despite the very difficult situation back in their country, or in exile, to speak about the "revolution." The interviews, a few face-to-face, and the rest over Skype or WhatsApp calls, and follow-up with text messages, were carried out in Arabic, or with a combination of Arabic and English. One Zoom interview was done in French with the leader of a small NGO in Sanaa. I finally established a contact on the Archipelago of Socotra, and over the months during which I was finishing the book (December–July 2020) I was in regular contact with an activist in Hadibo at the time when infighting between southern factions broke out. This "direct" access gave personalized touches to an analysis that otherwise relied on gray and journalistic literature.[50]

In Tunisia, access was easy and took place over three different periods: July 2015, January 2016, and June–July 2016. These journeys, done in moments of social tension (summer 2015, a couple of weeks after the Sousse attacks, and January 2016 at a time when protests were taking place in Kasserine), constitute in themselves an exercise in radical representation. My presence, with previous exposure to work on and with civil society in Palestine but originating then from the USA, was rarely anodyne, especially in the less central zones. My presence in Siliana prompted two brief police interrogations, and my passage through Tataouine presented the occasion for interviewees to vent their anger with Western donors (the topic of my research on civil society had probably given the impression to some of my interlocutors that I was working for a foreign donor or governmental agency). I was able to quickly move out of the capital city, where one could get the impression that Tunisia is doing fantastically well. Moving slowly from the south of the country (Medenine, Tataouine) to the north (Bizerte) and from Tunis to Siliana, via local minibuses, or *louages*, eating in little *sha'abi*, popular restaurants, or at street food stalls, and interacting in part Arabic, part French or Italian, allowed me to have a sense of immersion away from the large, international, and touristy cities of Tunis, Sousse, La Marsa, or Gamarth, where many foreign researchers confine their movements.

---

[50] Because of the civil war since 2015, I have relied on videos posted on YouTube, e.g. the channel by Ammar Basha with videos from 2011 until 2018. Some of these videos may now appear partisan, since he reports on what he can see in Sanaa, but they document the grim reality. The work of street artist Murad Subay' (www.muradsubay.com) or the long reporting analyses by Robert Worth, who traveled extensively in the country in 2011 and 2018, have also been helpful to capture the mood on the ground.

The material quoted about Tunisia comes from 58 in-depth interviews that I carried out in 2015 and 2016.[51] Five interviews were carried out in Arabic, two in English, and the rest in French (where the latter means that most of the discussion took place in French, but with occasional sentences exchanged in Arabic). I used a nonrandom or purposive sampling to identify a variety of actors involved in civic actions.[52] Most of the respondents are persons with an openly political profile, e.g. members of political parties or local public figures (NGOs, coordinators of local campaigns), ranging in age from their early 20s to 70s. To avoid the "activist fallacy," I have distinguished people supporting campaigns from association members (the former were usually not as demanding in terms of their commitment and direct contact with other persons), and listed people involved in advocacy (often with a clearer view of the legal intricacies and thus more likely to be familiar with legal hurdles in strengthening representation) as distinguished from party members. The exact breakdown in terms of their profile is the following: Seven interviews with advocacy persons, 29 with associations (three of which are charitable associations), six with campaign organizers, eight with party members, and three with journalists. Six meetings were conducted with international donors. Thirty-nine interviews were made with men, 19 with women.

The sample does not claim to be representative of the whole array of political opinions: All Islamists I interviewed were *Nahdaoui* respondents, i.e. members of Ennahda, namely eight interviews, but none were self-declared Salafists. The roster offers different political opinions, from the far-left (Popular Front) to the (center-)right (Nidaa Tounes), including Islamists and *azlam* (what the Egyptians call *feloul*), i.e. remnants or supporters of the former regime.

The sample is much more representative of Tunisian political geography: I interviewed people from Bizerte (3), Siliana (6), Tunis (17, with

---

[51] I have done 58 interviews with 53 different persons, meaning that five persons were interviewed twice. Five additional interviews were conducted with persons at the crossroads of academia and NGO consultancy work, whose views were not taken into consideration for the following empirical parts. Most of the contacts were initiated from my own research, via internet searches.

[52] For a discussion of methods, and interview sampling, see Clark & Cavatorta (2018: 109–121, in particular 115 for the question of recording). The semi-structured interviews included general questions on their involvement with civic engagement (or with a party) and the nature of the "transition," leading to more personal questions about their involvement and experience with the "revolution" and its aftermath.

an additional 3 in the Greater Tunis area, such as La Manouba), Sousse (4), Mahdia (1), Sfax (7), Mahares (1), Djerba (6), Zerzis (1), Medenine (6), and Tataouine (3), covering 9 of the 24 governorates existing in Tunisia. Notwithstanding the usual depiction of Tunisia as a homogenous country, with a rich and long history of urban life from the Punic centers such as Carthage to the Arab and Mediterranean heritage cities along the coast (Djerba, Sfax, Monastir), each region has its own specific relation with the hinterland. It was important to meander in different parts of the country.

People were identified from websites, online publications, public databases about Tunisian associations,[53] or from references in Tunisian dailies. As public personalities, they have agreed to answer my questions and to appear in this book to convey their and their peers' opinions. Part of the sample was obtained by snowball sampling, but an overall effort was made to reach out to peripheral parts of the country, outside of the capital-area or from the northeastern coast, where the most developed and urban centers are concentrated. Additional sources gathered during field visits include: official documents (e.g., draft laws, new lists of municipalities), press articles, pictures of graffiti that I gathered from field visits, and journal-style notes after spontaneous encounters on the streets (with high school students, street sellers, newspaper merchants, etc.). Except for a few train rides along the coast to Sfax, most of the travel from city to city was done through *louages*, allowing for spontaneous contact with Tunisians.

For the parts on Yemen, I gained access to empirical material documenting the civic engagement in and after the 2011 Uprisings via other means. Between 2011 and 2013, when I was part of a research network from the Graduate Institute for International and Development Studies in Geneva, I helped organize two international meetings with civil society activists after the 2011 Uprisings, one in Amman (April 2012) and the other in Cairo (February 2013). Since then I have regularly been in touch with Yemenis, some who attended the National Dialogue Conference (NDC), but who have all followed the spiraling violence as it washed away their collective democratic efforts. From the East

---

[53] There are different online sources on associations. Two were helpful to spot exact contact details: the site https://jamaity.org/ ("My Association" in Arabic) and the *Toile des Associations pour le Civisme et le Développement*, with a rich network of associations in the south, whose website ceased to be active, but whose profile can be found on the Internet Archive at: https://web .archive.org/web/20130809000354/http://tacidtn.org/.

coast in the USA, I was fortunate to interview a few Yemeni exiles in New York and in Washington, and to benefit from the opening of a diplomatic representation of the Southern Transitional Council in the US capital, which is the diplomatic antenna of the putative new country of "Southern Arabia."

The analysis comes from a dozen interviews with Yemeni activists and from primary online sources, in particular the material that the NDC generated during its period of intense work in 2013 and 2014. Even if the NDC documents have mostly been taken down from the NDC website, with a simple search via the parent directory, I was able to download a larger set of 250 documents that were put on the NDC intranet.[54] These include reports presented to one of the nine working groups, mid-term reports, and a draft of the final constitution. The bulk of these documents are in Arabic. I have therefore made extensive use of these documents to recreate a sense of the debates about the key themes of this paper, namely decentralization and federalism, and which actors were the most involved or critical of the process of drafting a new constitution. Interviews with persons involved with the NDC and the political transition have been done mostly in the last two years, but a couple were done in 2013.

Doing interviews about past events in a country facing war is difficult. Ideally it should not be done. But because of material and a few interviews I had done in 2012 and 2013, I felt I had to complete the work and offer an interpretation of the Yemeni democratic ferment. This is because the country is generally omitted from the comparative literature on the Middle East and North Africa (MENA) and because people keep fighting for a recomposition of the collective body despite the hardship. I acknowledge a possible bias in the geographical origins of the people interviewed between November 2017 and October 2019 with people who believed (and generally still do) in the centrality of the National Dialogue, and a majority from the north (either from Sanaa, Ibb, Taiz, and their hinterlands). Despite efforts to reach out to Huthis in the north, I could not elicit a response over email or social media. To be fair, it was a time when these portions of Yemen were facing violent military operations. But, late in the writing of this book, I managed to interview one

---

[54] The website of the NDC was unplugged recently, but most of its content can be found on the Internet Archive: https://web.archive.org/web/20130402041407/ http://www.ndc.ye/.

person working in Huthi-held areas and three persons from the south: representatives of the Southern Transitional Council (STC) in Washington (January 2020) and an NGO activist from Socotra from December 2019 onward. The interviews I did with Yemenis were either conducted in Arabic (6) or in English (6), with a late additional interview in French. Transcriptions of these interviews were made in a unique language, French for Tunisia and English for Yemen, in order to code the voluminous material, with the help of the software *Atlas.ti*.[55] Portions of text in square brackets are my own additions to correct a sentence, translate a word, or paraphrase content deemed too elliptic.

Additional comparative material on the Arab Uprisings and their aftermaths was collected over multiple years. All of the textual and visual analysis was done with the help of the software *Atlas.ti*. A couple of books collecting rich visual material (caricatures, graffiti, slogans, etc.) were particularly helpful in reconstituting the dynamics of the revolutionary intentions and moments. The special issue of *Arabian Humanities* coordinated by Mermier (2020) on contemporary Yemeni literature in the context of the war, as well as analyses of literary production (e.g. Al-Rubaidi 2018b), and translations of short novels or poetry capturing themes of this book provided other valuable empirical sources for the second half of the book. In total more than 350 documents, from transcriptions of interviews to pictures I took while traveling Tunisia, and from videos documenting Arab protests to pictures assembled in published books, provided "evidence" of a non-elite, bottom-up, alternative political imaginary.[56]

---

[55] Different phases of coding with *Atlas.ti* allow for breaking down the compound facets of citizens' engagement and contribute to a grounded theory of our understanding of radical forms of activism. On grounded theory, see Mattoni (2015).

[56] The book covers events until 2021, a decade after the outbreak of the Uprisings. It therefore leaves out developments that took place in 2022, but the themes and theses of this book remain valid, as the reader will discover in Part III.

A final note on spelling, transliteration, and diacritics for the Arabic terms. In the core text and for the sake of legibility, I have used a simple transliteration from Arabic, keeping the *'ayn* with the closed 'and the *hamza* with an open '. I have adopted simplified spellings for names that are now common in English (Sanaa, Taiz, etc.). Diacritics will only appear in footnotes, captions of images, and bibliographic references that exist only in Arabic.

The Making of Latent Citizenship

Introduction

Part I deals with the slow rhythm of state-making. It revisits the Euro-American account of citizenship as a peaceful process of enlarged franchise. It combines a relational account of the advent of political modernity in Europe and in the Arab Middle East with a diachronic account of state–society relations. It discusses the impact of external encroachments on institutions of coercion (police, army) and of representation (limited civic participation, tiered citizenship in parliaments). It identifies the international roots of limited citizenship in the Middle East.

Chapter 1 discusses the pre-colonial and colonial epochs. Chapter 2 concentrates on the post-independence period, and explains why citizenship never fully emerged in the Middle East as it did in advanced capitalist polities. Yemen and Tunisia share the characteristic of being remote provinces of the Ottoman Empire, with lasting center–peripheries fragmentation. Both endured less invasive forms of French and British colonialism, yet both were exposed to three forms of external encroachments: colonial, imperial, and capitalist, which insidiously weakened the social life of citizenship in these polities.

Finally, Part I revisits the dominant social theories of violence (Foucault, Elias, Weber, and Tilly) in light of an enlarged and relational frame of analysis: If Europe is considered the place where social relations were pacified thanks to an extension of the political franchise (citizenship) and through a process of reduced violence (the Foucauldian disciplining process), this is because the Middle East encountered more violence and extreme forms of encroachment. In light of these *connected* sociologies of citizenship, Part I re-assesses in a critical-colonial manner these dominant theories of violence and proposes the idea of uneven distribution of violence to capture inequalities, at the macro- (European and Middle East) and meso-levels, with police and army operating differently in the Yemeni and Tunisian territories.

Key Dates, Actors, and Institutions: Tunisia

1705–1955	Husaynid dynasty rules over Tunisia, a province of the Ottoman Empire
1856	A new capitation, the *mejba*, replaces an older tax imposed by the Ottomans
1861	A Grand Council is established in Tunis. First form of political representation
1864	Massive rural revolts against the *mejba*, crushed by Ottoman army
1881–1955	French Protectorate
1881	Signing of the Bardo Treaty generates rebellions in Sfax a few months later
1938	April 9: French police violently crush Tunisian nationalist protests
1952–1954	*Fellagha* resistance in the south and western part of the country after the assassination of UGTT leader Ferhat Hached
1956	March 20: Independence
	Monarchy abolished and Habib Bourguiba is chosen as Prime Minister and, later, President
	August 13: Women gained substantial rights with a new Personal Status Code
1987	"Medical coup" against Bourguiba. Zine El-Abidine Ben Ali becomes President
1991	Barakat Al-Sahel plot uncovered (a coup allegedly prepared by Islamists)
2008	Significant protests in the mines of the Gafsa and Rdayyaf regions

PSD	*Parti Socialiste Destourien*, ruling party under Bourguiba
RCD	*Rassemblement Constitutionnel Démocratique*, ruling party under Ben Ali, also called *Tajammu'*, "Rally" in Arabic
UGTT	*Union générale tunisienne du travail*

Key Dates, Actors, and Institutions: Yemen

1538–1635	First lasting presence of the Ottomans in Yemen
1839	Britain captures Aden. Governed from India until 1967
1849–1918	Second Ottoman occupation of (northern) Yemen. Sanaa taken in 1872

1859–1869	Construction of the Suez Canal
1911	Imamic–Ottoman condominium (Treaty of Da'an). Recognition of the Mutawakkil Kingdom of Yemen, ruled by Zaydi imams in the northern highlands
1918	Ottoman withdrawal from Yemen. British troops fail to take Hodeida (north)
1947	Establishment of a legislative council in Aden
1962–1970	Civil war in northern Yemen. Republicans (with Egypt's support) opposed to the Zaydi monarchists. Victory of the Republican side
1963	October 14: Start of the anti-colonial campaign in Southern Yemen
1967	November 30: Independence of Southern Yemen. Short internecine war between the two main anti-colonial factions: the NLF prevails over the more urban and labor-oriented FLOSY
1974–1977	Ibrahim Al-Hamdi, President of the Yemen Arab Republic (North), encourages local development associations (LDAs)
1978	Ali Abdallah Saleh becomes the fifth President of the Yemen Arab Republic
1990	Unification of the two Yemens as the Republic of Yemen (ROY)
1994	Short civil war opposing a secessionist wing of the YSP in the South to the North. July 4: Victory of the North
2004	First war in the Saada region, north of Yemen. Beginning of the Huthi movement
2010	President Saleh grooms his son as his successor in a constitutional amendment

FLOSY	Front of Liberation of the Occupied Southern Yemen
NLF	National Liberation Front, a rural-based Arab nationalist front that prevailed in the years after the creation of Southern Yemen in 1967. Become the YSP
YSP	Yemeni Socialist Party, established 1978. Ruled South Yemen (People's Democratic Republic of Yemen) until 1990
GPC	General People's Congress, ruling party established in 1982 by Saleh

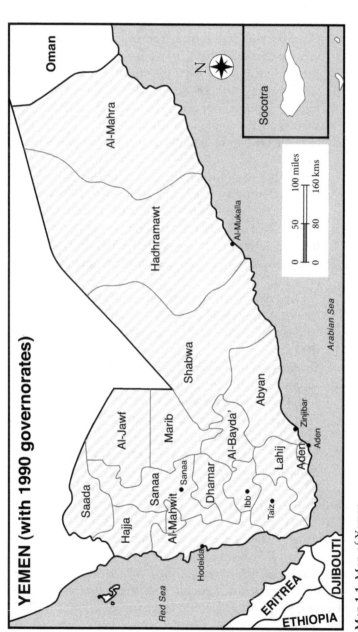

Map 1.1 Map of Yemen.

TUNISIA (with governorates)

Map 1.2 Map of Tunisia.

1 | Revisiting the Foundations of Citizenship: The Colonial Era

1.1 What Is in a Name? Citizenship, Violence, and Participation

No good sociological work or theory can emerge without a substantial historical grounding. Let us take a few steps back in the coming two chapters to deal with the "problem" of citizenship in the Arab Middle East before 2011. In this section, where I adopt a slow pace analysis, I will explain why latent citizenship has been the norm in the contemporary Middle East, rather than "citizenship" tout court like in Europe. In the Introduction, I suggested that demands for new representations – cultural and political – have been reconnected in a democratic manner with the management of violence during the 2011 Arab Uprisings. If these elements have been re-articulated, why were they disconnected or apart in the first place? To understand this, I propose to revisit, in a relational manner, the history of *state–society* relations, some key elements of *citizenship*, and the dominant theories that connect the management of *violence* to the issue of citizenship. This will reference the Middle East from the early colonial period, but with an eye on Europe as the region that influenced the thinking behind all of these concepts, and as the source of power and domination in and over the Middle East from the nineteenth century onwards.

Introducing Europe in this chapter does not mean taking it as model, nor as a normative yardstick.[1] What follow are ideal-types, modelized accounts of how granting rights to residents of a polity occurred in a variety of ways and with different constitutive, at times discriminatory, elements. Using such simplified paths to citizenship is meant to

---

[1] Here, I speak of "Europe" because the countries that were directly involved in the making of the modern Middle East are European. Later I will use "Euro-America" and "the West" to refer to the presence of the USA as another source of external influence.

revisit some doxas, or unquestioned truths, in both regions: Citizenship is inclusive and universal in Europe, according to the dominant political theory literature on advanced capitalist and liberal states, while it is defective and/or imperfect in the Middle East. I question this dichotomy of presence/absence and shed light on complex entanglements between European "citizenship," management and theories of violence, and forms of encroachment on the Middle East. These entwinements will have lasting detrimental consequences for civic participation in the Middle East, while they will be conveniently forgotten or omitted in core European theories of violence, and of the civilizing process. Like Gurminder Bhambra (2014), I hope to support "connected sociologies" that also work on "connected histories," with the ultimate goal of a better and thicker understanding of citizenship. This will be done by reconstructing the slow process of state-formation. Other large historical distortions, that undermined the prospect for equal citizenship, have existed elsewhere in the world, for example the legacy of slavery in Africa, the Caribbean, and the Americas (Bhambra 2015a; 2015b; 2019). In the Middle East, the key defining characteristic has been the impact of external encroachment and its impact on social, possibly also racialized, stratification, and on the management of physical coercion.

I do not take citizenship to be a narrow set of rights as a positivist might, but consider instead the larger historical and regional context that has given a certain coloring (repressive) and content (latent and at times negative) to the idea of Arab citizenship.[2] Additionally, relinking citizenship to violence sheds light on the unquestioned expectation that coercion can only be managed by a small body of institutions under the control of a reified thing called a "state," whose close association with a social body, society, citizenry, or whatever term is used to denote the masses or people is left out of the picture. In a nutshell, how are citizens, rather than formal state institutions, involved in drawing the border of what is a "legitimate use of physical coercion"?

One could offer a simpler account of Arab citizenship by showing the origins, debates, and legal evolution around the term "citizenship" in the MENA region starting from the current legal frames at play.[3] But

---

[2] Citizenship can be defined as "a set of equal entitlements and obligations vested in individuals with respect to the state" (Poggi 1990: 40).

[3] For such an approach, see Davis (1997), Butenschon, Davis, & Hassassian (2000), and Joseph (2000). Butenschon, Davis, & Hassassian (2000: 4) defines citizenship as the "contractual relationship between the state and inhabitants

this would amount, in my view, to describing the proverbial finger pointing at the moon, rather than looking at the moon in its entirety. Here the moon represents *the social life of citizenship*, by that I mean not only the legal and formal aspects of rights and duties (the positivist "finger"), but also the practice of pushing for more civic participation or negative forces resisting equal treatment. For example, the 1991 Yemeni Constitution affirmed equal citizenship for all, yet the practice and intensity of discrimination against various groups, in particular the *muhammashin* ("marginalized," in Arabic, also called *akhdam*, servants), has been repeated and virulent (Christiansen and Al-Thawr 2019: 125; B. Hall 2017). Thus the law does not reflect the practices and the social norms on the ground, hence the need to also study revealing informal sites of interaction. To return to the image of the finger and the moon, the finger is like a study of a proxy of democracy or citizenship, say an article of the constitution (equality in the Yemeni Constitution) or a narrow instance of citizens' life (holding an election). One can instead look at the moon, by concentrating on the much larger processes, contexts, and historical forces behind democracy – what I call the social life of citizenship.[4]

The social life of citizenship also means building an understanding of the transregional forces that allow for the emergence of citizenship relationally on both shores of the Mediterranean, and of the global forces that impact Arab citizenship. "Social life" also captures the less visible, sometimes contradictory actions that indicate a propension for civic engagement. This approach takes citizenship as "a practice of contestation through which subjects become political" (Bhambra 2015b: 107), with a specific focus on social groups and subjects who were historically marginalized or the object of predation by external actors. The "acts of citizenship" can be enactments of citizenship as they "instantiate constituents," even subjects who have often been considered strangers or outsiders (Isin & Nielsen 2008: 17, 37–38).

---

under its jurisdiction," which is, for me, too narrow: For example, the historical processes that brought these various states and jurisdictions into being are marginally discussed.

4 Other scholars have called this "citizenship work" (Bijl and Van Klinken 2019: 191) or "acts of citizenship" to move away from the actor-centered approach (with a person bearing rights conferred by the state) to the deed, the series of actions that give substance to "citizenship" (Isin & Nielsen 2008: 2).

The standard narrative is that modern states replaced the ancient regime systems of monarchies or feudal powers with a new form of authority, called legal-rational. Modern state formation contributed to a depersonalized type of rule replacing the personalism of absolutism. The new technique of power has been said to be introduced by a social contract, that is the image of a body of people constituting itself or creating, out of the many, a collective body who would entrust state authorities to rule over it. That contract, clearly a foundational myth that excluded many, vested the modern Leviathan with "legitimacy": it protected the population from a situation of war against all and organized the allocation of resources to perpetuate this protection of the collective whole. State-formation has been the equivalent of the "gradual monopolization of the legitimate means of violence with at its core a negotiation around the exchange of protection against taxation" (Kartas 2016). Laws and judiciary bodies sanctioned the details of how the social "contract" and mutual obligations were to be organized to cover the entire collective as equally as possible. Objective law (in the Weberian sense of the term) and bureaucracy replaced the personal authority of the *ancien régime* (the epitome of *subjective* law) and delegation to trusted vassals or deputies of the monarchs. This process coincided with the growing scale of commercial exchange favored by the isomorphic forces of capitalism, an economic system that needed predictability and stability to expand beyond the borders of domestic trade, thus replacing mercantilism as the dominant theory of economic exchange. That is the Weberian story of rationalization and modernity in the eighteenth and nineteenth centuries in which religions play only a minor role.

From the late nineteenth century until the decolonization period after WW2, each state acted in a concerted manner to re-shape the entire international system of sovereign states, in a manner that favored imperial expansions. This system consisted of a minimal delegation to a supranational body to facilitate peaceful exchange around the globe, the spread of commercial treaties at the international level, and the general outreach of commercial courts at the national level to guarantee that global trade and capitalist expansion.[5] The function and perception of law also changed during this gradual and difficult

---

[5] For such an account of the entanglements of capitalism, market, courts, and state, see Beaud (2002: 19–29).

transformation: From an imposed, often arbitrary, type of law under feudalism, absolutism, and the *ancien régime*, we moved to modern state law that became increasingly respected as people recognized the law was just rather than merely imposed.[6] In other words, with the advent of modernity (not an unproblematic transition, as we will see below), the justification for accepting laws shifted deeply: we moved from a situation of *jus quia jussum* – "it is law because it is ordered, commended" – which was typical under the *ancien régime*, to a setting of *jus quia justum* –"it is law because it is just" – under "modernity."[7]

As far as the management of coercion is concerned, the historical evolution was that a judicial process, distinct from the executive and the legislative, would provide oversight in a standardized application of laws. The latter generated the expectation of a similar result by any tribunal, whose sentence would then be enforced by security institutions such as the police and detention centers. With the consolidation of larger territorial entities, another institution of coercion, the army, gradually disappeared from domestic politics, and its task evolved towards the safeguarding of external borders. This process ensured a tormented and ferocious period of internal or civil wars that peaked with a forced homogenization of the population's profile, be it in religious, ethnic, or linguistic terms.

In Europe, the modern state took the specific form of a nation-state, that seemingly good or "natural" fit between "a people," imagined or forced, to share similar cultural traits (a language, a common ethnic origin, the same religion, or all of these) and a territory. Decades if not

---

[6] The recognition for the right to self-determination of the colonies was delayed to after WW2. The League of Nations was an imperial organization and it took the UN General Assembly resolution 1514 of December 1960 to put an end to the argument that colonized nations displayed "lack of preparedness" for independence.

[7] Poggi (1990: 29). I put quotation marks here to show that one has to take this narrative, here a historical reconstruction of "progress," with a pinch of critical salt. Indeed, as we will see below, that narrative suffers from a tunnel vision perspective and neglects relational and violent processes outside of this "modern core." Modernity occurred not only at the institutional level (state and capitalism), but also at a philosophical and individual level. On that account modernity helps in understanding how individuals developed a critical stance towards heteronomous authorities, or forms of power that could not be questioned until then (religion, absolutism, racism, etc.). In short: "to be modern is to quarrel with modernity," according to the quip of John G.A. Pocock (quoted in Cooper 2005: 277, fn. 24).

centuries of wars, mass forced conversions, or other coercive measures, not to mention mythologies and distortions in official historiographies, were essential to the "creation" of these nation-states. But the narrative, often couched in terms of a "contract,"[8] is that citizens were gradually given protection and formal rights in exchange for their willingness to remit part of their income through taxation and to fight for the preservation of their state and the defense of their territory. Citizenship, understood as the ability to exercise political rights, was originally only for a happy few, usually landed or propertied (white) males, able to pay a certain amount of tax, the censitary or elective franchise.[9] Qualified suffrage remained in force in many European countries throughout the nineteenth century, with many "marginalized" groups (women, the poor, enslaved and later manumitted people, etc.) facing duties (e.g. to serve in the army or to support war efforts) but bearing almost no political rights. To the gendered bias favoring men over women, one should not forget the broader impact of racialized privileges for white people over people of color under colonialism.

European peasants were turned into citizens by national education, military conscription, and social struggles when they joined the ranks of urban workers and the industrial proletariat.[10] Through strikes, decades of demonstrations, and demands for equality, second-class citizens and marginalized groups were gradually enfranchised, finally giving substance to the principle of "equal suffrage." But the massive participation in WW1 and WW2 of young men and women and of people of color (a shortcut to describe generally colonized subjects) led

---

[8] Contractualism emerges as a dominant theory with authors such as Locke, Hobbes, and Rousseau precisely at a time when modern states were emerging as the new norm. The grammar of a contract, or the way out of nature into a commonwealth or civil society (back then synonymous with the state), permeates liberal understandings of citizenship, understood as obligations, often gendered, between the state and its citizens.

[9] See, e.g. Bhambra (2015b: 105) for a discussion of the biases of "citizenship" against non-white and non-propertied persons.

[10] In the USA, it was migrants, at least those passing legally as whites, who became citizens by laboring a land that they were told belonged to nobody, and by embracing the "Manifest Destiny" of expanding the western frontier. Violence is also at play there, but is more individual, with the frequent isolation of the westward "conquest." After WW2, soldiers were rewarded with more or less free education in the USA, under the terms of the G.I. Bill, and desegregation that had started in military units in wartime gradually spread, not without difficulty, in the whole of American society, generating upward social mobility.

to a slow expansion of the franchise, or generated an initial impetus toward the recognition of their full political rights in the colonies. France mobilized 800,000 colonial workers and soldiers, some of whom asked for some form of representation after 1918 (Adi 2018: 90–91). West Indian soldiers fighting for Britain in Italy in 1918 also called for Caribbean independence because of the unfair treatment they encountered while in Europe. A later leader of the Trinidadian independence movement, Arthur Andrew Cipriani (1875–1945) established the first Caribbean League after West Indian soldiers were not given the same compensation as European soldiers in Taranto in 1918.[11]

There were also infamous cases of equality being violently denied after WW2. In French Algeria, on the day of armistice in May 1945, the 300,000 Algerians who had joined the French Liberation Army celebrated with French colonists the defeat of Nazi-Fascism. But when they used their own Algerian flag to celebrate, French police repressed these nationalist celebrations, leading to the killing of more than 40,000 Muslim Algerians in the towns of Setif, Guelma, and Kerrata (Benatouil 2020; Brower 2009; Fanon 1961/2004: 38). V-Day in Algeria is commemorated as "the carnages of 1945" (*majazir 8 may 1945* in Arabic). Acts of citizenship thus have different connotations on the two shores of the Mediterranean. They evoke also distinct memories that have a racial fracturing line: French Algerian communists condoned the massacres and "vilified the activists as fascists, despite the fact that the French army and settler militias killed many thousands of Muslim Algerians in a brutal campaign of repression" (Krais 2021: 114).

Industrialized economies responded to workers' pressure, while modern political and economic exchanges, via the state and the market, yielded a modicum of equal opportunities. These states still discriminated heavily against women, former enslaved and indigenous populations in the USA, Muslims in France, etc. Yet in one way or another, the standard narrative about the legitimacy of modern states – one might say the dominant fiction considering the atrocities committed in the twentieth century by European "modern states" – is that a handful of

---

[11] Cipriani later merged this soldier-based complaint with that of trade union activists, and paved the way to self-determination in the Caribbean region. See C.L.R. James (1932/2014) and Hinds (2012: min 24 of the video).

security institutions (police, army) were seen or presented as the legitimate bearers of physical coercion "protecting" a (culturally) homogenous
"nation," with the market serving as the less cumbersome venue to
allocate and distribute opportunities for economic development.[12] A
combination of economic opportunity, of the democratic effect of military
involvement in wartime, and of education contributed to an equalization
of citizenship in the twentieth century.

Political leadership of Euro-American states, with a degree of citizens'
and workers' involvement, *successfully articulated* the *means of coercion*
with the *means of interpretation* (culture, education) and protected
private ownership over the means of production (Poggi 1990). Such
a *result* of articulation did not happen out of the blue. There was more
than top-down liberality in the emergence of the modern state: There
were many instances of push back from below to demand more inclusion
or to fight for the definition of the regime that should inhabit this state.
Pierre Rosanvallon (2013) terms the result of such pressures the
"reformism of fear": Out of the anxiety of ruling elites in front of mass
mobilizations, or to undermine the influence of revolutionary ideologies
(anarchism and communism in particular) and of reformist programs
(socialism), concessions were made, allowing for the inclusion of portions of these demands.[13] The "social question" in the nineteenth century (Chartists, Luddites, Blanquists, socialists of all sorts), the fear of
international solidarity on the eve of WW1, and the spread of professional Leninist revolutionaries after this conflict, as well as the scattered
nationalist upheavals in colonies in 1919 and after (Irish and Chinese
nationalist revolutions, the redrawing of the Middle East, etc.) are the
most relevant factors that forced incumbent authorities towards reformism and a substantial extension of the political franchise.[14]

---

[12] The relation between market and democracy is widely discussed in political
theory. Joseph Schumpeter's (1942) idea of democracy as the epitome of
political entrepreneurship is one of these formulations. Karl Polanyi's (1944/
2001) account of the *Great Transformation* and of the idea of dis-embeddedness
offers an important critique to this connubial of democracy and market.

[13] Bhambra (2015a: 267–270) criticizes Rosanvallon for his silence on the Haitian
revolution and on the shadow that the slave trade has left on the mark of
European "citizenship." Trouillot (1995/2015: 99) makes a similar observation
on Eric Hobsbawm, who only "scarcely" mentions Haiti in his *The Age of
Revolution: 1789–1848*. Rosanvallon's observation about the relational impact
of the "reformism of fear" remains important.

[14] Think of the introduction of women's rights in many countries (e.g. Hume 2016)
or some measures towards self-determination after WW1.

The end result of citizenship "thus means that individuals at large possess (among others) specifically political capacities, interests and preferences, the exercise of which allows them to affect to a greater or lesser extent the content of state activity" (Poggi 1990: 28). So does the ideal type of the modern state, with democratic regimes as the "main game in town" for the political system, inhabit the form of the modern state.[15] The link between democracy and the modernity of the state (in particular whether there is an automatic connection) is still the object of wide debate.[16] This link is generally proposed because of elective affinity between the depersonalization of authority (Lefort's famous image of an empty seat)[17] and the democratic principle of power rotation. The necessity to strike a balance between different visions and social coalitions when it comes to disputing the control over the means of production (with capitalist actors forced to limit their greed in front of the power of the working classes' number and threat to disrupt, nationally or internationally, production and/or surplus extraction) forced the states to manage antagonism and protect some sense of pluralism. T.H. Marshall (1941/1992) has offered the standard account of citizenship, seen as a multi-tiered expansion of political, civic, and social rights in Europe. This idealized model, however, does not account for the colonial realities, nor does it address the condition of women, migrants or racialized subjects at large.

1.2 Missing Articulations, Encroachments, and Latent Citizenship

The modern Middle East did not experience a similarly "inclusive" transformation of citizenship. Let us elaborate on this thesis of an absence of citizenship, though it would be misleading to adhere

---

[15] The modern state is not automatically democratic. It can also be autocratic (Russia under Putin, Egypt under El-Sisi), monarchic (Morocco or Saudi Arabia), communist (Soviet Union), or totalitarian (Nazism in Germany). The main difference is that democratic regimes, including the variance between liberal and socialist, i.e. reformist types of democracy, guarantee pluralism and promote a unique degree of citizens' participation.

[16] For example, with theories of agonism, populism, or the diagnosis of post-democracy.

[17] The empty seat signifies the move away from markers of certainty (e.g. religion, traditional beliefs) and the end put to a situation of inherited authority (such as in monarchies). Instead, various groups constantly vie to capture the seat, but they are always replaced by new contenders (the unpredictability of modern democracy).

wholesale to a narrative of defective citizenship, simply because it does not look like that which took root in Europe. The Middle East is not alone in being described with a denunciatory tone that too often claims that non-European or non-capitalist societies lack the cultural fundaments, typically of liberal values,[18] for citizenship to emerge. Other area specialists from Asia, Africa, and Latin America have warned against these essentialist, culturalist, and Euro-centric interpretations, whereby only Europe or the Anglo-Saxon world harbor and defend a developed and multi-tiered form of citizenship, or "have" a "civil society."[19] Instead, many have shown that elements of citizenship can be found in these "peripheral" parts of the world. It simply does not match the content and form that "citizenship" took in Europe. If the T. H. Marshall or the Rosanvallon recipes could not produce inclusion and enfranchisement, it was not for cultural reasons but because of different social structures (stratification and/or non-homogenous populations),[20] dissimilar paths to class formation, and other structures of political economy (regime of property, etc.), all of which were particularly amplified because of massive processes of encroachment.

For example, scholars of the Middle East have shown the burst of civic activism, transgressive proposals to impose an egalitarian, republican order, or radical democracy (Chalcraft 2016: 198–277; Khuri-Makdisi 2010; Jakes 2020: 137, 184, 235) in the early decades of the twentieth century. However, these moments failed to produce suitable conditions to transform informal demands into representative democracy, sustain ephemeral citizens' acts, or anchor aspirations for political, social, and civil rights in new laws or a new political order. The next chapter will defend the simple thesis that the social life of citizenship of what is now called MENA was rich and vibrant. In particular, in the last third of the nineteenth and the first few decades of the twentieth centuries, quite revolutionary experiments in self-government were

---

[18] See Gellner's (1994) idea of the "modular man."

[19] See Bijl & Van Klinkel (2019) or Forment (2003) for a criticism of the defective theses in Asia or Latin America. I have tackled such narratives in Challand (2009) with regard to the absence of civil society in the Arab world and with regard to citizenship in Challand (2017).

[20] On the impact of diversity in Muslim majority society thinking about political leadership, see Masud (2005). On class formation in the Middle East, see Halperin (2005), and on class formation and democracy in general, see B. Moore (1969). Colonial rule by difference also deepened the tendency of colonial subjects to be seen as "irretrievably heterogenous" (Spivak 1988: 284).

implemented or called for by intellectuals and self-made political leaders in the region. Yet, democratic life sputtered in the twentieth century, and ruthless post-independence states prevented the emergence of rich, participative movements and thus the spread of citizenship (Meijer 2014; Challand 2017). The difficulty in manifesting democracy is best explained in terms of *hegemony* (that is the style of leadership based more on consent than on force or coercion) and of *various forms of encroachment* that altered the process of state-formation in the region. The rest of this chapter explains these phenomena.

First, let us dwell for a moment on the issue of articulations and on certain concepts that Italian thinker Antonio Gramsci made popular.

A Gramscian perspective is illustrative for three reasons. First, the literature that uses Gramsci's conceptual tool box sums up the problem of state–society relations in the Middle East in an elegant and complex manner: state and society are not automatically in opposition, but they can overlap and complement each other.[21] Second, the distinction that Gramsci draws between the two types of state, a repressive and an ethical state, will open ways to reconnect our apprehension of "the state" to democratic theory. Third, the Gramscian idea of concatenation and hegemony will serve as a springboard into the next part of the book, where we will discuss three facets of representation and analyze the nature of the democratic demands of 2011.

The late political scientist Nazih Ayubi provided the best summary to the problem of state–society relations in the Arab world from a Gramscian perspective.[22] Writing at a time when political scientists worried about the strength or weakness of states,[23] Ayubi (1995: 3) argued that the Arab states "are not strong, because they lack the infrastructural power that enables states to penetrate society effectively through mechanisms such as taxation," and because "they lack

---

[21] For Gramsci, the state can either be oppressive or the source of emancipation (via civil society) for the oppressed classed. It is not automatically bourgeois, as it is for Marxist-Leninist intellectuals. This explains why Gramsci became so relevant for political theory later in the twentieth century, and for the new left in particular. Brennan (2006: 239) identifies the recasting of Gramsci as a "radical refinement of Marxism" by Bobbio in the late 1960s as a turning point for the growing interest in Gramsci.

[22] I am quite confident that his analysis of Arab states is very much relevant for the Middle East as a whole, as many features described by the late Ayubi apply as well for Turkish, Kurdish, and Iranian politics.

[23] On these themes, see Skocpol, Evans, & Rueschemeyer (1985).

ideological hegemony (in the Gramscian sense) that would enable them to forge a 'historic' social bloc that accepts the legitimacy of the ruling stratum." It is because of this ideological weakness and the lack of unforced support from the population that state institutions become "fierce" or "ruthless," all terms that Ayubi prefers to the normative and loaded concepts of "strong" or "weak" states. For Ayubi, the Arab state is all muscle, imposition, or in Gramsci's terms it is a gendarme or corporatist repressive state (*stato carabiniere*), rather than an ethical state (*stato etico*).[24] The state is not an emanation of the community (as it should be for the Sardinian writer, who viewed state–society as one and the same, at least in its virtuous, socialist version) but instead embodies the interests of the bourgeoisie or of only a few social groups preying on state institutions and who are able to use the "legitimate" means of coercion against their own citizens. There is no coalescence between different social groups, or between the society and the state (coalescence is *iltiham* in Arabic,[25] a term close to hegemony, that is the complex unity of leadership and domination). Citizens do not share the "internalized consciousness and worldview of the state" (Ayubi 1995: 6), which would lead to a situation where the pacified state–society relations emerged as they did in Europe (because of the necessity to reconcile demands from the liberal bourgeoisie and from the working class). So is Ayubi's diagnosis. But why do Arab states lack this ability of coalescence (*iltiham*) or hegemonic rule?

The monumental work of Ayubi, which clusters different historical trajectories of state-formation in the Arab Middle East, explains this lack of articulation between the three means of control (means of coercion, of production, and of interpretation)[26] as the result of joined internal and external factors. For the latter, he lists colonial distortions, as well as a certain degree of cultural alienation with the form of the modern state (Ayubi 1995). Regarding the internal factors, Ayubi acknowledges that the economy has often developed along the lines of local interests

---

[24] The first formulation of this distinction in Gramsci dates from 1917. See Gramsci (1952: 76).

[25] Ayubi (1995: 6) and Salamé (1987). The Hans Wehr Dictionary (Wehr 1976) defines (727) *iltiḥām*, as "close union; cohesion; conjunction, connection, coherence." The term comes from the root verb *laḥama* (to mend, to patch), which, in its fourth form, means to "join in battle; to cling together; cohere; to be joined."

[26] See Poggi (1990) for a theoretical and sociological break down of power along these three lines. Stuart Hall's (2016) cultural sociology is also helpful to understand the roles of articulation.

(p. 105), or that bureaucracy was used in a clientelist manner and as a cushion for incumbent elites, and thus did not serve to defend the rule of law or anchor the legal-rational form of authority meant to protect citizens equally. In other words, bureaucracy in post-independence Arab states became the vector for personal privilege, and because of its immense size, like in the case of Egypt, a source of political inertia (Ayubi 1995: 102–105). Another internal factor stems from the state's inability to function as a social aggregator, or in Gramscian terms, as a political educator.[27] Ayubi follows the Moroccan historian Abdallah Al-ʿArawi [Laroui] for whom the Arab states may be "strong" in terms of "body" (i.e. certain apparatuses of the state), but the violence of this state is in reality an indication of its weakness and fragility. The state as a whole is weak because it lacks rationality and educational support (Laroui 1981: 146–158, 168, quoted in Ayubi 1995: 23).

Chalcraft, inspired by a neo-Gramscian interpretation of historical change as pulsated from below by "popular politics," concurs with Ayubi's main lesson on hegemony. In Arab societies, one cannot find hegemony, understood in Gramsci as the "spontaneous consent given by the great masses of the population to the general direction imposed on social life by the dominant fundamental group."[28] But this does not mean that politics is only "made" top down or by elites in charge of "the state." With his focus on informal politics and creativity, Chalcraft collects a rich series of episodes where Arabs, from below, have revolted and pushed for new forms of political participation that come close to what passes as "democratic action." This he terms "transgressive mobilizations" and distinguishes them from contained mobilizations for their ability to involve new social actors and propose new political paths and forms.[29] No doubt, 2011 was a moment of

---

[27] Ayubi (1995: 3–5). They also lack infrastructural power and ideological hegemony. Infrastructural power (as coined by Mann 1986) is the power that "enables states to penetrate societies affectively through mechanisms such as taxation" (Ayubi 1995: 3).

[28] As quoted in Chalcraft (2016: 30). Other components of hegemony are given by Guha: it is "a state in which a class establishes its dominance by relying more on consent of other classes than it does on coercion." Hegemony stands for a "condition of dominance such that persuasion outweighs coercion" (Guha as quoted in Chibber 2013: 35). A dominant social group can speak for the whole of the society in large part because coercion plays only a minor role.

[29] Chalcraft (2016: 191) characterized popular protests as associated "with dynamics of hegemonic contraction and expansion." This means "when authorities broke up existing sites of consent without replacing with new ones,

transgressive mobilization that involved creativity to contest the dominant political order.

The next chapter will deal with these episodes of "popular politics" (Chalcraft 2016). Citizenship *is* a practice and an ideal that local populations strive and have strived for, with or without the legal protections that usually come with citizenship. The environment and general conditions do not allow citizenship to be permanentized or consolidated. I will therefore concentrate on the main, general reasons that obstruct the substance and lasting manifestation of citizenship. A diachronic account of state–society relations and of the problem of violence is needed here to better understand the conundrum of citizenship–representation–violence, an issue that Ayubi did not engage with, instead focusing on the state as an organization and the "strength" of statehood. To create this account, I propose revisiting the impact of *external encroachments* on the region. The coming pages recount a geography of political exclusion that overlaps with what I call an uneven distribution of violence. The proposed alternative account of violence and representation will also lead us to question the dominant theoretical representations of citizenship and violence, so far presented as "standard narratives" or "foundational fictions," which we will question in greater detail below (Foucault, Elias, Weber, Tilly), in an effort to connect to the Arab experience of state-formation.

Talking about state–society relations in the region in a historical manner must start by identifying the origins of these states. Individuals and collectives of people have always existed, but they were only governed as large polities from the early modern period onwards. The question then is more about the "state" and when a central authority claiming obedience from a large community started appearing. For obvious reasons of space, I will not be able to re-narrate the variety of historical backgrounds that put contemporary Arab states in the orbit of what is termed the state system. Some are very old, such as Morocco, with monarchies ruling the region since the time of the original Muslim conquest; some are very new, such as the Gulf statelets, a British imperial invention of the twentieth century until their independence in the 1970s. Some were artificially created (typically in the Mashreq region, with the interwar Mandate period generating

and thus altered the existing balance of coercion and consent in favour of the former, protest was commonplace, especially in transgressive mode."

states with very little historical precedent, e.g. "Transjordan" or "Iraq") or ignored the right of large national groups (Kurds, Palestinians) to self-determination. Others have a long organic continuity, for example Egypt dating back to the Pharaonic dynasties, with scribes and bureaucrats helping to rule the territory for centuries, if not millennia.

Ayubi (1995: 99–132) has clustered the variety of experiences into four distinct paths of state-formation, namely the Egyptian, North African, Gulf, and Levant states. Even if Tunisia and Yemen, my two comparative countries, come from distinct paths in Ayubi's typology, I take their shared characteristic of being remote provinces of the Ottoman Empire as the basis for a similar path to state-making. They also share common features, such as being secondary to the priorities of the Sublime Porte (the Ottoman Empire), and both were impacted by French and British colonialism in a less frontal manner than say Algeria, Egypt, Palestine, or Jordan.[30] A very important difference between the cases of this book comes from divergent colonial policies, with lasting impacts on territorial rule: While France created a central bureaucracy during the colonial time in Protectorate Tunisia,[31] colonial rule in Yemen generated or heightened administrative and legal fragmentation. The issues of territorial and social fragmentations and the related obstacles for citizenship were important factors in the origins of the 2011 Uprisings for most, if not all, Arab countries (Chapter 3).

From this brief preliminary comparison, I hope to make clear that one needs to give considerable attention to external forces that might have prevented or altered the process of state-formation in the Arab Middle East. Ayubi sees colonialism, as well as the artificial nature of the idea of the state, as external factors. Before I discuss the idea of the "artificiality" of the Arab state, I propose considering colonialism as only one of three forms of external encroachments: colonial, imperial, and capitalist. These are the three ways or dimensions in which a series

---

[30] Yemen was also impacted by Ottoman colonialism, as argued by Kühn (2007; 2011), but in a rather superficial manner, as I will elucidate below.

[31] L. Anderson (1986); Perkins (2014). Even if legally a "protectorate" for the years 1881–1956, Tunisians speak of this period as *istiʿmār* (colonialism), and not as *manṭaqa maḥmiyya*, the technical term for "protectorate." For the long term impact of *istiʿmar*, see Al-Salhi (2017).

of external actors managed to intrude on the domestic process of state-making.

Encroachment means to intrude upon a person's or collective's territory or rights. To be sure, and throughout the globe, states have fought many wars to prevent such occurrences. This is because the distinctiveness of state power, or the capacity to rule by virtue of defending a state, is *paramountcy* and *ultimacy*. What does that mean? In the best sociological account of *European* state-formation,[32] Gianfranco Poggi (1990: 9) describes paramountcy in "particular as safeguarding a given society's territorial boundaries against aggression and encroachment from outsiders." Defending the integrity of its territory is paramount for any state, in particular for post-Westphalian, modern states. This capacity resides in another characteristic of state power, namely ultimacy in the use of violence. Says Poggi (1990: 9–10): "Violence – or the threat of it – appears as the facility of last resort in shaping and managing interpersonal relations, for it operates by causing sensations and activating emotions which all sentient beings experience, and which in their rawer forms do not even presuppose the quality of humanness in those on whom it is brought to bear."

What happens in a region such as the Middle East, where numerous entities encroach on the state's privileged right to rule or organize a unified institution of coercion? There are dozens of modern and contemporary cases where this happens in the Middle East: British colonial rule over Egypt, with nominal Egyptian autonomy and key functions (ministries of defense and the interior) under British control; British and then Israeli colonial control over Palestinians up to the present day; French annexation of Algeria as part of its territory in 1832; John Baggot Glubb's ("Glubb Pasha," a British officer) rule of the (Trans)Jordanian army between 1936 and 1953. More recently, we can think of the existence of Lebanese militias undermining the authority of the national army; the Sinai Peninsula, a substantial part of Egypt, where the Egyptian army cannot operate since the Camp David agreement; private security companies granted extra-territoriality around strategic assets, typically oil wells in many countries of the region. By expanding only slightly to include more-or-less coerced agreements or

---

[32] I insist on the fact that Poggi offers only an account of *European* state-formation, even if he describes his theorizing as a *general* account of state-formation.

leases, one can cite the large docking infrastructure granted to Russian and American maritime forces in Tartus (Syria) and the Persian Gulf; Turkish and Russian military bases in Sudan; Israeli bases in Eritrea; Chinese, French, German, and US bases in Djibouti; and the forced use of Yemeni waters in Socotra by the United Arab Emirates (Melvin 2019; Aggestam et al. 2009: 340–342). Are there as many instances of forced encroachment for advanced capitalist polities? We can think of "western" instances like Gibraltar, a British enclave in Spain, Ceuta and Melilla in Morocco, or Guantanamo in Cuba, but all are remnants of colonial or imperial times. If there are so many cases in the Middle East, what does that say about the process of state-formation there?

In my view these encroachments matter much more than the debate about the artificiality of the Arab states. They insidiously weaken the social life of citizenship in these polities. It is important to distinguish between different forms of encroachment. This has become urgent in light of some confusion in the quarters of "postcolonial" or "decolonial" studies that often simplify distinct or complex historical processes (e.g. conflating modernity with modernization; hypostatization of "colonialism" taken as a ready-made plan carried out by a state, instead of as a multi-tiered process of encroachment and domination). Colonialism is a distinct form to exercise an outsider's authority over another territory. It is often confused with capitalist intrusion or with the isomorphic pressure that capitalism exercises globally. And to make things more complicated, colonialism often comes with imperialism, but not automatically. Let us try to undo these concepts and provide clear definitions.[33]

One can identify a **capitalist mode of encroachment** as a situation in which private individuals or corporations establish a legal presence on an external territory and push for ad-hoc regulation for the privileged extraction of economic surplus in that territory, now known as a colony, and/or the refusal to respect local laws and institutions. This impinging presence and more-or-less legally coerced extraction can be done with or without the support of the capitalists' country or state of origin. For example, we will encounter Italian capitalist actors interfering in Yemeni politics in the early twentieth century without an explicit policy from the Italian government to establish an Italian presence there. We could also give the example of a landlocked, neutral

---

[33] Unless stated otherwise, the following definitions of forms of encroachment are mine.

country, Switzerland, with some of its famous citizens (Henry Dunant, the founder of the International Red Cross) or non-state actors (pharmacies or missionary groups), working to create colonies in Algeria or India.[34] It was often private actors impinging on primary resources and creating the first paths and activities for trade that made colonialism possible. In many historical cases, capitalist encroachment *preceded* colonialism, typically in the Middle East or in the sixteenth- and seventeenth-century Americas. But capitalist encroachment does not automatically generate colonialism. Think of the Brazilian case of Fordlandia, a large-scale project by the US car magnate Henry Ford (1863–1947) who tried to establish a rubber factory in the middle of the Brazilian Amazon between the late 1920s and 1940s (Grandin 2010). Ford, who was famous for his union-busting actions in the USA, made no secret that he would not tolerate the application of Brazilian laws on his Brazilian property, which he considered a de facto US territory. Hence, Henry Ford felt unfettered in his efforts to undermine unionization efforts, even by violent means, for example hiring thugs to intimidate workers (Grandin 2010: 70, 308). This is an example of capitalist infringement that undermines the exercise of workers' and citizens' rights in an otherwise sovereign country. Elsewhere, private chartered companies, such as the various West Indies Companies or the Dutch East India Company, enjoyed great autonomy and almost no legal oversight by, or accountability to, state organisms. Slavery, an institution with the most abject involvement in violence, was initially a feature of private entities, with "the state" looking the other way. But in all cases, capitalist encroachment needed legal mechanisms, be it consular protection for capitalist actors to operate in that alien territory, or the signing of treaties or agreements with local populations that resulted from a massive asymmetry of resources and arm-twisting.

The **colonial mode of encroachment** refers to a bundle of official policies and actions aiming at the (partial or full) political control of

---

[34] See Lüthi, Falk, & Purtschert (2016). On church and missionaries in the Middle East, see Makdisi (2009) or Vitalis (2006), who show the multiple connections within American families with some members involved in missionary or university activities in the Middle East while others were creating an extension of their mining and industrial activities in the region. One thinks of the Phelps-Dodge family, famous for the foundation of what is now the American University in Beirut, and their involvement in the copper and mining industry both in the USA and in Saudi territories and Cyprus.

another country in order to exact a privileged (for the metropolis) extraction of resources, and preserve access to land resources via selective migration patterns. It exerts its authority by heightening the rule of difference and by limiting rights for the local population. In Maxime Rodinson's (1973: 92) apt phrase, colonialism is "occupation with domination and emigration with legislation." Colonialism has existed in many forms and, in this definition, is moved forward by a sovereign state, which aims at subjugating another territory. The dichotomy of settler colonialism vs. franchise colonialism (one moving a population *en masse* from the metropole, the other focusing on trade and the movement of commodities) is misleading, especially when it associates France with the former and England with the latter. In reality, both empires used a variety of colonial forms. It is more accurate to think of colonialism on a continuum, on which one can locate settler colonies, *colonie de défrichement*, penal colonies, military colonies, *entrepôt* colonies, franchise colonies, and agricultural or plantation colonies (Stoler 2016). This is for the *forms* of colonialism. It is also important to underline the *objectives* or the *results* of these various forms of external intervention. The aim of colonialism is the "utter transformation of the colonized culture: the eradication of its structures of feeling, the subjection of the population to the colonizer's notions of legality and citizenship and the displacement of indigenous forms of religion, labour, patriarchy and rule by those of colonial modernity" (Lloyd 1999: 2). That additional definition encapsulates indirect or informal elements of colonial rule and makes visible the mental, linguistic, religious, racial, or cultural properties of colonial rule. In other words, if material and capitalist interests are an essential reason behind colonialism, there are other manifestations behind capitalism that can include symbolic domination, cultural annihilation and the coloniality of power.[35]

Finally, the **imperialist mode of encroachment** is the project ensuring the subordination of distant political economies to processes of accumulation in the core capitalist states.[36] Like colonialism, it is a set of

---

[35] The Peruvian intellectual Anibal Quijano distinguishes colonialism from "coloniality of power," that is the concern that "ways of being and thinking, such as the body and mind, labor exploitation, racialization and gender socialization," remain rooted in the "historical condition of colonialism." See Quijano (2014: 285).

[36] Hanieh (2013: 12–13 and 97), who also adds that imperialism is based on a dual tendency of competition and rivalry between global hegemons at the economic, political, and at times also military level.

policies proposed by a powerful state, but unlike colonialism, imperialism does not always necessitate the presence or direct involvement of the country of origin in that subordinated entity (a territorial takeover or, in the current lingo, "boots on the ground"). Thus, imperialism worked as an agreement among European powers when they agreed on racial criteria to justify mass enslavement, expropriation of land, and denial of rights even before they set out to colonize those purportedly inferior groups (Getachew 2019: 84). In Julian Go's (2012: 7) account, imperialism is "a sociopolitical formation wherein a central political authority (a king, a metropole, or imperial state) exercises unequal influence and power over the political (and in effect the sociopolitical) processes of a subordinate society, peoples, or space."[37] Go also notes that colonialism is not the only way to exert imperial influence over societies: Imperial influence can also take the form of "informal dependency, weak ally, or client," but imperial power has the means, historically through the military, to make sure that the vassals will stay in line with these imperial policies and strategies.

In this book, I will distinguish imperialism from neo-imperialism to indicate that the central might has moved from military and fiscal channels of imperialist subjugation (claiming unique control over a vassal) to new forms of intimidation, such as financial or cyber bullying, which take place by different powers acting at the same time (a different configuration from past imperialism, which was more of a zero-sum game). Historically, imperialism went hand in hand with colonialism and radiated from leading economic powerhouses (USA, Japan, Europe). Nowadays, neo-imperialism does not automatically rely on military power, but on massive financial and economic asymmetries. It follows a multi-directional map, rather than one based on the center–periphery logic of expansion, because of new economic powerhouses, in particular China and some Gulf states (Saudi Arabia and the UAE), competing for influence in North Africa, Yemen, and the Horn of Africa.[38]

Both colonialism and imperialism strive to subordinate another population's territory, but they benefit from different resources to do

---

[37]   Go (2012: 7, 10) states that imperialism comes with *imperial policies*, which are official and stated plans and practices by which power is exercised. They formulate various *strategies* and deploy multiple *tactics*, *techniques*, or *modalities* – sometimes unstated or unofficial – to realize their policies and extend or sustain themselves.

[38]   On these new imperial actors, see Hanieh (2013).

so. While colonialism flexes economic and political muscles, it is mostly the prerogative of imperialism to activate military might to achieve unique possession or control of a given territory. Colonialism usually comes with some form of coercion, as suggested by Martin Thomas (2012), but systemic exaction of violence is the appanage of imperialism. Thus, Italy could be considered an imperial force in its actions towards Libya, Eritrea and Ethiopia (Abyssinia) in the early twentieth century, but not when it comes to the presence of Italian actors in Tunisia or Yemen, where it is more accurate to speak of a capitalist mode of encroachment. As a result, imperialist modes of encroachment inflict much more direct and profound damage on native societies.

What do these definitions add to the texture of the argument about citizenship? They should make clear that encroaching powers[39] have leaned on a multiplicity of techniques of domination, many of which include force, violence, cultural discourses of difference, and civic denials: According to the logic of domination and the rule by difference, only "Europeans" were full citizens in these alien territories.[40] European, and later Japanese and American, encroaching powers have grown "at home" precisely because of sheer force and the abusive extraction of resources from the "peripheries." Thus, the "linear narrative" of enfranchisement and modern capitalist expansion acquires a new transnational and relational dimension.[41] All of a sudden, the Weberian thesis of the "spirit of capitalism" that, combined with scientific progress and "great discoveries," explains why European and Atlantic powers became a hegemonic block and eclipsed past Asian powers does not hold. Fred Cooper concludes that the "great divergence"[42] between Europe and other parts of the world

---

[39] The three modes of encroachment certainly overlap. They often express their effects in the shadow of one another, or with one anticipating or facilitating the work of the other. Various parts of the world have their own specificities when it comes to modes of, and impact of, encroachment: distance between the conquered territories and the metropolis; types of resources or strategic advantages at stake; degree of imperial rivalries; etc.

[40] On the idea of the "rule of colonial difference," see Chatterjee (1993: 16).

[41] See also the fascinating account by Laleh Khalili (2013) on the circulation of repressive anti-insurgency techniques in imperial times and their relevance in liberal politics, all the way to the present day.

[42] Namely the question as to why Asia and Europe were on par in terms of economic potential and development until the eighteenth century, yet one emerged much more powerful, economically and politically, two centuries later. See Pomeranz (2000).

ought not to be understood with an internalist, culturalist explanation (Weber's thesis, or Europeans' alleged superiority or supposedly innate inclination for "reason" or "science"), but rather should be set in relation to the European ability to *deploy fiscal-military power* and sheer coercion across the globe. Because of the European move away from mercantilism to capitalism, and then because of the destructive innovations set in motion by capitalist actors, colonies and empires emerged as a way to reinforce the novel advantage of "free lands" and forced labor (slavery) in the Americas. The end result of this process of colonial extraction was state-formation, not only to create an organic home for an invented nation, but mostly to protect global imperial advantages. For Cooper (2014: 120), it is the "Empire that made the British state, not the other way around." Paraphrasing this with the concepts presented so far, I would submit that it is capitalist first, followed by a combination of colonial and imperial encroachments that have not only made the state in Europe, but have also left in tatters the possibility of enfranchising, democratic relations between Arab societies and their states. This is important to bear in mind, for when one speaks of colonialism, one too often assumes an original plan prepared by a "state" (the British Crown, the French Empire, the Belgian monarchy). Private actors led the way for encroachment, and with colonial and imperial intrusion, the exchange of taxes for protection, which had been at the heart of feudal authority in the Ottoman Empire, was transformed into a clientelist pattern of fragmentation that favored European interests and deepened their involvement in the region. Obviously, knowledge, discourses of civilization or progress, and arguments about cultural maturity have also been part of the raw force of, or justification for, encroachment.

Let us now see how these forms of encroachments hampered the development of a democratic compact inside Arab polities, with a focus on Tunisia and Yemen.

1.3 Historical Accounts of Early State-Formation in the Middle East

The Arabic term for the "state," *dawla*, or more precisely its new meaning to describe a state, as opposed to the earlier meaning of dynasty, dates back to the first third of the nineteenth century, 1837 to be precise, if we are to believe Ayubi (1995: 22).[43] The new meaning to the term thus antedates European colonialism in the Arab worlds, which started in earnest as a full-fledged system with far-reaching regulations in the last third of the nineteenth century. It can therefore be argued that the idea of the modern state is not a cultural importation or imposition, as Badie claimed it was.[44] This does not mean that the "Arab states" had a clear form and content from the onset, nor do I minimize the cases of artificially drawn borders or cases of negated statehood by European mandatory powers in the post-Ottoman region, with Greater Lebanon carving out some territory from Syria, Palestine, Transjordan, and Iraq, or the denied Kurdish state.[45] But all contemporary Arab states had a historical kernel, or a basis of local administration that was already at play in the nineteenth century, and most Arab and Kurdish societies started developing a sense of nationalism toward the end of that century. Both countries under consideration in this book, Tunisia and Yemen, emerged from the rather lax control of the Ottoman Empire, which often delegated authority to a deputy alien in Tunisian or Yemeni society. It is around this minimal delegated authority that a "Tunisian" or a "Yemeni" state emerged. For the Ottoman North African entities, Lisa Anderson (1986: 65) speaks of garrison states, to which a growing body of bureaucratic and legal institutions was gradually attached to form a proto-modern state. Let us see briefly how these garrison states came into existence.

After the capture of Constantinople in 1453, the Ottomans conquered North Africa in the sixteenth century, with Sinan Pasha reaching Tunis in 1574 and Algiers shortly after. They posted vassals in Algiers, Tunis, and Tripoli, with the three Maghreb regencies benefiting from varying degrees

---

[43] In classical Arabic, for example in the Qur'an, the term *dawla*, whose roots mean to alternate, to rotate, to change periodically, is associated with the notion of dynasty, of rotating, alternative power, and has thus a very different root than the Greco-Roman root of *statis*, i.e. standing, staying in place. *Dawla* became synonymous with the (modern) state from the early nineteenth century onward.

[44] See Badie (2000) but also an opposite view in Bayart (1993).

[45] Even if there were no formal Lebanese, Palestinian, or Syrian states before the twentieth century, there were pre-existing administrative units and provinces within the Ottoman Empire that correspond, broadly, to these newly formed states. In Doumani's (1995) account of a nascent Palestinian bourgeoisie, one sees that the geographical space corresponding to historical Palestine already existed back in the early nineteenth century as a space of socio-economic exchange. In Salame's (1987: 8) apt phrase, "There are no *terra nullius*." It is therefore misleading to say, *in globo*, that Arab states are artificial entities.

of autonomy (Kartas 2016: 3). These local vassals held different titles: A *Bey* (an Ottoman title equivalent of "regent" or governor") ruled, from Tunis, a territory that corresponds more or less to modern Tunisia (then also called *Ifriqya* for "Africa"); there were two others beys, but called locally *deys*, with one based in Algiers commanding what is now Algeria, and the other in Tripoli for Libya; while a *Khedive*, or "viceroy" in conjunction with Mamluks, an exogenous military formation, was in charge of the Egyptian province of the Ottoman Empire. For Yemen, the Ottomans also delegated authority to a *vali* (governor of an Ottoman province), but in two distinct periods, first at the time of the maximal expansion of Ottoman trade with the Indian Ocean, namely between the 1538 and 1635 (Casale 2010: 64), and again between 1849 and 1911/ 1918 (Honvault 2012: 275). The second period ended in 1911 with the recognition of a Zaydi monarchy in the northern highlands, but Ottoman units remained there until 1918, when they withdrew from Arabia Felix. Some have argued that this second occupation amounts to a case of colonialism over northern Yemen by the Ottomans (Kühn 2007).

As in feudal structures, local authority was transmitted, providing approval by the Sublime Porte and a certain amount of tributes and presents to the Sultan, in a dynastic manner. "Rule by difference" (Barkey 2008) was a typical means of governance that the Ottoman sultan practiced throughout the empire, accepting a certain degree of autonomy in the remote provinces in exchange for the regular flow of taxation. Barkey argues that the Ottoman Empire could live so long precisely because it was built on, and included, diverse segments of its population and granted local autonomy to manage various parts of the empire. In other words, informality maintained the Ottoman Empire. But when it was forced to implement formal measures to promote the same standards in the mid-1850s, the Sublime Porte quickly reached the point of implosion. By and large, only inchoate state forms existed under the Ottomans in these two countries, with weak uniform administrative practices and Ottoman deputies only thinly recognized as legitimate by local populations.

In Tunisia, cities along the coast were expected to pay their dues, and raids were organized by the Bey twice a year to collect taxes in rural areas, in particular in the south of the country. It is estimated that 20% of the (garrison) state revenue of Tunis around 1800 was generated by maritime commerce and revenues from corsairs and privateering (L. Anderson 1986: 39). All 19 Beys who ruled Tunisia from the *qasba*, the walled old city of Tunis, were from the Husaynid dynasty, which lasted from 1705 to 1955 (Perkins 2014: 17, 130).[46] The Beys, like the Khedives in Egypt, were perceived as alien by the local population (Laroui 1982; Ayari 2016). This fed numerous quests for political change and eventually facilitated the rise of Arab nationalisms: Ottoman elites in North Africa, some of whom could not even speak Arabic, became the targets of attacks under growing nationalist aspirations. But these feelings were also exacerbated by the colonial endeavor and European brutalities.

Yemen was also involved with maritime commerce and custom houses in Mocha and Aden (Casale 2010: 64), and to a lesser extent in oversight over the cities of Taiz in the north and the hinterland cities of the Hadhramawt, which absorbed riches generated by trade between the Mediterranean and India, and from there to the rest of Asia. The Ottomans never managed to fully control the entire northern Yemeni provinces, with Sanaa only taken in 1872. In the first period of Ottoman rule in Yemen, an annual tribute was collected by the *vali* and sent not to Istanbul, but to the treasury in Egypt (Casale 2010: 64), and the main competitors were Portuguese traders who had established rival trading routes towards India. That shifted in the nineteenth century, with Britain as the main rival. In 1839, Britain managed to capture Aden, which they occupied until 1967, while the Ottoman Empire re-established its control over Mocha in 1849, and from there over Sanaa. Typical of Britain's franchise colonies, the Crown only controlled Aden and made alliances with local potentates, like the Sultan of Lahj or the Emirs of the Hadhramawt (a geographical space corresponding to late-twentieth-century South Yemen). It secured its rule through a policy of *divide ut imperes*, building direct relations with a large number of local rulers, whose claims they pledged to uphold (Dresch 2000: 37). This territorial breakup favored the existence of small armed forces acting locally and often preventing a larger national identification.

In Yemen, because of the competition between different historical figures, there was less of a process of organically growing Yemeni nationalism – as a matter of fact it emerged only later in the 1940s as

---

[46] They were surrounded by medinal elites with a traditional Islamic education in Zaituna, one of the oldest universities in the world and one of the historical hubs, with Kairouan, for the Sunni Maliki school of jurisprudence. Medina ("city" in Arabic) refers to the old walled city in historical towns of the Maghreb.

a result of other Arab nationalist projects in the Middle East. The *vali* appointed by Istanbul were bureaucrats and never established a dynasty, like the Husaynids in Tunisia or the Karamanli in Libya. Rather, intra-European competitions, in particular between Italy and Britain, led to factionalism in what would become North Yemen. The Ottomans, unable to take control over the entire mountainous regions of the north, had to accept a Zaydi leader, Yahya Hamid ad-Din, as an interlocutor thanks to the support he was able to muster within tribes from the northern Saada region (Brandt 2019b: 12). After various military skirmishes, the Ottomans signed a treaty with him and considered him the legitimate ruler of Yemen in 1911 in exchange for the continuous nominal rule of the Ottomans over the entire region.[47] Britain and Italy, by different means, tried to intervene in the north of Yemen, Britain by supporting Muhammad Al-Idrisi, the head of the rival dynasty in the Asir region (Dresch 2000: 31), and Italy by being the first state to recognize the sovereignty of Imam Yahya in 1912 (Honvault 2012: 278). This intra-European rivalry over the rights to commerce in the gray zones of the not-so-clearly defined borders between "northern" and "southern" Yemen (Dresch 2000: 219) was meant to establish trade monopolies between various parts of Yemen and the Red Sea. The most active Italian actors were not government officials but capitalist entrepreneurs (Blumi 2011: 91–115).

The emergence of a modern state in Northern Yemen in the 1930s is paradoxical in that its recognition by international actors (Saudi, Britain, and European powers) reinforced indirect encroachments: by creating modern institutions of control over borders to regulate the trading rights of this tribe or that foreign company, Yahya's imamate alienated parts of his own people. In the 1930s, with the Taef treaty, Yahya gave up three northern provinces to Saudi Arabia. The tribes affected took it badly: they supported Yahya against the Ottomans, then had to pay taxes to the Imam, and now were losing commercial advantages from the trade along the new Saudi border (Bonnefoy 2018: 55). Anthropologist Marieke Brandt (2019b: 12, 17) analyzed how these episodes generated long-term resentment in the north of the

---

[47] On the circumstances that led the Ottoman Empire to sign the Treaty of Da'an in October 1911, and to recognize the Mutawakkil Kingdom of Yemen, see Kühn (2007; 2011). *Al-Mutawakkil 'ala Allah* ("he who relies on God") has been the regnal name of Imam Yahya Muhammed Hamid Ad-Din since 1890 (Dresch 2000: 5).

country and how some tribes, in particular the Khawlan bin Amir, joined coups against the Zaydi imams in 1948 and 1962, with ramifications for the current civil war.

Indeed, some Yemeni groups resented certain agreements taken by their central authorities and generated the spread of smuggling activities. This impossible integration of the "peripheries" along the northern–southern and the Saudi borders is a classic problem for state-formation: Rather than building universal territorial control, the exercise of central authority precipitated peripheral resistance and, at times, episodes of armed conflict. Thus, Blumi demonstrates the existence of mixed and entangled local, national, and (British and Italian) imperial agency, and the long history of embattled central authorities that create the conditions for their non-acceptance by their own citizens. Blumi also forces us to rethink the idea that borders were always impositions by external actors: In the Yemeni case, some local actors, in zones of authority disputed by the Ottomans to the north and to the British Protectorate in the south, were able to tease out the competition between state and colonial actors to gain some benefits. "The borders of [Yemen] in the end were the results of bureaucratic reactions to indigenous agency" (Blumi 2011: 104).

After a rich period of territorial and maritime growth (the sixteenth to eighteenth centuries, but with little administrative unification), the Ottomans responded to the growing encroachments of European powers with standardized administrative measures and "defensive developmentalism" (Gelvin 2011: 71–86). The small-scale commercial challenges from Europeans dating back to the Capitulations became a growing headache for Istanbul, once Europeans grew economically. The sixteenth-century Capitulations became a huge breach for Europeans to exploit in the nineteenth century. These agreements, stipulated between the Ottoman Sultan Suleiman I (Suleiman the Magnificent) and French King François I in the 1530s, gave France the status of protectors of Christian minorities in the Ottoman Empire. What was initially a French privilege soon became competition among Europeans to obtain similar rights for their co-nationals. Each consul in the south and southeast Mediterranean managed de facto economic privileges. Local diplomatic protections for Europeans opened the door to mercantile and soon capitalist interactions. Increasingly in the nineteenth century, private gain and interests motivated consular actions. Thus, the capitalist mode of encroachment, made possible by diplomatic treaties, facilitated subsequent colonial and imperial modes of encroachment. In the same manner, military intervention was often carried out alongside indirect and direct colonial purposes.[48]

On top of the Capitulations, the origins of external encroachments into Beylical Tunisia and Khedivian Egypt are three-pronged. First, the territorial expansion by France into Egypt (1798) and Algeria (1830) titillated the spirit of other European powers, creating rivalries for control over the territories. Later, the British imperial policies to control navigation routes in and through the Mediterranean added to French colonial expansion. Thus, (French) Malta returned to British possession after the Vienna Congress in 1815, while Cyprus was taken from the Ottomans by Britain in 1878. No wonder that French and British capital were the most instrumental for the construction and appropriation of the Suez Canal, built between 1859 and 1869, which gave a much more direct route to Asia. Second, capitalist competition was combined with pressures to modernize state, educational, and military infrastructures. Faced with the speed of European expansion and success in the nineteenth century, Ottoman, Egyptian, and Tunisian elites all tried to emulate the European model of rationalism by establishing secular institutions of education and new military training schemes. They also sent their elites for training in Paris, Berlin, or London, precipitating a series of half-baked reforms that sped up the indebtedness of both countries. Imamic Yemen did the same a few decades later, sending some of its elites to Iraq and Jordan. Third, the regime of capitulations, with numerous consular offices and privileges, facilitated a gradual implantation of not only French and British, but also Italian and German interests in these countries. Europeans thus established an ineluctable economic (through debts) and commercial (via navigating routes) grip over weakened Ottoman authorities in the second half of the nineteenth century. Istanbul was forced to sign treaties favoring free trade for Europeans, sanctioning the increase of external encroachments over the region (Gelvin 2011: 158–164): immunities for British ships and its personnel, the right to purchases within the Ottoman Empire without taxes, and weakened Ottoman

---

[48] Keddie (1991) thus notes that the *marginal* advance of European powers (not only nascent industrial forces, but also colonial powers) was transformed into *decisive* power by thwarting peripheral countries' efforts to industrialize as well.

control on its monopolies.[49] France and, later, Italy increased their presence in the Mediterranean and soon encroached as well.

In Tunisia, the Ottomans tried to bolster their income and to extract taxation from the rural hinterland to cover the cost of these reforms (L. Anderson 1986: 54–55). To do so, the ruler made an alliance with the rural nobility, attempted to set monopolies on trade such as olive oil, tobacco, and salt, and established a standing army of local recruits. A new poll tax, the *mejba*, replacing older Ottoman taxes, was introduced in 1856 for regions outside of the five large urban centers of Tunis, Kairouan, Sousse, Sfax, and Monastir, a heavy taxation that provided 40% of the Beylical state budget (Ganiage 1966: 858–859). These measures generated splits within the population and resistance to the pressure of taxation, especially in the western and southern parts of the country. With de facto little extraction, irregulars supplemented the army for tax collection, which further alienated the population at large. Under Sadiq Bey (ruling 1859–1882), the building of a 22,000-strong army cost so much that rural revolts became massive in 1864 (Ganiage 1966: 859) and remain deeply anchored in the memory of Tunisians from the south of the country during interviews I carried out there in 2017.[50] All of these military reforms left agriculturalists and pastoralists embattled and with a bitter sense: rural and tribal leaders felt they were forced to send conscripts (L. Anderson 1986: 60, 68). To remedy this situation, the Bey granted some benefits to and coopted rural leaders (*qaʻid*, in Arabic). For a period, the situation improved, but the efforts to maintain internal peace came with patrimonialism. Bitterness remained strong for rural pockets (L. Anderson 1986: 77, 80; Perkins 2014: 61). The shift to commercialization gave profit only to the capital and a few notables. A constitution passed in 1861 introduced a modicum of

[49] For example, the 1838 Commercial Convention between Britain and the Ottoman Empire, as a result of the British help in ousting Mehmet Ali from Syria in 1838 (Gelvin 2011: 158–159).

[50] Mahdi Al-Ghamd, retired school teacher, interview in Tataouine, 01/03/2016. He connected the 1864 rebellions because of the doubling of the *mejba* (tax, in classical Arabic *majban*), with the resistance to the imposition of the French Protectorate in the period 1881–1889, and the *fellagha* resistance in the years between 1952 and 1954. He puts the center of Tunisia in the same situation as the south, when it comes to heavier violent repression. These memories are also evoked in the 2018 documentary *Voice of Kasserine* (IA 2018: minutes 20–26), around the insurgency led by Ali Ben Ghedhahem in the Kasserine region. On French colonial violence in Tunisia and the specific resistance in the southern and central parts of the country, see Bénot (2005: 159, 187–188).

representation with a Grand Council (*majlis akbar*) and unity of treatment of the Bey's subjects, but this legal reform turned out to be another instrument of central control. The courts were loaded, and the rural poor, peasants, and those not connected to the Bey or local elites were systematically discriminated against (L. Anderson 1986: 82).

Other hastily devised schemes, such as military modernization in Tunisia under Ahmad Bey (Perkins 2014: 19–22), resulted in expensive taxes that proved ruinous, just like in Egypt. The twelfth and thirteenth beys were under such a heavy load of debts that giving up to the French under the format of a protectorate was a modest face-saving result for them. In Tunisia, it was an ambush by a group of Algerians in February 1881 that handed the French a pretense to put a siege on the Bey's palace (Perkins 2014: 15). General Bréart marched on Tunis from the harbor city of Bizerte in the north of the country and obtained the Bardo Treaty of 1881. The Treaty acknowledged the Bey's sovereignty but placed "Tunisia external relations under the supervision of a French resident minister and its army under the command of a French general" (Perkins 2014: 17). Fragmentation in terms of the exercise of authority started at this moment, with the French having the upper hand in deciding where armed forces could and should be used and Tunisians at the wrong end of the baton. There was serious resistance to the French invasion from Sfax all the way to the south. It is not by chance that this unique act of resistance to the French military takeover of the country in 1881 took place in Sfax, the first town along the coast excluded from the *Tunisie utile* (see below), and the gateway to the deep south (Perkins 2014: 55). In July 1881, Sfax was heavily bombarded and eventually "taken by the French naval forces after a major battle" (L. Anderson 1986: 121), a massacre that left 800 to 900 dead. Colonialism in Tunisia, with the French Protectorate starting in 1881, was the result of capitalist pressure and imperialist competition against the Ottomans. It deepened the internal fracture with the south and the interior of the country.

In Yemen, the Ottoman Empire also proposed a new census to reorganize taxation as part of these defensive modernization policies. Measures included setting "a uniform system of administration, taxation, military recruitment, and education in order to ward off both the encroachments on the part of European imperial powers and separatist challenges at the domestic level" (Kühn 2007: 315). For example, actions were passed to unify legal practices and undermine personalized forms of authority embodied by the Zaydi traditions. This was supposed to be the role played by "largely secular" *nizamiye* courts (Kühn 2007: 316), but these courts had to be abandoned, a recognition by the Ottomans that Yemeni subjects would not be ruled like the more "civilized" Ottoman subjects in other parts of the empire (Kühn 2007: 317). But the Ottoman *vali* did not want to leave the Zaydi leader, a self-appointed Imam, to challenge the authority of the Sultan and agreed on some indirect forms to limit the influence of Imam Yahya. The 1911-signed "Imamic–Ottoman condominium" split sovereignty over courts (Zaydi judges appointed locally, but with the overall court in Sanaa) and created "sectarian" zoning, thus ending what Kühn (2007: 311) describes as the Ottoman colonial period in northern Yemen.[51]

The Ottoman Empire soon disappeared: After WW1 and the creation of the League of Nations, it was dismantled and replaced by successor states, or by mandatory powers ruling over post-Ottoman territories. Encroachment deepened radically in that new historical period. Let us now see how the social life of citizenship – first in Tunisia and then Yemen – fared after the downfall of the Ottoman Empire.

In Tunisia, French colonialism built a strong central administrative apparatus in Tunis, the capital city, but the lack of a system of political representation and the unequal spread of state institutions intensified during the pre-colonial, or Ottoman, times. The main difference is that the French favored the emergence of a variety of economic actors trying to move the country not only beyond rural surplus production, but also to industrialize certain sectors, in particular the mining sector. In neighboring Libya, Italian colonialism, which started a couple of decades later in 1911, almost totally obliterated the limited bureaucratic and administrative infrastructure on the Libyan coast in favor of the project of mass migration from Italy. In both colonies, French and Italian authorities shared the same strategy of punitive campaigns at the time of conquest and military rule in large swaths of the peripheral territory, and resorted to martial law in various moments to quell protests, in particular in 1911 in Tunisia (L. Anderson 1986: 142,

---

[51] For Kühn, elements of the Ottoman rule by difference and efforts to recognize but contain "native authority" justify the use of the term "colonialism." Not all Yemenis seem to agree with this trend in the historiography. A couple of persons interviewed mentioned some faults of the Ottomans, for example, fiscal injustice (*zulm al-ḍarība*), but did not use the term "colonization." Abdullah Al-Saidi, former Yemeni ambassador to the UN, interview in New York, 02/26/2019.

161). Eugen Weber (1976) famously argued that peasants were made into French citizens under the Third Republic. If in Europe it was through education and fighting wars that respective citizens' rights were created, in North African colonies, it was repression by colonial apparatus that generated lasting resentment against the state, in particular in rural areas (Perkins 2014: 61). In North Africa it was the gendarmerie protecting European economic interests that turned peasants into colonial subjects and indispensable cogs in capitalist modes of production. Let us see how the bitterness of the Bey's reforms turned into unequal citizenship in colonial Tunisia.

The first instance of violent encroachment is apparent through an application of Fanon's (1961: 37) famous statement of a world divided into two, with the "frontiers shown by barracks and police stations." Martin Thomas' (2012) detailed story of police and gendarmerie forces in colonial Africa shows that the location of these barracks and police stations were not random, but followed capitalist interests in defending private investments and sites of surplus extraction: the map of exaction of colonial violence in Tunisia overlaps quite directly with that of mines, industries, and large agricultural properties. In Tunisia, most of these barracks were placed at the heart of the phosphate mines, in the interior province of Gafsa and in its administrative seats such as Kasserine (Thomas 2012: 41; 89–140). Another example of class differentiation and the gradually racialized unequal treatment among residents of Tunisia[52] is the so-called "colonial third," a measure introduced by France after WW1, which granted a 30% higher salary to French workers based in the Tunisian Protectorate (Yousfi 2015: 26). Tunisian workers not only did the hard work, but they also faced stricter police control, were paid less than their European co-workers, and in the agricultural sector, they were paying more taxes than Europeans.[53]

Second, the central authority of the Tunisian state exacted violence through uneven territorial deployment and ethnic profiling. During the Protectorate years, the Bey, still the nominal ruler, had to foot the bill of the security expenses incurred by French police forces (Thomas 2012:

---

[52] See Challand (2020). Racialization is functional to the administration of difference: a presumed essential difference, at the crossroads of biological or civilizational determinism, explains the colonial distinction that France made in Tunisia (but also in Morocco) of a useful and a useless part of the territory.

[53] Perkins (2014: 61) notes that grapes, the "quintessentially European crop," were exempt from taxes, while dates and olives carried "additional levies."

114). Furthermore, the police and the *garde républicaine mobile* had no Muslims listed on their payroll. This repressive apparatus worked in collaboration with the roughly 200,000 settlers to police and prevent mobilizations in the productive areas of the country, notably around the phosphate mines in the center of the country, and in the coastal areas (Thomas 2012: 119–120). These regions, between Bizerte and Tunis, south all the way to Mahdia in the Sahel region, and the immediate hinterland were considered in French colonial times *la Tunisie utile* (the "useful Tunisia"). The rest was quipped as "*Tunisie inutile*" – the "useless part" of Tunisia, in particular the southern territories along the Libyan border, left pretty much untouched by capitalist transformation, and the western parts of the Protectorate, also called "the interior" or the "economically neglected interior" (Hartshorn 2019: 7).

The French took on the earlier neglect by the Beylical authorities towards the south of the country, which was only a problem twice a year, when authorities led semi-annual expeditions in these marginal areas to collect tax and tributes (L. Anderson 1986: 79). They also extended to Tunisia practices that were already in place earlier in Algeria, with a laxer application of law, e.g. the French turning a blind eye to the practice of slavery and slave-trading in the southern parts of colonized Algeria.[54] Important for this book (see Chapter 6 for a reference to the sit-in in El-Kamour in 2017 and 2020) is that these punitive campaigns were carried out by the army, rather than by a police force, that is, an executive arm connected *in theory* to the implementation of legal measures targeting all citizens equally, but which *de facto* targeted only the poorer segments of Tunisian society. In terms of inequality in the face of death and military exposure, one can also cite the fact that during WW1, Tunisia provided more soldiers per capita than Algeria (Thomas 2012: 117). In this instance as well, there was a clear and stated discrimination towards Muslim Tunisians: Registered residents of Tunis, the capital, as well as Tunisian Jews were exempted from conscription, leaving only Muslims, often from the poorer part of the Protectorate, in the army ranks.[55]

[54] Brower (2009: 167–168). A governor-general ruled from Algeria, under the control of the Ministry of War, with territorial divisions mirroring distinct military units in Oran, Algiers, and Constantine. See Brower (2009: 22, 167–171).

[55] Thomas (2012: 117). There was also a process of setting Jews and Black communities (called *chaouachine*) aside (Ganiage 1966: 860).

Third, the colonial discourse of a *Tunisie utile* deepened a fragmentation of the territory, with unequal access to state and police protection long after the end of colonialism. Outside of seizing the best agricultural land, like in the case of the Jemna Oasis in the 1930s (see Section 6.2), France saw little benefit in expanding its direct rule over the south of the country and along the Libyan border. The "non-useful Tunisia" was presented as the territory of the *fellaghas*, an Arabic term usually rendered as "bandits" in European languages to describe rural fighters that resisted French colonial policies.[56] France did not believe that these low-density population areas with low economic potential could be incorporated into agrarian capitalism or systematic economic exchanges. Thus, rather than extending a unified rule over the entire protectorate, or sending settlers deep into the south, Tunis cemented alliances with tribal groupings living on these borderlands in exchange for mutual alliances (the right to commerce along caravan routes for the Jefara tribes and the creation of buffer zones as border protection for the colonial regime) (Kartas 2016). This different modality of police administration was also used in neighboring Algeria, where the three departments (along the coast) were under civilian rule, while the south of French Algeria was under military rule (Kateb 2001; Brower 2009: 167). This uneven reach is not only territorial, it is also expressed in unequal legal protection between European settlers (benefiting from consular protections) and the native population. For example, Albert Memmi (1957/1965: 14) notes that the common religion of these European settlers provided the common, racialized basis for discrimination against Tunisian natives, even if the Europeans were not economically well off, for example poor Italian or Maltese settlers. Colonists and natives were pitted against one another through a system of indirect policing, with the French authority inciting settlers and *contrôleurs civils* to spy and report on Tunisians who were thought to be hostile to colonization (Thomas 2012: 118–120). The *contrôleurs civils* benefited from quasi extra-juridical power during the protectorate to enact colonial policies (Mouilleau 2000; Perkins 2014: 62). In a population of

---

[56] The term literally means "wood choppers," from *fallāq*, pl. *fallāqa*, a substantive derived from the verb *falaqa*, to split, to cleave. In Algeria the *fellaghas* led a very long anti-colonial war, while in Tunisia, they were only a secondary to the mostly political path towards independence that the first Tunisian President, Bourguiba, chose. I am grateful to Mondher Kilani for the clarification.

about 2.6 million at the time of the 1936 census, Tunisia counted 2.3 million Muslims, about 60,000 Jews, and 200,000 settlers, mostly French and Italians.[57] The Grand Council, established under Khayr Ed-Din, granted 44 seats to French Tunisians and only 18 to Tunisians. These two bodies, part of the same institution, never sat together, held separate meetings, and did not have the same rights: Tunisian natives were thus denied any vote on constitutional and political issues (L. Anderson 1986: 164): "Natives" were parked, so to say, in parallel and unequal institutions of representation. Moreover, Tunisians in the south and in the central mining regions faced harsher police and army brutality.[58]

Based on this short rendering of political life in pre-independence Tunisia, I propose viewing the impact of garrison-state formation and colonial rule in particular as characterized by a fundamental problem of the uneven distribution of violence. In my eye, the uneven distribution of violence refers to three different processes. The first instance resides in the actual use of violence and repression by coercive institutions (police, army): Some political subjects are more exposed to physical violence than others. The second component deals with the so-called legitimate use of physical force (or legitimate means of coercion). There as well, colonial authorities were spread unevenly across the territory, and post-independence authorities perpetuated such practices, consolidating past forms of marginalization. The third meaning of the uneven distribution of violence deals with symbolic forms of violence, and the continuous existence of "a pyramid of petty tyrants," with groups of powerful Tunisians oppressing some of their peers (Memmi 1957/1965: 17), and generating a new sense of cultural superiority along geographical identification and the bracketing of regional identities. In the next

---

[57] Thomas (2012: 381, fn. 5). Ganiage (1966: 857, 864) estimates that in 1856 there were 1.1 million Tunisians (500,000 living a sedentary life and 600,000 nomads), 30,000 Jews, and already 12,500 Europeans. In 1904, Tunis alone counted 55,000 Europeans, a majority being Italians (35,000), followed by 10,000 French and 8,000 Maltese.

[58] Mullin (2018) offers a detailed account of the repression in March 1937 and again in the period 1946–1956 in the Gafsa area. For her, these mining regions have "been central to the development of the security state architecture" and surplus extraction. Details she gives about the *Compagnie des Phosphates de Gafsa* (CPG), for example the fact that it has its own security apparatus, concur with the description I give of the "uneven development of coercion." Mullin, however, does not cover the independence era, something I do in the next chapter.

chapter, we will see how forms of regionalization and marginalization evolved during the post-independence decades, but in a nutshell, these forms of marginalization help us understand the cartography and unfolding of the winter 2010 and 2011 protests (Chapter 3).

Let us now dwell briefly on colonial Yemeni history and see how the social life of citizenship might have suffered from this period.

Overall, no egalitarian citizenship could emerge in the two Yemens. Instead, traditional principles of subjecthood (*ra'ya* or *ra'iyyah*) predominated (Dresch 2000: 24). Monarchical rule, with personalized authority that Messick (1993) describes in detail in *The Calligraphic State*, continued after the period of shared authority in northern Yemen well into the twentieth century. The taxes introduced under the last years of Ottoman rule have been perceived as the main form of colonial oppression (*"zulm al-dariba"* or tax oppression, in the words of one of my interviewees),[59] a feature that the Imam perpetuated well after the downfall of the Sublime Porte. When the Ottomans withdrew from Yemen in December 1918, the British first thought of occupying northern Yemen out of the port of Hodeida. Facing resistance, they instead handed control of the coastal region to a competitor of Imam Yahya, Muhammad Al-Idrisi, based in the 'Asir region (Dresch 2000: 28–31). Italians also tried to take advantage of the weakness of the Imamate. Via Eritrea, Italy took over in 1923 the small Hanish Islands along the Yemeni coast, over which the Mutawakkil Kingdom in the north could not assert control. In terms of the relation between taxation and "citizenship," the practice in the north until the republican era was characterized by a very peculiar but reversed fiscal institution, that of the Imam taking hostages. Rogers (2019: 84) describes the system in these terms:

The hostage system (*nizam al-raha'in*) has generally been credited with playing a key part in this gradual assertion of central control over tribal areas. By 1955, the Imam's court hosted some 2,000 tribal hostages ... . Hostages from leading tribal families served as leverage against tribal leaders, but the system also had allocative and educational functions: it tied the tribes to the Imam's court through stipends to the hostages' families and by providing education to future tribal leaders. Hostage stipends were generous and

---

[59] Al-Saidi, interview, 26/02/2019. Dr. Al-Saidi, on top of being the Yemeni ambassador to the UN in 2011, was also a legal expert on the late Ottoman period, and his expertise helped resolve the Eritrean–Yemeni divergence pertaining to the sovereignty over the Hanish Islands. See Dobelle & Favre (1998).

became an increasingly important source of income for tribal leaders during the 1940s and 1950s.

This system increased the personalistic relations at the heart of the Zaydi states, and like education, taxation was not universal, but it constituted another form of equalizing function within a limited group of Yemeni citizens. Only a few subjects (part of the social stratification of "tribes") were levied in the Imamate army, and no legal-rational authority existed. Justice was exercised locally by the *qadi*, an Islamic judge who would also educate a few children whose parents were sufficiently well off to pay for education in the *madrasa*.

In the south, Harold Ingrams, the British Colonial Resident, talked of about 2,000 separate "governments" in the Hadhramawt (Dresch 2000: 37). The British levied local, mostly underpaid troops (Lackner 1985: 19) and withheld political rights from local residents until the end of WW2. In the 1950s, the British assisted the sultans of Al-Qu'ayti (around Mukalla) and Al-Kathiri, in the Hadhramawt, "to develop government administration" that was supported by a Hadhrami Bedouin Army, made up in part of mercenaries (Yafi' tribesmen) and modeled on the Arab Legion in Jordan (Day 2012: 37, 39). This "army" numbered about 1,000 men by the mid-1960s, and helped the British to reach out into the remotest parts of the region by playing local rivals off against one another (Brehony 2011: 8). Foot soldiers were Arabs, and only the British would attain the rank of officers in that military corps (Mawby 2005). Closer to the time of decolonization, when skirmishes started to contest the British encroachment in Aden, the Aden Levies were largely "useless [as an] instrument of order" for Britain (Dresch 2000: 74). Following a spate of separate incidents in 1954, a host of levies "deserted or failed to act" (Dresch 2000: 74), a sign that there was nothing or very little considered "legitimate" in the deployment of the institutions of coercion.

In 1947, a legislative council was established for the first time in Aden, but there were no elections and very limited representation for the local population: half of the members of this council were nominated by Britain, and the other half were appointed ex officio. Only in 1955, under pressure from nascent Arab nationalists, did Britain open an electoral contest for four of the 18 seats of the council. As Lackner (1985: 20) notes:

The vast majority of the Aden population was disenfranchised: the only people who had the vote were British-protected subjects who had lived in Aden for seven of the last 10 years. This allowed Somalis to vote but disqualified Yemenis, with the result that only 21,500 were enfranchised out of population of 180,000. It was announced that in 1959, the number of elected members would rise to twelve to outnumber the five ex-officio and six nominated. The election was boycotted by the nationalists.

Citizenship was a very variable and exclusionary concept in southern Yemen.

The opening of an oil refinery in Aden in 1954 meant that the city and its harbor became more than just a coaling station on the way to India (Lackner 1985: 15, 18): it started a period of economic expansion unmatched by the Western and Eastern Protectorates, and Aden became the second busiest port after New York city in the 1950s (Bonnefoy 2018: 24). These inequalities generated contradictory feelings about unifying the various parts of what would become Southern Yemen: Nationalists wanted to expel British rule, as did the Imam, who opposed the idea of federation in the 1950s (Dresch 2000: 64). Britain preferred having Aden separate from the rest of the protectorates, and feared that the Eastern Protectorates would fall under the control of the Saudis. This eventually forced Britain to establish the Federation of South Arabia in 1963 and announce in 1964 that a federation comprising both Aden and the protectorates would be granted independence by 1968 (Dresch 2000: 99; Clarke 2010: 80–88). Nationalist pressure mounted, and Great Britain deployed more soldiers to secure Aden and the navigation routes, not from or toward India, since it had gained independence in 1948, but from the Gulf region (Dresch 2000: 101). After the nationalization of the Suez Canal by Gamal Abdel Nasser in 1956, Arab nationalist movements felt emboldened by the revolutionary and anticolonial spirit. Soon an anticolonial movement spread, and Southern Yemen obtained its independence at the end of 1967.

* * *

This historical account of proto-state formation in Tunisia and Yemen is quite different from the European paths charted earlier in the chapter. The variety of European encroachments, at times economic, at times military, created the conditions that prevented systems of representation and democratic enfranchisement from emerging. Tunisian Muslims and Yemeni subjects were considered *minus habentes*, and thus were not granted *equal* citizen rights: Europeans granted a few formal concessions, for example a timid form of political representation in the Tunisian Grand Council or the Aden Legislative Body, but these bodies were only "representing" a small urban layer of the local populations, and these institutions were fraught with deep discrimination and imbalances. Moreover, the quality of citizenship engagement on the side of the European settlers was also highly dubious: Albert Memmi noted that the attitude of colonial populations was only "remotely civic."[60] Many examples substantiate this accusation of a lack of democratic commitment from the colonists: European left parties and labor movements never flinched or objected to their salary privilege (the colonial third) that left Arab workers in worse conditions. Political parties never objected to unequal representation in local legislatures nor to the bloodbath in neighboring Setif in May 1945 (Krais 2021: 114). Violence was used in the most extreme manner against the local populations, even in manners that were caricatural, if we believe the description given by Albert Memmi in his *Portrait du Colonisé*: Since the colonized is presumed a thief, s/he must in fact be guarded against, and violence should even be used preemptively. Some laundry of the colonizer is missing? Then it *must* be a colonized person who stole it, even if he did not come close to the Europeans' property (e.g. Memmi 1957/1965: 90).

This makes us transition to the last section of this chapter to complete this *tour d'horizon* of the emergence of "citizenship," where I will tackle the dominant narrative about European citizenship. I propose revisiting the latter in a relational manner, i.e. in a way that takes international relations and the marked politics of difference and the demeaning of the colonial subject into consideration. This double journey, of Europe to the Middle East and from there back to Europe, is also a metaphoric journey that interlocks the inside and outside of citizenship, what I call the Moebius strip of violence and citizenship, to express how processes of state-making in Europe are actually connected to the fate of citizenship in the Middle East.

1.4 The Moebius Strip of Citizenship

The organization and management of violence by the state (the "means of coercion"), I suggested earlier in the chapter, have always been at the very heart of the development of citizenship in Europe. Yet very little is

---

[60] In Memmi's terms, "*le colonialiste est civiquement aérien*" (p. 98 of the original French, *Portrait du Colonisé*, 1956). The English translation only politely states that the colonist "is between two places" (Memmi 1957/1965: 68).

said about the multiple forms of encroachment on colonies or how the violence exacted in the peripheries was actually essential to the emergence of modern states and democratic citizenship in Euro-America.

Classical texts in historical sociology, from Michel Foucault (1926–1984) to Charles Tilly (1929–2008), or accounts of classical sociology, from Max Weber (1864–1920) to Norbert Elias (1897–1990), give almost no space to the non-European experiences of building state–society relations in the process of state-formation. These gaps have been increasingly criticized, but more conceptual work is needed to connect and suture these different ideal-types of state-formation around the globe, rather than just observing the absence of colonialism or imperialism in this or that author. Let me offer a brief synopsis of four of these dominant theories of violence (Foucault, Elias, Weber, and Tilly), and identify a few points on which to connect with the vicissitude of citizenship in the Middle East.

Michel Foucault's famous account of the emergence of the prison is probably the most discussed account of the reduction of public violence. In *Discipline and Punish: The Birth of the Prison* (1977), Foucault documents the shift away from the spectacle of public executions under the ancient regime to microforms of disciplinary power in modernity. Jeremy Bentham's panopticon is discussed in detail, but it is not the only point of relevance for this book. Gradually, in the eighteenth century, the visual component of punishment, with the masses witnessing the scene of the execution, was replaced by a new representation of justice exercised not to defend the sovereign monarch, but society as a whole (think of the *jus quia justum* described above). This shift coincided with the emergence of new scientific discourses of the so-called reformist thinkers (e.g. Cesare Beccaria), and with the fall of the *ancien régime*. It is not the sovereign (monarch) any more that can claim to be the victim of a criminal's action; it is society as a whole: "In effect, the offence opposes an individual to the entire social body; in order to punish him, society has the right to oppose him in its entirety" (Foucault 1977: 90). Foucault goes on to describe "the gentle way in punishment" (pp. 104–131), which he explains is the "art of punishing, [which] then, must rest on a whole technology of representation" (p. 104), such as the Lancaster schools, new rituals of justice, and the publication of new posters or texts to educate modern subjects. Foucault speaks of "penalty-effect, penalty-representation, penalty-general function, penalty-sign and discourse," as all interconnected by discursive formations and a project of organizing society (p. 114). The very representation of a different form of justice is at the core of the disciplining process of modernity.[61] Representation, for Foucault, is discursive, scientific, cultural, and its truths produced a new materiality. It is not about political representation, for Foucault is not interested, in his post-structural vein of inspiration, in the classical formation of political power.

But Foucault does not explain how power, outside of parallel regimes of scientific truths, is constituted as a whole historically and in *relation* to other powers outside of Europe, let alone if this process of discipline is valid globally. Instead one can read a circular statement that "at the heart of the procedures of discipline, it manifests the subjection of those who are perceived as objects and the objectification of those who are subjected" (Foucault 1977: 184–185). Furthermore, even if he notes that this new disciplinary power is connected to the necessity to shoulder economic and capitalist developments, nothing is said about how these new representations of modern power are influenced by gender, class, or racial processes of differentiation.[62]

The absence of colonialism and imperial violence is surprising for an intellectual who spent time in Tunisia and who followed the Iranian revolution so closely. Yet, like so many other Western European thinkers, the tendency to produce Theory (with a capital T) based on a few European cases, mostly French, with a few references to Italy, Prussia, and the USA in that specific 1977 book, is also at play for Foucault. Ann Stoler (1995: 35) has noted that, for example, "crucial elements of gender and empire are missing from Foucault's account of biopower," or how his theorization of the carceral archipelago remained mostly silent about violence and disciplining processes exacted in the colonies (Stoler 2016: 73–74, 85–89, 107). Medien (2019a: 5–7) highlights the ways in which Foucault's stay in Tunisia between 1966 and September 1968 exposed him to brutal state repression and how state institutions ("courts, cops, … military, and the state") were retrospectively described as "intolerable." Yet nothing

---

[61] It acquires a new visual and immaterial dimension. This does not mean that materiality has no importance for Foucault, for whom discourse was a reflection of the actual materiality of micro-managed spaces, of institutions "correcting" social or sexual "abnormalities." Walter Armbrust's (2019: 7–8, 33) apt identification of the politics of space in the Egyptian "revolution" shows the material connection between space and the formation of "heterotopia."

[62] For example, the military medals that stop representing the monarch but extol the virtue of military discipline (Foucault 1977: 170) are never discussed in relation to class or gender formation.

from the repression of the Tunisian student movement or his direct encounter with Third Worldism (and a certain eulogy of political violence) loops back into his writings. Some would later emerge in his *Collège de France* lectures, but only marginally (see Foucault 2008). The *critical-colonial* approach, that this book calls for, is largely absent from Foucault's rich theories.

But let us discuss briefly another classical account of the restrained space occupied by gradually disappearing violence, that of Norbert Elias.

Elias was recognized as the author of a monumental work of historical sociology late in his life. His *Civilizing Process* was published in German in 1939 but only gained attention when parts were translated into English in the 1970s. In 2000, when the entire work was translated, his approach generated much enthusiasm for its acute ability to describe prima facie remote practices such as the introduction of a fork to eat a meal in the late middle ages and the end of capital punishment in the nineteenth century. Elias' method is based on *sociogenetic and psychogenetic investigations* (the sub-title of the book), that is an individual-centered explanation of the gradual decrease in the use of violence and the increased presence of a polished retinue in public life. Such a narrow focus, rather than an institutional or macro analysis, explains a slow but deep transformation in the exercise of sovereignty culminating in the modern state. For Elias, who covers the immense period of European history between 800 and 1900, to understand the "macro" transformation in terms of violence–civility (with less of the former and an increase and publicly sanctioned presence of the latter over time), one needs to understand the micro-transformation from the level of elite groups, all the way down to the psychology of a few individuals.[63]

Another way to capture Elias' idea is to think in terms of the restraint that led to the modern state. This happened at both the psychological level, for example the taming of personal impulses gradually induced new

---

[63] Salvatore's comparative analysis of the Eliasian civilizing processes (he focuses on instances where Islam is a distinct source of civility) identifies the strength and the weakness of Elias: "the [European] state is able to integrate all emergent forms of social power into its authority in ways that ultimately make the transition from Leviathan to demos in the European cases . . . much more of a socio-cultural than a political process" (Salvatore 2016: 242). Thanks to Elias, we understand the micro-foundation and the engines of socialization behind the spread of civility, but the overall political contours and geography of these processes (are they separate from colonialism? reproduced in part in colonialism?) are still pretty much blurred.

public behaviors, and at the sociological level, for example how people become gradually accustomed to new norms. Thus, the process of civilization is an outward, gradual expansion of micro forms of restraint that paved the way, according to Elias, for the isomorphic emergence of modern states based on the monopoly of physical force. Examples of such micro processes, to be sure very slow in their affirmation, can be found in mechanisms of self-restraint and competition among individuals to reach higher levels of refinement. At the meso-level, one can imagine how aristocratic courts were gradually socialized into new norms of culture, civilization, and good manners, or, from there, how institutions representing a monarch were progressively coerced into restraint. One illustration is the forbidding of dueling (Elias quoted in Poggi 1990: 46) under the French monarchy: only the state could conduct warfare, and at a given point in French history even famous musketeers had to stop behaving as if they could take justice into their own hands. The monarch and later republican leaders could only be considered rightful by exercising maximal restraint and demonstrating that justice was exercised in a standardized manner for all. Thus, sociogenesis connects individuals, social norms, and the state, in a long historical process that "gradually impelled society toward this centralization and monopolization of the use of physical violence and its instruments" in the hands of the state.[64]

In Elias' view, civility is portrayed as a product of the centralization and monopolization of legitimate violence by the state that flows from interpersonal relations and well-policed manners. The civilizing process was gradually and isomorphically replicated, in a process of mimicry and competition, to appear as the most virtuous once a potentate had obtained a large territorial basis for his or her rule. Elias' narrative covers Europe as if it was a self-enclosed entity characterized by internal competition, but eventually the process of civilization won the day. It is as if this cycle of the taming of violence is self-propelling (Salvatore 2011: 805, 810), or at least we have a view of the diffusion from the center (Europe) of new norms of civility. For example, in one of the few sections mentioning colonial realms and reactions to the civilizing process, Elias states that "from the 19th century onwards, these civilized forms of conduct spread across the rising lower classes of

---

[64] Elias (1939/2000: xiii). It is important to note that Elias does not only emphasize a gradual decline in violence, but also the displacement of it by and within the state (with temporal and special enclaves). See Landini and Dépelteau (2017: 17, 62).

Western society and over the various classes in the colonies, amalgamat-
ing with indigenous patterns of conduct. Each time this happens, upper
conduct and that of the rising groups interpenetrate."[65] Elias is aware
(and he quotes many instances of this) of the instrumental use of "civilization" to justify colonization (e.g. pp. 43, 47), but he never decenters
his analysis to other sociogeneses than the ones he built for Europe.[66]

It would be unfair to reproach Elias because he did not study the high
degree of court refinement in the Ottoman Empire (after all, it is not
called the "Sublime Porte" by coincidence).[67] Or because he failed to
acknowledge concerns for *adab*, an Arabic term denoting the combination of intellectual commitment to the high arts (literature, poetry) that
is congenial in Islamdom with etiquette and codes of good manners that
have played a similar role in the promulgation of ruling consensus and
civility in Muslim empires (Salvatore 2016: 123–125). But a view of
expansive civility from a core (the courts in Europe) limits the Eliasian
project to the mutually constitutive links and interactions between different cultural traditions. In short: civility and the process of civilization
did not only flow from European history, its court system, and the
commercial-turned-capitalist rationality (Salvatore 2016: 239). It
existed in other historical blocks (e.g. in Islamdom or Japan)[68] but the
nexus was not oriented toward the system of citizenship that has been
enmeshed with the rise of legal-rational forms of authority so dear to
Max Weber, another influential theorist for historical sociology.

Max Weber's work on rationalization and *Lebensführung* (conduct
of life) is not too far from Elias, and as a matter of fact, Weber was

---

[65] Elias (1939/2000: 428). Elias here comes close to Simmel's idea of fashion,
which is constantly re-shaped by new tastes and norms and sustained by
bourgeois classes, leaving the lower classes with only the imitation of these
norms. See, e.g. "The tendency for the upper class to colonize the lower and for
the lower to copy the upper is more pronounced" (Elias 1939/2000: 430).

[66] Salvatore (2016: 246) argues that Elias is fully aware of the violent costs of
colonialism, insofar as conflicts were somehow internalized through the
arrangements and tensions of civility itself (which also released its own, mostly
symbolic, violence, e.g. through status) and were also generated by the
importation of an instrumental reasoning linked to surplus extraction.

[67] The Ottoman court, with similar high cultural manners, would be a natural
candidate for an explanation of the resilient empire, but this is not covered in
Elias. One article (Pfeifer 2020) deals with table manners in an Eliasian vein.

[68] This is also a point that Eiko Ikegami (2005: 23, 28) has offered in her study of
aesthetics networks and the making of the Japanese state, and thus connecting
civility with the organization of violence.

a great influence on Elias.[69] The main difference between the two authors is that Weber sustains that this conduct of life is a combination of cultural and material (read as economic) factors, best studied through the differences between religious ethics and forms of asceticism. Elias does not consider religious institutions as a source of civilization and concentrates instead on temporal power: courtly life impressing new mundane behaviors, such as the use of the fork rather than knives and communal spoons to appear more civilized (Elias 2000: 70). For Weber, bodily practices matter little per se, unless they are related to a worldview clustered around religious principles and forms of authority. In *The Protestant Ethic and the Spirit of Capitalism*, Weber (1920/1992) insists on the restlessness of the proto-capitalists who saw in new translations of the Bible a calling for a new behavior, that of investing in industrious activities. For Weber, the various steps behind modernity provided the occasion for certain Protestant sects to demonstrate their preferred, sustained form of this-worldly asceticism: Out of these daily practices arose benefits from the calculable and predictable profits made possible by more stable and regulated economic exchanges, in short, a complex evolution towards economic and legal rationalizations, which was in synchrony with a new form of power, that of legal-rational authority.

All in all, in this vein of classical sociology, different scales, the micro- and macro-levels, are used to understand developments (a sociogenesis) of the modern state in Elias, while Weber points at *Lebensführung* as cause for change. Both are prisoners of a certain cultural determinacy (norms of civility; religious forms of asceticism; elite cultural models), as opposed to a materialist interpretation. Elias does not address the sophistication of the Ottomans, which was known and admired as part of the European fascination with the East (Rodinson 1987), and Weber builds his sociology of non-European processes on recycled anachronisms, as if understanding ancient religions could help to understand contemporary *Lebensführung*.[70] The

---

[69] Even though Weber does not appear very often in Elias. Weber is only mentioned in the 1936 Preface (Elias 1939/2000: xiii) and in the 1968 Postscript. On some parallels between Elias and Weber, see Goudsblom (2003: 24–25).

[70] Islam entails a this-worldly form of asceticism, which according to Weber is a necessary condition for the emergence of modern capitalism, but the predominance of subjective law (what he calls "kadi justice," for *qadi*), rule by soldier-rulers, and patrimonialism are for him hurdles that have prevented the

problem is that, contrary to the spirit of capitalism, which Weber studies diachronically, Weber's analysis of Islam is made through the socio-economic structures that existed at the time of Prophet Muhammad.[71] It is as if "the Islam" that Weber studied was frozen in time with a total inability to adapt to new world situations.[72]

Finally, the last theory about the gradual domestication of violence is that of political sociologist Charles Tilly. Like Elias, Tilly sustains that state-making harks back to the middle ages, rather than being a recent modern artifact, and to the period of feudalism and intra-city competition when different lords or cities fought to establish a larger territorial hold. This rivalry, the Tillyan category of war-making, allowed for territorial expansion that gradually became state-making when one of these lords or cities managed to eliminate rivals within his or its territorial basis. Along with war- and state-making came the need to find resources to sustain these military campaigns, which Tilly distinguishes as either capital-accumulation or coercion-accumulation processes. In the latter formation, power is accumulated with military might (in my terms through imperial encroachment), while in the former, accumulation is made possible by institutional incentives favoring commercial exchanges (in my terminology, capitalist encroachment). Tilly gives the Spanish Empire as an example of the high coercion accumulation, and Dutch commercial expansion as an example of high capitalist concentration.

Here Tilly poses his Augustinian question of "what are states but robberies on a larger scale?" but offers a different answer. For theologian Augustine, the question was about monarchies, and the answer was that the only thing that distinguished state-making from robbery and war-lordism was the exercise of justice ("what are kingdoms if justice be removed, but robberies on a larger scale?," according to

spread of modern capitalism in Muslim-majority societies. See M. Weber (1978: 818–822) and Schluchter (1999).

[71] Furthermore, Weber balances a variety of internal and external factors to account for the spread of capitalism in Europe. But in his scattered sections on Islam, he only seems to offer internalist accounts for the lack of capitalism, e.g. the waqf and religious endowments that barred the emergence of a maximalist use of resources. See e.g. M. Weber (1978: 1092–1097). See also Turner (1974).

[72] A mistake that many contemporary "Orientalists" have reproduced and thus contaminated, by their narrow and instrumental Weberism (in modernization theories), the more laudable project of Weber himself of wanting, but never fully realizing, a comparative historical sociology. On Weber(ian research) as opposed to Weberism, see Salvatore (1996).

Augustine, as quoted in Poggi 1990: 6). For Tilly, state-formation succeeded because it managed to protect its citizens, but this protection came with extraction. War preparation led to the organization of bureaucracies, and from there to centralized state revenues in the (Western) European cases, and as such, it was war-making that enabled state-making because of the always larger logistical and extractive capability that those wars required. Once the states were large enough, included an interior pacified of rivalries, and built a robust army to protect the borders of this entity, the narrative in Tilly (1975) culminates with a situation of more-or-less pacified social relations,[73] and with specialized institutions in charge of coercion and tax extraction, which replaced war bounty and plundering. The specialization of violence ("war specialists" in the feudal era) was replaced with the modern state and what I would call an *equalization* of violence: the burden of carrying out war is no longer in the hands of a few warriors, as all men are forced to enroll in the military. Out of this incorporation, later also for women because of their role supporting the war efforts in industry or in terms of natalist policies, a growing sense of citizenship emerged. Thus, the exercise of coercion, first limited to territorial pockets engaged in war or conquest, was then replaced by police and army forces meant to protect the entire territory, its population, and the political and bureaucratic apparatus (the "state"). In a sequel, Tilly (1990) notes the intimate relation between coercion, capital, and the existence of European states, again with the emergence of a specific form of (capitalist) market and the establishment of a "European state system" (Tilly 1990: 161–165) that moved competition from the field of war and violent rivalries into the realm of economic antagonism and processes of cooperation.

We are back to some of the central tenets or bases for the dominant narrative behind (European) citizenship. But like Foucault, Weber, or Elias, little is said in Tilly about colonialism as a pre-condition, or as another pool of territories and humans out of which the extraction of resources and riches *also* made European state-making possible.[74] Tilly

---

[73] Tilly (1990: 56) speaks of the states' gradual "disarming of their civilian populations," and from there, conflictuality moves to the field of contentious politics, another key topic in Tilly's research agenda in the field of historical sociology (Tilly 2003a).

[74] Put differently, Tilly could have explored how access to colonies or non-European resources functioned as an intervening variable in the process of state-

notes the high level of European competition around empires, but it is almost as if the sea and navigation routes were just an extension of territorial rivalries to concentrate the accumulation of capital and credit-supporting resources; he did not take the colonies as distinct locations in which war-making was also at play, although this could have enriched and rendered his two-dimensional model of state-making more complex.[75] All of these theories replicate a form of methodological Euro-centrism.[76] They should instead be opened and connected to the historical process of state-making in the Middle East – and per extension to the other global "peripheries" (of Europe).

All of these accounts interweave an understanding of modernity evolving, not to say culminating, with the disappearance of war and violence. This is deeply unsatisfactory, as many have noted that modern institutions have been even more violent and barbarian than one could be led to believe when reading these theories of transformed violence. The systematic erasure of women's voices and property in early modern European history (Federici 2004), the racist annihilation of European Jews and other "minorities" during WW2, the murderous

---

making in Western Europe. For Tilly, the relation is the reverse: distinctive patterns of coercion as opposed to capital accumulation explain the type of imperial attitudes towards the colonies. The Spanish Empire (characterized by high coercion accumulation) is the only case where Tilly describes more-or-less explicitly the nefarious impact of colonization: Spain "devoted more of their energy to settlements, enslavement of the indigenous (or imported) labor force and exaction of tribute," while his characterization of French and British colonization is rather benevolent: "Britain and France entered the imperial game relatively late, and excelled at it by combining the capitalist and coercive strategies." See Tilly (1990: 94).

[75] The two dimensions of state-making are based on the distinction between an ability to accumulate capital as opposed to coercion. Thus, the concentration of capital vs. the concentration of coercive means (e.g. Tilly 1990: 56, 60, 132–133) overlaps with a two-pronged ability for taxation vs. the capacity for surveillance (p. 88). On navigation and intra-European competition, see Tilly (1990: 93). When talking about the violence of imperialism, Tilly notes the ruthlessness of the Portuguese, but this description serves to characterize the nation's attitude and risks taken at sea, not to describe the treatment of local colonized populations. See Tilly (1990: 91).

[76] Tilly (1990: 117) does mention non-European lineages of state-making with the Chinese example. But again, this is based on the central idea of war-making (not the uneven application of violence to different subjects), that allows or propels the process of state-making. In earlier work, Tilly (1975: 82) states that one should be careful with taking the European patterns of state-making as a fixed model out of which deductions could be made.

drive towards ethnic cleansing in the name of "nation-states" or empires, and ideas of purity are reminders that processes of civilization are not complete, and that the "pacification" of world society is a myth. Ayyash (2020: 34) notes that violence does not disappear with modernity, but it is made distant, or partly invisible. I would add that it is also differentiated in terms of gender and race.

Because the racialized component will be analyzed in some depth for the origins and motives of the Tunisian Uprisings of 2011, I will try to lift the veil to these very complex processes of differentiation. This is an initial step, and as Middle Eastern studies seem to finally be taking a critical racial turn, it is important to contribute to this new analytical lens. The same should be done for the gendered exaction and exercise of violence. Some elements are discussed in the coming chapters, but indications will point to a rich literature on gender and violence (e.g. Amar 2013; Salime 2014; 2015a). Recent debates that raged in French academic circles after the publication of two collective books on sexual violence in the colonies (Boetsch et al. 2019; Blanchard et al. 2018) indicate that more work is needed to understand how women have been the objects of pernicious violence across place and time. Christelle Taraud, one of the authors, thinks that it should be impossible to narrate colonial violence without addressing the sexual violence that has accompanied it.[77] To paraphrase Joas, "many continue to dream the 'dream of a non-violence modernity'" (Joas in 2003, quoted in Joas and Knöbl 2013: 2), and some continue to dream the theory of "less violence" or "civility" when brutal violence has left vulnerable subjects excluded from the "rights" offered by citizenship, when in reality it has been a self-granted set of privileges from and to the white propertied male (Wynter 2003: 260).

In this last section, I want to bring into dialogue the two parallel accounts of state-formation and make visible the origins and weight of capitalist, colonial, and imperial violence. This effort situates itself in the growing literature that questions cultural or political separation in some quarters of postcolonial studies. Ann Stoler's (2016) work on the simultaneous development in mid-1800s France and Algeria of camps and colonies and Gurminder Bhambra's (2015b; 2019) effort to

---

[77] See *Le Monde*, 11/17/2019, at www.lemonde.fr/afrique/article/2019/11/17/le-recit-de-la-colonisation-ne-doit-plus-faire-abstraction-de-la-violence-sexuelle_6019499_3212.html.

rethink how the Haitian Revolution or the consequences of slavery in the USA makes us apprehend citizenship not as principle of *inclusion* but one of *exclusion* are vital examples of this growing field. But we still need to reinforce a research agenda that does not subscribe to views of disconnects and gaps between different parts of the world. To avoid this separation (here as the view of fundamentally different political cultures), I propose to think metaphorically about violence as part of the same continuous stream of colonial impacts, that generate differentiated impacts around racialized or gendered formations.

Using the metaphor of the Moebius strip (a two-sided and four-edged piece of paper turned into an object that has only one side and one edge, see Figure 1.1),[78] I want to show how the two facets of the colonial origins of violence and even of theories of contained violence are continuous: What happened in the metropolis (the expansion of capitalism, pressure for enfranchisement) engulfed the colonies in some of its consequences, in the same manner as events or processes in the colonies also helped to shape the content of "democratic" life in Europe. Processes that are presented as declining in a European core (the decrease of public violence) are in reality expanding in the colonies

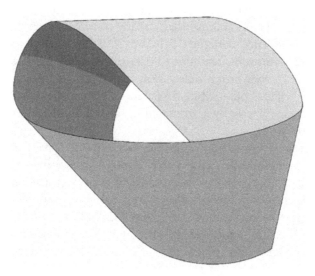

Figure 1.1 A sketch of a Moebius strip.

[78] Drawing by Leo Challand, courtesy of the artist.

and/or the peripheries where raw material and basic commodities are extracted. In a Moebius strip, there are never two faces that overlap, like in the new account of violence I propose here: rather the two sides are the same, continuous, even if they contain a twist in the paper. This image should help us keep in mind that there is no interior or exterior, no clear start or end point, and that geographical distance matters little. Similarly, policies and actions with increased violence on the colonial subjects are intimately connected to theory, in particular liberal democratic discourses and the process of civilization in Europe.[79] Later, we will also see how what seems to be a thing of the past (the racialized exclusion of Tunisian Muslims) continues to haunt the present with differentiated violence by the current Tunisian government against its own citizens that eerily echoes colonial practices.

The image of the Moebius strip allows us to come to grips with the interconnectedness not just of the two shores of the Mediterranean, but also of class-based and racial forms of exclusion and oppression, both in colonial and post-independence times. Following Balibar (2015: 9), I would like to suggest that an excess of violence in the colonies has been a necessary condition for capitalism to emerge. Without this, there would not be a "civilizing process" in Europe. To this excess of violence, one should add a racial component. Rarely acknowledged within Western theory, studies from the colonies have shown the many forms and instances of racist blind spots. To paraphrase Balibar, one could say that the excess of racialized violence in the colonies is necessary for capitalism,[80] and in Moebius terms, the illusion of liberal equality of chances of reaching a similar condition of full citizenship is in reality in continuity with the denial of these chances in the parts of the world that suffered systematic encroachments, such as the Middle East. Slavery was banned in the 1830s in Europe, yet the French colonial authorities allowed the slave trade to go on in southern Algeria for much of the nineteenth century (Brower 2009: 171). Law was unevenly applied

---

[79] I took the metaphor of the Moebius strip from Etienne Balibar (2015: xii, 73), but the idea of connecting theories of violence is mine. Agamben (1995) also uses the image to denote the lack of interior and exterior. I am grateful to Agnes Czajka for that additional reference. See also Bigo (2001).

[80] I do not address class-based violence because it has been the focus of 150 years of critical Marxist research. Gender should also be included, but I concentrate on the novelty of racialization. For the gendered component of violence and exclusion, see the critical work on social reproduction in a global perspective, e.g. J. Moore (2016).

"there" because it favored capitalist and colonial interests "here." A Moebius-type of approach lets forgotten episodes re-emerge and complicate the dominant narrative of liberal citizenship.

In terms of the *social life of citizenship*, I hope that I have made clear why it is misleading to study "citizenship" through only the holding of elections. In Europe, the social life of citizenship has been the result of bloody centuries of struggle, and there is agreement that it was in the making for nearly a millennium. In most of the Middle East, these processes were altered by European interference that started two or three centuries ago. It is therefore improbable to expect the same process of balancing, or articulating, economic, political, and symbolic aspects of citizens' rights and duties to emerge in so little time. In particular, the racialized forms of government and administration that Euro-Americans introduced or reinforced in the Middle East force one to account for the long denial of full enfranchisement in the metropole.[81]

European elites created a worldview and justification for the exploitation of racialized subjects (labor forces in the colonies) and criminalized subjects (Europeans forced to resettled there) whose role was to feed the process of raw material extraction and surplus production (Wynter 2003). The development of penal colonies to punish dissenters in the metropoles was synchronous with the incorporation of the peripheries in the new order of (agrarian, later industrial) capitalism (Ross 2008: 93–97). Balibar's formula could also be used to explain the invisibilization of the problem of social reproduction and of sexualized violence against women from the colonies and to obfuscate the uneven depletion of global natural resources and raw materials, an issue that Maria Mies (1987) addressed already in her powerful *Patriarchy and Accumulation on a World Scale*. Elsewhere, I have proposed a reading of the impact of racialization of certain parts of Tunisia (Challand 2020), in findings that echo research on differentiated forms of citizenship along the lines of *indigénat* and "non-universal subjecthood" (Saada 2013: 323, 333; Pitts 2000).

My hope is that the Moebius detours demonstrate that theories of citizenship or civility must be revisited in a transversal and relational manner. The idea of the Moebius image is to reconnect the two faces of

---

[81] On American entrepreneurs importing racialization into the Middle East, most visible in the mining and extraction industries (copper, later oil), see Vitalis (2006). Here again, private capitalist actors precede imperial encroachment.

combined and uneven civility and set them in relation with one another in a way that transcends geographical and temporal separations. As the two sides of the Moebius strip are in continuity, these two conditions of full and negative/latent citizenship are consubstantial.

To complement Foucault in a Moebius sense, one could say that the image of the panopticon rests on the crude and highly visible presence of the encroachers' authority. The more lenient, re-educative prisons in Europe were only one side of the coin, while the other side was made of the brutal elimination of dissent in the colonies proceeding more along the lines of the ancient regime of public torture and dismembered victims.

In Eliasian terms, the process of civilization, which could be applied to the highly sophisticated court life of the Ottoman Empire, was only one part of the story. In the colonies, because of the absence of the role model played by the nobility and courtesans, civility was less visible or foundational. Cruelty might have well been enshrined in new ruling and administrative measures rather than being shun by the courts or elites.

In Tillyan terms, if the legitimacy of the modern states in Europe rested on finding the equilibrium between coercion, extraction, and demands placed on citizen-soldiers, in the Middle East, the colonial distortions and the brutality of the fiscal-military power prevented the discovery of this point of equilibrium between state and society, or of just law (*jus quia justum*). In that part of the world (the Middle East, but by extension to the peripheries of Europe or the West), law remained arbitrary because it was imposed for the benefit of the European encroachers (*jus quia jussum*).

The dominant narrative of citizenship cannot be thought of in terms of an "equalization of violence," as Tilly suggests, as an expansive view of civility, or in the T.H. Marshall approach of gradually expanding political, civil, and social rights. I believe that Arab citizens would like to see such equalization happen, but up to this point in our analysis, we have seen that pre-colonial (garrison states) and colonial interventions and encroachments have created pockets of deep inequality. Gender, class, and race produced a priori conditions for exclusions in the colonies, as opposed to an illusion of universal enfranchisement in the metropoles. Let us now turn to post-independence in the Arab Middle East and see if the social life of citizenship had a chance to flourish despite these external influences.

2 | Post-Independence Aspirations, Security Custodianship, and Latent Citizenship

2.1 The Making of Latent Citizenship

Chapter 1 covered the straightjacket of state-formation inherited from pre-colonial and colonial times. The result has been, among others, fragmented geographies of civic participation. The excess of violence in the colonies enabled the actualization of some form of equal citizenship in Europe, while the Moebius perspective suggests that, as a result, the bases for citizenship in the Middle East are more unstable and precarious. Chapter 2 identifies contrasting dynamics within the MENA region, with democratic aspirations playing out in the arena of contention despite these original limitations: When did civic activism emerge in limited spaces and periods? What were the aspirations for citizenship? Why were they short-lived?

Contrary to the view that 2011 came out of the blue or through the sole power of social media, this book argues that 2011 revived older ferment for democratic participation and re-assembled social fractures that were deepened in the independence era. It is therefore important to understand what generated these upheavals, what limited them, and how domestic dynamics, not just external encroachment, contributed to democratic informal mobilizations. It also brings nuance to Bayat's (2017: xi) argument that the 2011 revolutions were "leaderless" and made of "unsettling novelties."

The thesis of the chapter is plain and simple but it has the merit to shake up the fundaments of doxas about citizenship in the Middle East. I take the doxa, namely that which "is beyond question" (Bourdieu 1977: 169), to be that there is no citizenship, or that it is defective, because we don't have the same T.H. Marshall (1941/1992) or liberal expansive approach to citizenship in the Arab world. The model of citizenship in Europe and advanced capitalist countries is liberal, and the literature affirms that this form of citizenship is functional, while the Middle East does not manage to conform to this exemplar or model (Turner 2000; Thompson [2002]).

Contrary to culturalist narratives, the social life of Arab citizenship has been in certain time and spaces rich and vibrant. In particular in the last third of the nineteenth century and the first 15 years of the twentieth, revolutionary experiments in self-government, mostly republican, were implemented by previously unorganized actors or theorized by self-made political leaders in the region. It was a space of rich conceptual exchange, be they intra-regional, cross-Mediterranean, or "South–South" influences. It often took the form of inchoate mobilizations. In a nutshell, it was a laboratory of early democratic or nascent republican politics that was gradually extinguished by the force of colonialism and imperialism, the straightjacket of "nation-states" in partly imposed borders, and the dominant ideology of state developmentalism after independence.

After a democratically creative period, politics in the region pivoted, from the mid-twentieth century, around new states, meant to "represent" a "nation," led by a new political elite reluctant to embrace pluralistic politics. As a consequence, this new period erased localized exercises of self-rule – a local republic in the Moroccan *rif*, or in the Lebanese mountains – and generated a search for homogeneity alongside ideologies of modernization and developmentalism. A situation of intense democratic ferment (that is, scattered positive elements that spearheaded democratic experiments) existed in an early incubating period at the turn of the last century, but it was blocked and suppressed for most of the decades prior to the 2011 Uprisings. The past relegation of, or bracketing of, this ferment, explains why 2011 exploded in the manner that it did. Chapter 3 will show that the Uprisings of 2011 generated substantial democratic demands thanks to the power of new articulations (the "three facets of representation"), but that each pocket of demonstration or dissatisfaction had a distinct history and a clear project. In the condition of latent citizenship, these seemingly isolated acts of contention could not reach the transformative effect they aspired to at the national level.

This chapter assesses why there have been repeated attempts to deploy principles of bottom-up civic participation since the end of the nineteenth century, and what the motives were for support or undermining what I call the "ferment of democracy" (Section 2.1). Section 2.2 explains other factors that have contributed to the condition of latent citizenship in the independence era, and Section 2.3 revisits the "civility paradigm" in light of the analysis of domestic Arab politics. The chapter concludes with an overview (Section 2.4) describing the situation in Tunisia and Yemen on the eve of the winter 2010–2011.

The proposed genealogy captures the dialectical relations between state and society and the reasons that led to scattered episodes of democratic ferment or ebullience at the turn of the nineteenth and twentieth centuries, and in the immediate years following independence. While there was a sociological change in leading political actors, transgressive mobilization was limited to small bursts. A very rich literature focuses on the hurdles to citizenship generated by colonial policies,[1] but these studies tend to "leapfrog" from the colonial time directly into the present (Cooper 2005: 17–18), without dwelling in the historical period after independence wherein Arab leaders had the possibility to right past wrongs. Because of the multi-directionality of flows that the model of the Moebius strip captures, I think it important to study the evolution of security institutions during the post-independence era. Domestic and international ideological factors, coupled with the materiality of the state (rent, foreign aid), have stifled civic participation in the second half of the twentieth century. For this reason, the following sections propose a periodization distinguishing the late colonial era (called Period I) from the independence and Cold War era (Period II). The uneven geographic distribution of violence in the colonial era is only partly transformed by the new nationalist ideology that was supposed to unify citizenship practices, but which remained fractured, often around security organizations, and had limited access to citizenship. In this context, a permanent custodianship by the security forces (Sayigh 2015) shut the door to political participation for the majority of Arab populations, a condition that generated a negative habitus for democratic participation.

2.2 Ferment of Democracy and Closure in the Age of Ideologies

The last few decades of scholarship on the modern Middle East have produced very fine studies reacting to decades of (neo-)Orientalist and distorting accounts of the region,[2] with approaches akin to social history

---

[1] Colonial distortions are discussed in greater detail for Syria and Lebanon (Thompson 2000), Jordan (Massad 2001), Algeria with French citizenship (Shepard 2008; Hannoum 2010), Egypt (Esmeir 2012), and Palestine (Giacaman 1998; Clarno 2017), to name some of the most important recent interventions.

[2] Orientalist in the second sense described by Edward Said in his eponymous book (Said 1978: 2), that is the ontological invention of the "East" imagined as the

or the history from below rather than top-down, elite-centered studies that dominated the field for most of the twentieth century. With a strong entry point in social theory, Charles Tripp's (2013) study of popular culture and resistance and John Chalcraft's (2016: 4, 6) more recent *opus magnum* on the complex role of "contentious politics" and the contributions made by spontaneous and informal movements are the most salient studies that have re-oriented the field away from a procedural, liberal, and previously modernist account of local politics. Historical studies have also engaged with radical groups vying to promote equality in the decaying years of the Ottoman Empire (Khuri-Makdisi 2010; Campos 2010; Thompson 2013: 13–88). Communist parties have also been the focus of important studies (Hilal & Hermann 2014; Budeiri 2010; Guirguis 2021), in particular how these parties have been de facto vehicles for the inclusion of marginalized groups in the first half of the past century, such as Shiites in Iraq, Kurds in Syria, or Palestinians inside Israel (Batatu 2004; Lockman 1996; Beinin 1990). Moreover, in the vein of global environmental and capitalist studies ushered in by Jason Moore (2016), Aaron Jakes (2020) also shows that pushes for market-driven political changes in Egypt were a *combined* effort by the British occupying force and the local nascent capitalist class, who together thwarted popular mobilizations.

With a view on a combination of domestic and international influences, I will discuss novel representational politics in these two periods.[3] These are ideal-types, i.e. typified, or idealized, schemes with the heuristic function of explaining complex empirical phenomena around issues of citizenship and violence. Within these different periods, each of which influenced the mobilizations of 2011 in their

systematic opposite of the "West." For the orientalist debate on democracy in the Middle East, see Sadiki (2004) or Harik (2006). Sadowski (1993) shows the futility of the shift from classical Orientalism to neo-Orientalism in the depiction state–society relations.

[3] Every periodization can be disputed. I will only note a certain convergence with other periodization efforts made by Meijer (2014) and Chalcraft (2016). Chalcraft also distinguishes a first historical period (1798–1914), labeled "Millenarianism, renewal, justice, rights and reform," from a second (1914–1952), "Patriotism, liberalism, armed struggle and ideology," a third (1952–1976), "National independence, guerrilla war and social revolution," and a fourth (1977–2011), "Islamism, revolution, uprisings and liberalism." In my reading, I share the first period and then lump the second to the fourth periods into Period II, the age of ideologies, which starts with nationalism (the second period in Chalcraft).

own manner, we will distinguish regional influences and factors from external ones. Thus, we put the metaphor of the Moebius strip to work, but also hope to limit the view that democratic politics is merely an extension of Euro-American practices.

First, *Period I* covers a very fluid and multi-directional process of identification, in part coupled with the advent of political modernity in the Middle East. Some events antedate the systematic European influences and reveal innovative local aspirations for civic emancipation. Chalcraft (2016) lists many examples of intra-colonial or intra-regional diffusion of popular politics in the first historical period he covers, namely between 1798 and 1914, a historical period where only very limited forms of political representation existed. As a consequence, these emancipatory political experiments, and ferment, did not survive long or break from their limited territorial basis. Yet these episodes are significant, for they were more than a revolt of commoners (*'ammiyya*) against a new tax, an administrative reform,[4] or a series of revolts interpreted as Islamic millenarianism and revivalism against the decaying authority of the Ottoman Empire or nascent colonial encroachments:[5] They also proposed new models of connection between subjects. The most emblematic example is the so-called Kisrawan Republic between December 1858 and July 1860, where a "force of Maronite commoners, under the leadership of a humble muleteer," Tanyus Shahin (d. 1895), revolted against their feudal lords in the district of Kisrawan, northwest of Beirut (Chalcraft 2016: 123–129; Thompson 2013: 37–60). Peasants revolted against local Christian lordly families and followed the lead of Shahin, who called this uprising a movement (*haraka* in Arabic). Self-reference was made to "the people" (*ahali*) to create a new political object, that of a republic, aimed at "reshaping the social order in Kisrawan through the mass, forceful, but non-violent appropriation of the means of production and the temporary eviction of the [local] shaykhs."[6]

---

[4] Chalcraft (2016: 67 68, 85, 88, 95) lists many examples of these small-scale *jacqueries*, or other Robin Hood-like episodes.

[5] On these, see Abd Al-Qadir's revolts in Algeria and Al-Sanusi's order in North Africa. Chalcraft notes that unlike subsequent Islamic modernism of the turn of the century, these revivalisms "paid little attention to the West" (Chalcraft 2016: 106–107).

[6] The notion of *al-saleh al-jumhuri*, popular welfare, was already articulated in 1840 in Mount Lebanon to oppose the unjust rule under a short period of occupation by the Egyptian Mamluk (Chalcraft 2016: 69).

Institutions of elected representatives from villages, calls to respect the proclaimed equality among Ottoman subjects,[7] and the modest participation of women in the revolt were pitted against the burden of heavy taxation collected by local shaykhs on behalf of the Ottomans (Makdisi 2000: 103; Thompson 2013: 42). This short-lived experience that described itself as a "republic" (*jumhuriyya*) was eventually crushed, as a result of the reorganization of the Druze and Ottoman elites, but also because of the "confessional coloring" that Shahin allowed to dominate the republic, and for self-appointing himself "Bek," "in flat contradiction with the egalitarian principles of the original uprisings" (Makdisi 2000: 124, quoted in Chalcraft 2016: 126). Other uprisings of commoners in the region occurred, but never with the same degree of transgressive-ness as the one in Kisrawan.

Another emblematic case of new republican mobilization was the Rif revolt in Morocco, which was taken as a source of intra-regional influence all the way to Syria years later. The Rif revolt occurred between 1921 and 1926 in the northern mountainous region of Morocco. The leader, Abd Al-Krim Al-Khattabi (d. 1963), was a descendant of an important Sunni lineage going back to one of the first Caliphs. He mixed Islamic heritage with the republican project and consciously tapped into Arab and tribal structures. Abd Al-Krim was himself a *qadi* (judge), used Islamic symbology on the flag, invoked religious edicts to justify his war orders, and called for allegiance (*baya'*) in a manner that supported the Arabophone population against European settlers as well as the Berbers. The movement called itself a formal republic (*dawla jumhuriyya rifiyya*, the "Rif Republic"), which included a parliament (*barlaman*) and an elected president (*ra'is*) (Chalcraft 2016: 233). Like a new, emerging state, coercion was centralized and monopolized: "A paid, trained, standing army was created with Abd Al-Krim as its commander-in-chief" (Chalcraft 2016: 124). In brief, a proto-state was in the making in part of Morocco, again debunking the idea that states in the Arab worlds or in the Middle East could only be artificial, external creations of Europeans or imperial powers.

Mixing different registers of morality, other protests of the early twentieth century tapped into Islamic notions of social justice, and articulated a proto-nationalist project. One can list here two

---

[7] This occurred with the Gülhane Edict of 1856. See Gelvin (2011).

developments in Libya, with the short-lived Tripolitanian Republic between 1918 and 1923 and Omar Al-Mukhtar's resistance from the 1920s until his death in 1931 to the Italian fascist rule of Libya, and the rural segments of the Great Palestinian Revolt against British and Zionist encroachment in Mandatory Palestine, around Izz Al-Din Al-Qassam (d. 1935). The attempt was to generate a larger imagined community by forging new horizontal ties. Abd Al-Krim's challenge was a thorn in the flesh of the Moroccan sultan, of the Alawi dynasty, but also of French and Spanish colonialism, which tried to coopt him. Abd Al-Krim was eventually crushed, but he was an inspiration to another anti-colonial rebellion, this time in Syria, then under a French mandate (Chalcraft 2016: 227). The Great Palestinian Revolt of 1936–1937 was so substantial that Britain faced the greatest counter-insurgency ever registered and had to take radical measures to quell it: It is often forgotten that the ill-fated Munich Agreement between Hitler and Chamberlain in September 1938 occurred because of Britain's need to free some of its troops to crush the Palestinian revolt – another example of the necessity to apply the Moebius strip of the uneven, yet connected, deployment of means of coercion across Europe *and* the colonies.[8]

In sum, all these rebellions were more than short fires. They articulated original forms of republican mobilization, with some secular components (principles of nationalism, representation), but also at times with religious sanctioning or references, and without automatic reference to European "models."[9] These examples of mobilization eventually failed, and the sociological explanation provided by Chalcraft helps us understand why this is the case.

Building on a Gramscian understanding of emancipation, Chalcraft notes that a sense of self-awareness must grow, often from cultural or religious programs, until a tipping point where disruptive mobilizations occur: In such creative moments, popular politics emerge from the

---

[8] An earlier occurrence of colonial rebellion impacting military developments in Europe is the Haitian revolution (1792–1804). C.L.R. James (1963: 374) connects the French naval defeat of Trafalgar in 1805 with the massive loss of soldiers during the Leclerc campaign in 1802 and 1803 against Toussaint L'Ouverture in Haiti.

[9] To be balanced, one should acknowledge that the crushing of these "republican" rebellions offered an opportunity for European powers to further encroach upon the regions, and precipitated confessional conflicts. See e.g. Thompson (2013: 38, 56–60).

ties that a few individuals, underprivileged groups, or new constituencies can create, and thus generate a larger and new sense of politicized consciousness. Such "historical blocks" can then challenge hegemonic power. The reading of hegemony, like in Gramsci, is two-directional: The task of the political incumbent is to retain their hegemony, understood as the "spontaneous consent given by the great masses of the population to the general direction imposed on social life by the dominant fundamental group" (this is Gramsci's definition, but written as such by Chalcraft 2016: 3), but when there is a "hegemonic contraction," the "failure of political articulation and the dessication of the site of articulations," then we are likely to witness a fundamental challenge from below.

Such a challenge, what Chalcraft describes as "popular politics," consists of new social groups that vie for leadership and fight not to simply reform the existing political arrangements, but to establish their own hegemonic project. He distinguishes between two types of disruptive mobilizations or contentious politics: namely the *contained* as opposed to the *transgressive* mobilizations. The former is more institutionalized, and is generally led by publicly recognized contenders or political actors (Chalcraft 2016: 24). Transgressive mobilizations stem from previously unorganized or apolitical actors. The more innovative force of the transgressive mobilization compensates for the lack of structures (Chalcraft 2016: 25).

The difficulty lies in explaining why, in certain cases only, popular politics really matters and re-shapes actual participation in the political system. Chalcraft thinks that crises arise when there is a desiccation of the sites of articulation. Politics, à la Gramsci, is about the ability to rule without force. To do that, *the rulers must be able to articulate* economic, political, religious, and cultural programs.[10] When these articulations fail to "speak to the masses," then authorities face the prospect of a political or social crisis. Put differently, the possibility of counter-hegemony arises because there is a tendency towards disincorporation of the dominant alliances previously put in place by the ruling elites.

Popular politics only works inasmuch as it succeeds in offering a new hegemonic project (sometimes disruptive and transgressive, e.g. a shift

---

[10] Stuart Hall (2016) elaborates also on the issue of articulations, as seen in Section 1.2 above.

from a feudal to republican order), creates alliances and new articulations, and explores creative means to incorporate new social groups. If this popular politics (either class or sectarian) fights only for its own cause, so to say, then it is doomed to failure because it cannot expand to other sectors of the society to make a lasting impact on the formal political system. I will add to Chalcraft's assessment that the force of new political imaginary is also an important ingredient in understanding how transgressive politics from below can succeed in democratizing parts of the political system.[11]

Each historical period has additional, contingent reasons why mobilizations are likely to succeed or fail. For Period I, Chalcraft sees that there is no fixed sense of what the "masses" are, and the lack of mass media and an independent state are additional factors that hampered radical experiments in this period. But the richness of these endogenous mobilizations demonstrates the presence and (limited) power of informalism. We will return later to this aspect in Period II.

Let us now look at *reactive* instances of innovation, namely cases where mobilization or forms for political expression followed or emulated international models in Period I. Among these, one can list constitutionalist episodes and the parallel emergence of new political concepts. Said Arjomand (2008) documents successful constitutionalist movements that emerged in the late nineteenth and early twentieth centuries. The first wave of constitutionalism, typically traced to the Ottoman reforms of 1876, or Egypt in 1882,[12] paved the way for a second, more profound wave of constitutionalist demands, namely the Iranian Constitutional Revolution (1906–1911) and the Young Turks' Revolution in 1908. In these cases, modern principles of citizenship trumped those of religious or confessional identifications. It was

[11] A political imaginary in itself cannot change a political system. It requires, first, new forms of content of self-representation that in turn translate, through sustained practices and/or new rituals in new forms of political representation. The second clarification is that the cases of collective actions and ruptures, discussed in this chapter, had a democratic component, but they could have also turned conservative or segmentary ("tribal") as opposed to inclusive and fully egalitarian, something that happened in part with the Tanyus Shahin revolt. Not all instances of popular politics or informal citizenship can be subsumed under the category of "democratic" breakthrough. They are, however, an important pre-condition.

[12] One could also add the Moroccan case after the signing of the protectorate in 1912 with a constitution passed by Sultan Abd Al-Hafiz (see Chalcraft 2016: 150).

a period that saw the triumph "of modern conceptions of pluralism over religious particularisms" and in which *shari'a* was actually contained rather than proposed as the basis of a new modern political order – legislation, or legislative power, was connected to the root *qanun* (law in the technical sense), not to that of *shari'a* (Arjomand 2008: 35, 39). In the Iranian case, Shiite clerics even took sides with the defenders of constitutionalism in their opposition to the dying Qajar absolutism and supported equality for Muslim and non-Muslim citizens (Cole 2006; Hairi 1976).

Such experiments were connected with a profound renewal of the vernacular political language. New concepts were adapted to Arabic. For example, new meaning was given to terms such as "party" (*hizb*), which until then had a pejorative connotation of secession or dividing faction(alism); "liberty" (*hurriyya*), moving from a limited understanding of being in a state of non-servitude to individual entitlement; and "voice" (*sawt*), to capture the novelty created by electoral politics. Probably one of the most significant semantic shifts has been the creation, conceptually, of the idea of citizenship. The Arabic *ra'iyyah*, a word that captures the notion of subject (it also means herd, flock), or "collective subjectivity" (Parolin 2018), was replaced temporarily by the more abstract *ri'ayyah*, to express the notion of custodian, or citizenship, but the main modern term is *muwatin*, i.e. a person connected to a *watan*, a nation.[13] *Muwatana*, the abstract concept of individualized citizenship, replaced – because of the democratizing effect of popular politics – the older term of *al-'amma*, the public or commoners in opposition to the privileged (ruling) classes (*al-khassa*) (Meijer 2014: 636). Like most societies confronted with political modernity in the nineteenth century, Middle Eastern societies built a positive (and often positivist) arsenal and conceptual equipment to deal with modern forms of representation, Islamists included.[14]

Pluralism was also seen on the mobilizational level where one sees, in this first period, identifications with class, political movements, and communities that were not yet constrained by national borders. Ilham

---

[13]   See Ayalon (1989: 36), Arjomand (2008: 36), or Chalcraft (2016: 161). Another term used in the modern context of post-independence states is *jinsiyya*, to describe nationality or "passport citizenship" (Davis 2000: 53).

[14]   In the words of one of the best observers of this historical period, Islam and modernity were in full dialogue, with numerous attempts "to reconcile modern values and Islamic faith" (Kurzman 2002: 27).

Khuri-Makdisi illustrates this in her study of radical militants spreading anarchist and socialist ideals in the southeastern Mediterranean basin. Italian or Greek anarchists based in Alexandria or Beirut connected to northern Mediterranean countries, Levantine networks shared resources with North African ones, and many radical Marxist intellectuals (many of them Jewish) felt unconstrained by what we now call the northern or southern shores of the Mediterranean: their horizons of inspiration spread throughout the Mediterranean basin all the way to Latin America.[15] Theatre plays, new monthly print media, and, later, cinema – all explorations of cultural representations – were the vehicles that shared visions of a new society in which women were invited to play a more political role. The fusion was not just about different (vertical) identities (such as religious and national), but also about the adoption of new meanings attached to the term "people" (*sha'ab, ahal*), which in that moment directly connected to the demands of the working class.

Inchoate republican politics spread like wildfire in the interstitial years after WW1, when European powers were absorbed with the conclusion of years of destructive and destabilizing wars, the revolutionary Bolshevik challenge, general strikes, Spartakist movements, and social republics in the heart of Western Europe. Hussein Omar goes as far as comparing the protests that erupted in much of the Arab world in that period as the "Arab Spring of 1919" (Omar 2019). In his words:

War-weary peasants staged sit-ins, removed railroad tracks and occupied buildings across Libya, Egypt, Palestine and Tunisia. By 1920, the tremors had spread to Iraq and Morocco, where guerrillas declared independence from the semi-colonised kingdom. Sudan was engulfed by protests in 1924. By 1925, Syria was in the throes of a full-blown war. The recently established RAF bombed Egypt and Iraq to put an end to the revolutions. Instead, the bombardment energised them. These uprisings have often been understood as isolated national revolutions, but they may be better thought of as a single (if protracted) wave that lasted from 1918 to the early 1930s, much as the Arab Spring movements that began in 2011 continue to reverberate today. The revolutionaries shared slogans, ideas, ideals and personnel.

The Moebius metaphor also makes visible the connection between these radical uprisings in the Middle East and race riots against

---

[15] Khuri-Makdisi (2010: 31–32). Though Marx's texts were of little influence. It is the anarchist tradition that received the most attention in the Levantine circles.

Egyptians based in the UK: Omar (2019) relates that Egyptians were targeted in the race riots that broke out in Manchester, Cardiff, and Liverpool, just as the episodes of violence in Algiers against the Edict Crémieux and the Paris Commune between 1870 and 1871 were connected.[16] Overall, the aspirations among Arab commoners, peasants, or rebellious city-dwellers and the incubator of democratic participation were gradually extinguished by a variety of factors. Like in Europe, these "internationalist" experiments were repressed, and the model of nation-states meant to take over the dismantled Ottoman Empire became the new norm. With European powers imposing the form and borders for many new state entities through the Mandate system, the Euro-centric practice of the "nation-states" became a straightjacket for radical experiments from below. The creativity of Period I came to an end and was replaced by the stifling power of ideologies, especially during the Cold War.

Period II (1920 to 2010) is described here as the "age of ideologies,"[17] and is not specific to the Middle East, but typical of the decolonization era, which witnessed the contrast between nationalist, socialist, and later religious ideologies. In the late colonial moment various nationalist groups emerged throughout the world to fight colonialism. But it is only after WW2 that these nationalist movements managed to rid themselves of European encroachments. Lebanon and Syria (1943) were the first, followed by the withdrawal of Britain from the mandates in Transjordan (independence in 1946) and Palestine (creation of Israel in 1948), and from the joint control of Sudan in 1956. Military coups in Egypt (1952), Iraq (1958), and Libya (1969) put an end to British-backed monarchies, while French possessions in the region obtained independence peacefully in Morocco and Tunisia (1956), and through a war of liberation in Algeria (1962).

Post-independence regimes "command[ed] a certain legitimacy and the support and consensus of the governed," with popularity taking

---

[16] Ross (2008: 93–97). Kristin Ross demonstrates that the revolutionary project of an immediate universal citizenship during the Paris Commune of 1871 (e.g. accepting Algerians, Italians, Poles, and other social pariahs, for example women prostitutes, into the new polity in Paris) was a way to break the mold of conservative nationalism and to resist social regimentation (p. 5). On the Edict Crémieux, see also Hannoum (2010: 131).

[17] For an intellectual history for Period II, see Hanssen & Weiss (2018). What they call the *Arabic Thought against the Authoritarian Age* corresponds to what I call the "age of ideologies."

root in the promise to "expand the substantive freedoms of the common people" (Ahmad 2006: 136–137). Hélé Béji (2008) eloquently describes how the decolonized encountered a quasi-metaphysical joy at the process of national liberation – one only need picture one of the famous moments, such as when Gamal Abdel Nasser and the Free Officers were surrounded by a swath of cheering people after the coup of 1952, or during the nationalization of the Canal in 1956, to realize this new symbiosis between the aspirations of the people at large and a truly new (both in national and sociological terms) leadership. Gamal Abdel Nasser and Abd Al-Karim Qassem, who toppled the Hashemite dynasty in Iraq in 1958, were from modest backgrounds (son of a railroad worker and son of a mail man), were described as *ibn al-balad*, "the son of the village," and symbolized the access laypeople had to power.[18] In 1964 Sudan experienced a revolution against the military rule of general Ibrahim Abboud (Suleiman 2012; Ottaway 2017: 25), which was also characterized by massive popular support. The composition of the revolutionary forces (workers, youth, women, professional groups, parties, and other civil forces) conferred upon it a democratic character, at least for its initial moments.[19] In short, the new idea and practice of the post-independence state, embodied in the new heroic leader and carried by the fervent populations, was about unity, about the direct involvement of the masses in politics. Walter Armbrust (2019: 9, 17) gives a name, *communitas*, to this stage and explains this sense of joint embodiment or fusion between the masses and their leaders at the time of independence: in a liminal moment, a sense of *communitas* and perceived unity emerged out of the collective interactions, but these ended in a moment of schism and eventually failed.

Three clusters of factors explain how democratic transformations moved from the stage of euphoria, and of the *communitas*, to a fractured state–society situation and the ensuing consolidation of latent citizenship. First, nationalism and competing ideologies generated a politics of "authenticity," which rapidly created a profound separation between the masses and formal state institutions. This often led to a strong party polarization, involving a ruling party on

---

[18] On this, see El-Messiri (1978).
[19] See A. Jamal (2021) for a long historical reading of the 1964 and 2018 revolutions against military rule in Sudan.

the one hand, and Islamist and leftist parties on the other. Second, the high number of wars and conflicts left the region with a deeply militarized political economy, with emergency regulations used frequently to curtail civic liberties. Third, the state, and its key institutions, became an object of predation. Out of more-or-less imagined threats, the availability of external non-tax incomes (rents) to fight these (ideological) wars reinforced a logic of resource accumulation at the helm of the state, generating profound inequalities within Arab societies. The three factors play out differently in each country, but a brief overview of post-independence Tunisia, and the longer account of the two Yemeni republics that emerged in the 1960s, connects to the general consideration about the links between violence and citizenship that constitute the focus of Part I of this book.

In Tunisia, independence occurred without a war. A resolute urban Arab elite, educated in the modern *Collège Sadiki* or *Lycée Carnot* in Tunis (Chouikha & Gobe 2015: 11), had emerged from the 1930s onward under the guidance of leader Habib Bourguiba. Republicanism was the preferred form, and when independence was obtained from France in 1956, the monarchy and the Husaynid dynasty were replaced by a presidential system. The main opponent to Bourguiba was Salah Ben Youssef (1907–1961), a leader from a traditional Zaituna-educated family from Djerba, who could count on the strong support of the *fellaghas*, the armed men fighting against colonialism in Algeria and Tunisia in the mid-twentieth century (Chouikha & Gobe 2015: 12–15). When the war in Algeria broke out in 1954, France used an iron fist against Salah Ben Youssef's guerilla forces in the south, who supported the Algerian revolution, but proved much more lenient towards the other nationalist leader, Habib Bourguiba. The latter was also more accommodating towards the French. In exchange for independence in 1956, Bourguiba granted France continued control of the city and harbor of Bizerte, north of Tunis, as a French territory, out of which it could patrol nearby Algeria (L. Anderson 1986: 236).

Despite the strong legitimacy that Bourguiba obtained in leading the nationalist movement to independence, he suffered from the rivalry with Ben Youssef, leading to an uneven deployment of state institutions, in particular in Ben Youssef's strongholds. With most of the republican elites around Bourguiba being from the coastal area, the south and the central regions of the country felt punished for their support of Salah Ben Youssef, who was assassinated in Frankfurt in August 1961, most probably with Bourguiba's blessing. This left a mark on the country's economy, with a less developed interior (the term we will use to speak of the non-Sahel, non-coastal areas of Tunisia). Bourguiba championed the view of equal nationalist developmentalism, but many political and economic benefits went to the president's home region until his fall from power in 1987.

Tunisia was spared the destruction of war, and thus the army played a more marginal role in contemporary history than it did in Yemen. Over time, two ideological blocks developed and challenged Bourguiba's authority. First, a strong leftist and Marxist movement organized, and it was soon rivaled by an Islamist movement (the MTI, *Mouvement de la Tendance Islamiste*), precursor of the Ennahda party (Burgat 1996). Bourguiba did not tolerate political opposition and imprisoned many Marxist and subsequently Islamist activists. Seeing how often military coups had deposed neighboring Arab leaders, Bourguiba developed misgivings about the army and preferred to lean on his ruling party, Parti Socialiste Destourien (PSD), for his three decades in power (1957–1987) (Bou Nassif 2015: 67). He grew increasingly autocratic but remained popular for measures that favored gender equality and the spread of education and literacy. A true pioneer among Arab republics, Tunisia adopted an unsurpassed code on personal status, granting equal rights for women and men in most areas of civil law and eclipsing Islamic prescriptions on polygamy, custody rights, and divorce only five months after its independence (Charrad 2001).

In Yemen, one has to distinguish two different trajectories: In the North, the civil war (1962–1970) that ended the Imamic Zaydi rule led to the preeminence of military leaders. In the South, the anti-colonial struggle heralded the unique case of an Arab republic ruled by a quasi-Marxist party that had ended British colonialism. What was common for both parts of Yemen was the vivid dissatisfaction of citizens in the early 1960s. Britain enacted a very limited condition of subjecthood, *ra'iyyah* (Dresch 2000: 76, 58) in Southern Yemen, so much so that an Arab historian went so far as to say that "Arab citizens were living at the margin of life in their own country" (Al-Adhal 1993: 80, as quoted in Dresch 2000: 58). In the North, opposition to Imam Ahmad grew in intensity in the 1950s. A famous pamphlet against Imam Ahmad first published in Aden in

1956 called for the creation of a republic in the North. Its title, significantly, was *"matalib al-sha'ab"* ("Demands of the People"), and the text was penned by future republican leaders in the north, Ahmad Nu'man and Muhammed Zubayri (Dresch 2000: 103–108). They promoted the ideology of the Free Yemenis by invoking their common ancestry, thinking of all Yemenis as "Sons of Qahtan" and thus in the frame of equality (Day 2012: 37). Nu'man (d. 1996), a teacher from Shafii in lower Yemen, and Zubayri (d. 1965), a judge from the Zaydi highlands, were the perfect combination to offer a "broad base" for unifying the republican movement (Bonnefoy 2018: 22). But the common feeling, in the North and South of Yemen, was that public resources had to be mobilized to eradicate poverty and create better conditions for mass political participation and not just that of a tiny minority. Appalling rates of infant mortality, high levels of poverty, double taxation, and insufficient funds for education in the 1960s were some of the reasons that made Yemeni citizens' expectations grow at the time of independence and republican politics (Dresch 2000: 111, 118).

In 1970, after eight years of civil war in the North, the Imamic rule was defeated by the republican side, which benefited from the support of the Egyptian army. All Yemeni presidents in the North, except Abdel-Rahman Al-Iryani, a *qadi* from the Shafii elite, came from modest origins and rose to power through the army ranks, just like Nasser, Qassem, and others of the new generation of Arab military leaders. In the South, the anti-colonial struggle prevailed, sending Britain packing its imperial bags in November 1967, but an ensuing internecine war opposed the National Liberation Front (NLF), itself made of different currents, and the more urban and labor-oriented Front of Liberation of the Occupied Southern Yemen (FLOSY). The NLF prevailed and ruled the new country, whose name changed from People's Republic of Southern Yemen to People's Democratic Republic of Yemen (PDRY) a few years later, under the helm of the Yemeni Socialist Party.

The rhetoric of Arab nationalisms and pan-Arabism could not hide profound rivalries. Libya and Tunisia announced their intention to merge into one single entity in the 1970s; talks of unifying the two Yemens also occurred in this time frame. Both failed to materialize (Bonnefoy 2018). Remaining as individual, separate countries, they became, at best, authoritarian corporatist regimes (Tunisia, Egypt), one-party regimes (Algeria, South Yemen), simple dictatorships with a strong military component (Iraq, Syria, and Libya), or a combination of the three (North Yemen). (We exclude here monarchies in the other half of Arab countries whose pretence for the defence of citizenship was never a priority.)

The presidents of North Yemen in the 1970s were Ibrahim Al-Hamdi (1974–1977), Ahmad Al-Ghashmi (Oct. 1977–July 1978), and Ali Abdullah Saleh (July 1978 to February 2012). All came from the same common rural areas around Sanaa and benefited from the same social ascension that only the military could give them.[20] They rose to the rank of officer during the civil war that raged between 1962 and 1968 and eventually put an end to the Imamate. Rogers (2019: 121–129) astutely notes that, with the civil war in the 1960s, these "violence specialists" came to the fore with another social group, the urban merchants, who were previously second to the Zaydi aristocracy (the *sada*) and the Shafii-trained *ulama* and *qadis*. Officers came to monopolize state authority, and merchants became important political players, in part because of their ability to provide war goods and basic supplies during hardship. With know-how amassed during the civil war and social networks comprised of military peers and tribal segments of the northern population, these two groups came to dominate political life in Northern Yemen. As Rogers (2019: 221) sums up, the civil war (and per extension the process of state-making) made tribalism vitally important in Yemen. In this alternative interpretation, state-making favored tribalism, rather than tribalism being an antagonist force to state-making.[21] In Southern Yemen, the original rivalry between the NLF and FLOSY, inspired by two different visions of Arabism, one pro-Marxist and the other pro-Nasserist, was replaced by regional rivalries between Hadhramis and people from the Aden and Abyan regions. Despite being a nominally socialist state, fears of regionalism and tribalism that had been supported by British colonialism turned the People's Democratic Republic of Yemen into a regime tightly and centrally controlled by the Politburo of the Yemeni Socialist

[20]   Ali Abdallah Saleh is from Al-Sanhan (as was Abdallah Al-Sallal, interim president during the Civil War) and Al-Ghashmi from Al-Hamdan. The other two Presidents, Al-Hamdi and Iryani, are from the governorate of Ibb. On Al-Hamdi and Al-Ghamshi, see Day (2012: 68).

[21]   Dresch (2000: 107–117) also notes that these tribal leaders moved "from relative obscurity under the last Imams" and emerged at the start of the war as "major figures" in the republican era. See also Brandt (2019b).

Party, the successor of the NLF and ruling party from 1978 onwards (Lackner 1985; Lackner 2016a: 142). The honeymoon between these new Arab military leaders and their populations lasted, maybe, a decade. In the initial period, much progress was registered, with full primary schooling established, and secondary and university level education promoted. Heightened standards of alphabetization were coupled with a push for the recognition of workers' rights and gender equality. Major infrastructure projects were projected. President Al-Hamdi, from the Taiz region, was very conscious in playing this line of development and progress. He is often seen as the champion of the cooperative (*ta'awun*) movement, with numerous local development associations (LDAs) building additional infrastructure (Carapico 1998). Al-Hamdi was a progressive politician, influenced by socialist ideas. He emphasized views favoring a civil state (*dawla madaniyya*) separate from religious, military, and tribal powers (Bonnefoy 2018: 189, fn. 23). But gradually, seeing the vast resources that the LDAs were able to muster, Al-Hamdi sought more top-down influence over them. He thus became the first President of the Confederation of Yemeni Development Associations, an umbrella organization for the LDAs (Lackner 2019: 101). He also established the Yemeni Military Economic Corporation (YMEC) in 1975 to provide "military cadres with access to cheap subsidized basic food and other commodities" (Lackner 2019: 232).

Al-Hamdi was open to talks of unification with South Yemen. However, his progressive politics and the prospect of a unified Yemen frightened Saudi Arabia (Bonnefoy 2018: xiii, 56). His killing was staged to discredit him and his legacy. Rivals from Upper Yemen, the Hashid and Bakil tribes, were probably behind his assassination, in cahoots with the Saudis. He was replaced by Ahmad Al-Ghashmi, a much more conservative figure, who was close to Hashid tribal leaders, but he was also killed a few months later (Day 2012: 68). Another military figure, Ali Abdallah Saleh, thus emerged as the new strong man of Northern Yemen in 1978. To help cement his grip on power, Saleh established the General People's Congress (GPC) (Day 2012: 69). This, and the manna from increased oil prices in the 1980s, provided new means to undermine the LDAs. It was not only a defeat for this model of self-organization but also the drying out of economic and social opportunities for women, teachers, and community workers, who had benefited from the boom of the *ta'awun* movement

(Lackner 2019: 271, 276). Instead, Saleh and the GPC boosted clientelism through state patronage, military networks in particular.

In all Arab countries, in the name of the "national revolution," dissonant voices were first corralled, and later simply suppressed. "When [these regimes] faced pressure from the disillusioned masses, they turned down the rightward, repressive road" (Ahmad 2006: 137). Citizenship quickly became hollowed out from its revolutionary substance in the independence period. Instead, the political space of participatory pluralism shrunk considerably; ruling elites again became more distant, to the point where one could speak of "negative citizenship" (Chouikha & Gobe 2015: 5), a more extreme form of what we called above latent citizenship. The exercise of collective freedom and impacts from civic activism pursued outside of the official party gradually became impossible in the Arab world. The little bottom-up participation that existed under colonialism was also impeded by national and domestic regimes that were more interested in self-preservation than pluralism and democratic agonism. To be fair, the context of the Cold War and the polarization pro-USA vs. pro-USSR, or the stance on the existence of Israel, either acquiescence or open resistance, also played a role in undermining democratic participation in the post-colonial era.

As the result of nationalism and the competition among ideologies leading to coups and assassinations, MENA has been the arena of *a high number of conflicts*. These are of different types: international wars, regional conflicts, and internecine armed struggles. The presence of Israel, an artificial construct made possible by British imperialism and the complicity of the West, generated nearly half a dozen of conflicts of the first type, with wars that implicated Israel in 1948, 1956, 1967, 1973, and possibly also 1982 ("Operation Peace in Galilee"). Other wars were either direct confrontations between two states (e.g. Iran–Iraq 1980–1988) or by proxies (Algeria and Morocco over the Western Sahara crisis), or war episodes (in Jordan, Lebanon, and Syria) because of Israel's effort to uproot the Palestine Liberation Organization. Many wars were of course fought because of natural resources, such as the control of oil (Kuwait and Iraq in 1990), water (Jordan, Syria, and Israel), arable land (Turkey and Syria), the tracing of borders (Egypt and Sudan), or phosphate and other minerals (Western Sahara, Morocco, and Algeria).

The horrendous list of internal violence – campaigns by Saddam Hussein to suppress Kurdish dissent in the 1980s and Shiite uprisings in the 1990s, civil wars in Algeria and Yemen in the 1990s, *les années de plomb* in Morocco in the 1970s and 1980s, the crushing of Islamist rebellions in Homs and Hamma in 1982 in Syria, and massive incarceration of communists and Islamists alike in countries such as Tunisia, Egypt, Sudan, and Iraq – have also left a profound mark in terms of intimidation and the prevention of civic participation. A multiplicity of regional wars and the presence of overdeveloped security apparatuses in many Middle East countries finished the business of turning the "legitimate" means of coercion into a repressive, rather than defensive, tool against their own citizens.

This situation of constant war-preparation fed ruthless authoritarian regimes. The state became an instrument for the accumulation of rents, facilitated by or involved with its executive arms, be it the police, intelligence forces (the *mukhabarat*), or the army that exacted violence against national subjects. The situation of oppression was so systematic in the region that Ali Farzat, a famous Syrian cartoonist, depicted the region as a gigantic prison, represented as a building having the shape of the Middle East (the flat roof of the building) and the walls being prison bars with ghostly populations trapped inside.[22]

The high number conflicts generated competition to secure weaponry and political support that ensured each country would remain aligned with the interests of one of the world super powers. This produced militarized and *mukhabarat* states whose second nature was to criminalize any form of activism and bottom-up mobilization that could threaten the regime. The reach of the military was so vast in certain countries that some have even spoken of "militarized key economic activities" (Hartshorn 2019: 70–71). In a country like Egypt, the military was a distinct societal block, even competing with Islamic and secular development associations and charities for the distribution of aid (Sayigh 2012). Forbidding any step forward while dispensing constant rhetoric about progress, anti-imperialism, or revolution: such was the modus operandi of Arab republican leaders who leaned on military and police institutions to secure their rule. In so doing, however, they hastened "permanent custodianship" by the security forces over the state.[23] This process generated a habitus of

---

[22] See www.ali-ferzat.com/ar/comic/id/271.html.
[23] I take the phrase permanent military/security custodianship from Yezid Sayigh (2012: 3). In this report, Sayigh analyzes how the Egyptian Army is not just above the law, but "above the State."

negative or latent citizenship. Habitus, for Pierre Bourdieu (1977: 76), is the social interface between individual and the collective (or the fields of social action), which leads to "the tansformation of the past effect into the expected objective." It is also defined as the "system of durable, transposable dispositions, structured structures predisposed to function as structuring structures" (Bourdieu 1977: 72), which in this case, means that conditions for civic participation were severely limited by the fear of the military and autocratic rulers.

Most states in the Middle East have a battery of legal artifices to limit public action and to further solidify the habitus of latent citizenship. On the top of this list are emergency or martial laws, followed by various measures of impunity for security and police forces. Finally, there are strict laws limiting freedom of association (licensing as opposed to registering new associations) and freedom of assembly, thus impeding freedom of expression and demonstrations. The state of emergency is often the result of, or the revamping of, colonial legal artifice. In Israel, the Military Emergency Regulations that the government used to prevent the movement of the Palestinians citizens of Israel inside the Green Line between 1948 and 1966 was a simple extension of the British laws that governed Mandatory Palestine (Hajjar 2005: 42; Pappé 2011). What is shocking to non-MENA readers is to learn that states of emergency have often been in place for decades, although this legal artifice is meant to be used only for short periods when warranted by instability or a threat to national security. In Egypt, it was in place from the assassination of Sadat in 1981 until February 2011. In Algeria it was enforced from February 1992 until early 2011. The state of emergency has been in place in Syria even longer: It was initially called after one of the numerous Baathist coups in 1963 (Yassin-Kassab & Al-Shami 2016: 18) and was systematically prolonged under spurious grounds of the threat represented by neighbouring Israel, with which Syria is still technically at war. In 2000, a timid civil society movement emerged after the death of Hafez Al-Asad and called in vain for the repeal of the state of emergency and martial law, amnesty for political prisoners, and the recognition of political pluralism (Yassin-Kassab & Al-Shami 2016: 17). It failed.

The synchrony in repealing such laws in Egypt, Algeria, and Syria is not lost to the reader: in Egypt, Mubarak proposed the change as a last-minute measure before being forced to step down; in Algeria, Bouteflika declared the end of the state of emergency on February 24,

2011, also to take some wind from the sail of the growing popular protests (Boumghar 2019: 52), while in Syria, it was the fear of regional Arab uprisings that eventually pushed the regime to call off the state of emergency on April 21, 2011, along with the abolition of the Supreme State Security Court (Yassin-Kassab & Al-Shami 2016: 47).

The fight against so-called terrorism aided the length of these measures. Whether as an excuse to crack down on Islamist opposition, or as a result of the American "global war on terror," it allowed additional legal mechanisms that would destroy civil liberty from the late 1990s onwards. In Yemen, Egypt, and Tunisia, the fight against Islamist threats or Al-Qaeda justified sending hundreds if not thousands to prison, where they would meet the other "ideological" enemies, i.e the communists rotting in jail from earlier purges. In Tunisia, the radical left that had been the main historical opposition to Bourguiba and then Zine El-Abidine Ben Ali were gradually freed in the 1990s when the Islamists started filling cells.[24]

The declared objectives of many Arab regimes of fighting Islamist and/ or jihadist factions hide other projects. Jean-Pierre Filiu (2015) documented how "contemporary Mamluks" (the nickname he gives to militarized state leaders in Arab countries in reference to the professional soldiers turned politicians or administrators in the Ottoman Empire) have been playing with the fire of fomenting jihadi seditions in order to preserve their control over the "Deep State." Much of the violence in the Middle East results from complex and multiple manipulations by a secretive club of military or intelligence-gathering institutions: Reactions to jihadi violence, according to him, are best explained by a fine understanding of local political tensions, regional learning and borrowing tactics from neighboring political regimes threatened by popular protests, and global motives in trading "commodities" (such as information on global terrorist groups) to international donors (typically the USA, but potentially also European states after being the object of attack by groups such as Al-Qaeda, or later ISIS) (Filiu 2015).

As a result of these wars, militarized societies, and competition for external rents, the state became an *object of domestic predation* from the 1980s onwards.

---

[24] See Ayari (2016), who also narrates how the left was given a certain freedom providing that they would entertain the ideas that the Movement for the Islamic Tendency, the forerunner of Ennahda, was a threat to Tunisian national identity.

What does that mean? Rather than being a neutral venue for competition between different groups, the state is increasingly seen as an occasion to accumulate more wealth for those running its institutions (Tripp 2001), leading to a different state–society compact. State–society relations, as seen in the previous chapter, are considered possible because of an increased process of differentiation, the rotation of personnel in charge of the state bureaucracy, greater efficiency due to specialized entities caring for a single domain, and checks and balances between different segments or layers of a polity. There was very little of this in the Middle East, where small elite cliques in charge of the state were able to prevent any form of pluralism and bottom-up mobilizations, thus preventing the democratic effect of contention, understood here as the degree of unpredictability that co-constitutes democracy (the empty seat of Lefort, or the fact that no one knows who will be the winner of the next round of elections). Coupled with the bonanza of oil, pushes to liberalize economies ("*infitah*" policies) from the 1980s onwards, and the structure of external rents outside taxation (both from the Soviet Union and the USA) only deepened the distance between local Arab elites and their citizens. The reality in the Middle East, like much of the Third World, was the emergence and consolidation of a "state bourgeoisie" (Ahmad 2006: 139). By that, Eqbal Ahmad means that a thin layer of influential political actors preyed on the state to reinforce and perpetuate their authority. "The power of the state bourgeoisie was derivative from the state; its expansion depended on the expansion of state power and functions. Hence its vested interests and compulsions would be toward expanding the state machinery" (Ahmad 2006: 139). In the post-independence era, these elites became local agents of capitalist expansion and spearheaded resource extraction in the national peripheries, replacing, but also perpetuating in new guise, old colonial structures of center–periphery in their own quest for "development." For these reasons, discourses of "internal colonization" would emerge both in Tunisia and Yemen, generating demands for equality and the end of the political center's privileges in 2011.

Foreign "aid" did little to deepen the small space for pluralism and civil society participation that emerged with great fatigue when the ideological confrontation of the Cold War receded in the 1990s and early 2000s. Aid, usually understood as official development assistance, has evolved enormously in the last decade, and an overview of the latest trends in aid will show that aid is not automatically a benevolent or stabilizing factor. In reality, aid pouring into the region has increasingly taken a militarized or securitized form, undermining the possibility for sounder, gradual development as a basis for stability. Despite widespread talk of "exporting democracy," it seems as if Western money has not bought democracy in the region, but rather its repression (Challand 2011). Counting total American aid, both military and economic assistance for the period 2005–2010, one finds out that in the MENA region, 93% of American aid for Israel is military-based, 76% for Egypt, 53% for Turkey, and 45% for Iraq.[25] And indeed much of what counts as "foreign aid" in the USA is in reality military aid. For example, the flow of American aid for Yemen increased from US$67 million in 2009 to 250 million in 2011, but the vast majority of this was military aid.[26] USAID came to an agreement with the Yemeni government and its Ministry of Planning and International Cooperation to provide US$121 million over three years. Work was to be done with the USA Department of Defense (Pentagon) in Yemen, which uses "community-based development" projects to "counter violent extremist activity" from Al-Qaeda in the region.[27] The question is, of course, whether local citizens truly benefit from such support.

Even if democratic aspirations remained vivid and burst at a few sporadic times,[28] the social life of citizenship was phagocyted and sclerosed by the ad nauseam official state rhetoric of progress, Arab Unity, anti-imperialist struggle, or the threat of an Islamic takeover. Bread riots in

[25] Percentage of Military Aid in Cumulative American Aid (2005–2010). Source: author's compilation. Information on American aid can be found in the so-called *Green Book*, a report on "Overseas Loans and Grant" published by USAID since 1945. Its latest version is available at https://pdf.usaid.gov/pdf_d ocs/PBAAJ833.pdf.

[26] Only the USA counts military aid as "aid." On other technical aspects of aid, see Challand (2014).

[27] Figures taken from a 2010–2012 USAID report on Yemen, still available at htt ps://web.archive.org/web/20120313111524/www.usaid.gov/locations/mid dle_east/documents/yemen/USAIDYemen2010-2012Strategy.pdf. Stephen Day (2012: 255) discusses the militarization of aid under Obama and the nefarious choice of the West: looking the other way when President Saleh was crushing democratic demands.

[28] Lisa Wedeen's astute analysis of authoritarian regimes in Syria and Yemen reminds us that it is not only citizenship that is sporadic, but that the state as such is characterized by an intermittence of power (Wedeen 2008: 68–75), using ornamental trappings, spectacles and scenography compelling citizens to act "as if" this central authority was fully respected (pp. 16, 24).

Tunisia or Egypt in 1977, 1978, 1983, and 1984 were quashed by repressive tools and emergency laws.[29] In Yemen, there were protests about the increased price of bread or of diesel in 1996, 1998, and 2005. More than 50 people died in 1998 and again in 2005 (Lackner 2016a: 150). In short, Arab states face a recurrent *democratic deficit* that translates to growing social inequalities, suspended or split parliaments, constitutions superseded by states of emergency, a mockery of the rotation of power in republics, long-standing dictatorships, or a deliberate series of obstructions to make sure that the legislative could not act during such crises.[30]

From the perspective of the masses, of the people, the state is seen to be neglecting its duties to assist the population. In Yemen, the failure of the government in consolidating basic institutions of education, roads, and health led people to repeat "*mafish nizam*," "there is no system!" (Bonnefoy 2018: 12). The state is "an empty shell … subject to patrimonial processes that encouraged corruption and the personal enrichment of its leaders" (Bonnefoy 2018: 31). In Tunisia, the state is commonly perceived as a coercive and arbitrary body raising tributes that go to the benefit of a ruling elite that is itself perceived as alien to the rest of the society (ICG 2019). These negative perceptions influence the actions of citizens. For example, many Yemenis "minimize the composition of their household [during census], fearing that the statistic could be used to set up a system of taxation" (Bonnefoy 2018: 182, fn. 32).

In sum, the situation of Arab states was best captured by Burhan Ghalioun. In his 1991 book *Le malaise arabe. L'Etat contre nation*, the Syrian sociologist[31] posited the following diagnostic: The domestic Arab predicament comes from the opposition between the state and society. Because key organs of the state never really became a channel for inclusion, participation in redistribution, be it through the bureaucracy used as a channel for clientelism[32] or through the military and the

---

[29] For an account of the violent repression of the 1978 and 1984 bread riots, see Khiari (2003: 18, 21, 70).

[30] This was the case in 1992 Algeria when President Chadli Benjedid dissolved the parliament shortly before resigning himself, paving the way for the military to take over the command of the country, via the *Haut Comité d'Etat*. See Boumghar (2019: 46).

[31] He became a leader of the Syrian opposition after the outbreak of protests from March 2011 onwards.

[32] See Ayubi (1980). The politicization of bureaucracy hampered the emergence of a rich party system and stifled the expansion of the kernel of Arab civil society that had emerged at the turn of the nineteenth and twentieth centuries.

"deep state" (Filiu 2015) to preserve a small clique of people in power, the state has remained alien to Arab populations. It never benefited from a high degree of legitimacy or acceptance (Ghalioun 1991), nor did it manage to generate wide and inclusive articulations that are necessary for social coalescence (*iltiham*). The "rule of law" was only rarely rooted and enacted, and even constitutions were thin documents that were often drafted to suit the profile of a leader,[33] rather than charting fundamental political principles. "Specially constituted courts" and other ad hoc measures taken by the executive rendered constitutional guarantees of an independent judiciary moot (Ahmad 2006: 134). Even if there were timid forms of civic participation, Tunisians and Yemenis could not shake off the habitus of latent citizenship.

2.3 Revisiting the Civility Paradigm

Faced with these denials of citizenship, numerous instances of military and police exactions, and the use of the state's "legitimate" force against its own citizens, it becomes urgent to expand on the initial assessment and criticism of the "civility" thesis and the idea that there can be such a thing as "the legitimate use of physical force within a given territory" in the Middle East. I will also discuss a couple of authors who have reflected on the specificities of the colonial and post-colonial predicament when it comes to citizenship.

In the Arab world, there is a long and distinguished intellectual tradition on violence, civility, and political order. After all, Ibn Khaldun (d. 1406) developed a full theory on civility (*tamaddun*), civilization (*'umran*), and forms of political regimes. One work, the *Muqaddimah* (2005 [1402]), which many consider exemplary of sociological thought (Chabane 2003; Alatas 2014), builds on these concepts. Ibn Khaldun preannounces Weber's idea that cities are essential components for the new emancipatory socialization when Ibn Khaldun identified the vital connections between city, civility, and a stable form of government.[34] The scholarship on Ibn Khaldun is vast, but

---

[33] This view of "*ad personam* constitutions" is the thesis of Tunisian jurist Kais Saied (La Presse 2018: iv). Saied became the President of Tunisia after the November 2019 elections.

[34] There is no civilization (*tamaddun*) without city (*madina*), both terms that come from the same Arabic root. On state, sovereignty, and civilization, see e.g. Tlili

tends to be tainted with Orientalist shortcuts (e.g. Gellner's [1981] famous idea that there is such a thing as a "Muslim Society" and that Ibn Khaldun had identified group solidarity, '*asabiyyah*, as one of these core stabilizing "mechanisms" for (all?) Muslim societies) or focused on parallel, rather than transversal or dynamic, analyses of political systems. Tlili (1972) offers a rich reflection on civilization and progress, and a comparative analysis of North African societies with ideas developed in the nineteenth century by French thinker François Guizot, but treats the two regions as if they are totally separate from one another. Let us see how contemporary thinkers have tried to tackle the symbolism of civility or the interconnections between hyper-militarized polities from a relational viewpoint.

First, let us start with Albert Memmi (b. 1920). The Tunisian-French intellectual's production dovetails with that of Frantz Fanon, both in terms of the period of dying colonialism, during which they offered their incisive analyses, and the relational understanding of the effects of colonialism. They are living examples of the power of hyphenated identities, able to read the relational ills of metropolitan and colonial societies alike. Colonialism makes both the colonizer and the colonized; there is not one without the other, in terms of language, manners, laws, and the seemingly paradoxical need for one another. To paraphrase Ashis Nandy (1983: 1), colonialism is a state of mind that connects and impacts both the metropole and the conquered territories. For the criticism of civility, I will only tap briefly into Memmi's description of the colonized and the strong presence of military symbols in the post-independence era.

Memmi noted the fascination that military garbs and khaki had for so many politicians after independence in the Arab world.[35] In Memmi's judicious formulation "history today [at the time of independence] wears a military uniform" (Memmi 1965/1957: 96, 124). The empirical reality of a new historical generation of leaders donned in military clothes has been read in various manners. For those adopting a culturalist explanation, often with condescending views, this was

---

(1972: 141). See also Amri (2008) and Alatas (2014) for an application of a Khaldunian sociology to our contemporary societies.

[35] The same can be said for many instances of Third World politics if one thinks of the military fascination in many Third Worldist movements, and in various radical movements in the 1960s, such as the Black Panther Party, or mythologies of "people's wars" around the time of the Vietnam war.

evidence that only "strong men" can rule "native societies." For main-stream political science of the modernization period, the sociology of the military on top of politics was a necessary evil to "transition" into a more stable (but not automatically democratic) order (Huntington 1968). But in line with the image of the Moebius strip and the uneven development of violence, this fascination for military outfits can be seen as an occasion for the finally liberated masses to adopt the same symbols of executive power that they had been deprived of for so many decades (Memmi 1965/1957: 95, 96). One will remember from above how security forces in colonial times were only used to quell resistance, with almost no participation of locals in the actual police forces. Wearing khaki now sends a message to the rest of the world that independence leaders or radical groups must be considered as full peers of the "first world" directors. (This self-realization, another possible instance of the equalizing role of institutions of legitimate force, being on par in terms of coercion with former colonial rulers, soon, alas, came with a new tendency to usurp power.)

Elsewhere, Memmi observes the tendency for the psychology of the colonized to be trapped by distortions that the colonizers introduced in dozens of their policies. Memmi (1965/1957: 135, 140, 142) observes the difficulty of building robust educational institutions in the post-independence era, precisely because the denial of good education for the "natives" was a cornerstone of the colonial playbook. Memmi also evokes the continuing geographies of exclusion after independence: the persons likely to be forced out of their livelihood in the colonial period were the *fellagha* (Chapter 1), now joined by the *fellahin*, peasants, forced by developmentalist and industrialization plans to resettle in *bidonvilles* and poor urban neighborhoods (Memmi 1956: 146).

Eqbal Ahmad (1933–1999), a prominent Pakistani intellectual, offered general lessons on the consequences of limited or distorted governability in the postcolonial worlds (Ahmad 2006: 128–141). He describes the predicament of the Third World at large, but he recounts many examples of violent governance from the Middle East. He breaks down the "post-colonial systems of power" into seven different types, one that preserves a democratic life (in the "elective-parliamentary system"), two that are simply descriptive (the "ascriptive-palace system," for monarchies, and the "Marxist-socialist system"), and the other four have a political char-acterization: the "dynastic-oligarchic system," the "pragmatic-authoritarian system," the "radical-nationalist," and the "neofascist system" (Ahmad 2006: 129–130). These ideal-types yield fluctuating realities. He notes, in a 1981 text, that a democratic polity is often "replaced by a military, frequently neofascist government precisely at the time organized popular interests begin to gain ascendance through the electoral process" (Ahmad 2006: 132). Within the state bourgeoisie described above, elements of the ruling party and the military tend to lock down access to state resources and thus generate a profound rift with the masses. Due to the relative weakness of local industries, the oligarchy in power has "an independent material base" with statism, and the presence of "foreign development aid" makes them more attuned to the interests of the (former) metropole than their own population. In this configuration, "such a state is not merely a subsidiary but a suspended state, inherently incapable of endogenous development" (Ahmad 2006: 160).

The "neofascist state" is also a pathology (a term he uses explicitly) for many Third World countries. He lists 1950s South Korea, Iran, Nicaragua, and "new comers" in that sinister category of the 1960s and 1970s, with Brazil, Greece, Indonesia, Uganda, Zaire, and Chile. One could easily add a majority of Middle Eastern countries when he describes the widespread uses of organized terror: repression can occur anywhere (rather than in military barracks or prisons) but with less "visibility"; dissidents are disappeared; journalists are barred from accessing secrete detention camps; there are "safe houses" where torture takes place, or mass graves (Ahmad 2006: 143). The reason why Eqbal Ahmad calls these regimes neofascist and not fascist is that they are the "product of dependence" and are "sustained by a symbiotic relationship to the external metropolis," but also by "corporate concentration" (Ahmad 2006: 145, 148). Like aid, this shadow sponsorship hints at a new revamped form of encroachment, not direct or punitive, but influencing the course of action by local leaders who strive to maintain firm control. None of these leaders are charismatic, or are able to "perform the political functions of aggregation, communication, and socialization" (Ahmad 2006: 148). In terms used elsewhere in the book, articulations between different classes or political projects cannot occur in these regimes. No meaningful citizenship or civic participation can emerge. The chilling international alliance for "national security" or stability (quite essential in the age of ideologies that Ahmad described) replaced direct encroachments, but in the same manner prevented the emergence of informal conditions for democratic participation.

From Eqbal Ahmad's Third World typologies of state power and focus on structural factors of state-centered class formation and capitalist encroachments, one can now move to Steven Heydemann's (2000) study of the relation between violence and limited civic engagement. To this day, his edited volume *War, Institutions and Social Change in the Middle East* remains the most substantial effort to connect Tilly's historical and political sociology to a detailed comparative study of war and state-formation in the Middle East.

Heydemann (2000) elucidates another aspect of the missing link between demos and state. In his introduction, which draws parallels with the Tillyian insight of state-making as war-making in Europe, Heydemann demonstrates that it is not futile to try to compare two very idiosyncratic paths of European state-making, a process based on the relevance of revenue-collection and that culminated in gradual enfranchisement. Whereas in Europe war preparation led to the organization of centralized state revenues, in the (Arab) Middle East, the opposite is true: The organization and structures of state revenues, in particular the importance of (military) aid during the Cold War and the existence of oil rent, influenced and encouraged patterns of war preparation (Heydemann 2000: 22–24). In Europe, once a powerful warlord emerged, he was able to extend his territorial basis and thus gradually to pacify social relations or equalize the institutional presence of coercion, to use the term I proposed in the previous chapter. Over time, typically in the eighteenth and nineteenth centuries, the sovereign delegated the function of coercion to legal-rational institutions or new disciplinary mechanisms, and developed an interest in keeping a peaceful status quo with former enemies. In the Middle Eastern ideal type of state-making, domestic pacification or equalization rarely occurred: Arab statehood became a vector for personal enrichment and the consolidation of personalized power for a few dictators who would not hesitate to go to war to solidify their grip on power. Western military forces, usually kept in barracks under civilian command, differed from their Arab counterparts: the latter repeatedly stepped out of their barracks and vied for power, turning their weapons not only against external enemies but also against their own citizens, and maintained a strong presence of military involvement in governance. Thus, the large number of wars and the hypertrophied presence of *mukhabarat* (security and intelligence units) are key reasons for the democratic deficit in the Arab worlds: There cannot be equality in front of death (a substantial element of democracy) if Arab leaders play with the lives of their co-nationals, seen as cannon fodder or dispensable lives, in order to cement their hold on power.

These are the main findings described by Steven Heydemann. Other chapters in the book provide additional in-depth critical observations on violence and civic enfranchisement. Some demonstrate that the compact between coercion and enfranchisement has also been at play in certain polities, similarly to Europe, and that it would be a mistake to see the Middle East as, yet again, just the reverse of Europe. For example, Yezid Sayigh has documented how armed struggle in Palestine has been a cornerstone of Palestinian national identity (Sayigh 1997) and functions in an analogous manner to certain European countries as an aggregative factor for class, regional, and religious identities. The main difference in terms of state-formation is that Palestinians have obviously been denied their own aspirations for self-determination as a result of the multiple encroachments that started in the late Ottoman period (economic encroachment), followed by imperial encroachment in the Mandatory period, and the current colonial encroachment by Israel.

Next we move on to the hypotheses of sociogenesis or cultural formation of states formulated by Weber and Elias. First, a certain sociology of Islam has tried to extrapolate, from a few scattered passages, what the two German intellectuals would have said in terms of the relation between Islam, civility, and *Lebensführung*. Bryan Turner has been the most prolific author to apply Weberian insight, in particular with his books in the 1970s, but the core of these writings deals with the puzzle of modernity and capitalism, with no interest in democratic life. More recently, and in a way to criticize the typically 1990s Orientalist focus on Islam and democracy, Armando Salvatore (2011) has offered stimulating thoughts on the possible application of the Eliasian theme of civility to the Middle East. He notes that the Eliasian hypothesis of a gradual *polissage*, or move to more policed and refined manners, fails to see that some of the more recent processes of "state formation" in the Middle East are taking place under very different constellations than the European tradition. Salvatore notes that the Eliasian condition of sovereign states is increasingly difficult to reach there. He suggests that it is better to think of the international arena that shapes state interactions in the Middle East as "a post-Westphalian context," a situation in which powerful forces at play act to *prevent*, rather than *support*, state-building or maneuver more towards state-unbuilding, rather than state-formation. For the first instance, one can list denied statehood in Kurdistan, Palestine, or Western Sahara, while Libya, Iraq, Yemen nowadays, and Afghanistan are instances of state undoing.[36] Furthermore, Salvatore (2011: 810) notes that the over-securitization of the Middle East has "enfeeble[d] even more the residual capacity of the region's postcolonial political elites to influence the social bonds and civic connections at local level. These communities in turn become ever more disconnected from official politics, thus further undermining the fragile mutual ties between state apparatuses and citizens."

Cihan Tuğal (2017) concurs with the impact of undermining sovereignty identified by Salvatore, but adds an essential additional point. For him, it has become totally *passé*, after neoliberalism, to sustain the assumption that a Middle Eastern state can have a legitimate monopolization of violence. The attacks on 9/11 and the ensuing "war on terror," combined with neoliberal reforms, have precipitated the surge of "nonstate warriors" (Tuğal 2017: 77). Whether due to community policing (think of Shiite policing as distinct from the Iraqi army or police), the rise of private subcontractors, or counter-insurgency as a method of population management (Tuğal 2017: 79), the notion of the state as the normal depositary or organizer of the means of physical coercion has become a hollow concept. Set in relation to the notion of encroachments, one can see how "legitimate" violence and civility do not sound congenial to Middle East realities, again not because of some intrinsic Arab or Muslim conditions but in large part because of relational factors.

In conclusion, we can see that there is a growing scholarship that fills the gaps in the literature of "civility" or "reduced violence" from the ongoing process of state formation in the Middle East. The effort made in this book so far has followed the paths chartered by Gurminder Bhambra (2014) and her call to establish *connected sociologies* and by Ann Stoler (2016) to shed light on the impacts of imperial formations and the present effects of "ruination" and gradual decay.

The important lesson here is that if Arab states turned violently against their own citizens, it cannot be explained only in reference to

---

[36] For a crude description of the hypocrisy of the international community in "failing" a Palestinian state, see Sayigh (2007).

colonial or external influences. Nor can it be understood in isolation from these post-independence developments. The lack of legitimacy by ruling elites is a mixed problem, combining historical intrusions (Ottoman governance and colonial fiats in co-opting a given group) with sovereign political decisions taken by post-independence Arab regimes. Gradually, in fear of losing their grip on the economy, bureaucracy, and resources, or of losing to (frequently) Islamic oppositions, republican Arab leaders turned state institutions, typically coercive ones, against their own citizens and reinforced the control of the one-party system, while monarchies, notably the Gulf Cooperation Council, established self-defense pacts that were instrumental in crushing or limiting democratic aspirations in the region. These developments generated a habitus of latent citizenship, with people being afraid to criticize their leadership and feeling forced to pay lip service to the rhetoric and ideology of nationalist unity. Let us see in this last section how Tunisia and Yemen had similar yet different problems of tamed civic participation and regionalism in the years preceding the 2011 Uprisings.

2.4 The Question of Marginalization in Tunisia and Yemen by 2010

Dozens of books have explained the detailed dynamics in the year leading up to the fall of Presidents Ben Ali and Saleh. In this final section of the chapter, I can only offer a summary of the historical canvas of exclusion that was in part inherited from patterns of state-formation and related to contention around security issues. The core take-away from Part I is that significant marginalization was embedded in structures of uneven regional development, in particular of institutions of coercion, that favored a small oligarchic group of rulers, often connected to security institutions. The only way in which this straight-jacket could be shattered, or at least challenged, was for the masses, or bottom-up forms of participation, to act at the micro-level and to re-enact the condition of democratic ebullience that existed, as I have tried to show above, in earlier historical moments. It is therefore important to recap what these spaces of political fragmentation and symbolic disregard for certain groups have been in Yemen and Tunisia, and what are the respective specificities of latent citizenship.

In terms of the *commonalities*, both countries gradually adapted to the requirements of market expansion, with laws and administrative measures introduced precisely to allow for the demands of a capitalist economy from the 1960s onwards and later for the expansion of neoliberalism in the last decades of the twentieth century. As a result, both faced mounting pressure from international financial institutions (Ifis) and the donor community to adapt to neoliberal reforms or structural adjustment programs, which had a negative impact on civic participation, a feature documented by a variety of scholars.[37] In Tunisia this opening was spearheaded by growing economic relations with the European Union and the Barcelona Process, a project initiated in 1995 to create a free trade zone by 2010 (Krichen 2016: 65). The main result was a period of de-statalism (*"des-étatisation"* in French), which replaced a state-led developmentalism that had often taken the form of state-cooperatives (Krichen 2016: 30). In Yemen, the leverage of financial institutions was expressed in the increased securitization of foreign assistance and aid.[38] Both countries had long-standing dictators (from 1987 for Ben Ali and 1978 for Saleh), a very corrupt clique around these presidents, profound territorial inequalities that only deepened with post-independence politics and with complex institutional ramifications, and intra-elite rivalries.

For more than a decade, critiques of international development aid to the Middle East have been tangled up with critiques of the market, in particular its neoliberal variant (Mitchell 1999; Hanieh 2013). Many have observed that neoliberal restructuring has led to popular demobilization, an NGOization of civil society, the growing control of NGOs by transnational elites, and ultimately the consolidation of autocratic regimes throughout the Arab region (Hanafi & Tabar 2003; Guazzone & Pioppi 2009: 325, 330, 347). In Kienle's (2001) apt phrase, the politics of liberalization led more to de-liberalization

---

[37] For Tunisia, two essential books capture the issues of control and this deliquescence. Hibou (2011: 10) demonstrates how the entanglements between credit and bureaucratic surveillance in Tunisia produced "the force of obedience." Khiari (2003) captures a much more fluid situation, that of the gradual undoing of the civic trust under Ben Ali.

[38] Yemen was less systematically confronted with World Bank and IMF requests than Tunisia because of its geographically and economically marginal situation (Bonnefoy, Poirier, & Mermier 2012: 208). Lackner (2019: 232) notes that the IMF did push for privatization in 1993, which led to the façade of the "liberalization" of YMEC, which became the Yemen Economic Corporation (YEC) from 1993. On YMEC, see below. For Tunisia and neoliberal restructuration, see Murphy (1999), Khiari (2003), Cassarino (2012), Krichen (2016: 65).

than to democratization and was a "grand delusion." In the two countries, neoliberal reforms and "hollowing out" of the state actually reinforced the grip of a small clique of elites who coordinated such "privatization" and the accompanying delegation of authority to local entities. So the "absence" of the neoliberal state (Hibou 2004) is a myth: the security apparatus' custodianship was never challenged. To the contrary, it was even reinforced, with security actors benefiting from access to the economic sectors.

Neoliberal "success stories," like Tunisia under Ben Ali (Cassarino 2012) or Egypt under Mubarak (Mitchell 1999), were in reality artificial. Using a variety of tricks, including unloading debts onto public workers in Egypt (Soliman 2011: 44–45), selling enterprises to just-retired generals or security personal in a process of phony privatization in both countries, spurious repackaging of financial "growth" also in both (Mitchell 1999), and falsifying statistics in Tunisia, neoliberal policies only accelerated the concentration of economic and political power in the hands of a happy few. In the Jemna Oasis, mentioned in the Prolegomenon, the state-controlled entity that had taken over the farm after independence leased the Oasis to two private investors in 2002. These investors had strong ties with Ben Ali's security sector (Mahmoud 2020: 16). The farmers in Jemna, who had faced what Bourdieu and Sayad (1964: 4) called the "war machine" of colonial agrarian policy during colonial times, when the best land of the Oasis was "developed" for the exclusive benefit of French settlers, received very little of the promised trickle-down benefits from the 2002 "investment." Like other Arab populations, they did not dare protest against these new owners, with connections to the Ministry of the Interior. With neoliberalism, external encroachment shifted from the Cold War model of direct influence to more covert or indirect forms. Spaces of privileged economic exchange were removed from public purview through international investment schemes, leaving new spaces for international influence in these liminal areas baptized Qualified Industrial Zones or Free Trade Zones (P. Moore 2005). The demand for more social justice with the Arab Uprisings shed a crude light on the tensions generated by two decades of intense economic liberalizations and the widening gap of social inequalities these programs generated among Arab societies (Armbrust 2011; Hanieh 2013; Akcali 2016).

A last general commonality that did amplify anger among Yemeni and Tunisia protestors in 2011 was the institutionally kleptocratic nature of both regimes. The Trabelsi clan in Tunisia, from the wife of President Ben Ali (Ottaway 2017: 54–55), and the extended family of President Saleh in Yemen had developed a rapacious network of control over public institutions and exerted racketeering pressure over private economic actors. In Tunisia, one institutional tool that Ben Ali and his party, the RCD, which had replaced the Destourian Party of Bourguiba, used to enrich themselves was the famous bank account "26.26" that every worker was pressured to feed, with voluntary donations, to promote "national solidarity" (Hibou 2015: 106). Leila Trabelsi and her kin, like the infamous Sakher El-Materi, were later accused of systematic embezzlement and corruption, with some describing Tunisia as ruled by "the mafia dictatorship of Ben Ali-Trabelsi" (Ayeb 2011: 467). In the 2004 elections, RCD members took 152 of the 189 Parliamentary seats. Ben Ali was re-elected with 94% of the vote (Ottaway 2017: 39) and built a new ring of security protection for his family, the Presidential Guards, that responded directly to the Presidency and not to the Ministry of the Interior. Thus the "hegemony of the security sector emerged from the single-party state and the transformation of the presidency into a dominant administration under the Ben Ali regime" (Kartas 2014: 376). The confidence that the President placed in the Presidential Guard, led by Ali Seriati, "was a source of humiliation for the other security services. These services were in effect banned from deployment in the neighborhoods of the Ben Ali and Trabelsi families (Carthage, La Marsa, La Goulette, and in the vicinity of the airport" (ICG 2011: 11)). This example shows that uneven deployment of coercion need not to be a problem for a large territorial portion of the country (the "south" or the "interior"), but can also occur at the micro-level, when it intersects with class differentiations.

In Yemen, Saleh used a military institution to distribute perks to its members and to extend the patronage network of his party, the GPC. Saleh stated in 1992 that the armed forces were "the party of all the parties" (*hizb kulli l-ahzab*, as quoted in Dresch 2000: 192). He knew how to handle protests – bread riots or otherwise – with a combination of firm (or even deadly) force, dispensed through his deputies, and his own personal interventions as the proponent of compromises (Lackner 2016a: 150). Dresch (2000: 201) lists Saleh's numerous kin who became business tycoons, among them his sons, nephews, and two sons of his political ally, Shaykh Abdallah Al-Ahmar, Speaker of the House and leader of the Islamist party (Islah; see below). These young men ran no less than 300 companies – at least that was the case in the late 1990s (Dresch 2000: 201), but Lackner suggests that this number grew even higher in the years leading up to the 2011 protests (Lackner 2019: e.g. 207). In the former South, some cutbacks made in the early 2000s in the name of neoliberal reforms, in particular among teachers and former military of the Southern army, generated growing dissatisfaction (Caton, Al-Eryani, & Aryani 2014: 128), while in the north, Saada faced grueling rounds of wars (2004–2010).

If we now turn to the *dissimilarities* between the two countries, different degrees of military involvement in politics, distinctive openings to pluralism, and the degree of territorial and social fragmentation emerge as the main points of attention. In Tunisia, Ben Ali took power through a "medical coup" in November 1987 (invoking the frail health of Bourguiba to depose him). He was all too aware that the military could foment another coup against him (Khiari 2003: 87). Ben Ali rose socially as a military officer, but his real clout came from his role as director of the *Sécurité Nationale* (National Security), "the main branch of the country's secret police," to Minister of the Interior, and from there to the post of Prime Minister, which he occupied in November 1987 (Bou Nassif 2015: 68). Kartas (2012) explains how as President Ben Ali pitted the security services of the military against those of the Ministry of the Interior. Later, he even created an independent security service, which included the Presidential Guards, within the President's Office, reporting directly to him, rather than to the army Chief of Staff or the Minister of the Interior. The share of the budget allocated to the military shrunk from 5.1% in 1988 to 4.3% in 2011. Even the Ministry of the Interior's share of the budget, still much larger than that of the army, gradually dropped from 8% in 1988 to 6.5% in 2011 (Bou Nassif 2015: 75). Bou Nassif does not indicate the share allocated to the President's Office, but that proportion most probably rose during the years of Ben Ali's presidency.

Another major difference has to do with the attitude of the regime towards Islamist factions. In both countries, the main opposition forces are Islamists and self-avowed socialist forces: in Yemen, this translates to the Islah party (more details below) and the YSP, and in Tunisia, to Ennahda, the Popular Front, and other Marxist formations. The chiasmus of tolerance involved an increased bias towards the Socialist Party in Yemen, in particular after the 1994 civil war, and a growing acceptance of the leftist opposition in Tunisia, which was gradually released from prison to grant a veneer of pluralism. The other dimension of the chiastic tolerance is the attitude toward the Islamists. The main Islamist party in Tunisia, Ennahda, whose precursor was the MTI (Burgat 1996), was banned under Ben Ali and harshly repressed. An alleged military coup involving Islamist officers was uncovered in 1991, the so-called Barakat Al-Sahel plot, but it turned out to be a manipulation within the security services to have a free hand to crack down on Islamists, which kept its presence underground.[39] In Yemen, President Saleh leaned indirectly on the Islamist Party Islah. Rumors have it that this party was actually created with his blessing just before the first post-unification election in order to split the vote from the YSP. Saleh's party, the GPC, always won the majority of seats in parliament, but he considered Islah a powerful ally, not a coalition partner: The Speaker of the House of Representatives in Yemen, Abdallah Al-Ahmar (d. 2007), was one of the founding members of Islah and a prominent tribal figure. Saleh, from a lesser tribal group, needed to pay homage to the social power of Al-Ahmar, the paramount shaykh of the larger tribal confederation, the Hashid. This alliance was a typical tactic used by Saleh to control a very fragmented Yemeni society, by playing alliances or supporting the enemy of his enemies, as we will discuss below regarding Saleh's attitudes toward the Salafi and Zaydi movements.[40]

A third difference: freedom of expression and censorship of the media diverged greatly in the two countries. Republican Yemenis benefited from a relatively free press and a quite consolidated freedom of expression. This does not mean that at times intimidation or even political killings did not take place under President Saleh (e.g. the 2002 killing of Jarallah Omar, a leader of the YSP).[41] But it was not a problem of freedom of speech: it had rather to do with the impunity granted around the president and the absence of judicial independence. In Tunisia, where levels of literacy are much higher, the regime had to use various techniques to make sure that the media would sing the tunes the regime wanted. But the end result was that, by 2010, freedom of the press in Tunisia was ranked among the lowest globally (El-Issawi 2012).

---

[39] Two events pushed toward the eradication of the Islamist movement in the early 1990s: the burning down of an RCD office at Bab Al-Swika and the discovery of a winged arm within the MTI. See Ayari (2016: 152).

[40] Dresch (2000: 201). This system of "tribal" alliances went on until the death of the paramount shaykh in 2007. Thereafter, his two sons had recurrent moments of open rivalry, trying to split economic and political control (Day 2012; Lackner 2019: 129).

[41] https://merip.org/2002/12/the-death-and-life-of-jarallah-omar/.

Select macro-indicators (Tables 2.1 and 2.2) and a graph (Figure 2.1) of population growth also indicate some fundamental differences between the two countries. One, Tunisia, has a rate of urbanization close to that of advanced capitalist societies, and the other, Yemen, is still firmly anchored in rural settings, and features a faster pace of demographic growth. As I have shed light on the importance of (militarized) aid, the contrast between the rather modest amount of official development assistance (ODA) allocated to Tunisia (US$776 million, an average of US$65 per capita) and that of Yemen (US$3.2 billion, or US$110 per capita) is most relevant when compared to the share of aid in the gross national income, 2% vs. 12%. Rent, non-taxed income, is vital for Yemeni politics.[42] The figures quoted here are from USAID, which counts military aid as "aid," while other countries of the Organisation for Economic Co-operation and Development (OECD) exclude that form of support. Comparing the figures for civilian aid only, the figures (for the actually disbursed amounts in 2017, like the USAID figure) are US$386 million in Tunisia vs. US$1,269 billion in Yemen.[43]

Table 2.1 *Basic indicators for Tunisia and Yemen*

	TUNISIA	YEMEN
Income Cat. (World Bank)	Low middle income country	Low income country
Population	12m (1.1% annual change)	29m (2.3% annual change)
Urban / Rural	69% / 31%	37% / 63%
Land size	155,360 sq. km	527,970 sq. km
Development Assistance – Net ODA (USD)	US$776 million per year	US$3.2 billion per year
Development Assistance – % of gross national income (GNI)	2.01%	12.07%

Source: https://idea.usaid.gov/.

---

[42] All figures valid for 2017.
[43] See OECD Development Assistance Committee (DAC) reports: www.oecd-ilibrary.org/development/data/oecd-international-development-statistics/oda-official-development-assistance-disbursements_data-00069-en.

Table 2.2 *Selected detailed indicators for Tunisia and Yemen, compared to MENA region*

	TUNISIA	YEMEN	Avg. MENA
Employment in agriculture (percent of total employment) (modeled ILO estimate)	15	35.5	11.7
Global Food Security Index (0–100, 100 = best environment)	60.9	28.5	61.5
Government expenditure on education as percentage of GDP (percentage)	6.6	5.15	4.34
Human Capital Index (HCI): Learning-adjusted years of school	6.3	4.1	7.47
Primary completion rate, both sexes (percentage)	95.1	72.3	93.3
Global Gender Gap: index score (0–1, higher is better)	0.65	0.5	0.61
Access to electricity (percentage of population)	100	79.2	96.8
Climate Risk Index, (low score=higher risks)	82.3	66.2	102
GDP per capita (current US$)	3,400	944	16,000

Source: https://idea.usaid.gov/.

Table 2.2, which compares Tunisian and Yemeni data with the average figures for the Middle East region, indicates that both countries have larger agricultural sectors than the average rate for the region, but agriculture accounts for more than a third of the total employment in Yemen, which has a much larger rural population. With water resources running low due to its overconsumption for the cultivation of *qat*, and the need to import "nearly three-quarters of the food needed to sustain the nearly 30 million people" (Bonnefoy 2018: 10), Yemen is facing an acute environmental crisis, here captured by the food security index. This crisis will only intensify considering the war situation of the last five years and rising demographic pressures (see also Figure 2.1). The gender gap is also very pronounced in Yemen, a country that invests little in education and is far from reaching a high rate of completion of primary schooling. Only 8% of Yemeni women have some secondary education, as opposed to 24% of men (Brehony, Lackner & Al-Sarhan 2015: 18). The International Labour Organization (ILO) determined that Yemen has had one of the lowest female labor force participation rates in the world (Al-Ammar, Patchett, & Shamsan 2019: 22).

Like other low-income countries, the rate of demographic growth is much higher in Yemen than in Tunisia, a low-to-mid income country with limited growth. If both countries had 4 to 5 million inhabitants in the 1950s, the gap between the two countries has reached a staggering difference, with an estimated 30 million by 2020 in Yemen as opposed to 12 million in Tunisia.[44] In terms of north and south divide in Yemen, the estimate is that a quarter of the total population lives in the former South, and three-quarters in the North.[45]

Let us now turn to a detailed description of the geographies of marginalization in these two countries. Since Tunisia was the first Arab country that toppled its dictator, we will start there.

In Tunisia, like its neighbor Algeria, protests started when basic food prices shot through the roof. It is therefore not a "revolution of the

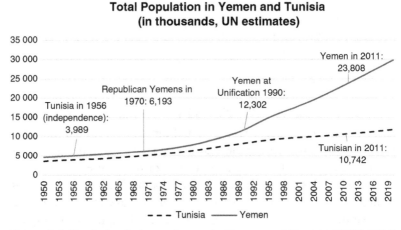

Total Population in Yemen and Tunisia (in thousands, UN estimates)

Figure 2.1 Total population estimates in Yemen and Tunisia (1950–2020) Source: United Nations, Population Division, *World Population Prospects 2019*, at https://population.un.org/wpp/Download/Standard/Population/.

---

[44] For the estimate total population, see the figure of the UN Population Division: https://population.un.org/wpp/Download/Standard/Population/. The last census in Yemen was done in 2004 and counted 5 million Yemenis in the former South and 14.6 million in the former North. See data of that census at www .statoids.com/uye.html.

[45] Estimates are from Lackner (2019: 274).

bloggers," one sparked by Al-Jazeera, or a revolution of the jasmine, as is often said, because the "revolution" did not start on the shores of the Mediterranean where jasmine grows, but in the semi-arid zones in the center of the country (Ayeb 2011: 470). It started with a strong class component concerning underpaid workers and massive unemployment in central Tunisia, an uneven institutional presence of the leading trade union, and a vivid rural–urban divide. In Yemen, with a faster demographic growth, these questions of fluctuating food prices and state subsidies created recurrent instabilities, which would come to play an important role a couple of years after the start of the 2011 Uprisings. This historical geography has already been contoured earlier, so we will only dwell on three aspects: violence and coercion; the geography of poverty, and the formation of an elite within these urban–rural parameters.

Continuity is the keyword.

Above, the geographical split recounted in terms of security was described as the uneven distribution of violence, or means of coercion. France, like the previous Ottoman authorities, used punitive campaigns in the country to extract taxation and did not deploy regular police and gendarmes in the south. Instead it delegated authority to *qa'ids*, strong men. President Bourguiba perpetuated the colonial management of its borderlands. To weaken the internal opposition of the Youssefists (supporters of Salah Ben Youssef), Bourguiba chose not to deploy state institutions equally throughout the territory. He opted instead to perpetuate the informal colonial agreements with tribal leaders (Kartas 2016). The subject was taboo under Bouguiba and Ben Ali, but post-2011 Tunisian studies have given the name "internal colonization" to the continuing policies of marginalization, or *tahmish*, that the Tunis bureaucracies have maintained since independence toward the south and the interior of the country (Al-Salhi 2017).

In terms of administrative "legitimate violence," municipalities were established in a vast majority of the territory at the time of independence. Yet a large number of Tunisians, typically in the south of the country, knew no municipal authority, remaining thus under the direct control of the Ministry of the Interior for a long period after independence, a problem that some call the absence of a universal municipalization.[46]

---

[46] One impact of the 2011 Uprising has been the introduction of full municipalization. See Chapters 5 and 6.

Policing tasks over the southern territories that were delegated to "local tribes" turned into a privileged role played by the *haras watani*, or *Garde Nationale*. In exchange for recognition of their political grip in the rest of the country, Presidents Bourguiba and Ben Ali treated turning a blind eye over smuggling in these parts of the country as de facto official policy (Meddeb 2015a). Both presidents, who originated from the Sahel region and were therefore quite socially distant from the southern constellations of authority, were also happy with this compromise, granting near autonomous rule in exchange for a pacified south. This, over time, cemented a deep fragmentation of the national territories, with some regions treated better than others (Daoud 2011). This differential treatment of the various parts of the country also led to unequal representation in the army and at university. An old practice that allowed richer families in the Sahel region to "pay their way out of military conscription" (Meddeb 2015b) resulted in a majority of soldiers coming from the impoverished interior regions (Grewal 2019: 262). At university level as well, youth from the coastal urban areas are over-represented: most of the university-trained students come from the Sahel in an unbalanced manner of 2:1, while the two parts of the country (Sahel vs. the rest) have a ratio of 1:1 in terms of overall populations.[47]

Geographer Habib Ayeb recounts an anecdote from early in Bourguiba's presidency that illustrates the benefits that his region of origin, the coastal area, would reap economically. During a visit to the interior town of Tozeur, famous for its dates, a peasant asked Bourguiba why his government did not build a sardine factory in Tozeur. Puzzled as to why sardines should be brought 250 km inland to be manufactured, the Tunisian President asked the peasant: why?

---

[47] Al-Salhi (2017: 557). "Coastal urban areas" refers to Greater Tunis and the Sahel, which in current administrative language and statistics corresponds to the Tunis region and the center east (*wasaṭ al-sharqī*). In 2013–2014, there were a total of 221,000 university students in the two macro-regions of the Tunis region and center east, as opposed to 56,000 students in the universities of the "western" and "southern" regions, i.e. counting the student population in Kairouan, Jendouba, Gabes, and Gafsa (Al-Salhi 2017: 557). However, in these administrative categorizations, Sfax appears alongside Sousse and Monastir. If we add Sfax to the "west" and "south" (as it was the "capital of south" during colonial times), recreating the *Tunisie utile* vs. *Tunisia inutile*, then we have an imbalance of 193,000 vs. 94,000 students, thus a 2:1 ratio in favor of the "coastal urban areas," when the total population for these two large regions ("coastal urban areas" vs. "west" and "south") are more-or-less 1:1 (5,243,000 vs. 5,740,000), based on the 2014 data of the Tunisian Statistic Institute (www.ins.tn/).

The answer was: *"Si l'Hbib* (Mister [or lord] Habib), but the distance between Tozeur and the sea did not prevent the construction of a date factory in Monastir" (the city of the President, situated on the east coast of the country). The story does not tell what happened to this unfortunate peasant. However, the anecdote does show that there are two Tunisias: one, the Tunisia of power, money, comfort and "development," which covers the coastal areas, particularly the capital city and its upper-class suburbs and the Sahel (including the Gulf of Nabeul, Sousse and Monastir) and, second, the marginalised, poor, submissive and dependent Tunisia (of the south, the centre and the west). (Ayeb 2011: 470)

The second continuous element is the geography of marginalization, which inherits a great deal of the more-or-less explicit racism and condescending attitudes of the French Protectorate toward the central and southern parts of Tunisia, that is the hinterland between the coast and the Algerian border (from the "center") and the part south of Sfax. This region is also called "the interior," as opposed to the coastal area lying between Bizerte and Sfax. The more-or-less indirect forms of racialization within contemporary Tunisia are still related to capitalist extraction of surplus, and to the colonial divide between the center and peripheries. Concentrating on urban cities of the coast and the north to favor the exploitation of richer agricultural land, the French protectorate generated, and the post-independence governments maintained, a split that imagined Tunisia as two regions. The French used the town of Sfax as a bridgehead to colonize the interior and southern parts of the country, inviting the local bourgeoisie to purchase land and large olive tree plantations in the south. Still now, Sfax is dubbed "the capital of the south" and absorbs surplus workers from tedious manual labor – often that of women – in the southern olive fields. Phosphates from the central regions of Gafsa or Rdayyef are still shipped by train to Sfax, leaving miners in these central regions asking why they do not benefit more from the hard labor of extraction. Moreover, Sfaxis, proud of their much more direct resistance to the French colonial project, are also upset about the pollution that the main site of phosphate transformation, the SIAPE, generates locally, while the capital city, Tunis, reaps the benefits from this extractive and transformative process.[48]

---

[48] Author's interviews with three Sfaxis making similar observations.

Another central actor in the 2011 Uprising is the UGTT, the main national trade union. Since its formation in 1946, the UGTT has been very strong in the south. Most of its historical leaders, Ferhat Hached or Habib Achour to name only two, are from the Sfax area (the island of Kerkenna, to be precise). These leaders continue to hail from southern zones, liminal areas where capitalism has only partially encroached and where the institution earned its historical credibility by fighting French colonialism (Yousfi 2015: 20). The UGTT grew in spaces involved in capitalist extraction (e.g. in the phosphate mining region and in Sfax, where it is refined at huge environmental cost), as well as spaces on the fringes of French control. Thus, and with a paradoxical historical twist (the return of the south to the fore, in a way), the UGTT benefited from loose direct control in the south of the protectorate granted by the colonial authorities. It is well known that the top leadership of the UGTT was later largely coopted both by Bourguiba and by Ben Ali, and was thus unable to criticize the regime for its lack of development in the interior.[49] Yet, the historical hub of the UGTT has remained in the south and peripheral sections, sections that would be instrumental, as we will see in the next chapter, in spreading the protests in December 2010 and January 2011 (Yousfi 2015: 61–64).

This discussion of the UGTT's historical role demonstrates that direct racialized violence of the colonial period (the 1881 Sfax massacre for the town's refusal to accept the French protectorate; the inconsistent presence of "legitimate means of coercion" during the colonial era; mixed policies targeting the *fellagha* resistance while granting privileges to the few tribes living in the southern and eastern borderlands; etc.) turned into *indirect* violence in the independence era. The post-independence state moved to a more structural and symbolic form of violence that targeted the same marginalized parts of the population and denied them a role in building a modern Tunisian state (Challand 2020). Saheli and *Tunisois* elites repeated colonial discourses of a *Tunisie utile* after independence but with a new rhetoric of development and industrious zeal, opposed to endemic poverty of the south.[50] In practice, political recruitment was conditional on being a citizen

---

[49]   Omri (2016) defends the view that the UGTT retained a substantial independence, even during the Ben Ali years, notably by supporting cultural dissidents.

[50]   For this reason, I have preferred talking of the marginalized interior, rather than "poverty."

from the coastal areas, from Bizerte to Mahdia (Ayari 2016: 29), and people from Sfax and all of the regions that are south and west of this city did not have much access to the metaphoric pie of jobs, resources, and economic opportunities. A renewal of political elites started in the last three decades of the Protectorate and continued after 1956, but people like Habib Bourguiba and many of his republican peers stemmed from the Sahel region, from coastal towns between Tunis and Mahdia (Hammamet, Enfidha, Monastir, Sousse, Msakin, Moknine) and embraced a modernist ideology of nation-building, undermining ancient forms of authority, notably religious ones.[51] The main opponents to Bourguiba around the time of independence were what Ayari calls *"extra muros,"* i.e. people from the internal regions, such as Sidi Bouzid, Gafsa, or Medenine, and who were not born or socialized in the walled cities of the historical towns of Ifriqiya.[52] *Extra muros* people were judged as lacking refinement, civilization, and ability to cultivate certain secular dispositions. Out of this space came the strongest support for Ennahda[53] and pan-Arabist movements and a great deal of resentment against central authorities.

Let us now turn to Yemen. The existence of two sister republics for the period running from the 1960s until 1990 requires that we assess how the uncontested leader of post-unification Yemen, President Saleh, established centralized control over resources and power. While in

---

[51] Zaituna, also rendered as Zitouna, is one of the oldest universities in the world and was one of the historical hubs, with Kairouan, for the Sunni Maliki school of jurisprudence. Under Bourguiba, a staunch secularist, it was turned into a mere theology faculty. See Ghorbal (2012: 91) and Chouikha & Gobe (2015: 19).

[52] Ayari's (2016) sophisticated sociology of militancy identifies four "social-identity origins of activists": the first group of elites is that of the medinal elites, those attached to the Ottoman Bey and his palace; the second group, the *medinaux*, i.e. people from the historical urban centers, the *medina*, but with different cultural and educational capital; the third group is the *"publiciens,"* or post-independence literati, that is people who accumulated social capital from dual-language education (French and Arabic); while the fourth category is the *extra muros*, i.e. people who come physically from outside the medinas, or outside of urban centers.

[53] The sample of activists assembled by Ayari (2016: 71–72, Tableau 5) reveals that 45% of political activists with an *extra muros* social origin are Islamists. These four clusters of social origins are ideal-types, as some individuals straddle different categories, or geographical locations could harbor two different types or waves of activism.

Tunisia the geography of power remained almost untouched in the post-independence period, in Yemen one has to assess regionalisms and the differentiated impact of physical coercion in much more fluctuating terms. Consideration of factors related to political economy is necessary to understanding how different power games have been at play. While in the case of the town of Marib regionalism evolves around the oil economy and a soft patronage system, the trend for southern separatism and the Zaydi revival around Saada involves crude force and episodes of war.

From the 1980s onward, the presidential family also started assuming key military and governmental functions throughout the country, a process that Stephen Day (2012) has documented in great detail. Marib, a region long overlooked by Sanaa until the discovery of oil in 1984 (Day 2012: 71), faced extractive measures from Saleh and his tribal connections, which, like Taiz, would limit these cities' and regions' autonomy. The revenues from the hydrocarbons extracted in Marib contributed significantly to the state budget, yet the area lacked basic services, such as electricity, proper schools, and hospitals (Alwazir 2016: 176). People of this central interior region demanded a better redistribution of the oil income, but all they got from Sanaa was more political appointees close to Saleh: 75% of the political appointments in the Marib region were given to people from the Upper highlands (Day 2012: 71). Furthermore, the former independence of the tribes in the Marib, Shabwa and Abyan governorates was lost, with the central state intervening to assure control of resources and avoiding cross-border smuggling (Bonnefoy 2012a: 111). By the end of the 1980s, "the average citizen in Taiz, Ibb and Al-Bayda contributed more than twice what citizens on the highland plateau around Sanaa contributed" (Day 2012: 70, 82). Marib was not paying more tax; it simply did not receive investment back from Sanaa. On the other hand, Yemenis from the Upper highlands (the Hashid tribal heartland) evaded taxation by exerting violence on the staff of the tax authority if they were too insistent (Day 2012: 70).

Patronage and crony capitalism soon had the upper hand over the past power of remittance resources controlled by the LDAs, which had been important in a region like Taiz. The LDAs ceased to be a real force for local governance, and with Saleh's grip on power now firmly established, local self-governance was permanently hampered. Pro-government tribalism thus generated resentment in the Marib and

Taiz areas.[54] Saleh also used the YMEC to spread his kleptocratic reach. The YMEC acquired massive assets, including land, real estate, and a range of monopolistic import licenses (Lackner 2019: 232). With liberalization in the mid-1990s, the YMEC became the Yemen Economic Corporation (YEC), but the clientelist patronage role of the organization remained untouched.

In the former South, feelings for regionalism took the form of separatism, which grew from the first years of unification and the short civil war in 1994. Political economy factors are related to the end of the Soviet Union and to a perceived process of internal colonization by the former North of Yemen in the years after 1994. One last fundamental issue is the high degree of internal fragmentation. The YSP, the ruling party in the South, has been drawn into bitter leadership rivalries, which overlapped with old regional cleavages. In 1986 a blood bath decimated half of the YSP leadership, leaving thousands dead in the following weeks. One of the military officers, Abed Rabbo Mansur Hadi, the current Yemeni President, originally from Mudiya in the Abyan province (South), left Aden at that time. He later became the deputy of Saleh in October 1994 (Mermier 2012: 49). With the collapse of the Soviet Union (1989–1991), Southern Yemen lost not only political support, but also important revenues. Ali Al-Beidh, the secretary general of the YSP, accepted the project of unification with the North, and in May 1990, the Republic of Yemen (ROY) was established as a unitary republic. Al-Beidh became the Vice-President of a reunified Yemen, Sanaa became the capital, and Aden was given the honorific title of "economic capital."[55]

Parity between North and South was guaranteed in the body tasked with writing the new 1991 Constitution and in the transitional government (Mermier 2012: 43). For the first legislative elections in 1993 there was genuine mass participation, with a multi-party parliament contesting each of the 301 constituency-based seats. At the time, Carapico (1993: 139) described this period as characterized by "unfettered public debate and discussion that ... represents the advent of organized mass politics in a region where political power has long

---

[54] We remember that Taiz, the heartland of the LDAs, is where alternative social organization in the form of villages had, "to a large extent, supplanted the tribes" (Bonnefoy 2018: 23).

[55] Haydar Abu Bakr Al-'Attas, President of the PDRY between 1986 and 1990, became Prime Minister after May 1990. See Mermier (2012: 43).

remained a closely held family affair." Popular participation in politics was animated despite an unclear political line and growing rivalries between the former ruling party of the North, the GPC, and the YSP. Women, who had more political deputation in Southern Yemen (5–6 women in a 111-strong legislative council; Lackner 1985: 118), could only count on two women in the 301-member Parliament elected between 1993 and 2003, and only one since then (Al-Sakkaf 2018: 140; Carapico 1998: 149). Citizenship practices were alive in this new phase of Yemeni history, but the social conservativeness of the north started to extend its grip over the entire country.

In 1993, Al-Beidh lamented the fact that the political system born of unification had federalist trappings, but did not have the formal component (an upper chamber, in this case the Consultative Assembly, *majlis al-shura*, was only a consultative body for the president) (Carapico 1998: 194–195). Despite a seven-point agreement meant to share power equitably between the North and South (in particular in the army) in October 1993 and the "Amman Agreement" signed by the GPC and YSP to institute "administrative and fiscal decentralization" in February 1994 (Detalle 1994), a segment of the YSP called for secession. A short but grueling civil war broke out that lasted between May 5 and July 7, 1994, with the North crushing the secessionist Southern movement.

The manner in which power was redeployed after the victory of the North in 1994 is reminiscent of what allowed Saleh to come to power in the 1970s. Saleh added the support of the Islamist party Islah to his small circles of privileged connections. After unification, Saleh used Islah, the Yemeni branch of the Muslim Brotherhood, to counteract the influence of the YSP. Islah was guided by the paramount leader of the Hashid tribal confederation, Abdallah Al-Ahmar. After the 1994 victory against the South, "all pretenses to conceal the presidential family's monopoly of military power were abandoned" (Day 2012: 137). Saleh let Islah, its ally against the YSP in the Parliament, run the south of the country, with a systematic plundering of resources, particularly in Aden. Southerners had complained about the more than 150 YSP leaders killed by Islamists in the early years of unification, 1990–1993, but the post-1994 reality saw no real improvement (Amira Augustin 2015: 11). For instance, false land deeds were forged by Northerners to claim ownership over land in the South, and positions of authority in security institutions were monopolized by people from the North (Day 2012: 138, 142, 143). Saleh entrusted people from his own tribe, the Sanhan, and village to key positions. Thus, Ali Muhsin (b. 1945) became military commander of the central region, while two maternal uncles of Saleh became commanders: one of the Hadhramawt and Shabwa provinces, and the other of the southwest region of Aden (Day 2012: 137).

The accusations of "internal colonialism" grew in the former South. Civic protests formed in the early 2000s. These protests were resolutely non-violent and underlined the inequalities that the discharging of hundreds of soldiers and officers from the South had on the entire population. In mid-2005, a cluster of southern army officers who were illegally dismissed after the 1994 civil war coalesced with unemployed youth and many others and formed a new movement called Hirak (Arabic for impulse, or movement) (Dahlgren 2014a). In July 2007, thousands gathered in Aden to recall the July 1994 invasion and looting. From that time, various southern leaders, many in exile, proposed a break with the model of the unitary state, with some favoring secession, and others a form of federalism (Mermier 2012: 52–54). Hirak established catalogues of grievances that would soon find resonance with the 2011 Arab Uprisings. Federalism has always been the minimal concession that Hirak wants to snatch from Sanaa, but many argue that secession (an untellable truth) is the only real way to obtain self-governance. A number of Saleh's policies, over the years, paved the way to the growth of Hirak in the south: northern dominance in privatization, land grabs, the destruction of flourishing industries during and after the 1994 war, and the use of military campaigns against Al-Qaeda to repress the southern movement in 2008 (Mermier 2012: 45; Bonnefoy 2012a).

In 2004, Saleh also had to face another regional crisis, this time in the north of the country around Saada. In substance, the symbolic elements of an age-old confessional identity (Zaydi) and of resentment against a hegemonic Hashid tribal domination and over-centralization of power by Sanaa are as important as political and economic factors for understanding what would become the Huthi question. In Section 1.3, we discussed how the northernmost tribes of the Khawlan bin Amir confederation were aggrieved by the Imam's heavy taxation and the loss of historical territories with the 1934 treaty (Bonnefoy 2018: 55). During the civil war in the 1960s, these tribes rejected the authority of the Imam and joined the republican side

(Brandt 2019b: 12, 17). Yet, throughout the republican era they were never rewarded. The same problems of marginalization described for the Taiz, Marib, and southern regions after 1990 occurred for the Saada population. Reducing this Saada–Sanaa fracture to confessionalism is misleading: the bulk of all these three tribal confederations, Khawlan bin Amir, Hashid, and Bakil, are Zaydi.[56] While the Hashid and Bakil alliance had the lion's share of power from 1990 onwards, there are more mundane and material reasons, such as access to water and subsidized oil, tax pressure, and lack of infrastructure to explain the growing rift between the population of the Saada region and Sanaa. The militarization of the Saada rebellion amplified the rift, which turned into six rounds of wars for Saada between 2004 and 2010.

Like in Marib, Saada was almost always left out of the state's generosity (Dorlian 2012: 75–76). A journalist in 2005 noted that "the province of Saada has only encountered the power of the Yemeni republic through missiles and tanks," not with infrastructure (Nabil Al-Sufi, quoted in Dorlian 2012: 76). The Saada region counts less public infrastructure, with only two hospitals for 700,000 inhabitants (Dorlian 2012: 76). In 2003, 27% of the population of Saada lived from the selling of qat.

This material backdrop needs to be combined with post-unification politics and the growing monopolization of power by the alliance between the two main parties, the GPC and Islah. In 1990, scores of new parties emerged. One of them, the Truth Party, Al-Haqq, was a party formed by Zaydi intellectuals. It gained two seats in the 1993 elections. A firmly republican party, it opposes the aristocratic privileges of the *sada* (also called Hashemites) and stood against the effort of Sanaa to erase the cultural legacy of the Zaydis. For instance, Saleh appointed Salafi predicators in historically Zaydi mosques in Saada and forbade a specific Zaydi holiday (*'eid al-ghadir*) (Dorlian 2012: 80). By promoting anti-Zaydi discourses throughout the 1990s, government officials further fanned the flames of confessional tensions in the country. Saleh allowed the creation of a Salafi institute in Dammaj, a small village outside of Saada (Bonnefoy 2011: 54, 57). Salafi–Zaydi

---

[56] The sectarian component of the opposition between the Huthis and President Saleh emerged only a few years before the 2011 protests. On this, see Dorlian (2011), Fraihat (2016: 39–42 and 45–48), and Yadav & Carapico (2014). According to Bonnefoy (2011: 2, fn. 1), 35% of the Yemeni population are Zaydi.

rivalries took an even more unpleasant turn in the late 2000s, with violent actions around the Salafi center, with Salafis accusing Zaydi Shiism of being a Jewish plot (Bonnefoy 2011: 274, 266).

In this context, a group close to the republican party Al-Haqq called the Young Believers (or Believing Youth, *al-shabab al-mu'min*) emerged in the Saada governorate. While Al-Haqq remained rather elitist and respectful of the political process (Bonnefoy 2011: 269), the Believing Youth were more turbulent. After splits in 1997 and 2002, a member of the Al-Haqq party, Husayn Badreddin Al-Huthi, created a distinct, more political movement fighting corruption and social injustices. Hussein Al-Huthi has been credited as being the real leader of Zaydi revivalism (Dorlian 2011: 184; 2015 :62). When a first round of hostilies between the military and dissenters against Saleh's army in the Saada region took place in 2004, the rebellion took on the name of the recently killed Hussein Al-Huthi. The Saada wars, with six rounds of destructive clashes between 2004 and 2010, gradually came to be called the Huthi wars.

The founder of the Huthi movement was not justifying his movement in confessional terms. He was attacking the problem of social injustice and the political arrogance of those in power, *al-mustakbirun* in Arabic (Dorlian 2012: 73; 2015: 72). The movement grew in strength, building on Hussein Al-Huthi's "agenda calling for equality of all groups and sects and for the end of patronage and corruption" (Lackner 2019: 158). Saleh waged six rounds of military campaigns against the Huthis and sent his deputy, Ali Muhsin Al-Ahmar, to lead these difficult military operations.[57] Nasty scorched earth tactics were used by Muhsin and his Firqa units,[58] especially in the fifth and sixth wars for Saada, which saw the intervention of Saudi troops on the side of the Yemeni army (Dorlian 2015: 66). Another episode fanned the flames of tribal rivalries, when Hashid tribes violated the sacrosanct territorial sovereignty of another tribe, the Khawlan bin Amir. Many representatives of the Huthi movement come from this territory. Anthropologist

---

[57] Some say that Saleh sent him to the north to sideline him and make more space for his son to come to power, thus reneging on a deal that Ali Muhsin and Saleh would have done to support each other at the time when the latter became President in 1978. Ahmad Ali, son of President Saleh and Chief of the Republican Guard, was able to score a quick victory in the Muhsin–Saleh rivalry during the fifth Saada war (Dorlian 2011: 188).

[58] On the power of the Firqa brigades, see ICG (2013a).

Brandt (2019b: 12) notes that the Khawlan bin Amir tribes have joined the Huthi movement, either as tribal members or as *sada* with ancestry in the Khawlan territory, and that nowadays most of the country is ruled by people from the Khawlan networks (Brandt 2019b: 12), like the people of Sanhan had ruled the country under Saleh for three decades.

The hardships in the entire northern regions were massive at the end of 2010: About 300,000 people in the Saada governorates, that is 40% of the governorate population, were internally displaced.[59] The smuggling of weapons, qat, medicines, and also drugs grew out of dire economic necessity in the north. Qat, the main cash crop, helped fuel the armed rebellion (70% of the land cultivated in the Huthi regions was dedicated to qat in the late 2000s) (Radl 2019: 19). With water resources being so scarce (and with 90% of water consumption going into agriculture, 2% for industry, and 8% for household)[60] people started digging wells deeper and deeper, increasingly requiring the activation of pumps. In this context, weapons and gasoline smugglers became important local figures. One of them, Fares Manaa, will play an important role in the next chapters.

Although very distinct, the two regional struggles helped each other at a distance: The relative success of the Huthi rebels emboldened the south to continue its protest movements and to demand the reinsertion of civilian and military employees that had been forced to retire after the 1994 civil war (Day 2012: 227–228). Conversely, the Huthi benefited from the attention that Saleh had to give to the tensions developing in the south in 2009 and 2010 (Brandt 2019a: 28). The southern Hirak were discredited by their association with the presence of Al-Qaeda in the Arabic Peninsula, while the Huthi rebellion in the north was presented as a primarily sectarian, Shia threat to the entire Peninsula. Saleh's regime thus used the confessional conflict card to muster new forms of support, from the USA (Dorlian 2012: 72; Brandt 2019a).

In the four to six years before the Uprisings, Yemen was locked in limbo, and the frustration of the citizenry grew to unparalleled levels.

---

[59] For Radl (2019: 20) the figure is between 287,000 and 317,000 internally displaced persons (IDPs). In the 2004 census, the total population of the Saada governorate was 695,033. Census figure from www.statoids.com/uye.html.

[60] The same sources estimate that Yemenis have only access to $87m^3$ per capita per year, as opposed to the $1,000m^3$ that the WHO suggests for normal yearly water consumption (Brehony, Lackner, & Al-Sarhan 2015: 14).

The death of Saleh's ally, Shaykh Abdallah Al-Ahmar, in 2007 further complicated the balance of power. Various civilian groups described as politically liminal (Yadav 2011) organized against the extent of tribalization in formal politics. Like in Tunisia, multiple forms of marginalization overlapped: women (who lost much of the benefits of more egalitarian socialist measures, in particular the guarantees of the 1974 Family Law; Lackner 2019: 204), youths left out of the patronage system, former military members of the South, and low status groups (the so-called *muhammashin*, Arabic for "excluded"), all faced social discrimination.[61] In November 2005, a new opposition coalition front emerged, called the Joined Meeting Parties (JMP).

The work and formulations of political scientist Stacey Philbrick Yadav (2011) are very helpful to clarify the difference between the two countries and the specificities of the Yemeni case. Yadav documented the assembling role that the JMP and the post-partisan nature of a new movement, that is, a trend in political parties to transcend identities of "class, tribe, regions, gender and ideology," that emerged in the decade 2000–2010 (Yadav 2011: 551). These new articulations were "a necessary antecedent of the [2011] revolution" (Yadav 2011: 551), something that did not exist in Tunisia, where the RCD was controlling civic and party political life.

The Joint Meeting Parties, *ahzab al-liqa' al-mushtarak*, is a cluster of parties that realized that without a common commitment to establish an anti-GPC block, nothing would change in Yemen.[62] The JMP had Islah, the quite pragmatic Yemeni Muslim Brotherhood party, at its core.[63] It also includes the YSP – still somewhat popular in the south – and three other minor parties (Al-Haqq, the Unionist Party, and the Popular Forces Union party) (Browers 2007). In a document published

---

[61] The *muhammashin*, also referred to with the pejorative term *akhdam* ("servants"), whose numbers have been estimated for 2016 to be 3.5 million (UN figures of the "Special Rapporteur on Minority Issues," UN Human Rights Council, quoted in http://sanaacenter.org/publications/analysis/7490). According to Bonnefoy (2018: 129) the *muhammashin* only represent 2% of the population. For a fine description of the *muhammashin* condition, and how they are racialized, see B. Hall (2017: §§ 16–18).

[62] www.aljazeera.com/indepth/spotlight/yemen/2011/02/201122814145398633 7.html.

[63] The work of Clark (2004), Schwedler (2006), and Browers (2007) is essential to comprehend the inclusion of Islamists parties into the formal realm of politics in Yemen.

in September 2009 and entitled the Preparatory Committee for National Dialogue ("PCND"),[64] the JMP listed, among its key demands, federalism as a way to generate a more equitable power distribution in the whole country (Zyck 2014: 3). The expression "National Dialogue," which re-emerged in 2012, had its origin in this document and called for informal talks to loosen up the grip that President Saleh had on the country. Both the JMP and Hirak speak the same language of federalism, but the objectives are different: The JMP wants to undo the monopoly of power of the GPC and return to political pluralism (the name "Joint Meeting Parties" is no coincidence), while Hirak concentrates only on the southern question, so much so that federalism could be synonymous with a "federal state," but with only two regions (*iqlim*), north and south (Mermier 2012: 62).

* * *

In conclusion, this chapter has demonstrated that civic vitality is part of the history of the contemporary Middle East. It has been stifled for a diversity of reasons, ranging from old geography of uneven domination in the pre-colonial and colonial eras, a problem of uneven use of coercion, to post-independence policies that have favored the control over state institutions by an oligarchic clique, many of whom have a military or security background. Furthermore, the chapter has argued that inchoate mobilizations and a new political vocabulary have historically emerged in support of republican ideas: From the horizontal alliances of Tanyus Shahin to the cross-class and status alliance of the Krim in the Moroccan Rif, cross-cutting alliances emerged, but these loose mobilizations can easily die out (Chalcraft 2016). During the age of ideology, in particular post-independence, developmentalism, feminism, and other egalitarian projects were genuine projects that generated hopes for expanded enfranchisement. But the encroachments of the Cold War, with its sponsorship of militarized rulers, turned these expectations into vacuous promises serving to legitimize an increasingly corrupt and entrenched elite. They also generated skewed state–society relations and brutal repression against Middle Eastern citizens, a repression that was increasingly delegated to private security actors. The privatization of security encouraged by the diktats of neoliberal policies absolve de facto state institutions of accusations of human

---

[64] https://yemenvision.wordpress.com/category/summary/.

rights violations (Hever 2018: 3) and thus show that there is something valuable in Tilly's model of the equalization of violence, but which could not happen in the Middle East.

Typical of those Arab states with a deep security state, Yemen took the form of a neo-patrimonial state,[65] that is a superposition of a male-dominated network over state institutions, with President Saleh's kinship entourage entrusted with key military and economic functions. One of his sons, Ahmad Ali Saleh, was leading the very powerful Republican Guard, and viewed the brigades he commanded as "his personal property" (ICG 2013a: 3, 7, and 10). Various nephews of President Saleh were also trusted with top security or business positions.[66] The political system of representation was totally stalled, with presidential and legislative elections postponed a couple of times in the late 2000s and a Parliament under the control of the GPC, which had vassalized a series of small, formerly independent parties.

In Tunisia, as Lisa Chomyak (2014) has astutely argued, the "archi-tecture of resistance" to Ben Ali has a longer history than accounts that focus on unexpected or "out of the blue" revolution suggest. This architecture also has a geography whose origins date back to the nineteenth century. The economically neglected interior, the institu-tional marginalization of certain collective actors (Yousfi 2015) and of entire regions, in particular the southern, central, and western regions, as opposed to the concentration of wealth and power along the Sahel coast (Ayeb 2011: 469), and processes of elite-formation, with differ-ent social origins granting better access to power (Ayari 2016), have offered explanations of the socio-economic fragmentation in Tunisia. Those who had access to neutral grounds outside of the country were able to organize inchoate forms resistance. Two examples of this. First, the platform of opposition parties and associations called the "October 18 Committee for Rights and Freedoms" (*hay'at 18 oktuber lil-huquq wa al-hurriyyat*) was established in 2005 and took advantage of a large international conference in Tunis to draw attention to the dire

---

[65] On neopatriarchy in general, see Sharabi (1988).

[66] Yahya Saleh (Lackner 2019: 142) was in charge of the Central Security Forces in charge of fighting AQAP (Al-Qaeda in the Arabian Peninsula). Two other nephews, Tareq and Tawfiq, acted as leaders in a far-reaching economic conglomerate, called Schlumberg (Lackner 2019: 142, 215, 257–258). In sum, a small layer of "kleptocrats," whose "status [arose] from connection to central power," was running a country still characterized by enormous economic disparities (Lackner 2019: 207).

situation of anyone who was critical of Ben Ali's regime (Hajji 2006: 4; Dahmani 2015). Pushing aside ideological divides, these organizations called for the realization of fundamental rights in Tunisia, such as freedom of expression and association and the release of all political prisoners. Second, the significance of the Rdayyef mine protests in 2008 and early 2009 was amplified through networks of solidarity in Nantes. These French connections allowed for the mediatization of the protests (Gobe 2010: 19), a technique meant to shame Ben Ali's government, and which would be used again in December 2010 after the self-immolation of Mohammed Bouazizi.

Let us now see how the 2011 protests made the management of coercion a central point of democratic political contentions and how the various components of informal politics succeeded in creating distinct participatory paths in the reform of security.

Informal Revolutionary Practices (2011–2014)

Introduction

Part II occurs against the backdrop of fast-paced events with demands for deep changes. The Arab masses in 2011 reinvented *political representation* by gathering and occupying public squares. In and around these spaces, they also invented a new imaginary, a different path to *cultural representation*, in which the people (in Arabic, *al-sha'ab*) imagined for themselves a new role in punishing past tyrants and in defining a new, more democratic, and less violent system. They projected images in which they act as rights-bearing citizens involved directly in state activities. The dynamic self-representation generated a new habitus capturing a sense of civic responsibility through the management of state coercion. This habitus, instantiated by a new force of assembled and empowered people, *vis populi*, emerged in stark contrast with the depiction of latent citizenship in the Arab world, but amplified earlier examples of transgressive popular mobilization.

The informal step towards cultural and self-representation, *taswir*, is only a preliminary method of synchronizing the presence of the many. It does not construct a new form of democratic order in itself, but generates the conditions for future actions. It is at this point that *tamthil*, or political representation, comes in. Only when a certain form of *taswir* capturing the novelty of these revolts remained possible, open-ended, and skeptical of the past uses of violence could the principle of political representation (*tamthil*) be re-thought and experienced along new lines and take new, more democratic, forms (Chapter 3).

The symbolism of violence and the concerted non-violent actions constituted a mirror of past geography of the uneven distribution of violence and of the long winding processes that had generated negative and latent citizenship, from the colonial to the post-independence era. Both Tunisia and Yemen faced a series of crossroads, or forking paths, that led to reforms and not to profound revolutionary changes. The dynamics within the security sector reform proved to be a litmus test for the revolutionary dynamics. While the strength of *vis populi* was vividly felt in the first months of the Uprisings, its presence was overshadowed by deeper processes of elite regrouping, and inhibited by barriers erected around these reforms by political parties, which limited the extent of the democratic reforms in both countries (Chapter 4).

Key Dates, Actors, and Institutions: Tunisia

2005	Formation of the October 18 Committee for Rights and Freedoms, with common requests from secular and Islamic oppositions
2010	
Dec. 17	Self-immolation of Mohammed Bouazizi, and ensuing protests in the interior regions of Tala, Kasserine, Menzel Bouzayene, and a few days later in Medenine
2011	
Jan. 11	The protests reach the coastal cities of Sfax and Sousse
Jan. 14	Ben Ali flees the country. Fu'ad Mebazza becomes interim president the next day
Jan. 17	Formation of the first Ghannouchi government (Ghannouchi I)
Jan. 23–27	First occupation of Qasba Square (Qasba 1)
Jan. 28	Ghannouchi II government
Feb. 18	Appointment of Yadh Ben Achour to the Political Reform Commission
Feb. 25	Second occupation of Qasba Square (Qasba 2)
Feb. 27	New government under Essebsi
March 15	Ben Achour Commission becomes the Higher Authority for the Realization of the Objectives of the Revolution (HAROR)
April	Additional members are added to the HAROR

Oct. 23	100 parties, 34 coalitions, and 11,700 candidates vie for a seat in the ANC
Nov.	Formation of the Troika, the governing coalition that rules until end of 2013. Moncef Marzouki is chosen as President

2012

March	Salafi militants plant their black flag on Manouba university and cultural venues
Spring	Nidaa Tounes, a secularist party, is established by Essebsi
Nov.	Marches in Siliana

2013

Feb. 6	Killing of Choukri Belaid
July 25	Killing of Mohamed Brahmi
August	Start of the National Dialogue
Sept.–Dec.	Quartet negotiates the end of Troika rule and of the constitution drafting process

2014

Jan. 26	Final vote at the ANC on the new constitution
Dec.	Beji Caid Essebsi wins the second round of the presidential election

ANC	Constituent National Assembly (2011–2014)
ARP	Assembly of the Representatives of the People (Legislative, 2014–)
HAROR	Higher Authority for the Realization of the Objectives of the Revolution, Political Reform, and Democratic Transition (also Higher Authority)
Quartet	Informal alliance between four associations (UGTT; the Tunisian Confederation of Industry, Trade, and Handicrafts [UTICA]; the Tunisian Human Rights League [LTDH]; and the Tunisian Order of Lawyers) pushing the Troika to accept the National Dialogue. Later winner of the Nobel Peace Prize
Troika	Three-party coalition that ruled after the election of the ANC until Jan. 2014

Key Dates, Actors, and Institutions: Yemen

2011

Jan. 11	Start of the Uprisings. Some encampments to last until April 2013
Feb.	Twenty protesters are killed in Aden
March 18	Massacre in Sanaa
May	Battle of Taiz
June 3	Bomb leaving President Saleh gravely injured. He is treated in Riyadh
Sept.	Saleh returns to Sanaa
Nov. 23	Signing of the GCC Initiative and the Implementing Mechanism
Dec. 7	Government of National Unity (GNU) formed. Mohammed Salem Basendwa is new Prime Minister
Dec. 24	Start of the March of Life, converging from different cities towards Sanaa

2012

Jan. 21	Parliament grants immunity to Saleh
Feb. 21	President Hadi is elected as interim president for two years
March	Hadi establishes the "Committee on Military Affairs"
Summer	120 military are killed in two attacks in Sanaa (100 in May; 20 in August)

2013

March 18	NDC inaugurated
April	The *sahat* movement in Sanaa disbands

2014

Jan. 26	NDC publishes its final recommendations

AS-Y	Ansar Al-Sharia (Yemen): an insurrectionist movement affiliated with AQAP
AQAP	Al-Qaeda in the Arabian Peninsula
GCC	Gulf Cooperation Council, a club of six monarchies imposing its mediation on Yemen
Islah	Muslim Brotherhood-type of party, with a tribal component

JMP   Joint Meeting Parties (coalition of opposition parties, such as Islah and YSP)
miliyuniyyat   "million people" marches organized in the former Southern Yemen
NDC   National Dialogue Conference

3 | *The Three Facets of* Vis Populi: *Re-articulating Active Citizenship*

3.1 Timing, Spontaneity, and Re-assembled Exclusions: The Three Facets of Representation

One morning, the Italian women working in the rice fields refused to bend their backs and work uninterruptedly for a corrupt and forceful master. After having talked silently and complained about it, they finally engaged the system of inequity and, together, ascertained their collective strength.

The parallel to the Italian rice-weeders evoked in the *Prolegomenon* of this book is no exaggeration, despite the romantic aura that does not capture the courage it took. From "every morning" to an exceptional "one morning," the rebellious Arab masses stood up and shook the yoke of latent citizenship. With a sense of urgency and direct confrontation of the corrupt regime (*al-nizam*), and at times with violent actions against apparatuses of repression (a police station, the Ministry of the Interior, the offices of the ruling party stormed, torched, or vandalized), "the people" (*al-sha'ab*) acted across most Arab states in quasi synchrony with a similar demand: the people want the fall of the regime (*al-sha'ab yurid isqat an-nizam*).

While there remains disagreement as to why 2011 came with its flow of uprisings at this specific moment in time, and not two years earlier or five years later, the scholarship tends to agree that there were multiple triggers and causal factors behind them.[1] A series of factors and immediate triggers generated small-scale protests, but the reaction of the different regimes contributed to the upscaling of the protest movement. It soon became unstoppable, in particular at an age where the power of

---

[1] The Conclusion comes back on this point. Identifying a unique cause (neoliberalism, robbed elections, spike in food prices, relative absence of conflicts, growing presence of social media, the spread of satellite news coverage, etc.) remains unsatisfactory because each national protest had some specificities that do not fit the homogenizing narrative.

images, an interrupted flow of news coverage, and citizen journalism have become so widespread. Whatever the proximate causes, the 2011 Uprisings are the by-product of the *relational* interactions between disgruntled but politically aware masses and repressive regimes who lazily thought that applying the usual rhetoric (external threat, foreign manipulation, risk for stability, etc.) and repressive recipes (use of the baton, shutting telecommunication, combined with a few carrots to contain spiking prices of basic commodities) would work. It did not.

One morning, people stood up and by doing so affirmed their collective power and force that confronts the iniquitous violence and repression of a corrupt regime. Vis populi *appeared with its full force because of its ability to project and enact a new collective imaginary, a new sense of subjectivity that demanded new forms of political representation and respect for the sovereign power of the demos. It reversed the symbolic order, with an active citizenship replacing old grievances with new collective projects, and replaced the uneven distribution of violence with a project of equality across national spaces.*

This chapter tackles a number of sociological and theoretical puzzles around the theme of *vis populi*, the force, strength, or will of the people: What exactly is the "people," since it is not a sociological category, but only a political one? What made possible the articulations between distinct, unrelated sociological groups that had encountered different types of marginalization and/or oppression? What is the relation between the informal and formal, when it comes to the impact of mass mobilization and revolutionary dynamics? What exactly is spontaneity? What is the relation between spontaneity and revolutions? How can the *vis populi*, which is partly a collective reaction to past state violence, be a basis for a democratic order? Why did I maintain in the Introduction that the two forms of representation (cultural and political) are (to be) connected to the theme of violence? And to which violence are we referring?

This part of the book captures dynamics that occurred during phases of high tempo or fast paced civic activism and democratic change. There is a price to pay in this choice of offering a comparative gaze or sustained look at different countries' or regions' dynamics: nuances will disappear at times, but my hope is that the enchasing of micro-scenes (e.g. a poem performed in public, a graffiti, or a poster) into a broader historical backdrop will help elucidate how democratic and innovative these episodes have been, and how inspiring for social and democratic theory these "events" have been and remain.[2] I will focus on informality, social roles, space, and democratic theory in the context of the proposed relational perspective (the Moebius strip).

While details on Yemen are offered later, the bulk of the chapter leans toward Tunisia, for which I have been able to amass significant amounts of my own primary sources, alongside a rich series of secondary sources, to illustrate the phenomenon of democratic mobilizations in the two years before the self-immolation of Mohammed Bouazizi. As this book also intends to offer a general reading for the (Arab) Middle East, I will also occasionally, as in earlier chapters, mention a few examples from Egypt, Syria, or Palestine, where similar themes and mobilization sequences occurred. As a result of the effort to generate a theoretical perspective, commonalities in these countries will trump differences and specificities across them.

In 2011, all Arab countries witnessed protests where "the people" resisted past exclusions and re-assembled as an imagined *and* acting one. The connecting element or force is what I call the three facets of representation: an energized ability to project a new *demos* or collective force (*taswir*); a demand for new democratic political representation (*tamthil*);[3] and a frontal, at times destructive, confrontation of the past repression by the state. Once *articulated* these three facets produce the *vis populi*, the force, will, or strength of the people, or of the many. This provides in turn a counter-hegemony bringing coalescence (*iltiham*) across social and geographical spaces and actualizing a sense of shared civic responsibility.

Something happened, something that philosopher Cornelius Castoriadis called "spontaneity," but in a very specific sense. A new wave of transgressive mobilization à la Chalcraft (2016) engendered a call for profound political changes and democratic demands. The vibrancy of all-out mobilizations, collective effervescence, or liminal energy in early 2011 led to a new cartography of civic identification and laid bare the past ruthless policies of incumbent regimes to prevent democratic participation in the name of security or the threat of war.

---

[2] I share the view of my colleague Robin Wagner-Pacifici (2017), who defines events not as a distinct moment, but as based on restlessness. Unlike her focus on mediation and media, I concentrate more on the connective practices.

[3] I leave the German *Darstellung* and *Vertretung* out of this chapter. In the Introduction, where the concepts were presented in relation to Marx's and Said's discussion of representation, it made sense to have both Arabic and German.

The foundation of the pyramid of power, so to say, where citizens are supposed to provide the bases for democratic and state participation, had been forcedly vacated by corrupt elites and dictators. Not by coincidence, as we will see, the masses convoked much energy and effort to occupy certain symbolic locations and strategic institutions. The force of their presence signified, sometimes in a dynamic and converging manner, their *return* to the center stage of political participation. Attention will therefore be given to space, the new meanings of "a people," the politics of presentism, and the emergence of new subjectivity. Such formulations, with so much "newnesss," might yield the impression that much was invented from scratch. It was not fully new. It re-assembled older elements to spontaneously generate a new social compound, and offered a new method, that of direct and self-representation, which snowballed throughout the Arab world. The visual component of the "revolution" was not just the politics of a few images, their aestheticization or commercialization, what Negar Azimi (2016: e.g. 336–337) powerfully debunked in the Egyptian case and described as "ready-made revolution." The visual and expressive components of the Uprisings, caravans, graffitis, chanted slogans also expressed the "texture of everyday life" (Azimi 2016: 351) and choreographed a double movement between the peripheries and margins of political life until the end of 2010, with the expectation that the tremor of the revolution in the capital cities would then produce a wave of reforms throughout Yemen and Tunisia.

Spontaneity for Castoriadis (d. 1997) is not what comes into being from nothingness with no relation with the past. In a foundational text, Castoriadis (1976) tried to understanding how in a "short life-span, the Hungarian revolution posited new organizational forms and social meanings" (p. 7). For him, "every important historical action is spontaneous precisely in the pristine meaning of the Greek word: *spons*, source" (p. 11). The *source* of this creation was the "activity of the Hungarian people – intellectuals, students, workers" (p. 8) – and typically of the post-Marxist ideas that animated Castoriadis in this phase of his intellectual life, it is not an *already existing organization*, say a party, that organizes people or that inculcates from outside a political consciousness. "The revolution is exactly that: the self-organization of the people. . . . Self-organization is here *self-organizing* and consciousness is *becoming-conscious*. Both are *processes*, not *states*." In an Aristotelian vein, Castoriadis concludes that "spontaneity is the excess of the result over the causes" (p. 11). This does not mean "simply" that something anew emerges from collective mobilization, a "thing" that proponents of the "new social movements" identified four decades ago as a new identity in the making (Touraine 1977; Melucci 1995). This excess of the result is not a reified or clear-cut entity called "a social movement." Rather, out of contentious or even agonistic politics, one can see a bundle of new social roles, a new subjectivity, and a political awareness that spills over from a localized arena. This crystalization comes from the self-organization, from the still unclear and uncoordinated activities. Inchoate generates the formal. Gradual awareness generates political consciousness. New imaginal and critically assertive self-representation[4] engenders new forms of political representations. Informal does not mean dis-organization: it can also mean a choice to resist bureaucratization or hierarchization of struggles (Leach 2009). And in the context of the fragmentation and marginalization identified in the previous chapter, informality can also become the best way to bring to the fore previously silenced grievances.

Informal mobilization and articulated demands, what I detail below as "three facets of representation," do not equate with the theme of prefiguration.[5] Prefiguration is the term used in social movements to suggest that the way in which a given movement organizes itself and its internal discussions announces, or embodies, a new blueprint for the society or the polity at large. Informality here is different because it is much larger than one or a multitude of "social movements" (if such a thing exists): it is what allows for the (temporary) articulations between different segments of a lived and embodied, re-configured social body. I would propose that informality is even needed in the context of post-colonialism and of latent citizenship as the only transitory way to offer paths for a democratic reset. It is this informal sphere of engagement, in micro-processes of convergence and specific locations of violence, that the power of and by the people (*demo-cracy*) can be observed.

Informality also captures the quality of propositions made around new possibilities for managing state coercion. While numerous acts of destruction did occur in the early phases of the Uprisings, the way that violence was "seized" by the people generated a new discursive space

---

[4] I take the phrase imaginal politics from philosopher Bottici (2014).
[5] See, for a general discussion, Leach (2013) and for an example Maeckelbergh (2011).

and a common call to dislodge authoritarianism. These flows and movements serve also to stitch together different parts of the country and of its population.

The essence of a democratic society is the ability to articulate differences and to actualize these articulations in everyday life. For this reason, I will make reference to the diversity and the surplus of social roles that emerge in these revolutionary moments of spontaneity and auto-realization, of auto-organizing. Like Chalcraft's (2016: 15–21) criticism of the monolithic or reification of the social movement literature for its belief in the existence of a "movement" (we are better off by speaking or analyzing contentious politics), I also believe that the collective self-awareness – the vignette of Khiari (2016) in the Prolegomenon of people struggling as a whole, rather than just separate individuals – arises in the activities of "the people" and of the constituent groups that form it.

The idea of social roles that I propose is related to visions of internal equilibrium and division of labors with a system,[6] but also on creativity and the generation of new spaces and realms of civic engagement. I thus hope to create a bridge with democratic theory, but without the formal institutions that validate civic engagement (election, participation in deliberative fora such as a legislative assembly) that is generally the focus of "political theory." To be a responsible and active citizen means engaging with a variety of activities, some of which are outside the regular, regional, professional, or other scope of daily social engagement. Below, I will refer to "social roles" to capture the multiple dimensions of activism, without having to be a formal member of a social movement, a club, or an association. By participating in spontaneous and collective actions, individuals shape new meanings and new awareness. Activism in this book is not about self-appointed members of a given movement, association, or NGO. Instead, civic or

---

[6] The idea of social roles has been associated for too long with structural functionalist social theory, à la Talcott Parsons (d. 1979), where sub-systems, typically individual, social, and cultural, are integrated and contribute to the system stability. I strongly depart from the foundation of this social theory, which does not question how norms come into being and which does not care too much about power from below, or democracy, even more so in a postcolonial context. I would also underline that mine is not a social theory, but a theory of revolutionary moments, where "spontaneity is the excess of the result over the causes" (Castoriadis 1976: 11), not a system in equilibrium as Parsons' imagined society was "functioning."

democratic activism is lodged in everyday life; it is the practice that Castoriadis identifies as the *spons*, the source for revolution. Activism is informal and is one of the bases for democratic order. It of course needs to be structured and institutionalized at some point ("movements" cannot last forever), but some of it must remain enshrined or embodied in everyday practices and not just in institutions of deputation or in institutional accountability of checks and balances.

This, finally, connects to the dynamic theory of Gramsci around culture, class-consciousness, and political action. I creatively rely on Gramsci's intellectual system as a concatenation of different realms of action that creates the basis for an emancipatory and revolutionary move. Gramsci's full philosophical system[7] has been termed a theory of praxis, mixing culture and politics, coexisting with reflections on etymology and literary criticism, and independent ideas on Marxism. These elements are the basis for the complex and dynamic system of thought that strives for universal emancipation, or at least for the "subalterns," a Gramscian codeword for the proletariat and working class.

The non-European settings under focus in this book, where marginalized subjects of history are not only (white male) workers, but various social groups, women, racialized subjects, migrants, and cannon-fodder to Western capitalism, warrant a neo-Gramscian extension of this theory. But to avoid creating ad hoc categories that could generate cultural essentialisms, I will not call them "subalterns," or people whose voices are generally not included in official archives, but citizens or actors of civic acts who express political views. This a way to show the common objective of enacting and creating a democratic order, a civic praxis, that can be witnessed from below.

Contrary to the post-structural and post-modern turn in social science that focuses only on "culture," I take it from Gramsci that cultural emancipation goes with a profound work on (political) education and ethical commitment toward freedom. Put in the geometrical terms of the proposition of a *vis populi*, culture is only one of three corners of a triangle that, as a whole, sets a path for democratic representation in the Middle East. Cultural self-representation (*taswir*) must go with

---

[7] For an overview of Gramsci's theory, see Coutinho (2012). For an extensive discussion of Gramsci's frames of analysis applied to North African politics, see Gervasio & Manduchi (2020).

political representation (*tamthil*), with a view toward making the institutions of coercion accountable to the people, and to thus having the force of *vis populi* come to life. The neo-Gramscian twist is that education and ethical transformation are not only about class identification, but also about the civic engagement of the many, the multitude, the people. I also speak of neo-Gramscian approaches, because the focus of these pages is on democratic theory, not a refinement of revolutionary theories, which very often follow a Marxist-Leninist pattern, or a quite narrow postcolonial approach that sees resistance as a limited, defensive process of sabotaging the "public transcript" (Scott 1990). À la Asef Bayat (1997: 56), the informal politics of this book deals with the effort "to move forward and improve their lives," possibly even fight for democratic mobilizations.[8]

The emancipatory power of 2011 was consubstantial with the new subjectivity that emerged from the series of protests. This subjectivity mixes the individual sense of citizenship with a redefined and reinforced collective identification. The praxis is mutually constitutive: the aggregation of individual's efforts erased the past sense of collective inertia, and the omnipresence of the term "*sha'ab*," "the people" in Arabic, in turn, led individuals to act again overtly in a political manner. The informality of this collective mobilization manifested itself in the relatively marginal role that structured civil society organizations played in the outbreak of 2011.[9] I define subjectivity as a dynamic process in which the interplay of individual and collective self-understanding and interactions becomes constitutive of a social imaginary and translates into shared sentiments and joint aspirations.[10] Such a process is based on a form of internalization of certain ritualistic, bodily practices and disciplining interactions (Ismail 2007;

---

[8] James C. Scott is also too rational a theorist, as if subjects are involved in limited calculation, weighing costs against benefits. Bayat is right in claiming that force of necessity moves street politics to a much deeper level. There is thus an offensive, creative, possibly also poetic resistance in informal politics. But I try to go a step further than Bayat (1997: 58), who claims that informal politics do not aim at the state. I argue that it does, and that the core of *vis populi* is all about capturing the state to generate a democratic social contract that encompasses the means of coercion.

[9] Which I called in a 2011 article "the counter-power of civil society" (Challand 2011). I expand now to informal politics and *vis populi* to ground this reading in democratic theory, but there was an agreement already back in 2011 that the "banner" of organized civil society was hardly raised during the revolts.

[10] This is my definition, which is an adaptation of Ismail (2007: 7; 2011).

2011). But the new habitus of *vis populi* also offers a space for externalization, and an interface at the crossroads of individual perceptions and collective action whose effect is to remove the old structures of latent citizenship.[11] Thus, a certain dialectical relation, for example between the internal motives of mobilization and the external factors, or between spontaneity and organization, springs to the fore and becomes apparent in the revolutionary moments and praxes.

The Tunisian case illustrates that tendency: most of the main national trade union, the UGTT (the French acronym for the Tunisian General Labor Union), had been placed under control of the ruling party in the last decade of Bourguiba's rule, a trend that only intensified with Ben Ali (Khiari 2003: 69ff., 185ff.). Yet, it has been noted that without the informal space or refuge (*malja'*) that the UGTT could offer demonstrators because of the historical legitimacy of an institution that had been at the forefront of the independence struggle, the protests that followed the death of Mohammed Bouazizi would have probably died by the end of December 2010 (Yousfi 2015: 33–34). Omri (2016: 71–73) also maintains that the UGTT had historically provided for confluency (*tarafud*) between trade union and oppositional activities, and also did so in key moments in 2011. Due attention is thus given to places used for the mobilization, the more-or-less symbolic spaces that large assemblies of people chose to use, as well as flows of mobilization. This attention does not flow from a hypothetico-deductive effort in identifying variables. Rather it is an invitation to locate a possible series of informal factors, among others, in the 2011 Uprisings. I shall argue that these spaces and flows of mobilization are mirroring the past articulations of exclusion, both colonial and post-independence, and it is these *old* themes that provide *new* impetus for an active citizenship.

Yemenis and Tunisians both claim that they have initiated the waves of protests of the "Arab Spring" and that dynamics had been launched before January 2011. There is little point in dating the exact start,

---

[11] For Bourdieu (1977: 86, 76), the habitus is "a subjective but not individual system of internalized structures, schemes of perception, conception and action common to all members of the same group"; it is a "socially constituted system of cognitive and motivating structures," which is able to induce gradual social and political change. Ismail (2011: 990) notes how subjectivity includes also a relational component, in particular the humiliations by Egyptian police forces that helped generate a sense of inter-subjectivity during the Arab Uprisings in 2011.

relating, for Tunisia, to one of the December 17, 2010 immolation of Mohammed Bouazizi, or to the 2008 Gafsa mine (Gobe 2010; Mullin 2018), or to the common opposition platform of October 18, 2005 (Krichen 2016: 84); or, for Yemen, the sit-ins of Aden, Taiz, or Sanaa to earlier simmering protests and demands for decentralization in the south, in particular the Salvation Agreement (*wathiqat al-inqadh*), a collective call by different southerner leaders to establish a federal Yemen back in 2008.[12] These earlier episodes of contentious politics matter (they flagged the terrain of social fractures), but it is difficult to argue that they were the *actual* start, or a direct trigger to the "2011" protests.

The broader point is that the two regimes had lost total legitimacy, and that the existing formal structures of representation, such as parties, trade unions, and the largest civil society associations, had been either coopted or bought out by the kleptocratic regimes, or they were unable to offer social coalescence (*iltiham*). Tunisian intellectual Aziz Krichen captured the situation in terms of two contradictory dynamics at loggerheads: an upward, progressive dynamic of change from the populations against a regressive and repressive dynamic led by elites caught in deeply entrenched divisions (Krichen 2016: 69). In Stephen Day's (2012: 16) words, "the government of united Yemen [post 1994] became an illegitimate form of internal control exercised by President Ali Abdallah Saleh and his closest associates from the northwest highland region surrounding the capital Sanaa." Yemenis and Tunisians were increasingly making demands related to economic justice and citizenship empowerment: federalism or decentralization in Yemen; realization of fundamental rights in Tunisia, such as basic freedoms of expression and the release of political prisoners (like the "October 18 Committee for Rights and Freedoms"). In Yemen, the deadlocked fight for more autonomy in the south, with the birth of the Southern Peaceful Movement in 2007, the death of a key tribal ally of President Saleh, Shaykh Abdallah Al-Ahmar, in December 2007, or the Huthi rebellions in the north of the country had, at a distance, given new energy to tackle the increasingly illegitimate rule of President Saleh. Only informal movements would be able to break the deadlock (Yadav

---

[12] Baligh Al-Mikhlafi, in Cairo, formerly active in youth campaigns, interview via Skype, 09/18/2019. On the variety of southern reform propositions, see Mermier (2012: 59).

2011). All efforts via formal political channels of participation in the few years before 2011 had been in vain. Informality and spontaneity reshuffled the cards in a decisive manner.

The following reconstruction of timing and spontaneity builds on a combination of secondary sources and interviews I collected about Tunisia and Yemen. As the Roman saying goes: *verba volant, scripta manent* – spoken words fly away, written words remain. While words, chants, and slogans are vanishing into the air, printed sources, pictures, and graffiti have the advantage of remaining available for historians and social scientists. It remains hard to give the exact date for some of the material, especially graffiti. As a result, the following pages might collect "soundbites" from different moments, or revolutionary phases, of 2011 or 2012. Some might even be from 2013. But this can be justified for two reasons. First, this part of the book deals with the revolutionary moments (2011–2013), where I identify common themes and dynamics where informalism and new articulations demand democratic changes. One can debate endlessly whether the message of a slogan (e.g. "The people want the fall of the regime") changed its meaning fundamentally, say between early 2011 and mid-2012. But it is clear that the slogan gained its impetus and political traction in the extraordinary moments of January 2011. Second, as Chapter 4 deals with the push back against the revolutionary objectives and identifies contrary dynamics in the same period (2011–2013), the two phases are shown to be intertwined or dovetail with one another. Hence an overlap between the two phases of "revolution" and "counter-revolution" is unavoidable.

Let us now see how the aggregative and transformative dynamics played out in Tunisia.

3.2 Undoing Past Tunisian Fragmentation and Making Revolutionary Demands

Why are spaces and flows of mobilization mirroring the past articulations of exclusion, both colonial and post-independence? In this section, I will retrace an ideal-type of the Tunisian protests while putting stress on new meanings of "the *people*," underlining the symbolism and informalism of *spaces* and how "*violence*" was at play in the two or three months of the protests, i.e, from mid-December 2010 until February or March 2011, when it became clear that it was more than a rebellion against Ben Ali and also an *en bloc* rejection of the ruling RCD party and the whole corrupt system of power.

3.2.1 The People

Al-sha'ab was the ubiquitous name given to the converging flow of protestors. Under that umbrella term, a whole array of groups started mobilizing. Initially these were only local or sectorial rallies.

Youth were the original force of the 2010 protests. As an interlocutor from Tataouine, a poor city in the southeast of the country summed up, "it was originally the revolution of the poor and of the youth."[13] They were also the most vulnerable assembly of bodies that faced the initial brutal repression of the Ben Ali regime. Mohammed Bouazizi offered his life on December 17, 2010, but many others in small towns from the center of the country died before he succumbed from his injuries on January 4. The first "martyr" of the 2011 Uprisings was Mohammed Ammari (age 26), who fell under the shots of live ammunition fired by the police.[14] This took place on December 24, 2010 in the little town of Menzel Bouzayene, but protests were erupting in the same days in Meknassi, Tala, Kasserine, Kef, Medenine, and Gafsa.[15] Subsequent public inquiries demonstrated that snipers, from police or military units, were active in the first month of the revolution, targeting young protestors, mostly male.[16]

A brief geography of protests below (see Section 3.2.2) will qualify the presence of youths in the 2011 revolution. But the sociological components were rather clear: the lack of jobs, the bias of police forces targeting youths,[17] and other generational rifts, with the youth finding an opportunity with the 2010 and 2011 protests to take their lives into their own hand. The youth revolt against the corrupt system was also a rebellion against the authority of their families. A young female Nahda supporter decided to return to Tunis shortly after the revolution broke

---

[13] Ali Béchir, NGO leader, interview in Tataouine, 01/03/2016.

[14] Video posted by Tunisian Reporters, www.youtube.com/watch?v=pidhj83-Ols.

[15] See my interviews with people in Siliana and Medenine. See also Yousfi (2015: 70) and Alsaleh (2015: 24).

[16] *Nawaat* reports the grim details of the death of Amine Alkarami, aged 27, in Bizerte on January 17, 2011. See https://bit.ly/3rCrxIK.

[17] Based on a critical summary of the findings of Lamloum & Ben Zina (2015), I have discussed the term and definition of "youth" in another text (Challand 2015). See also Laiq (2013).

out in 2011, despite the warnings of her parents, members of Ennahda who had spent many years in jail under Ben Ali. Her parents feared she might encounter the same fate. Despite the warnings, she could not hide anymore abroad and decided to engage openly in politics to fight for her own autonomy.[18] The rebellion against patriarchy and neo-patriarchy seems to have been a truth whatever the class backgrounds of the youth involved, since many of my young Tunisian respondents confided going against the advice of their parents.[19] Thus, youth is defined more by a status of relative autonomy (vis-à-vis older gener-ations and family structures) than by an age bracket.[20] Disgruntled young Islamists also pushed for the overthrow of some of the imams who had been officially appointed by the state under Ben Ali (Merone, Sigillò, & De Facci 2018).

Youth overlaps with unemployed. Unemployment in the Arab world at the time of the protests was very high; prospects of getting a job even with a completed high school certificate, let alone a university diploma, were as dim as the degree of social justice exercised by Arab neoliberal governments. Tunisia was not an exception. Clientelism was so strong in the regions of the center, around the mining basin of Gafsa (Ayeb 2011: 468), that many youths chose the desperate route of out-migration. With the revolts of 2010, the unemployed felt that the late December 2010 demonstrations were an opportunity to pressure for a job and ham-mered the first slogans of the revolutions. It was not (yet) about political rights: it was about bread, social justice, and challenging the thieves and corrupt people around Ben Ali. The main initial slogan for street protests in December 2020 was: *"al-tashghil istihqaq ya 'isabat as-sarraq"* ("a job is a right, you pack of thieves").[21] The "system," *al-nizam*, became the later focus of popular protests. A professional of NGO work

---

[18] Fatma Toumi, Nahdaoui militant, interview in Tunis, 05/31/2016. In her words: *"se cacher ou être de retour."* Sawaf (2013) suggests that even if the youth liked to think of itself as autonomous during the revolutionary moments, there was a widespread language of kinship in 2011 and 2012 that suggests that patriarchy was still at play. Sawaf's study is on Egypt.

[19] I have similar accounts by ostentatiously bourgeois militants (who picked fancy cafés or neighborhoods of the capital for the interviews), and by lower middle class and lower class individuals. For a detailed analysis of the poor youths and their support for the surging Salafi groups, see Merone & Cavatorta (2012), Merone (2015).

[20] On definitions and characteristics of youth, see also Herrera & Bayat (2010).

[21] As translated in Beinin (2015: v). See Ayari (2011: 24) for the French *"l'emploi est un droit, bande de voleurs!"*

observed that, in his hometown of Sfax, the first wave of mobilizations came from the neighborhoods that were the most underserviced, with less public infrastructure, and where the only encounter with the state came through police control.[22] Not by chance, the first organizations that stepped up to shoulder the demands of the youth and unemployed were either the main national trade union, the UGTT, or the workers' party. For example, the demonstrations that started in the southern city of Medenine on December 24 and 25, 2010 took place in front of the UGTT branch.[23] A couple of days later, before the judges and the bar association endorsed the wave of protests in the first days of 2011, the PCOT (*Parti communiste des ouvriers de Tunisie*) was the most vocal political faction to criticize the regime. As a result, the local spokesperson of this party, Ammar Amroussia, was arrested in Gafsa on December 29, 2010 (ICG 2011: 8).

The forgotten and the peripheral. By these terms I want to shed light on segments of "the people" that fall beyond the accounts concentrated on urban centers and on the capital (where media and journalists covering the protests were located). There are many types. The contrast in terms of overall poverty in the south with the much richer (touristic) cities along the coast is striking. The three people I interviewed in Tataouine, a pensioned teacher, the coordinator of a civic platform, and a state employee, for example, were all adamant in reporting that "since the time of the Bey," their part of the country was asked to pay tax to the center but would see no benefits from the state (see Chapter 1). This continued under colonial rule and later under Bourguiba, when oil revenues would fall into the state coffers and not trickle down back to the southern regions, where people were forced out of their economic livelihood (e.g. pastoralism) because of the militarized pockets around the oil fields in the south.[24] Deep disparities exist between the Sahel and the interior. The Sahel accounts for 85% of the country's GDP and 80% of industry, while the interior contains 50% of the country's oil, gas, and water resources and 70% of wheat

---

[22] Fathi Belhadj, international NGO, interview in Sfax, 01/05/2016.
[23] Béchir Souidi, party activist, interview in Medenine, 01/03/2016. The same is true for the early Sfaxi demonstrations.
[24] Mahdi Al-Ghamd, retired school teacher, interview in Tataouine, 01/03/2016. He stated that the contemporary situation of Tataouine mirrored that under the Bey, in the late nineteenth century. Similar statements are heard in the documentary on Kasserine (IA 2018).

production.[25] But what I call "the forgotten" can also be villages not too far from a richer urban center. One example, Sidi Ali Shebab, 10km south of the Bizerte sea resort, will be discussed in Chapter 5, indicating how "center–periphery" fractures are multi-scalar.

Last, in this general characterization of the people, are semi-formal networks. It is not that all protesters in 2010 were individual atoms and all of the sudden "became" a "collective" or "the people." There was a large share of spontaneity and informality, and the population at large was present in these protests. Women and men were active, probably with more men than women in the first sub-group, the youth. Otherwise, the gender balance was rather equal, something that is visible in books such as *Dégage* (2011), which shows pictures of dozens of these initial protests. This balance was due to the well-entrenched equality laws and measures taken by the post-independence Tunisia governments.[26] But in this midst of semi-formal networks that were pivotal in spearheading the protests were various abeyance networks. Choukri Hmed (2012) has described with great precision such networks in the case of Sidi Bouzid.[27] The immolation of Bouazizi was not unique in Tunisia, but it was the only one that captured international attention, because activists and citizen journalists were swift in spreading videos and information about the street vendor (Hmed 2012). During the January 1 protests in Menzel Bouzayene, the organizing nucleus was made up of UGTT activists, members of the Union of Jobless University Graduates (UDC in its French acronym), and high school students with commitments to Arab Nationalism and radical left politics. Thus all were prepared, possibly even trained, for direct action (Hmed 2016a: 76). Another instance of this indirect facilitator for popular mobilization is the loose connections that existed among opposition parties that had not been coopted by the Ben Ali regime. For example, a young journalist who took to the street in Tunis against the

[25] Kherigi (forthcoming). For more on the rural origins of the uprising, see Gana (2012), Ayeb (2011), Daoud (2011), and Meddeb (2020). Without specification, the term "interior" designates the western, central, and southern regions of Tunisia, as opposed to the Sahel region.

[26] On women's movements in and after the Arab Uprisings, see the very rich Sadiqi (2016).

[27] See also Gobe (2010) on the Rdayyef protests of 2008 in the Gafsa region. The term "abeyance," made popular in social movements studies by Verta Taylor (1989), helps to capture how dormant networks or past associations or protestor groups become active again after years, if not decades, of inactivity.

will of his parents on January 11, 2011 noted how important the *Plateforme du 18 Octobre 2005* had been for his parents: he realized that this platform was providing common objectives across various segments of the population and that these common political demands allowed activists to "desectorialize" and create new immediate convergence in the revolutionary Tunisia of 2011.[28]

Only with all these constitutive elements can we understand how central and mutually reinforcing the symbolism of "the people" was during the Tunisian revolutionary moment. The people, often decried as an "empty signifier" after Laclau's famous formation, was in reality extremely significant for the protests and for the protestors themselves. For outside observers, protests and people are mutually exchangeable, and this exchange allows for an economy of sociological analyses like the one I have just proposed. But for demonstrators, "the people" become a rallying cry for signifying (and enacting) who was now in charge politically: It is not the regime anymore, as it increasingly becomes the target of the "revolution," but the people. It is not the supreme political leader, Ben Ali, that is absent, but the people. Hence the widespread joke about the internet error "Error 404: not found": Tunisia suffered major internet censorship, and thus Tunisians were used to encountering this "error" message when browsing online. In the heat of the revolution, the "error" was now connected to Ben Ali himself, who was not be seen or heard for much of December or January and who suddenly departed the country like a thief on January 14, 2011. The seat of power was empty. The people eclipsed also the ruling party, which disappeared all of a sudden, and the police force that hid and let the brunt of the storm pass by, thus making "the people" the temporary bearer of the means of coercion and of policing function. This chiasmus amplified the meaning of the new civic habitus.[29]

The symbolic self-representation of the people emboldened further protests. One of the most revealing pictures of this initial period is from Egypt. A rather old, probably poor Egyptian man is seen carried on the shoulders of an exuberant crowd in Tahrir Square. He holds a laptop that airs footage from Tahrir itself. Everybody shouts and erupts in joy

---

[28] Khalil Klai, journalist, interview in Tunis, 06/06/2016.
[29] R. Porter (2016; 2017: 272) also talks about these reversals in the Yemeni case. More on their meaning in the Conclusion.

as the live Al-Jazeera coverage (recognizable from the logo of the TV channel) announces that President Mubarak has resigned.[30] The picture captures the quasi literal elation that Egyptian peoples felt when seeing their own protests as having succeeded in dislodging the tyrant.

In Tunisia, like in all Arab countries, the symbolism of the people is expressed also through the massive presence of the national flag, or of maps of the country. An early account of the January protests in Tunis recalled that:

> The national anthem, not *"Allahu akbar,"* was the dominant rallying cry, and the women were both veiled and unveiled. The tone of the protests was rather one of reappropriating patriotic language and symbols: Women and men lay in the streets to spell "freedom" or "stop the murders" with their bodies and worked together to tear down and burn the gigantic, Stalin-style portraits of Ben Ali on storefronts and street corners. (Marzouki 2011a)

Later, in the ex-post narration of the protests, a young Islamist activist told me that after the revolution, all the work she does in academia and as a political activist was "a gift she does for her country."[31] A second person interviewed stated that once people came together, once all segments, secular or Islamists alike, of Tunisia assembles, it was the "strength of union" (*"il y a eu union des forces"*).[32] Rather than a president keeping Tunisians divided, drawings or slogans expressed the unity and dignity of the Tunisians. For example, in a poster one sees President Ben Ali depicted as a fat rat eating the people's wealth and resources, symbolized by a loaf of bread, now half eaten by the rodent.[33] On a graffiti that was documented in different places of Tunisia and different moments, one could read *"Al-sulta lil-sha'ab"* (Power to the people!").[34] Another graffiti stated that "Tunisia had won," as it became the first Arab democracy (Lacquaniti 2015: 60).

---

[30] I am grateful to Walker Gunning, a former student at NYU, for identifying this picture, which can be seen at www.wsj.com/articles/BL-BPB-3563, "Celebrations Follow Resignation in Egypt," February, 2011.

[31] Toumi, interview, 05/31/2016.

[32] Anis Khenissi, youth activist, NGO leader, interview in Medenine, 01/04/2016.

[33] With the caption: *"al-ra'is al- far,"* "the president is the rat." See Dégage (2011: 127).

[34] For the variant "the authority belongs to the people," see Dégage (2011: 131) and Lacquaniti (2015: 38): Later, in 2012, the slogan became: "Revolution taken away from the people? Where is freedom?" (Lacquaniti 2015: 33).

The people are variegated. It knows it is, but this common name allows for de-sectorialization, coming together, and the articulation of multiple partisan and class differences. The name "people" is what articulates the economic, sociologic, and political differences among Tunisians. It therefore becomes sacralized with all the danger that this entails.

Time to see how a brief investigation of the spaces in which protests snowballed allows us to unearth new dimensions as the ones described under "the people."

3.2.2 Spaces

By "space" I speak of a variety of geographic (a place) and more abstract locations, different types of space and the symbolism they entail, as well as location in which collective protests started and moved fluidly.[35] I will illustrate the polysemy of space over the following pages, and again in Part III, where I propose the evaluation of the revolutionary legacies and the contested meanings of decentralization.

Before discussing the political geography, it is worth observing how people insist on reclaiming public space – a hallmark of social movements, in particular in the left traditions (Pigenet & Tartakowsky 2014), and which had a great international success after the Arab streets indicated the path for occupy movements across the world (Werbner, Webb, & Spellman-Poots 2014). The Arab multitude (Kilani 2014: 39) called on expressing its control over the streets with a common slogan (Figure 3.1), "*al-shari' mulkna*," i.e "the street belongs to us," or in the more directive form "*ihtilou al-shawari'*," "occupy the streets!" (Lacquaniti 2015: 42). Once these physical spaces were won and occupied, the agglutinative effect of the protests could start.

The early marches took place where they could. The collective indignation the day after the self-immolation of Bouazizi converged on the market place of Sidi Bouzid because it was the natural location for the weekly market. Organizers, part of the network of abeyance described by Hmed (2012: 44), also capitalized on the fact that it was a school holiday and mocked a theme of the Ben Ali presidency that had made of 2010 the "year of the youth." Thus, the space and fortuitous presence

---

[35] For a discussion of space and places in mobilizations, see Boutros (2017).

Figure 3.1 "The street is our property" ("*al-shāri' mulknā*"). Tunisia 2013.

of a large cohort of students and youth gave a broader dimension to the local protests.

Once the protests spread in neighboring towns, dissenters sought protection in front of an institution that was deeply rooted in the south, the UGTT. Hela Yousfi describes the sense of "refuge" (in Arabic *malja'*) that the UGTT provided to the initial protests, a sense that was confirmed by interviews done in the peripheries. In Tataouine, one of the interviewed persons, a teacher, told me that, over there, the UGTT is a shelter, or a roof for all.[36] In Medenine, as noted, or in Siliana as well, the first protests timidly occupied some space in front of the branch of the UGTT.[37] Some buildings, or squares in front of them, provided a shelter. Others functioned as lightning rods for the popular anger, as we will see in Section 3.2.3. A knowledge of prior demonstrations and scuffles with security forces allowed young protestors to prepare escape routes and dissipate in the street, when the tipping point of mass support had not yet been reached.[38]

Inquiring about the geography of the protests and their flows from one point to the other, I encountered typical examples of

---

[36] Abdelhamit Al-Khatib, NGO leader, interview in Tataouine, 01/03/2016.
[37] Various interviews in Medenine and Siliana confirmed this point.
[38] Klai, interview, 06/06/2016. This person refers to the *Passage de la République*, a square that has many escape routes, making it almost impossible for police forces to arrest protestors.

ethnocentrism, namely the belief that the protests that occurred in the
town of the interviewee were most likely decisive in toppling Ben Ali:
the interior knows to have initiated the wave of protests; and the people
in the coastal towns, Sfax, Sousse, or Bizerte, feel that the game was
over for Ben Ali and the Trabelsi clan once the demonstrations gathered
steam in these respective places. Giving credence to the above-cited
argument about the "forgotten" component of the "people," the
people of the interior are the ones with the more correct description
of the chronology and geography of the 2010 protest: "It all started in
Sidi Bouzid, then Gafsa, then Kasserine and finally Sfax."[39] Once the
smaller protests reached the coastal cities, they had enough momentum
to threaten the regime. It also had acquired legitimacy because of the
brutal repression and death of dozens of protests, in particular the
massacres in Tala and Kasserine on Jan 8, 2011 (see Ayeb 2011: 474;
Hmed 2015: 87; IA 2018), all of which generated indignation and
urban solidarity with the forgotten and marginalized regions of the
country. Each in her or his own regionalism, the interviewed persons
saw the mass popular support in the south for the 2010 and early 2011
protests as the clear result of past marginalization.[40]

By and large, the Tunisian revolution started as an upheaval of the
rural and mining parts of the country, all political and economic margins
as described in Part I. Ayeb (2011) marvels that many still call the
Tunisian revolution the "Jasmine Revolution," when this plant does
not grow naturally in these parts of Tunisia. To signify the rural and
stricken origins of the Uprisings, Ayeb proposes to speak of the "alfa
grass revolution," from the name of a type of esparto grass that grows
around Sidi Bouzid and the central regions. Until January 8 or 9, 2011,
Ayeb claims, the protests were only from these rural areas disregarded by
the state or from their administrative centers (Gafsa, Kasserine). If the
protests picked up from January 11, on the coastal towns, it was only in
poor neighborhoods of Tunis (e.g. Ettadhamen, Ibn Khaldun) (Ayeb
2011: 474), Sfax, Sousse, or Bizerte,[41] that these protests happened.
Only from January 12 did it become a truly cross-class and mass protest.
From that date onwards, it became a middle-class affair, with *twitterati*,

---

[39] Khenissi, interview, 01/04/2016.   [40] E.g. Souidi, interview, 01/03/2016.
[41] In Bizerte, the location of the initial protests was not in the city center where rich
hotels are located, but on the cutting street moving away from the sea front at
the Hippocamp roundabout. Tareq and Ghassen Ben Barka, charitable workers,
interview in Bizerte, 05/24/2016.

young urban bloggers, now pacing the charge against the regime. New refuge and protection were given by the National Bar Association (Gobe & Salaymeh 2016) and the entire leadership of the UGTT (Yousfi 2015: 70–71), as opposed to only a dissident regional leadership in December. The protests became less about social justice, more about dignity and liberty. Then, the regime was the target, and larger political demands were made. It is only at this moment that the 2011 Uprisings can be said to be social media revolutions, not before. The twitterati, bloggers, and citizen journalists articulated and amalgamated different demands and gave a new international visibility to the protests. They thus helped internationalize what were very local and national campaigns. But the initial impetus for self-representation came from the rural, lower-class segments of Tunisian society.

This does not mean that the geographic "margins" and the sociologically marginalized stopped being part of the protests. The poorer segments did not trust the move taken by the political establishment after the sudden departure of Ben Ali. Protests continued for a couple of weeks, sometimes for as long as a month. On Tuesday January 25, 2011, in Gabes, a coastal town halfway between Sfax and Medenine, there was a mass protest with a clear message: "You stole our wealth. You won't steal our revolution!"[42] "Poverty" is only the result of the center's greed. The next day, a large demonstration took place in Sfax in the vicinity of Bab Al-Bahr (January 26, 2011), with women and many youths on the front lines (Dégage 2011: 224). More sophisticated slogans and stylistically elaborate graffiti (Figures 3.2 and 3.3), some couched in gender terms, appeared on the walls of Tunis, for example, "*sawt al-mara' thawra*," "the voice of the woman is the revolution" (Lacquaniti 2015: 68). They evoke particular identities, but point to a culminating overall, universalist (Marzouki 2011b), objective, that of a full revolution. Other stencils evoke the refusal by women to be categorized as secularist, religious, or Islamist (Lacquaniti 2015: 67; Figure 3.3).

The spaces moved and the geography evolved. But these movements did not stop with the abdication of Ben Ali and his flight with his wife to Saudi Arabia, where he died in 2019. Rather, the movements

---

[42] A slogan that plays on the pun *tharwatna* ("our wealth"), *thawratna* ("our revolution") (Dégage 2011: 224).

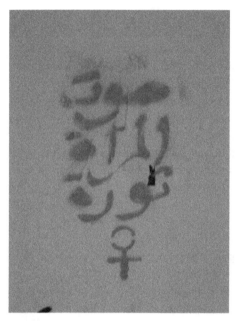

Figure 3.2 "The voice of the woman is the revolution" ("*ṣawt al-marā' thawra*"). Tunisia 2012.

Figure 3.3 "Don't classify us!" ("*mā taṣnifnīsh*"). Tunisia 2012.

intensified. Let us look at the micro-reality of this. Chains of humans were formed either to protect a space of protests or sit-in (e.g. in Qasba, but this has been documented in Tahrir Square in Egypt as well), or people choregraphing a slogan, for example, people sitting on the ground to form the phrase *"Tunis hurra"* ("Tunisia is free").[43] The movement can also take the form of an iteration or repetition: "new revolution" (Lacquaniti 2015: 35), or the more political slogan "permanent revolution" (*thawra mustamirra*) or in the imperative form *"thur"* for revolt! (imperative of the verb *thara*, to stir, to revolt) (Lacquaniti 2015: 43).

The movements intensified at the macro-level, with a multi-directional flow of information leading to a new social imaginary of the entire country. A whirl of caravans started being organized from the peripheral towns to the capital after the fall of Ben Ali, bringing more detailed knowledge about the bloody repression in early January but also an awareness of dire living conditions. Before 2011, Tunisians of the Sahel could live believing the nationalist myth of Bourguiba and Ben Ali of a unified, homogenous country. In reality, people lived in siloed areas, a perception that was easily controlled by the regime because of the abysmal level of freedom of information in the country. The significance of these *décloisonnements*, de-siloeing, was not lost to many of the people interviewed, for example, citing evidence of new Facebook pages sharing information relative to the struggles throughout the country.[44]

Such de-siloeing, or reconnection of formerly contained sub-units or parts, had political consequences for the formal institution, as we will see in the next chapter. It also had important consequences: Caravanes, i.e. organized travels by bus, for example, from one Tunisian town to another moved first to the capital, but also, in the second phase of the revolution, back from large cities to the margins. Thus, on February 6, 2011, residents of Tunis went to Sidi Bouzid as part of *"caravane du remerciement."*[45] It is now possible for forgotten segments of Tunisia

---

[43] For a picture, see Bottici & Challand (2012).
[44] E.g. Klai, interview 06/06/2016.
[45] Dégage (2011). There are multiple actors involved in these caravans, as it is a phenomenon that continued well after the revolutionary moment. Sigillò (e.g. 2020: 119) shows Islamic charities adopting the form in order to distribute goods, but Michaël Ayari sees in these later caravans a form of paternalism from the center.

to utter their name, to state their presence in the heart of the large coastal cities. Be it a tag on a wall of the rich suburb of Tunis, La Marsa, with the French and English "TUNIS LIBRE! KASSERINE VICTORY," or with a chant "*hana ga'din*," "we stay here," but with the q pronounced softly as a g, as people from the interior do (*ga'din* instead of *qa'idin*), meaning that the people from the south or center are here to stay (Lacquaniti 2015: 28). The vengeance of the *gaf*, from the pronunciation of the letter *qaf*, is a nutshell summary of the history of the past oppression and victory of the marginalized people in the 2011 revolutionary moments (Allal 2016; Daoud 2011). The irruption of the unemployed youth from the interior in the capital was an erasure of the old colonial *Tunisie utile*.

The regionalism, however, cedes full ground to a sense of re-discovered national unity. The national anthem was sung everywhere, and the historical meaning of the text, a poem written by Abu Kacem Chebbi (1909–1934) under colonial occupation, acquired a new one: a famous verse known to all students in the Arab world (Chebbi's poem was widely taught during the heyday of Arab nationalism) acquired a new life with and after the Tunisian revolution (Hanafi 2011). One of Chebbi's verses, "The people have broken the chains of oppression," galvanized the imaginary of a suddenly unified mass. The poem reflected new priorities: The people taking power, occupying streets and hereby claiming ultimate authority became the radical source of a nation acting in concert and targeting illegitimate violence.

3.2.3 Violence

Dealing with the theme of violence is the third step in this chapter that studies new radical representations. Figures 0.2–0.5 reveal a popular imaginary that sought to topple the illegitimately unequal and uneven application of repressive violence against citizens. Like space, violence has a multiplicity of meanings. I present these facets to complete the journey of this revolutionary moment, and as a way to establish a richer paradigm and understanding for the concept of *vis populi*.

The discourses of a non-violent Arab Spring and/or of a flowery Jasmine revolution in Tunisia are profoundly inadequate and an insult to the many victims. For Tunisia, the number of casualties was already in the hundreds of dead and injured by the time Ben Ali fled the country. An official inquiry, called the Bouderbala Commission, named after the jurist Tawfiq Bouderbala, concluded in April 2012 that 338 persons died during the revolutionary period and more than 2,100 people suffered injuries.[46] Nearly 80% of the deaths were the result of police actions, the rest being victims at the hands of the military or during fires that occurred during mutinies in prisons or detention centers (86 deaths). 96.5% of the casualties are men, and 82% of the victims are below the age of 40 years old. Only 3.5% of the fatalities are women, but the proportion of injured women increases to 11% (Bouderbala 2012: 26), suggesting that women also took great risk to demonstrate and act with the rest of the protestors, as illustrated for example in Figure 3.4. Sixty-eight percent of the injuries occurred in the first month of the revolution, while the majority of the deaths occurred after the departure of Ben Ali.

Figure 3.4 Young woman with pony-tail and Molotov cocktail. Tunisia 2012.

[46] The full report, more than 1,000 pages, with the detailed list per governorate and per date, can be found at www.leaders.com.tn/uploads/FCK_files/Rapport %20Bouderbala.pdf. It is quoted below as Bouderbala 2012. See also Chapters 4–5.

It was violent and also relatively limited: Bouderbala (2012: 25) found out that only 14 policemen (*"quwat al-amin"*) and 5 military were killed during the protests. The brutality committed by the police forces stems from the regime's preferred choice of letting violence speak against democratic demand, a choice that has had a long history, as we have seen. The acts of violence by the "people" were mostly geared at key institutions and almost never led to the death of people. There were numerous cases of physical destruction that came with *vis populi*, but these acts indicated indignation with symbols of authoritarianism: police forces, customs offices, and buildings of the ruling RCD party.

Ayeb (2011: 474) narrates that when the protests spread out around Sidi Bouzid on December 18, 2010 a new strategy emerged: demonstrations were organized "at night to harass the security forces." The police, in a few locations with the help of military snipers, used a heavy hand, and dozens fell in the cities of Kasserine, Regueb and Ben Aoune (30 km from Sidi Bouzid) between 8 and 10 January (Ayeb 2011: 474). In Sfax, my interviewees confirm that violence happened in the poorer neighborhoods of a city that had sprawled in the last decade due to internal migration and high rural unemployment in the south and center, while in Bizerte these violent confrontations with the police took place away from the more protected touristic centers along the Corniche.[47] On January 10, 2011, demonstrations reached the city of Greater Tunis through neighborhoods such as Ettadhamen and Ibn Khaldun, where "most of the inhabitants, generally of modest means, come from poor or marginali[z]ed regions" (Ayeb 2011: 474). Other published witness accounts, for example of a young intern in a hospital of the periphery of Tunis, recall the vicious injuries inflicted on the face (the eyes were targeted by snipers) or on the legs of protesters during protests on January 13, 2010.[48] There is thus a geography of violence that overlaps with disadvantaged socio-economic backgrounds in these fatal clashes.

This geography of protests explains also why particular buildings were targeted. In the south, where the security forces were less present and relied on the National Guard (*haras watani*) to police the region

---

[47] In Bizerte, the clashes took place around the intersection between avenues Omar Mukhtar and Amir Abdel-Qader. Ben Barka, interview, 05/24/2016; Belhadj, interview, 01/05/2016.

[48] A doctor from Tunis also stated that many injured were coming from Ettadhamen and Sejjoumi, poorer parts of the capital. See Dégage (2011: 84).

where there is a lot of trade in contraband, the population targeted out of anger *the* institution that is seen as the most unjust: the customs offices (*Diwanat*) was the institution that would confiscate vehicles and other goods that were sequestrated during smuggling operations along the Libyan border. In Medenine and Tataouine, the *Diwanat* were stormed by protestors between January 11 and 13, 2011 in the hope of finding goods "stolen" by the state.[49] In Sidi Bouzid, but also in Sfax, protests were started in front of the building of the National Agricultural Bank, involved in lending schemes that had ruined small land owners, permitting rich Tunisians to buy at discounted price small plots of land that had fed for decades families like that of Mohamed Bouazizi (Ottaway 2017: 69).

Another site of destructive violence or vengeance, this one common to the entire country, has been the office of the ruling party, the RCD (or *Tajammu'*). The RCD was more than a party: it also organized collects of public funds for "national development" projects (the famous account "2626"), and served to organize surveillance cells meant to spy on Tunisians (Hibou 2011). Dozens of these centers, along with rich villas of the Ben Ali and Trabelsi family, were stormed, looted, and torched on and after January 14, 2011. The description used by interviewed persons to qualify these acts of violence are highly instructive: posters put on Tunis' walls mocked the regime's propensity to disqualify any opposition or dissent as "terrorism" by reverting the accusation that it was indeed RCD leaders who were actually the source of terror in Tunisia.[50] Graffiti denouncing the stifling control of the RCD had amassed, both politically and culturally. Thus, an RCD building in the Greater Tunis area that served as a cultural center was at one point defaced with paintings and Molotov cocktails. It is no wonder that this action and its ironic commentary were later celebrated by a stencil portraying a young woman ready to throw a Molotov cocktail: this type of violence was a safety valve.

If and when destructive violence occurred at the hands of the protesters, they targeted buildings, cars, police files, or the property of the corrupt circle surrounding Ben Ali and Trabelsi. Violent acts did not

---

[49] Various interviews in Medenine, Zerzis, and Tataouine.

[50] Inspired by US Westerns, the "Wanted" poster captures two RCD leaders (Al-Hadi Bakkoush and Mohammed Al-Gharbani) with the description "*irhabin min al-tajammu'*," "The Terrorists from the RCD" underneath (Dégage 2011: 145).

target the people in charge of these institutions themselves. These acts retained a democratic dimension insofar as the protestors acted with an expressed understanding that they were done not for a personal, particularistic, or localized interest, but for the greater, collective good. These acts of civil rebellion were also "a more effective way in achieving their end" (Morreall 2002: 143, see also 131) of denouncing the rotten nature of the entire political, social, and political system.[51] *Vis populi*, with its strong symbolic and performative components, suggested direct popular sovereignty over the means of coercion and demonstrated that the incumbent authorities had lost their moral claim to legitimate authority. The "people" *suggests* a self-limiting or self-restraining power in its *symbolic representations* (slogans, drawings, stencils, marches, and other informal actions), but *enacts* direct political representation through non-violent action.

From January 11 onward, it became clear that the demonstrations acquired a national dimension. The police force, thought to have a total workforce of 200,000, suddenly disappeared. Provocations occurred against police buildings. Four-hundred police stations were targeted between February 2011 and February 2012,[52] mostly in derelict zones where usually only the repressive face of the state was seen by local residents, for example, with the station in Ettadhamen being burnt down on January 11, 2011 (Yousfi 2015: 72). With policemen nowhere to be seen in the cities outside of Tunis, the army was called to step up. On that day, protestors in Tunis passed in front of the feared Ministry of the Interior, on Bourguiba Avenue, and the sheer fact that they were allowed to march so close to the center of repressive power was already considered a victory by young protestors.[53] Security forces would still exact brutal violence on the night of Ben Ali's departure, but after that, there seemed to be a drop in police violence.

The next chapter will describe the official policies and measures taken to reform the security sector as a response to the pressure applied by the demonstrating masses, but there emerged a moment where the institutions in charge of coercion seem to have disappeared. The army

---

[51] I take some formulations from John Morreall's (2002) chapter dedicated to the issue of the "Justifiability of Violent Civil Disobedience."

[52] Ottaway (2017: 98). An ICG report on Tunisia indicates the same number of attacks on police stations. It also reports that 12,000 individuals were arrested for looting, assault, or attempted murders (ICG 2013b: 1, note 1).

[53] Khenissi, interview, 01/04/2016 and Klai, interview, 06/06/2016.

was out on the street, to protect vital institutions, but, under the order of the Chief of Staff, it engaged only in minimal policing function, thus averting a blood bath on January 14, 2011.[54]

What is fascinating about this short window of time is that in these few days – ranging from three or four days in certain places, to a maximum of ten days in other places – there was a moment of extreme and generalized civility. Having no police on the streets could have meant looting and possibly the pursuit of personal vendettas. Very little of that happened. The peaceful moments could be expected in certain areas where tourism is the main source of income for the population, but it happened across the country. In Midoun and Zerzis, two beach resorts near Djerba, people told me that for three or four days around January 13, 2011, there were many peaceful marches, a few provocations directed at policemen in their offices from afar, but all of this happened in a friendly, restrained mood. In Sfax, where violence had occurred a few days before, there was a moment of lull and suspension. An observer told me: "All behaved nicely on the road, people yielding to each other, and an overall sense of fraternity was tangible throughout the town." For him, it was significant (*"notable"*) that the population would not exact easy violence or "vengeance."[55] Another actor, who left his town of Zerzis, in the south, close to the Libyan border, to be part of the decisive Tunis protests in January, noted the spontaneous sense of community: "People would offer food or milk to small groups patrolling the streets at night, out of fear of some people or police attacking the neighborhood."[56] Anthropologist Mondher Kilani discusses a similar instance in which the neutralizing effect of the collective against violence was unequivocal. A poster plastered in a small town of the interior stated: "The night passed. Dawn came. The shots . . . tac . . . tac. The people came out to take care of the neighborhood . . . and thieves suddenly left" (Kilani 2014: 94, his translation). This can be read as a double reference to the *vis populi*: First, the poster recalls the

---

[54] The army itself contributed to the mythology of the peaceful army that refused to shoot on the demonstrators. There were serious and brutal reprisals by some security segments on the night after the departure of Ben Ali.

[55] Belhadj, interview, 01/05/2016. In his words , *"c'est notable que cette population a été capable de maîtriser ses sentiments de violence ou de vengeance."*

[56] Khenissi, interview, 01/04/2016. Other people think that these popular committees were paid by rich people to protect their neighborhood. Amira Yahyaoui, NGO leader, interview in Tunis, 05/30/2016.

moments of pacification, and second it can serve as a reminder of the power of the neighborhood's people in defending themselves against thieves.

This is the *communitas* that Walter Armbrust (2019: 6) describes in his *Ethnography of the Egyptian Revolution*. The material I have accumulated for Tunisia indicates a similar short-lived situation there. Evoking the instances of extreme civility discussed above, one person involved in that type of experience (for him, in the capital) told me that he wished he had a remote control, of sorts, that, like for TV, would allow him to pause and keep these moments "of maximum solidarity" and of citizenship in action to last forever. "Alas," he noted, "after 15 days where citizenship was tangible … [party] politics as normal resumed," and people returned to normal life.[57] French researcher Amin Allal (2011: 53), who did fieldwork in the Tunisian neighborhood from which the police disappeared entirely on January 2011, concurs that these extraordinary and fluid moments entailed the "germs," the nucleus of politicized civic action. This, he notes, is particularly true for young people, from the ages 15 and 17, who represented about 40% of the unemployed people, those between 20 and 24 years old. The youth were eager to take over police stations as if to revert the order of political control. Police files on local people were burned in Bab Jdid, in the old city of Tunis, and youth were heard chanting "Now everything can restart" (Allal 2011: 58). Allal notes that the youth knew that this was a naïve statement, but they took solace from this extraordinary moment. Between January 15 and 16, these youths organized vehicle checkpoints in collaboration with civilian policemen to make sure they were not carrying guns in the trunk (Allal 2011: 58). In various parts of the country, demonstrators turned over to the army guns that police forces had left (ICG 2012: xx; 2015: 8). The reversal of control over such spaces, now characterized by shared civic engagement from both civilians and policemen, was particularly

---

[57] Khenissi, interview, 01/04/2016. "*Pendant 15 jours c'est la solidarité maximale que j'ai vue entre les Tunisiens. Tu vois, je descends le matin et le mec dit: 'Tu as du pain? Tu as du lait? Je te le donne.' Pas de soucis. Tout le monde surveille sa cité. Tout le monde s'aide. Les femmes amènent à manger aux hommes qui font la veille. Puis commence la politique et tout rechange. Ça a été très bien: ces quinze jours que j'ai vécus ont été inoubliables dans le sens de la solidarité. Jamais je [n]'ai vu les Tunisiens aussi solidaires, extraordinaires. Mais après … . J'aurais aimé avoir une télécommande, comme à la Télé et faire 'PAUSE !!!! Restez comme ça!' La citoyenneté était là, pendant 15 jours.*"

astonishing in neighborhoods that had usually exhibited inimical relations between the police and the youth.[58]

The temptation is great to idealize these moments of extreme civility.
There were also naïve expressions of support for the army that had
replaced the police in Tunis. For example, flowers were placed on tank
turrets, grateful letters placed on tanks, etc. (Dégage 2011: 71). The next
chapter will revisit this narrative of the benevolent army standing, like in
Egypt after the fall of Mubarak, against the over-present and hyper-violent
security forces. But these expressions of support for the army and of
extreme civility also had the tangible effect of enacting a collective identity
of citizens in action and shouldering a political project that demanded
democratic changes. The storming of a security building to burn files that
the political police had gathered on citizens over years can be considered a
democratic form of violence because these actions came along with other
proposals for reorganizing the management of coercion itself. If an isolated
group loots private property, or intimidates other citizens in order to gain
economic advantages, it is (petty) criminal activity and does not qualify as
vis populi, which consists of law-preserving (law of the demos) and as law-
making action (law that places the collective and pluralist good of the
demos at the heart of legitimacy). *Vis populi* is force (or persuasion) and
collective will all in one. It is not violence as destruction (*violentia*), but
does invoke symbolic elements of it.[59] It is a space, at times physical, where
specific protests gather or, at other times, a semiotic space where people
disclose the ruthlessness of past violence or call for a socially just use of the
means of coercion. For this reason, this dimension of physical and collective force (*vis populi*) relates to the issue of representation (cultural or
political) and can be democratic because it is an *autonomous, spontaneous*
representation of the sovereign power of the people.[60] Of course, *vis*

---

[58] Allal (2011: 60). I have also heard indirect reports that people *prevented* the
destruction of files that the RCD held on certain Tunisians, in the hope that these
documents would be helpful for establishing justice after the revolution. I am
grateful to Nathanael Mannone for this tip. Bloggers and activists also report
that the police destroyed some files themselves (Chebbi 2016).

[59] As stated in the Introduction and in line with Ayyash (2020), I do not take
violence to be only an instrumental (destructive force), like Arendt (1977a) or
Tilly (1978). Nor do I see it as a phenomenon that emerges within a limited space
of encounters or antagonisms between police and social movement actors
(McAdam & Tarrow 2000).

[60] As one recalls, for Castoriadis, a democratic society can only exist when it self-
institutes, and autonomously chooses its own representation.

populi is related to the theme of coercion, and thus goes beyond moral persuasion, non-violence, popular force, civil disobedience, and the influence of the masses. But it is a *program*, very often expressed in a visual, graphic, and/or embodied manner.

Vis populi is different from revolutionary violence because the self-reference to the demos, namely a kaleidoscopic people (the many, the multitude), coupled with articulated demands for social justice, civility, and inclusion, is itself a reminder to all that violence should not be exacted for the advantage of a small group (say, a revolutionary group, the proletariat, in Marxist-Leninist understanding). The enfranchisement of subalterns, of the marginalized, of racialized subjects, is thus the means for ending the tyranny of corrupt leaders ("the regime").

Like the politics of space, the affirmation of this collective identity, or the enactment of this *communitas*, requested a quasi-protective constant re-iteration and rituals of coming together under the theme of a newly founded power. For example, the theme of fear (*khawf*) was mentioned in many chants and slogans: the wall or barrier of fear had been broken by the massive and national presence of marches. Slogans turned these words into certainties now inscribed on walls. For example with the chant: "*la khawf, la ru'b, al-sulta mulk al-sha'ab,*" "no fear, no awe: the power belongs to the people," was written twice on a Tunis wall, probably close to the Ministry of the Interior in Tunis, as an exhortation to continue demanding the end of repression (Lacquaniti 2015: 38).

Kalamti Hurra, "My Word is Free," one of the songs of Amel Mathouthi, discussed in the Introduction, illustrates the emergence of a collective "we." The limited positionality and experience of the artists opens up to the expression of a plural "we," "I am the voice of those who are not dying / We build out of iron some fragile clay." This, and many other examples, demonstrates that cultural representations (*ta'bir* or *taswir*) are one step forward, but that they remain very fragile projects.

3.3 *Vis Populi*, Presentism, and New Democratic Subjectivity: The Case of Siliana

The case of the Siliana mobilization offers a thick description of *vis populi* and illustrates how a higher moral claim is enacted by an assembled force of local citizens. In their manifestation of unity, and through their exercise of physical restraint, the people reaffirmed themselves as sovereign. Their determination and restlessness in confronting the illegitimate use of coercion also carved out channels through which to reorganize the political system.

A rather marginal wave of protests that took place in November 2012 in the town of Siliana became a new point of reference to new democratic mobilization in Tunisia. Nearly two years after the start of the revolution, and a year after the election of the National Constituent Assembly, the ANC (more details in Chapter 4), Tunisia was gripped by a new wave of struggles between local authorities and the resilient power of the capital. Many feared that the ANC was not working fast enough to enshrine the demands for more social justice and direct popular participation in a new constitution. Sporadic episodes dotted the landscape throughout 2012 to oppose the power of the central authority, in this case, the role of the governor, the person in charge of dealing with budgetary and security decisions in each of the 24 governorates, but was still appointed by politicians in Tunis. Siliana, located equidistant from the Algerian border and Tunis, is the eponymous capital of one such governorate, situated in a rural hinterland with almost as many tractors as cars.[61] It exemplifies the plea of the historically marginalized Tunisia that is dependent on the leadership from the coastal area (Chouikha & Gobe 2013: §67). Small-scale protests had simmered for a couple of days over the handling of a trade union complaint by the gubernatorial team.

In November 2012, after a first local general strike to remove the private secretary of the governor, clashes erupted on one of the two main boulevards, right in front of *qasr al-wilaya*, the main governorate building. Silianans feared that the ruling coalition, a three-party coalition called the Troika, was entrenching its grip on national politics.[62] The authorities refused to free a handful of locals who had been detained after protests in April 2011 (Yousfi 2015: 210) and organized small protests on November 26 and 27, with demands

---

[61]   The town has 44,000 inhabitants. For information on the municipality of Siliana, see https://web.archive.org/web/20190319193712/http://baladia.mar sad.tn/Siliana/Siliana and Al-Bawsala's website, at www.albawsala.com/en/pro ject/marsad-baladia.

[62]   Ottaway reports that the main party in the Troika, Ennahda, was engaged in a vast campaign to appointing thousands of new civil servants (4,500 according to Ottaway), the majority coming from its ranks. The Siliana episode occurred during that wave of appointments, making the position of the governor and of his team a very sensitive issue (Ottaway 2017: 108).

now to remove the governor (Chouikha & Gobe 2013: §69). On Wednesday November 28, the protest turned more vociferous and confrontational. The police responded with brutal force, using buckshots against the protestors, leaving 300 wounded and blinding at least 16 people.[63] Outraged by the violence and the non-responsiveness of the Troika government, locals set another protest at the same place for Friday, with the same demand that the Governor leave his job, using the same one-word slogan *"Dégage!"* (*"Leave!"*) that had been so effectively used against Ben Ali and other Arab dictators.[64] Yet, that day, a totally new form of demonstration kicked in. Rashid, a member of a local cultural association, present that day, described to me the movement as follows – I have added emphasis on terms capturing the high degree of informality and the manner in which separate projects merged into a larger political protest:

I don't know who had the idea, but *all of a sudden*, people started moving out of the town. It was all *spontaneous*. We left the city. People felt that *symbolically* leaving the city was a strong message to the Governor [who wants to stay in place]. Some youths are in front. They are the ones who have organized spontaneously the march. *In the beginning*, it is symbolic, [we are meant to walk] only a small distance. But *then more and more* people joined. It was incredible! Women were in front and everybody followed. [There were] lots of women. They were in front. Even more when we passed in front of the hospital [which is the last building on this main street, about half a mile away from the Governor's Palace]: The female nurses, with their white blouses, came out and joined us. [He laughs]. Incredible. People walked 11 km outside of the city, although it was meant to be a symbolic gesture![65]

Historically, episodes of collective mobilizations in most Arab countries ended with shots fired by the police, or more baton and repression. Yet, after the 2011 Arab Uprisings and what most Tunisians still call their "revolution," people in Siliana remained resilient in their determination to uphold their demands and not bow to police violence. Not only did they turn the table by responding peacefully to the old-fashioned governmental use of force, they

---

[63] The people I interviewed mentioned 30 people who lost their sight. The other figures come from ICG (2013b: 43).

[64] The term, although of French origin, is a fully Tunisian word, equivalent to the Arabic *irhal!* chanted in other Arab countries.

[65] Rachid Kharroubi, cultural association, interview in Siliana, 06/01/2016.

creatively and relentlessly connected the symbol of emptying out the space in front of the formal political power (the governorate) with a unified assertion of their political unity ("everybody followed") and their unique role as the sovereign in a democratic system.[66] What is a governor if s/he does not have people to administer? Eventually, in light of the symbolic victory scored by the Silianans and the cost of a disastrous use of violence against demonstrating citizens, the Troika replaced the local governor and heeded the calls of the protestors.

To be sure, social media probably played a role in the walk-out march of Friday November 30, 2012, with calls and pictures posted on Facebook or other online platforms leading to a fast snowballing effect. But the virtuous force of collective mobilization did not need a grandiose urban setting, like in the Qasba of Tunis or Tahrir Square in Cairo. It needs collective practices, continuous efforts by people to carry on the themes of the 2011 mobilization, and at the very heart, it needs to reverse the old formula of Arab politics: instead of latent citizenship and a ruthless state apparatus, the Siliana episode was about the direct involvement of male and female, young and old, poor and middle-class citizens, and called for the end of autocratic repression. Informal civic engagement, such as the march out of Siliana in November 2012, is not a definitive solution for a more democratic polity, but it is a preliminary and necessary step for profound political changes.

Siliana was not an isolated, contained incident: similar types of protests have become a way to criticize non-democratic political institutions. During periods of fieldwork in Tunisia in 2015 and 2016, many people I talked to in various parts of the country made reference to Siliana, or when asked about it, immediately recalled

---

[66] This episode recalls events from the times of the Roman Republic, when the tribunes of the *plebs* left Rome, thereby expressing their disagreement with the Senate and the aristocracy. Livius narrates a few of these episodes, which also appear in Machiavelli's writing to suggest that the people in arms are a key constituting element of the polity. See Lacore (2013) who builds on the metaphor of the body by comparing the role of the *plebs* as an organ of the whole body. Pedullà (2018) gives a more robust resonance to the idea of a politically active and creative people (in Roman times, the *plebs*, through their tribunes) that mobilize around the theme of violence. He calls this *political conflictualism*. See also Barthas (2010: 265) for a discussion of the Machiavellian idea of the people in arms.

these episodes and referred to them as "*ahdath al-rash*" – the events of
the buck-shots (*al-rash* is the Arabic name for buck-shots or shotgun
shells). All shared the same outrage at the use of force to harm and
injure protesters there and expressed admiration for the innovative
march out of the city.

Visual traces, in this case graffiti, evoke the burgeoning new political
imaginary that has stuck since the Siliana protests. Figures 3.5 and 3.6
are tags made in Tunis, the capital city, a few months after the march,
probably early in 2013.[67]

Figure 3.5 is a palimpsest of political messages that sums up recent
Tunisian turmoil and some of its key actors. First, one can identify the
initial red tag, just underneath a plaque indicating that it is a building

Figure 3.5 "Did you see us?" ("*shuftūnā?*"). Tunisia 2013.

[67] These pictures are taken from the publication by Lacquaniti (2015: 52).
Reproduced with her authorization.

Figure 3.6 "Ministry of buckshots" (*"wazīr al-rash"*). Tunisia 2013.

hosting one section of the powerful UGTT. The red graffiti in Arabic rhyme reads: *'isyan, 'isyan, yasqut al-tughiyan*, with a signature of JFP, which can be rendered as "Disobedience, disobedience [until] tyranny falls!" This call for disobedience is from the *Jeunesse Front Populaire* (JFP), the youth section of the Popular Front, a coalition of left-leaning and Marxist parties. It is not clear if the tag is a general opposition against tyranny or whether it is connected to a specific episode. The second layer clarifies the answer: The black silhouette has a name on her/his chest:[68] "Siliana" (in Latin letters). One eye is covered with a black strap, most probably to cover an injured eye (remember that at least 16 people were blinded by police buck shots). The black person asks, in the bubble, *"Shuftuna?,"* which in colloquial Arabic means, "Did you see us?" The dark piratesque silhouette, combined with the caption, can be read as a reminder that the ghost or shadow of these violent episodes is not disappearing ("you see us, so don't forget us") and is haunting those willing to reassert tyranny ("see, we stood up

---

[68] It is hard, and probably also beyond the point, to identify the sex of the person. It is not clear if it is a hairdo or a turban that explains the bulky head.

against old-fashioned police repression"). It could also be black humor, with those who were blinded in these episodes of November 29, 2012 asking whether they are actually seeing, a rhetorical question to the onlooker. This is another reversal of what I will describe in the following chapters as radical representation and here demoscopic violence: the blind can see and the seeing are blinded (by a tyrannical government).

Figure 3.6 adds another twist to the fateful episode of Siliana.[69] The tag states in simple red words: *"wazir al-rash,"* "Ministry of the Buckshots."[70] Contrary to Figure 3.5, there is no explicit reference to Siliana, but this use of unjustified police repression remained engraved in the collective imaginary as a symbol of illegitimate use of violence. The term *"al-rash"* [buckshots] of Siliana became a metonymy for the larger Tunisian and, by extension, Arab predicament of the unaccountable use of extreme violence on innocent citizens. Thus, Figures 3.5 and 3.6 resonate with the disfigured visage of Khaled Sa'id in Egypt (see Introduction) and Yemeni victims (see Sections 4.2 and 5.4) who reappear in a new form to call for accountability against those who ordered the disproportionate use of repressive violence.

A last example of this demoscopic violence and its long-term Moebius origins comes from a two-color graffiti in the capital Tunis. The main part of the stencil, in black paint, makes a reference to a historical national holiday, the Day of the Martyr (*'eid shuhada'*), which is celebrated in Tunisia on April 9.[71] It commemorates the dark episode of anticolonial struggle of April 9, 1938 (in Arabic, *"ahdath 9 afril 1938,"* or "the events of 9 April 1938") when 20 Tunisian subjects were killed by colonial police during a protest demanding the end of the mockery of parallel deputation to France and the creation of a local Tunisian parliament (Perkins 2014: 107–108). April 9, 1938 is a pivotal day in cementing the demands of Tunisian nationalism against the French protectorate. Interestingly for us, the stencil does not use the expected reference to martyrdom,

---

[69] Reproduced in Lacquaniti (2015: 56). She also confirmed that this picture was taken a few months after the Siliana episode, in March 2013. Picture taken near the tram stop of *Passage de la République*, Tunis.

[70] There is another smaller tag, reproducing the contours of the Tunisian map, partly hidden under manifestos, and which reads (in black): *"akhdam, tunis aham,"* "Serve [or work]! Tunisia is more important!" This is a call to work and not respect one of the UGTT's calls for a general strike.

[71] For a reproduction of the image, see Lacquaniti (2015: 47).

but speaks of "a citizen." The stencil reads: "*huna 'unnifa muwatin tunisi. yom: 9 abril 2012,*" "Here a citizen was badly beaten. Date: 9 April 2012." The verb "was badly beaten" or "was treated severely" is the same root as violence in Arabic, *'unf.* The date is a reference to the day when riots shook various cities in Tunisia after the Troika government (see next chapter) had prevented demonstrations in front of the Ministry of the Interior in Tunis. Heavy crowd-dispersal techniques were used on that day to disperse the demonstration in the capital, and as a result and in solidarity, new riots occurred in other parts of the country.[72] A third line of the same stencil (with the same font, but now written in red) added in Tunisian dialect the intimation "Don't hit me!" (Lacquaniti 2015: 47).

Again in these visual elements and their relational content (past events with current affairs), we have all the ingredients of a rejection of the long roots of latent citizenship. It is a "citizen" not a martyr who is beaten; the date, April 9, evokes the colonial struggle but links with current police violence; the continuous existence of graffiti criticizing police brutality demonstrates that a more open turn has taken place in Tunisia. The iteration of multiple statements, with the commemoration of a "citizen beaten up," added to the plea to the police "Don't hit *me!,*" the reader of this graffiti, are all elements that have been described and discussed as part of the facets of representation and violence. If we know that the other cities that protested in solidarity with Tunis were Gafsa, Sidi Bouzid, and Ben Guerdan, all cities of the interior, we can also find another illustration of the multi-directional and relentless politics of informal, yet collective, mobilization. But without the historical detours of Part I, it would be impossible to understand the multiple meanings of the stencil, let alone capture the post-2011 revolutionary message.

Two supplementary principles reinforce that of *vis populi*: presentism and a new democratic subjectivity.

A new subjectivity has emerged through the Arab protests that will make it relevant for future political change. In the Arab Uprisings there emerged a new sense of citizenship expressing itself through a closer fit of the people's aspirations with the functioning of the state. It represents a caesura between the age of ideologies discussed in Chapter 2 and

---

[72] See the report, dated April 10, 2012, www.tunisienumerique.com/tunisie-accr ochages-entre-citoyens-et-forces-de-lordre-dans-plusieurs-villes/117031.

the revolutionary moment that pivots around a different philosophy of the present. All Arab protests can be defined as the unfolding of an accrued sense of civic involvement geared at acting *hic et nunc*. The notion of the present, I argue, is the fulcrum upon which this new subjectivity can be raised and articulated and out of which *vis populi* becomes manifest. By putting the present at the heart of the protests, different layers of the population reclaimed a direct connection to politics. Until the moment of massive protests and encampments, the people had been denied the capacity to occupy the present and were barred from acting together and performing what Palestinian film-maker Elia Suleiman called poetic justice, meaning a justice that is made now.[73]

This new sense of political subjectivity went together with a differ-ent attitude towards time that I will call "presentism": more than calls for the end of the regimes, more than calls for bread and dignity, all of these protests expressed the capacity of different layers of the popula-tion to reclaim the present moment and to articulate, out of this recaptured momentum, new political demands aimed at changing the future. The argument, connected to the new political subjectivity, is that until then, the people had been denied the capacity to occupy the present and were barred from acting together: it is this philosophy of presentism and of restlessness that is at the core of the Arab Uprisings.

To speak of such a temporally immediate reclamation, I suggest the term presentism. Frustration soared so much in nearly all Arab coun-tries to the extent that the youth were literally disowned of their present and future (Herrera & Bayat 2010). Meanwhile, others became alien-ated by the bleak future offered by patronizing elites and dictators who instrumentalized the fear of Islamist violence and mayhem. The revolts have been about breaking these distorted mirrors and occupying the present moment.[74]

---

[73] Elia Suleiman, as per his endorsement to Hamid Dabashi (2012).
[74] See also Bamyeh (2013) for the techniques of discussion and deliberations and the adherence to presentism. Dialogue arose from people, like in the case of the extreme civility and the "pause" moment in Tunis, or in the Egyptian streets, in particular in the heart of Tahrir Square. Presentism is thus a method: "After all, at the time, the most apparent and important aspect of the revolution to its people was the content of their mutual speech and not the result of the revolution. ... This is because the dialogue of the revolution proceeds at the pace of the revolution and alongside it,

In Tunis, actors occupying Qasba Square, in front of the Prime Minister's office, in January and February 2011, were involved in activities resembling artistic workshops and political assemblies: people wrote lyrics and song, debated how to arrange the little space in the Qasba, and talked of how to organize these very discussions. But the larger questions were about the organization of society, and how all these exchanges *now* could become the alternative bases for a joint political *future*.[75] Not all were artists versed in singing, not all were architect-citizens, politicians, or organizational activists. But out of these sustained, presentist exchanges, people endorsed new social roles. To go back to Castoriadis' (1976: 11) idea that "spontaneity is the excess of the result over the causes," we see here how spontaneity in a revolutionary context leads to a questioning of the social environment, cultural artifacts, and political participation and to a reconnecting and articulatation of them into a new political program that synchronizes collective actions. Amin Allal's (2011: 58) conveyed a chant that captures this idea: "Now everything can restart."

This illustrates the definition of subjectivity given above, with the dynamic and relational process that allows for a new habitus to undo past structures of top-down violence and which deferred all civic action. Salwa Ismail's analysis of some of the Cairo graffiti that emerged in January 2011 suggests the dialectical structuring of immediate injunctions, and the emergence of new subjectivity. One of these graffiti, in a street adjacent to Tahrir Square, stated:

> Starting today, this is your country
> Do not throw rubbish. Do not pay a bribe
> Do not falsify a document. Do not submit to injustice and tyranny
> Complain about any institution that falters in the performance of its work.
> (Ismail 2011: 989)

Starting today . . . This is where people focusing only on formal changes might lead us to miss or dismiss the transient components of the revolutions. For indeed, people in Tunisian, Yemeni, or Egyptian streets have uttered similar projects: Occupy the streets! Revolt! Do or don't do certain things now! The re-appropriation of the present

---

whereas the result of the revolution remains uncertain, if not unknown, before we arrive at it." Such dialogue, in his words, "needs immediacy" and contributes to a "constant need of self-discovery" (Bamyeh 2012: 39).
[75] Othman Khaled, civic campaign leader, interview in Tunis, 01/10/2016.

entails a deeper process that connects society and state. Presentism, in other words, is also about claiming one's own autonomy. I am autonomous if I am at the "origin of what will be" (*archè tôn esomenôn*, as Aristotle used to say), and by being spontaneous and autonomous, the polity indicates to the usurper and incumbent elite that they must yield to the objective of the "people."

The multiple examples seen from Tunisia were not about vacuous, individualistic subjectivity but about democratic demands. There is more than just self-referential or celebratory cultural representation, otherwise interim Prime Minister Beji Caid Essebsi would have not asked state employees to erase the political slogans and graffitis in Tunis (Lacquaniti 2015: 26), as the Supreme Council of the Armed Forces did in the streets of Cairo in 2011 (Shalakany 2014). These chants and stencils repeatedly call for *muwatana* (citizenship) or "the people want a parliamentary system" ("*al-sha'ab yurid nizam barlamani*"; Lacquaniti 2015: 41), and the masses mobilized or expected symbols that reflected their demands for political inclusion.

One revealing instance of the depth of the demand revolves around the motto inscribed on the state's coat of arms, and which evolved at key historical moments of the country. From 1959 until 1963, the coat of arms read: "*hurriyya, nizam, 'adala*" ("Freedom, Order, Justice"), while with Bourguiba from 1963 until 1989, the motto read "*nizam, hurriyya, 'adala*" ("Order, Liberty, Justice"). After the revolutionary demands of 2011, the term "Freedom" was put in first place again, in the following sequence: "*hurriyya, karama, 'adala, nizam*" ("Freedom, Dignity, Justice, Order"), a new version which is now guaranteed by the 2014 Constitution.[76] Is the insertion of "dignity" only paying lip service to the momentum of 2011? Or is it an indication that the collective political imaginary gravitates now closer to the requests of the people? Only the future will say.

3.4 Dynamics in Yemen: Social Outcasts Occupy Center Stage

The Yemeni protests started around mid-January. Even before the Tahrir mobilizations had gathered momentum on January 25 in Cairo (Carapico 2013a), the country was reacting angrily at Saleh for pushing, at the end of 2010, for constitutional amendments that would

---

[76] Dégage (2012: 177). For the new motto, see article 4 of the 2014 Constitution.

allow him to remain in power beyond the stipulated limit of 2013.[77] But the real wave of encampments started when Mubarak was forced to resign on February 11. On that night Taiz protesters organized their own encampment called *sahat hurriyya*, Freedom Square. In Sanaa, the eponymous encampment of the "Revolution for Change" started a week after the occupation of Tahrir in Cairo. The choice for the location of the protestors' camp in the capital city of Sanaa, close to the university campus in the north of the city, resulted from the early occupation by pro-regime stalwarts of the largest public square downtown, called Tahrir Square like in Egypt. To avoid any ambiguity with this place, connected as it is to official republican history (the National Museum, celebrating, among other things, the toppling of the Imamate, is located on the side of Sanaa's Tahrir Square), people christened this alternative camp by the university in the north of the city as *Maydan Al-Taghayyir*, "Square of Change." In Hodeida, the largest city in the Tihama, the encampment chose the name "Garden of Change" (*Hadiqat Al-Taghayyir*), and Aden opted for the same name as in Taiz. Hajja and Saada, to name the largest cities, also had vibrant sites of protests.[78] In Sanaa, the encampment spread along large streets, which let people speak of the space as the "first kilometer of dignity" and "land of freedom." Similar locations across the country were alternatively referred to as a place (*sahah*), camp or encampment (*mukhayyam*), or sit-in (*i'tisam*) (Alviso-Marino 2016: 35; Al-Rubaidi 2014).

The same dynamic of cross-sectional, multi-generational, and cross-class alliances as seen and documented in protests in Tunisia was also present in the Maydan Al-Taghayyir, as they were in Cairo, Tripoli, or Manama. The main difference with other Arab countries in 2011 was that the Yemeni regime managed to organize its own anti-protest encampment, in *Maydan Al-Tahrir*, and later along Seventieth Street

---

[77] R. Porter (2016: 59). For a timeline of the evolving protests, see interview given by Abdulghani Al-Iryani (March 17, 2011) on Al-Jazeera, www.youtube.com/watch?v=SbAYKYpG924. In substance, larger demands for the resignation of Saleh emerged only after February 11.

[78] The now defunct blog, "Yemen 4 All," aggregated reports from various towns (Wiacek 2012: 348). The site was hacked and is not accessible anymore. Readers can still find examples of reports, e.g. at http://yemenrightsmonitor.blogspot.com/2011/03/ (for Haja), or https://web.archive.org/web/20120608015444/http://yemen4all.com/index.php/news/2011-06-26-10-52-48, for a report from Saada.

and Square (*Saba'in*) (Al-Rubaidi 2014). These pro-regime protests lasted as well and evolved on many aspects as a mirror of the pro-revolution camps. If the latter insisted on non-violent rhetoric and measures (with a cordon of people checking that no arms were brought in the encampments), the former had hired thugs openly defending the regime (Alviso-Marino 2016: 47). One chanted to Saleh, "*Irhal!*" ("Go away"), the other responded "*lan yarhal*" ("he will not leave [office]!") (Alviso-Marino 2016: 48). Their interconnected fate was also visible in a ready made sculpture in Taghayyir Square, where revolutionary groups turned the burned car used by pro-regime thugs to ram into the first campers into a memorial, by placing upon it a plaque evoking the new resistance and struggle (Alviso-Marino 2016: 35). The symmetry of a divided city (north–south)[79] was in homology with the political paths envisaged by both sides: peaceful vs. violent intimidation, the power of many vs. survival of the one, Taghayyir vs. Tahrir.

In a society that remained stratified even after the rise of republican egalitarianism, with *akhdam* (servants, better called *muhammashin*) at the bottom, tribesmen in the middle, and urban merchants and *sada* on the top (Bujra 1971), the fact that people from all walks of life demonstrated was quite significant. The first months of 2011 saw "day after day, with special energy on Fridays, in cities and towns across the land, men, women, and children agitated against dictatorship and the politics of violence" (Carapico 2013a: 102). Women were conspicuously present from the onset (Caton, Al-Eryani, & Aryani 2014: 121), and future Nobel Peace Prize winner, Tawakkol Karman, made a name for herself through her fiery speech (Finn 2015). *Muhammashin* took the microphone on the platform established near the encampments (B. Hall 2017). At first, youth activists from the south of the country were eager to make connections with their northern brothers and sisters trying to unseat President Saleh (Dahlgren 2014a). Youth formed the original core of the campers: Carapico (2013a: 112) described the demographic bulge of the occupiers as

fifteen- to thirty-year-olds who had never known another leadership: university students, graduates, dropouts, and wannabes grasping for hope for a better future. ... These "peaceful youths" enlivened the experience with

---

[79] Al-Rubaidi (2014: 27–28) describes this north–south symmetry along Zubairy Street as connected to the long, Islamic history of Sanaa as a sanctuary, *hijra*, which prevents massive confrontations and forces compromises.

music, dancing, poetry, readings, posters, street art and collective gestures of defiance, such as fifty thousand pairs of clasped hands held high. The call to prayer became a call to civic engagement, and mass prayers became a form of civic disobedience.

Huthi supporters from the north joined the protests in the capital, with a strong and very pragmatic delegation of youths called Youth Resistance (*Shabab Al-Sumud*), which was happy to mingle with other Yemenis stubbornly dedicated to toppling the tyrant Saleh (Dorlian 2015: 64). Tribal representatives later joined the encampments and contributed to the democratic debates a craft of its own, the reading and performing of poetry specific to Yemen, as we will see below (Caton, Al-Eryani & Aryani 2014: 130–133). Opulent instances of cultural and self-representation combined unity with a message for political change, even if it was a wide variety of actors who delivered these representational practices. The composition of these encampments was, in the words of an observer: heterogenous urban youth, people from governorates who had flocked via tribal networks, workers and unemployed people, middle and upper classes, low castes, but also sympathizers of the southern Hirak and Huthi movements (Alviso-Marino 2016: 59–60). This contradicts flatly those who described the Yemeni revolution as a mere intra-elite struggle.[80] The Yemeni encampments went on for the whole year, lasting, in certain locations, until 2013 or 2014.[81]

Taiz, located halfway between Sanaa and Aden, became the "epicenter of the democratic *intifada*" (Carapico 2013a: 113). It was also a historical center for the cooperative movement of the 1970s, the era of progressive policies under President Al-Hamdi, not to mention a place of refuge for dissidents of the south and thus a place for debates between Hirakis, northerners, and more progressist intellectuals (Lackner 2016b: 22). Taiz was also a very important location because of the weight of historical and symbolic marginalizations. The town and its surrounding region are famous for producing the intelligentsia and for their urban character. Mermier even compares the Taizis as the Yemeni "Benjamin

---

[80] The argument is made for example by Frison-Roche (2015).

[81] Alviso-Marino (2016: 64) indicates that the camps disbanded in 2013, when the National Dialogue Conference (NDC) started, but according to R. Porter (2017: 267), a few tents in Sanaa's Taghayyir Square, lasted until 2014. In both cases, the timing of the encampments is in synchrony with the democratic debates of the NDC.

Franklins and protestant sects": they are arduous at work, and in study, have an army of teachers for the rest of the country, and the surrounding province is one of the most fertile regions of the country, with an industrious and prosperous city of 500,000 people, for a total population of 2.5 million in the governorate (Mermier 2012: 48, 50). Yet, they have been given the pejorative nickname of *burghuli* by their Yemeni peers – a term whose meaning is disputed but seems to indicate people who are "half-way" (between rural and city and between plains and mountains) as opposed to fully established (Planel 2012: 128). Even if generally more well off than the rest of Yemenis, Taizis resent their marginalization in top decisional jobs (very few are high ranking in the army, for example) and dislike the system of tribal connections that President Saleh built over the years (Planel 2012: 127, 134).

Logically, Taiz functioned as a magnet for various discontented groups that found in it a fertile ground for their revolutionary program. In that city in particular, Al-Hamdi's modernist rhetoric for a civil state (*dawla madaniyya*) was revived in 2011 (Bonnefoy 2018: 189). Jumping from, or connecting, the 1970s to 2011, the same rebuffing of military, religious, and tribal powers connected the Taizis with pro-southerners and anti-Islah supporters. In Taiz, there was a "large youth contingent that identified as southern and socialist, the likes of the Al-Ahmars personified the antithesis of the kind of revolutionary 'civility' [*madaniyya*] they were seeking to promote" (R. Porter 2017: 269). A sundry iconography echoing the period of the 1970s, either with the socialist themes of the former Southern Yemen, or with references to the progressive politics of the Al-Hamdi era, popped up in these encampments in early 2011 (Alviso-Marino 2016: 35). Southern Yemenis, who suffered the humiliations of the 1994 civil war, found support there.[82] Taiz was thus an important place for the flourishing of the principles of presentism, *vis populi*, free expression, and a new democratic subjectivity in Yemen.[83] As the principles are overall similar to what has been described until now, I will only list short examples.

---

[82] In the parliamentary elections of 1993, Taiz was the only governorate that sent a combination of YSP, GPC, Islah, and independent deputies (Day 2012: 119). Aden and Taiz were also under-represented in ministries. For example, in 2007, out of 33 leading roles held in ministry delegations in Aden, 27 are occupied by northerners (Mermier 2012: 47).

[83] www.youtube.com/watch?v=8MdKsH36e-M, Yemen: another day in the heart of the revolution يوم اخر في قلب الثورة. Youth protesters are heard saying that Taiz is

First, the power of coming together and presentism was particularly noticeable for a very fragmented (in part due to the orography) and conservative society. The protests started on January 17, 2011 modestly, with 1,500 people, and January 27 with 15,000 to 20,000 people (Lackner 2016b: 20), but by February the two main encampments, in Sanaa and Taiz, hosted up to 100,000 people, a remarkable feat for towns or catchment areas of around two million people (Caton, Al-Eryani, & Aryani 2014: 121). A high and steady number of protestors expressed a collective desire for change.

The presence of many women constituted a second proof of the new force behind these protests (Al-Sakkaf 2018; Strzelecka 2018). A leader of Islah, Mohammed Qahtan, acknowledged how pivotal the women's mobilization was in 2011 in these terms: "To see those endless waves of women protesting in the streets left no option for Yemeni men but to rush to the streets as well and do their part in supporting the uprising and demanding regime change" (quoted in Fraihat 2016: 206). Feminine presence was used as an argument by people resisting the demands for democratic changes to discredit the protests: how can women be on their own out in the streets, and for some even camping at night in these sit-ins? The presence of women was a lightning rod for reactionary forces, and served to discredit as "effeminate" (*mukhannatha*) the entire protest movements, in particular the one in Taiz (Planel 2012: 129). But self-rules were established to cut short these attacks. Protestors devised new strategies to preserve some gender separation: women prayed or sat in different spaces, a separation marked in certain instances with a simple rope or string.[84] The subsequent support of many tribal groups for the protest movements, with the enactment of gendered use of spaces (more below) helped to stem these moral attacks and reaffirmed the legitimacy of the protests.

Third, even if tribal and religious morality are often represented as undermining the action of citizenship in Yemen, these massive and aggregative protests "opened up new spaces for new discussions about all relevant religious, social, and political issues" (Al-Rubaidi 2018a: 40). Some were already debated, but now with a new momentum and influence on a scale yet unseen in the country. Yemeni

free, while Taghayyir Square in Sanaa has become a prison. Video published 02/07/2012.
[84] See pictures by Jameel Subay (2012: fol. vii).

intellectual Abdulsalam Al-Rubaidi (2018a: 41) noted that the "incredible general tendency towards secular criticism of religious and social norms in Yemeni life [resulted in the decline] in popular and intellectual faith in the viability of the traditional Yemeni model of polity." In 2011, Yemeni people expressed skepticism and started questioning taken-for-granted ideas, values, and practices. Faith in political parties, even oppositional ones that had been instrumental in generating cross-partisan alliances (Yadav 2011: 554), was altered, and people felt the need to keep a distance from the power of the JMP and from its main party and hegemonic presence in Sanaa, Islah (Alviso-Marino 2016: 53). Women were particularly keen on calling for a civil state (*dawla madaniyya*) (Alviso-Marino 2016: 63).

Fourth, and as a result of these new themes that were the object of intense debates and scrutiny, actors from different origins stitched together different demands. Thus, bodies such as the "Civic Coalition of the Revolutionary Youth" or the "Coordinating Council of the Youth Revolution for Change" were established in the Sanaa encampments and some worked on the publication of a broadsheet.[85] The blog "Yemen 4 All," now inactive, and specific pages on Facebook collated and published reports, images, videos, and lists of demands proposed in the various towns. Calls for a state that is for all its citizens and "across categories of distinction" (social, demographic, geographic, political, etc.) (Yadav 2011: 556) were heard from all corners of the country. Like Armbrust's observation from Cairo's protests, a "sense of unity forged through such *communitas*," namely protests that "brought together youth activists of both genres, armed insurgents of the Huthi family . . ., southern movement members, factions of the Yemeni Armed forces and prominent tribal figures" (Yadav 2011: 557). Parties and pro-Islah tribes mattered, but informal actors, whom Yadav (2011: 557) calls "liminal groups," such as youth, women, marginalized, and population groups such as the Taizis, were as important.

"Spontaneous" in 2011 Yemen did not mean that the protest erupted out of thin air, but rather that people were being the source of their own actions. Presentism also became a new mode of expressing a new subjectivity. In the local capital of the island of Socotra, Hadibo, the

---

[85] See Subay (2012: fol. ix), Wiacek (2012), or the blog of *Noon Arabia,* http://notesbynoon.blogspot.com/2011/09/demands-of-yemens-peaceful-youth.html.

population picked up trash littering the streets. The following episode, taking place in Hadibo, the capital of the archipelago of Socotra, is reminiscent of the scenario of extreme civility encountered in Tunisia in early 2011, combined with presentism and culminating with a new political identity:

Demonstrators took it upon themselves to pick up the plastic bags, cartons and other garbage layering the streets of Hadiboh – accomplishing in one day, pointed out [activist] Fahmi 'Ali, what "the Environment" had failed to do in a decade. (One of the [UN-led activities] did sponsor a trash removal project in the mid-2000s, which worked somewhat effectively, and did encourage several Hadiboh cleanup events, carried out primarily by its own staff and the army. The difference is that, then, Hadiboh residents watched as "foreigners" cleaned their streets; this time, the youth and shop-keepers participated more fully and the streets remained relatively garbage-free for three months.) [. . . Thus, people] espouse a collective, local responsi-bility and a self-governance of sorts, in other actions – and precisely through the act of taking on the government – Socotrans are professing and perform-ing their national (Yemeni) identity and citizenship. (Peutz 2012)

Vis populi took on a variety of forms and, as in Tunisia, adopted a relational content. To the corruption, thuggery, and ruthlessness of President Saleh and his entourage, protestors opposed demands for justice and expressed their determination to reject the fear of the regime ("we will not fear your bombs," as quoted in Caton, Al-Eryani, & Aryani 2014: 136). For past injustices, the people demanded punish-ment and refused proposals of presidential immunity (Caton, Al-Eryani, & Aryani 2014: 123–124). The youth in Change Square in Sanaa declared: "We brought our pens and words [here in the Square] to end corruption [and . . .] to bring Ali Abdallah Saleh to court."[86] The improvised monument mentioned above, made with the car that had been rammed into anti-regime protestors, became a symbol for non-violence and for the rejection of the oppressive regime.

Anthropologist Steve Caton, a specialist of Yemeni poetry, conveys the power that tribal poetry, in particular *zamil* and *balah*, as poetic forms used in public environments and with a certain degree of impro-visation (Caton, Al-Eryani, & Aryani 2014: 130–133), have had in the

---

[86] See min. 1:00 from the video of Ammar Basha, called "Yemen: One day in the heart of the revolution", يوم واحد في قلب الثورة. Video published 05/06/2011, at www .youtube.com/watch?v=Jj59JAK6I4A.

2011 protests. Caton and his two co-authors (2014) note that tribes have a moral obligation to use non-violence and moral suasion before using violence to redress a tort they have suffered.[87] *Zamils* are staged between feuding parties and on public display, where the convincing power of literary prowess can serve as a suitable exit and reconciliation. *Zamils* (and in a few instances, longer poetical *balah*) were chanted as new tribal groups joined encampments in 2011. With these texts and the staged uses of the space, poems functioned as "challenges" to Saleh (Caton, Al-Eryani, & Aryani 2014: 129). To the risk and reality of fragmentation that Saleh's policies had sown in the past decades, *zamils* expressed the strength of a "unified nation" (p. 127), unity also enacted by a group of tribesmen marching together while chanting these rhymes), and Yemenis expressing their will to have "their heads held high" and "in dignity" (p. 140). One of these poems captures the connective elements of poetry (from "I" to "we" facing an abject "you"), and the immediate shift of power that is performed in the collective performance and repetition of these rhymes:

The Land of Yemen, Its People Revolted (poet unknown)
Tell our government I have a new one
    Injustice has crossed the line and the land of Yemen, it's a nation revolting
    . . .
    Listen to my advice and obey, no we will not fear your bombs
    even if machine guns rain
    This is an order you must obey, your people command and you must obey (as reproduced in Caton, Al-Eryani, & Aryani 2014: 136)

The next chapter will discuss the details of these demands, but a core demand by Yemenis was to end the personalistic, fragmentary, and repressive use of violence by Saleh's clique. Coercion was used selectively to mount six wars in Saada against the Huthis, in the north, or to repress the secessionist aspirations in the south, and imprudent alliances were made by Saleh with Al-Qaeda to undermine his domestic enemies. Pressure from below to end this instrumental use of violence by the incumbent regime met some success in the first months of 2011, but the price paid by the protestors was high. The Yemeni Uprising was not a

---

[87] Dresch also accounts the political role of these *zamils* in the pre-revolutionary period, for example, how *zamils* served to criticize the Sanhani control and concentration of power, or the growing political role played by his son Ahmad. See Dresch (2000: 98, 192, 202).

non-violent promenade. Indeed, essential to the momentary success of the revolutionary moment in Yemen was the defection of key allies around President Saleh: GPC leaders, officials of the Yemeni republics (ambassadors, ministers), and a few military figures. Among these, Ali Muhsin, whose Firqa Brigade[88] defected in March 2011, shortly after the bloodiest act of repression against the peaceful protestors, is listed as a key turning point, but one that would bring its own host of complications during the attempts at reforming and democratizing the security forces. Huthis who had joined the Taghayyir Square were not particularly pleased to see their former oppressor now being their protector. Some Huthi loyalists remained in Sanaa, but rapidly, from March onward, the Huthis in the north took advantage of the torments of President Saleh to seize Saada. They saw a unique occasion to take revenge against Saleh, but also against Hashid irregulars who had been sent to help Muhsin crush the fifth and sixth wars in Saada (Brandt 2019b: 16). In the south, what had been the most durable non-violent movement since its inception in March 2007, Hirak, prepared for an alternative course of action in light of the growing repression (Alviso-Marino 2016: 43).

The number of victims on the March 18 attack in Sanaa reached 51 dead with hundreds injured. The shockwave that this planned massacre caused was enormous, and after that, Saleh was increasingly isolated: Muhsin defected, and many tribal groups stopped supporting the President and joined the ranks of the protestors. The then Yemeni Ambassador to the UN, Dr. Abdallah Al-Saidi, told me: "The day after the massacre of 51 people, I tended my resignation. For me, this was proof that Ali Abdallah Saleh could not reason anymore. I knew that his regime would fall."[89] Dr. Al-Saidi also noted that the three reasons why Saleh had already lost support in the last decade of his reign were all security-related: his dangerous game of limiting Al-Qaeda only at times; the use of the Huthi wars to marginalize Ali Muhsin; and his ineptitude in dealing with the increasingly organized protests among former South Yemeni officers.

---

[88] On the First Armored Division, Al-Firqa, led by Ali Muhsin during the wars in Saada 2004–2010, see Heinze (2015: 6) and Transfeld (2016).
[89] Abdullah Al-Saidi, former Yemeni ambassador to the UN, interview in New York, 02/26/2019. A dozen other Yemeni ambassadors resigned (Bonnefoy 2018: 48; Poirier 2020: 186), while tribal leaders who had supported Saleh waited a few more months to cast their lot with or against the protestors.

Overall, the Yemeni "revolution" was stained by many more fatal casualties than in Tunisia. The 238 dead of Tunisia are small in number in comparison to the estimate of the post-Saleh unity government, published at the of 2011, with more than 2,000 dead.[90] Even if peaceful means were deployed by the protestors, the incumbent regime could for a long time use total repression. There were fears that an all-out war was about to erupt in June 2011 when leaders of the Hashid tribe clashed violently with Saleh's son, head of the Republican Guard in Sanaa (Bonnefoy 2018: 37).

But the collective force of the people eventually toppled President Saleh, forced to resign in December 2011, with an interim president elected in February 2012. The election was only a superficial show, for there was only one candidate who could run, namely Abed Rabbo Mansur Hadi, the Vice-President who had served nearly two decades as a docile deputy of Saleh. This episode of a "transition" steered from above and abroad by the Gulf Cooperation Council (GCC, an intergovernmental union of six monarchies wary of seeing republican ideas of equality spread in the Gulf region), which will be discussed in the next chapter, signified also the danger of Saudi and Gulf counter-revolution. When I asked a prominent northern intellectual, from the Taiz region, which term we should use to qualify the 2011 Yemeni revolution, Zaid Alwazir responded, without hesitation "*inqilab al-khalij*," the "coup from the Gulf."[91] The democratic legitimacy, in this answer, was taken away by a new form of external encroachment: Gulf monarchies preying on Yemeni weakness, as we will see in Chapters 4 and 5. But for younger participants in the Uprisings, the name they prefer giving put the stress on the youth and generational rupture: the 2011 Uprising was *al-thawra al-shababiyya alfain-wa-ahdash fil-yemen*, or the "2011 Youth Revolution in Yemen."[92]

* * *

[90]   Subay 2012: ix. According to Lackner (2016a: 163), the number of demonstrators killed in 2011 was limited to 270. In light of the acrimony around the sole encampments of Sanaa, it is doubtful that this figure is accurate. For an overview of the tensions around the first months of the 2011 protests, see the sobering short documentaries produced by Yemeni film-maker Ammar Basha on his YouTube channel: يوم واحد في قلب الثورة [*Yemen: One day in the heart of the revolution*] and which captures different moments of the encampments, march for life, and protests in the various parts of Yemen.

[91]   Zaid bin Ali Alwazir, intellectual, interview in Fairfax, VA, 06/26/2019.

[92]   Al-Mikhlafi, interview, 09/18/2019. Muhammad Khalifa, civic campaign and youth NGO leader, in Socotra, interview via WhatsApp, 12/29/2019.

By 2010, all movements on the front of citizenship had been stalled. But by the beginning of 2011 a sudden energy, channeling past discontent, led to a wave of revolutionary protests that toppled Presidents Ben Ali and Saleh. The facets of cultural and political representation were aligned with the collective force of the people, or *vis populi*, demanding the respect for the sovereign power of the demos with regard to coercion and security matters. A new articulation of past marginalization and exclusions powered a reimagined and unified mass as "the people" into front stage. The strength of the mobilization, the power of the symbols chosen, and the restless enactment of an active body of citizens led to what an acute observer of North African politics termed "the end of the security social pact" (Boumghar 2019: 35). A new state–society compact was proposed as a way forward by the numerous and repeated demonstrations and public actions in Tunisia and Yemen throughout 2011 and part of 2012.

Contrary to the dominant definitions of political science, this state was not "an organization which controls the population occupying a definite territory is a state insofar as 1) it is differentiated from other organizations operating in the same territory; 2) it is autonomous; 3) it is centralized; and 4) its divisions are formally coordinated with one another" (Tilly 1975: 20). The state, in this revolutionary moment, was a collective, a human community claiming the sovereign power over its principle institutions ("we are a new government," as mottos or graffiti both in Tunisia and Yemen expressed), and enacting a democratic control, or at times a counter-power to the institutions of coercion. As we have seen, past brutalities by the police and army were rejected and replaced by a mostly non-violent model of informal and spontaneous actions from below. This form of state corresponds to the Gramscian model of an ethical state (*stato etico*) opposed to the gendarme state (*stato carabiniere*) (see Chapters 1 and 2). It was a state for, and with, a people, and the proposed political form was one based on the praxis of emancipation and struggle from below, and on collective aspiration for re-found unity, equality, and equity of the means of coercion.

The motto of the Tunisian revolution was eventually shifted in the sequence described above: Freedom, Dignity, Justice, Order. The choice favored by protestors was not a mere "freedom and dignity"; rather it also entailed a commitment to equity, and in Yemen, as in the case of the Dignity March (Yadav 2015: 145), rejected offers of impunity for Saleh. And the choice of words did not call for a revolutionary *tabula rasa*: "order" remained a cardinal principle, with Tunisians handing guns that police had left in their state to the army (ICG 2012: xx; 2015: 8). *Vis populi* is not synonymous with destruction. It is an informal compass that guided collective action in Yemen and Tunisia to move away from repressive and unjust coercion. It can be said to be democratic because the new articulations it proposes are in favor of inclusion, of aggregation, and for creative solutions that favor the interests of the many, as opposed to one unique set of actors (be it a party, a tribe, or a region).

In Tunisia and Yemen, people did not call for abolitionist measures, or radical shrinking of security forces. Like in other Arab states, the demand was to neutralize *excessive* violence (in particular against marginalized groups), to make all citizens equal in front of institutions of justice and coercion, and to bring to justice the corrupt governing figures. As a result, the social life of citizenship regained new vitality in 2011. The fight against corruption, nepotism, the ills of structural adjustments, and stolen elections were triggers that motivated hundreds of thousands of protesters to pour onto the street. But none of these, I think, formed the basis or the bedrock on which a new more just political order could be established as a whole. Put differently, the visible force of the *vis populi* is a much broader theme on which Arab masses expected a new social contract to be established. An economic reform, or a re-run of a stolen election, or a campaign to uproot corruption would have never contributed to the reformation of such reinvention and self-discovery of united populations as we witnessed in most Arab countries in 2011.

Vis populi, the collective force of the people, is different from nonviolence or civil disobedience. The latter are often sectoral, limited, or collective interventions. *Vis populi* is much more powerful because it is connected to a broader system of cultural representation (the auto-institution of society, à la Castoriadis) and questions the legitimacy of political representation. The project of *vis populi* places the demos at the heart of the management of the state, and questions the fundaments of the legitimacy of the laws that sanctioned past uses of violence. In short, it is not a band aid, or sectoral reform; it proposes an alternative democratic order.

The strengths of the revolutionary moment, presentism, *vis populi*, and the articulating power of informalism will remain forever enshrined in the collective imaginary. But there is no doubt that these strengths will be weaknesses for formal institutions of power and for incumbent actors who will prey on the self-centered presentism and the evanescent cultural effervescence of encampments, marches, and protests. The task of the next chapter is to illustrate the counter-revolutionary dynamics in the initial two or three years of the revolutionary moments. The democratic path charted by the 2011 protests was *legitimate* because it emanates from the force, or collective will, of the people and from social coalescence. The question now is: Could this new order be made *legally* binding? How can this *informal* collective force create a new binding *formal* political order defending equity, equality, and social justice? What happened in Tunisia and Yemen when these principles of a just management of coercion became the objects of formal political reforms?

4 | *Revolutionary Crossroads: Security Reform and the Limits of Informalism*

4.1 Was Ending the Permanent Security Custodianship Ever Possible?

In both Yemen and Tunisia, pulsating revolutionary dynamics brought the key actors to successive crossroads, leaving them limited options and forcing them to choose a pathway that informal and revolutionary groups did not automatically want to take. In Tunisia, the political actors confronted the bifurcation: revolution or reform. For Yemen, the forking path offered the choice between a pacted reform or an implosion of the political process with the possibility of civil war. In both cases, the demand for *vis populi* reached a point where formal institutions simply denied the pursuit of a democratic revolutionary trajectory. In Tunisia, this hurdle was raised by political parties and older elites, while in Yemen, security forces and their leaders acted as the "spoilers"[1] of the political opening and reformist process in Yemen. Therefore, we can see that at these crossroads, the force of informal mobilization reached its limits.

Yet, pursuing the focus on informalism allows us to revisit events and processes that international relations and political science tend to attribute to the camp of failed revolutions. Often, the focus has been placed on nominally existing *organizations* or political entities (political parties, trade unions, civil society organizations, etc.) and their qualities (abilities to establish linkages, coalitions, governmental alliances). This literature has many merits but its premises are based either on positivist or substantialist grounds (civil society is reduced to civil society organizations, NGOs, political actors able to generate horizontal or vertical linkages) rather than on relational ones, or it fails to

---

[1] A technical term in conflict-transformation and peace-keeping to identify actors, often within the armed groups, who have not given their (full) consent to a "transition" or post-conflict agreement and who have the ability to ruin the peace-keeping, or here, the democratizing, efforts.

capture the creative aura of the new imaginary, the assembling force of informal constellations that might re-appear later.

It is also unusual to explore the security-democracy nexus from the side of the collective imaginary rather than pursue a study of organizational change (ministerial changes, new chains of command within the army, etc.). But informalism in these pages captures best the existence, around the various crossroads made explicit in Tables 4.1 and 4.2, of fluid coalescing points, or the possible crystalization of common democratic expectation that aimed at ending the "permanent security custodianship" that characterized Arab political systems (Sayigh 2015). We will try to give more substance to the democratic meaning of "dialogue," decentralization, and self-management. These form a block of a new political imaginary, which – like Sewell's (1996) famous study of the shift from culture to structure during the French Revolution, rather than an anodyne event, the taking of the Bastille – generates new expectations of political participation, and new ways to rethink the link between soldiers and citizens in the long run.

In Yemen and in Tunisia, the commonality of the occupation of particular places (e.g. city squares, marches, and Qasba protests) will be more than obvious. It is in these locations that imaginary spaces of cooperation generated tactical innovations (Boutros 2017), new articulations for political participation, and even new constitutional projects. Space, in line with Sewell, is an ally for those advocating democratic change or even, perhaps, revolutionary demands. It will be in these spaces that informalism is put to a litmus test of democratic participation: These mobilizations remain democratic in their transforming potential only if they are transparent, performed in concert with a variety of groups, and with a view on the collective good. In cases where spaces are occupied for instrumental gains, for the advantages of one political faction only, and with the intention to harm others, then these acts of informalism cease to contribute to *vis populi*.

For Yemen, the first country we will discuss in this chapter, we focus on the period from April 2011 until the end of 2012, while for Tunisia, we will analyze a few processes in which self- and political representations evolved towards larger political enfranchisement, as well as security reforms that began in February 2011 and which were largely abandoned by 2015. The tenor and pace of security reforms, as will become apparent below, explain the choice of these dates, but the

preparation of a new constitution was a commonality for both countries where diverging paths had to be taken.

Though Yemen obviously has experienced a volatile period, there
was a much more revolutionary situation in Tunisia, namely a moment
where a condition of dual power was possible, with some calling for
a *tabula rasa* and the abolition of (most) existing structures of political
representation and a rebooting of all the administrations and
bureaucracy.[2] Quite rapidly, two months after the fall of President
Ben Ali, revolutionary advocates were outpaced by the reformists,
but substantial changes were made and negotiated in the security
sector. This was made possible because of early arrests of senior intelligence and police cadres, and the rather neutral role that the Tunisian
army played in January and February 2011. All of this allowed
a vigorous expression of the *vis populi* as the alternative basis for the
refoundation of a new social contract.[3]

In a nutshell, I want to show that the nature, cohesion, and degree of
reforms made by security actors explain the degree to which *vis populi*
has been able to force the foundation of a new (securitarian) social
contract in the two countries. By *cohesion*, we think of the degree of
unified institutional command in a few (Tunisia) vs. a myriad (Yemen)
of sites of leadership and the ability to incite change after the 2011
revolutionary moment. By *degree of reform*, I mean the pressure (high
in Tunisia, low or deflected in Yemen) exacted by formal political
actors and the exemplary democratic impetus from below, with the

---

[2] Ottaway also uses the frame of dual power to compare the Tunisian with the
Egyptian 2011 Uprisings. But he misleadingly describes the dual power as the
struggle that "two distinct blocs of contenders" wage to control the state
(Ottaway 2017: 10). In Tunisia, he sees the two blocks polarized between
secularists and Islamists (p. 93). Such a divide had initially little purchase in the
revolutionary dynamics, but existed later in 2012 and 2013, as I will show in
Section 4.3. Dual power refers here to a theory of revolution where the old
regime's legitimacy is simply considered dead and in which no gradualist, legalist
reform can be the path for a profound transformation of the governing
structures. A new revolutionary body, claiming to carry the legitimacy dissolves
previously existing institutions. A situation of dual power occurred for a few
months in the Soviet Revolution in 1917 when the Bolsheviks claimed to have
power over the entire political process.
[3] I am aware of the criticisms about the social contract from a gender and racial
perspective that Carole Pateman (1988) and Charles Mills (1997) have
elaborated on. Here, the security social contract is democratic and hence
legitimate for as long as it is controlled by the varied force of *vis populi*.

ability to exercise alternative functions of protection against unjust coercion (*vis populi*).

4.2 Yemen: "No Voice Rises above the Sound of Battle"?

In Yemen, the fully revolutionary model of a *tabula rasa* was never an option because each camp – at least three, as we will see – was coerced into being militarily organized. External sponsors intervened to quell the democratic pretense, with the Gulf Cooperation Council (GCC) imposing itself as the *supra partes* mediator. But despite the extremely volatile situation, Yemen's transition did not collapse into a civil war for nearly four years. Thus, the term "Yemeni model" was used by international actors such as US President Obama, who believed that a very peculiar process of political transition was taking place there. Albeit steered from above, from the perspective of the international community, the Yemeni transitional model had to be embraced because, unlike the Libyan and Syrian cases, the path for discussion had managed to avoid a descent into civil war (Lackner 2016b: 14). In reality, the situation in Yemen was extremely fragile and volatile from the onset, and it is quite remarkable that pushes for democratic participation lasted for three years, with an inclusive round-table discussion, the National Dialogue Conference, which proposed adopting a federal constitution. *Vis populi* in Yemen had a harder time expressing itself, but it was nonetheless an active force.

Table 4.1 offers a synthetic overview of the main crossroads in each circumstance. Each term from the second column faces its corresponding hurdle or barrier in the third column. Thus, the first three lines can be read as opposing the virtuous politics of the places (*sahat*), to groups organizing violent actions and waging "battle" (*ma'raka*) against them; or the revolutionary youth using new connecting media in contrast to the propaganda of the Ministry of Information or of old tropes of political participation in Yemen. When listed in square brackets, the item is a more indirect source of democratic mobilizations – for instance, the recognition offered by the UN Special Envoy to the revolutionary camp was in turn confronted by tribal alliances who maneuvered to undermine their efforts. The Table presents dynamics as cleanly separated, but the reality is also a messy overlap between the two columns. Let us now look at the details of this particular dynamic.

Table 4.1 *Forking paths of the three facets of radical representation in Yemen*

	Vis Populi / virtuous spaces	Barriers
Cultural representation	*Sahat* (places) Connecting media Revolutionary youth [UN Special Envoy: Recognition]	"Battles" of Sanaa, Taiz, Aden Ministry of Information Old tropes of mobilization Informal alliance with tribes
Political representation	Legitimacy of masses National Dialogue Conference (NDC) Transitional governing council [UN Special Envoy: transitional justice]	Legality and institutional continuity Pacted transition (inadequate GCC Initiative design) GPC & JMP
Security	Peaceful Movement (South) "Military Committee" Moderate to high pressure for change	Crushing and killing protestors Spoilers in the security sector Deflected pressure for reform

In 2012, a UN report estimated that President Saleh had amassed a personal fortune of $62 billion by diverting public funds of various kinds (Dahlgren 2015). He had perfected the use of discourses against his enemies to pit one against another and decried their escalating conflicts as "terrorism." In turn, and as a result, he secured significant funds to carry out "counterterrorism" operations (Day 2015) and extended state control over the allocation of the country's resources. Saleh also knew how to use his or his allied forces' armed groups, be they thugs, *baltagiyas* like in Egypt (Lackner 2016a: 157), or regulars in the army, to crush popular protests and encampments. The process of intimidation against non-violent protesters went so far that the protestors had to organize their own armed groups, popular committees, or security forces within or around the encampments.[4] Even after his

---

[4] On the People's Protector Brigade in Taiz, see Yadav (2011: 560).

removal from power, Saleh remained in the country and used his vast assets to undermine all the progress generated by the popular pressure. The intermittent periods of Al-Qaeda insurrection in the south of the country also posed a serious threat to the ability of Yemenis to organize and demand democratic rights. Saleh and, later, President Abed Rabbo Mansur Hadi leveraged these episodes of terrorism to undermine popular committees and to create the illusion that governmental forces were irreplaceable. Yemeni film-maker Ammar Basha, in a series of short documentaries capturing the meaning of revolutions in different cities,[5] illustrated the different facets of the protests: The first two episodes were centered on Sanaa and Taiz, which already had a palpable tension and had seen violence used against demonstrators. But the third episode, which moves to the south in the first weeks of 2012, captured the horrible destruction inflicted on the region of Abyan, in particular its capital Zinjibar during a war against an Al-Qaeda affiliate active in the area. This affiliate, Ansar Al-Sharia (AS-Y) captured the region in 2011 in an operation that forced at least 28,000 people to flee to Aden and to live there in terrible conditions for months.

In cities where conflicts had not yet emerged, the courage of the protesters and the vibrancy of the demands for change, the end of corruption, and the respect of political rights, illustrated during long months of sit-ins, demonstrate that *vis populi* was a central aim of protestors. Cultural self-representations of the revolutionary legitimacy opposed state propaganda with videos or newsletters posted by young Yemenis from different towns through the Coordination Council for Yemeni Revolutionary Youth (CCYRC) (Alwazir 2016: 173). "Live-ins," not simply sit-ins (Lackner 2016a: 160), describes this unique experience in the Arab world. Yemen saw the longest continuous protests in the Arab world, from January 2011 until mid-2013. Youth groups[6] organized encampments in most large cities, produced broadsheets, organized marches, and published blogs and videos documenting the government's responses to the protests.[7]

---

[5] See Ammar Basha's seven documentaries "In the heart of the revolution" posted between 2011 and 2016 on the "Thawrat al-Shabab" YouTube channel. See also Basha (2012a; 2012b) and Carapico (2014) for a rich interview with film-maker Basha.
[6] Basha stated that "the 75 percent of the protesters [were] under the age of 25." See Carapico (2014).
[7] On these media and coordination platforms, see Wiacek (2012); Grabundzija (2015).

To a certain extent, Yemen can be considered an outlier to the Arab proverb "*la ya'lu sawtun fawqa sawt al-ma'raka*," which can be translated as "No voice rises above the sound of battle" (as quoted in Mallat & Mortimer 2016: 7). We will now see how the clamor of the battlefield silenced some democratic voices, in particular after 2015, but despite the instrumental killing and stoking of violence from 2011 to 2013, Yemenis remained obdurately dedicated to the project of *vis populi*, which in this first phase was understood as a flow of poetry, news, and information to denounce the loss of legitimacy of Saleh's regime. Lackner is right to insist that what these Yemenis achieved is indeed revolutionary: 2011 had "a significant constitutional and evolutionary aspect and amounted to a revolution – of a unique kind" (Lackner 2016a: 142). The movement had political objectives that, although ill-defined, called for a fundamental transformation of the country's political system (Lackner 2016a: 142).

To contain the strength of the popular protests, two parallel processes, pushed by two different sets of actors, emerged around April 2011. Each generated its own dialectic path. The first effort came from the main opposition party block, the JMP, which positioned itself as the true defender of the popular protests. The JMP opted for the path of legality, calling on President Saleh and his party, the GPC, to negotiate a transition deal. The deal would be limited to the existing governing bodies (parliament, unity government, new president) and validated by parliamentary fiats rather than popular referendum or plebiscite. No new "revolutionary" body meant to "represent" the Yemeni streets and encampments would be called into existence, a very important difference with the Tunisian case, as we will see below.

To force Saleh's acceptance, the JMP relied on the sponsorship of the GCC, the powerful club of Gulf monarchies that had already organized a concerted response to substantially quell protests that had taken place from March 16–18, 2011 in Bahrain (Matthiesen 2013). In April, a first draft of a GCC Initiative emerged, indicating that the revolution could be reduced to an elite-led transition. Protesters, dissatisfied, pushed for renewed street actions. They felt that the JMP and in particular Islah, the Islamist party which was the strongest component in the JMP, were hijacking the revolution. As a result, new slogans targeted not only Saleh's corruption, but also the barriers that political parties represented. In Sanaa, by the end of April, youth assembled in Change Square were chanting, "No to politicking [party politics], no to political parties! Our revolution is the revolution of the youth!" The chant also targeted tribes and their ambiguous stance in the youth revolution, with the formulation "No to tribes, no to parties! Our revolution is a youth revolution."[8] The legitimacy of a number of the encampments was now facing a second, systematic challenge, this time organized by Saleh and his shadow armies. After a first round of defection on March 19, the day after the Day of Dignity Massacre, Saleh had to organize a different response, since many camps and live-ins were now protected by defectors[9] and tribal groups close to Islah (Caton, Al-Eryani, & Aryani 2014). Saleh used snipers, hired thugs, and special forces that remained faithful to him (e.g. Central Security Forces). In response, the revolutionary forces deployed a combination of non-violence resistance, a determination to expand participation, and their own armed responses.

The more Saleh hit, the more determined people seemed to be. The more violence waged against the people, the louder and more unified their voices. At this point, the mantle of legitimacy that Saleh had used for decades, presenting himself as the sole guarantor of stability, passed to the shoulders and creative force of the youths' live-ins and marches. This generated a space for a political imaginary that transcended local realities and objectives or, in Yadav's (2011: 556–557) terms, a *communitas* across categories of distinctions was formed. Leaders coordinating the protests and flow of news called for national solidarity, giving revolutionary names to each of the weekly mass protests: a Friday in April would be called "Martyrs' Friday." May 6 was deemed a "Day of loyalty with southern people"; and May 13, after the first attacks on Taizi youths, became a "Day of loyalty to Taiz" (Day 2012: 284).

The dialectics between the particular (a location: the south, Taiz) and the more general (solidarity across the nation) emboldened the revolutionary groups and dynamics of converging pressure on the corrupt regime. Southern protestors deliberately refrained from using southern flags or chanting secessionist slogans in 2011 (Amira Augustin 2015). A truly national identity – a novelty according to many observers – seemed

---

[8] For the formulation *lā ḥizbiyya, lā aḥzāb, thawratnā thawrat al-shabāb*, see Alviso-Marino (2016: 62) and Alwazir (2016: 171). The slogan *lā qabīla, lā aḥzāb, thawratnā thawrat al-shabāb* is cited in Yadav (2015: 145).
[9] 12,000 soldiers had defected by April, plus 30,000 army troops already under Ali Muhsin. 2,000 Republican Guards under the command of Saleh's son Brigadier General Ahmad Ali defected between May and early July 2011 (Day 2012: 292).

to emerge from the dialectics of popular protests against Saleh's ignomini-
ous response and from the rejection of a legal, pacted transition.[10]

But the protests soon came to a forked path. Two prominent Islahi
members, Hamid Al-Ahmar, son of Shaykh Abdallah, and the very
conservative religious leader, Abdelmajid Al-Zindani, instrumentalized the encampment movement for their own purpose (Al-Sakkaf
2011; Bonnefoy 2018: 59; Alviso-Marino 2016: 64). They also used
slogans that discredited the tribal credentials of Saleh (Dorlian 2012:
79). The case of Taiz illustrates this movement, yet another dialectical
evolution that will have a lasting impact on the democratic process, the
oscillation between non-violence and active armed self-defense.

We have seen that Taizis were nicknamed and derided for their urban
and supposedly sophisticated habits. An old word, *burghuli*, contain-
ing a sneering connotation, "weakling," was chanted by young thugs
intent on demoralizing Taizis. Saleh's men beat them with batons and
provoked "Taizis to abandon their moral high ground and fight back"
(Worth 2011). Protesters were more rigorously nonviolent than elsewhere in Yemen and objected by chanting fervently the national
anthem (Worth 2011) to show that patriotism was not the monopoly
of "gun-toting highland tribesmen" (Day 2012: 99). On May 29, late in
the night, thugs backed by Saleh attacked the encampment, burning the
protestors' tents, leaving almost 20 dead and injuring dozens more. The
attack came to be called the "battle for Taiz" (*ma'rakat Ta'iz* in
Arabic). This confirmed what many Yemenis had feared: Saleh saw
the democratic uprising as a greater threat to his power than Al-Qaeda
(Worth 2011).

The episode of Taiz occurred as Saleh was trying to undo another
threat, that of legality. By late April, the GCC had already asked Saleh to
step down. Initially, it seemed as though he would resign, but eventually
he refused because the JMP had requested that Saleh be denied legal
immunity (Day 2012: 284). On May 22, he made his intention to remain
in power known, opting instead for open confrontation. The decision
nearly cost him his life. On June 3, an incendiary device exploded in
a mosque in Sanaa where Saleh was attending prayers. Thirteen people

---

[10] Rafat Al-Akhali, former minister, interview in Oxford, 09/19/2019. He believes
that until 2011 Yemenis were experiencing only regional or local identities, but
2011 brought them closer to a collective sense of national identification. Al-
Akhali is from the Taiz region.

died in the attack, and Saleh escaped with serious burns and injuries that required intensive treatment in Saudi Arabia.

With Saleh gone, but without his resignation, the streets again came alive. Throughout the summer, a new slogan was sung over and over: "The people demand a transitional governing council" (Day 2012: 288), with a proposal for a new parliament, involving revolutionary youths, overseeing a technocratic government, the writing of a new constitution, and the immediate dismantling of the national security system.[11] Paradoxically, the use of violence by Saleh prompted the UN to become involved with the "transition," which eventually opened a space for revolutionary youth at the discussion table. The UN General Secretariat ordered the UN Mediation Support Unit (MSU) to offer assistance and deescalate the situation. Jamal Benomar, a British United Nations official with Moroccan origins, was appointed as UN Special Envoy to Yemen and worked through the summer with the GCC discussing transition scenarios (Zyck 2014: 1, 4). He should receive at least some of the credit for incorporating the street legitimacy into the political processes, even if it took until March 2013 for that component, the National Dialogue Conference, to start.[12]

By late September Saleh made a surprise return to Yemen. He tried again to impose his authority over the country, but his time and credibility had expired. The GCC revised its April offer, which had not included a provision for legal immunity, and granted more generous terms of resignation for Saleh. At last, on November 23, in Riyadh,

---

[11] The detailed program can be found on the blog of *Noon Arabia*, an anonymous female blogger, at http://notesbynoon.blogspot.com/2011/09/demands-of-yemens-peaceful-youth.html. Alwazir (2016: 174) also discusses the 13 concise points of the revolutionary youth. Revolutionary youths articulated similar demands already at the end of March. See video posted on March 31, 2011 on the platform http://yemenrightsmonitor.blogspot.com/2011/03/. In min. 1:50 of the video (available at https://youtu.be/yEfCzz43lrc), one can hear the demand to disband the Ministry of Information.

[12] Frison-Roche, a French legal expert dispatched by his government during the time of the NDC, negatively judged Benomar's role. He was also very condescending toward the entire revolutionary process, attacking Tawakkol Karman and the NDC (Frison-Roche 2015: 3, 5, 10, 13, 14). He is conveniently silent about the French corporate actor Total and its interest for Yemeni oil (Frison-Roche 2015: 24). Yemenis have noted that Frison-Roche's preference for a centralized state, as opposed to a federal regime, might have to do with French oil giant Total's need to efficiently renegotiate natural gas contracts (Bonnefoy 2018: 152).

Saleh agreed to hand over power, but for the revolutionary groups the outcome was bittersweet.

The result was disagreeable on at least four counts. First it meant that the international community had come to see the Yemeni transition as an extra-constitutional process that limited the core of the future negotiations to two parties or factions: the GPC of Saleh and Islah and its allied parties in the JMP.[13] The revolutionary groups could claim no representation at the table, and the two aggrieved regional groups, the Huthis and the Hirakis, were not even mentioned in the "political process" ahead. Second, the "democratic revolution" was to have no mechanisms of accountability and transparency in the GCC Initiative. Point 4 of its Introduction stated that, "the GCC Initiative and the Mechanism shall supersede any current constitutional or legal arrangements. They may not be challenged before the institutions of the State."[14] Third, and in relation to the second point, this lack of accountability was even stronger for the military and security reform, where presidential authority was the sole decision-maker. Finally, in exchange for his stepping down, Saleh secured full impunity for himself and his family (Fraihat 2016: 41, fn. 1).

Within weeks, the first phase of the transition was completed. A Government of National Unity (GNU) was established on December 7, with a strict power-sharing arrangement that gave 50% of the seats to the GPC and 50% to the JMP, and included a massive cabinet comprised of 34 ministries. Islah was now calling the shots: the person chosen as Prime Minister, Mohammed Salem Basendwa, was an experienced but weak political figure, whom Islah knew would be docile enough (Lackner 2016b: 36). On January 21, 2012, the Chamber of Deputies extended Saleh's legal immunity to his entire entourage and staff. Saleh handed presidential power to the deputy he himself had chosen years ago as Vice-President, a meek figure from the ruling GPC party, Abed Rabbo Mansur Hadi. The Parliament also approved the unique candidacy of Hadi for the presidential election

---

[13] The term "the two parties" refers to the National Coalition (General People's Congress and its allies) as one party, and the National Council (Joint Meeting Parties and their partners) as the other.

[14] The Initiative and the Implementation Mechanisms, as well as all UN Security Council Resolutions discussed below, can be found in the section "Yemen" of the UN website: https://peacemaker.un.org/.

and held an election on February 21, 2012, with Hadi securing 99.8% of the vote.

Having been betrayed by the JMP, which had been the first protector of the youth, and crushed between the imposed path of legality introduced by the Saudi government and the brutality of Saleh and of his henchmen, the live-ins and encampments resorted to new tactics. In late December 2011, the protestors reasserted their claim to legitimacy by organizing the so-called March of Life, a cluster of marches which began in the main cities of northern Yemen (Taiz, Ibb, Hodeida) and eventually converged on Sanaa. Like the caravans in Tunisia, these marches refused control by a few political parties. Protesters were attacked numerous times on their way from Taiz, but nonetheless they carried on, making their voices heard – voices above the sound of the battlefield. As one of the organizers, Ryadh Al-Same'e, commented, these marches breathed fresh life into the Uprising: "This is a new revolution which caused the silent group in Yemen to come out. We saw many people coming out from their homes and joined the Life March" (as quoted in Basha 2012a).

Overall, the double countenancing strategies of the GCC and of a marginalized Saleh only worked to a certain extent. It is really remarkable that despite the adversity and the very harsh economic circumstances, the Yemeni revolutionary groups managed to preserve a distinct space for democratic inclusion. One of these spaces was the National Dialogue Conference (NDC), whose preparatory work was spearheaded in 2012 by the Liaison Committee. This body was made up of eight members, five of them representing the five leading parties, and three of them being informal representatives, one for youth, one for women, and one for civil society. Dr. Nadia Al-Sakkaf, a member of this Liaison Committee, whom I interviewed, confirmed that serious efforts were made to bring the Huthi and Hiraki members on board.[15] This preliminary step of connecting the main constituent groups of the "revolution" was fundamental to generating an inclusive and

---

[15] Nadia Al-Sakkaf, member of the NDC Presidency, in London, interview via WhatsApp, 09/21/2019. On behalf of the Liaison Committee, she met with Abdelmalik Al-Huthi, the hardliner leader in Saada.

The daughter of a respected Yemeni intellectual, Al-Sakkaf had made herself a name as a journalist and editor of the bi-weekly *Yemen Times* newspaper and eponymous community radio station. She was also a Member of the Technical Committee, and of the NDC Presidency, and former minister of Communication 2014–2015.

representative process. The Liaison Committee was replaced by a larger Technical Committee, made of 25 members selected by President Hadi, two of whom had to be women.[16] The NDC eventually met between March 2013 and January 2014, and will be discussed in Chapter 5, since it became entangled with the outbreak of a civil war. The preparation of the NDC was also sidelined by President Hadi's priority to reform the military and security sector.

The establishment of a "Committee on Military Affairs for Achieving Security and Stability" was, with the NDC, the second phase of the Implementation Mechanism foreseen by the GCC. There was a brief overlap in the mandates: The Technical Committee established a list of 20 demands, sometimes called the Twenty Points or confidence-building measures, many dealing with questions of coercion and security. Among these demands were apologies to the population of Saada and of southern Yemen for the brutal military campaigns; the reinstatement of personnel forced into retirement after the 1994 war, in particular former soldiers; the return of confiscated land in the south; and the release of all those imprisoned since the start of the revolution. President Hadi agreed to these demands, but for the most part, these turned out to be empty promises.

There were great expectations that Hadi would undercut Saleh's grip on the security apparatus.[17] Hadi activated the "Committee on Military Affairs for Achieving Security and Stability," subsequently referred to as the Military Committee. But its architecture and objectives were too insulated to have a chance of succeeding. One of the key conditions for revolutionary transitions to yield a stable and more democratic outcome is that a majority, if not all of the key actors, agree from the outset to

---

[16] Al-Sakkaf, interview, 09/21/2019. The Technical Committee is also referred to as the Preparation Committee.

[17] "Security apparatus" means the conjunction of Defense (including the army and its two powerful units, Firqa and Republican Guard, plus the air force and navy) and the Ministry of the Interior (policing, paramilitary, and intelligence services) (ICG 2013a: 1, fn. 2). In the Ministry of the Interior, two bodies are important: The Central Security Forces, a unit led by Yahya Saleh, a nephew of Ali Abdallah, and which was behind the attacks on protestors in March and May in Sanaa and Taiz (ICG 2013a: 8); and the *Quwat Najda* or Rescue Forces, led by Abdullah Al-Qawsi, a person close to Ahmad Ali Saleh (ICG 2013a: 8). The main intelligence unit, the National Security Bureau, in charge of anti-terrorism, was headed by Ali Al-Anisi, with Ammar Saleh, a parent of the former president, as number two. On the nepotistic relations in the security sector, see Transfeld (2016).

a minimum set of objectives and then find ways to implement these. In Yemen, nothing of the kind was agreed upon. The Military Committee reflected the state of the security forces on the ground: fragmented and accompanied by the continuous presence of Saleh and other sub-groups (regionalist, tribal, or insurrectional Islamist) who were able to foment violence or to force loyalty from foot soldiers.[18]

For an entire year the Military Committee worked without any input from the revolutionary groups who asked for a civil state (*dawla mada-niyya*), a new form of government that would undo the military and hereditary character of Yemeni power.[19] In other words, the Military Committee remained a separate issue, with no women or youth representatives and hardly any civilians involved. The military reform was fraught: it did not have a clear end point, it was being sabotaged by the "spoilers," and Hadi had limited space of action to impose his will. If civil war was to be averted, the security reform should have been the "absolute priority" of the political transition, with neutrality over the command of the two ministries, new non-partisan military leaders, and compliance with legal, political, and financial oversight (Sayigh 2015: 2).

Hadi adopted too modest an approach, the "salami-slicing approach," taking very limited and discrete actions one at a time (Lackner 2016b: 11, 39). And when he did make decisions, he hesitated, for example when deciding to restructure the armed forces in the Defense Ministry.[20]

In March 2012, Hadi appointed 14 senior members of the security forces – all men – in this Military Committee. It was broken down into three sub-groups: a presidential sub-committee, and two technical committees, one in the Ministry of the Interior (also in charge of the intelligence units) and the other in the Ministry of Defense.[21] For most

---

[18] Gordon (2012) discusses cases of preemptive purges in the Republican Guard instructed by Ahmad Ali and by Yahya Saleh in the Central Security Forces.

[19] Bonnefoy & Poirier (2012: 136–137). The two French authors define the civil state as "a project for a new society organised around the demand for the rule of law, strong principles of social justice, and the protection of fundamental freedoms, but also for the people to exercise control over the state and politics."

[20] By Defense, we refer mostly to the Firqa units, established in the 1980s and known to harbor pro-Muslim Brotherhood sympathies (ICG 2013a: 4), and the Republican Guard, under the command of Ahmad Ali, the son of Saleh. This committee had the support of the USA (ICG 2013a: 16).

[21] Hard to reform because under the influence of US and Jordanian intelligence security.

of 2012, the two technical subgroups made the bulk of the decisions, while Hadi limited his subcommittee to a few interventions. It was the least domineering of the three groups mostly because Hadi, at its helm, was actively trying to avoid becoming entangled in unnecessary conflict (ICG 2013a: i, 15).

From February to July 2012, Hadi pushed for a modest change of security leaders. He rotated only two dozen senior commanders (ICG 2013a: 15) and did not remove any of the influential members of Ali Saleh's network. For example, Tariq, a nephew of the former president, had his post reassigned twice, once in February and again in April. Instead of being demoted or pensioned, he was simply relegated to the Hadhramawt. Ammar Saleh was removed from his position as deputy head of the National Security Bureau in May. Hadi put forward other successful security reforms to increase police accountability and restructure parts of the Ministry of the Interior (Sayigh 2015: 5). But on the international front, Hadi continued the drone attacks that the Obama administration wanted (Bonnefoy 2018: 63). Stopping these attacks would have not only increased Hadi's and his government's credibility, it would have also bolstered their independence from all the regional and international actors keen on perpetuating the narrative that Yemen was fragile and unstable, and helped him break the Moebius strip of delegated violence from afar.

Hadi knew that he commanded very limited loyalty in the security forces and that he was vulnerable to the strength of key spoilers. In one instance during August of 2012, Ahmad Ali Saleh sent soldiers from the Republican Guard to oppose Hadi's plan to subsume some of these soldiers into his newly established Presidential Protection Units. A couple dozen of Ahmad's soldiers tried to storm the Ministry of Defense, leading to shootings and the death of two civilians.

One had to wait until December 2012 to see Hadi's boldest move: he clipped the wings of two arch enemies inside the Defense Ministry – removing Ahmad Ali Saleh and Ali Muhsin at the same time, and disbanding their respective and feared Republican Guards and Firqa Units.[22] The idea was a good one in terms of security reform: by undermining the institutional basis for personalized leadership in

---

[22] ICG (2013a: 21). Hadi was seen moving against Ali Abdallah Saleh and not doing enough to curtail the growing power that Ali Muhsin retained as head of the most competent and equipped Firqa units (Lackner 2016b: 16).

each of these units, Hadi aimed to organize military troops based on a logic of a unified national command. This would achieve the goal of the unification of military forces under a singular national command, but still allow for necessary sensitivity to local contexts. The reform proposed the creation of two new regions, with now seven, instead of five, regional military units. Later, the 2015 draft of the constitution, which was built on a federalist distribution of competencies, developed this point, embracing equal geographical representation and rotation of leadership rather than siloed security forces. The proposal echoed slogans chanted by a group of police officers who had complained about the diverted objective of the security forces under Saleh and the private use of public institutions: "We are the soldiers of the people, not the soldiers of Qawsi" (Qawsi being the head of Rescue Forces, a unit from the Ministry of the Interior).[23] Police should protect the entire country, all its people, not the interests of a few people.

Subsequently, Hadi began working toward the development of a Presidential Protection Unit. This new entity responded directly to the Presidency (as opposed to the two ministries of the Interior and Defense) in order to reduce the risks of in-fighting and lack of loyalty of the army. But Hadi opted for people from his region, Abyan, to take these new security positions (Lackner 2016b; 2019), raising suspicion that despite taking measures that could provide modest change at the top, Hadi was essentially promoting his personal networks. The fact that the Presidential Protection Unit was placed under his son's (Nassar Hadi) control did not elude his critics. Once again, security appointments were made to protect the regime, not the people (ICG 2013a: 20).

Breaking down the system of patronage (Lackner 2016b: 11) at the heart of Saleh's authority was a Herculean task. At a time of economic difficulties and volatility, Hadi was forced to cut benefits, a decision which was highly unpopular with soldiers and their commanders. Republican Guards, the Central Security Forces, and the National Security Bureau not only were better equipped, but had better benefits,

---

[23] As quoted in Gordon (2012). Qawsi reportedly brought out armed tribesmen to confront the dissenting officers. On the "parallel revolution" in the security and private sector (strikes against key economic organizations run by Saleh's family, see also the blog entry of *Noon Arabia*, at: http://notesbynoon.blogspot.com/2012/01/yemens-ongoing-and-parallel-revolution.html.

including access to hospitals and housing; dismantling these units in December of 2012 meant losing large chunks of support in the Defense Ministry.[24] As a result, any change in terms of administrative practices (standard reporting, equal treatment and pay) was immediately resisted within the existing organizations.

Foreign influences also cast a long shadow over the reforms. The main international sponsor of the security apparatus, the USA, did not want to lose its local allies in the fight against Al-Qaeda: Joint drone attacks continued after the revolution. The modest results of the Military Committee charted a path for deeper reforms, but too many spoilers were able to prevent their implementation. For example, a battalion of the Yemeni army launched military attacks against Huthis in the Amran province in spring 2014 with no approval of the Ministry of Defense and of the presidency, fueling a cycle of clashes in the north (Dorlian 2015: 67, fn. 18). Furthermore, the influence of Islah and Saleh over tribal militias undercut the work of Hadi to generate his own military basis (Lackner 2016b: 18), and Saleh retained strong influence in the lower ranks of the military (Transfeld 2016: 157).

So far, we have concentrated on the political process and on the transition seen from the political centers, in and around Sanaa. To an extent voices rose above the sound of battle, but with limited impact. What about places outside of Sanaa, the center of political power? We will briefly deal with the realities in the south and in the north of the country during the period from mid-2011 to early 2013, when the NDC started its work.

In the south, many remained doubtful about the opportunities for revolution. Live-ins, camps, and marches continued, but the initial sense of unity among protestors vanished quickly in the second part of 2011. Islah organized its own camp in Aden called Freedom Square. Revolutionaries and Hirak members had their own camp in Martyrs' Square in the working-class neighborhood of Al-Mansura (Basha 2012b). In June 2012 the Mansura encampment was destroyed by Hadi's troops following their clearing of the Abyan region from Al-Qaeda's presence.[25] Since 2012, *miliyuniyyat* brought citizens of the

---

[24] ICG (2013a: 5, 7). The National Security Bureau had triple the budget of other intelligence units (ICG 2013a: 8), and the Central Security Forces had unlimited and unaccounted access to weapons and general supply before 2011 (ICG 2013a: 8 and 11, fn. 53).

[25] https://globalvoices.org/2012/06/24/yemen-attacks-on-southern-yemen-jeopardize-national-dialogue/, June 24, 2012.

former South together, but the rituals and colors waved did not match the patriotism of the Yemeni flags and symbols. The color blue, from the old Southern flag, re-emerged, indicating a specific "transition" in the south: self-rule or secession.

Elsewhere, southerners were preoccupied with the Islamic insurrectionism of Ansar Al-Sharia (AS-Y), a subgroup of the Al-Qaeda network. The group had taken control of Zinjibar, the capital of the Abyan region, in May 2011, and subsequently the rest of the region along with a portion of the Shabwa governorate by September 2011. Southerners wondered why the military – at the time it remained under Saleh's command – left the regional capital so quickly, leaving their weapons and vehicles behind for AS-Y to recover (Basha 2012b). Popular committees were formed to fight the Islamists (ICG 2017), but in the beginning these efforts found little success. After the election in February 2012, a military campaign was coordinated by Hadi, and collectively, Yemeni citizens and institutions managed to oust AS-Y by May 2012 (Brehony, Lackner, & Al-Sarhan 2015: 11, 12). The popular committees that joined Hadi's military campaign represented a double-edged sword: On the one hand, they helped liberate the region, but, as they established their own alternative source of resources, they also contributed to the further fragmentation of the institutions of coercion.

Another episode illustrates the weight of selective violence in the revolutionary process or in the democratic transition. On January 1, 2013, at a time when the final selections of the NDC members were taking place, two leaders of the Southern Peaceful Movement (Hirak) were killed by snipers in Ataq, the regional capital of the Shabwa Province.[26] For southerners, the deaths were Hadi's responsibility, illustrating yet again his indifference towards southern lives. The event was a watershed moment for Hirak, which found increasing popular support and sudden disinterest in the "political process" of Sanaa. The National Dialogue became the object of virtual and physical attacks in the south. People literally said that the NDC was the "Sanaa Dialogue" and NDC advocacy billboards in the south were taken down or vandalized. The Dialogue tents, intended to explain the NDC's mechanisms to the

---

[26] On the killing of two Hirak activists and other episodes of violence against southerners, see https://stcaden.com/news/7887 (published September 17, 2017).

general public in the form of open meetings, were rejected in the south, including the Hadhramawt.[27]

In the north of the country, a similar lack of interest in the political process prevailed. The situation in the northern governorates had not improved significantly after the start of the revolution. People were still awaiting aid for reconstruction after the sixth Huthi war (August 2009–February 2010). The scorched earth campaign had left the region even more impoverished (Radl 2019: 20). Chemicals had been poured on the ground, rendering the soil inapt for cultivation, fuel shortages made pumping water all the more laborious, and agricultural production suffered as a result. The region was facing a terrible situation, and its people were deeply bitter about it.[28] The little money that people could make was from *qat* cultivation, arms smuggling, and trafficking along the Saudi border (Brandt 2019a).

In March 2011, Fares Manaa, a tribal mediator well-respected in the north, but also an arms smuggler whose background was presented in Section 2.4, was appointed governor in Saada (Brandt 2019a: 28). With Saleh out of power, the Huthis exerted a blockade on a Salafi center in Dammaj, just outside of Saada, between November 2011 and January 2012, and occasional fighting with Islah members broke out in the Hajja province throughout 2012 (Dorlian 2015: 66). The majority of the population around Saada and in the neighboring governorates did not like the GCC Initiative, which had excluded them, and saw the NDC as being more legitimate. This explains why the Huthis participated in the work of the NDC under the name of a new party, Ansar Allah, as we will see in the next chapter, but with growing distrust for President Hadi.

The various forking paths in Yemen were profoundly impacted by deteriorating economic conditions. Efforts were made to improve the architecture of the security forces, but these came much later and in a more timid manner than in the Tunisian case, as we will now show. Additionally, a rich vein of foreign aid – a total of US$8.49 billion to alleviate the hardship – only materialized six months after its promise in September 2012. The international community did not help much and effectively allowed the fox into the hen house by permitting the IMF and

---

[27] Nadia Al-Sakkaf's personal communication, September 2020.

[28] On the bitterness in the north and Huthis, see Ammar Basha's video "4th Day in the heart of the revolution-Saada," الشمال- الثورة قلب في رابع يوم, video published 03/18/2003, at www.youtube.com/watch?v=5itps3kKU8o.

the World Bank to carry out a rapid credit scheme when basic subsidies receded,[29] rather than working to undo the "long-standing tensions around the Arab social contract" (Furness 2020: 72). Donors were not keen on disbursing so much aid, using the excuse of instability to postpone payments, thus precipitating a vicious circle of contention between different groups.[30]

4.3 Tunisia and the Limits of Reforms

In the Tunisian revolutionary context, the theme of "security" is either scarcely discussed or analysts convey the simple view that the Army's peaceful intervention, under the command of General Rachid Ammar, preserved the non-violent nature of the Tunisian "revolution."[31] These accounts barely scratch the surface and attribute too much power to a few key organizations (the Chief of Staff of the Army or a Higher Authority in charge of the "transition"). The reality is more complex, with various iterations of popular pressure and a web of committees playing important roles. I will now deal with a much more detailed account of the entanglement of armed and security forces (police, special units) in Tunisia, and of their institutional reform, connecting them to the double movements of the *vis populi* described in Section 3.2. We will see that, far from an isolated decision by General Ammar, Chief of Staff of the Armed Forces, one has to take into consideration the complex security dynamic that Ben Ali had set in motion a few days before departing the country on January 14, 2011. Furthermore, the historical analysis of economic and territorial fragmentation conveyed in Chapters 2–3 must be connected to the dozens of new committees, initiatives, and coordinating platforms that gave a clear impetus for the *vis populi*.

To illustrate these subdividing or forking paths (continuity vs. rupture; changes pulsated by formal or informal institutions; etc.), I propose breaking down the Tunisian case into the following

---

[29] Two UN resolutions, UNSCR 2051, in June 2012, and UNSCR 2140 in February 2014, deal with aspects of economic reforms. See also Lackner (2016b).

[30] Email communication with Dr. Nadia Al-Sakkaf, September 2020.

[31] He is said to have refused the order of Ben Ali to shoot on protestors. Brooks (2016: 121) makes Ammar the de facto power broker, which is an overstatement of his role in the revolution. Jebnoun (2014) gives a much more limited account of Ammar's role.

questions, which I will then address: How did a last-minute concession made by Ben Ali limit the institutional path towards political reform? How was the security sector reformed in the year after the fall of Ben Ali and to what extent did it favor more democratic forms of accountability? And finally, how was the main party in power after the October 2011 elections, Ennahda, forced to alter its course of governing after the targeted killings of oppositional figures in 2013? I will touch briefly on the Salafist use of violence, and on the idea of Islam's sacred authority. This last step clarifies the limited compatibility between *vis populi* and non-secular principles of sacrality.

Table 4.2 offers a synthetic overview of these diverging forces – that is, the dichotomous opposition between principles meant to accelerate or slow down civic and democratic life after the revolutions. Some of these pairs and institutions (legitimacy vs. legality; NCPR vs. Higher Authority) are discussed in the following pages, but others (e.g. *haybat al-dawla*, the principle of "prestige of the state") will be examined in Chapter 5.

How did concessions made by Ben Ali in his last days in power limit the path towards institutional political reform? How did the people resist attempts to protect legal continuity? Any revolutionary situation that does not turn into a civil war is by definition a struggle between legality or legitimacy, or between continuity (of existing laws) and ruptures. In Tunisia, these tensions gradually shaped the path to the election of the ANC on October 23, 2011.[32] There were conflicting views and deep political antagonisms at play. Some wanted radical, revolutionary measures, but others maneuvered to favor legality and only partial change. It is thus far from clear that the 2011 protestors wanted *only* the rule of law, as Bellin & Lane (2016: 1) have argued, or that the transitional bodies were smoothly put in place in February and March 2011 (Hartshorn 2019: 133). One should assess critically the depth and feasibility

---

[32] They were also dichotomous principles that split organizations at their very core. For example, within the UGTT, there was a consensus-oriented wing that opposed an insurrectional current (Chouikha & Gobe 2013). Within the Islamist party, Ennahda, some voices favored the legality of the ballot box while others insisted that the party should cede to the legitimacy of the streets, in particular when they were put under intense popular pressure in 2012 or 2013. The Higher Authority is listed twice in Table 4.2 because some aspects of its formation and work enabled democratic accountability, while others functioned as a barrier to *vis populi*.

Table 4.2 *Forking paths of the three facets of radical representation in Tunisia*

	Vis Populi / virtuous spaces	Barriers
Cultural representation	Legitimacy Caravans, Qasba Unity (across country) Unity because diversity	Legality *Haybat al-dawla* (status/ class barrier) Salafist sacrality Unilateralism despite diversity
Political representation	Constitutional Assembly National Committee for Protection of the Revolution (NCPR) [Higher Authority]	Slow and divided parties One party in charge (before July 2013) [Higher Authority]
Security	Reshuffling inside Ministry of the Interior Dismissal of political police Inquiries	Regrouping Ennahda's hubris

of the revolutionary project: To what extent were popular commit-tees, spontaneous municipal elections, occupations of collective land as in the case of the Jemna Oasis, or Leagues for the Protection of the Revolution (LPR) committed to the principle of *tabula rasa* the systematic undoing of existing institutions in the name of the people's and revolutionary legitimacy?[33] Or were these bodies will-ing to work with the existing legal and constitutional frames and thus accept a gradualist path towards reform?

The task of this section is to avoid taking the reformist path for granted, and to keep the romanticization of revolutions at arm's length. It focuses first on decisive turning points after the sudden departure of Ben Ali on Friday, January 14, 2011, and proposes an assessment of the forces at play. We then shift our attention to the management and use

---

[33] For an overall account of these tensions, see Gobe (2012), Chouikha & Gobe (2013), and ICG (2011: 12; 2019: 5). On the occupation of Jemna, see https:// autogestion.asso.fr/jemna-intervention-de-tahar-etahri-president-de-lassociation-de-sauvegarde-des-oasis/ (January 9, 2017).

of violence, to realize that *vis populi* can slip into non-democratic tendencies. The discussion of the security reform will also clarify the limits of the power of the "*peuple acteur*," or "acting people" (Gobe 2012).

The short answer to the reform or revolution question is not *refolution*, like many have proposed, but simply reform, for three reasons: First, it is mostly the principle of legality that prevailed in 2011. For example, the Higher Authority for the Realization of the Objectives of the Revolution, Political Reform, and Democratic Transition, in short Higher Authority or HAROR, whose origin is discussed below and which functioned as a mini-parliament from March 15, 2011 onwards, was the by-product of one of the last decisions made by President Ben Ali. Second, hardly any new institutions created in the wake of popular protests had a direct say in the political future of Tunisia. Instead, former politicians and long-standing political parties took the lead, while academics and leaders of pre-existing NGOs were appointed to head this or that transition commission. The notable exception is the National Council for the Protection of the Revolution (NCPR), which fought for the logic of revolutionary rupture, but even there, a significant section of its members accepted being integrated into the Higher Authority (ICG 2011: 20). Third, a quick look at the politics of naming indicates that reformists won the day. As we know, revolutions only accept their own logic and push for a situation of dual power pitting the older order to a new one based on revolutionary rupture. We can think of past revolutions: Haiti's Revolution of enslaved peoples in opposition to the continuity of white planters' ownership; the French Revolution that dismantled the *ancien régime* in the name of citizenship; or the Russian Revolution, with the proletariat dictatorship and the Marxist-Leninist principle of the party vanguard imposing their will. The fact that the HAROR, the main collective body running the "transition" in Tunisia between February and the election of the Constituent Assembly in October, entails both concepts of "Reform" and "Revolution" indicates the victory of the reformist camps.

Without going too far into the details, let us see how, in a matter of two months, the reformist and legalist side managed to prevail over the revolutionary forces.

To avoid a vacuum of power and avert a constitutional crisis after the departure of Ben Ali, the Constitutional Council called on article 57 of the 1959 Constitution to appoint the President of the National

Assembly, Fu'ad Mebazza, as interim president. His appointment took place on January 15. Two days later, the head of the previous government, Mohammed Ghannouchi, was asked by Mebazza to form a new government, of "National Unity." The latter included mostly members of the ruling party, the RCD, and a few new ministers from the authorized opposition. Prime Minister Ghannouchi (unrelated to the leader of the then-still-illegal Islamist party Ennahda, Rachid Ghannouchi) also announced that there would be an election of a new president by July 24, thus recognizing the 1959 Constitution, which set a six-month time-limit on holding a presidential election in the event a sitting president is permanently incapacitated (Gobe 2012: para. 3).

These measures were clearly not enough for Tunisians who sought a complete end to the rule of the RCD. As a result, on January 23, 2011, a "Freedom Caravan" (*qafilat al-hurriyya*) left the towns of Sidi Bouzid and Menzel Bouzayene, where the first martyrs of the revolution had perished.[34] The caravan of protestors converged with other Tunisians who opposed Ghannouchi's government at Qasba Square, in the old city of Tunis, where many ministries are seated. Qasba 1 had begun. The occupation lasted from January 23 to 27, culminating in the resignation of Ghannouchi's government (Yousfi 2015: 102–103; Hmed 2015, 2016b) and the forceful removal of protestors by police forces (ICG 2011: 14).

The next day, Ghannouchi formed his second transitional government, Ghannouchi II. Only a few despised RCD ministers were sacked: Ahmed Fréa, Minister of the Interior, and Mohammad Jegham, a former Defense Minister (ICG 2011: 14), were replaced by independents, for example, judge Farhat Rajhi was appointed the new Minister of the Interior. The two legislative chambers were dissolved on February 9, and legislative powers were handed to the interim president (Ben Achour & Ben Achour 2012: 720). This second transitional government lasted one month, slightly longer than the first. Then on February 27, it was forced to resign by a new wave of marches, caravans, and encampments called Qasba 2,[35] which had begun in

---

[34] See Chouikha & Gobe (2015: 82). Hmed (2016a: 79) has a map of the zig-zagging route that the caravan adopted to draw more support.

[35] There is also another Qasba sit-in, called Qasba 3, demanding the departure of Essebsi in July, but it was not successful. See Lacquaniti (2015: 33). Hmed (2016a: 74, fn. 5) locates this third attempt in April 2011. For some, only the

earnest on February 20. This time, a new revolutionary coalition, the NCPR, the National Council for the Protection of the Revolution (which is different from the Leagues for the Protection of the Revolution), shouldered the informal efforts of the *people acteur*. That alliance made it possible for the people to gain some form of political representation in the Higher Authority. But to understand this development, one needs to go back to the last days of Ben Ali's presidency and two of his famous televised speeches.

On January 10, Ben Ali offered a modest promise to calm the popular protests, which had at that point become fairly widespread, reaching much of Tunisia's urban coast. Ben Ali promised the establishment of three commissions of inquiry (Yousfi 2015: 72). One was called the "Higher Commission for Political Reform," the second the "Extortion and Repression Commission," and the third the "Embezzlement Commission" (ICG 2011: 14). All three were called into existence on January 13, 2011 by Prime Minister Ghannouchi,[36] but their chair and members were formally appointed only *after* the departure of Ben Ali, on February 18, 2011. Thus, legality and continuity prevailed over the logic of revolutionary ruptures; these bodies were decided by Ben Ali and RCD leaders, and had no teeth, so to say, as they were not thought of as decision-making bodies.

With the Decree-Laws of February 18,[37] a prominent lawyer, Yadh Ben Achour, who had resigned from the Constitutional Council in 1992, was tasked to lead the first commission. The second investigated the violence committed by the regime since December 17, 2010,

---

first caravan, that came from the south and center of the country, had the connecting, democratic elements. Michaël Ayari, security expert, interview in Florence, 05/28/2019.

[36] ICG (2016): 2. Yousfi (2015: 72) places the origin of these commission on January 10. An ICG report speaks of January 13, while Chouikha & Gobe (2015: 79) sustain that these commissions were proposed by the legal opposition on the morning of the fateful Friday, January 14. This does not alter the fact that these three bodies were established when Ben Ali and the RCD were still calling the shots.

[37] These decrees-laws (DL) replaced laws in the period that followed the dissolution of the legislative in February and the suspension of the 1959 Constitution on March 15, 2011 (Ben Achour & Ben Achour 2012: 720). DL 2011-6 deals with the Ben Achour Commission, DL 2011-7 with the RCD corruption accusations, and DL 2011-8 with the Bouderbala Commission. On all these procedural steps, see Ben Achour & Ben Achour (2012), Chouikha & Gobe (2015: 84), and ICG (2011).

and became known as the Bouderbala Commission, drawing its name from its leader, Tawfiq Bouderbala, a former president of the Tunisian League for Human Rights. The main player at this point was the Ben Achour Commission (also called at the time "Higher Commission for Political Reform"), in charge of preparing presidential elections.

However, another informal group, the January 14 Front, had also made a name for itself by issuing a similar demand. The group, made of leftist parties and activists, was formally established on January 20. It called for the dissolution of Tunisia's major political institutions, for example the parliament and the High Council of Justice (*Conseil supérieur de la magistrature*), and they demanded that an election of a new constituent assembly take place within 12 months (Gobe 2012: §4). For this group, no revolutionary legitimacy could be preserved outside the radical solution of *tabula rasa*: dismantling all the existing political institutions. Within weeks, additional powerful associations and parties adhered to the project. Segments of the UGTT and of the Bar Association, as well as two political parties, Mustapha Ben Jaafar's Ettakatol and Ennahda, became part of a larger project called the National Council for the Protection of the Revolution (NCPR), which was established on February 11. Gathering 28 organizations in total (Gobe 2012: §5), the NCPR positioned itself as a shadow government or counter-parliament (ICG 2011: 13), and the sole carrier of the revolutionary legitimacy. And unlike its competitor, Ghannouchi II, the NCPR required that all new official appointments be confirmed by way of a democratic process, with the consent of its members.

Two differences between the January 14 Front and the NCPR should be underlined at this point. The former was a reaction to the early 2011 protests and was following a radical Marxist agenda of clear-cut revolutionary change. The latter, the NCPR, can be considered a continuation of the October 18 Committee for Rights and Freedoms, the network that emerged in 2005 (Ottaway 2017: 94). It encompassed pretty much all opposition parties, Islamist and secular alike. It was therefore not party-oriented, but value-oriented: it asked what the future of Tunisia should be once Ben Ali and the RCD were no longer in power. This pre-commitment to alliance-building, less constraining than coalition-building, might explain why the reformist path was chosen once the NCPR later became an integral part of the Ben Achour Commission.

Rumors that the former security elites were plotting against the new Ministry of the Interior and the reluctance of Ghannouchi II to outlaw the RCD emboldened both the NCPR and new popular protests. Street pressure worked, since the government decided on February 21 to dissolve the RCD (ICG 2011: 17). The NCPR saw these protests as evidence that its demands were legitimate, and organized local antennas across the entire country. Organizers of the Qasba 2 and the NCPR called for a massive protest on Friday 25, with the slogan "*i'tissam hatta yasqut al-nizam*," "Sit-ins until the regime falls." With 100,000 people in Tunis, this was the largest demonstration during the entire revolutionary period (Gobe 2012: §6; ICG 2011: 17). Prime Minister Ghannouchi was replaced by Beji Caid Essebsi, a former minister under Bourguiba and a member of an old elite Tunis family whose status comes from its association with the Bey. His familiarity with Tunis' elite circles but distance from Ben Ali informed some of his executive decisions in 2011.

For Eric Gobe (2012), the victory of Qasba 2 was also the retreat of the *peuple acteur*. New arrangements were made by Essebsi and Mebazza to guarantee that there would be no interference from older RCD elites and to deliver on the demand for a timely election of a constituent assembly, first scheduled for July 24, then rescheduled to October 23 (Gobe 2012). But many of these decrees of Essebsi and Mebazza also worked to hollow out the demand for a direct, or at least vigorous, representation of the people and the NCPR in the interim bodies. Two instances clarify this.

The first case arose with a seemingly technical decision clarifying the powers of the interim president and of Prime Minister Essebsi. As we saw before, the legislative chambers had been suspended and their powers delegated to the executive. On March 23, the Decree-Law 14 suspended the 1959 Constitution (Ben Aissa 2016: 59), which was replaced by a new "Provisory Organization of the Public Authorities." The power to issue decrees became the exclusive domain of the presidency, only requiring a consultation with the broader government, with no parliamentary oversight (Ben Achour & Ben Achour 2012: 722). Many pre-revolution legal provisions continued to be in force, in particular Law No. 67-29 (passed on July 14, 1967) concerning the organization of the judiciary, the High Council of Justice, and laws on police deployment.[38]

---

[38] Hanlon (2016: 204) discusses the ambiguity of Law 1969-4, "Police Law," which allowed the police force to be used in a manner that contradicts basic democratic rights of assembly.

Legal frames of the past, including on issues of coercion and the exercise of justice, remained pretty much intact (Ben Aissa 2016: 56). The preamble of this Decree-Law also made clear that there could be no legitimacy from the streets or from the groups carrying the flag of the revolution: It stated that the Tunisian people are the sovereign and that this "sovereignty is to be exercised through *elected* representatives chosen in a direct, free and fair suffrage" (Ben Achour & Ben Achour 2012: 723, my emphasis). Furthermore, the preamble brackets all other procedures, declaring that the "will of the people during the 14 January 2011 revolution will express its full sovereignty within the frame of a new Constitution."[39] It is as if the political process moved in a single leap from January 14 to the future constitution, as if no conflicts could arise as to how to define this popular sovereignty and the path to drafting a new constitution.

The second case illustrates, in much more graphic and geographical terms, the forced crossroads of the post-Qasba 2 process. The names of the appointees to the aforementioned Higher Commission or Yadh Ben Achour Commission were published on March 15. The appointment of some members occurred without consultations, which created a malaise (ICG 2011: 19). The Higher Commission was now called the Higher Authority for the Realization of the Objectives of the Revolution, Political Reform and Democratic Transition, in short HAROR. In its first session, on March 17, it counted 71 members and was criticized for its lack of representativity. It was composed of jurists and political figures from the urban coastal area: It entailed almost no representatives of the interior and no youths (Gobe 2012: §11). The NCPR added pressure on the Higher Authority to modify its membership, which it did on April 7, adding 84 new members corresponding to these underrepresented groups and regions, as well as 12 new parties, 18 trade union and associations leaders, and families of martyrs from the revolution (Gobe 2012: §11). This round of inclusion also proved to be the NCPR's own crossroad: Some were co-opted into the extended Higher Authority, since it was guaranteed to have powers akin to those of a parliament, with oversight over the executive and the possibility of proposing new

---

[39] Ben Achour & Ben Achour (2012: 723). The full decree-law (DL), made of the preamble and 19 articles, was published in the Official Journal (JORT) on March 25, 2011, p. 363.

decree-laws. Other members of the NCPR refused to join (ICG 2011: 20).

This negotiation to expand the Higher Authority did not occur under the direct pressure from the street or the two Qasba sit-ins, but out of the spirit of concertation within the NCPR and the actors involved in the October 18 Committee. From April onwards, one cannot find any more national demands based on ideas of *tabula rasa* and the sole logic of revolutionary legitimacy. All new decisions were based on the mechanisms that flowed from the legality and reformist principles of institutional compromises: the establishment of the High Electoral Committee (ISIE, *Instance supérieure indépendante pour les élections*), the preparation of the October elections, and the reform allowing simple registration of associations were all conducted by formal organizations or done with a view on the parties' interests, with increasingly tokenistic representation afforded to the aggrieved populations that had driven the Uprisings.[40] Furthermore, the core of the security reforms was handled by people who, if not Ben Ali insiders, had been working at the heart of security institutions during the preceding decades: For example, Caid Essebsi and Fu'ad Mebazza had both been Interior or Defense ministers, and their decisions had little form of concertation with the camp of the revolutionary rupture.[41]

The Tunisian transition was now evolving on the common principles of the October 18 Committee: protected freedoms, legalization of all political parties, and amnesty for political prisoners. The spirit of this broad consensus provided the basis for the Republican Pact that the Higher Authority adopted in June 2011, and which has been said to be beneficial for the later writing of a new constitution. Despite periods where the secular–Islamist polarization was strong, Ennahda accepted all the principles of the Republican Pact and showed an overall willingness to act in alliance with other political formations, assuaging the fears of secularist Tunisians that Islamists would seek power on their own (Ottaway 2017: 82).

We can now turn to the second question, the assessment of the security reforms, where we will identify a similar modest movement

---

[40] For example, political parties chose the modality of elections with proportional representation as a way to undermine the expected hegemony of Ennahda (Gobe 2012: §15). On electoral politics, see Gana & Van Hamme (2016) and Ottaway (2017: 77–81).

[41] Moncef Kartas, academic, interview in New York, 11/17/2019.

of popular pressure expressing a desire for a revolutionary rupture and a gradual regrouping of the security establishment.

"Security" is a loose term that encompasses army and police, and matters pertaining to ministries of the Interior and Defense. But as we saw in Chapter 2, presidential guards, special units under the direct command of the Presidency, have also deepened the control of the *mukhabarat* over state and population. In Tunisia, the Army is said to have protected the revolution and to have allowed the neutralization of the rogue security leaders who worked as the core protection around Ben Ali until January 14. While there is some truth to those assertions, the reality is more complex.

The Army had been historically sidelined under Ben Ali, for fear that it could organize a coup against him, just like he did against former president Bourguiba in November 1987. The Ministry of the Interior and Presidential Guards, who reported directly to Carthage, the presidential Palace, benefited from greater financial support than their military counterpart. Thus, when the Army was asked to crush the protests and thus help the police on January 10, 2011, old resentments quickly resurfaced. The rather small army, with only about 18,000 soldiers, plus 20,000 staff, and less key equipment than the other security forces,[42] wondered why the National Guard and National Security Police, whose ranks were then publicly estimated to reach 150,000 persons (ICG 2011: 11), were not able to handle the wave of protests. The military, whose only real deployment had been peace-security missions in Africa with the UN, did not want to take sudden risks for a president who had clipped its wings and given the best benefits to the 5,000 soldiers of the Presidential Guard, who were under the command of the closest security person that Ben Ali trusted, Ali Seriati (ICG 2011: 11). As Risa Brooks (2016: 112) puts it, "A military with little investment in the regime will also have little incentive to come to its defense."

The head of the Army, Rachid Ammar, is said to have refused Seriati's order to shoot the protestors on January 14. In reality, he only ordered his soldiers to put on a red beret instead of protective helmets: both the Army and the National Guard (*haris watani*) have

---

[42] The Army controlled only 4 of the 12 helicopters in the Tunis area, the rest being deployed by the police (Ministry of the Interior) and Presidential Guards (ICG 2011: 11).

green uniforms, but by instructing Army soldiers to don red berets, Ammar could be sure that his units could be distinguished and would be *seen* as siding with the protestors (Jebnoun 2014). In short, Ammar and the Army took advantage of a fluid and unclear situation after the departure of Ben Ali to settle some scores with old foes. It is Seriati who brought Ben Ali to Tunis airport, where he departed to Saudi Arabia, and it is Seriati who acted as the general of the generals (ICG 2011: 11) even if he had no authority to give orders to the Army or to the regular police forces (who are under the command of the Ministry of the Interior). The Army proceeded to arrest Seriati immediately, but they did not notify the public of his arrest, allowing rumors to spread about him, saying that he had access to weapons, or that he had fled to Libya to get support to crush popular rebellions.[43] By doing this the Army could reap enormous political advantage by being perceived as the protector of the "revolution" while maneuvering to discredit the vast security networks of Ben Ali within the Presidency and in the Ministry of the Interior. With Ben Ali and Seriati out of the picture, these "deep security state" bodies were headless and left pitted one against the other with no one able to instill centralized order.

Noureddine Jebnoun's (2014) fascinating study shows that it was less a "refusal" to take orders from the Army than it was the broken chain of communication among key security figures and the military (Presidential Guards, ministries of Defense and the Interior, and different domestic security organizations) that explained the rather peaceful transition. But the Army was also involved in preventing the collapse of key state institutions and did resort to lethal force when necessary. For example, between January 14 and the end of Qasba 2 on February 27, the Army killed more civilians than the police (respectively 37 and 24) (Bou Nassif 2015: 81). It also used its military tribunal with no coordination with civilian tribunals, something that would in part backfire for the quality of the democratic reforms of the security sector, as we will see in Chapter 6.

So what did the post-Ben Ali governments manage to do to bring democratic accountability on these various security networks? We can identify four types of measures: removals; arrests; administrative reforms; and new hires. But all show some lasting influences of Ben

---

[43] Kartas, interview, 11/17/2019. On rumors spreading among the population, see Allal (2011: 59).

Ali security personnel, leading to rather modest results (Sayigh 2015: 16).

First, there were different waves of removal of RCD and top-brass security leaders. Prime Minister Ghannouchi removed Ahmed Fréa and Mohammad Jegham, ministers of the Interior and of Defense, respectively, on January 27. On February 1, the new Minister of the Interior, Farhat Rajhi, conducted a mini-purge, with 34 high security officers, among which were the heads of National, General, and Presidential Security, pensioned.[44] There were also institutional reshufflings. On March 7, the State Security Department, which was "especially dreaded by the population," was formally abolished (Brooks 2016: 118). This was accompanied by the promise in the Ministry of the Interior to end "all forms of organization akin to a 'political police,' be it in its objectives or practices" (Gobe 2012: fn. 48). A month into the Essebsi government, Rajhi was replaced by Habib Essid as Interior Minister, a person who was more palatable to the establishment than Rajhi.[45] By April, another 50 cadres were fired.[46] Up to 4,000 personnel from the Presidential Guard were said to have been dismissed after the revolution (Hanlon 2016: 197).

Second, a few arrests and trials were organized during the first few months of the new government's rule. However, these sentences never exceeded a few years.[47] Abdallah Kallel, a high dignitary of the RCD, former interior minister between 1991 and 1995 and 1999 to 2001, and president of the upper parliamentary chamber, was arrested in March 2011 for syphoning off public and RCD funding. He was then deferred to a military tribunal for his involvement in the Barakat Al-Sahel affair (see Chapter 2), where he was sentenced to four years in prison. Ali Seriati was arrested for helping Ben Ali flee the country, and

---

[44] Gobe (2012: 47) and Kartas (2014: 381); www.france24.com/fr/20110202-tunisie-ministre-interieur-limoge-responsables-securite-incidents-milices. Sayigh (2015: 17) lifts that number to 42 senior Ministry of the Interior officials put in mandatory retirement, including 26 members of National Security.

[45] Habib Essid had been *chef de cabinet* of the hardline anti-Islamist Interior Minister Abdallah Kallel under Ben Ali. He "wielded considerable influence among the informal networks within the ministry and the security sector in general" (Sayigh 2015: 18).

[46] Kartas, interview, 11/17/2019.

[47] Sayigh (2015: 25) mentions other cases (two former interior ministers, five directors general of the Ministry, and several mid-ranking and senior security officers) of security officials put on trial – by military courts – but their sentences were lowered on appeal in summer 2012.

later charged by two military tribunals for leading the repression in Kasserine, Tala, and Greater Tunis during the revolution. He was sentenced to 20 years in prison.

Third, administrative measures were taken in summer 2011 to relax the grip of the security custodianship. The Higher Authority managed to set the new Election Committee, the ISIE, free from interference by the Ministry of the Interior, making the electoral process a truly independent process with no "security" interference (Ben Achour & Ben Achour 2012: 725). In July, Lazhar Akrémi, a delegate for reforms in the Ministry of the Interior, proposed a series of measures to reform the police into a public service rather than a wholly repressive tool. The proposal recommended training, or a peaceful re-booting of security staff, and opened internal dialogue between newly formed police syndicates and the Ministry (Gobe 2012: §37), a topic to which we will return. But the most important reforms took place only after the technocrat government of Mehdi Jomaa in January 2014 succeeded the joint rule of three parties, the Troika, who governed Tunisia after the October 2011 elections. It is in this context that Ridha Sfar, State Secretary for Security Affairs, initiated the most substantial administrative reform since the revolution.[48] The Directorate General in charge of National Security was short-circuited, and Sfar established instead an inter-ministerial structure, coordinating, and thus forcing, the different units to open further.[49]

Fourth, and finally, new staff and fresh, non-partisan blood was brought in to replace the demoted persons at the start of the revolution. On February 1, seven new heads were hired to lead National Security departments, with ranks of DG, *directeurs généraux*. This came after rogue RCD security members within the Ministry of the Interior had stormed and threatened Minister Rajhi and Army Chief of Staff Ammar on January 27, 2011 (ICG 2011: 16). To the surprise of everybody, even to the most informed security experts, it turned out that the total staff on the Ministry payroll was actually way less numerous than the figure of 140,000 to 200,000 that were estimated. In reality only 49,000 police officers were on the payroll (Brooks 2016: 118). This meant that staff there were over-worked, doing double, if

---

[48] Moncef Kartas is not sure whether the reform had fully developed plans *and* the capacities to implement the proposed changes. Email communication with author, 09/16/2020.
[49] Kartas, interview, 11/17/2019.

not triple shifts, and that more employees were needed to meet the international policing standards. Twelve-thousand new recruits were rushed to training in the months that followed the revolution. But this new cohort received only a superficial training and did not receive enough attention to profoundly alter the organizational culture (Hanlon 2016: 198).

In comparison with Yemen, which undertook staff removal, reshuffling, and inter-ministerial restructuring only a year after the start of the protests, the Tunisian security sector underwent very quick reforms. Arguably, many of the measures discussed above were a direct result of the street pressure and of *vis populi*, and the positive impact of these decisions could be felt almost immediately in civic life in the Maghreban country.[50] It would, however, be misleading to consider these changes revolutionary ones. They were partial reforms with mixed results and a lack of detailed planning, and quite rapidly, some regrouping at the top undid the governmental reforms that had been introduced in response to the sit-ins of Qasba 1 and 2.[51]

The mixed blessings of the first security measures pertain to the military tribunals and to the establishment of syndicates for police and internal security officers and staff (ICG 2015). The application of military jurisdiction (we will remember that the Army was the institution that remained untouched during the revolution) eventually backfired: The accused were able to question the legality of these tribunals used to try non-military personnel or accused of charges that should have been brought to a normal, civilian court. A number of members of the Ministry of the Interior managed to escape accusations in the following years on these grounds.[52]

Political priority shifted away from security reforms with the October 2011 elections. A coalition of the three largest parties, Ennahda, the CPR, and Ettakatol, emerged from the ballot box and

---

[50] On top of the full independence guaranteed to the ISIE, the intimidation of the more radical fringes of the UGTT and labor movements ceased: freedom guaranteed to hitherto illegal political parties in March meant that radical activists in the labor movement and in the NCPR were free to discuss publicly their political lines (Gobe 2012: fn. 32).

[51] Kartas speaks of the security reform as a "remaining aspiration," abandoned as it was by political parties and advocacy NGOs (Kartas 2014: 380).

[52] Kartas, interview, 11/17/2019. See also Brooks (2016: 125) for a discussion of how the competence and independence of these military tribunals were questioned.

replaced Essebsi and Mebazza as interim authorities. Three co-presidents were distributed among the three largest parties of the Constituent National Assembly, or ANC: Moncef Marzouki, from the CPR, the party with most second seats, became President of the Republic; Mustafa Ben Jaafar, from Ettakatol, the third party, was in charge of the ANC Presidency; and Hamadi Jebali, from Ennahda, the party which won the plurality of the vote, became Prime Minister. The ANC passed a temporary or mini-constitution on December 16, 2011 (_Loi-Constitutionnelle_ 2011-6) (ICG 2016: 5, fn. 22). The mini-constitution set the parameters for the distribution of power across the ANC, which eventually came to exceed a one-year time-limit restricting its mandate, and went to function instead both as a constituent assembly and as a parliament, checking the work of the government.[53]

Polarization across parties and between the Troika and the opposition surged rapidly after the elections. Many feared that Ennahda could actually run the country as it pleased because the mini-constitution handed real power to the Prime Minister, a Nahdaoui.[54] Furthermore, the ANC needed a two-thirds vote to topple the government, which meant that the Prime Minister could govern even without a majority (Gobe 2012). All these agreements, pushed for by the Troika, put an end to the politics of broad consensus that had characterized the transition since the installation of an expanded Higher Authority.

Participation in the elections had been good, but not stellar, a sign that "the people" had grown tired of the games of political parties. Fifty-two percent of the population registered for the election, and the ISIE managed to guarantee a free and fair election, with parity between men and women on each election list and guaranteed eligibility and voting rights for all Tunisians, whether resident in Tunisia or abroad (Ben Achour & Ben Achour 2012: 724–725). The lowest rates of voluntary voter registration were from the historically marginalized regions, Tataouine (39%), followed by the governorate of Jendouba (41.95%), and Medenine (44.10%). Within the Greater Tunis area, the

---

[53] The mechanism for the approbation of this new constitution was based on two types of vote: article by article (majority) and then a final global vote: if there were not two-thirds in support of the final text, then there would be a popular referendum (Gobe 2012: fn. 55).

[54] Under this transitory or mini-constitution, the President would have mostly ceremonial responsibilities.

poorest sector of the capital city, Tunis 1, had a registration rate of 41.26% (Gobe 2012: §40). The geography of the results was telling: Ennahda obtained 89 seats out of 217, and was thus the largest national party. Yet, in the zones where the revolution started, the Islamist party was at its lowest and was largely overtaken by independent lists running as the "Popular Petition" (*al-'arida al-sha'abiyya*). Gobe (2012: fn. 61) noted that the voters from the central regions had been drawn to Hechmi Hamdi, who vocalized their frustration against the Sahelian elites. The second largest party in the ANC was the CPR, whom many saw as representing the historical line of nationalist leader Salah Ben Youssef. They won 29 seats, securing them almost entirely in the south. The third largest party was Ettakatol, which obtained 20 seats, mostly in the coastal areas (Sahel), netting the support of the urban voters with higher education (Gobe 2012). The Troika was not simply a coalition of Islamist and secular (CPR and Ettakatol) parties, it also covered smaller and rural regions, underwriting a claim to national representation, and hence to legitimacy, which no other party alliance could have produced.

The developments after the formation of the Troika in December 2011 led to very opaque moves. Ennahda, the party that won most seats in the Constitutional National Assembly (ANC), was leading the government and took over the Ministry of the Interior. To offer some guarantees to other factions, the party retained Habib Essid, the Interior Minister since March 27, 2011, in the capacity of Security Advisor to Prime Minister Hamadi Jebali. The fear for most secular parties was that Ennahda would use its governing role to seek vengeance for decades of torture, arrest, and repression against the Islamist movement. While Ennahda had an ambiguous attitude towards violence, as we will discuss in the next page, it did not enact any significant security reforms, neither deepening the trend towards more democratic accountability of the security forces initiated in 2011 nor stopping these developments. The new Interior Minister, Ali Larayedh (Ennahda) was in a tense standoff with the police syndicates,[55] who were known for harboring strong anti-Islamist views.

---

[55] The police unions are a direct by-product of the revolution. They committed to foster a "climate of trust between citizens and security forces" and to operate as a "republican police force" (Gobe 2012: fn. 49 and 50). The two main syndicates are the SFDGUI (from its French acronym, for Syndicate for Officers of the General Directorate of Intervention Units), created in July 2011, and the SNSFI (National Syndicate of the Forces of Internal Security), established in

The ANC had a slow start in its work drafting a new constitution. Pressing political matters demanded the Troika's attention, and the expressive dynamic of the revolution seemed to give way to monotonous governmental work, reinforcing the fear that Ennahda and its allies were more concerned with entrenching their political position than the democratic process anchored in the demands of 2011. Now Ennahda was claiming that the real legitimacy was not that of the street, nor of the "revolutionary actors," but that of the ballot box (Gobe & Chouikha 2014: §§6, 9, 39). As the strongest national party, Ennahda felt it could deflect all the criticism, something it did with hubris during the last months of 2012 and into the beginning of 2013.

Let us now discuss the third sub-question on the limits of reforms and *vis populi* in Tunisia. How did people respond to those acts of violence committed by Islamists, Salafists, and popular committees, in short, by non-state actors? How did coalitions and parties that had been part of the effort of *vis populi* respond to the challenges of targeted killings or threats against individuals and institutions? How did Ennhahda minimize violent threats to political order in Tunisia?

Tunisia, like Yemen, has faced uphill economic difficulties since 2011 as a result of halted economic production following labor strikes and a sudden drop of touristic activities associated with an increase in acts of violence by growing Salafi-jihadi groups. By February of 2011, there were also individuals and non-state actors committing acts of violence, looting, and ransoming on highways, alongside mass attempts to cross the Mediterranean and cross-border smuggling; these activities made it difficult for governing bodies to address the most pressing reforms. And the revolutionary politics cast a mysterious fog over the intentions underlying the violence and thefts. But two clusters of non-state violence occupied the attention of the Tunisian public and of the new governing coalition from the summer of 2011 onwards: the Salafist insurrection and the so-called Leagues for the Protection of the Revolution (LPR). And Ennahda, who might have had the capacity to intercede as the main governing party, approached the situation with indifference, leading these two, ill-matched groups to

May 2011. The former counted 23,000 members in 2015, including the Presidential Guard union, and the latter 8,000 members. For some, the rapid and robust organization of these syndicates has played a significant part in slowing down the pace or calls for transitional justice, something we will discuss in Chapter 6.

reach a dangerous tipping point during the summer of 2013, as we will see later.

"Salafi" is the name given to a group of puritanical Islamists calling on Muslims to follow the teachings of the first community of believers. In public discourse, in particular by governmental forces, "Salafis" are typically associated with "terrorism," but this rhetoric hides a variety of actors. They are described as scripturalists, and many Salafis in the Arab Middle East follow a quietist path (Meijer 2014: 635; Bonnefoy 2011). In Tunisia, the Salafi network is made of a quietist branch and of activist groups, one of which was led by Seifallah Ben Hassine, better known as Abu Iyad. The spread of Salafi ideas should be read in mundane sociological terms: many of its adherents are very young individuals, mostly male, who grew up in the poorest of urban peripheries (Merone 2015; 2016). The largest Salafi movement was Ansar Al-Sharia, not to be confused with the Yemeni version, a sub-group of Al-Qaeda. The Tunisian Ansar Al-Sharia (AS-T) was established in April 2011, in the wake of the liberalization of political parties (ICG 2013b: 31, fn. 66; Torelli, Merone, & Cavatorta 2012). Tunisian Salafism has strong domestic roots, with a base in poor neighborhoods characterized by the presence of very few political structures, parties, or associations. Most self-declared Salafists after 2011 had been political prisoners jailed under the anti-terrorist legislation of Ben Ali and released in March 2011 as part of the political amnesty (Merone & Cavatorta 2012). A study on political prisoners at the time of revolution revealed that nearly half of them are between 25 and 30 years of age (48% of the total), and 39% are working class (Merone 2015). It is from these milieus that Salafis grew, and this generational profile (many who grew up with absent parents who had been themselves imprisoned for their militancy within the ancestor of Ennahda, the MTI) explains why the Salafis and Nahdaouis have a love–hate relationship: The latter recognize the plea of the younger Salafis, but in a paternalistic manner. Salafi youths also distrust the pragmatic approach of Ennahda and its older generations in charge, willing to strike an alliance with a political formation such as Nidaa Tounes (Sigillò 2016: 97).

Salafis were a source of violence and potentially also of political chaos with which Ennahda had to deal. Salafis destroyed the Afric-Art cinema in Tunis in June and a couple of weeks before the elections in October, 200 Salafis tried to torch down Nessma TV after the screening of the film *Persepolis* (Ottaway 2017: 102; ICG 2013b: 2).

Other episodes in 2012 showed that Ennahda was not willing to do much to curb the aggressive activism of the Salafis. On numerous occasions, the Salafis planted their black flag, first at La Manouba University on March 7, 2012 and later on Avenue Bourguiba at the heart of the capital on March 25 (ICG 2013b: 2). They clashed with trade unionists in Sfax on March 11, and trashed a hotel selling alcohol in Jendouba in May (ICG 2013b: 3). The Troika government remained largely inactive and did very little to contain these Salafi attacks. Ennahda hesitated to crack down on Salafis for fear that it would give them an aura of martyrdom. Others accused the more conservative fringe of Ennahda of playing a double game of criticizing the Salafis but letting them act freely, since Ennahda also harbors very conservative members, close to the scripturalist position of AS-T.

The situation reached a point of no-return when two leftist leaders were gunned down by unknown assailants who were thought to be Salafi militants: Choukri Belaid on February 6, and Mohamed Brahmi, on July 25, 2013 (Yousfi 2015: 207). The episodes resonated with other instances where Ennahda showed too much leniency toward violent actions committed by the LPR.

These LPR were heirs of protection committees that citizens organized spontaneously in their neighborhoods or towns throughout the country. They emerged after the police, having realized that Ben Ali's system had crumbled, vanished. The Army being spread thin after January 14, basic security could not be guaranteed everywhere, and thus people organized their own police of sorts. These were tailored to local realities: in some places they were made of people of the neighborhoods; in other places, like in the capital, it was organized by the wealthier population paying people to patrol the streets; or it was made up of protestors from outside cities who were offered a shelter on top of the sit-ins in Qasba, and were given food for helping to secure a given neighborhood at night.[56]

The LPR were originally apolitical, marked by the same converging and blending effects as the Uprisings. With the reformist–revolutionary fronts solidifying during the period from January 17 to April 7, 2011, that is, from Qasba 1 until the expansion of the Higher Authority to 155 members and the thus de facto end of the NCPR (see ICG 2011: 20), these LPRs were invested in by the Tunisian Workers' Communist

---

[56] Anis Khenissi, youth activist, NGO leader, interview in Medenine, 01/04/2016. Amira Yahyaoui, NGO leader, interview in Tunis, 05/30/2016.

Party (PCOT), which hoped to capitalize on the informal, revolution-
ary groupings. But with Ennahda legalized in March, it was the
Islamists who got a better footing in these LPRs and gradually sur-
passed the PCOT's influence (Chouikha & Gobe 2013: §59).
Benefiting from cells (re-)activitated throughout the country,
Ennahda became the most influential political party in the LPR.

The initial function of these leagues, self-protection in light of the
collapse or strategic retreat of the police forces, stopped with the stabil-
ization of the country, now on a path of steady reforms. As a result, some
ceased to function, but two new objectives were said to take root in the
remaining groups. Some were active in petty crime (selling alcohol,
racketeering, connections with contraband networks), while others
would function as an indirect arm of one political faction or another
and found work intimidating political rivals. Only a tiny minority of
these leagues were ever formally registered as associations.[57]

In 2012, the leagues close to the Islamists were involved in some acts
of violence. Secular opposition parties, journalists, and the UGTT were
the main target of these LPRs. Two violent episodes functioned as
a lightning rod among Tunisians on the *dérive*, dangers that LPRs
now out of control represented for democratic life. On October 18,
2012, under rather murky circumstances, the coordinator of Nidaa
Tounes,[58] Lotfi Nagdh, was killed during clashes with members of the
Tataouine LPR (Chouikha & Gobe 2013: §§8, 21; Cherif 2013). The
silence of the government generated national outrage. The episode in
Siliana, where a majority of people retreated from the town (discussed
in Chapter 3), occurred in this ebullient context. The people of Siliana
refused the repressive baton and buckshot of the state,[59] but they also

---

[57] An umbrella organization at the national level was registered formally in
June 2012, but only a few local branches did register, in Kairouan and in Gabes
(Chouikha & Gobe 2013: fn. 67). The LPR of Kram was known for its brutal
and Islamist leaning (Cherif 2013), and those in Ettadhamen, Zahra, and
Hamam Ennef all acted illegally. See Nawaat (2013).

[58] During the spring of 2012, a coalition of secularist politicians established Nidaa
Tounes ("The Call of Tunis") under the leadership of Essebsi. This new political
formation, which included old regime people, captured the support of many
deputies of the ANC who were disillusioned with the Troika and the slow pace
of the constitutional work.

[59] Hanlon (2016: 201–202) speaks of the Siliana birdshot as "an improvement,"
since the state did not use live ammunition. I think the present analysis, with the
relational and contextual information, shows that the improvement is *not* the
use of buckshot, but the confident and positive attitude of the people in Siliana.

never engaged with the instrumental use of violence by the LPR: they preferred a non-violent and direct way of expressing their own forms of self-representation and redefined new contours of *vis populi* as a praxis. Siliana thus acquires more relevance in a context where some actors engaged in killings and physical destruction.

Another case, a few days later on December 4, involved a Tunis branch of the LPRs. On that day, the UGTT held an annual nationwide commemoration in remembrance of the assassination in 1952 of its founder, Ferhat Hached. The Tunis gathering, which took place in front of the UGTT main office near the old town, was assaulted by members of the League, leaving 26 injured people (Nawaat 2013). From that moment on, the UGTT and other parties, such as Ettakatol, called for the systematic dismantling of these LPRs; likewise, a small Islamist party with 10 members in the ANC and led by Nejib Hosni, also called for the dissolution of all the LPRs (Gobe & Chouikha 2014: §§15, 17). Again, the coordinated response by various formal and informal actors, like the parties and the UGTT, indicated that violence was not acceptable.

The regional crisis in July 2013, when a military coup occurred in Egypt, forced Ennahda and the Troika to change course of action. Ennahda knew that it had no other choice but to relinquish power and accept the transition to a technocratic government. The Egyptian Armed Forces, under the guidance of its commander in chief, Abdel Fattah El-Sisi, led a coup against President Morsi, from the Muslim Brotherhood, on July 3, 2013, sending a clear signal to all Islamist parties in the Arab world that their days at the helm could be numbered. The massacre that occurred in Cairo on August 14 when several hundred Morsi supporters were killed in Rabi'a Square more-or-less coincided with rumors of a possible coup by the security and armed forces in Tunisia against Ennahda. This added pressure to the Ennahda leadership and its coalition partners, Moncef Marzouki and Mustapha Ben Jaafar.

The Troika bowed to the combined pressure of opposition parties, inside and outside of the ANC,[60] and Tunisians resumed mass protests and sit-ins in front of the Bardo, the seat of the Parliament. In August, the

---

[60] On July 26, a National Front (FNS, Front du Salut National) was established between Nidaa Tounes and the Popular Front. It called for the formation of a National Salvation government and a speedy end to the constitution drafting (Chouikha & Gobe 2015: 95).

Ministry of the Interior outlawed the Salafi Ansar Al-Sharia-Tunisia party (Gobe & Chouikha 2014: §35). To make clear that he would not be held hostage to Ennahda's ambiguous formulations in the draft constitution of April and June 2013, Mustafa Ben Jaafar suspended work on the constitution.[61] Moncef Marzouki also engaged with civil society actors to form a national dialogue and discuss ways to wrap up the work of the ANC in a cross-partisan sprit, and bring calm to a tense security situation in the country. This national dialogue, not to be confused with the Yemeni NDC, became known as the Quartet, and was composed of an alliance between the UGTT, the Tunisian Confederation of Industry, Trade, and Handicrafts (UTICA), the Tunisian Human Rights League (LTDH), and the Tunisian Order of Lawyers. After weeks of negotiations, the Quartet and the Troika agreed on a roadmap that led to the end of the constitutional drafting process and the formation of a technocratic government in January 2014.

After very tense summer months in 2013, a reestablished sense of consensus and trust, thanks to the Quartet, allowed parties to set aside their differences. Ennahda gave up more assertive formulations for key articles of the constitution. The new Constitution was adopted with a crushing majority of 200 votes in favor, four abstentions, and twelve opposed on January 26, 2014 (Ottaway 2017: 109). Armed forces and internal security forces became constitutionally mandated to act "in conformity with the law and in the service of the public interest," with "total impartiality," and to ensure the "respect of freedoms" (articles 17, 18, and 19).

A new Prime Minister, Mehdi Jomaa, took charge of a technocratic government, with Ennahda now out of power. Parliamentary and presidential elections followed in October and November 2014. An intense presidential campaign opposed the incumbent Moncef Marzouki to Essebsi, the leader of Nidaa Tounes. Essebsi won in the second round. With his move to the Carthage Palace the security reform process, already on pause when Ennahda was caught in a standoff with the police unions, slowed down definitively. Two appointees of President Essebsi were responsible for this: Rafik

---

[61] The draft version of April 22, 2013 generated a heated debate on the absence of reference to freedom of consciousness (Gobe & Chouikha 2014: §24). The June 1 version included a controversial reference to gender complementarity instead of equality. On an assessment of the final draft of January 2014, see Gobe & Chouikha (2014: §27).

Chelli, the new State Secretary for Security Affairs, and Abderrahmane Belhaj Ali, assigned to a function that had been previously discontinued, the Directorate General of National Security. Belhaj Ali, who served before the revolution in the Presidential Guard, made a significant come-back under the presidency of Essebsi. He allowed many of the pensioned security officials who worked under Ben Ali back into service.[62] The reforms introduced by Ridha Sfar, State Secretary for Security Affairs, were also cut short after December 2014. The years 2014–2015 saw a gradual regrouping of old RCD and key security figures. Ali Seriati's sentence to 20 years in prison was reduced on appeal to a period of three years, and by May 2014, he was already free.[63] Eighty judges dismissed during the revolution were later reinstated after having successfully demonstrated the illegality of their dismissals (Ben Aissa 2016: 60–62). The lack of pressure from political parties and very few legislative initiatives to force the transparency and democratic accountability of security institutions allowed security actors to circumvent reforms, to re-organize, and to defy, ultimately, civilian control (Kartas 2014: 374, 384).

4.4 Conclusion: *Vis Populi* as a Law-Making Mechanism?

What can we learn from the comparison between Tunisia and Yemen? By 2013, the countries are on somewhat similar paths: both have avoided the pitfalls of civil war (unlike in Syria or Libya) and of a total military crackdown on democratic protests (as in Bahrain or Egypt), with various informal coalitions managing to get their voices heard and to continue demands for greater democratic accountability of the political system and of the institutions of coercion to the people. They have both engaged with some reforms in the security sector (with varying success), and both "transitions" have rapidly bracketed demands for revolutionary breaks or *tabula rasa*, preferring an incremental path of reforms.

Yemen would soon precipitate into a civil, then a regional war, and Part III will highlight reasons why the two countries' paths diverged. But what kept Yemen and Tunisia fundamentally on par and on the path to

---

[62] Kartas, interview, 11/17/2019. Kartas believes that at least 40 (out of 48) are re-integrated under Chelli and Belhaj Ali.

[63] Former Interior Minister Abdallah Kallel was freed in July 2013 (his original four-year sentence had already been reduced to two years).

some democratic reform has been the formation of a new collective imaginary, the force of *vis populi*, and the double movements of the popular protests that refused recourse to killings and violence. This "permanent repository of resistance and repertoires of contention" (Alwazir 2016: 186) has been a force with which Tunisian and Yemeni political elites have had to reckon on multiple occasions. Security reforms may have not gone far enough, but at least the pressure never ceased, like it did in Egypt when protesters too readily accepted the Army as the guarantor of the transition.[64] In terms of political representation, informalism promoted by non-party actors generated innovative inputs, rooted in fluid and multi-directional spaces of participation. That has meant that these informal coalitions of protestors should be consulted, and are considered just as valid a source of political representation as established political parties, trade unions, etc. The successful intervention of the Quartet in Tunisia and the refusal of the people in Siliana to respond to unjust repression were instances in which informalism charted a path forward, while in Yemen, the March of Life or the use of specific locations (e.g. Taiz) to assemble different constituencies have preserved important spaces for civic cooperation. The stubborn, yet non-violent requests for more political representation from the interior in Tunisia (with regions getting access to the HAROR) and from Huthi and Hiraki militants in Yemen showed how the "people" articulated an awareness of space that rejected past (colonial and post-independence) spaces or tropes of marginalization.

The next chapters will deal with the political relevance of these imaginary spaces, and show how these would lead to either open conflict, as in Yemen, or to a redeployment of older elites, in Tunisia. The battle around decentralization will constitute the new phase of the dialectic of state–society relations in the two countries in question. It will also test the limits of informalism.

As we wrapped up Part I with a theoretical consideration on the nexus civility–citizenship, I would now like to draw lessons from the

---

[64] El-Raggal offers an analysis of the democratic scrutiny over surveillance institutions in Egypt. He shows how the "main security and intelligence apparatus," the State Security Investigation Service (SSIS), was stormed by protestors in the first weeks of 2011, an event that sadly produced new alienation for Egyptians who handed SSIS files to the Army, rather than to new civilian bodies (El-Raggal 2019). In Egypt the pressure of informal politics ceased too soon.

empirical material, with some theoretical reflections on violence. This time, I would like to use the metaphor of the Moebius strip to pause and ponder the actual interconnections between various parts of the world, so that social and political theory can learn from, and be enriched by, the historical events of the 2011 Arab Uprisings. The thesis is that Arab citizens generated a new collective politics *around* violence, rather than engaging directly *with* violence, which can enrich the existing debates between democratic theory and violence.

My contention regarding the democratic potential of the protests described so far is that the actions and praxis of the "people" or of the "multitude" combine, rather than contrast, law-preserving and law-making. In their manifestation of unity, the people recall that they are meant to be the sovereign, and by demonstrating their force and restlessness in confronting the illegitimate use of coercion by "the state" or incumbent regime, they indicate ways in which the means of coercion could be re-organized. As we have seen from examples in Tunisia and Yemen, the "people" *suggest* self-limiting or restraining power in *symbolic representations* (slogans, drawings, stencils, marches, and other informal actions) but *enact* direct political representation in action. They criticize the use of violence by state entities but refuse to perpetrate physical destruction (except on buildings, police files) or the killings of persons. *Vis populi* is the force, the will of the people, not the violence of the people. If and when destructive violence did occur in Yemen (thugs employed by former president Saleh to beat peaceful protestors) and Tunisia (LPR actions in 2012, Salafi violence), the assembled masses refused to condone these actions and expressed a firm commitment to non-violence. In a situation of looming violence (e.g. the possibility of a military coup in the summer of 2013 in Tunisia), informal alliances showed resilience and demonstrated a pluralist commitment to peacefully negotiating a way out of a crisis.[65]

The Tunisian Quartet brought gravitas to the situation and in 2015 was awarded the Nobel Peace Prize for its "decisive contribution to the building of a pluralistic democracy in Tunisia in the wake of the [2011]

---

[65] The July 2013 coup in Egypt, after the mass petition organized by the *Tamarrod*, cannot be described as an expression of the *vis populi*, since civilian actors collectively abandoned political responsibility to the military and allowed violence to be used directly against a very large portion of the population in support of the Freedom and Justice Party and the Muslim Brotherhood.

revolution."[66] But one should never forget that the Quartet was just an expression of the principle established in early January 2011 in order to topple Ben Ali: an informal alliance of quite different political actors that managed to come together and press collectively for change. Without the creativity and stubbornness of various segments of Tunisian society that stood behind all the revolutionary and reformist pressure in early 2011 and which foregrounded and inspired more inclusive mechanisms of representation, the Quartet might never have been able to achieve what it did in 2013.

[66] Taken from the official press release by the Nobel Committee, which qualifies 2011 as the "Jasmin revolution." See www.nobelprize.org/prizes/peace/2015/press-release/. For a criticism, see https://publicseminar.org/2015/10/just-a-peaceful-quartet/.

PART III

Embattled Revolutionary Legacies (2014–2021)

Introduction

Courte and *longue durées* interlink again for this last part of the book, which brings us all the way to the present. As the partisan version of the song *Bella Ciao* recedes in the background and gets gradually overplayed by the slow complaints of the rice-weeders, so do the creative and democratic expectations and articulations of the disinherited and marginalized citizens of Yemen and Tunisia, whose voices are deafened by the actions of military and "strong man" leaders. Formal institutions of representation became barriers to the democratic proposals from below for Tunisia, while in Yemen the breaking out of a regional war since 2015, with three entities claiming to have legitimacy to form a government (the Huthi movement in Sanaa, Hadi and his cabinet ruling from Riyadh, and the Southern Transitional Council in Aden). This part compares processes of decentralization and efforts to keep the security forces accountable to the democratic demands of the people.

Chapter 5 shows that elements of transgressive mobilization still coexist along contained mobilization. The new sense of citizenship that expressed itself through a closer fit of the people's aspirations with the functioning of the state is shown at play in the issue of federalism in Yemen and decentralized, everyday practice in Tunisia. In both countries, artistic visions rhyme with civic expectations and a profusion of social roles enacted by citizens. The preservation of the new political imaginary became another way for Yemenis to engage with "high" or "formal" routes of politics, even within the civil war.

Chapter 6 documents how formal politics creates moving sands in which informality ceases to be an efficient democratic tool. We witness the re-emergence of the "strong man" syndrome, and the growing marginalization of the younger generation of 2011 by the authorities. In Yemen, the three-way civil war is best understood with reference to neo-imperial powers that discursively reduce the political process on the ground to that of shallow sectarian conflicts and security-threats. Formal (military) actors accelerate these trends, and even when they claim support for democratic renewals and popular sovereignty, they all precipitate territorial fragmentation that makes Yemen increasingly look like it did in the early twentieth century: a series of statelets, with mercenaries and fragmented means of coercion that befit the agenda of other powerful regional actors. In Tunisia, everyday actions around mundane spaces, even sidewalks, have become the occasion for differing political visions to emerge. Thus, despite encouraging signs in the sphere of transitional justice, security and economic actors have found ways to thwart demands for accountability. Even President Kais Saied, elected in 2019 with slogans taken from the 2011 Uprisings, emerges as a barrier for democratic and judiciary reforms, after his "coup" of July 2021.

Key Dates, Actors, and Institutions: Tunisia

2014

Jan. 26   A new constitution is approved by the ANC. A technocratic government led by Prime Minister Mehdi Jomaa replaces the Troika

Oct.   Parliamentary elections for the ARP

Dec.   Presidential elections: Beji Caid Essebsi defeats incumbent President Moncef Marzouki in the second round

2015

Jan.   Coalition "Ni-Na" (Nidaa Tounes and Ennahda). Habib Essid is chosen as Prime Minister

March   ISIS attacks on Bardo National Museum

June   Attacks on tourist resorts in Sousse

Oct.   Nobel Peace Prize awarded to the Quartet

2016

March 7   ISIS attacks on Ben Guerdan leave 70 people killed

May   Tenth Congress of Ennahda, sanctioning the specialization thesis

Aug.   Youssef Chahed replaces Essid as Prime Minister

Nov. 17   IVD starts its work, with hearing aired live on prime time national TV

2017

April Protests in Tataouine region and encampment at oil-producing site of El-Kamour

May *Manich Msameh* ("I won't allow") protests in Tunis against draft law on economic reconciliation

June El-Kamour agreement with the government

2018

Jan. 8–11 Violent protests against food price increase. One demonstrator shot in Tebourba

April 26 ARP passes the law on municipality

May 6 Municipal elections

July 3 Souad Abderrahim (Ennahda) is chosen as mayor of Tunis, first woman to hold the post

2019

July. 25 Death of 93-year-old President Beji Caid Essebsi

Oct. Legislative elections for the ARP. Ennahda and Nidaa Tounes score bad results

Nov. 17 Presidential elections: independent Kais Saied defeats Nabil Karoui in the second round

2020

Feb. Formation of a new government under Elyes Fakhfakh

Sept. Presentation in the ARP of a new government under Mechichi

2021

Jan. President Saied refuses to recognize the new government

July 25 President Saied invokes article 80 of the Constitution to take full power for 30 days

ARP Assembly of the Representatives of the People (legislative)

IVD Truth and Dignity Commission, from the French *Instance Verité et Dignité*, led by human right lawyer Sihem Ben Sedrine

Key Dates, Actors, and Institutions: Yemen

2014

Jan. 26 NDC publishes its final recommendations

Feb. Region Committee sets the border of the six future federal regions

March–Dec. CDC works on the NDC recommendations to propose a new constitution

July 29 End of fuel subsidies under IMF and World Bank pressure

Aug. Ansar Allah organizes mass protests in the north

Sept. 21 Sanaa taken by Ansar Allah, with the help of Ali Abdallah Saleh

Sept. 22 Peace and National Partnership Agreement (PNPA)

Nov. New government, under Prime Minister Khaled Bahah

2015

Jan. 17 Official draft of the federalist constitution published

Feb. Huthi coup (also called "constitutional declaration"). Hadi flees to Aden

March–July Aden besieged by Huthi troops. Creation of the Southern Resistance

2016

May Diplomatic negotiations in Kuwait. Prime Minister Bahah sacked. Ali Muhsin becomes Vice President

Aug. North: formation of the Supreme Political Council (SPC). Power sharing agreement between the Huthis and the GPC

2017

May 11 Creation of the Southern Transitional Council (STC), eyeing secession in south

Nov. 30 STC nominates its legislative arm, the National Assembly

Dec. 4 Ali Abdallah Saleh is killed after having turned on the Huthis

2018

Jan. Standoff between STC and Hadi's government, and the latter is expelled from Aden

April UAE troops land on Socotra

Dec. Negotiations in Stockholm (Hodeida truce)

2019

Aug. STC and Security Belt Forces eject Hadi's government a second time

Nov. Riyadh Agreement. STC is now formally recognized by the GCC as a governmental partner, along with Hadi loyalists

2020

April 25	STC declares a state of emergency and self-rule over the south
June	Fights between STC and Hadi in Abyan and in Socotra
Dec.	Hadi's government returns to Aden

2021

Spring	Battle for Marib, producing a stalled situation between Huthi and troops loyal to President Hadi.
CDC	Constitution Drafting Committee (successor of the NDC)
UAE	United Arab Emirates
KSA	Kingdom of Saudi Arabia
SBF	Security Belt Forces

5 | Two Tales of Decentralization

5.1 Federalism in Yemen: Source of War or Continuation of the Democratic Pressure?

According to John Chalcraft (2016), popular politics in the Middle East reached a novel point in 2011, with transgressive mobilizations pushing for a democratic redefinition of the republican political systems. The new articulations proposed by popular protests were put to the test of "new institutional forms" (Yadav 2011: 551) and were gradually contained. This chapter analyzes the interplay between space and civic activism, ranging from actions contesting spaces for inclusion in municipalities in Tunisia to street artworks in Yemen, two countries where decentralization was officially on the agenda after 2014. This concatenation of participatory expectations, that is, this chain of mobilizations and of political projects that flowed from the imaginary of the 2011 Uprisings, persisted despite very significant national security setbacks.

Ideas about decentralization are not entirely novel in Yemen, with earlier calls heard in the 1990s and early 2000s (Alwazir 1998). Discussions concerning a federalist project in Yemen between 2013 and 2014 performatively did what they were supposed to do, namely, assembling different views, including those regarding a regionally equitable distribution of leadership positions within the armed forces, *as long as they were in the hands of informal political actors*. As soon as the constitutional template drafted by actors who had gained legitimacy in 2011 was handed to President Hadi, federalism became a direct cause for war and for the implosion of the democratic political process.

In Tunisia, the form of decentralization adopted with the 2014 Constitution was new, but it responded to the *longue durée* geography of marginalization and recast debates about participation in novel ways. Those concatenations relied on a diversity of social roles

283

assumed by lay citizens, and on the artistic creativity of the Yemeni and Tunisian peoples.

We will first focus our analysis on Yemen by going back to the creation of the NDC in March 2013, and follow through all the way to the start of the civil war.

Like the moon and the finger invoked in the Introduction, assessments of the NDC can be reductive: Some see it as an important cause for the civil war (Shuja Al-Deen 2019; G. Anderson 2019), but if one takes a more holistic view, one perceives the NDC as an important symbolic space that has kept hopes for democratic changes in Yemen alive. According to Chalcraft's typology, even if the NDC was a contained form of mobilization, it still harbored elements of transgressive mobilizations. The NDC was an opportunity to engage with the "structural tensions" between the center (Sanaa) and the different peripheries under Saleh, in particular the Saada wars and the southern secessionist movements (Bonnefoy 2013).

In 2013 and 2014, efforts to produce a new constitution were spearheaded by the NDC – active between May 2013 and January 2014 – and finalized by the Committee for the Drafting of the Constitution (CDC), which was active for exactly one year from January 2014 to January 2015. Despite serious legal flaws, most conspicuously regarding the mandates of these two bodies,[1] substantial and increasing resistance in the south, and a disconnect from harsh economic realities, there was rather widespread support amongst Yemenis for the re-foundation of the Yemeni Republic as a federal entity.

Because of its origins (the only part of the GCC Initiative that involved revolutionary groups), its architecture (an alternative parliament with seats guaranteed to non-organized political factions), and its mandate (establishing non-binding recommendations for a new constitution), the NDC generated new expectations that were shared well beyond the circle of its participants. For example, citizens and soldiers from Hodeida, the marginalized region of Tihama on the west coast, were heard complaining about fuel shortages and overdue pay in 2013. Their hope was not that the government or the parliament would address their concerns, but that the NDC would do so.[2] But, contrary

---

[1] I have proposed a detailed analysis of the NDC and cultural expressions of support for the federalist project in Challand (forthcoming).

[2] This was taken from Ammar Basha's documentary, "5th Day in the heart of the revolution," ليمن: يوم خامس في قلب الثورة, video published 10/24/2013, at www .youtube.com/watch?v=6SWBDoSBe3I.

to the Constituent Assembly in Tunisia, it was never the NDC's responsibility to address such affairs. Yet, the people of Hodeida nevertheless pinned their hopes for immediate action and democratic reforms on the NDC. Furthermore, the NDC gave a voice to those youth that became political and directly engaged with political elites (Alwazir 2016: 175). The NDC pieced together not only about 16 different parties and representative groups' inputs, but acted as a temporary representative body that captured the attention of a majority of Yemeni lay people. The new social imaginary of 2011 (social justice, rule of law, *vis populi*) and of the NDC (new spaces for participation of the disenfranchised) left a profound and positive mark, in particular for the young generations. In hindsight, the NDC appears as an illusion of democratic change, but one which generated new socializations and expectations across the demos – from hitherto largely silenced social groups (women, *muhammashin*) to aggrieved regional entities (southern and Huthi movements, but also representatives from Taiz and Marib). It also regenerated older debates on federalism, which were genuinely endogenous to Yemeni politics and society and not just a technical import favored by a few international experts (Challand forthcoming).

After the appointment of two preparatory committees (G. Anderson 2019: 317), two Presidential Decrees laid the legal bases for the NDC in September 2012 and for the nomination of its members. The NDC could lay out a new vision for the future of the country, but the proposals it would make were not legally binding: The task of drafting a new constitution fell to another committee, the CDC, which would build on the work of the NDC. For many, inside and outside of the country, the creation of a classical round-table type of institution (Arato 2016), meant to discuss the broad contour of a new constitution, was an important symbolic victory: Clearly, the NDC was the more legitimate representative body in this phase of Yemeni politics, and this legitimacy was understood as the more viable guarantor of a democratic outcome than the Government of National Unity (GNU).

Because of the pressing focus on the security reforms, the Presidency was slow in finalizing the extensive list of participants in the round-table discussions. The NDC was formally called into existence on March 18, 2013,[3] and given a six-month window to propose its

---

[3] The date was chosen to honor the memory of the 51 persons who were killed in Sanaa during the massacre of March 18, 2011.

recommendations. The round-table gathered 565 participants, half of them coming from the south, where the most pressing political issues and the more concretely articulated demands for reforms were made. To lead the Dialogue, an NDC Presidency was formed, with nine members representing the six largest parties.[4] Nadia Al-Sakkaf, a woman representing the three "revolutionary groups" (women, youth, and civil society), Abdullah Lamlas, the leader of the Presidential Quota, and President Hadi himself completed Presidency.[5]

Sixteen blocs or constituent groups proposed solutions to the political problems of the country. The logic of representation followed that of party lines, with the GPC (and its allies) securing the largest quota of 131 members, followed by Hirak with 85 representatives. Islah sent 50 members, the YSP 37, Ansar Allah (the Huthi party) 35, and Nasserite Popular Unionist Party 30. Six other parties were given four or seven seats (e.g. the newly formed Salafi party, Al-Rashad). Fixed quotas of 40 each were allocated to bolster the presence of independent women, youth (defined as below 40 years old), and civil society organizations, three constituencies that had played a massive role in the 2011 mobilizations. President Hadi appointed an additional 66 members, listed as "presidential quota."

This representational configuration demanded a reconsideration of who or what could be counted as a political actor in Yemen: not just new parties, like Hirak and Ansar Allah, but new and historically marginalized groups otherwise excluded from formal politics until that point. For example, the *muhammashin* (literally "marginalized," lower caste) sent one delegate, Noman Al-Houthaifi (B. Hall 2017). One delegate might seem small given the size of the community, but it was a considerable achievement given the history of the *muhammashin*'s lack of formal representation in Yemeni institutions. It allowed them to place quota demands on public administration and demand an end to specific forms of discrimination, in particular in the workplace, and in terms of access to education.[6] For women, the NDC guaranteed

---

[4] For a list of parties and informal groupings invited, 16 in total, see Lackner (2016b).

[5] The NDC website has ceased to be operating. The information about its Presidency can be found on the Internet Archive, at: https://web.archive.org/web/20210816005450/http://ndc.ye/page.aspx?show=92.

[6] Christiansen & Al-Thawr (2019: 116). They only have temporary contracts in public administration and have no rights to pensions. Statistics on marginalized groups tend to systematically lower their numbers. Kendall (2018: 76) makes a similar observation for the official census data related to the Mahra

new and vastly superior spaces for participation, and UN Envoy Benomar would send back to invited parties any proposed lists that failed to reach the requirement of 30% of those nominated being women.[7] Compared to the regular Yemeni parliament, where only one woman sat as a deputy, the high percentage of women NDC delegates, 40% of the total delegates, with a reasonable number of them assuming a leading role, deserves particular attention.[8]

The work of the body was organized in plenary sessions alternating with nine working groups, the most important concentrating on the southern question and on the Saada, or northern, dispute. There was widespread international support for the work of the NDC. But it also had opponents and inherent tensions. The model of "respectable political voluntarism" with unexpected levels of "political maturity" was, according to the account of Laurent Bonnefoy (2018: 36, 38), a longtime observer of Yemeni politics, contrasted with the economic and security deterioration in the rest of the country, when the NDC met at the high-end Movenpick hotel in Sanaa. Another disconnect was related to Ansar Allah, whose delegates participated in the NDC deliberation, but which was involved in armed actions against the tribal components of Islah in Hajja in 2012 and Amran in 2014 (Dorlian 2015: 66, 69, 72).

Ansar Allah was partly in, partly out, depending on the current of the Huthi movement, which ranged between a pragmatic republican wing and a hardline Zaydi revivalist faction (Lackner 2019: 158). The Hirak bloc had the lowest rate of party attendance in the NDC plenary sessions. An analysis of list of attendees shows that Hirak filled 69.2% of its seats during a sample of plenary and working groups sessions, while Ansar Allah had a rate of presence at 72.7%, while all other parties and informal groups (youth, women, and civil society) filled their seats 80% to 95% of the time.[9]

---

governorate, in the most eastern province of the country. B. Hall (2017: §§25, 37) discusses the tension that arose within the *muhammashin* community during the NDC.

[7] Nadia Al-Sakkaf, member of the NDC Presidency, in London, interview via WhatsApp, 09/21/2019.

[8] Lackner (2019: 140). For a full list of members, see NDC website, section *"tamthil"* ("representation"), at https://web.archive.org/web/20130805160150/ http://ndc.ye/ar-page.aspx?show=68. See also a more detailed discussion in Challand (forthcoming).

[9] Percentage expressed in terms of attendance vis-à-vis allocated seats. Author's analysis of presence lists, with a focus on 11 out of the total 87 lists of presence,

Southern Yemenis viewed the NDC with distrust, largely seeing the process as a barrier – if not an enemy – to their aspiration for autonomy. According to the long-term observer of southern Yemeni political life, Susanne Dahlgren (2014a), "it was difficult to find anyone in Aden who believed in the National Dialogue." Most of the southerners sitting in the NDC, whether as YSP members or as representatives of Hirak, were appointed by President Hadi, and thus in agreement with the premise that the NDC had to preserve Yemeni unity. This was not what most people in Aden and in the Hadhramawt aspired to. In 2014, a leader of the Southern Peaceful Movement in Aden estimated that 90% of the former South opposed the NDC (Amira Augustin 2015). The leader of the Hirak bloc at the NDC did propose a federalist solution, but only on the condition that a future federal Yemen would be made of two regions only, the former North and the former South, with a referendum allowing for self-determination in the southern part after five years. This option was nicknamed the Sudanese model (where South Sudan emerged as an independent country away from Sudan), but this was not an acceptable option for the GCC and President Hadi (Brehony, Lackner, & Al-Sarhan 2015: 22). The Hirak leader stepped down and was replaced by another southerner close to Hadi (G. Anderson 2019: 319).

However alienating it may have been to some, especially in the early stages, the NDC managed to offer several innovative and groundbreaking proposals three months after its launch. I will also argue in the last chapter that protests, marches, and cultural events organized at a subsequent time in the south have replicated the NDC's ideas about self-determination and as way to overcome internal divisions. So even if the NDC was not seen as a legitimate round-table for many southerners, it generated a cascade of new spaces for participation in the south, kept the principle of *vis populi* alive, albeit in altered forms, and combined both transgressive and contained forms of mobilization.

roughly a list of presence every three weeks, from April 2013 to January 2014, taken as a sample of the entire period of work for the NDC. The parties with the highest rates of attendance were the Nasserite Popular Unionist Party and the YSP (89.7%), Islah (87%), and the GPC (80.2%). The members directly appointed by President Hadi had the lowest rate of participation with an attendance rate of 65.7%. Source: Presence lists found on the NDC website, now on the Internet Archive at https://web.archive.org/pdf/search/www.ndc.ye-/ndc doc/.

By June, in its "mid-term outcomes," the NDC had identified essential reforms.[10] Many of these recommendations evolved around guaranteed protections for citizens and significant restrictions placed on the security sector at large (as opposed to only military reforms), and fell within the contours or parameters of the principles of *vis populi*. For example, the NDC requested official apologies for all violations against citizen rights, including pledges that such violations will not be repeated, the prohibition of the establishment of any military or paramilitary groups, and the formation of a supreme independent council, which would be tasked with protecting the rights of all citizens, *muhammashin* included. The NDC also called for an independent legislature with the power to execute supervisory functions without external interference from the executive of the military, and they called for the "removal of party control of state administrative institutions." In order to put democratic limits to the security custodianship, and to prevent regional privileges of a fragmented body of intelligence and army groups, the NDC called on the development of "military doctrine for armed forces derived from constitutional principles so as to become a national and professional army" (Mid-Session Outcomes: Point 18; hereafter NDC 2013: 18), and it asked that the engagement of "the armed and the security forces" would "derive from compliance with the constitution and the law" (NDC 2013: 19), indicating that this had not been the case previously. The NDC also requested a "rotation system to all commanders of the armed and security forces" be applied to all current commanders in order to meet the NDC's newly articulated criteria regarding the seniority, competence, and qualifications of military officials, as well as their goals concerning national representation (NDC 2013: 54). These newly proposed forms of accountability were thus intended to cover all fronts of civic life, address past grievances and acts of violence, and deal with foreseeable issues related to the legislature and security forces.

Finally, the NDC reiterated a popular demand for the reinstatement of benefits for all southern retirees and northern governorate soldiers (NDC 2013: 49 and 50) who had been removed from pensioners lists. The NDC placed the northern and southern questions on equal footing

---

[10] The Mid-Session Outcomes, dated July 8, 2013, can be found on the Internet Archive at https://web.archive.org/web/20140726110035/www.ndc.ye/page .aspx?show=102.

in this case, and requested concrete "actions to reestablish trust between the people and the military, security, and intelligence services" (NDC 2013: 57). These requests were drawn from the Twenty Demands issued in early 2012, demands which signaled a continuity with the *sahat* and large marches of late 2011. Representatives of the civil society sector felt their input was valuable, albeit with different degrees of successes.[11] It led to memorable moments, for example, when Amal Basha, a female leading voice in the human rights sector, publicly and successfully challenged Sadiq Al-Ahmar, the paramount shaykh of the Hashid confederation, over the appointment of a woman as chairperson of the Saada working group during a session covered live on national TV (Strzelecka 2018: 61; Stephan & Charrad 2020).

Despite a rather slow start, and some skepticism as to whether the NDC was a sideshow to the GCC's political process, the NDC managed to finalize a trove of constitutional recommendations. On January 26, 2014, which, by coincidence, was the day Tunisia adopted its new post-Ben Ali constitution, the NDC passed a final document, listing 1,578 proposals. The NDC recommended founding a federal state, with new institutions, e.g. a Constitutional Court and new mechanisms to ensure a "broad national partnership, representation of the regions and enable citizens to exercise their political rights and participation in governance."[12] But on key issues – for example, the number of federal regions, regional borders, and mechanisms to distribute oil revenues – the NDC remained silent, as no full compromise could be found.

The process of drafting these constitutional recommendations regenerated political debates and provided a welcome space for new political figures against the power of patriarchy. Many were women: Amal Basha, Bushra Al-Maqtari, Samya Al-Aghbari, and of course Tawakkol Karman (Strzelecka 2018: 58). Younger generations have not hesitated since to openly criticize historic leaders (Amira Augustin 2018; Al-Rubaidi 2018a). The increasing visibility of university-educated professionals has been saluted as a by-product of the 2011 events (Strzelecka 2018: 67): Nadia Al-Sakkaf, in the NDC Presidency,

---

[11] Baligh Al-Mikhlafi, formerly active in youth campaigns, in Cairo, interview via Skype, 09/18/2019.

[12] Taken from the Final Communique of National Dialogue Conference, dated 01/ 26/2014, p. 11. Available at https://web.archive.org/web/20210711151011/ht tp://www.ndc.ye/ndcdoc/NDC_Final_Communique.pdf.

and Rafat Al-Akhali, who joined as technical adviser to the GNU, were later appointed ministers at the end of 2014. Even the new Salafi party, Rashad, which participated in the NDC, seemed to have learned the ropes of pluralism and political compromise, as Kuschnitzki (2018: 209, 222) has argued.[13] A form of federalism, with new regions and a proposal for more equitable redistributions of resources in places like Marib, Socotra, or Al-Mahra, was widely discussed in Yemen during the time of the NDC.

The process of broad, inclusive deliberation of the NDC was derailed once its mandate was completed, with political parties imposing their will and ready to throw away compromises made in the NDC. The CDC, whose task was to pick which of the 1,578 proposed articles would make it into the draft of a new constitution, worked behind close doors. President Hadi was also heavily involved in breaking the cooperative spirit of the NDC when he proposed a map for a new federal Yemen made of six regions. The attempted top-down imposition of this plan drew the ire of both northerners and southerners, and when combined with a deteriorating economic situation in the summer of 2014, led to an overall downward spiral into armed confrontation. Asked about her greatest disappointment in her experience as an independent sitting in the NDC Presidency and involved briefly in the Bahah government (Nov. 2014–Feb. 2015), Information Minister Nadia Al-Sakkaf said it was "the politics of the parties [which] would surpass the national agenda of the Yemenis. Even if it meant ruining the country, the parties decided things that they thought were right for them."[14] She felt a bitter disappointment that all the work of the NDC was washed away by the interests of a few political groups.

Why did the six-region map that Hadi proposed in February 2014 (see Map 5.1) generate so much animosity among NDC participants? Aside from a few southerners in the NDC and many in the Hadhramawt region (Lackner 2019: 183), the real Hirak – again, in contrast to the NDC Hirak – were infuriated by the six-region proposal put forward by the Region Committee (G. Anderson 2019: 320). First,

[13] Lackner (2019: 158) also argues that a few members of Ansar Allah, such as Ali Al-Bukhayti, proposed compromise with the revolutionary groups, calling for a "participatory state" (*dawlat al-sharaka al-waṭaniyya*) and a "second republic" (*al-jumhūriyya al-thāniyya*), thus opposing a restauration of the Zaydi dynasty. On earlier debates about federalism, see Alwazir (1998).
[14] Al-Sakkaf, interview, 09/21/2019.

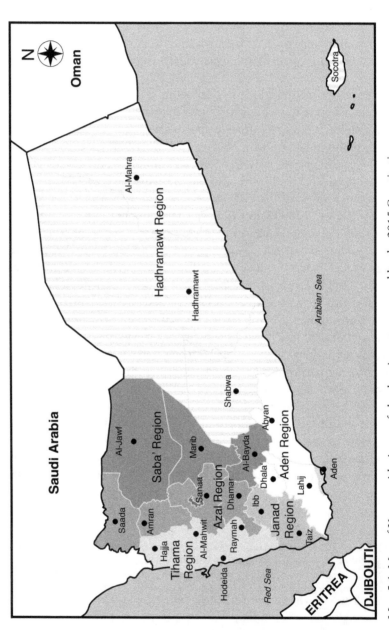

Map 5.1 Map of Yemen with six new federal regions, as proposed by the 2015 Constitution.

Hirak feared that, with the proposed two regions for the south, old cleavages and regionalisms would re-emerge in that part of the country (Lackner 2019: 183). Secondly, some southerners were incensed that the country's main economic resources – the oil from the Hadhramawt and the gas pipeline running to the port of Balhaf (in Shabwa gover- norate) – would be separated from the Aden region. Thirdly, separatists feverishly opposed this division. But it should be noted that others in the south, Hadhramis in particular, who have historically always exhibited strong desires to tread their own path, saw this federal map as an opportunity to create distance between themselves and power- brokers in the urban centers of Sanaa and Aden (see TYR 2019; Lackner 2019: 18).

The Huthis also had ambivalent attitudes toward the map. One the one hand, a new region in the north, called Azal, was carved out to guarantee some regional power for the Upper Yemen Zaydi popula- tion, and thus some degree of autonomy from Sanaa. The reason for the dissatisfaction for Ansar Allah lay in the border drawing of this region, which did not grant access to the Red Sea, turning the province into a landlocked region. The Huthis objected to the borders of the six regions, not to federalism as such (Brehony, Lackner, & Al-Sarhan 2015: 9; Thiel 2015). For this, they mostly concentrated their political efforts on Hadi, whom they considered to be weak and to have dwin- dling legitimacy.

Once the regions were defined, the CDC worked to give institutional substance to this federalist map and mission. Its work was done in isolation, however, with much less representation for the historically aggrieved regions. The momentum from the NDC was thus lost. The unresponsiveness of the government, a very dire economic situation, and pressure from the IMF to cut fuel subsidies at the end of July 2014 (G. Anderson 2019: 322) proved to be the end of the more-or-less peaceful political process. Three sets of non-governmental actors pre- cipitated the path towards an all-armed conflict: the Huthis, former president Ali Abdallah Saleh making a political come-back at the end of 2014, and Hirak. This Thermidorian phase (Heydemann 2015: 2) ushered the return of strong (military) men in the Yemeni "transition."

The Huthis, led by the demagogy of their leader Abdelmalik Al- Huthi, launched massive protests in the north of the country because of the end of fuel subsidies. Surfing on the wave of popular protests, Ansar Allah and the various popular committees supporting the Huthi cause marched on Sanaa (Brehony, Lackner, & Al-Sarhan 2015: 10). Former president Saleh sensed that this was a golden opportunity for a political come-back and struck a deal with the Huthis, his former arch-enemies.[15] Saleh had not taken well the removal of his son, Ahmad, from military command, and was willing to obstruct the transition in whatever ways possible. The combined masses of Ansar Allah and armed units loyal to former president Saleh were too powerful for Hadi's troops, and Sanaa was taken by September 21, 2014. The real Hirak in the south felt that the more the crisis amplified in Sanaa, the more legitimate their preparations for secession were in the south.

The Huthis, after the capture of Sanaa in September, demonstrated that they were fine with the federalist solution as long as they were included in a revamped government alongside the representatives of Hirak. In exchange for the withdrawal of Huthi militias from the streets of Sanaa, Ansar Allah requested the resignation of the entire government of national unity (GNU) (Brehony, Lackner, & Al-Sarhan 2015: 10). President Hadi had to accept Ansar Allah's terms. He signed the Peace and National Partnership Agreement (PNPA) on September 22, 2014. The preamble of this document explicitly endorsed the outcomes of the NDC and was full of reference to the objectives of the 2011 Uprising. The PNPA requested the appointment of political advisors to President Hadi from both Ansar Allah and Hirak, immediate measures to alleviate the costs of living (in particular fuel subsidy), and the execution of the "outcomes of the Saada Working Group of the National Dialogue Conference." Interestingly, in the six-page document, the NDC is mentioned 15 times, the term "consultation" six times, yet the GCC Initiative is not mentioned even once.[16]

As a result of the PNPA, the Huthis appointed one presidential advisor, Ali Al-Sammad. Likewise, Hirak nominated Yasin Al-Makkawi, an Adeni intellectual, but one who hardly represents the movements of contemporary Yemen.[17] Following negotiations

[15] Since Islah, and the tribal component under Sadiq Al-Ahmar, had defected in February 2011, this new alliance between Saleh and the Huthis signalled the recomposition of old northern Zaydi alliances, not as a sectarian project, but as a social identity with a historical claim to authority over the north. This is the interpretation, with hindsight, of Abdulghani Al-Iryani (Sanaa Center 2020).

[16] Demands made in articles 2, 3, and 11 of the PNPA. Full text available at: https://peacemaker.un.org/.

[17] Older southerners remember that another Al-Makkawi acted as political adviser to the British when Aden was a Crown Colony. See Dahlgren (2014b).

between President Hadi and his two new advisors, a new government was established with Khaled Bahah as Prime Minister. Many of the fresh figures who joined as ministers came into their positions by way of revolutionary and NDC involvement.[18] These and the language of the PNPA indicate how revolutionary legitimacy temporarily had the upper hand over the formal stipulations of the GCC Initiative, which, we will recall, listed only Hadi's government, Islah, and the GCC as formal actors in charge of the "transition."

After the fall of Sanaa, southerners felt caught between the rock of an alliance between Ansar Allah and Salah on the one hand, and the hard place of the Hadi–Islah alliance of governmental power. It would mean either a return to conservative highland tribalism and religious bigotry,[19] or the deepening of the fake reform of federalism with Islah in charge of governmental matters. Both of these were entirely unpalatable options, and a rejection of the principle of a civil state. The new facts on the ground, with the Huthi takeover of Sanaa propelled the full secessionist agenda forward in the south as the only viable option. A massive march was organized in the south on October 14, 2014. A federal Yemen receded further down the agenda in the south since it was seen there as a new iteration of internal colonialism by the north.

Hadi pushed for the finalization of the constitution, a complete draft of which had been circulating since January 4, 2015.[20] Ansar Allah exerted intense pressure on Hadi to change the federal map. Until mid-January 2015, federalism was fine for Ansar Allah (Thiel 2015). But when federalism came into conflict with Ansar Allah's political aims, the Huthi party reneged on article 2 of the PNPA – which insured consultation with the two regions aggrieved – and even turned on the Southern Movement a few weeks later.

Furious that Hadi did not cede to Ansar Allah's request to redraw the inner border of the Azal region, Huthi loyalists kidnapped President

---

[18] Al-Sakkaf, interview, 09/21/2019, and Rafat Al-Akhali, decentralization expert, interview in Oxford, 09/19/2019. See also the proposed appointment of Gabool Mutawakkel, a member of a new party, *Al-Watan*, established in January 2014 by revolutionary youth (Alwazir 2016: 186).
[19] This mixture had left 150 southern intellectuals killed by Islamists in the early 1990s, and had expropriated vast land and economic assets from southerners after the 1994 civil war (Amira Augustin 2015; Lackner 2016a).
[20] On the release of the first full version of the draft, see www.saba.ye/ar/new s382937.htm (January 4, 2015, in Arabic). For the final draft of the Constitution, see Sources.

Hadis' Chief of Staff, Ahmad bin Mubarak, on January 17, 2015, the day Hadi authorized the dissemination of the Constitution with the planned six regions. A tense stand-off ensued. Hadi and the Prime Minister were placed under house arrest by Ansar Allah on January 22, 2015. One of the Ansar Allah leaders of the NDC, Ahmad Sharaf Al-Din, was assassinated in the same period, prompting a spectacular round of retaliations in February, when the house of the late Shaykh Abdallah Al-Ahmar was destroyed in Al-Khamri – a direct hit carried out by Ansar Allah at the Hashid tribal confederation (Dorlian 2015: 73).

Hadi and his Prime Minister both resigned, a move which resulted in a constitutional crisis. Following these resignations, the Huthi movement carried out what amounts to a coup on February 6, 2015, when they issued a unilateral constitutional declaration, establishing a five-person Presidential Council. A new government was formed under the form of a "Supreme Revolutionary Council" with branches throughout the north of Yemen, and a Transitional National Council made of 551 members claimed to replace the parliament (Lackner 2019: 162). The Huthis had no legal authority to make these decisions, but with Saleh's support, the awkward allies felt they could cross this Rubicon, claiming now governmental and executive authority over the whole country.

The political process (referendum on the new constitution, with ensuing elections for a new president and parliament, and for the implementation of decentralization through new regions) imploded in March 2015. The main actor of the GCC, the Kingdom of Saudi Arabia (KSA), refused the resignation of Hadi and mounted a military campaign, and with the support of nine other Muslim-majority countries around the GCC, started bombing Huthi and Saleh positions. Since then, the country has been dealing with a civil war coupled with a regional war.

As of 2021, the civil war still opposes Hadi (and his loyalist government) to the Huthi alternative governing bodies. After December 2017, when Saleh was killed by the Huthis, the civil war sporadically turned into a three-way domestic conflict, with southern secessionists, grouped around the Southern Transitional Council (STC), taking arms against Hadi's government and its military leader, the pro-Islah Ali Muhsin, and mounting their own military operations. After a couple of diplomatic missions by the Saudis in 2019 and 2020 to patch the disagreement between Hadi and the STC, which was given a seat at the table with the Riyadh Agreement of November 2019, Hadi is again considered the legitimate source of authority in the south, even if he governs from a foreign capital, Riyadh.

The regional component of the war comes from the fact that Huthis had launched attacks into Saudi territories, as well as the Saudi accusations that Iran stood behind the Huthis. Now, while it is true that Iran has provided some support to Ansar Allah and the Huthi government, saying that the war is the result of Iranian meddling in Yemeni affairs would be a gross simplification and would erase all the history of marginalization and internal tensions within Yemen already described. It would also play into the GCC's rhetoric of there being a risk of state collapse, or state failure, which has allowed it to sideline all the people's democratic aspirations in Yemen (Al-Eriani 2020).

Let us now turn to Tunisia, where decentralization, not federalism, was on the agenda after the passing of a new constitution in January 2014. There, the tale of decentralization is not as grim as the war that erupted in Yemen, and despite generational and legislative barriers, everyday politics in Tunisia reveals a continuous expression of *vis populi*, the proliferation of social roles, and small-scale civic initiatives.

5.2 Civic Activism in Tunisia: New Spaces, Social Roles, and the Pushes for Decentralization

Tunisia closed two important chapters of the revolutionary period in 2014. On January 26, the ANC voted for the new constitution by an overwhelming majority, thus replacing the constitutional law ("small constitution") it had adopted in December 2011. In the fall of the same year, legislative and presidential elections renewed the top-tier political personnel. The trend toward increasingly contained mobilization, which started during the work of the ANC, became, once again, the norm under the presidency of Essebsi and the new parliament, the ARP. Beji Caid Essebsi, from a prominent Tunisois family, won with 56% of the vote, which mostly came from the north and the Sahel region, and defeated the interior's candidate, who had been President between December 2011 and December 2014, Moncef Marzouki. The ARP inaugurated a five-year legislature, with an awkward coalition between the two largest parties. Nidaa Tounes, Essebsi's party, won the majority of the seats, 86, with Ennahda finishing second with 69.

The following section illustrates how the two forms of contained and transgressive mobilization (Chalcraft 2016: 24–25) overlap within a gray zone of bottom-up activism and controlled top-down political change.[21] A myriad of informal practices demanding civic involvement in politics is documented around new participatory spaces. These micro-initiatives are often located at the level of municipal decisions, but also entail a connective dimension of transnational solidarities, with projects of joint citizenships with other Arab and also European citizens. The Moebius strip, in this informal configuration of everyday politics, becomes the vector for a new positive and participatory politics. This section conveys the multiple points of view vis-à-vis the post-2014 trends and challenges of Tunisian politics, and tries to make sense, away from clear-cut judgments of the "failure or success" of the Tunisian "transition,"[22] of what *has become* of the radical demands of 2011.

I chose to assess the evolution of *social roles* in Tunisia. In particular, I will concentrate on the years 2014–2018, when decentralization was discussed throughout the country and enacted with the May 2018 municipal elections, the first time in Tunisian history where every adult, regardless of gender and geographic location, could cast a vote in municipal council elections. I want to suggest that a plurality of social roles, enacted in new spaces, and in the cultural realm, connected Tunisians to the political process. This informality of civic engagement often got lost in the narratives about the post-revolutionary years in Tunisia.

The idea of "social roles" is not without imperfections. Yet it is a prompt to realize that social roles are always multiple and played out situationally. In Hank Johnston's (1995: 224) terms:

The social actor typically assumes a role with incomplete information about other interactants and often incomplete information about the institutional requirements of the role itself. The actor also brings a unique assemblage of skill and experience to the role that imparts an additional indeterminacy. As

---

[21] For Chalcraft, *contained* mobilization is about publicly recognized actors entering the arena of contention, while *transgressive* mobilization sees previously unorganized or apolitical actors with more innovative and sporadic tools disrupting normal politics, including what counts as the arena of contention.

[22] The term "transition" reflects the dominant language used in that period, 2014–2018. See Introduction.

imprecise as the concept of role may be, there nevertheless are continuities and a certain boundedness to the various roles that each social actor plays and in lieu of an alternative, it remains a useful concept.

Thus, roles are not always clearly defined, and depending on the moment and context of the interaction, role postures can vary and produce inconsistent statements. An example is an interviewee who had explicitly denied the revolutionary nature of the 2010 Uprisings while speaking in the role of a social scientist, but then suddenly started speaking of "counter-revolutionary forces" when switching to the role of a mere lay citizen. Speaking of multiple and at times interchangeable social roles thus allows us to avoid what I call the "activist fallacy."[23]

Social roles were not always *acted out* or *performed* with the immediate political intent of questioning and renewing forms of delegation or representation. Much of the revolutionary effervescence also brought forward a burst of creativity, with tags, graffiti, posters, collages, or videos posted online. One could see an "unleashing of playful imagination" around collective and mass mobilization that contributed to the emergence of a "partial new social order ... symbolically represented through practical action" (Barker 2001: 184–185). This was true for Yemen and Tunisia, and would re-emerge in other Arab countries towards the end of the 2010s.

Examples of everyday life practices illustrate the effort to sustain a capacity for radical self-representation. In brief, these practices are about *enacting citizenship* (new forms of socialization, use of theatre as civic education, etc.), *pressuring local authorities* and the central government for decentralization and devolution of power, and keeping the *symbolic repertoires* of 2011 (marches and slogans) alive. In all these cases, one can observe a new constructive component of the Moebius-like citizenship, with a dialectic between local and translocal forms of solidarity, which connected hitherto fragmented spaces into united spaces of participation. Again, Siliana and other small towns will be one of the privileged spaces in which a new social life of citizenship can be documented.

In Siliana, during a visit in June 2016, I could spot graffiti recalling the motif of wrath against the regime. Instead of *"al-sha'ab yurid isqat al-nizam,"* "the people want the fall of the regime," the tag in the center read *"al-sha'ab la yuridkum,"* namely "the people do not want you."

---

[23] See Introduction, Section 0.3.

The vagueness of the plural "you" is hard to interpret, but the location of the graffiti, on a cross street from the municipality, could hint at the rejection of the authorities appointed by the central government, as we will see below. A couple of blocks down, on a crossroad at which the bi-weekly market takes place, another graffiti offered a radical rebuke of this secular view of politics where the "people" are meant to choose. In that second graffiti, "*la wila' ila'llah*" sustains that there is "no loyalty but to God's" (or no one is allowed to rule but God).[24]

The tag "The people do not want you" contained a message to the municipality. It is also an allusion to a famous case of mass mobilization that took place at the end of November 2012. The divide in the text of the graffiti of "us" as "the people" vs. the plural "you" refers to a cycle of protests against the governor. Siliana was one of the municipalities shrouded in controversy after the central government dissolved the *Délégations Spéciales* and reasserted central authority through the governor. Grievances against the representative of Tunis, the governor, piled up and generated protests in front of the governor's building on November 2012. These led to the extraordinary march six miles out of the town by a quarter of the local population, which I described at length in Chapter 3.[25] Since then, Silianans have been on the look-out and kept pressure on their local authorities.

For example, the Siliana branch of the Social and Economic Rights Tunisian Forum, better known in Tunisia through its French acronym, FTDES, organized a coalition of various NGOs to ask for more accountability from the governor's office.[26] This type of initiative has been widespread in Tunisia. Abundant meetings have taken place throughout the country since the passing of the 2014 Constitution, inviting citizens and NGOs to participatory workshops discussing the budget and five-year development plans. There have been countless proposals and realizations to use new technologies to guarantee clearer

---

[24] This is probably a reference to the Qur'an (*Sura* 4, verse 59): "Obey Allah and obey the Messenger and those in authority among you" ("*wa wuli al-amr minkum*"). Such debates on who to obey, God or human authority, has led quietist Salafis in many Arab countries to *not* contest worldly authority, as long as the ruler is a Muslim. For a discussion of this doctrine in the Yemeni context, see Bonnefoy (2011: 262).

[25] For a detailed account of the events, see the report (in Arabic) of FTDES (2013). Rachid Kharroubi, cultural association, interview in Siliana, 06/01/2016 and Akrem Yakoubi, NGO member, interview in Siliana, 06/02/2016.

[26] Yakoubi, interview, 06/02/2016.

oversight and opportunities to report inefficient bureaucracies.[27] Many Tunisian NGOs and small civic fora have supported participatory budget planning in a host of municipalities. During a presentation organized by a forum of citizens of Djerba, questions were raised about possibilities to organize regional funding to palliate problems of internal migration, and different issues involving local unemployment.[28] For example, the most active NGO at the national level, Al-Bawsola ("the compass" in Arabic), established a specific website, called "the observatory," with data for the entire territory. All the information is in Arabic, indicating that this is not a window-dressing exercise for the international donor community. It aims to bring systematic transparency on all the public data available on each municipality in Tunisia.[29]

At the micro-level, the sense of belonging with a commitment to improving small things at the local scale is repeatedly expressed. Unwilling to be ensnared by party politics, the founder of a cultural association in Zerzis stated: "[if I have to work with people from the] left or right, I don't care! What I want is to lead small actions for the good of my city. People in associations should be worried about that. If you want to work for the sake of the community, Welcome! [Do it!]"[30] In the south, I saw how the former RCD building in Midoun was turned into the "House of Associations" (*dar al-jama'iat*). But apparently, this was not enough. A graffiti had barred the terms *dar al-jama'iat* and replaced them with *dar al-sha'ab*, "House of the People." Thus, some of these initiatives are putting their foot in the official authorities' doors, including municipalities and governorates, but also asking for transparency and reliability from NGOs.

A comparable sense of moral obligation to carry the legacy of the revolution forward emerged during the founding assembly of a network of Tunisian, Moroccan, and French associations working for the defense of the rights of migrants. This transnational network is entitled Immigration, Development and Democracy (IDD), which can

---

[27] We could cite numerous initiatives: i-Watch (www.iwatch.tn/); *Baladiaty* ("my municipality," www.facebook.com/baladiaty.tn/), Al-Bawsola (www.albawsala.com/en/project/marsad-baladia), etc.
[28] Adbelhamid Ghribi, civic campaign, interview in Djerba, 01/02/2016. The conference organized involved a member of the 2011 transition government, former minister Houcine Al-Dimassi.
[29] Chaima Bouhlel, program manager, NGO, interview in Tunis, 06/07/2016.
[30] Anis Khenissi, youth activist, NGO leader, interview in Medenine, 01/04/2016.

be seen as a positive side of the Moebius strip of democracy. One member of the FTCR (Fédération des Tunisiens pour une Citoyenneté des Deux Rives), which launched the IDD initiative, insisted on including an explicit reference to social justice as a cardinal and operating principle in article 9 of that network's founding charter. "Since Tunisia came out of a revolution based on this principle, it seems an obligation for us to insist and carry these revolutionary themes," one of the FTCR members argued.[31] The location chosen for the establishment of this network, Mahres, a small town south of Sfax, far from the political centers of Tunisia, was also symbolically important. Transnational networks of Tunisian migrants in France and throughout Europe, which represent 1.3 million Tunisians (i.e. 10% of the total Tunisian citizenry), have been lobbying to be granted a consultative role in Tunisian politics.[32] Another project of the FTDES also buttresses solidarity with European countries through a film festival it organizes yearly in the southwestern town of Rdayyef. With the help of a German foundation, Rosa Luxemburg Stiftung, the festival devotes the lion's share of the films to issues of social justice and solidarity.[33] The social life of citizenship, in this case, is vivified by circulating north–south energies. In a way, the year 2011 helped to turn the Moebius strip into the purveyor of constructive and inclusive elements to the social life of local citizenship. Al-Bawsola, the NGO working on transparency and accountability, was established by a young female returnee who had fled to France after her cousin, Zuhair, a famous dissident blogger in the early 2000s, was arrested by Ben Ali's regime and died a few years later from the torture he had undergone. Her family, which also includes a judge who was critical of the regime, hails from the Tataouine region, but militated from Tunis after the revolution.[34]

Regional solidarity has also been connected with local efforts. A small charitable organization (with a religious overtone) in Bizerte, Ahl Al-Khayr (People of Goodwill), generates small revenues by

---

[31] Observation raised by a member of the FTCR during the *assises* in Mahres, 06/03/2016.

[32] www.nawaat.org/portail/2016/06/06/tunisians-abroad-dissatisfied-with-proposed-representative-authority/. The FTCR had also organized support for the strikers in the mining region of Gafsa in 2008 (Gobe 2010: 19).

[33] The Rencontres du Film Documentaire de Redeyef has been held every year since 2014.

[34] Amira Yahyaoui, NGO leader, interview in Tunis, 05/30/2016.

offering baking lessons to the women of Bizerte and its surrounding villages, and by collecting food from local markets and supermarkets, notably during Ramadan and *'eid al-adha*. It organizes small caravans of solidarity from Bizerte into poor rural communities. They also run projects with teenagers to clean the streets in the less touristic zones of Bizerte, creating occasions for interaction with people from different outlooks.[35] The founding members of Ahl Al-Khayr were also involved in a Maghrebi caravan of solidarity for Palestine back in 2014, with participants from Morocco, Algeria, and Libya, which managed to reach Gaza. Back to Siliana, Rachid, the founder of a cultural center, prides himself on multiple projects, including one that cooperates with a nationwide association called *"kulluna tunis"* (*"We are all Tunis"*) and with Mediterranean networks that enhance cultural exchanges and political debate around the links that the Mediterranean offers, beyond the hope of migration.[36] Two editions of the World Social Forum (WSF) that met in Tunisia, first in 2013 and then in April 2015, are also worthy of attention in this rubric of expanded space for enacted solidarity. The WSF have been held as pilgrimages for the alterglobalization movement since the late 1990s, and the choice to hold meetings in Tunis was more than symbolic. It was an occasion for international activists to connect with Arab peers. But the Tunisian community that converged on Tunis was comprised not only of left or center-left constellations of militants. Part of a 10-organization strong delegation, young (self-declared) Islamist individuals joined the debates in 2013 and 2015. They interacted in workshops pertaining to solidarity with Palestine, but also took part in workshops dealing with citizenship, equality, and social justice.[37]

In all these examples, social justice for *all* Tunisians is paramount. A small, apparently trivial event illustrates how an imagined sense of belonging offers an example of reciprocal interaction between communities and governing authorities. In the spring of 2015, a couple of associations and sponsors from Bizerte offered to help a small village, Sidi Ali Shebab, organize a festival of fava beans, an agricultural

---

[35] Tareq and Ghassen Ben Barka, charitable workers, interview in Bizerte, 05/24/2016. On Ennahda using this type of connective activities, in particular during Ramadan, see Sigillò (2020).
[36] Kharroubi, interview, 06/01/2016.
[37] Achref Wachani and Riadh Mastouri, charitable workers, interview in Tunis, 07/25/2015 and 07/23/2015.

product of that region that grows in abundance in the spring. The three-day event included games for youth, a donkey race, and a cooking competition. It was a big success with many people from surrounding towns attending, including deputies of the ARP. A small income was generated, and in the eye of one of the sponsors, it was a rich occasion for youths to interact rather than remaining closed off in cafés or at home.[38] Following the festival, villagers asked the government to replace the signpost with the name of the town at the entrance of the village, a post which had been vandalized many years ago when Ben Ali was still in power. Under Ben Ali, villagers preferred not to go to the government for even a small favor like that one; people simply wanted to avoid feeling like they owed a corrupt regime. But in 2015, when the festival managed to attract so much success and therefore a sense of pride from the inhabitants, they decided that the time was ripe for actually putting their town back on the map (and on the road) of Tunisia: "Before people were mocking us [because of the absent road sign indicating the entrance of the village]: we had no identity."[39] Thus, a modestly virtuous sense of belonging to a place could again be connected to larger state politics via the presence of regional deputies attending the festival. Belonging, here, entails more than just words.

Improvisational theatre is another example of reconnecting social roles, in this case with an enacted commitment to the defense of underprivileged groups. A project was set up by a collective of urbanists in the Greater Tunis area, with the objective of thematizing inequalities of resources and the unequal use of public space. Starting from the premise that the revolution started on the very inequalities between the interior and the Sahel (what the organizer called "spatial inequalities"),[40] the association, whose name is Municipalité Efficace ("Effective Municipality"), decided to role play at the micro-level the three municipalities, with some actors playing a fixed canvas in contrast with the open and thus improvised interaction of the public. How can municipalities improve access for all of their residents to basic services, commercial centers, and, possibly, leisure time while promoting transparency and efficacy? The play, originally organized with the municipality of Medjez El-Bab, a small town 60 km west of Tunis, was

---

[38] Yassine Annabi, NGO leader, interview in Bizerte, 05/23/2016.
[39] Annabi, interview, 05/23/2016.
[40] Othman Khaled, civic campaign leader, interview in Tunis, 05/26/2016.

thought of as a form of civic instruction on the rights of residents and the obligations of municipalities, combined with an occasion for officials to engage with attendees, a group of actual residents. The endresult is a work on the transparency of information and the use and allocation of resources by the municipalities. It generated a pact on what needs to be improved, through the forming of panels agreed upon during the play. Thus, a *visual representation* of common objectives comes as the fruit of self-acting and self-representation in real-time interactions with city-officials.

Other examples of theatres, in a recreational or civic educational vein, seem to assuage the desire for political activities. Theatre festivals in Le Kef (March 2016) and Medenine (April 2016) were very successful, offering "public spaces and the possibility to gather, meet and discuss" (Carnevale 2016). Acting was also improvised, like small flash mobs. A short-lived campaign in the winter of 2016 by young women in Kairouan and Houmt El-Souq (Djerba) consisted of temporarily occupying cafes, a type of public/commercial space where only men are normally allowed (women go to *salons de thé*, tea-rooms).[41] The message in using public space is one about social roles, namely that women ought to be considered full members of the public, with equal rights. This reverberates with the example of a female Nahdaoui militant, who requested anonymity. She refused the clothing diktats of her father at home and engaged with full spirit and energy in her political militancy for the Islamist party.

The symbolic components of these multiplied social roles expressed exasperation toward municipal institutions. For the period under consideration here, 2014–2018, a majority of municipalities were still under the control of an appointee of the Ministry of the Interior.[42] It took enormous pressure for the government to pass a new law on local authorities. All of the small initiatives I have documented in this section were connected with the popular discontent vis-à-vis centralized power. All the governments of this period used the legal regimen for socalled *Délégations Spéciales* (*niabat khussussia*, "Special Delegations")

---

[41] On this campaign, called "*nahnū aydan lanā al-haqq fi-dukhūl al-muqāha*," "We also have the right to go into cafés," see www.lexpress.fr/actualite/monde/afrique/en-tunisie-des-femmes-protestent-a-leur-facon-contre-les-cafes-pour-hommes_1768879.html, or www.wepostmag.com/djerba-des-femmes-sinstallent-dans-un-cafe-pour-hommes/.

[42] Besma Omezzine, party activist, interview in Sfax, 06/05/2016.

to assert the prominence of centralized authority. An old law from the 1970s dealing with representation at the municipal level (*"loi organi-que sur les municipalités,"* Loi 75) was used profusely after January 2011. After the revolution, the transitional governments dissolved a majority of the 264 municipal councils. That allowed them to get rid of the direct control of the RCD and pro-Ben Ali cronies, but it also left Tunis and the Ministry of the Interior in charge of appointing these new temporary municipal authorities.

Many Tunisian citizens had great hopes for decentralization, as promised, among others, in article 131 of the new Constitution, which guarantees administrative and financial autonomy to local collectivities. Article 141 foresees that establishment of a high council of local authorities with a location outside of the capital, to contribute to further deconcentration of authority in a country that suffered from a highly centralized power structure. For the first time in Tunisian history, all Tunisians were guaranteed the right to be represented in municipal structures. Before the passing of new administrative measures and laws on local collectivities in 2018, 20% of the population was not "municipalized," and thus did not have access to the same services of the state (the right to interact with local police, to elect municipal delegations, etc. – the uneven distribution of coercion identified in Part I). Despite the claim by all the governments to carry the mission of the revolution, it took seven years to actually turn this promise of universal citizenship in municipal matters to full fruition.

In May 2016, when I was doing fieldwork in Tunisia, the government finally released a first draft of the code on local collectivities. The new law foresaw the creation of 86 new municipalities.[43] In general, the project was received with a great sense of satisfaction: in the south, it meant that citizens would have civilian authorities to deal with local issues (and not the Army and the Ministry of the Interior as in the past), and cities that had absorbed a large number of rural migrants were given new means to organize their territorial coverage. The governorate of Sfax, in particular, which absorbed hundreds of thousands of new residents coming from the interior regions in recent decades, added six new municipalities to the 13 previously existing.[44]

---

[43] The creation of these 86 new municipalities was confirmed by governmental decree No. 2016-602 (26 May 2016). See Belhadj (2019: 25).
[44] I am grateful to Souhail Belhadj and Hela Yousfi for discussion of municipalities in the decentralization process.

Yet, the draft of the new law, which started to circulate in the summer of 2016, was full of contradictions, with one hand giving power to these decentralized entities, and the other reclaiming a form of central control. Most notably, people lamented a dearth of fiscal measures to generate direct resources for the municipalities, and the continuation of centralized control over local police. Such contradictions were not lost on the four members of the special delegations I interviewed, in Bizerte, Siliana, Sfax, and Midoun.[45]

There was a clear reluctance by the national leadership to implement the decentralization agenda. The Tunisian governments of Habib Essid and Youssef Chahed, the two Prime Ministers under President Essebsi and the ARP, dragged their feet in finalizing this law, without which no municipal elections could take place. Eventually it was the EU and international donors' pressure that broke the deadlock (Belhadj 2019). On April 26, 2018, the ARP finalized the last details of the law on municipalities, and just a few weeks later, on May 6, the first post-Ben Ali municipal elections finally took place. Section 6.2 will explain how municipalization coincided with the return of "strong men," but in fact the initiatives that Tunisians proposed and implemented to give meaning to decentralization were extremely varied. Whether these initiatives really impacted the timeline of decentralization is highly disputable. But they demonstrated that many citizens in Tunisia, women and men, young and old, took it upon themselves to occupy civic spaces. This was not an impulse from above, from the parties, nor from the Parliament. It was only seldomly done with the help of local NGOs or foreign donors. Citizens acted spontaneously and mobilized their own resources and social capital to generate public debates and direct action.

5.3 National Prestige and the Resistance of Artistic Creativity

Tunisia and Yemen are now on opposite paths, with Yemen torn between three warring factions, and Tunisia continuing, at a much slower pace, with the politics of "reforms" and "transition." This section compares civic and artistic creativity. In both countries, national actors tended to refuse to acknowledge the critical work

---

[45] E.g. Foued Guechaï, party activist, *Délégation Spéciale* of Houmt El-Souq, interview in Midoun, 05/29/2016.

made by artists. Various episodes oppose the unfettered power of cultural criticism to the authorities of elders, and of male political leaders. *Vis populi* is partly relegated to the margins, but a variety of examples show continuity as well.

One vignette captures the generational and institutional hurdle discussed in greater detail in Chapter 6. After the revolution, the municipality of Siliana tried to develop a new space inside its main building, at the entrance of the town, to be more welcoming to its residents. Thanks to a small grant from a European donor, 30,000 dinars (about US $14,000) were used to renovate and make the waiting room more welcoming, with seats, leaflets about resources for citizens, and new screens displaying essential information. A new team in the municipality chosen to replace the pre-2011 council oversaw the renovations, while the secretary general of the municipality, a political boss from the time of the RCD less enthusiastic about these innovative ideas, used all kinds of procrastinating measures to obstruct the realization of the new space. He refused to sign and delayed the authorization for the work. Eventually, the project was implemented to the apparent satisfaction of the population.[46] But for the secretary general, this project has no purpose, stating that the scheme was meant to be "for kids" ("*pour des gamins*"), not for "real citizens." This echoes the language of presidential candidate Beji Caid Essebsi in the second half of 2014, when he introduced in his speeches the idea of defending the "dignity of the state" (*haybat al-dawla*).[47] This notion of restoring "prestige" is a direct testimonial on the clash of cultures of representation: on the one hand, the new waiting room meant to accommodate citizens *inside* official state premises, while on the other, the reiteration of an excuse for exclusion, in the name of restoring prestige, status, or (as in Siliana) maturity.

The trope of patronizing superiority by an older generation was also seen in Yemen. The symbols of nationalism muzzled the aspiration of a new generation of citizens. For example, in the south of Yemen, the practice of democratic self-representation by a younger generation turned into an exercise in political recapture by the emerging militarized

---

[46] I rely on Rachid Kharroubi's testimonial, Siliana, 06/01/2016. I could see, one day, the queues of people expecting to solve a bureaucratic problem formed in front of the municipality in the early morning before the actual opening.

[47] Zemni (2016). See also www.alaraby.co.uk/english/politics/2014/12/20/essebsi-and-tunisia-the-nostalgia-for-past-glories.

elite. Here I will make the relationship between *vis populi* and southern civic activism explicit, but I want to draw attention to the evacuation of the presentist component of *vis populi*, and how this removal was enacted by the invocation of old tropes of political mobilization.

With the collapse of the constitutional project, and the march of the Huthis on Aden in the spring of 2015, it became clear to many citizens of the south that federalism was not a viable option. Secession has been advocated for in two sorts of events, mass marches (*miliyuniyyat* in Arabic, for the supposedly "millions" of people marching) and by *fa'a-liyyat*, "agitprop" events that mix cultural celebration with big street parties (Amira Augustin 2018: 101). Both forms employ rituals to piece together a common narrative. These events have been wrapped in the symbolism of self-determination, the revival of the old Southern flag, and the collective memory of the South, especially around the 1963–1967 anti-colonial struggle and the 1994 war. Dates for important rallies and events that are chosen by political groups in the south, like Hirak and the STC, all pivot around three dates: October 14, November 30, and to a lesser extent April 27. The date October 14, 1963 marks the start of the movement towards independence from Britain, and the event was romantically commemorated during the massive march on that same date in 2014, a moment widely understood as a turning point towards southern independence.[48] November 30, 1967, the date of independence from Britain, was commemorated in a special manner in 2017: the 50th anniversary of Southern Yemen's independence coincided with the establishment of a new legislative, the National Assembly for the STC.[49] Finally, a particularly important *fa'aliyya* took place on April 27, 2014, commemorating the start of the 1994 war and the process of internal colonization by northern elites.[50]

---

[48] For example, mourning the death of the fighter (*munāḍil*) Abdallah Ahmad Huru, a figure who fought against the British, Aydarus Al-Zubaydi makes a reference to the October 14 Revolution in Dhala', with the direct superposition of the current battles between the STC and the Huthis in Dhala', and the actual initial episode of the 1963 anti-colonial insurrection against the British. See https://stcaden.com/news/12227 (June 24, 2020).

[49] Amira Augustin (2015: 12) reports that on November 30, 2014, southerners had already toyed with the idea of southern independence but the fruit was not ripe yet.

[50] See Amira Augustin (2014). For the symbolism of the dates chosen during the 2000s protests, with reference to the brutalities by Saleh when Hirak was in its embryonic stage, see Mermier (2012).

The dance of parallel dates conjugates cultural representation with new political aspirations. They marry *taswir* with *tamthil*, or cultural practices with political representation. *Fa'aliyyat* and *miliyuniyyat* reactivate a collective southern identity, which generates its own dynamic intertwined with principles of 2011. In *fa'aliyyat*, "anyone, male or female, young or old" can go "onto the stage to recite poetry, make a speech on Southern independence," or evoke historical episodes of the Southern past (Amira Augustin 2018: 101). Music and collective songs bring about a sense of collective effervescence. The pro-secessionist TV channel *Aden Live*, operating from Beirut, has been ripe with depictions of northern Yemenis as annoying, crassly uneducated, and profiteers always using violence.[51] Intergenerational exchanges and interactions (family recollection of past memories of the PDRY) have been said to play a role in cementing a distinct southern identity in the open (Amira Augustin 2018: 101). These rituals are also a space for citizens to express their commitment to the project of their own state.

Thus, *vis populi*, albeit embodied in a variety of actions since 2007, was at play at in various moments in the south after 2014. To a certain extent, especially for people living in the south, denunciations of encroachment by the north (the idea of "occupation" or internal colonization) expressed a democratic aspiration. The cultural manifestations (*fa'aliyyat*) helped socialize new citizens and taught them how to express their political commitments. They also galvanized popular hopes to build a new, democratic south, open to the world, and neutralize unaccountable violent groups such as Ansar Al-Sharia (AS-Y) and Al-Qaeda offsprings, which have operated mostly if not uniquely in the south of the country.

But all these elements also hide actual tensions. The *fa'aliyyat* can also be seen as public occasions to teach southerners to express their unconditional loyalty to their leaders, away from the horizontal and participatory mode of organization of Hirak during its initial years. The overemphasis on the colonial period and the 1994 war in all these mass events reveals that the agenda was set by an older generation of politicians. Younger participants were also excluded by another

---

[51] On the famous character Dahabshe, see Amira-Augutin (2018: 100). Day addresses both the symbolism of Dahabshe (Day 2012: 147, 149) and of the Upper Yemeni accent, *lughat al-nakhlit* (pp. 98, 99, 152).

development, which connects to the infightings in Sanaa between September 2014 and February 2015 and the growing militarization of the country. As a result, Hirak's internal tensions became exacerbated. According to Amira Augustin (2015: 12), the two small wings of Hirak that argued for continued cooperation with Sanaa (one for federalism, but with only two regions, the so-called "Sudanese model"; the other for pressuring Hadi into a more inclusive attitude toward the south) were definitively outmaneuvered by a "vast majority" of Hiraki supporters preferring "full independence and the end of cooperation with Hadi's *sulta*" ("authority," or in this case, government). The increased militarization of all these southern demonstrations and the role that a few middle-aged males played in armed stand-offs slowly left the very young and the female constituencies within Hirak without a voice.

Issues of "security" and problematic alliances within the STC connecting military with Salafi leaders will be discussed in the next chapter. The limited, yet important role played by a few advocacy NGOs in the context of a militarized Yemen drawn into a regional and a civil war mattered. Even if this type of action belongs to "contained" mobilizations, it preserved the main aspirations for a civil state and the civic expectation for accountability of the coercive forces. In particular in the north, it has been important that NGOs document the war atrocities committed by the KSA and its allies – often indiscriminate bombings – but also to document human rights and international humanitarian law violations by Huthis and Saleh supporters. Unlike in Tunisia, where civic work gravitated around (new) municipalities, Yemeni associations resumed the long tradition of self-help and community work that existed notably in the 1970s and early 1980s (Carapico 1998). Other initiatives were taken by new NGOs, working on issues of human rights and accountability.

In Yemen, the nature of the GCC Initiative and the collapse of the process in 2015 meant that there could be no formal mechanisms for accountability and transitional justice. The 2015 draft constitution did include six articles on transitional justice and national reconciliation, in the Transitional Provisions (Chapter X), but the text was never put to a vote. Hence, the burden of accountability for violent action fell on the shoulders of associations. Various centers and platforms have worked relentlessly to document war crimes, to complain about irregular detentions and collective punishments, and to call on international actors to end their support for the Saudi coalition and their aerial attacks.

On the NGO front, we can list the work of *Mwatana* ("Citizenship" in Arabic). With its network of researchers located in various governorates, *Mwatana* has produced resounding and finger-pointing reports demonstrating international involvement in war atrocities. It publishes an annual report called *Without Accountability*,[52] as well as other detailed reports. For example, in interviews collected in 20 Yemeni governorates between May 2016 and December 2019, *Mwatana* documents the squalid conditions of detention and numerous abuses of citizens' rights and of war laws. The 90-page document entitled *In the Darkness* emulates international standards of human rights organizations documenting such violations.[53] A 2019 report titled "European Responsibility for War Crimes" documented how Italian and German arms wiped away a family of six during an airstrike by the Saudi/UAE-led military coalition in Deir Al-Hajari in northwest Yemen a few years earlier.[54] Its chairwoman, Radhya Almutawakel, was declared the winner of the Anna Politkovskaya Award, for her determination to defend the fundamental rights of Yemenis.

Another small organization, *Nabdh*, Arabic for "Pulse" (the full name is "Pulse for Social Justice Organization")[55] generates projects to protect vulnerable groups and people affected by the war. It was established in July 2013 in the Taiz area and taps into a long tradition of local self-help. Since the start of the war, it has mobilized displaced people with very local job-creating projects. Typically, collective work is done on restoring pavements on damaged roads, rebuilding health centers and schools destroyed during military engagements, and offering first aid and civic education. The modus operandi is that of direct action and collective action to find funding locally, that is either from the collectivity or through remittances sent by parents or friends living abroad.[56] With the so-called "Pilot" project, *Nabdh* seeks voluntary participation in municipal matters. For the founder of this small NGO, engaging with the three warring parts – the Huthis, Hadi's government, and the STC in Aden – with the same developmental model shows that Yemenis have the ability to use power at the local level, be it in villages

---

[52] https://mwatana.org/en/without-accountability.
[53] Published in June 2020. See https://mwatana.org/en/in-the-darkness/.
[54] https://mwatana.org/en/european-responsibility-for-war-crimes/.
[55] www.facebook.com/psjoYemen.
[56] Interview with Bachir Al-Mohallal, NGO leader, Sanaa, interview via Zoom, 02/23/2021.

or in the parts of the governorates most affected by the conflicts, in order to restore civic interactions.[57]

The context of the wars and the absence of a clear governmental authority generates opportunities for associations to fill in the void, but it also means that patriarchal social structures often emerge as the basis for collective action. Section 6.2 will discuss the potentially corrosive effect that these structures have for citizenship rights. The work of a small civic forum on the Socotra Islands echoes the experience of *Pulse* and of local engagement, but with a focus on civic education. The "Yemen Foundation for Renaissance and Development of the Socotra Archipelago" runs small workshops for the youth, male and female, cleaning actions, and courses on political participation and awareness of the need to preserve the unique ecosystem of the archipelago.[58] Its founder, who obtained a PhD in Algeria, also partners with the Socotra College of Education and Socotra Community College to run events and offer English or French languages classes.

During a period of violence on the islands in the first days of June 2020, when clashes occurred between Hadi loyalists and supporters of the STC, Muhammad Khalifa's association activated its network of "elders" to promote *sulh*, traditional reconciliation.[59] His engagement with the NGO, but also his role as a person teaching in the local community college, made him part of the "coalition of elites" in Socotra who invoked the archipelago's tradition of pacifism. A few days later, a joint declaration was issued by this group of elders calling on everybody to respect the leadership of the "sages in the pursuit of mediation." The statement was then published on local Yemeni news websites, with a joint call for "development, not clashes."[60]

National or local prestige often seems to lay in the hands of "elders," traditional community leaders (Yemen), or of a presidential candidate

---

[57] *The Pulse* website states "The importance of the communal effort increases in societies where the formal institutions lack the credibility. Thus the family bonds gain more value and the individual resorts to his primary bonds and relations to achieve his goals." Taken from: web.archive.org/web/2022020604 0456/https://psjo.org/moreProject.php?id=16.

[58] Interview with Muhammad Khalifa, civic campaign, in Socotra, via WhatsApp, 12/28/2019 and 06/07/2020. He is also Chairman of the Network of Young Academics in Socotra.

[59] Khalifa, interviews on 06/07 and 06/11/2020.

[60] See https://qishnpress.com/localities/394/, "Socotra wants development, not conflicts" (in Arabic, June 2, 2020).

(Essebsi in Tunisia). There are also continuous efforts to defend pluralism and equality in the face of violence and war. In Yemen, one has to
read between the lines of artistic and literary creativity to find ideals of
equal participation (Al-Rubaidi 2021). In Tunisia, the forms of mobilization inspired by the idea of *vis populi* continue, but come with a risk
when addressing political criticism and the ensuing backlash too directly.

The first symbolic example comes from the northern town of Bizerte,
which was the last military base that the French maintained in Tunisia
even after independence, and which was the place of a horrifying and
failed military campaign led by Bourguiba in July 1961 to reclaim the
city. The French military, with better equipment and high ground,
crushed the rebellion, which ended in a bloodbath and hundreds of
dead Tunisians. On October 15, 1963, the French finally left Bizerte.
Every year, on that date, a ceremony is held in Bizerte to commemorate
the martyrs in the presence of the highest state authorities.

In October 2013, for the 50th anniversary, a group of associations
decided to organize a protest, knowing that the President, Prime
Minister, and the like would attend. This was the perfect venue to air
local grievances and put the question of unemployment, in particular
youth unemployment, on the agenda for the executive's attention. To
illustrate how protests convey demands that are connected to violence
and popular wrath in front of political inaction, it is best to report
verbatim the account of the event by Yassine Annabi, the leader of an
association active in sustainable development:

> You know that every year on October 15th, the President and Prime Minister
> come to Bizerte for Martyrs Day. Usually, they come to pray and then leave
> the city. We [a group of associations] decided that this would be a day of
> wrath, not a day of celebration. Youth on that day [in July 1961] sacrificed
> themselves to free Tunisia and make it an independent state. But today
> youths are the walking dead: they are without job, without future, without
> income! Politicians should be coming for the living, not for the dead ones! So
> we decided to express our solidarity. From the Martyr's Cemetery to the
> [building of the] representative of the state, our governor, we formed
> a human chain, to represent and express our wrath by marching in front of
> the governor's building in Bizerte. [We knew] the official parade would pass
> here. We played the card of mediatization.[61]

---

[61]   Interview with Yassine Annabi, Bizerte, 05/23/2016. My translation from
       French. On the association, DERB, see www.facebook.com/association.derb/.

The police, hearing of the plan for a joint manifestation, tried to prevent it. A couple of days before the event, the governor attempted to placate the project by trying to find a compromise with the associations to stop their plan, with compensation for a few jobs here and there for youths. They refused because, time and again, the governor had failed to do his job of creating large job-schemes for youths of the region. This echoes the statement of an activist in Djerba using the axiom according to which to gain something (like new rights), you have to be in the offensive (*"il faut attaquer pour avoir son droit"*).[62]

In the second example, old patterns of repression as a response to critique are combined with the ability to confront diffused violence and social taboos. The burst of creative activity, in cartoons and critical artworks, is not likely to disappear in Tunisia because of the taste that most citizens acquired for freedom of expression. In January 2016, Dalinda Louati, a young female artist, made a drawing criticizing the dangerous pollution generated since the 1950s by the phosphate industrial plant in Sfax, the SIAPE (Société industrielle d'acide phosphorique et d'engrais). To evoke the danger, Louati represented the chimney of the industrial plant as the continuation of a gun, hidden in the ground (see Figure 5.1).

Louati was arrested for this harmless piece of art.[63] A quick but vivid campaign of solidarity helped her out of detention, but a signal was sent that even indirect, cultural representations of radical demands (here the request to close the SIAPE and protect the environment, but with the SIAPE also being a symbol of the carelessness of Tunis when it comes to the quality of living in Sfax) are now the object of intimidation. Why did this piece of work draw the ire of the authorities while other Facebook posts, which are much more aggressive and directed at key political figures, remained without a response by the police? Such selective repression puzzles more than one in Tunisia. The leader of the association who narrated the protest of Bizerte above believes that only those with the right connections, such as those with a prominent father, the right political clout, or the right social capital, are let off the hook. Without giving names, he mentioned the son of the family of a martyr of the 1963 events in Bizerte, who published trash talk on the

---

[62] Interview with Hassen Jribi, association member, interview in Djerba, 01/02/2016.
[63] See the Tunisian daily *Le Quotidien*, 01/13/2016, p. 27. I am grateful to the artist for additional information provided about her art work and this episode.

Figure 5.1 "The death factory" (*"L'usine de la mort"*). Tunisia 2016.

web with full impunity, while another young man was arrested for a couple of days with no charges for an improvised harmless sit-in in front of the governorate.[64] The criterion of having the right connections (the proverbial Arabic *wasta*) to strong men or not explains the different attitudes toward criticism.

In Yemen as well, the political commentaries made by street artists generated some controversies. Murad Subay', born in 1987 into a family of modest means in Dhamar and an English student at the university of Sanaa at the time of the revolution, has become quite famous as a street artist in recent years. He has advanced a "politically-involved and humanist discourse which, in its attention to matters of justice, human rights and his pacifistic perspective" has gathered support in Yemen and abroad (Bonnefoy 2018: 163). His first project, which started in early 2012 with a campaign disseminated through Facebook, was quite innocuous, called "Colour the Walls of Your Street," an effort to mingle abstract art with people's discussion about the use of public spaces in Sanaa. More openly critical of the recent past, he then launched a campaign called "The Walls Remember

---

[64] Interview with Yassine Annabi, Bizerte, 05/23/2016.

their Faces," in which faces of persons who have disappeared due to government repression since the 1970s where stenciled on walls.[65] For the first time, and emboldened by the NDC's discussion of the issue of the disappeared, families of the disappeared spoke out and, in coordination with a human rights organization, stenciled more than 100 *desaparecidos*' faces on walls in Sanaa, Ibb, Taiz and Hodeida (see Figures 5.3 and 5.4).[66] A small documentary shows how the campaign stirred deep emotions and contributed to a synchronization of various temporalities, connecting the 1970s and 1980s to the time of the revolution and its aftermath: drawings of people were defaced again, but Subay' and his team repainted them. One of the disappeared persons was even found alive (Bonnefoy 2018: 163), suggesting the power of the arts to bring people out of oblivion and of synchronizing past times of military repression to the Yemeni present.[67]

As soon as the civil war broke out, Murad Subay' disparaged the "twelve scourges" of Yemen, among which were sectarianism, poverty,

Figures 5.2 and 5.3 Mural stencils by Murad Subay'. Yemen 2012.

[65] https://muradsubay.com/2013/12/25/9808/ or www.instagram.com/muradsubay/.

[66] https://almadaniyamag.com/2017/07/04/2017-7-4-graffiti-creativity-and-influence/.

[67] See also the video by Benjamin Wiacek on the campaign of the 100 disappeared Yemenis: www.youtube.com/watch?v=HBeLL1wqZM4 (December 13, 2021, English).

Figures 5.2 and 5.3 (cont.)

corruption, civil war, and bombardments by foreign powers. In a style reminiscent of Banksy (Murad is now often nicknamed "the Yemeni Banksy"), Subay' denounces targeted killings and declares that "civil war is suicide" (*"al-harb al-ahliyya intihar"*) (Bonnefoy 2018: 164). One famous drawing depicts a Yemeni child with a paper plane facing a threatening bomb flying at him, or a girl tagging the wall under the presence of an armed drone marked "Made in USA." She asks: "why did you kill my family?"[68] Or a little girl watering a flower growing on the bomb, a piece of art drawn on rusted metal pipe surrounded by litter, called "Mortar Rose."[69]

Writers and poets have also for some time combined a series of themes around democratic participation, pluralism, and civil rule, and increasingly with the disrupting effects of the war, together. Intellectual and writer Bushra Al-Maqtari maintains that "the revolution is not limited to places. The revolution is the pen. The revolution is the change" (quoted in

---

[68]   www.poetryfoundation.org/harriet-books/2013/12/people-of-yemen-protest-drone-strikes-through-graffiti-and-poetry-.

[69]   https://muradsubay.com/campaigns/ruins/imag0307777777777777777/. Another street artist who has engaged with political commentary is Thiyazen Al-Alawi. Using graffiti in the bustling streets of Sanaa, he launched a campaign called "Street Caricatures," which engages with political and economic issues and events in a cynical manner and "allows the audience to engage with his work." See https://almadaniyamag.com/2017/07/04/2017-7-4-graffiti-creativity-and-influence/.

Strzelecka 2018: 60). Al-Maqtari hails from Taiz, the city that still harbors a yearly commemoration of the "2011 Revolution." In that town, the anniversary of the revolution is celebrated on February 11, the day Egyptian President Mubarak resigned, which was also the first day upon which encampments started in the city. As recently as 2020, the youth of Taiz were said to carry the "torch of the glorious 2011 revolution," with thousands of young people marching in the city.[70]

Marching in public spaces, where it has become difficult to express support except for one of the warring parties, has been replaced by online campaigns. Virtual spaces of debate include not only online blogs and magazines, but also literature. In these spaces too, the themes of the revolution and the call for a civil state gradually ceded space to the theme of war and the cost of the destruction for Yemenis. *Al-Madaniya* is one of such new spaces that has been active since 2017. This online magazine is a platform for Yemeni art, culture, and civil society. Funded by German foundations, it has the expected themes for international donors, but it also acts as a platform for young artists (writers, musicians, poets) to showcase their art work in Arabic. The notion of awareness or consciousness (*wa'y*) encountered in the revolutionary years (Al-Rubaidi 2014: 31; R. Porter 2016: 64; 2017: 271), as the enabling connector between different groups, is now alive in literary production.

On the subject of literature, Al-Rubaidi (2018b) notes that 83 novels were published in Yemen between 2005 and 2015, which is more than in the 70 years between 1927 and 2000. The outpouring of cultural creativity is significant, but the content of these novels is also highly revealing of a change in attitudes when it comes to politics and civic participation: Scholars of Yemeni literature underline how many books are now tackling difficult issues of regionalism, confessionalism, or race (*muhammashin*) with vigor (Mermier 2020; Al-Rubaidi 2018b: 3–4). Regionalism, south and north, or social cracks between lower and upper Yemen, is tackled in recent novels by Ahmad Zayn and Nadya Al-Kawkabani (Al-Rubaidi 2018b: 6). Even the NDC became

---

[70] See the report made on Yemen Shabab TV (Yemen Youth), available at: www .youtube.com/watch?v=ysTbJvO2fW0: "Sons of Taiz carry the torch of the Glorious 11 February Revolution" (February 11, 2020). Atiaf Alwazir (2016: 186) also believes that informal youth participation after 2011 has created a "permanent repository of resistance and repertoires of contention with which political elites will have to reckon."

the object of a utopian novel narrating the quest for a new president that would correspond to the demands of 2011 and the recommendations of the NDC, which in the novel assumes the form of the new Yemeni constitution. The novel, *Saghira's Laws*, was penned by Wajdi Al-Ahdal. Saghira is the name of the woman chosen to be the new president and elevate Yemeni politics to the high ground of good governance. "The novel demonstrates that the goals of the 2011 popular uprising require strenuous work, patience and difficult decisions to achieve" (Al-Rubaidi 2021). The name *saghira* is also an adjective for "small" (in the feminine or in the plural), which might also be a pun on the small and mundane steps that passing laws and choosing a new president require. In the last chapter, we will come back to recent Yemeni literature and the hidden messages it conveys in this war-torn society.

5.4 Vulnerable Articulations

This chapter has argued that social roles in everyday practices in Tunisia, and to a lesser extent creative artistic creation in Yemen, have sustained those novel articulations of new forms of civic participation and criticism, which otherwise have become bogged-down during the Yemeni and Tunisian "transitions." Through an analysis of small anecdotes, street graffiti, testimonials from lay citizens involved in low-key campaigns, activists of new cultural associations, and local politicians from different parts of Tunisia, and of visual and literary art in Yemen at a time of an all-out war, I proposed a different assessment of the revolutionary legacies, which relocated violence in relation to cultural and political representation, *vis populi*. I contend that a critical attitude is perceptible and aims at anchoring pluralism and equality within Tunisian and Yemeni society, in particular when it comes to restrain the use of violence. Even if one has to read between the lines (Al-Rubaidi 2021), or interpret mundane gestures, like the occupation of the terrace of a café in Djerba, a graffiti in front of the municipality in Siliana, or stencils of Yemeni *desaparecidos*, it is possible to see how citizens are able to express a desire to open up political systems and criticize the regrouping of central authorities with their own means.

When conducting research in Tunisia between 2015 and 2016, I encountered numerous small episodes of daily life that were subject to intense debate. Everybody lamented the unruliness that exists on the streets: people try to jump the lines at red traffic lights; sidewalks are invaded by illegal street sellers; badly parked vehicles bar passage for pedestrians. Time and again, in *louages* (the collective mini-buses), or on Tunisian streets, one could hear that "things were better under Ben Ali." Others were less drastic in their assessment of the past, and noted that the dreamlike harmony of the revolutionary moments, where everyone seemed to yield to other drivers, and people stopped at traffic lights even when they were not operating, seemed to have definitely disappeared.

Rather that jumping to hasty conclusions about setbacks or failures of the Arab revolutions, I have taken these daily experiences as attempts by Tunisians to renegotiate social roles in a more democratic manner. People complained a lot? Maybe they felt more like citizens entitled to speak, now that they are protected by freedom of expression. People behaved differently in the turmoil of the revolutionary moments? Maybe because the old social roles determining who felt entitled to exercise authority, especially through informal privilege, have been radically questioned. Municipalities have been slow or reluctant to open their space of interactions with their local subjects? The use of new spaces by various initiatives, such as political theaters, to express their opinion have kept pushing informally and from below for actual deconcentration of power.

In Yemen, two democratic potentials have been identified. First, these evocations of 2011 and/or of the NDC are evidence of a rupture with past patterns of Yemeni politics. Helen Lackner (2016a: 142, 167) is therefore right to suggest that for all its horrors since, the 2011 episodes must be considered revolutionary for Yemeni history because it made a majority of Yemenis actors of their own political fate and introduced a fundamentally different, critical, political discourse. Second, these evocations reveal that even those with little social capital or with no connections to one of the leading political parties, or connected to the right personalistic or tribal networks, now dared to speak the language of genuine enfranchisement. That the depository of these demands was the NDC suggests that a new political imaginary emerged, connecting people of lower class or political extraction, and put them on a putative equal footing.

To use metaphors put to work in Part I, I want to come back to Gramsci's idea of articulations and to the spatial metaphor of the

Moebius strip. For Gramsci, articulations are essential ingredients for popular mobilizations. In the neo-Gramscian perspective, one that takes as its political objective democratic transformation rather than a working-class revolution, these articulations are what allow hegemony to emerge. These articulations are multiple, rooted in everyday life, and connect with various constituencies and regions that have been left out for decades during the republican periods in Tunisia and Yemen. They have targeted issues of education and civic participation, but also underlined the necessity of maintaining pressure on the security sector for increased transparency. These articulations have often been proposed without the help or mediation of formal organizations, be they parties, NGOs, or parliaments. The people have continued to be their own source of action, a source largely influenced by the modus operandi (a new consciousness, insistence on diversity, etc.) and the repertoires of cultural expressions (marches, caravans, etc.) set in motion in 2011.

With regard to the Moebius strip, some of the actions, in particular in Tunisia, have added a novel translocal and transnational sense of solidarity. The social life of citizenship is now influenced by campaigns of solidarity across the countries of North Africa, all the way to Gaza. The joint citizenship initiatives of Tunisians based in France (or elsewhere in Europe) and in Tunisia itself are important examples of some positive legacies of these revolutionary principles. In Yemen, the impact of the war has debilitated the capacity for positive creative alliance and instead, as we will see in Chapter 6, has generated new forms of imperialist encroachment.

6 | *Strong Man Syndrome and the Resubjectivation of Citizenship*

6.1 Security, Wars, and Neo-imperial Encroachment

Gradually, everyday civic actions are gripped by arguments about security, national threats, or, in Yemen, by the reality of the regional war. To a large extent, the variety of social roles recede into the old forms of latent citizenship. The strength of the habitus of *vis populi* is weakened by resurging fault lines and the new doxa of securitization. The non-violent path is silenced by the destruction of a never-ending conflict in Yemen, while in Tunisia it finds few occasions to manifest its revolutionary project. The articulated multitude is also reduced by an increased sense of compartmentalization. Rather than a gender-inclusive assembly of people proposing common paths for political decisions, we see strong men, be they military, security leaders, or old male politicians, regrouping and taking the lead.

Tunisia remains more open to democratic politics not only because an informal alliance (the Quartet) avoided the prospect of a military coup in the summer of 2013, but also because its geographical location, at a distance from the Gulf region, kept it from becoming ensnared in Arab neo-imperialisms.[1] A general sense of improvement is registered by most in Tunisia, with a growing separation of power and more guarantees for basic freedoms.[2] Yet there are numerous delays in the implementation of the transitional provisions passed with the 2014 Constitution, leaving the country without a Supreme Judicial Council or a Constitutional Court, and heavy partisan disputes around the High Electoral Committee. The return to the state of emergency at the end of 2015 has also cast a shadow for citizens and associations.

---

[1] This does not mean that there were no moments of influence from the Gulf, with, for example, a widespread rhetoric about fears of Qatari interference in support of Ennahda. But the impact of Algeria's support for the Tunisian security sector against the growth of jihadi Islamists neutralized these influences.

[2] A sense that was largely shared by the people I interviewed in Tunisia.

Challenges to transitional justice, the presence of "strong men," and everyday expectations of "order" will constitute the bulk of the empirical material around Tunisia in this chapter.

For Yemen, the focus will be on fragmentation and external encroachments, which have been virulently at play. Arabia Felix, which was for decades a backyard of Saudi politics, also became the object of predation for the United Arab Emirates (UAE). I see the current Yemeni crisis as being best explained by referencing neo-imperialism, as distinguished from the older form of imperialism (Part I). Military might still matters in Yemen nowadays, with American and also European bombs dropped on the country, but the new imperial forces rely on an abundance of indirect means to exert pressure: claims of humanitarian interventions in support of a "failed state"; rhetoric about assistance for long-term development in Socotra hiding the strategic presence of the UAE; the power of discourses that shape the apprehension of a very complex three-way civil war in Yemen; all the way to the targeting of Yemeni livelihoods.

Conceptually, the chapter pays attention to the issue of articulations, understood as a "form of a connection or link that can make a unity of two different elements under certain conditions. It is a linkage which is not necessary, determined, absolute, and essential for all times; [. . . and which] requires particular conditions of existence to appear" (S. Hall 2016: 121). Stuart Hall's understanding of articulations echoes the neo-Gramscian themes evoked throughout this book. Here in Chapter 6, the focus will be on how these articulations have been adversely affected by the rise of the security forces, the reassertion of a business mentality, and strong man syndrome, all at the expense of civilian rule, voluntary participation, and a combination of women, youth, and the marginalized making demands for equality. As a result, external actors, corporate power, and formal institutions undercut bottom-up participation and transitional justice initiatives. The stories told below, covering developments until the summer 2021, are not about a total shutting down of civic engagement. Notable efforts occur in both countries to keep the articulations working, with rather symbolic actions in which the principle of *vis populi* continues to work (*Sayyeb Trottoir* in Tunisia; symbolic victories for Yemeni associations in the field of accountability).

One observes a resubjectivation of social roles to past and more restrictive patterns of civic interactions. Political representations in both countries face the syndrome of the "big men" or "strong men," phrases used to characterize the loss of hope in pluralism, articulation, and new social contract replaced by the hope that one person, an old male political or military figure, may come and take the lead in "saving" the country. Rim Naguib (2020) captured this tendency with the phrase "patriarchal nationalism" in her studies of Egypt under President El-Sisi. This gendered expectation about political leadership is certainly at play in Yemen and Tunisia and has pushed women back into a passive role in politics.[3]

This last chapter starts with the issues of security, war, and terrorism. The conditions that these three themes create resemble what has already been described in Part I, but with notable novelties: A new discourse of security and stability, which suits both domestic and international agendas, has replaced the colonial "benevolence" and/ or the Cold War projects of modernization. A new geography of imperial encroachment arises in the twenty-first century, with the growing might of the Saudi and Emirati monarchs supported by cohorts of African and South American mercenaries. We will first discuss the reasons why Tunisia reinstated the nefarious state of emergency, and then move to Yemen's implosion in the last four years.

* * *

Describing Tunisia since the 2014 elections is complex and challenging: it is a return to the past but with new actors and institutions, and a party system that seems to block any democratic progress. One metaphor that captures this situation is the comparison to a half-full, half-empty glass.[4] It is a period with a ruling coalition, made principally of two arch-enemies,

---

[3] Naguib (2020) shows that male–female gender binaries overlap with military-ruled and civilian-ruled individuals, as do opposing discourses of "salvation" to "untamed participation." It resonates with Sharabi's (1988) concept of neo-patriarchy identified in his seminal, yet much clearer gender focus. Patriarchy refers to the diffuse social attitude of males exerting authority with no consideration for women. Neo-patriarchy applies when these attitudes are instrumentalized by formal state or governmental institutions or individuals. In Tunisia, with the suspension of the Parliament by President Kais Saied on July 25, 2021, we see another aspect of neo-patriarchy: Throughout the first six months of the year, the President invoked the lack of female ministers in the cabinet proposed by Prime Minister Mechichi, leading to a growing institutional paralysis. Eventually President Saied suspended the Parliament and dismissed the entire government and has since accumulated additional power, well beyond what the 2014 Constitution would allow him. More on the "coup" of July 25 below.

[4] Less generously, it has been described by Nadia Marzouki (2015) as "Tunisia's rotten compromise."

Nidaa Tounes and Ennahda, both claiming to maintain the legitimacy of the revolution but delaying reforms, and of the return of corrupt politics as usual (Meddeb 2015c). Coalitions, fragile and short-lived at times, have been the new norms in Tunisia since the end of 2014, with eight cabinets presented to the ARP for confirmation since February 2015.[5] Such volatility hinders in-depth political and economic reforms, but also anchors pluralism and rotation in the Tunisian political system. Each of these parties adopted measures that were opposed to the ideas and expectations of *vis populi*, with the clock turned back on many of the security sector reforms.[6]

Essebsi, an old state apparatchik, made no mystery of his support for the return of many former RCD members into the fold of his party, Nidaa Tounes. With his son, Hafez Essebsi, groomed to become the new party leader, the President re-played many cards from the pre-revolution period. He openly lamented the loss of presidential power that the 2014 Constitution introduced, and reappointed many security leaders from the Ben Ali era.[7] The alliance with Ennahda, without which he could not govern, and which was based on his determination to avoid the Egyptian path of a military coup, was what prevented a full return to the pre-2011 situation. This awkward coalition between an arch-secularist party and an Islamist party harboring various currents was unique in the long-run transformation of Arab politics.

For Ennahda, placing second was a convenient situation after the 2014 elections.[8] Contrary to 2011, Rachid Ghannouchi's party was the second largest faction in the parliament, well behind Nidaa Tounes, which won the contest. Even when it was the largest single party in

---

[5] There have been five Prime Ministers seeking approval by the Tunisian legislature, one whose cabinet was never approved by the Parliament in January 2020 (Habib Jemli). The four others who have been Prime Minister are Habib Essid (February 2015–August 2016), Youssef Chahed (August 2016–February 2020), both appointed by Essebsi, while Elyes Fakhfakh (February–September 2020) and Hichem Mechichi (since September 2020) were appointed by President K. Saied. Prime Minister Essid reshuffled his cabinet in January 2016 and Chahed twice, in September 2017 and November 2018. Mechichi's cabinet was never approved by President Saied, leading to the constitutional crisis of the summer of 2021.

[6] Michaël Ayari, security expert, interview in Tunis, 05/30/2016. He speaks of these security reforms as "an ersatz of an ersatz of the initial revolutionary demands."

[7] See Section 4.3.

[8] On the issue of Islamist strategies to be second, see Brown (2012).

parliament, after some defections within Nidaa Tounes, Ghannouchi preferred to remain a minor coalition partner, and never claimed key ministries, such as that of the Interior, which it had held during the Troika period. Instead Ennahda embraced the same politics as Nidaa Tounes, condemning political violence and giving priority to boosting its democratic and *salonfähig* credentials. For its tenth congress in May 2016, Ennahda rolled out the red carpet for President Essebsi, and committed to civilian politics by calling for a turn towards specialization (*takhassus*), with a formal separation between political activism (betrothed to the party Ennahda) and *da'wa*, religious predication, which was now left to its loosely affiliated associations (Sigillò 2020; Gana & Sigillò 2019). The growing institutionalization of Ennahda left many more radical and conservative fringes disaffected. Ennahda lost many voters, as we will see below, especially among the youth, with a fair number of Tunisians, an estimated 3,000, straying closer to the Salafi networks, preferring to exit and take up arms in Libya or Syria.[9]

The volatile context in Libya, with its own civil war, and the presence of at least two active ISIS (*Da'esh*) branches, gave Essebsi the occasion to adopt an iron fist. In part, the proverbial fight against terrorism in the Arab world was a genuine concern. Attacks were carried out on Tunisian ground by the Islamic State. But it was also an excuse to shun the path of democratic changes, with negative consequences for civic life. The violent acts by *takfiri* Islamist groups started in July 2014, with attacks along the Tunisian–Algerian border in the Mount Chaambi area (14 soldiers killed). In 2015, ISIS conducted three bloody attacks: first in March, when 20 European tourists were killed and dozens injured during an assault on the Bardo National Museum; in June, when nearly 40 people were gunned down in a tourist resort on the beaches in Sousse; and finally, in November, when a bus carrying members of the Presidential Guard was attacked in Tunis, leaving 12 soldiers dead.

In Ben Guerdan in March 2016, armed Islamist groups from Libya infiltrated the country and wreaked havoc on a small border city. Fifty jihadists, a dozen members of the security apparatus, and seven civilians were killed. This dark period between 2015 and 2016 constituted

---

[9] Fabio Merone (2021) argues that the new hegemonic block invoking the revolutionary banner of Islam is the Salafi youth, who are willing to enact their version of a purified and anti-corruption state through violence.

the peak of *takfiri* jihadi attacks, but subsequent explosions in the capital city, for example in 2018 and 2019, all generated tighter security measures. All these led to the re-emergence of the infamous state of emergency, characteristic of republican histories in Arab countries for so long. President Essebsi applied the measure to the entire country after the November 2015 bus attack. Under this legal measure, the Ministry of the Interior regained latitude to forbid assemblies and censor media. Cultural and public activities must obtain an official authorization from the Ministry of the Interior (Hmed 2016b: 139). The state of emergency has been prolonged every six months since 2015, and the current President, Kais Saied, renewed it in December 2020 and again on July 24, 2021, a day before his bold move to concentrate power into his own hands after a deleterious political stalemate with the Parliament and the difficulties generated by the COVID-19 crisis in the country.[10] Thus in two days, with different legal artifices, Saied extended limitations on basic rights, and through the so-called "emergency clause" (article 80 of the Constitution), froze parliamentary activities for 30 days, removed parliamentary immunity, and dismissed Prime Minister Mechichi.[11]

Truth be told, the violence is not only from the Salafi-jihadis nor from the international *takfiri* jihadi networks. Every winter, typically around periods of commemoration of the revolution, young and unemployed people organize marches in the interior regions. Their anger has often led to violent clashes with the police, and a few deaths occur every year. In the last round of bread and job protests to turn

---

[10]   www.aa.com.tr/fr/afrique/tunisie-l-%C3%A9tat-d-urgence-prolong%C3%A9-de-six-mois-/2088702. Accusations of threats to national security have been used quite frequently in the last few years, in particular under Prime Minister Chahed, who used alleged "dossiers" against critical voices and politicians threatening his claim to succeed Essebsi as the next Tunisian President. Security became such a prominent and guiding theme for even apparently unrelated reforms that observers of the decentralization issue noted how the "security consensus" drove the agenda of rearranging local authorities (Belhadj 2019). This also affected the presidential campaign in 2019, when one of the leading contenders, Nabil Karoui, a former Nidaa Tounes member who established his own party to run against Chahed, was under arrest during most of the campaign (Gobe 2020: §§27–30).

[11]   It should be underlined that article 80 does not allow for the suspension of parliamentary activities. As a matter of fact, it requires the ARP to remain "in a state of continuous session." It is clear that Saied overstepped his prerogative on July 25, 2021. For this decree, see www.pist.tn/jort/2021/2021F/Jo0672021.pdf.

deadly, in 2021, one young man was killed in Sbeitla, near Sidi Bouzid, in January 2021, during the celebration of the tenth anniversary of the revolution,[12] but every January since 2016 has seen dozens injured in these commemorations/clashes. The problems of underemployment and of youth unemployment are acute and explain a recurrent discontent and summering insurgency in the interior.[13]

The geography of these protests and sources of armed responses to Islamist violence should be familiar by now. Interventions in the name of "security" can often hide a persistent territory of "spatial inequality."[14] If in the political center of the country, namely the Sahel, protests are comparatively rare, in the interior, one can still perceive the effect of the habitus of the force of the multitude, the *vis populi*. The remarkable expressions of regional solidarity during the military intervention in the El-Kamour protests in 2017 illustrate this resilience.

According to sociologist Hamza Meddeb, who has researched extensively the disinherited regions along the Algerian and Libyan border, by 2020 inland provinces went without the corresponding share of the national resources: 50% of the country's oil, gas, and water resources, 70% of wheat production, and 50% of olive oil and fruit production all come from the portions of Tunisia described historically as "useless Tunisia," or the interior. Yet two-thirds of public investment has been allocated to the coastal Sahel region, a continuation of the Bourguiba and Ben Ali policies (Meddeb 2020). The western governorates of Kasserine, Kef, Jendouba, and Gafsa (and to a lesser extent Sidi Bouzid), along the border with Algeria, and which are home to nearly 1.8 million Tunisians, have also seen a sustained insurgency,[15] which

---

[12] www.lorientlejour.com/article/1249560/manifestation-devant-le-parlement-a-t unis.html.
[13] Meddeb, compiling FTDES reports, suggests that the increase of social protests (demonstrations, sit-ins, and occupations of land or state buildings) is noticeable in the marginalized regions away from the Sahel region. In Kasserine, the number of violent protests rose from 4,400 in 2015, to 8,700 in 2016 and 10,400 in 2017. In 2018 and 2019, the number receded to around 9,000 episodes.
[14] As worded by Othman Khaled, civic campaign leader, interview in Tunis, 01/10/ 2016.
[15] The insurgency in these regions originates from socioeconomic marginalization and relative deprivation. It targets objectives deemed to be the source of injustice (army, police stations). It is quite distinct from what are generally labeled "terrorist" activities, namely attacks with a disproportionate use of violence targeting civilians or peaceful areas.

has been linked to limited socioeconomic opportunities and poor access to education and healthcare (Herbert 2018).

From March to June 2017, protests erupted over the control of oil production in the El-Kamour region, in the governorate of Tataouine. Protestors demanded 3,000 new jobs, and asked for the creation of a regional fund to redistribute part of the oil revenues back to the southern regions.[16] Despite promises for decentralization and of greater distribution of financial resources to the regions, the capital city kept all of the oil bonanza. The protests started in Tataouine, the administrative center of the governorate, and then morphed into an encampment next to the strategic oil pumping facility of El-Kamour. Campers pitched their tents in this desert region for two months and successfully disrupted the flow of oil toward refineries in the north. The protests were peaceful, based on the 2011 methods of sit-ins and collective deliberations. However, Chahed's government refused to negotiate. After weeks of stalemate, Essebsi sent the army to re-open the oil pipeline on May 10. A few days later, and with the reinforcement of the National Guard following the defection described below, one protestor had died at the hand of the security forces on May 22.[17]

What is peculiar about this repression is not the refusal of the government to negotiate, but the fact that the army, and not a police unit, was sent to remove the protestors. The army, whose mission is to protect the borders of the country, had refused to support Ben Ali in January 2011, which had led to the characterization of the army as a central pillar for democratic political reforms (as we saw in Chapter 4). Some might claim that the exceptional use of the army to crush the protest was justified by the "national interest" (restoring the flow of oil revenues). Yet, in this case, the President sent the army, not unlike the punitive campaigns under the Ottoman and French colonial authorities that has been launched in order to subdue the peripheries refusing to pay their dues to the Bey. El-Kamour should also be seen in light of a tendency to stigmatize the population of the deep south as unruly, unpatriotic (as they are said to be infiltrated by Libyans) – in

---

[16] The protest's organizational committee wanted 20% of the region's oil production revenues and a development fund for Tataouine. For a timeline and the demand in 2017, see https://nawaat.org/2017/05/27/timeline-el-kamour-and-the-states-security-response/.

[17] Gobe (2018). The National Guard reports to the Ministry of the Interior, while the Ministry of Defense is in charge of the Army.

brief, as *fellagha* – a national threat that only the army can tackle. When set in relation to patronizing comments heard in the capital around that time against people of the south presented as *gu'r* (the dirty peasants, as opposed to the people with a *baldi*, i.e., urban and educated backgrounds),[18] one can actually glimpse a continuity in the arrogant attitudes of the current Tunisian authorities all the way back to the demeaning comments from colonial times about "useless Tunisia."[19] Thus the pattern of repression in the Tataouine region in May 2017 evokes, prima facie, a return to the old use of state violence against the margins.

The second notable twist in this episode is that dissent occurred within the ranks of the army and gave a second breath to the protest movement on May 20. Political scientist Sharan Grewal, who has accumulated remarkable sociological data on the Tunisian military since 2011 and proposed original lessons on coup-proofing, narrates an interesting detail. A few days after the Carthage Palace sent the military to force the reopening of the site on May 10, protestors managed to shut the oil valve in El-Kamour again on May 20. This happened because of defections in the Army and soldiers siding with the protestors (Grewal 2019: 259). The momentum swung back to the side of the protestors, and finally, in June, with the mediation of the UGTT, the strikers won a symbolic victory, forcing the government to accept the creation of 4,500 jobs, and massive investments, in the region.

Pausing for a moment on the details of the May episodes reveals the presence of informal articulations of solidarity and the limited, but symbolically strong importance of army defection. It also indicates how the mentality of security actors has changed after 2011. First,

---

[18] In French, *les bouzeux*. I am grateful to Michaël Ayari for pointing at these derogatory comments against the people of the south. See also Ayari (2016: chapter 1) for a description of the various stigma reproduced after independence against the rural population. See Hmed (2016a: 76) for the resentment of the marginalized interior against the Sahelians, and Challand (2020) for a discussion of racialization in Tunisia.

[19] Hibou, in her rich political sociology of Tunisia, notes similar traits of resilient asymmetries within the territories and the symbolic prominence of the continuity or reinsertion of older "*beldi*" elites (elites from the historical urban centers) a few years after the revolution. See Hibou (2015: e.g. 149; Hmed 2016a: 76). *Baldi* and *beldi* refer to the same socio-geographic origins, or urban educated people.

the logic of solidarity at play concerns both army soldiers and low-ranking officers who hail from the same neglected interior as the workers at the oil facilities (Grewal 2019: 259, 262). For the first 10 days of the Army's presence in El-Kamour, intense discussions must have taken place between oil facility workers and soldiers, leading to some members of the army who were meant to protect the pumping station looking the other way and allowing protesters to regain access to the facilities on May 20. Re-shutting the oil valve amounted to something similar to the January 14, 2011 episodes, where the army lent indirect support to the protestors: refusing to take orders from the President in a show of aggregated solidarity with the interior regions, who demanded economic redistribution and political equality. Put differently, the focus in the phrase *vis populi* is here less about the force (it was easy to turn off the valve, once the army looked the other way), but about the assemblage that *vis populi* entails here: strikers of the oil facilities, citizens of Tataouine, and soldiers in the army turning a local stand-off into an issue of national justice.

To understand why the Army as a whole, rather than just a few soldiers, become accomplices of the sit-in (indeed many high-ranking Army officers expressed dissent with Essebsi's orders in media),[20] one has to revert to the relative strength of the Minister of the Interior over the armed forces during and after Ben Ali (see Section 4.3). After the 2011 revolution, the share of the budget for the army increased, compensating for the marginalization under Ben Ali, who had preferred his own Presidential Guard. But Grewal notes that 2017 was the first year where the budget for the Army was cut, indicating Essebsi and Chahed's return to the Ben Ali preference for the Ministry of the Interior when it came to security questions. There was thus a corporate interest of the army that was enmeshed with the specific soldiers' decision to let the protestors storm back into the oil facility and shut the oil valve (Grewal 2019: 259–261). This act allowed them, in turn, to re-articulate demands for national solidarity and equity for the disinherited and impoverished regions along the lines of "security," or of *vis populi*.

With hindsight, the victory of the El-Kamour protestors was actually modest. Since the June 2017 agreement,[21] the government has balked

---

[20] Grewal (2019: 260) notes how various army officers expressed support on social media for the encampment throughout May 2017.

[21] www.businessnews.com.tn/accord-signe-entre-le-gouvernement-et-les-sit-inneurs-del-kamour,520,73021,3.

at implementing the creation of a regional development fund. It has postponed, and continues to do so, the creation of new jobs, generating new rounds of protests, similar to the winter protests that occur every year nationally. For the Tataouine region, the cycles of clashes erupt around the month of June, when demands for the implementation of the June 2017 promises are reiterated.[22]

In this case as well, the glass (of oil) can be seen half-full or half-empty. Some small economic successes come with a modest enactment of *vis populi*: The Army's refusal to be an accomplice of the center's kleptocratic tendency has given a new space for geographic discontent and for new calls for social justice to emerge. Below, the Oasis of Jemna will illustrate another aspect of these partly maintained articulations, this time in relation to land resources. However, let us now turn to Yemen and the fragmentation of the armed forces there.

* * *

In Yemen, the destructive spin of the two-tiered conflict has also affected most articulations between the three facets of radical representation. The regional conflict has accelerated the return to the fore of military or political leaders with dubious and corrupt backgrounds. Concerns about "transitions," or national reforms, become relegated in this three-way scramble for military and strategic resources, which range from access to harbor cities, oil refineries, and food supplies, to the indirect power bestowed by international support. This section offers a general overview of the state of fragmentation in the security sector, and of the architecture of power that the three factions, the Huthis in the north, the supporters of the legitimate government and of Hadi, and of the STC in the south, have tried to implement. Section 6.2 will deal with the sociological analysis of strong men politics.

In 2014, the combination of a deteriorating economic situation and of the opaque finalization of the new federal constitution had pushed the Huthi–Saleh alliance to storm Sanaa in September. A few months later, in January, their military action put a definitive end to the project of a six-region federal constitution. The Huthis crossed the Rubicon in March 2015 when they marched on Aden, the city where Hadi's government had taken refuge. The siege on Aden, which ran from

---

[22] New protests occurred in June 2020 in the Tataouine region; see www .france24.com/fr/20200622-tunisie-nouveaux-heurts-%C3%A0-tataouine-o% C3%B9-les-manifestants-r%C3%A9clament-des-emplois.

March to July 2015, forced Hadi and his cabinet to escape via Oman to Saudi Arabia. The UN Security Council authorized aerial bombings under the auspice of the GCC to force the Huthis back to the pre-February 2015 situation.

From 2015 to early 2021, there has been little progress on the military front, with the Huthis proving the more resilient force. Institutionally, two competing governments controlled different parts of the country: President Hadi maintained a rocky alliance with Yemenis from the south, and a Huthi authority ruling from Sanaa in alliance with Saleh. Hadi governed from Riyadh for most of the last six years. These long periods of absence justified calls for self-rule by the STC in the south, leading at times to internal STC–Hadi battles in Aden. Such was the case for most of the period 2017–2019, and again May and June 2020.[23] In November 2019, the Southern Transitional Council signed the Riyadh Agreement and formed a joint government with Hadi.

The military battlefield thus included a struggle for diplomatic recognition. Hadi, elected in February 2012, has remained the sole legitimate head of government for the international community. His followers are the loyalists. Due to the Huthi military success (they control most of what was North Yemen, except for Hodeida and the Marib regions), they have been invited to the international negotiation table, an important development for them since they are a recognized negotiating party.[24] The STC has also leveraged their military force (they were able to withstand the Huthi offensives in the Dahla' and Taiz regions in 2019) to become a diplomatically recognized entity.[25] On

---

[23] Beginning in May 2020, a new round of attacks on Hadi's troops occurred in the Abyan region, and from June onwards, attacks were carried out in the Socotra Islands, leading to fratricidal fighting among southerners. See https://qishnpress .com/localities/473/, "Members of the Socotra Committee call on ending the conflict" (in Arabic, June 10, 2020).

[24] Hadi negotiated with the Huthis in Kuwait (April 2016), and in Geneva and Stockholm (December 2018). On the eve of the Kuwaiti negotiations, Hadi sacked Prime Minister Bahah and appointed Ali Muhsin as his Vice-President (Bonnefoy 2018: 51). Bahah was replaced by Omar bin Daghr, a less popular leader.

[25] Hadi tried to orchestrate a return in November 2018, but that effort was short lived. The official STC website (https://stcaden.com/) never misses the opportunity to showcase diplomats visiting Aden and high-level meetings that Zubaydi has with diplomats and heads of state. See e.g. https://stcaden.com/ne

April 25, 2020, the STC declared a state of emergency and self-rule over the south (*idarat dhathi fil-junub*).[26]

As these lines are being written in 2021, Hadi is still governing from distant Riyadh. The STC and Hadi currently present a common front against the Huthis. Hadi is institutionally and politically weak: his only legitimacy comes from the support of the Saudis and the international community, with former US President Trump attempting a last push to designate the Huthis as a terrorist entity in the dying days of his Administration. When some of Hadi's ministers returned to Aden on December 30, 2020, the Huthis were able to launch a multiple-missile attack on the airport. By chance, the airplane had not stopped at the usual terminal, and a bloodbath was avoided.[27] Paradoxically, this attack might have helped Hadi to regain some legitimacy, as members of the cabinet would be seen facing the same dangers as Yemeni civilians. With the new Biden Administration putting pressure on the Saudis to find a diplomatic rather than a military solution to the conflict,[28] a new turn could have happened. But the Huthis, trying to capitalize on the momentum, organized what could be a final assault on Marib, an oil-rich region, in the spring and summer 2021. Marib is also the last pocket of territory where the remainder of the Yemeni army, under the guidance of now Vice-President Ali Muhsin, is based. The formally marginalized region of Marib could be the winning prize of the civil war, and its fate could decide the future of Yemen.

This stunning development has to do with the fragmentation of military might and the parallel existence of different armies. Let us look briefly at the organization of political and military authority in the different camps. We will start with the Huthi camp, and then move to the south.

In Huthi-land, it is now the Supreme Political Council (SPC) that governs. The SPC's President, Ali Al-Sammad, was killed by a Saudi missile in April 2018, and then replaced by Mahdi Mashat, a person close to Abdelmalik Al-Huthi, the demagogic leader of the eponymous

---

ws/12034 (June 1, 2020) reporting on a French diplomatic visit to Aydarus Al-Zubaydi.

[26] See https://qishnpress.com/localities/587, "UN: Taking state institutions in Socotra by force is extremely dangerous" (in Arabic, June 25, 2020). The article refers to UN Envoy Martin Griffiths.

[27] https://sanaacenter.org/publications/analysis/12947 (January 19, 2021).

[28] See "New U.S. Yemen envoy meets Yemen president amid fresh efforts to end war," at https://perma.cc/ZG4M-GFU3 (February 11, 2021). The meeting between Tim Lenderking and Hadi took place in Riyadh.

movement. In December 2017, the alliance between Saleh and the Huthis came to a brutal end. Saleh, who had regained a partial control over Sanaa, felt he could make a full come-back by playing the card of the diplomatic connections that his son, Ahmad, had while living in exile in Abu Dhabi. Aware that the Huthis were *personae non gratae* for the international community because of their ideological alliances with Iran and Hezbollah in Lebanon, Saleh accepted an offer made by the UAE, expressing his willingness to turn his back on the Huthis and help to restore control over the country.[29] He was killed a couple of days later, on December 4, 2017, by Huthis who considered him a traitor.

Two Saudi bombings killing scores of civilians galvanized the northerners' determination to support Ansar Allah and Huthi claims to power. On October 8, 2016, the Saudi-led coalition bombed a large funeral hall in Sanaa, leaving 157 dead.[30] Two years later, in August 2018, a school bus was targeted by another coalition attack, leaving 44 children and 10 adults dead in Dahyan, northwest of Yemen (Worth 2019). Debris from the bombing proved that US weapons were used in the attack, giving new meaning to the *sarkha*, Ansar Allah's motto, and kickstarting US Congress pressure to stop American support for the Saudi war.[31] In these circumstances, and in a society "marked by anti-Americanism and the fight to free Palestine," the *sarkha* and other slogans echoing the anti-imperialist chants of Hezbollah in Lebanon "ensured them [Ansar Allah] a certain popularity" (Bonnefoy 2018: 39). But this degree of "legitimacy" should not serve as a cover for the brutalities and basic violations of citizens' rights committed by the Huthi government since it took over most of the north at the end of 2014.[32]

---

[29] www.aljazeera.com/news/2017/12/yemen-houthi-saleh-alliance-collapse-1712 04070831956.html (December 4, 2017).

[30] See Ammar Basha's video: "Yemen: The Great Crime", الجريمة الكبرى :اليمن, video published 02/16/2017. It was recently blocked on YouTube. It can be seen on the Internet Archive, at https://web.archive.org/web/20171125204844/https://www .youtube.com/watch?v=nRhYkssz50M.

[31] *Ṣarkha* means "scream" in Arabic. Painted in red, blue, and green on a white background, the motto is ubiquitous in northern Yemen. It reads: "God is great, Death to America, Death to Israel, Curses on the Jews, Victory to Islam." The movement's official name, Ansar Allah (partisans of God), is also printed everywhere (Worth 2019).

[32] The Huthi authorities have also executed people involved in acts of treason, with no trials.

The Huthi movement, which had after 2004 capitalized on the tyranny of Saleh's regime and developed its unique brand of calls for social justice (Bonnefoy 2018: 39), became increasingly tyrannical with the population it governed. Its leaders arose because of their involvement with security issues. For example, Fares Manaa, a known arm struggler, described in Chapter 3 (Brandt 2019a: 25), was the governor of Saada between 2011 and 2014, and became a state minister in the Huthi government in October 2016.[33] Abdelmalik Al-Huthi, the ideologue and leader of the movement – who had used the atrocities of the Saudi bombings to whip up internal support – displayed no tolerance for internal dissent (Brandt 2019a: 23): many intellectuals, human rights organization leaders, and possibly also moderate Huthis have been killed in the regions under Huthi control (Heinze 2015: 5, 7). French historian Samy Dorlian, specialist of the Zaydi revivals, relates a revealing anecdote about the shifting terrain of legitimacy. The term *mustakbirun*, used to denote the "arrogant powerful ones" (Dorlian 2012: 73), had been the preferred term of the historical leader of the Zaydi Al-Haqq party, Husayn Al-Huthi. The term was originally used in 2002 to express rejection of Sanaa and Saleh's corrupt power, with the influence of the Iranian rhetoric of denouncing imperialism and glorifying the revolutionary downtrodden. With the six Saada wars, the term was propelled by the movement fighting corruption and social injustices (Dorlian 2015: 62). However, since the Huthis' rise to power in 2014, now many Yemenis use the term *mustakbirun* to criticize Ansar Allah leaders because of their own political arrogance.[34]

In the south as well, the warring context has precipitated the end of the Southern Peaceful Movement. With the Huthis marching on Aden in 2015, Hirak was swallowed and reinvented as Southern Resistance

---

[33] His name was even proposed to head the Ministry of Commerce. See www
.lemonde.fr/proche-orient/article/2016/10/07/au-yemen-la-guerre-devient-
economique_5009846_3218.html (October 7, 2016).

[34] Dorlian (2015: 72). Another problem for the Huthi political leadership is the
difficulty in sustaining tribal alliances (Brandt 2019b). The Huthis and Saleh,
when acting in concert between August 2014 and December 2017, were
militarily unbeatable because of their ability to muster tribal support for their
offensives against Hadi. Some of the Hashid tribes, faithful to Islah, fought back,
and this led to ample tribal fragmentation in the Upper highlands. The tribal
splitting grew deeper after the assassination of Ali Abdallah Saleh. Joining the
Huthi movement does not mean believing in the ideology of Husayn or
Abdelmalik Al-Huthi, but is often connected to very local rivalries, generational
divisions, with older tribal leaders supporting Hadi and the simple tribesmen
supporting Ansar Allah (Brandt 2019b: 15).

(*al-muqawama al-junubiyya*), made up of young men in popular com-
mittees, various local civilian militias, and former soldiers (Amira
Augustin 2015: 13). The Southern Resistance achieved a very import-
ant victory in July 2015 when it broke the Huthi siege of Aden. In large
part it has been equipped and trained by the military forces of the
Kingdom of Saudi Arabia (KSA) and the United Arab Emirates (UAE)
(Amira Augustin 2015: 14; Heinze 2015: 4). It was led by Aydarus Al-
Zubaydi, a military man who rose to prominence during the siege.
Twenty-seven at the time of the short 1994 civil war, Al-Zubaydi was
one of the officers in the older Southern army (Amira Augustin 2015).

Aydarus Al-Zubaydi, one of the leaders benefiting from Emirati
endorsement, was appointed as Aden's governor by President Hadi in
the first weeks of 2017.[35] That did not stop him of accusing the loyalist
government of corruption and inaction in the south. In this context, the
diverse secessionist groups across the south came together to establish the
STC (Dahlgren 2019). Unhappy with this criticism, Hadi dismissed Al-
Zubaydi in April 2017. This prompted a new round of *miliyuniyyat*. On
May 4, 2017, the people in the south expressed support for Al-Zubaydi,
and an "Aden Declaration" was promulgated, charting the path forward,
yet without declaring full independence.[36] On May 11, 2017, a Southern
Transitional Council (STC, in Arabic *al-majlis al-intiqali al-janubi*) was
established with Al-Zubaydi as its chairman. The STC awaited
November 30, 2017, in homage to the establishment of Southern
Yemen in 1967, to establish a National Assembly (*jama'ya wataniyya*)
as its legislative body. Jointly, the STC and the National Assembly have
since been adopting measures for self-administration, but are eagerly
awaiting the right moment to declare independence.

The STC's ultimate aim is the foundation of a new country called
Arabian South (*al-junub al-'arabi*).[37] In theory, this future state is

---

[35] Abdulsalam K. Mused and Ahmed Muthana, STC representatives to the USA,
interview in Washington DC, 01/19/2020.

[36] See STC's Political Vision (2019: 25–29). The Aden Declaration constitutes the
governing reference for the STC itself (founding members, role), sets out the basic
principles for an independent federal southern state (p. 29), and describes the role
of its external (p. 25) and internal direction (p. 26). In 2018 it opened international
representative offices in five countries, three in Europe (Berlin, Sheffield, and
Moscow), one in Washington DC, and one in Cairo (Amira Augustin 2019: 35).

[37] See e.g. the statement issued on the STC website: "Southern Transitional
Council issues an important political statement," August 15, 2019, available at
https://stcaden.com/news/10116.

meant to be a federal state connecting the southern governorates. Practically, however, disagreements abound. People from the Abyan and Shabwa regions continue to distrust Adenis, while Hadhramis want to decide what to do with their own oil resources.[38] The STC is firmly rooted in Aden, but the competition between the KSA (interested in the network of oil pipelines) and UAE interests in the port infrastructures of Aden and Socotra has exacerbated intra-southern rivalries. Some have called for the recreation of older sultanates, while Mahra, in the east, does not want to be included in this new country.[39]

The fragmentation of the security forces remains the real issue. The military component of this intrusion does not bode well for the possibility of an ebullient or democratic *vis populi*. The new situation of multiple conflicts has undermined the possibility of unifying the security forces under one single roof. With KSA and UAE officers training Yemeni units, a new layer of sub-national military divisions blossomed. The three most notable are the Hadhrami Elite Forces, Shabwa Elite Forces, and the Security Belt Forces in the Aden region (Dahlgren 2018; ICG 2017). The speed with which the UAE formed and trained these units is testimony to Abu Dhabi's strategic interest in rising up to the rank of regional actor in order to be able to measure up to, and possibly also to undermine, Saudi hegemony.[40]

The names of these security groups, or military units, indicate a localized security response: the Shabwani Elite Forces, active in Shabwa, have focused on Al-Qaeda insurrectionalists, while the

---

[38] Rafat Al-Akhali, decentralization expert and former minister, interview in Oxford, 09/19/2019. He mentions the antagonism between Shabwa and Aden.

[39] Colonial era sultans of the Hadhramawt made a come-back of sorts in September 2014, when the former Qu'ayti sultan called for the creation of a State of Hadhramawt (Day 2015: 41, fn. 13; 2012: 176). Mahra has received generous support from the Saudis, who transformed the local airport into a military base. See Kendall (2018), TYR (2019) and the report "The March on Mahra", available at https://sanaacenter.org/publications/the-yemen-review/7 955 (August 5, 2019). Susanne Dahlgren (2019) believes that "in Yemeni historical terms, the STC political coalition – representing rural peasants and sultans to urban entrepreneurs and socialists – reflects a far greater compromise than any yet seen in the South's history. Still, the divisions on the ground mark possible hostilities between people whose long-term aim is the same."

[40] Sanaa Center (2020: 15); Salisbury (2020). Although the UAE announced on October 2020 that it had ended its military involvement in Yemen, evidence suggests otherwise, with proxy actors continuing to support the direct military interests of the UAE. See www.middleeasteye.net/news/uae-yemen-conflict-deeply-involved-experts-say (February 22, 2021).

Hadhrami Elite Forces, with 10,000 members, are under the joint military command of the KSA and UAE, covering the eastern governorates. The Security Belt Forces, *Hizam Al-Amni*, were established by a presidential decree in May 2016 to cover the Aden area (TYR 2019; Amira Augustin 2019: 35). Some of these units are even paid twice, by the Hadi and UAE governments.[41] This localization raises questions about how coordinated these entities are, and about how a lack of unified command might speed up the process of territorial unraveling.

The Security Belt Forces are part of the coordinated Saudi military campaign, but in 2019 and 2020, they turned their guns against their own employer – or at least one of them. In August 2019, after a drone attack killed the powerful Aden-area commander and dozens of new recruits of the Security Belt in Aden,[42] the STC ousted the internationally recognized government. The move prompted Martin Griffiths, the UN Special Envoy to Yemen, to denounce the moves by the STC to take control of state institutions by force. He warned of the consequences of further Yemeni fragmentation (TYR 2019: 19).

This breakup is certainly and eerily reminiscent of the colonial past in the south, when Britain organized and armed small army units in the 1950s and 1960s.[43] Another resurgent practice is the importing of mercenary soldiers. In the nineteenth century, Yafi' tribesmen were brought in to expand the base of power of the Hadhrami Bedouin Army (Day 2012: 39). Nowadays, mercenaries come from Sudan and Central Africa, and even from Colombia. In 2016, there were initial reports of Sudanese "boots on the ground," and then reports were confirmed in April 2017

---

[41] On the UAE-backed Security Belt Forces, see see "Inflated Beyond Fiscal Capacity", a policy brief by the initiative "Rethinking Yemen's Economy", available at https://devchampions.org/publications/policy-brief/Inflated_Beyon d_Fiscal_Capacity/ (September 13, 2019). The journalist Robert Worth (2020) provides a revealing portrayal of Mohammed bin Zayed Al Nahyan, crown prince of Abu Dhabi and leader of the security forces in the UAE.

[42] The leader was Munir Al-Mashali, aka Abu Al-Yamama. The missile was most likely launched by Huthi units, but the STC blamed Hadi's government for its inaction in securing the environment around the Jalaa military camp. The government had some reports of possible attacks, but took no measure. See TYR (2019: 6–7).

[43] The British established the Hadhrami Bedouin Army and provided military assistance to the sultans of Al-Qu'ayti and Al-Kathiri "to develop government administration and the rule of state law" in the 1950s and 1960s (Day 2015: 37, fn. 15; 2012: 37). This seems to be the template for the present-day Hadhrami Special Forces and the Security Belt, which act in concert with the STC.

when five Sudanese soldiers were killed in fighting alongside Saudi troops (Schmitz & Burrowes 2018: xcii). The lesson from the involvement of foreign mercenaries is that Yemen is no isolated conflict on the fringe of the Arabic Peninsula; it is instead well embedded in the new landscape of neo-imperial violence. Sudan and Colombia illustrate two facets of the twenty-first century "security" issues and of neo-imperialist encroachment.

Sudan is thought to have been contributing at least 10,000 troops to the Saudi-led coalition at any given time since 2017 (Tubiana, Warin, & Mangare 2020: 33). Even though Sudan recently underwent its own popular protests and toppling of Sudanese dictator Omar Al-Bashir, the new Sudanese leadership reiterated Sudan's long-standing commitment to the Saudi coalition. The dead Sudanese soldiers came from the same paramilitary forces, the Sudanese Rapid Forces, used to crush democratic protests back in the Sudanese capital of Khartoum in June 2019 (see Conclusion). They were paid generously by Abu Dhabi and Riyadh – with an alleged one billion US dollars deposited at the Sudanese Central Bank in 2015.[44] The commander of the Sudanese Rapid Forces, Mohamed Hamdan Dagalo, better known as Hemeti, has benefited from unchecked power in Sudan because of the rent he has brought to Sudan (Majdoub 2019a). We will meet Hemeti again in the Conclusion for a last illustration of the Moebius strip.[45] But the power asymmetry between Sudan, a demographically rich low–middle-income country, on the one hand, and two high-income countries, like Saudi Arabia and the UAE, on the other hand, is so vast that cashing in on dubious military operations in an alien country gives Sudanese leaders no qualms.

The presence of Colombian mercenaries and efforts to bring in Senegalese and Central African soldiers (Bonnefoy 2018: 69) can be explained differently. Private corporate companies set up in the UAE, managed by Erik Prince, founder of Blackwater Worldwide, are also said to be bringing Colombian mercenaries to Yemen (Bonnefoy 2018: 153). Unlike with Sudan, this circulation of violence specialists is not connected to state channels or to public coercion institutions, but is structured via private capitalist networks. Benefiting from the total

---

[44] See www.al-monitor.com/originals/2015/11/sudan-saudi-arabia-war-yemen-houthi-economy.html (November 23, 2015). The figure matches a later estimate of the yearly payment made to the Sudanese mercenaries deployed in Yemen. See Tubiana, Warin, & Mangare (2020: 33).

[45] On Hemetis's connection to Yemen, see www.aljazeera.com/news/2019/06/sudan-rsf-commander-hemeti-190605223433929.html (June 6, 2019).

absence of democratic accountability in the two Gulf countries, these networks undermine the social life of citizenship in new ways, and represent a new instance of the Moebius strip.[46]

Yemeni livelihoods are put directly at risk due to the cynical actions of the Gulf monarchies. Taking over the port of Aden, and having a base in the archipelago of Socotra, which is located nearer to the Horn of Africa than to mainland Yemen, are strategic goals for Abu Dhabi.[47] The Emirates deployed troops to Socotra in April 2018, generating fear among locals that they would lose what little autonomy they had gained, having recently acquired governate status in 2013 (Peutz 2018). According to Dahlgren (2018), "in addition to a permanent military base," the Emiratis plan to build Zayed Residential City, "a large-scale commercial development plan" that threatens the "fragile flora and fauna of Socotra's unique natural habitat. … But even more, [local] population has had no say in the plans and are unlikely to reap a fair share of any profits" (Dahlgren 2018). The fragile and rare ecosystems – which Socotris have preserved with great care – on the island that has been listed a UNESCO World Heritage site (Peutz 2018), are now at risk.

The Emiratis had hoped to capture another port, Hodeida, in the Tihama region.[48] The port handles at least 70% of the food and medicine imported into Yemen, and the Huthis depend on customs duties on that trade for much of their revenue. The Saudi coalition mounted a campaign to encircle Hodeida and thus force the Huthis to sue for peace on their terms (Worth 2018). That plan failed, and the Stockholm Agreement in December 2018, albeit fragile, lifted the siege on Hodeida, with the "redeployment" of troops to the outskirts of the city (Sanaa Center 2020: 6).

Saudis and Emiratis have also targeted fisheries, food, and rural livelihoods, prompting Martha Mundy, an anthropologist who has covered Yemeni food production and agriculture since the 1970s, to suggest that these attacks are deliberate (Sowers 2018). With vegetable farms, poultry production, and fishing boats (220 fishing boats have been destroyed in a precise bombing campaign) the object of systematic and clearly targeted

---

[46] On privatized security in the Middle East, see Tuğal (2017) and Hever (2018).

[47] On Djibouti, see Introduction.

[48] For Abdulghani Al-Iryani the Saudi–Emirati rivalry is in part about access to the Indian Ocean, which gives a way out from the chokehold of the Hormuz Straight. According to Al-Iryani, the UAE's interest in the Yemeni harbors is a tactic to prevent the Saudis from having control over them (Sanaa Center 2020: 14).

attacks, food insecurity is growing rapidly. Food prices have skyrocketed, generating dependency on foreign (Gulf) aid[49] and additional waves of internal displacement. As of March 2021, 20.7 of Yemen's 29 million people are considered to be in need of humanitarian aid, over four million Yemenis are internally displaced persons, and 80% of the population have been displaced for more than a year since the start of the civil war.[50]

6.2 Strong Men and Generational Conflicts

What does this (re)turn to securitization in Tunisia and of a full war in Yemen mean for this book's themes? This section wrestles with the making of a new symbolic order rooted in questions of security. In the two countries, one can witness a re-siloeing or regeneration of spatial inequalities and the resubjectivation of individual actors that are the antithesis of the creative forces unleashed by informal actors in and after 2011. Resubjectivation means that the abundance of social roles enacted and sustained in Part II were gradually abandoned, and people have been sent back to their previous roles, that of precarious (or latent) citizens awaiting for decisions to be made on their behalf. If spontaneity and "the excess of the result over the causes" were the constitutive tropes in the period 2011–2014, resubjectivation signals the end of this connecting imaginary, a return to repressive violence and the fragmentation of social and political spaces. This also coincides with the return of regional and international sponsors dictating the terms of politics, and thus, the shelving of civic participation based on the deliberative and aggregative modalities. We will start with Yemen.

How does a situation of multiple wars allow for the revolutionary principles of autonomous and inclusive articulations to operate? In Yemen, like in Tunisia, the generational gap and the reaffirmation of older types of political representation are the common hurdles. More specific to Arabia Felix are the very significant setbacks for women, the abandonment of socialist ideals by the YSP, the unique role of military specialists, and the rhetoric of international actors mobilizing themes of "security" and "stability." In the absence of operating civilian authorities (bureaucracies, political parties, associations) and the predominant role

---

[49] On February 26, 2019, *The Guardian* reported that more than half of the US $2.6bn aid to Yemen was actually pledged by countries involved in war, namely the KSA and UAE. See https://perma.cc/6E3S-KFSU (February 26, 2019).

[50] Figures from March 5, 2021. See https://reporting.unhcr.org/yemen.

played by armed force leaders, war generates its own reality and a new symbolic order. In Pierre Bourdieu's sociology, symbolic power breeds symbolic violence because the people's dispositions are "attuned to the structure of domination of which they are the product," in this case the reality and disruptions of war. People are also the "victims of symbolic domination" (Bourdieu 2001: 41) because they are prey of the invisible symbolic power surrounding them (Bourdieu 1983: 170). This is captured by the support that people are forced, consciously or not, to give to their military leaders. In these conditions, the articulations or sources of coalescence (*iltiham*) enacted by a moving and assembled people are destroyed. The following considerations about the exclusions of women and youth and the loss of debating spaces, and through them, of the unifying principles of 2011, shows the centrality of patriarchal nationalism (Naguib 2020) and of the strong man syndrome in these new processes that undermine the social life of citizenship. This is apparent in the south and in the north, but also in the practice of an actor, the Yemeni Socialist Party, which was active in both parts of the country, in particular in a central region with a long history of self and civilian rule, Taiz.

Used to secularism and ideals of egalitarianism during the period from 1967 to 1990, civilians from the South have reasons for disillusion that the STC ceded so much space to men, soldiers, and Islamists. Women in the "Arabian South" have complained that the *miliyuniyyat* were for men, while women watched them on TV from home (Dahlgren 2019). Despite the promise offered in its political vision to grant at least 30% of seats to women in decision-making positions, only three women are listed among the original 25 leaders in the STC.[51] Instead, Aydarus Al-Zubaydi, the STC leader, is surrounded by men, such as the very conservative Hani bin Breik.[52] Even in the rather harmless realms of online mobilization, the website of Hirak has ceased to be updated since the Aden Declaration of May 2017,[53] referring now to the STC website (https://stcaden.com/) as the "official" website. Why could a movement not coexist along a more structured governing body? The two are not mutually exclusive. Maybe

---

[51]   See See the official document of the STC called "The Political Vision", dated 2019 (see Sources). On women's participation, see section "Principles of rights and freedoms," pp. 30–31. Women thus occupy only 12% of the STC executive seats. Author's analysis of documents and video presentations of the STC on its YouTube channel, at www.youtube.com/c/STCSouthArabia/videos.

[52]   Hani bin Breik, Vice-President, should not be confused with Ahmed Sa'id bin Breik, a Major General who is the Chairman of the National Assembly.

[53]   www.southernhirak.org/2017/06/aden-historic-declaration.html.

it is part of the trend in many Arab countries that witnessed the 2011 Uprisings and a flurry of civic initiatives but whose online platforms gradually unraveled with civil wars and increased infighting.[54] The malaise is that spaces for participation and gender equality have been reduced.

Another historical institution of the south that abandoned its role as a party open to civilian politics is the Yemeni Social Party. Yemeni writer Bushra Al-Maqtari noted the failure of the YSP, not just in south, but in other parts of country. In Taiz, the YSP had upheld "socialist or progressist ideas," but has recently been heard touting a "very conservative agenda" instead (Al-Maqtari 2021). Her words capture the corrosive effect of state power on the YSP:

The party has ceased its endorsement of just causes that side with the common citizen's basic needs and civil rights, and it has failed to voice a clear stance against threats that could fragment the country. The YSP's moral degradation becomes more pronounced when contrasted with its historic legacy and its political literature. Instead, by maintaining a low profile …, the party took a passive and ambiguous stance with regard to key intellectual and social issues. Its focus appears to have been carving for itself a zone of political safety, in return for some of its leaders receiving positions in state institutions. (Al-Maqtari 2021)

Furthermore, with the STC taking over Hirak, youths have lost their voice and the older generation has trampled past promises. Older leaders within the YSP, such as Ali Al-Beidh or Abdulrahman Al-Jifri, have remerged as political contenders and organized meetings in Cairo and London to discuss federalism as demands were placed on Saleh's crumbling power in 2010 and 2011. After 2014, some of these historical figures returned to Aden. But many southerners, in particular younger citizens, are uncomfortable with these old leaders. Generational distrust further exacerbates Hirak's internal divisions (Amira Augustin 2018), as does YSP leaders reneging on principles that had been agreed upon at the National Dialogue Conference (Al-Maqtari 2021).

The only aggregating force that has brought southern Yemenis together has been the negative force of military resistance. The logic

---

[54] This is true for the entirety of Yemen, not just in the south. Two other web-based initiatives from the revolutionary period have ceased to exist: the blog "Yemen 4 All" in 2013 and the Yemeni Revolution Electronic Coordination, which published a coordinated newsfeed and Facebook page (e.g. the News on Yemeni Revolution, www.facebook.com/EngYemenNews/about/) in June 2015, three months after the start of the bombings.

of militarization has become the new doxa, the unquestioned and unquestionable truth (Bourdieu 1977: 169). The STC is now in the hands of the military, of tribal leaders, and of a peculiar brand of Salafi-nationalists. The council has gained institutional legitimacy and, in the process, has largely eliminated the role of many historical leaders of Hirak. The military functions as a symbol of unity – marking a return to the time of 1950s independence in the Arab world – and this can be seen on the STC's website and in all its press releases; both are full of military reports and of references to military titles (e.g. "the leader commander Aydarus Al-Zubaydi" or "Maj. Gen. Al-Zubaydi").

Hani bin Breik, the STC Vice-President, is a militant Salafi extremist who does not hesitate to stir sectarian hatred and social divisions in the same extreme manner as Al-Qaeda (ICG 2017). He has also trusted military command to a "handful" of Salafi leaders, some of whom have been accused of murder and running secret prisons (TYR 2019: 6). Many in southern Yemen are concerned about the Security Belt's violent practices and about their close alliance with the Emiratis (Dahlgren 2019). In 2020, a wave of shoot-and-run killings of southern imams accused of being closed to Islah seems to be the work of the STC or some other powerful Emirati security service.[55]

Militarization and direct resort to killing are obviously prejudicial to efforts of alliance generation in all parts of the country. In the north, a similar logic is at play in the territories controlled by the Huthis and the SPC, and we have discussed the rise to power of violence specialists, the cases of political assassinations, male-only authorities, and death-sentencing of journalists.[56] The country is also united in the variable rhetoric of "crisis" and "security." Ansar Allah connects its own vision of security with the necessity of resistance to Saudi aggression. For Hadi loyalists, priority is given to the protection a fragile state. International actors involved in the conflict use the pretext of "humanitarian intervention."

---

[55] According to Amnesty International, *Islahi* activists in the south have been subject to a manhunt, with numerous disappearances and many tortured in illegal detention centers (Dahlgren 2018). See Elisabeth Kendall's unparalleled knowledge and twitter reports on Yemen (e.g. https://twitter.com/Dr_E_Kendall/status/11548074 36785721351, for a tweet on the killing of imams, June 26, 2019) and Worth (2020).

[56] https://twitter.com/Dr_E_Kendall/status/1260875326885965824 (May 14, 2020).

All these are oxymoronic reformulations: people opposed to these visions are brushed aside and have no say. All parties contribute to sustaining symbolic violence. Violence is not only physical destruction but also symbolic: this means erasing or delegitimizing anyone who supported or defends the habitus of *vis populi*. New sociological actors (women, youth, the marginalized, etc.) who entered the political state are made voiceless, and the rituals of this multitude of bodies in informal spaces of civic participation are denied. With the rallying cry of the *sarkha*, the Huthis reinforce the perception of a Huthi–Iranian alliance, which erases the legitimacy of the claims of the people from the Saada and northern governorates who are calling for decentralization (Brandt 2019b).

For Kamilia Al-Eriani, the rhetoric and epistemology of security concerns invoked by international and regional powers vis-à-vis Yemen have generated a culture of apprehension and disengagement from the issues of participation (Al-Eriani 2020: 1142). For the Yemeni scholar, foreign actors thus contribute to "de-democratization," described as the "tendency to authorize [security] intervention for the purpose of undoing or undermining rights … for equal political inclusion and democratic politics" that arose after 2011 (Al-Eriani 2020: 3; 18). Talks of "security threats" or the constantly evoked risk of a "state collapse" abound in the gray literature produced by think-tanks, which are more mouthpiece for hegemonic international actors than actual on-the-ground researchers with non-state actors interested in democratic reforms.[57]

For agencies and NGOs working on the ground, going through security intermediaries is a necessity. The conflict has amplified the gate-keeper function of militias or security actors for the distribution of aid. In Ansar Allah-held territories in the region of Hodeida, Mareike Transfeld (2019) has demonstrated the increasing role played by the *aqils*, delegates of state authority at the community level. These persons, all male, function as a link between state security providers and the community, and in the context of war play a dual role:

Under Ansarallah-rule, the Aqil continues to play a vital, albeit a changed role. According to interviews with Aqils, as well as observations of YPC [Yemen

---

[57] The trend was already present in some of the gray literature on the National Dialogue and the 2015 Constitution, betraying quite a paternalistic top-down interpretation of politics. The NDC is described uniquely as a rent-seeking exercise that allegedly detracted NDC members from "real" preoccupations (Frison-Roche 2015: 17).

Policy Center] researchers, Aqils – next to distributing propane gas and humanitarian aid in the communities – have become particularly important with regards to mobilization of fighters for Ansarallah and sharing intelligence with supervisors. The position of the Aqil before the take-over of Ansarallah can be briefly described as a community figure that is associated with providing services to and functioning in favour of the community, while acting as a link to state institutions. In the Ansarallah system, the Aqils are empowered by Ansarallah and work as informants and as a mechanism of control, but have less authority to serve the community. In short, Aqils have become more powerful; they are, however, seen as spies by the communities and are less trusted. (Transfeld 2019)

This is an example of a system, military but also discursive, around ideas of "security" that multiply the presence of strong men in the absence of a central state. In one of the few interviews I could do with a Yemeni NGO, one operating in the highlands between Taiz and Dhamar, it was clear that the state is nowhere to be seen in these moments of uncertainty.[58] Priority is given to filling in the gap left by this absence. The NGO, called Pulse (or *Nabdh*), supports local initiatives that provide a small source of revenues for internally displaced persons (IDPs), for example, by rebuilding roads, bridges, or schools destroyed during the war, or creating small funds to pay local teachers. To avoid the partiality that foreign funding might bring, the NGO is acting mostly as a mediator and facilitator with the authorities and political factions. Villagers organize their own financial means, generally from remittances from Yemeni relatives working abroad, and chip in to support one of these initiatives.

How does this relate to the issue of strong men? To make the work of the association possible, the NGO has no choice but to go through Ansar Allah, Islah, and GPC leaders. This means that lengthy discussions are needed to show that the work on the ground will not favor one warring side over the other. After that, the NGO has to obtain the authorization of the traditional authorities, *shaykh*, *qadi*, and *aqil*, who are all male figures, without whose approval citizens would not be allowed to start their work.[59] In that setting the work of "civil society" is not only deeply affected by political economy factors (war, remittances), just like Sheila Carapico (1998) identified long ago, but it also needs the active blessing of traditional male figures of authority, whom my interlocutor calls euphemistically

---

[58] Bachir Al-Mohallal, NGO leader, in Sanaa, interview via Zoom, 02/23/2021.
[59] Al-Mohallal, interview, 02/23/2021.

"pilots."[60] In the heartland of the cooperative movements that started at the time of President Al-Hamdi (see Section 2.2), this is a bittersweet development. Despite the war, local associations are providing basic services, but this also means the erosion of the principles of civilian rule (*madaniyya*).[61]

* * *

In Tunisia, strong men are also present as national symbols and in the implementation of the decentralization agenda. While not as drastic as in Yemen in terms of economic effects, with economic and discursive flows under the control of neo-patriarchal military order, the power of these symbols contributes to the resubjectivation of Tunisian citizens. We will discuss two examples. The first deals with the politics of commemoration, where we see a geographically differentiated disregard for the monuments of the 2011 revolution. The second case shows the imperfect impacts of the 2014 constitutional changes with regard to decentralization and universal municipalization.

Considering how frequently politicians speak of the spirit of 2011, it is surprising how few monuments have been built. In Tunis, the only new official monument that has emerged in the center of the capital evokes not so much the memory of the "fallen revolutionaries" of 2011, but rather that of the 12 Presidential Guard members killed in the November 2015 attack by ISIS. There is a reference to the 2011 revolution, but the "Place 14 Janvier" (*sahat 14 yanyar*) is a trafficked roundabout, with no statue or monument, but just an ordinary street sign. The real landmarks of Tunis' foremost central space on Avenue Bourguiba still celebrate strong men and security forces, not the people. Let us describe this awkward relational celebration of male power (see Figure 6.1).

---

[60] Al-Mohallal, interview, 02/23/2021. Clausen (2020) notes that the World Bank-sponsored Social Development Fund, a similar type of initiative meant to help villages and remote communities, encountered mixed results before the start of the war. Work on the ground required coordination with the Ministry of Finance and a de facto veto right for the GPC (Clausen 2020: 120–124). See also the report by Al-Mohallal & Stadnicki (2020).

[61] Al-Mohallal, interview, 02/23/2021. Nevertheless, Al-Mohallal sees some light at the end of the tunnel. The model of self-help has been replicated in all parts of the country, not just in Huthi and Islah-controlled areas (where the NGO is mostly implanted), but also in the south. The STC now favors the emergence of "popular committees" (*lijān sha'abiyya*) that are based on the same approach of strong men mediating the work of local self-governance. Thus, local governance could produce a common idiom for future national dialogues.

Figure 6.1 Three monuments in central Tunis. 2016.

Figure 6.1 (cont.)

The strong men are three presidents from the Sahel region. First, the presence of Ben Ali still looms large, since the obelisk-shape clock tower has remained at the center of the crossing of the large avenues (Avenue Bourguiba and Mohammed V, heading north). Ben Ali's predecessor, Bourguiba, himself made a return in May 2016, under the form of an equestrian statue that had been moved to a less important part of the city by Ben Ali after his medical coup in 1987 (to occupy the spaced opened by the vacated statue, Ben Ali built the obelisk). It is Essebsi, the third President, who decided to move Bourguiba's statue back into the city center. He used the plaque placed on the sculpture's new pedestal to glorify his own executive rule: the space left for Essebsi's signature is much larger than the reference to *al-za'im al-Habib Bourguiba*, the "great leader Habib Bourguiba."[62] Another element of the celebration of strong men is constituted by the memorial honoring the 12 Presidential Guards killed in the bus bombing of November 2015. This monument,

---

[62] Author's observation and translation. See also the article in the Tunisian daily Al-Shorouq, "*Al-'awda al-thāniyya li-'al-za'im'*" ["The second return of 'The Leader'"], section politics, p. 6, June 2, 2016. The sculpture had been placed in La Goulette for over 20 years.

a sober stone block with the names of the victims, is largely inaccessible to the public since it is adjacent to the Ministry of the Interior, which itself has turned yet again into a highly protected building. Ben Ali, Bourguiba, and Essebsi overseeing the return of former security leaders in the Ministry of the Interior: the triangle – or square – of security men is perfect.

The "Place 14 Janvier" (*sahat 14 yanyar*) roundabout, halfway between the obelisk and Bourguiba's sculpture, could not make for a starker contrast: The non-memorial, a street sign, is poorly kept, with posters and ads glued on it, while the strong men's memorials are made from well-kept marble stones and with the necessary elevation that such monuments usually entail. Freudian interpreters of these various monuments would not miss the meaning of the vertical elevation that two of these official monuments have, while the popular evocation of *Place 14 Janvier* is flat and mundane, just like the choice of renaming a section of the large northern highway in Tunis "Mohammed Bouazizi." "Dignity" is granted in this instance of memorialization only to the formal state (actors), not to the informal, connecting, and articulating power of the masses. Only males are celebrated in all these monuments, amounting to a celebration of patriarchy that makes the roles that women and Tunisians at large played in the revolution invisible.[63]

Outside of the capital, and in particular in the south and the interior, the memorialization of the popular revolts of 2011 is conspicuously different. Outside of Tunis, I have seen monuments that have some pride of place and are well-kept and seem to be respected by the population. None of the monuments I saw outside of the center of Tunis had been defaced or vandalized. In the popular neighborhood of Bizerte (away from the touristic center) and in Siliana, not far from the famed palace of the governor, two simple but well-kept monuments commemorate the local victims of the January 2011 upheavals. Simple plaques on each of these two monuments indicate "Street 14 January 2011" in Bizerte and "Square for the Martyrs of 4 January 2011" in Siliana. Also, the south of the country, for example in Midoun and Zerzis, has large monuments commemorating 2011 in

---

[63] It is also notable that Moncef Marzouki, President between 2011 and 2014, whose family historically comes from the south of the country, has been excluded from these spaces.

central roundabouts, one dedicated to the "Freedom Revolution" and the other to the "2011 Martyrs."[64] In Midoun, the former RCD headquarters was rechristened as *"dar al-jama'iyyat,"* "House of the Associations," with an official, larger sign over the main entrance to advertise the new function of a collective space for cultural associations, NGOs, and citizens' movements. When I visited Midoun again a few months later, a new title had been sprayed next to the main entrance to the building: *"dar al-sha'ab,"* house of the people."[65] Evidently, people continue to reclaim spaces that they fought to take away from the RCD and the Ben Ali regime.

The second example of political resubjectivation that evokes the half-full, half-empty glass metaphor stems from the process of universal municipalization. Redesigned municipalities were one of the institutions meant to guarantee the democratic accountability proposed in the 2014 Constitution. However, a brief overview of the municipal elections in May 2018 shows how old apparatchiks have remained influential.

As seen in Section 5.2, the ARP finally passed the law on municipalities on April 26, 2018. On May 6, the first post-Ben Ali municipal elections took place. The result of these municipal elections needs to be read at different levels. In general, it has been interpreted as an electoral defeat of the political personnel (Gobe 2019: §18), preannouncing why two anti-system presidential candidates would end up in the second round of the presidential elections in 2019. About 33% of the votes went to independent lists, and the two governing parties, Ennahda and Nidaa Tounes, finished respectively second (28.64%) and third (20.85%).[66] Souhail Belhadj's (2019) comparative in-depth study of municipalization in four socio-geographic contexts (Ettadhamen, Medenine, Kasserine, and Sfax) suggests that despite efforts by the center to use the municipal elections and regionalism to assert their national basis, the effort either failed or produced mixed results. Local coalitions managed to resist the efforts of the big national parties to impose their lines, and in some instances, these elections contributed to breaking the hegemony of male political leadership. For example, a few

---

[64] Visits in May 2016.
[65] Author's observation in Midoun, May 2016. Visits in January and May 2016.
[66] Figures taken from Gobe (2019). For maps of all the municipalities, see https://na waat.org/2018/05/06/est-ce-quil-existe-une-carte-des-communes-tunisiennes/.
For details of the election results, see http://tunisieelections.org/lists-overview.

weeks after the elections, the municipal council of the capital appointed the first ever female mayor of Tunis.[67]

But by and large, citizens were less than enthusiastic about these elections. Turnout was very low, with only a third of electors voting. Citizens expressed their frustration with political representatives and the central authorities alike. The massive presence of local bureaucratic elites on the electoral lists deterred many from voting (Kherigi forthcoming). It is therefore important to underline the generational and institutional gap around the municipalization issue. It is not youth who stayed away from the election out of indifference, but also the bureaucratic barriers with older apparatchiks calling the shots in municipal affairs that prevented youth from participating electorally (Belhadj 2019: 14; ICG 2019: i, 2). Although she was writing about the process of decentralization before these elections, Béatrice Hibou (2015: 117–119) perfectly captured the paradox of these new public tools meant to expand the common good: the preferred path was, ironically, a very centralized and technocratic vision of decentralization.

In terms of social roles, these elections sanctioned a shrinking tendency observed throughout the country. Women represented 47% of the elected persons but obtained only 19% of mayoral seats. Youth, defined as those under 35 years, who represented 52% of all candidates, managed to get only 37% of the municipal seats.[68] Compared to earlier elections, the 2018 municipal elections have deepened the trend towards a more lackluster political representation. The first post-Ben Ali parliament in 2011, the ANC, was host to a rich array of socio-professional profiles: Many young activists acceded to the benches of Bardo, teachers and artists adding to former exiles, journalists, and trade unionists. The second parliament, the ARP elected in 2014, was much more monotonously composed of business (wo)men and party apparatchiks.[69] The 2018 elections further pushed youths and non-professional politicians further to the sidelines, with businessmen grabbing a majority of seats.

[67] Souad Abderrahim, elected mayor on July 3, belongs to the political bureau of Ennahda (Gobe 2019). At the national level, 66 women were chosen as mayors, as opposed to 282 men, so just under 20% of mayors are women. See https://web .archive.org/web/20200624013504/http://www.tunisieelections.org/mayors-res18.

[68] Results taken from: www.isie.tn/elections/elections-municipales-2018/ and htt ps://blogs.mediapart.fr/salah-horchani/blog/130518/tunisie-elections-municipales-2018-breve-analyse-et-palme-d-or.

[69] Besma Omezzine, party activist, interview in Sfax, 01/06/2016.

This also raises the question of diversity in other sectors of civic life. In terms of gender equality, electoral laws in 2011 required that there be alternating male and female candidates on all of the electoral lists, a practice that has continued since. But the intangible barriers of patriarchy have been creeping dangerously back and undermine the reality of gender equality. Even the UGTT, which provided the actual initial space for the formation of marching protests in December 2010 and January 2011, suffers from a deafening absence of women in the higher echelons of the organization: 47% of affiliate members of local trade union cells of the UGTT are women, yet the latter represent only 5% of the leadership positions, despite internal elections during the December 2011 Congress in Tabarka (Yousfi 2015: 159).

Through associations and local campaigns, women remain very much active. Associational struggles engage with issues of gender equality much more consistently than formal political parties. In 2018, numerous demonstrations took place after the release of a report on gender inequalities in Tunsia by the Commission on Individual Liberties and Equality (COLIBE) (Gana & Sigillò 2019). But even if there was a strong polarization along secular–Islamist lines, associations of both broad camps did much more than the actual parliament to push the debate forward. On the issue of gender equality for questions of inheritance, ARP deputies, from Ennahda, Nidaa Tounes, and all the way to the Marxist Popular Front, have sided against a proposal to make inheritance gender equal.[70] Ennahda used the logic of specialization, introduced in its tenth congress, to push back against these measures through its network of associations (Gana & Sigillò 2019). The consensus among all parties of the ARP was to bury the parliamentary discussion,[71] a dynamic that was also favored by the election of independent Kais Saied as President, someone with clear socially conservative views opposed to this form of equality. Sporadic marches are organized by associations that want to keep the issue alive, but Tunisians have become disillusioned with the ARP's ability to take decisions. The only fast decisions that the

[70] See www.jeuneafrique.com/742549/politique/tunisie-divergences-a-larp-aux-premieres-discussions-sur-legalite-dans-lheritage/.
[71] See https://lapresse.tn/44189/nesrine-jelalia-directeur-executif-de-bawsala-un-consensus-de-non-decision/ and https://lapresse.tn/70542/egalite-dans-lheritage-saied-ne-revient-pas-sur-sa-position-et-insiste-sur-la-clarte-du-texte-coranique/.

Parliament is able to take are those pertaining to the private economic sector.

The 2011 Uprisings never came close to toppling capitalism or profoundly altering the structures of economic production and redistribution. Put bluntly, the Arab Uprisings have instead *enhanced* the connectivity of cheap Arab labor to capitalist surplus extractions (Ayari 2011). This is a widespread analysis in Marxist readings, with Adam Hanieh (2013) illustrating the amplification of circuits of productive labor (with intensified flows of migrants inside the Arab world) [72] or of commodity and financial services post-2011.[73] If the Arab Uprisings managed to create new social roles, it was also in the field of the economy, with a new layer of contenders acting on motives of rentierism (i.e. non-productive labor). The structure of the market and financial-monetary circuits remained unaltered, with even more intense regional and international flows of capitalist penetration (see also Allal 2016) from the Gulf region (Hanieh 2013), Turkey, Europe, and the USA, and in some places, like Sfax, with African or Indian entrepreneurial circles.[74] This partial opening explains, for some, why Ennahda and Nidaa Tounes have been sitting in a coalition, ruling the country between 2015 and 2019. But from a class perspective, the older generation making the main decisions inside Ennahda is simply a collaboration in a pragmatic manner with its secular counterpart to guarantee access to a share of the economic pie.

The business and entrepreneurial aspect of the Tunisian "transition" is a general problem. Hmed (2016a) argues that the entire political class is subservient to financial and economic elites. Right before Ramadan in 2016, the ARP hastened the passing of a law reforming the banking sector[75] in a way that was unparalleled. Why were there only two months to pass that law, but more than two years to finalize the laws

---

[72] His book was written before the acute crisis of asylum and migrant seekers across the Mediterranean, be it through Italy (from 2013 onwards) or through Greece (in 2015 and 2016).

[73] The Gulf states, all monarchies, have played a silent but immense role in crushing the revolutionary (republican) aspirations of the Uprisings.

[74] Hacem Kamoum, campaign leader and businessman, interview in Sfax, 06/04/ 2016. Indian companies have recently invested in Tunisia, in particular in the phosphate and pharmaceutical sector. See http://kapitalis.com/tunisie/2016/05/ 27/le-vice-president-indien-ansari-en-tunisie-les-2-et-3-juin/ or http://kapitalis .com/tunisie/2016/03/04/tunisie-inde-des-opportunites-non-encore-exploitees/.

[75] See *La Presse*, various articles published in May and again in June 2016.

pertaining to decentralization, and no conclusion to the legislative debates on inheritance equality? This interpretation of the Arab Uprisings as a purveyor of capitalist integration with the multiplication of rent-seeking actors seems to dovetail with the reality of a business mentality in which there is a gendered division of labor with males in charge of "real politics," protection of the economic and security sectors. Meanwhile, women take the crumbs of a few symbolic positions of leadership, leaders of associations and NGOs. Transitional justice will illustrate just that, in Section 6.3 below.

The politics of NGOization, so often criticized, probably has a downside with respect to *representation*. Associations and campaigns are partly shaped by the sociological profile of their leaders, which leaves out the actual political subjects about whom they speak. Thus, the informal sector (here understood in opposition to institutions and organizations involved in legislative and policy-oriented processes) is at pains to retain that informality once it becomes professionalized. Their discourse also entails a class component, with positions of NGO leadership depending on social capital that often elude young citizens. But the association sector, which has boomed since the revolution,[76] offers many job opportunities to Tunisian youths and university students. With regard to the transnational connectivity, and the idea of a virtuous Moebius strip, Tunis has since 2003 become a hub for many Arab NGOs that were threatened and/or forced into exile from their countries. Tunis has been a host for Egyptian, Syrian, and Libyan rights organizations, in the same manner as Cairo, Amman, and Beirut have become a new basis for Yemeni organizations.

6.3 What Remains? Smaller Spaces, Same Habitus

The spaces around democratic actors in Yemen and Tunisia are clearly shrinking and are being "colonized" by the presence of older male leaders and by new forms of encroachment. But the habitus of 2011 and of the *force of the people* is still operating. The habitus, we recall, is

---

[76] There were about 6,000 official associations at the time of the revolution, the vast majority being RCD-controlled organizations. The number of registered associations had jumped to 18,500 by June 2016, and to 23,900 by April 2021. The numbers are taken from the official clearing house on associations, IFEDA (Centre d'information d'études et de documentation sur les associations). See http://www.ifeda.org.tn/stats/arabe.pdf.

a "system of durable, transposable dispositions, structured structures predisposed to function as structuring structures" (Bourdieu 1977: 72). A habitus is a collective, sociological interface connecting individuals to social structures. The specific habitus of *vis populi* was the new subjectivity, the process of creating new civic linkages, which served to exteriorize a vividly active sense of citizenship. It was "a structuring structure," pushing for democratic participation, decentralization, and enfranchisement of the multitude. The "structured structures" of security, of strong men, and of traditional authorities that regrouped after 2015 have stifled this habitus. These antagonistic structuring structures are in an asymmetric opposition and the politics of security, professionalization, and strong men have much more inertia and organizational resources, not to mention the power of one single man, President Kais Saied, who can suspend the Parliament, take over interim control of the Ministry of the Interior, appoint ministers, including the Prime Minister, with no consultation whatsoever with the Parliament, and arbitrarily assign opponents to house arrest or ban their travels.[77]

This last empirical section on Tunisia and Yemen presents a twist, a complication, or a partially maintained articulation for democratic accountability in the realm of violence. Without these analyses, one would default to reductive narratives of "success" or "failures." It is better to think of these twists as flows in long-term dialectical relation between state and society, on which external factors play an influential role.

Let us start with the IVD, the acronym from the French name of the institution (Instance Verité et Dignité, or in Arabic, *hai'at al-haqiqa wal-karama*), which was meant to spark a public reckoning with past state violence, like the Truth and Reconciliation commissions did in South Africa or Morocco. In Tunisia, there was a great hope in the principle of transitional justice, but the forked path between reformism and gradual change (Chapter 4) and the return of security men contributed to the feeling of a mountain giving birth to a mouse when it came

---

[77] These are some of the unaccounted measures that President Saied has taken after his "coup" of July 25, 2021, although the article invoked by Saied (article 80) is cleared marked for other situations, such as war, or "imminent danger threatening the nation's institutions or the security or independence of the country." *Violence and Representation in the Arab Uprisings* covers developments until mid-2021, but President Saied has only intensified his power grab since.

to assessing the work of the IVD. The interests of the large parties – protecting economic interests – prevailed over the citizens' expectation of a recognition by the state of the crimes it committed over decades against its citizens. A gendered division of labor also explain the mixed feelings that observers note in their studies of the IVD's work.

The Constituent Assembly kickstarted the creation of the IVD when it adopted a law on transitional justice in December 2013.[78] The body, a national commission made up of 15 members, received the mandate to uncover the atrocities committed by the Tunisian state from July 1955 all the way to December 2013, the date when the law was passed.[79] The Parliament appointed intellectual Sihem Ben Sedrine at its helm. Ben Sedrine had founded a prominent human rights organization, the Conseil National pour les Libertés en Tunisie (CNLT) in the late 1990s, and was not shy about criticizing the lack of independence of the judiciary and state brutality. Her network of activists and associations was influential in pushing for swift reforms in the Ministry of the Interior in 2011, when Rajhi was appointed the new minister during the second Ghannouchi government. She was the perfect person to deal with transitional justice and accountability, and many expected that Ben Sedrine would be able to fulfill the mandate of the IVD.

The IVD was officially established on June 6, 2014, but it took nearly two years of intense negotiations for the new parliament to agree on the financial resources that it would receive. In November 2016, it launched emotional public hearings, with live TV coverage, in which testimonials of victims and families of victims could speak openly about past state crimes. For a moment, Tunisians could witness a real process of reckoning with past violence and felt as if the IVD would manage to do what the "transition" and politicians had failed to do. Sixty-two-thousand individuals lodged complaints, with 40,000 citizens audited during private hearings.[80] In more than 300 instances, regions of Tunisia, which were given juridical personality to claim the status of region-victim, presented arguments against past attempts by state authorities to marginalize their parts of the country (Gana 2020).

---

[78] For an overview of the mandate of the IVD, see the Internet Archive at https://web.archive.org/web/20210117001022/www.ivd.tn/livd/mandat-de-livd/.

[79] See ICG (2016: 13–16). For a brief overview of the content of this final report, see https://lapresse.tn/84824/justice-transitionnelle-un-bilan-mi-figue-mi-raisin (January 19, 2021).

[80] https://news.gnet.tn/23386-2 (November 21, 2019).

The IVD submitted its final report on the last day of 2018 and was officially dissolved on May 31, 2019. The IVD proposed to refer 1,400 persons to specialized tribunals and proposed a state arbitrage that would allow the government to recover 745 million dinars lost in massive corruption and embezzlement schemes. But all these recommendations depended on the actual ministries and tribunals to follow suit. After the dissolution of the IVD, a silently concerted reaction by these state institutions meant that there has been almost no consequence. Thus, the expected sum of 745 million dinars has amounted in practice, two years later, to a meek 12 million dinars restituted to the state treasury.[81]

Why were so few cases brought to justice and so little money from the project of economic reconciliation paid out? The three connected reasons are related to the exhaustion of the revolutionary period: First, the framework of reformism, as opposed to the logic of *tabula rasa*, took some of the punch that a full-fledged transitional justice program could have had. Second, the awkward alliance between Nidaa Tounes and Ennahda meant that the priority was given to economic reconciliation, not to transitional justice. Third, Essebsi's agenda to return to a strong presidential power with a gendered understanding of authority interfered substantially with the agenda of the IVD. Let us unpack these reasons.

First, the parameters of the IVD were the by-product of earlier reformist decisions taken in 2011 and 2012. Acknowledging some culprits and finding a limited number of scapegoats were the dominant goals in the first two years. We also remember that by the end of 2011, the Ben Ammor Commission had already collected 10,000 complains about embezzlement under Ben Ali, with 400 of them being deferred to competent authorities. By 2016, no decisions had been taken by tribunals, and many observers complained of a lack of collaboration in the justice sector (ICG 2016: 2, fn. 5). Another body, the Bouderbala Commission, investigated the violence during the revolutionary period and deferred the cases to military tribunals, but as we have seen (Section 4.3), only a few of the people sentenced to jail remained there after a process of appeal. Many state officials were also simply reinstated in new governmental functions under Essebsi. Thus, when

---

[81] www.webdo.tn/2021/02/16/ivd-la-valeur-des-operations-de-reconciliation-seleve-seulement-a-12-md/.

the IVD came into full action, in 2016, many decisions pertaining to "transitional justice" had already fallen under the jurisdiction of tribunals with no political will to proceed with the accusations. In a way, revolutionary justice could not come from the reformist path chosen in 2011.

Second, the alliance between Ennahda and Nidaa Tounes was more than a parliamentary or governing agreement. It was an alliance of old political leaders who were more than willing to look the other way to preserve stability, and to continue sharing control of the economy. This allowed Nidaa Tounes to neutralize potential political opponents by threatening to use criminal complaints for various crimes of corruption, embezzlement, or threats to national security against them. On its side, Ennahda preferred not to look too much into its own use of violence in the 1980s and 1990s, as it had committed various bomb attacks, so as to remain a trustworthy or respected political partner. This convergence of interests for both parties, called pragmatism in politics, explains why the ARP was reluctant in supporting the IVD effort, refusing to hand it the financial means to lead investigations, and pulling the plug on the IVD in 2018, with only a few prosecutions having been carried out. The IVD died following a shameful procedural vote in the Parliament in June 2018, before Ben Sedrine would conclude all the hearings and receive all the necessary documentation from the state bureaucracy to corroborate testimonials.

Third, Essebsi used presidential prerogatives to divert political attention away from the work of the IVD. This meant supporting alternative economic initiatives, and the security sector as a whole, while the IVD was trying to identify mechanisms or individuals that had contributed to state violence. On the economic policy front, and with the help of the ARP, Essebsi chose to pull the rug from under the feet of the IVD by further reducing the scope of transitional justice, by proposing a draft law on economic reconciliation in July 2015 (ICG 2016: 19). In substance, the law would allow people accused of corruption in the past to evade judicial trouble, in exchange for a voluntary payment made to the state. This was seen by some as an indirect blessing being given to the former economic elites of Tunis and the Sahel, which had been weakened by the revolution (ICG 2016: 19, 26–27). On the issue of state violence, Essebsi's presidential prerogatives represented further unsurmountable hurdles for the IVD: the latter's demands to access documentation, archives, or testimonies from the Ministry of the Interior were denied.

Moreover, access to police archives to document decades of brutal surveillance over, and treatments against, Tunisians were also denied. Even the military tribunals, which were tasked with judging former police and security officials for the use of violence during the revolution under the Bouderbala Commission, refused to hand over the minutes of the trials to the IVD. Gana's cunning analysis of the IVD's limited ability to engage with the 220 files regarding the region-victim status promoted an expanded understanding of social rights, but it could do nothing to ensure that tribunals would take a position.[82]

Connecting the dots of Essebsi's electoral campaign about the defense of the "dignity of the state," with the memorialization of Tunis' central square, along with issues of economic reconciliation, one can see a gendered understanding of public authority that resonates with Bourdieu's theory of masculine domination within state structures (e.g. Bourdieu 2001). On the one hand, the core functions of the state (justice, budget, army) are under masculine control. This is manifested by Essebsi, through his choice to celebrate a certain image of Bourguiba, the political-military leader on his horse, and by his alliance with Ennahda in Parliament to find ways to accelerate bank reform and economic reconciliation. On the other hand, the state deals with "soft" governmental issues, education, social policies. In this case, the IVD commission was led by a woman, but with very little financial and organizational support from the police and security sectors.[83]

Tunisians were no fools and saw clearly that the president and the ruling coalition were betraying any prospect for transitional justice. In 2017, when the battle between the full-steam IVD and the government was raging, protesters took to the streets. The draft law on economic reconciliation, pushed forward by Essebsi, galvanized youth and activists and generated a campaign called *Manich Msameh* ("I will not forgive" or "I will not tolerate it" in Arabic). The campaign demanded that accountability, justice, and anti-corruption remain a central priority of the government (Allal 2016: 17–18). It occurred more or less at the same time as the Tataouine and El-Kamour sit-ins. For this reason, new slogans developed around the issue of oil revenues. This new

[82] See Gana (2020), who discusses how the December 10, 2013 article granted legal subjectivity for regions.

[83] In line with Bourdieu's theory, Wacquant (2010: 201) distinguishes "the feminine 'spendthrift' ministries" in charge of health, housing, welfare, and "the masculine side" of government, in charge of budget, security, and justice.

campaign, *Winou el-Pétrole?* ("Where is the oil?," meaning where is the bonanza from the proceeds of oil selling),[84] created such a stir on Facebook and Twitter that the government was probably forced into the June compromise in Tataouine.

Let us move to two final examples of very localized campaigns that illustrate the dialectic relations between democratic efforts to reclaim public space and the effect of reaffirmed patriarchy in Tunisia. The first example is about a popular initiative by a high school teacher in Sfax to guarantee fair and equal access to streets and sidewalks. The project resonates with Tripp's discussion of the politics of space in Tunisia,[85] but when put in relation with another, much more isolated, campaign leader one realizes how little it takes to lose a well-meaning project to a much more ambiguous discourse of "security." The second initiative will deal with the Jemna Oasis, where continued resistance from below finds a way through the requalification of the land reclamation through a new law allowing new forms of economic–public partnerships.

Zied is a very popular teacher in one of the *lycées* in Sfax. In August 2015, he launched a small campaign on Facebook calling for the freeing of sidewalks from irregular street sellers, abusive parking habits, and illegal encroachment on public places and spaces by cafes and restaurants. The page he created on Facebook is called *sayyeb ettrottoir*, a mixed rendering of Arabic (*sayyeb* for "free," "clear," "get off from") and French *trottoirs*, for sidewalks. It gained publicity among students and gradually caught the attention of hundreds and then, after a couple of months, thousands.[86] The initial intention of the project was to emulate the sense of public occupation of 2011.[87]

What started as an impassioned outcry after seeing so many handicapped or elderly persons unable to use the sidewalks as they were

---

[84] www.opendemocracy.net/en/winou-el-petrole-oil-and-accountability-in-tunisia/.

[85] Tripp (2015: 6) argues that the "Tunisian revolutionary moment and its aftermath have opened up spaces that can provide a framework for the agonistic politics associated with democratic possibility." While in agreement with him that spaces matter, their civic use might not always generate democratic practices.

[86] The Facebook page announced 44,000 members in July 2016, 61,000 in 2020, and just over 100,000 in 2021. See www.facebook.com/groups/SayebTrottoir/about/. It is now called *Sayeb_Etrottoir*.

[87] Zied Mellouli, campaign leader and teacher, interview in Sfax, 01/03/2016 and 06/03/2016.

taken over by cars and illegal café terraces became a vector for civic education with his students and other schools in Sfax. Sidewalks around these establishments were refurbished, painted in white and red (as if a red carpet had been rolled all the way to the entrance of the Habib Thamer Institute where Zied teaches). With a graffiti rendering of Michelangelo's God giving life in the Sistine Chapel, here God's finger pointed not to Adam's, but to a trashcan, precisely to teach the basics of urban civility. Media attention started in local newspapers, was picked up by a regional radio, and soon spread to the national media. The teacher-turned-civics-teacher quickly became a national and soon international icon.[88]

He seems to enjoy the numerous media appearances, which are easy to track on Al-Jazeera or European media. Every other day, he posts pictures of new abuses: a house whose owner built an extra room on a sidewalk, a street light turned around so that the bulb does not illuminate the street but the back-yard of a private house, rapid overnight construction of an illegal kiosk, etc. More and more, his calls have become morally tinted. Rather than repeating the usual slogan of "keep the sidewalks free," he soon added calls for the respect and strict enforcement of the law. New hashtags such as #*satr al-trutuar* or #*tracage_obligatoire_des trottoirs* (which would be #compulsory_demarcating_of_the_sidewalks) indicated a more determined approach.

Before I returned for another round of interviews, I discovered that the motives of Zied's campaign had generated interest outside of Sfax. New hashtags, sometimes in Arabic, sometimes in French, flourished but with very different connotations: "#*tabbaq_al-qanun*" (#Apply the law!)[89] or #*Soyez Fermes!* ("#Be firm! Call on the state to intervene"). The promoter of these pages does not simply call upon the civic virtues of his compatriots, but expects the state to intervene, apparently with an iron fist.[90] The initial trust in people's capacity to represent and solve their own problems

---

[88] Mellouli, interview, 01/03/2016. His campaign occasionally got him into trouble: he was beaten up at least twice, apparently by thugs on behalf of shop or café owners who had been accused of illegal infringement on public space in his social media postings. Other intimidations happened in the spring of 2016 as well.

[89] www.facebook.com/hashtag/%D8%B7%D8%A8%D9%82_%D8%A7%D9 %84%D9%82%D8%A7%D9%86%D9%88%D9%86? source=feed_text&story_id=1064495343658078.

[90] Some pictures of abusive constructions posted on the Facebook page garnered praise for Zied and his followers.

seems to have faded away, conveying another example of the paradoxical expectation that the solutions must come from the central state. Tunisians I questioned about *Sayyeb Trottoir* had mixed feelings about this campaign. The person who organized the municipality role play mentioned above was unhappy that the *Sayyeb Trottoir* campaign failed to address the structural reasons for the encroachments on urban sidewalks: Had the municipalities provided clear spaces for itinerant sellers to operate, or had authorities simplified procedures to obtain a permit, for a fruit vendor in Sidi Bouzid, for example, then maybe one would not be confronted with this endemic abuse of public space.[91] For him, it is not just a question of equal access to public spaces (the elderly, children, or handicapped persons should be able to move freely on sidewalks without parked cars); it is also unequal access to public services and to mixed commercial and cultural centers that explains why sidewalks will be respected in richer neighborhoods, but less so in poorer and marginalized portions of cities.

One staunch supporter of the *Sayyeb Trottoir* campaign is a young founder of an association in Bizerte. He openly calls himself one of the *azlam* (the "villains"), a nickname given to supporters of the old RCD regime. He created a similar page for his hometown called "Bizerte_Cleaner" (sic). There, the gloves are off: pictures of people parking along the *corniche* in the touristy part of the city are accompanied by deprecating comments, such as "Animals"[92] or "We don't want you!" The social role assumed by the promoter of this page is not that of a concerned citizen: It becomes that of a self-appointed defender of justice taking the power to judge others in moralizing terms, or happily calling for the police forces, or even the army to restore order. One photoshopped picture shows a series of misparked cars being crushed by a tank. The parallel to President Essebsi's push to reestablish the prestige of the state (*haybat al-dawla*) is clear here.

This last example, which has nothing to do with the spirit of Zied, the founder of the campaign in Sfax, shows that use of public spaces does not automatically warrant that positive ethos of mutual respect or "new webs of interaction" that revolutions are said to "embed" (Lawson 2016: 113). Thus, we see a worthy civic campaign in one

---

[91] Othman Khaled, civic campaign leader, interview in Tunis, 05/26/2016.
[92] www.facebook.com/313256785524131/photos/a.313972982119178.10737418 30.313256785524131/498048540378287.

town turn into a call for tough security and a return to patriarchy in another city. The same idea of "protecting space" can be interpreted in a virtuous civic way in one place, but it can also inspire others to justify authoritarian leadership over very mundane issues, like car parking. These are tree different habituses that each emphasize different state–society relations in the use of public space. Indeterminacy is in effect.

Let us conclude our Tunisia journey with a possibly positive final development for collective mobilization at the Jemna Oasis. The reader will remember the caricature of the Prolegomenon, issued in 2016, at a time where the government (during the presidency of Essebsi) tried to divide claimants against one another (see Figure 0.1). The origin of the Jemna struggle is old, going back to colonial times, with all the ingredients of marginalized interior regions, latent citizenship during the republican period, and the connective mobilization of January 2011. At that moment, a collective occupied the 185-hectare date-producing oasis for months and petitioned the post-revolutionary authorities for the return of collective ownership (Szakal 2015). Here what could be a final solution to the Jemna struggle, a compromise, happened not through the recognition of past mistakes by state authorities, but through an awkward and indirect loophole created by a new law on social and economic solidarity. Let us look at the details of the Jemna affair and its territorial-democratic symbolism.

Claims of dispossession of collectives good in Jemna date back to the time of the French protectorate.[93] French capitalists saw the opportunity to turn this small oasis into a profitable enterprise and to expand the colonial presence to the southwest of the country, 600 km from the capital. In the 1920s, the *Société Commerciale et Agricole du Sud Tunisien*, a French company, was created and took land from locals. With independence, President Bourguiba launched a large plan to nationalize land, and granted control of former colonial properties to state-owned cooperatives, in this case an entity called STIL. The families originally owning the land purchased it back from the Republic in June 1964.[94] Yet in the 1980s, seeing how profitable it was, the government reneged on the purchase,

---

[93] I rely mostly on accounts given by local residents and later collected and turned into a small documentary *Jemna: Al-Karāma fī 'Arājīnhā*, loosely translatable as "The Palm Trees Are Jemna's Dignity." www.youtube.com/watch?v=gRRsdpl5 WqA, *Nawaat* (documentary in Arabic, posted July 11, 2015).

[94] This is from the documentary. Other accounts claim that in the 1960s the government sold the land without majority approval of Jemna's management council, the *Conseil de Gestion de la Localité de Jemna* (Szakal 2015).

gave the 1964 amount of money back with no adjustment to the increased cost of living, and forced state property back on the oasis. The state-owned company, STIL, was in charge of the oasis until 2002 when the government leased the oasis to two private investors, one of them being the brother of the former general inspector of Ben Ali's national guard (Mahmoud 2020: 16). Here is yet another instance of connections to the security state leading to good business in the period of latent citizenship. In January 2011, and with the support of the Leagues for the Protection of the Revolution (Szakal 2015), the youth of Jemna, most of them unemployed and landless, organized a sit-in, occupying the space in front of the STIL building for 99 days, collecting food and funds, and airing radio programs to raise awareness about collective rights over the land. The occupation movement ultimately wanted to reclaim the oasis as belonging to the local community.

A long battle to assert who were the rightful owners of the 185 hectares began. The claims of the youth that it was communal land were not fully correct, but in the spirit of 2011, and given the disappearance of many of the corrupt elites along with Ben Ali, there was a genuine hope that Jemna could be run in a collective manner, without state interference. Production after 2011 has been organized collectively, and the resources drawn from the sales went to build new infrastructure for the workers' community, with a new school building and a permanent market structure, and a temporary insurance scheme, since the oasis, in conflict with the state, could not receive social security benefits. All the governments that the Jemna collective met with kicked the can down the road. They refused to recognize that past governmental decisions, in the 1980s or in 1964, were tainted by state corruption, while at the same time acknowledging that there had been multiple locals involved in those transactions. The government of Habib Essid then changed course and tried to negotiate with each single individual involved in the former collective farm. Khiari's (2016) drawing, with people crawling in different boxes, captures that moment of the Jemna process where some individuals seemed willing to obtain a separate financial compensation as opposed to fighting collectively for the wholesale right to cultivate the land in a cooperative mode. (Khiari also makes a larger point about Tunisian politics' inability to articulate coalitions to resist the slowing down of reforms under the Nidaa Tounes–Ennahda government.) Eventually the strategy of parcellation or fragmentation pursued by the Tunis authority faltered, and the fear of seeing small private properties replacing a collectively-run oasis receded. The collective remained united in various court hearings, buying more time for the number of employees to grow to about 129 in 2015 and 150 in 2016, with thriving annual benefits from the collective farming of dates.[95] Still, the government did not want to recognize the entity representing the farmers.

The creation of the Association for the Safeguarding of the Oasis of Jemna (ASOJ) subverted the Essebsi government's plan to force small individual owners to sell. In 2016, the government decided to block the association's assets, arguing that it should dissolve and become an agricultural cooperative. ASOJ refused because the move would de facto recognize the state's right to manage the land (Aliriza 2020). The limbo in which the Jemna collective has been (Mahmoud 2020) seemed to come to an end in 2019. First a new president, Kais Saied, came to power with a program meant to deconcentrate power and build strong local authorities. Second, the ARP was discussing a new law on Social and Solidarity Economy (SSE), favoring mixed public–private arrangements, "which produce goods, services and knowledge that meet the needs of the community they serve, through the pursuit of specific social and environmental objectives and the fostering of solidarity" (Odone 2019). Aliriza (2020) discusses how the new law, eventually passed at the end of June 2020, could be the way for the Jemna Oasis to gain legal recognition and take a step toward the new state policy. But the association remains distrustful of President Saied's suggestion of handing the ownership of the date farm to the local municipality, since collective ownership would be abandoned.

The Jemna struggle for the commons is not finished even as these lines are being written. Nevertheless, it condenses many of this books' themes. Historical dissatisfaction with privileged access to land under colonialism, and through connections to the security apparatus later on, contributed to the revolutionary moment in Jemna in 2011. Those pushing for collective farming met the usual rollercoaster of problems: central authorities reluctant to cede some modest form of power, the use of judicial struggle to break the unity of the movement, all the way to threats of expropriation. The margins are still neglected by the post-revolutionary governments,

---

[95] "Tunisie/Jemna: l'Etat jaloux d'une ONG qui le dépasse." See article on the Internet Archive, at https://web.archive.org/web/20200805223023/https://new s.barralaman.tn/tunisiejemna-letat-jaloux-dune-ong-depasse/ (October 26, 2016).

but they also refuse, as in El-Kamour, to be made docile subjects. The fact that the association continues representing the farmers and their families bears witness that not all is bad with the world of associations and NGOs. The same can be said about the "opportunity" that occurred with the passing of the law on SSE. It is, on the one hand, a project pushed forward by international financial actors promoting some neoliberal accommodation to the logic of the market and private leadership. But as Sigillò & De Facci (2018) aptly note, these SSE schemes did represent "a small revolution." On the other hand, the scheme fostered a space of articulation between national and local priorities, and enabled a non-negligible source of financial support for small local associations, in this case from the disinherited interior of Tunisia, via partnerships with international associations and donors. Last but not least, the SSE schemes enabled a new type of conversation about the long-term protection of environmental resources and social rights (Sigillò & De Facci 2018: §22). Jemna inhabitants have retained their collectivist project, but they were forced to hook it up to the new and international language of a "solidarity economy."

* * *

In Yemen, NGOs and cultural representations have become the few remaining channels through which to express demands for political transformation.[96] Occasionally, associations make references to accountability, the rule of law, and local governance. A battle for transnational influence is waged through media wars and the import of mercenaries, but also from below by NGOs calling for accountability. But the need to adapt to the war situation trumps most considerations. Obtaining interviews with campaigns and with association leaders in Tunisia was generally straightforward. In Yemen, finding people involved directly on the ground proved much more difficult. The two associations I engaged with had much more serious problems to solve than responding to a Swiss sociologist based in New York. One Yemeni, leading an association based in Sanaa since 2019, had to deal with the grim reality: Our Zoom appointment in February 2021 was postponed because his operation officers had just been assassinated in front of his home. With another interviewee in Socotra, I could almost live through the actual clash that opposed the pro-Hadi and STC factions in a tense standoff in June 2020. My phone was constantly

---

[96] An argument also made in the case of Syria by Wedeen (2019).

buzzing from a cascade of images and press-releases that my contact in Hadibo was sharing over WhatsApp in the month of June 2020.[97]

NGOization in Yemen cuts both-ways, like it does in Tunisia. It is too simplistic to reduce associational work to political docility to the donors' agenda. Humanitarian aid is easily political, as we saw from the example of the *aqils* in Hodeida, but the two associations interviewed, in Taiz and in Hadibo, work with very limited budgets, in large part to prevent politicization of aid. They also extend a very long Yemeni practice of self-help and local governance (Carapico 1998). For Bachir Al-Mohallal, his work in small villages is also a way to prevent the fatalism of war. Aware of the danger of having to work through traditional authorities, he appreciated the larger benefits that accrue once the *skaykhs* are on board: it is easier to get women and younger people involved de facto and to restart teaching, rebuilding a small health dispensary, or offering a small job to IDPs.[98]

Spaces of critical engagement exist in the media sphere. The larger share is, however, dedicated to sustaining the symbolic order of "security" and "protection" against enemies, as well as to hagiographic descriptions of military leadership. In the list of flagrant cases of propaganda, we can think of Huthi's flagship media network, *Al-Masira*. Barrels of ink have been spilled suggesting that Iran is pulling all the strings in the northern part of the country, and is behind all the missile attacks from Yemen on Saudi targets.[99] Actual Iranian influence is mostly limited to the media, with the Huthi's flagship media network, *Al-Masira*, receiving Iranian support (H. Porter 2020).

---

[97] In a much-reduced scale, the study of associational work at a distance, compounded with the distancing imposed by the COVID-19 pandemic, resonates with the work of French anthropologist Marine Poirier (2020), who was forced to do fieldwork on Yemen from Egypt and who offers wonderful material about the new use of spaces, tribal connections, and charitable work. She has followed two tribal leaders in Cairo since 2015, one in a gated community and the other in the city center. The first (Shaykh A) had decided to join the "revolutionary camp" in 2011, and created a new party that sent seven delegates to the NDC. In Cairo, he has turned his cultural and social capital to become a prized expert in peace and mediation for the international community. The second (Shaykh B) has remained faithful to Saleh and to the GPC. After the death of Saleh, he chose to support Hadi and was elected in April 2019 as President of an extraordinary session of the Yemeni Parliament in Seyun (Poirier 2020: 191–195).

[98] Al-Mohallal, interview, 02/23/2021.

[99] Arm smugglers in the north have easy access to weapons or missile parts without having to go through Iran (Sanaa Center 2020: 13; Brandt 2019a: 25–27).

Since its creation in 2012, the network has mimicked, and worked in close relation with, *Al-Manar*, the TV station of Hezbollah. Indeed, both operate from Lebanon and produce slick promotional materials for the Huthi's military funding campaign and their military propaganda. Internally, these war-mongering campaigns have left pragmatist Huthi leaders marginalized (Lackner 2019: 158). Media have failed to report on the unresolved cases of critical intellectuals assassinated on the streets of Sanaa (Glosemeyer 2015).

There is a media war between all the factions, and each party tries to present the opponent's military campaign as the vilest and most illegitimate. The official news outlet of Hadi's government does not even speak of the Huthi army (*al-jaysh*), but of "*al-milishiat*," militias. The war against the Huthis is characterized on the pro-Hadi news agency Saba as the "war of the Huthi militias," and Huthi militias are portrayed as beneficiaries of support from "Tehran mercenaries" ("*murtaziqat Tehran*").[100] Saudi bombings are depicted as a "campaign" or "initiative" in support of Yemen on Sabanew.net, a pro-Hadi website, while Saudi bombings are deemed terrorism, aggression, or cowardice on the Huthi-run, saba.ye website.

But certain actors refuse this siloeing logic and flip back the content of these terms and discourses to keep democratic articulations alive. From a Gramscian perspective, culture has remained one the few places wherein to build counter-hegemony, now that revolutionary aspirations have been shelved. For example, young artists and intellectuals, whom we encountered earlier, turned the logic of war and of militias on their head, even when profoundly marked by the war.[101] For example, the street artist Murad Subay' drew a "militia prisoner" in 2019 (*sijin al-milishia*) in a style that evokes the fate of all Yemenis. The illusion of one militia being better than the other is denounced in this small art project,[102] as in other murals by Subay', where he denounces killings and torture, or the foolishness of a war driven by outside parties.

Literature and the theatre nourish and maintain a space that bridges the reality of war with cultural expression. These exchanges sustain a space of civility, an "intermediate zone of social relationship between the intimate and the hostile" (Ikegami 2005: 28). This has occurred with theatre plays,

---

[100] See www.sabanew.net/viewstory/63668 (June 25, 2020).
[101] Ammar Basha, whose videos have often been discussed in the book, is now obsessed with the violence of bombings.
[102] https://muradsubay.com/2020/05/07/99820/.

a tradition that has been kept alive in Aden despite the very dangerous situation there since 2015,[103] and in numerous examples of Yemeni literary production. To take Al-Rubaidi's (2021) formulation, one has to read between the lines to be able to see how the imaginary of a pluralist Yemen is still alive, even in 2021. Authors tackle this issue and the effect of wars, but they also comment on the return of dictatorship, the corruption that single leadership generates, and the price that critical voices have to pay.[104] Poetry and novels preserve a voice for women (see the novel *Saghira's Laws* penned by Wajdi Al-Ahdal with a woman chosen as president)[105] and for the *akhdam* and the low castes. "The humanistic vision in this focalized perspective lies in the very act of giving a voice to the *akhdam* . . . in view of their general voicelessness in Yemeni society. . . . The central message of the novel is to humanize the dehumanized image of *akhdam* in Yemeni society" (Al-Rubaidi 2018b: 15).

The contrast between the disaffection of the progressist rhetoric and policies of the YSP (Al-Maqtari 2020; 2021) and the content of novelists' interpretation of the socialist era in the South, or of the Al-Hamdi era in the Taiz region, is stark. Yemeni scholar Al-Rubaidi (2018b) analyzed six recently published novels, and his findings overlap with the argument presented in this book about symbolically preserved spaces for civic articulations and the habitus of *vis populi*. The 2015 novel by Ahmad Zayn, *Steamer Point*, set in the late 1960s, reflects on the lost opportunities of the post-independence project but poses similar questions about missed chances in the post-2011 south (Al-Rubaidi 2018b: 6–7). The same deflecting technique of talking about the past to address the current ordeal is used in Nadya Al-Kawkabani's novel *My Sanaa* (2013). The novel narrates an episode in 1968, during the Northern civil war, but it is a political commentary on the post-2011

---

[103] In Aden, the Khaleej Aden Theater Troupe resumed the tradition from the socialist times in 2005, a small troupe tries to keep a long tradition of political criticism through plays alive https://almadaniyamag.com/2017/08/08/2017-8-7-amr-gamal-theater-in-wartime/ (August 7, 2017).

[104] For examples of poetry disrupted by war and bombings, see S. Jamal (2020), Al-Mughni (2020). Bushra Al-Maqtari's (2020) powerful short story narrates the last moments of a young woman, Sara, who died in a mortar attack against a shop in Taiz. In a 2019 novel called *The Country of the Commander* (*Bilad al-qāʿid*), Al-Muqri disparages the living legacies of dictatorship, even after a revolution. See also Baqays (2020).

[105] The Yemen Policy Center recently offered a summary of the novel, with a debate about the relevance of the text. See www.yemenpolicy.org/saghira/ (January 8, 2021).

euphoric revolutionary discourse, and the weight of regional antagonisms between Taiz and Sanaa (Al-Rubaidi 2018b: 9). Finally, the most
recent novel by Ahmad Zayn, *A Fruit for the Ravens*,[106] mixes Aden's
past, a harbor for Arab revolutionaries in the 1960s and 1970s, with
the shattered hope of the 2011 revolution (Sayf 2020).

The novels analyzed by Al-Rubaidi "set new horizons for their
readers' imagination of a better life." It is a vision of "a multi-faceted
and tolerant society in a country where many people went to the streets
in 2011 in order to not only topple an autocratic regime, but also to
recreate a new social and political system that would have social justice
at its heart" (Al-Rubaidi 2018b: 17). He speaks of the

dialectical relation between the texts and the dominant, yet disorganized,
feelings of the masses post-2011 [that] implicates the fact that literature reflects
wide-spread societal emotions (in this case, uncertainties and insecurities)
beneath its technically organized narrative form. ... An abstract conceptual
alternative homeland is juxtaposed with the real homeland; the cosmopolitan
and open city with a city occupied by radicalism, poverty and military forces;
and the literature with its beautifully dreamed up spaces with the everyday
politics of nepotism, violence and marginalization. (Al-Rubaidi 2018b: 17)

Sociologically, the richness of this literary detour is not only about the
content, but also about the generational struggle that these authors
embody. The authors studied by Abdulsalam Al-Rubaidi all belong to
the era of the post-1960s revolutions, born respectively in 1958, 1966, and
two in 1968.[107] For Al-Rubaidi (2018b: 16, 18–19), these writers' aim is
"to provoke new ideas for the establishment of a new way of life in Yemen.
[They are] yearning for a new subjectivity, and worldly forms of representation to recognize the vast human and social diversity in the country."

6.4 Narratives of Return and Dialectics of Change

The narratives of return in Yemeni literature are actually a hope for
a peaceful Yemen *future* based on civilian and democratic rule. These
are alas the exception. Instead, we have the dominant narratives of
securitization (in different forms) in Tunisia and in Yemen, all of which

---

[106] The book, *Fākiha lil-ghurbān*, was published in 2020 by Al-Mutawāssiṭ
(Milan).
[107] Muhammad Al-Gharbi 'Amran was born in 1958, 'Ali Al-Muqri in 1966, and
Nadya Al-Kawkabani and Ahmad Zayn in 1968.

propose a return to a *past* of latent citizenship, but which is better captured with the phrase "precarious citizenship." It is therefore dangerous to simplify our own narratives about the political processes in Tunisia and Yemen. They are not entirely failures; it is not a sectarian conflict in Yemen;[108] it is not simply a question of stability or security. Tunisia is not the "only success" of the Arab Uprisings, as we so often hear – and the power-grab or coup by President Kais Saied in summer 2021 is here to remind us that a return to autocracy in this North African country is not entirely out of the question.[109] Narratives adopted in the scholarship at large are never innocent. They may orientate the apprehension of the complex political struggles in the two countries. Or they may preserve the efforts of articulations between an unjust past and a better future that the 2011 presentism proposed.

Tunisia and Yemen both harbor small positive spaces of participation. But the effects of the re-masculinization and re-militarization of power are detrimental for women and marginalized groups. While it is apt to observe tendencies to regroup the exercise of authority as modelled by past images and alliances (the statue of Bourguiba, a north–south divide in Yemen, a return to a Zaydi rule),[110] we should not erase the dialectical interplay between formal and informal politics, and state–society relations that have been profoundly influential, albeit in the realm of symbols and of imaginary. The final conclusion of the book will elaborate on the meaning of this "dialectic."

The remarkable legacies of 2011 are not appreciable in the grand scale of things. Yemen is at war, and Tunisia still awaits to have its Constitutional Court appointed and a regional administration organized. However, this does not mean that small scale practices and

---

[108] As Dorlian notes, saying that there is a sectarian rift between the Zaydi and Shafii communties is playing the tune of Saleh since early 2000s. It is this type of official rhetoric that has literally *created* the actual Zaydi revival. Zaydi people increasingly felt they were the object of public interpellations about their identity in the 2000s, a process that *made* them become openly Zaydi, for example joining Al-Haqq or the Believing Youth, even if "being Zaydi" did not mean anything to them prior to these interpellations (Dorlian 2012: 84–88).

[109] By October 2021, Kais Saied had twice extended the suspension of the parliament, when article 80 allows to do it only for 30 days. In 2022, he even pushed for an entirely new constitution, hastily written and with no parliamentary consultation.

[110] In Yemeni intellectual Abdulghani Al-Iryani's crisp rendering, the Huthis have recreated Saleh's system without Saleh (Sanaa Center 2020: 4).

everyday expressions will not make a difference in the future. In Yemen, local governance might be a natural space to argue for decentralization or for a return to a federal Yemen. In Tunisia, people debate about sidewalks or mobilize for collective farming. They are also able to vent their anger with the failure of local police or call directly on the President's or Parliament's responsibility without fear of repression. One person interviewed in Midoun noted the flagrant shift from callous and rude police forces before 2011 to courteous policemen since then.[111] In Medenine, another Tunisian I interviewed said that "the fear of going into a police station has vanished because people know that they have the right to complain without fear of being harassed."[112] The documentary *Voice of Kasserine*, produced by the international NGO International Alert in 2018, corroborates this view. A member of a civil society organization can be heard saying: "We have produced a citizen who is no longer afraid of the police, who no longer allows the police to rule and whose job is to protect him" (IA 2018: minute 37:20). It is notable that all these witnesses come from regions in the interior. The example of solidarity between the protestors in El-Kamour and part of the Army is a novel twist that was made possible by 2011 and its attendant revolutionary effervescence.

The politically and constitutionally tense situation generated by President Kais Saied's suspension of the Parliament on July 25, 2021 currently hinges on this undecided balance between defenders of pluralism and power-sharing mechanisms, on the one hand, and supporters of a strong man supposedly able to fix the economy and address the dire sanitary situation after the outbreak of a second wave of COVID-19 diseases, on the other. Initially, many Tunisians saw the bold move of President Saied, invoking article 80 of the Constitution to dismiss the Prime Minister (Hichem Mechichi) he had selected himself, and to suspend the ARP for 30 days as a strong, but necessary medicine:[113] The two arms of executive power (presidency and the government)

---

[111] Hassen Jribi, association member, interview in Djerba, 01/02/2016: "The relation with police has evolved substantially with the revolution. Before, they could arrest you. Now, they say: 'Hello! How are you?' It has changed."

[112] Mustafa Abdelkabeer, human rights NGO leader, interview in Medenine, 01/04/2016.

[113] Many applauded the presidential initiative, with popular celebrations in the streets following the announcement and the positive reception of many media outlets, in particular from the secularist side. It was a bizarre alliance of support from the underprivileged regions of the interior and the south, and from the

were unable to break the deadlock over the confirmation of Mechichi's cabinet that had lasted since January.[114] The dire economic and sanitary situation, with a new outbreak of COVID-19 cases, provided the perfect excuse for Carthage, the presidential palace, to invoke extraordinary power at the end of July. The initial push back against what amounted for many to a coup (the President can only activate article 80 in case of serious threat to national integrity, e.g. a situation of war, and with the consultation of the Parliament) was quite robust. The President dismissed all criticism, called on the Army to prevent parliamentarians returning to Bardo, and even placed former political leaders, including former Prime Minister Chahed and presidential candidate Nabil Karoui, under house arrest. He also appointed, with no parliamentary oversight, his own security advisor, Ridha Gharsallaoui, to the position of acting Minister of the Interior, and took measures to steer important judiciary decisions.[115]

For a few weeks, it looked like President Saied was strong enough to intimidate his detractors. Even his most vocal opponent, the Islamist party Ennahda, backpedaled in early August, dropping the accusation of having performed a "coup," calling instead for a gradual return to national dialogues and the establishment of a roadmap with a clear timeline for the return to power sharing with a regular government and an in-session parliament. But new revelations that Saied had been preparing his "coup" months before the excuse provided by a chaotic sanitary situation related to COVID (Hearst and Ullah 2021), and the extent to which Saied seemed ready to run against many principles of the Constitution to ascertain control over security forces (police and National Guard are under the control of the Prime Minister rather than the President, who is the head of the Army only)[116] emboldened a more assertive campaign of civil society

more affluent neighborhoods of the capital city, where many people abhor Ennahda.

[114] The ARP did approve Mechichi's cabinet in January 2011, but President Saied refused to finalize the investiture, invoking a lack of women's representation in the executive. A few months later, it became clear that the real issue was the selection of the Minister of the Interior.

[115] See the report by *Tunisie Numérique*, "Qui est Ridha Gharsallaoui?," https://www.tunisienumerique.com/tunisie-qui-est-ridha-gharsellaoui-le-nouveau-ministre-de-linterieur/ (July 29, 2021).

[116] A member of the suspended Parliament, Yassine Ayari, accused Saied and those supporting him of facilitating the emergence of a "populist military monarchy" and undoing citizenship. See www.businessnews.com.tn/yassine-ayari-annonce-quitter-lassemblee,520,110628,3 (July 28, 2021). An earlier

and political parties in September 2021. Saied plays the card of street legitimacy (he is still very well viewed among the disinherited parts of the interior, because of his electoral promises to give more power to local authorities, and in the high bourgeoisie of Tunis, seeing him as the new bulwark against Ennahda), but he has been under mounting pressure to respect the Constitution[117] and allow for the creation of the much awaited Constitutional Court, whose creation he himself, along with many politicians in the last years, had refused to facilitate during his standoff with Mechichi and the parliament in the spring of 2021.[118] The future will tell which of the two sides retains the upper hand. Saied has never hidden his taste for a strong presidential system, in which local authorities are asked to take direct decisions, as long as they mirrored the will of this strong President.[119] On the other hand, the fact that the early protests against the July 25 "coup" evolved from an Ennahda-only affair to a much larger and articulated campaign,[120] bringing civil society actors, a growing number of political parties, and intellectuals together in calls for civilian rule and respect of the Constitution, was an encouraging sign that the legacies of the 2011 Uprisings had not entirely vanished.

In Yemen, artistic and literary spaces are among the few forums where Yemenis can express their views. NGOs and human rights

statement made by President Saied in April 2021, during Tunisia's Security Day, arose the suspicion that Saied was particularly unhappy with the situation in which the control over the security forces is shared between the presidency and the Prime Minister (in charge of the Ministry of the Interior). On April 18, Saied stated that "the president is the supreme commander of the military and civilian armed forces." See a Reuters report, at www.reuters.com/world/tunisian-president-draws-security-powers-into-dispute-with-pm-2021-04-18 (April 18, 2021).

[117] A leading voice in the field of human rights, Amna Guellali, head of Amnesty International North Africa, has accused Kais Saied of "butchering the Constitution." See www.lemonde.fr/afrique/article/2021/09/28/tunisie-le-charcutage-de-la-constitution-represente-une-menace-pour-les-droits-humains_6096308_3212.html (September 28, 2021).

[118] See Reuters: "Tunisian President Resists Parliament's Bid to Create Constitutional Court," www.reuters.com/article/uk-tunisia-politics/tunisian-president-resists-parliaments-bid-to-create-constitutional-court-idUSKBN2BT1PF (April 6, 2021).

[119] On this populist risk, see ICG's March 2020 Briefing Nr. 73 "Avoiding a Populist Surge in Tunisia," at www.crisisgroup.org/middle-east-north-africa/north-africa/tunisia/b73-tunisie-eviter-les-surencheres-populistes (March 4, 2020).

[120] At the end of September, 2,500 demonstrators showed up in Tunis, with many parties and associations in opposition to the President.

occasionally score a victory. In February 2021, an alliance of Yemeni and European NGOs succeeded in documenting the use of Italian bombs in bombings in Yemen, eventually forcing the Italian government to suspend its arms delivery to Saudi Arabia.[121] The map of Yemen and of its numerous armed groups is dangerously reminiscent of the colonial period. But saying that this is due to domestic factors only (e.g. the inability of Yemeni citizens to cooperate peacefully) would miss the deep and highly transnational forces that have led to this fragmentation. The habitus of *vis populi* needs articulations to be sustained and renewed by numerous actors and through specific processes (S. Hall 2016: 121). Yemenis and Tunisians alike continue to operate to that effect in El-Kamour and Jemna, in Yemeni novels, and in the civic work organized by small associations. These episodes cannot carry the day and outweigh the rigidity and passivity of formal structures, but they retain principles of presentism, a new pluralist subjectivity, and a fundamental connection between cultural and political representation, on the one hand, and demands for the democratic management of state violence on the other.

---

[121] In January 2021, the Italian government banned the selling of weapons produced by RWM Italia S.p.A., a subsidiary of the German arms manufacturer Rheinmetall AG, to Saudi Arabia (Il Manifesto 2021).

Conclusion

هدنة

"في الهدنة سنذهب إلى "ديقة الدبابات"

ونرمي لها

فتات الخبز

Truce

During the truce we will go to the "park for tanks"

and will throw them

bread crumbs

Aref Hamza, *Du bist nicht allein* (2018: 79)

To wrap up our historical and comparative journey, a focus on the title of the book is again needed. The relationship between coercion and citizenship, between violence and representation, in the Arab Middle East was reconnected in a particular way in 2011. The metaphor of the Moebius strip conveys how citizenship emerged in Euro-America because of extractive capitalist and imperialist asymmetries that undermined the social life of citizenship in the Middle East. During the independence eras, and due to a combination of domestic and Cold War factors, citizenship in the Middle East remained limited to a latent form. In 2011, citizenship reached a turning point, however: the burst of creativity and its demand for new channels for political participation, decentralization in particular, proposed paths for equal protection by, and restrained use of, the means of coercion. In so doing, this burst of transgressive democratic mobilizations in the Arab worlds has assembled a unique form of cultural and political representation.

Does the reference in the epigraph to a bittersweet poem, throwing bread crumbs at tanks, indicate that wars and military destruction have washed away all hopes for democratic participation? Does it suggest that channels for political representation are irredeemably closed, with poetry and art remaining as the only ethereal conduits for democracy and deliberations? Indeed, 10 years after the "revolution," contentions are wide open in Tunisia, and in war-torn Yemen, diplomacy will have to trace novel paths towards military de-escalation before any agreement for power-sharing can be reached.

Because of the type of sociology put to work in this book (historical and relational sociology), and because we consider the presence of radical representation a litmus test for democracy, this poem could be a source for mild optimism. Despite the bitter gesture of feeding tanks, the poem indicates resilience, with hope of a return to normal life, feeding birds instead, and playing with children. *Hudna* (truce) in Arabic is very close to the state of permanent peace (*salam*). Elliptic as poetry can be, it can also be critical of all the actors – domestic and external alike – that have turned gardens, playgrounds, and parks into a depot for lethal war machinery. The text can thus be interpreted as a critique, in the full sense of the term.[1]

"Radical representation" is the shortcut used in this book to remind the reader that the three facets of cultural and political representation and the publicly sanctioned use of physical force must be articulated together and, as such, are the basis for a democratic Middle East. The historical journey from the nineteenth century to 2021 indicates that there have been repeated moments in which radical representation emerged. Here I follow John Chalcraft's (2016: 318, 325, 329, 374, 432) idea of alternating moments of disruptive and transgressive mobilization in the popular history of the Middle East. My contribution is to add specific focus on the articulations of such transgressive mobilizations, or, in my terms, of radical representation, in relation to the means of coercion, and the resources that informality and spaces offer for these articulations. Because of the distorted form of modern citizenship in the Middle East, which sought to emulate the pacified appearance of social relations north of the Mediterranean, there has been, historically, an uneven distribution of state violence that persisted from the pre-colonial and colonial eras through to the independence and republican eras (1950s to 2010).[2] The 2011 Uprisings were an

[1] Critique defined originally by Max Horkheimer (1937/1972: 219, 233) as an intervention to liberate human beings from the circumstances that enslave them, here the unjust violence, and per extension, citizen prisoners of the *mukhabarat* state. The poem can also be read as a defeat: a garden made to commemorate the tanks, the victory of the unjust rulers, and the forced subjugation of the people.

[2] The Moebius strip has the merit of making visible what seems actually a separate process or feature: one side visible, the other invisible unless one persists and connects metropoles and colonies. This book feeds into a growing literature that

attempt to recompose territorial, sociological, and symbolic fragmentations in a way that envisioned solutions for equality before the security apparatuses, and equal access to social, cultural, and political rights. *Vis populi*, the forceful will of the people, contributed to a synchronization of the spaces and times of political participation, rejecting claims of the immaturity of the marginalized segments of Tunisia and Yemen. It also generated a unified basis for democratic demands, a claim that had, until 2011, never emerged on such a scale in Arab history. The third part of the book explained why Yemen and Tunisia, which had been until then on a parallel path of comparison, took divergent routes.

This conclusion now ties loose threads raised earlier in the book together. In particular: Why 2011 and not another moment? Why did Tunisia and Yemen follow divergent paths after 2013? What does a comparative frame of analysis add to the production of knowledge. What does "*vis populi*" add to theories of (non-)violence? Why did informality matter so much in the making of the 2011 Uprisings, and less so in their aftermath? And why is this poem in the epigraph an indication of an evolving dialectic of state–society relations?

First, the question of why the Arab Uprisings occurred in 2011 and not at another moment. Kurzman (2005: 125) has warned us of the dangers of retrospective prediction, preferring instead his "anti-explanation" as a way to explain why "protestors overcame their fear of state repression" in 1978 Iran. After having explored distinct explanations for the outbreak of the Iranian revolution (in terms of resources for mobilization, as well as cultural, economic, and military causes), Kurzman proposed instead an anti-explanation, because of numerous anomalies limiting the validity of these separate variables. This book has focused on Yemen and Tunisia, but much of its analytic lens could have been applied to Syria, Egypt, Libya, or other Arab republics. In each case, idiosyncrasies would complicate a single narrative or "explanation" about triggers and precipitating factors affecting the development of each of these 2011 Uprisings. Instead, for Kurzman (2005: 166), we are better off with a "reconstruction [of] the lived

brings back to the center of Euro-American attention their own hideous pasts and abominable practices of necropolitics (Mbembe 2003), racialized surveillance (Browne 2015), control of sexuality (Stoler 1995), sexual violence (Boetsch et al. 2019; Blanchard et al. 2018), and discriminatory if not racist regimes of migration control (Shepard 2008; Haney Lopez 2006).

experience of the [revolutionary] moment." Similarly, I have tried to explain all the confusions, forked paths, and limited choices that actors, formal and informal, have faced in the two countries through a historical reconstruction of those actors' lived experience. The book explored similar yet competing overarching hypotheses of expansive cultural representation, of the bottleneck that formal political channels of representation created, and the limited reforms of the Tunisian and Yemeni security sectors.

My own "anti-explanation" has focused on the role of informalism, which is imagined as the straw that broke the camel's back of authoritarian regimes in 2011. The Uprisings in 2011 were different from earlier mass revolts – 1934 in Tunisia against the Protectorate policies, bread riots that rocked Tunisia in 1978 and 1984 (Khiari 2003: 18, 21, 70) and Yemen in 1996, 1998, and 2005 (Lackner 2016a: 150) – because they culminated in much larger assembled frames and repertoires. Other simmering factors led to political disputes around heightened regime corruption, the mobilization of the margins in Tunisia (Gafsa mining protests in 2008) and Yemen (Huthi wars since 2004 and the Hirak building support since 2007), as well as the desiccation of the sites of articulation for the ruling elites.[3] All these provided additional spaces for informal campaigns to be amplified. As Chalcraft has argued in *Popular Politics* (2016), the possibility of counter-hegemony arises because there is a tendency towards disincorporation of the dominant alliances previously put in place by the ruling elites. Informalism was a way to respond to years of flagging legitimacy and loss of alliances on top of the state. It is informalism that proposed new visions and assembled sectors of society left out by decades of elites promoting their own interests over those of their subjects. Other contingent triggers, such as spikes in food prices at the end of 2010 (because of floods in Australia) and a relative absence of military operations throughout the Middle East (Challand 2011) amplified the noise from disarticulated and still compartmentalized informal complaints. Once the genie was out of the box, with one dictator ousted in Tunisia on January 14, the same demands for removal of dictators spread, sustained by enormous media coverage, to Egypt, and then to Yemen and Libya.

---

[3] For example, President Saleh hastily grooming his son as the next President.

I have argued that under the condition of latent citizenship that had solidified during the republican era, only informalism was able to break the deadlock. Spontaneity is generally understood as something occurring unexpectedly, and out of the blue. In this book, spontaneity has been taken etymologically, as Castoriadis (1976) suggested: informal networks, clicking with one another, with this perfect storm of contingent and organized grievances, became their "own source." They tapped into networks of abeyance in Tunisia, connecting youth militants to media resources in France (Hmed 2012), and initiating a cascade of protests using the UGTT's office space for protection (Yousfi 2015: 33–34). In Yemen, Yadav (2011: 551) captured perfectly how a post-partisan movement that transcended identities of "class, tribe, regions, gender and ideology" emerged in the decade 2000–2010. This informal building up had a *history*, a *geography*, and even an *ecology*. The events of 2011 did not happen out of the blue. Self-representation burst into the open and linked pre-existing regional anger and resentment against the ruling elites.

What is remarkable is the similarity of the force of synchronized demands in the two countries in the first months of 2011: agrarian roots of the margin's revolts;[4] disaffection of (segments of) the army; key towns (e.g. Sfax and Taiz) becoming pivotal spaces for connecting margins to the center; civic investment by a younger, less politically experienced generation; revolution as "the excess of the results over the causes" (Castoriadis 1976: 11), with multi-directional movements in spaces, new vocabularies, and new critical methods of self-representation; bursts of *taswir* calling for new *tamthil* through proposals to democratize the security forces; imaginal reversals of who has power;[5] predominantly reformist paths rather than revolutionary break ups; the existence of national dialogues with informal alliances putting pressure on the transition; all the way to the simultaneous passing of constitutional texts on January 26, 2014.

---

[4] For the sake of brevity, I invite the reader to use the final index to identify references to all of these factors.

[5] I take the term "imaginal politics" from the philosopher Chiara Bottici (2014). Note that the French philosopher Jacques Rancière (2006) also explores the relation between political and cultural representation through the idea of staged or theatrical disruptions and contestations that reveal the realm of "the sensible." He also defends the view of an active and intelligent "people," or of a knowing plebeian subject. On Rancière, see Lievens (2014: 5).

Important dissimilarities remain.[6] Yemen, because of its orography, and the deep mistrusts of the north and the south for centrally administered reforms, has less possibilities to enact multi-directional solidarity. In Tunisia, solidarity caravans from the peripheries to the center and back, and from the Qasba to the peripheries, have been vectors for connecting demands and reinforcing the sense that decentralization and reforms of the security sector were vital. The closest action to this in Yemen is the March of Life in December 2011 and January 2012, which sustained collective pressure for immediate reforms, but given the harsh economic and ecological situation around Saada, and Al-Qaeda insurrectionary presence in the south, the synchronization and enactment of a multiple "people" broke down. The NDC revived these hopes in 2013, but it was partly hollowed out by the maneuvering of the largest political parties. The presence of much more conservative Islamist actors (Al-Zindani, one of the key leaders of Islah) in one of the driver seats of the transition, while also in alliance with army defector Ali Muhsin, meant that this very significant spoiler alliance of military–social conservatism could deflect pressure for civilian rule coming from the streets. Salafis in Tunisia also had little congenial points with the imaginary of a *vis populi*. For them a secular or civil state, *dawla madaniyya*, was not an option. The difference is that Salafis in Tunisia had little access to political salons and were institutionally isolated. Many opted for the exit, leaving Tunisians to take up arms in Libya or Syria in search of their own hegemony (Merone 2021). In Yemen, social conservatism is much more deeply rooted and accepted: thus Islah leaders did not have to bother too much with the demand for pluralism and inclusion once the NDC was over.

Why did the reformist path and *vis populi* somehow stall around 2013 and 2014? Independently of the specific circumstances in Yemen (worsening economic situation, opportunity for secessionists in the north and south to organize militarily, the return of Saleh) and Tunisia (political assassinations, fears of a coup), there are common difficulties. International financial pressure mounted on both countries: cuts to subsidies provided by the IMF, renegotiated loans from the World Bank in Yemen and Tunisia (Lackner 2016a: 159; Yousfi 2019),

---

[6] See again Tables 2.1 and 2.2 (Section 2.4) with basic differences in terms of demography and macro-economic indicators.

lack of consistency from the donor community in providing financial support to the security sector and in supporting civil society, and deepened sectorialization (Kartas 2014) and/or neoliberal depoliticization (Armbrust 2019; Carapico 2013b). Furthermore, Egyptian developments in the summer of 2013, with the military ousting of Islamist President Mohammed Morsi, limited the space for pluralistic maneuvering. This episode initiated a return of the prioritization of "stability" over democracy, and of realpolitik over the optimism of anchoring democratic accountability in the security sector. The Egyptian military had limited patience for reformist creativity and economic redistribution. Thus, new types of encroachment arose gradually, undermining domestic processes, and allowing the return of the "security custodianship" (Sayigh 2012: 3) and the Thermidorian moment (Heydemann 2015: 2).

Vis populi was an ambitious project, and informalism has not been able to sustain the multi-sited struggle for a post-securitarian social contract. If one really wants to use the language of success or failure, informalism was a total success in 2011; it then lost momentum because of the weight and disempowering force of those structures in charge of the "transitions" (the GCC initiative; the HAROR; a Troika; a GNU in parallel to the NDC; etc.) during 2011 and early 2013. From 2014 onward it became a failure, but a relational failure, because *formal* actors (technocratic power, parliaments, political parties, old and strong men in power) deliberately thwarted the enormous potential for democratic change. Let us not forget that building equality, civil rule, and justice is not something that occurs overnight. It is a long effort that formal and informal actors cannot perform on their own.

Democracy is not only about elections, constitutions, and a multiparty system. Informal actors have contributed greatly to generating and cementing additional spaces in which new civic experiments can be formed. To paraphrase Manal Jamal's (2019) work on political settlements, the presence of informal political praxes enriched proposals for democratic reforms, including in the security sector. For example, the involvement of Yemeni soldiers who defected and collaborated with the revolutionary groups also generated new political alliances between 2011 and 2013 (R. Porter 2017). The same happened years later in El-Kamour in 2017, in the south of Tunisia. The high degree of inclusion and synchronization of spaces and demands made by informal actors

impacted political consciousness.[7] As I will show below, this transformative potential is still alive, because of the state–society dialectic
and the ensuing new forms of connecting practices.

Let us now reflect on the comparative frame of analyses chosen for
this book. Arabia Felix and *Ifriqya* are in-depth case-studies on which
I have built. Elements of this comparison could match what political
scientists describe as the method of similarity, while other historical
and empirical materials suggest the method of difference. Throughout
the chapters above, I have shown how two different countries (with
different rates of illiteracy, rural–urban divides, homogenous–sectarian
fragmentations) had similar outcomes (2011, push towards decentralization), but I also placed emphasis on factors that explain the implosion of Yemen set in contrast with partially democratized coercive
institutions in Tunisia.

Beyond these features, I hope this book will contribute to rethinking
the politics of comparison based on an accrued sensibility for the
margins,[8] issues of coercive asymmetries, and the risk of sanitized
theories of citizenship. In my view, theory is not the abstract effort of
"raising up" the level of analysis from *empiria* to concepts. The Greek
"*theoria*" originally meant watching and observing (Wolin 1968: 319).
Because *theorists* in ancient Greece were ambassadors sent by the city-
states to observe *other* city-states, comparison was built into *theoria*,
the reports of these ambassadors, from the start.[9] *Seeing* was also
central back then, because the ambassadors – theorists – were given
the best seats in the theaters, where they were conveyed for

[7] A point also described by Arato (2016), in particular the mechanism of
round-tables as a stepping stone in the process of constitution drafting. For
Jamal, the quality of post-conflict settlements flows from the degree of inclusion,
which in turn generates a space of overlap between civil and political society
actors. "Shifting sites of contest" are crucial, she adds, as "individuals move from
one site to another, inextricably politicizing the link between them" (M. Jamal
2019: 18, 222).

[8] Tunisia and Yemen have rarely been studied in a paired comparison. Tunisia has
gained enormous attention in the recent Anglo-Saxon literature, but is often
paired with Egypt (see e.g. Hartshorn 2019; Beinin 2015). Nathalie Peutz (2018)
and Laurent Bonnefoy (2018) deserve particular praise for showing the long
history of interconnections of Yemen, whose society has not been as isolated and
unspoiled as is often repeated in the literature.

[9] I am grateful to my former colleague at the Scuola Normale Superiore, Anna
Magnetto, for the interdisciplinary panel "Diplomazia e risoluzione di conflitti
nel Mediterraneo Orientale: Antichità e Mondo Arabo contemporaneo," Pisa,
May 16, 2019. The standard work on *theoroi* is Rutherford (2013: 142–155).

observation. The literal application I have made here of the Greek term has led to a constant focus, in these pages, on the politics of visibility generated by self- or cultural representation, and on efforts to blind people or silence their political message. Because of my position in Euro-American institutions of knowledge,[10] I can become the mediator for these visual experiences, conveying to the readers a graffiti that was placed strategically in front of the municipality in Siliana, the politics of space behind the memorialization of strong men, the 2011 Uprisings in Tunis, or the fate of the murals of Murad Subay' about the 101 disappeared Yemeni. Many more images, graffiti, and sounds that have been missed, defaced, or destroyed could have been added.[11] Thus, this book has been "doing" theory simply by conveying a different type of material. The comparison has also been generating theory by setting the two cases in relation to European and Ottoman modes of encroachment that have historically taken colonial, imperial, or capitalist forms, and have thus tackled issues of state-formation with a much larger comparative lens. Currently, Europe, the USA, and Gulf country actors infringe on the Middle East in old and new ways, capitalist and neo-imperial ones. A new politics of visibility and of confronting hegemonic discourses and representations of the region is at play here. Theory-making needs to adapt to these evolutions.

As a result, this book is not only about the Middle East, nor is it about Euro-American theory that plunders "facts" from the Middle East to produce a new theory on the political and semantic meaning of violence. It does "do" theory, but it is rooted and informed directly by the expression of the people "there." To be sure, scholarly narrative, historical or sociological, will always involve a filtering effect. There is also a tradeoff between in-depth study of one country and giving equal treatment to two countries. Both have advantages and inconveniences. If we try to apply the analytic lens developed here to other countries too strictly, one might again encounter the anomalies that Kurzman (2005: 165) identified when trying to apply a too monocausal interpretation of the Iranian revolution. But in my view radical representation generates,

---

[10] The book project was realized when I held faculty positions at the University of Fribourg (Switzerland), the New School in New York, and the Scuola Normale Superiore in Florence.

[11] Al-Rubaidi (2014), Werbner, Webb, & Spellman-Poots (2014), Lacquaniti (2015), Alviso-Marino (2016) entails very rich additional visual material for the two countries. On defaced murals in Sudan, see Salomon (2020: 338).

with its focus not only on two countries, but also on the politics of theory production and comparison across time, a critical and self-reflexive component that allows us to rethink the links between epistemology and actual political struggles.

The politics of the external gaze on, and theorization about, the Middle East is very often problematic. It has a simple name, Orientalism. It has been criticized from Said (1978) onward from many angles (Mitchell 1988; Harik 2006; Bonine, Amanat, & Gasper 2012). For decades, the ensuing association of "violence" and "MENA" generated essentialist statements on "fundamentalism," cultural resistance to modernity, autocracy, absence of civil society, and the like (Sadowski 1993). Thus, suggesting that the Middle East can be a source of democratic theory, furthermore, based on the willful force of the people (*vis populi*) will come as a shock for some. And that it is its own source will surprise many, but not those working on the history of the region.[12] Below I will say more about violence, democracy, and *vis populi*, but indeed, an understanding that combines a broad non-violence with the evocation of the people's sovereignty over the means of coercion is one of the bases for establishing democratic foundations for Arab polities. The historical narrative of Part I shows that political modernity is not alien to local societies of the Middle East, and that creative and transgressive politics has been simmering for decades. The year 2011 gave a new dimension to the social life of citizenship. Arab peoples did not ask to manage the means of coercion themselves, nor did they destroy these institutions. They did express their rage at decades of oppression, but also indicated that there should be a concerted, pluralist, and region-sensitive democratic control over the security forces, be they national armies, praetorian guards, ministries of the interior, or police forces.

The relational flip of this coin of violence has been that citizenship "in the north" have benefited from a most cruel and exploitative limitation of civic participation "in the south."[13] The connected sociologies of

[12] Chalcraft (2016: 317, 339, 347) shows repeatedly how intra-Arab as well as "global South" references bolster republican movements. Kurzman (2002) deals with the influence of modernity on Islamic intellectuals, while Jakes (2020: 188, 235) denotes the inchoate Egyptian protests against the 1907 financial crisis.

[13] I use these terms rather than Euro-America and the Middle East to suggest that this is a matter of concern for current debates on the putative links between the global north and the global south.

intellectuals such as Gurminder Bhambra and Syed Farid Alatas have influenced the final thoughts I would like to share on the device of the Moebius strip. The "magic" of the Moebius strip lies in making the idea that political processes in the MENA regions are disconnected to those of Euro-America obsolete. It reduces the gap for, and complicates the politics of, comparison. For example, on the issue of physical pressure, the book should have made clear that non-violence might work in advanced capitalist societies because there has been a much longer and thicker social legacy of citizenship there, with multiple forms of accountability for security apparatuses and effective *habeas corpus* protections. In the Middle East, some authors of the edited volume *Civil Resistance in the Arab Spring* (Roberts et al. 2016) correctly insisted that the strength of the Arab uprisings "derives from long traditions of civil resistance in the Middle East" (Mallat & Mortimer 2016: 23). But this chapter does not sufficiently question the illegitimate nature of Arab states, and of their ruling elites. A narrow view of non-violence as theorized in liberal contexts (Bedau 2002) is not enough in this context, and *vis populi* puts its fingers on the need to rethink the entire edifice of citizenship and of state–society relations.[14] The liberal modalities of non-violent engagement in Euro-America that underpin the *Civil Resistance* book are not the same in autocratic regimes, and a more assertive, radical type of demand is indeed needed because the formal channels for civic participation were inexistent until 2011. "Western" non-violence influenced certain pinpoint practices in 2011, but the proposals for democratic re-articulations were specific to the region, indeed an informally coordinated response to the history of state repression. This radical representation multiplied spaces for participation and unleashed a vibrant social life of citizenship.

The Moebius strip reduces the gap, but still retains a sense of difference between Euro-America and the Middle East when it comes to encroachment. While one side has the upper hand, the other is vulnerable. Be it in the old imperialist form of direct subjugation, or in the current more indirect pressure of neo-imperialism, the Moebius strip moves security actors in manners that underscore unequal participation and distribution. In Ottoman and colonial times, punitive military

---

[14] Thus, one of the chapters of the book suggests that protestors should be strategic and "make more limited demands" (Mallat & Mortimer 2016: 28). This is a very liberal approach that assumes that this type of selective strategy can function in the Middle East, and which obdurate non-violence resistance for several years after the crackdown in Bahrain.

campaigns were waged to facilitate tax extraction from agriculturally rich parts of the country. In the independence era, these geographical inequalities morphed somehow, but discourses of internal colonization could be heard in both countries (Al-Salhi 2017; Day 2012). In recent years, it has been Yemeni livelihoods that have been the target of Saudi and Emirati pressure (Sowers 2018), while in Tunisia, the interior continues to protest against oil wealth trickling down only towards the capital. Thus, the Moebius strip of unequal violence is connected to specific ecologies and to lopsided protection or access to them.

It might seem that my use of the Moebius metaphor is one-sided, bringing attention to the negative, exploitative elements and works seamlessly in different contexts and temporalities. Such has not been my intention. The dominant attitudes of European empires are undisputed, and they occupy a large portion of the Moebius paradigm. The latter captures an important part of, but not the whole, story behind the connection between violence and representation. There are many instances where the Middle East is its own origin for virtuous citizen practices. This is the case for past instances,[15] and for the present. The year 2011 was exactly that: a source of *global* inspiration for democratic rebellions against growing inequalities, a source for new methods of collective action in Africa, Asia, and Europe, all the way to the Wall Street and Oakland occupy movements. The Arab 2011 was a conveyor belt of radical representations for the globe (Werbner, Webb, & Spellman-Poots 2014) and inspired new theories of the multitude (Hardt & Negri 2013) and of postanarchism (Newman 2015), to name only a few examples. There have been other instances of a constructive connection between Arab acts of citizenship, such as the Maghrebi solidarity caravans going to Gaza. The Moebius strip is evidence of an evolving dialectic of state–society relations that are not only limited to the confines of national borders.

To diminish the false impression of a seamless Moebius band, I would recall the harsh power differential at play. The capacity to say that there is a relation (say colonial) is also power. The Moebius strip comes with the focus on breaks and continuity that exist in all historical sociology. *Violence and Representation* has shown multiple threads of continuity, within the geography of marginalization, and

---

[15] See Haleh Davis & Serres (2018) on how a certain self-understanding of "Europe" was invented in North Africa. See also Bottici & Challand (2019).

techniques for preserving central power despite a veneer of decentralization in the sociology of actors involved at the helm (strong men,
military leaders, elders). It has also identified breaks, with three historical periods (first early citizenship, followed by the age of ideologies,
and finally 2011), a motive that allowed new social actors to take
a leading role in politics (violence specialists in Yemen; new educated
elite from the Sahel in Tunisia).

The theme of continuity and change (or rupture/discontinuity) has
been central in historical sociology[16] for understanding the productive
interconnection between culture and structures. William Sewell's
(1996) famous account of certain episodes of the French revolution
dovetails with our own account of violence: Originally, the taking of
the Bastille on July 14, 1789 was not an important event, yet it has
become the date celebrated by French citizens as the quintessence of
republicanism. Over time, this very minor event became a cornerstone
of French political culture because subsequent episodes in 1789, such
as the Great Fear and the abolition of the privileges on August 4,
"effected the definitive rearticulation between the new metaphysical
principles of the state and the juridical organization of social life"
(Sewell 1996: 874). Sewell's account of temporality is essential, for it
captures the constituted and constituting components of events. These
are chains of episodes in which existing structures, understood as "sets
of cultural schemas, distributions of resources and modes of power,"
are gradually transformed, because events are gradually recognized as
such by contemporaries, with then durable transformation of structures and dislocation of normal life (Sewell 1996: 842, 843, 845). An
Egyptian scholar noted this fleetingly eternal quality of the graffiti in
Cairo: They were constantly whitewashed by the Supreme Council of
the Armed Forces after 2011, but their message reappeared a few days
later, or could still be somehow read despite the erasure. They "continued to communicate … [despite their] ostensible obliteration"
(Shalakany 2014: 359).

Sequences and concatenations have been discussed abundantly in
these pages. The temporalities are said to have been synchronized by
rituals in which "backward" parts of the two countries expressed
forms of presentism and demanded equality, where multiple efforts to

---

[16] E.g., see Skocpol (1979) and Tilly (1984; 2003a), but also many studies in the
vein of critical colonial studies (Shepard 2008).

reduce spatial fragmentation were at play, when the ordeals of the lower classes, women, and young men were, at least for a few months, given central attention in the exercise of self-representation, and when broken bodies became the symbol of found unity and strength (see Figures 0.2, 0.3, or 3.5). What Chalcraft describes as transgressive mobilization (and what I called the radical representation of *vis populi*) are additional instances of the dialectical effects of changes impacting individual and collective actors, and new social consciousness.

It is not by coincidence that this *vis populi* was swept under the rug by many not-automatically-allied actors who shared an interest in burying the radical democratic experiment. International actors quickly got cold feet vis-à-vis the radical change that *vis populi* could generate. These fleeting moments were seized as opportunities to regroup and reassert new encroachment. The upper middle and higher classes also found virtue in pretending to support "transitions" and "reforms," while knowing it was the best way of ensuring continuity. Certain caravans of solidarity became ways for urban rich people to reassert paternalism toward the periphery.[17] In terms of gender, Zakia Salime (2014; 2015a) underlined how in the early months of the Uprisings the focus moved away from the self-immolated bodies of the women of the shantytowns making collective claims, and toward urban *twitterati* women, and upper-class claims for individual rights. In Yemen the discourse of security and stability deflected attention away from the genuine aspiration for federalism, or at least for some forms of decentralization.[18]

It is because of this gradual silencing by hegemonic (international) players, as well as formal political and domestic formal actors, that the politics of self-representation have remained so essential: it is cheap, easy to disseminate. But it is also transient and in need of a receptacle with connections to institutionalized politics if this "culture" wants to influence "structures" like those described by Sewell (1996). All revolutions have phases of expansion and of retreat. Some events are exalted, others are the objects of *damnatio memoriae*. Graffiti come and go. To a certain degree, *vis populi* and all the revolutionary aspirations

---

[17] Michaël Ayari, security expert, interview in Tunis, 05/30/2016.
[18] Al-Eriani (2020) offers the most detailed account of this tendency. The texts of French expert Frison-Roche (2015; 2016) illustrate that danger of paternalistically denying to Yemenis their own choice in the future of decentralization.

described here and by other authors (Lackner 2016a: 142; R. Porter 2017; 2020) are increasingly omitted from recent accounts of 2011.[19] In the postcolonial context, such amnesia for democratically symbolic or foundational episodes is too frequent to be surprising.[20] I hope that documenting the concerted efforts for deep security reforms early in 2011–2013 and the remaining efforts by certain Yemeni actors – some transnational, from Yemen to Europe – to stop the use of Western weapons, will sustain the focus on the connections of violence and latent citizenship on the one hand and the reversed effort of *vis populi* and democratic accountability on the other.

The main elements of the dialectics between state and society are summarized in Table 7.1. The latter synthetizes the ruptures and continuities and the key concepts of this book. The focus has shifted from overall macro-accounts of state-making in Part I to the more micro-accounts of lived experience in Part II, while Part III can be said to be a meso-analysis, with an eye on micro-everyday practices, but also a perspective that zooms out toward the larger processes (encroachment, technocratic "reforms," or the power of discursive formations). Throughout the book, a relational sociology connecting north and south, translocal actors, and the articulations for regional self-expression was applied, connecting encroachment, citizenship, informal actors, and spaces.

The dialectical components mean that political practices have been altered by the experiences of the revolutionary moments. Despite the setbacks registered in Part III, there remained a "tacit knowledge," to take Chandra Mukerji's (2007: 61) phrase, regarding expectations and current forms of self-expression. New opportunities around decentralized political spaces correspond to the dialectic between "social beings" and a new "social consciousness."[21] Spaces of participation,

---

[19] Political scientist Steven Heydemann (2015: 4) maintains that the Uprisings have produced a "de-institutionalization," rather than transition or transformation. But what might be straightforwardly true for formal politics is less certain when looking at the message of the graffiti or of informal demands made by the Arab masses.

[20] See Trouillot (1995/2015) about the "unthinkable" Haitian revolution. Laurent Dubois, a historian of Haiti, notes that the "sale, impression or distribution" of any coins or medals depicting or "commemorating the politics and revolution of France" were forbidden in Haiti to prevent slaves from developing their own revolutionary project (as quoted in Reiss 2012: 101, 135). Not everybody should have the same ideas of equality and emancipation.

[21] S. Hall (1980: 63). Stuart Hall's cultural program, influenced by Gramsci, is particularly helpful here. See S. Hall (2016).

Table 7.1 *Diachronic and comparative overview of the key concepts*

	Part I	Part II	Part III
Focus	Macro processes Relational	Micro-articulations Relational	Meso-level analysis Relational
Encroachments	Overdetermining Ch. 1: pre-colonial and colonial impacts on taxation Ch. 2: Cold War securitization	Mostly bracketed	Reasserted TUN: neutralized security influences YEM: massive neo-imperialism
Citizenship	Latent Subjects	Fully active: from subjects to actors	Precarious
Representations	Ch. 1: inchoate political representation, little self-representation Ch. 2: post-independence state-led representation	Three facets of democratic representation: political and cultural representation concentrate on the issue of violence. New subjectivity	Fading articulations between cultural and political representations Discourses of stability eclipsing democratization. Symbolic domination of expertise Resubjectivation
Formal and informal actors	Ch. 1: imperial and colonial actors Ch. 2: oligarchy in independence era. Growing informal civic networks	Ch. 3: multitude of informal actors assembling a sense of the people Ch.4: political parties. Variety of social roles	TUN: Big men syndrome, coexist with everyday democratic practices YEM: Return of military actors
Spaces	Compartmentalized	Assembled and assembling	Incomplete decentralization Return to fragmentation

because they are perceived as just (*jus quia justum*) entail practical knowledge of self-reorganization, which is often denied by international and formal actors in these countries, who prefer the return to the earlier form of legitimacy (*jus quia jussum*, law or order because it has legally, centrally, or formally been mandated).

For example, regional identities are now reimagined not only in geographic terms (or sectarian ones, in Yemen), but are understood within their full relational context, and in a way that could underpin a new social contract. Federalism and decentralization are thus important pivoting points for this re-imagination. In Yemen, the Huthis and southerners are presented as the separatist outcasts by the GCC and the loyalist government, but they have worked to retain the legitimacy obtained for having stood against Saleh's kleptocratic clique. The way a six-region federal Yemen was presented in January 2015 triggered hostility, but it might still be a basis, either with six or 22 regions, for the future of Yemen.[22] In Tunisia, the interior has been resisting the resubjectivation that the authority from Tunis would like to impose on them. The timing of the protests in the last four years in the Kasserine region (January) differs from that in Tataouine (May–June), but it signals the significance of different events and demands social justice for all. This also indicates that the central authorities will not be able to govern over docile subjects like it did during the first republic.

Thus, despite the faulty implementation of decentralization, there remains an imaginary space that can help sustain current and future informal initiatives. In Tunisia, aspirations to push the capital to create regional structures of representations persist. In Yemen, literature and arts cling on to the ideas of managing diversity and social hierarchies in an inclusive and non-militarized manner. This general sense of decentralization is thus more than a formal plan to raise municipal taxes, organize local police, or identify intermediary and regional deputies. It is also a symbolic space that functions like the civility discussed in the Introduction. Eiko Ikegami (2005: 28) sees civility as "a ritual technology of interpersonal exchanges that shapes a kind of intermediate zone of social relationship between the intimate and the hostile." Historically, such a space has been called "civil society" in Europe,

---

[22] Even if the south secedes, ideas of federalism in the Arabian South will remain influenced by the different federalist options discussed between 2011 and the NDC recommendation in 2014. Yemenis do not want to return to the 2010 architecture of power, be it in the Saada, Aden, or Mahra provinces.

but Ikegami shows that elsewhere on the globe, in Tokugawa Japan, other mechanisms emerged whereby "private citizens" were able to enjoy "a certain degree of autonomy from the state" (Ikegami 2005: 19). According to her, in the Japanese context of the seventeenth through the late nineteenth centuries, cultural interactions and sociability provided the basis for civility, defined as "the cultural grammar of sociability that governs interactional public spaces" (Ikegami 2005: 19).

Informal participation in debates and practices, and in the defense of decentralization and security issues, has provided a similar, albeit fragile, function in the Arab context of Yemen and Tunisia. Informality has been at play in very diverse contexts: the mundane example of a new space within the municipality in Siliana, returning and evolving graffiti, the stubborn demand for a regional solidarity fund obtained in El-Kamour, civic theater plays in the Tunis periphery, the content of revolutionary tents in northern Sanaa in 2011–2012, or the Yemeni literature of Al-Rubaidi (2018b; 2021) are all small examples of the dialectic of gained space and of a new civic consciousness after 2011.[23]

The final remarks below, dealing with Sudan and Algeria, will show how the politics of re-assembled space have been at play for democratic protests beyond Tunisia and Yemen. But in various parts of the text I have spoken of the space or mechanism of reversal in using self-representation or of demoscopic violence. All these political reforms, the political murals or graffiti, and now the internet for those Yemenis who have almost no access to public spaces because of the war are imaginary spaces that active Arab citizens continue to occupy and populate with visions of pluralism. Thus, the pair *taswir* and *tamthil* (cultural representation and political representation) are connected by the method of disclosure: it makes another political path visible and tangible. The ghost-city of Siliana, whose population left the governor without purpose and without power of representation, the ghost-internet ("Error 404"), the connective symbolism of marches and

---

[23] Ian Hartshorn in his comparative analysis of Tunisia and Egypt labor organization focuses as well on elements of informal incorporation as an *explanans* for the different trajectories. For him, the varying degree of internal and external linkages, that the "constellations" of labor network, is an important resource. But in general, Hartshorn considers labor organizations as distinct, substantial entities. See e.g. Hartshorn (2019: 5, 160).

caravans are all moments where the people, the multitude, assembled in space. The presence of the people is affirmed through a double image: they are simultaneously present physically and virtually. The previous order, which the state and the powerful used to embody and was supposed to protect citizens, no longer exists.[24] The (images of the) people are now the sources of a new order. These new forms of representation and *vis populi*, the willful force of the people, achieved this dialectical twist not through physical destruction and violence, but by neutralizing the illegitimacy of the repression through imaginary devices: a song, a march out of the city, a micro-campaign using flash mobs. With this new social imaginary, new images of one's own identity were projected and circulated as the new basis for a connecting, not a divisive, collective action. It was largely based on a secular grammar of collective rights, accountability, and state–society relations.[25]

The strength of democratic claims[26] resides both in the formal and informal components of mobilization. Informality, in that sense, is more than what social movement scholars call prefigurative politics.[27] It is not about the creation of an idealized micro-society. Rather, informality is a space where articulations are tested, new ideas tried out, and new linkages generated. Everyday practice allows one to see how these ideas are understood by other actors. As we saw the idea

---

[24] I am grateful to Antti Tarvainen for rich discussions on this matter.

[25] Talal Asad (2015) disagrees. For him, to claim that 2011 was about citizenship is a sign of Euro-centrism. Instead, 2011 was the search for an alternative (religious) basis of morality. I concur with Jens Hanssen's (2019) observation on the matter (developed in a review of a work by Wael Hallaq). Saying that 2011 was all about a search for a "religious" basis of morality negates all the evidences presented here, or those discussed by Chalcraft, of numerous forms of contained and transgressive mobilization, the call for republican forms, and demands for equal rights in the contemporary Middle East. Islamists contended as well, but most of them agreed with the path of reformism. Some did affirm God's sovereignty, took arms in Yemen, or left the country for Tunisian *takfiri* jihadists, but many converged in marches and *sahat* movements in 2011.

[26] Whether these demands were always democratic in nature and intention will not be resolved here. Some actors might play the rhetoric of democracy to appear as legitimate, but without a firm commitment for this political form. For example, smugglers with more mundane interests have used calls for democracy. Moncef Kartas, security expert, interview in New York, 11/17/2019.

[27] Maeckelbergh (2011); Leach (2013). But here the focus will be on informal politics, and building on the hurdles of organization vs. spontaneity (Leach 2005; 2009).

of sidewalk civility, the *Sayyeb Trottoir* campaign from Sfax, was interpreted by another campaign leader in the town of Bizerte as a justification for a return of repressive policing of the streets, not a deepening of citizens' sense of responsibility. Yet informality reveals possibilities and also stumbling blocks: it is not the idealized basis for democracy, but it can test whether participative articulations are shared with other actors. The Bizerte actor was not proposing more collective action; he wanted punitive action from the state like under Ben Ali. In Jemna, the occupation of the date farm represented a test of social cohesion, with lasting demands for collective rights, and not just a thinly sliced amount of rights granted to a happy few (as the cartoon in Figure 0.1, "What are your values?" suggested). Women occupying cafes in the towns of Houmt El-Souq or Kairouan generated more public debate than stillborn legislative debates on inheritance equalities in the Tunisian Parliament ever did.

Finally, the number, the multitude, and the synchronized times and spaces granted a sense of security to these informal embodied practices. The presentism and direct action of Tunisians involved in the first caravan from the south of the country to the Qasba, or of the Yemenis participating in the March of Life between Taiz and Sanaa, represented more than promises for change in a remote future: these collective events provided protection and a collective sense of identity. They broke the fear of state repression, refused geographical compartmentalization, and proposed new methods for representation.

The "extraordinary" behind the people's action has been the focus of Asef Bayat's rich sociology of everyday politics. Bayat (1997) is right that the informal is needed to make revolutions possible, like during the Iranian revolution. He claims that informal politics do not aim at the state (Bayat 1997: 58). This book has argued that the extraordinary in the 2011 Uprisings consisted in linking creative and poetic methods with a quest for the state, or with a mandate to request that the state guarantee equal protection against violence. The humbling courage and incredible creativity of harmless and weaponless protestors in Yemen stripped the "regime of political legitimacy," "redistributing it to the revolution[ary camp]" (R. Porter 2020: 206). Tunisians from the interior, more than anybody in the country, can fully speak of the one-month period at the turn of 2010–2011 as "revolutionary." Their task was impossible under the earlier patterns of securitization. Their achievements became extraordinary. To undo decades, if not centuries of encroachments, new imperialist forces, the duplicitous attitude of the international community, willing to congratulate itself for Ben Ali's "democratic laboratory" but doing little to shoulder these democratic demands, was a grand realization.[28]

The bases on which security states were built were shattered; the emperor had no clothes on anymore. That is what *vis populi* did. "Violence" was present throughout the years after 2011 as a semantic space. These new representations generated democratic practices and favored informal civic engagement that mostly neutralized acts of physical destruction. For example, *vis populi* tried to harness and limit the power of security apparatuses. It also created a virtuous space of civility through ideas of decentralization and self- or local management, and initiated new cooperative relations with institutions of state coercion.

Vis populi is more than non-violence, of course, but it is also "less" than the use of political violence that occurs in revolutionary moments with dual power (the populist violence) (see e.g. Tilly 2003b). In the reformist paths of the Yemeni and Tunisian Uprisings, *vis populi* almost never enacted destructive violence. It used the moral strength of its pluralism to enact non-violent actions and to force a democratic foundation for the new social contract. Because of the history of the MENA, the profusion of wars, an overbearing state of emergency, profound inequalities in mortality, and the risk of being targeted by political police in everyday life (Bayat 2008; Ismail 2006), it has been impossible "to dream the dream of a non-violence modernity" (Joas & Knöbl 2013: 1) as a basis for political action. It is thus illusory to expect Arab actors to move entirely to an Arendtian view of power, with the plurality acting in concert and finding peaceful ways to iron out differences. Nor does *vis populi* mean that non-violence is out of the equation. The specificities of the regions require that the theme of violence be confronted and turned into a space of alternative discussions. Violence is everywhere in the Middle East. Ben Ali and Saleh used violence in the first weeks of the protests, but the demonstrators largely abstained from committing their own acts of violence. They did destroy

---

[28] Another theme of Bayat (2017) is "a revolution without revolutionaries." This view does not give enough credit to the numerous overlooked leaders (intellectuals, organizers in small section of a party or of a trade union, networks in abeyance, etc.). It also overlooks the failure of formal actors in shouldering these new extraordinary demands.

symbols of antidemocratic power (police stations, buildings of the ruling party, custom offices), but refrained from targeting the *people* in these institutions. In the case where violence was used by self-declared revolutionary groups, such as the Leagues for the Protection of the Revolution (LPR), or Salafi groups in Tunisia, a consensus arose that this was not the way forward and people turned their back on their violent actions. A few weeks later, legal norms emerged and outlawed these groups.[29]

Vis populi requires and sustains pluralism. The people does not exist as a sociological category, and when it did exist and was labeled as such by actors, it emerged precisely because of this sense of concert, of the articulated multitude. It was an act of radical representation, with an imaginary act of violence that would rid citizens of tyranny or of unjust exploitation. In the images in the Introduction, or in episodes described in Chapter 3, violence was made visible, but it did not mark state agents; it highlighted illegitimacy. Figure 0.4 portrays the necessary act of violence, killing the snake, which would free the country from being asphyxiated by Ben Ali and the RCD. Acts of destruction targeted, and demonstrations focused upon, institutions that sustained the fragmented geography (the *Diwanat*, customs offices in Medenine; the Ministry of the Interior in Sanaa; the Agricultural Bank in Sfax). Popular moments of violence occurred in a way that people would gain civic freedom and tyranny or unjust economic control over marginalized parts of the country would stop. *Vis populi* was not about calling for, or acting towards, the killing of other persons, but about enacting a higher moral ground than superseded and delegitimized authorities.[30]

In numerous instances, *vis populi* condemned political violence. It clearly refused the game of tension and escalation that would have discredited the entire movement. In Sanaa, after the massacre on the Friday of Dignity in March 2011, revolutionary youths called for the replacement of the Ministry of the Interior in charge of the police forces

---

[29] See the case of the Salafis outcast by the Troika under street pressure in 2013 (Gobe & Chouikha 2014: §35). The LPR were outlawed by Mehdi Jomaa's government in 2014, following the Quartet's and National Dialogue's decisions on the matter. See ICG (2016: 7).

[30] I am adapting the formulation of Morreall (2002: e.g. 138–140, 143), who discusses instances in which violence can be considered an effective tool of civil disobedience.

that beat up and threatened protests with their own Ministry of Information.[31] The new representation preferred by the Yemeni campers was generating true information about the repressive nature of Saleh's regime. It was not used to enact violence. The reversal was also captured by young men walking bare-chested to nearby checkpoints, while chanting democratic slogans (R. Porter 2017; 2020). When there were threats by Salafi groups on UGTT leaders, or by the LPR on journalists or intellectuals, the UGTT used its symbolic capital to organize peaceful collective protests, just like it did at the end of December 2010 when Ben Ali ordered the military crushing of the growing protests.[32]

Second, the reference to physical force and political violence did not constitute the basis for a new beginning. It only shed light on the illegitimacy of past state violence. It is not about a revolutionary *tabula rasa*, but rather about an attempt to resume republican politics, or popular politics from below. *Vis populi* re-assembles historical fragmentation and wants to distribute the means of coercion evenly across the country (think of the proposal made for equitable geographical representation in the various armed forces in the Yemeni federal constitution). Thus, the continuity-and-rupture approach applies here as well: The novelty of *vis populi* in 2011–2013 constituted a break with the post-independence republican era. The short slogan "Tunisia is a people, not a government" (*tunis sha'ab, la hukuma*) captures this idea: Rather than being simply the objects of governmental rule, Tunisians, but also Yemenis, want to be direct elements in and of politics.

The semantics of radical representation indicates that the people *are* the state if the latter is ruled legitimately. In Ross Porter's (2020: 207) terms, the 2011 revolution can be seen as "a form of securitization in its own right." There is an insurrectionary moment, but that is not the end point. *Vis populi*, in my view, is more than securitizing a revolution. It is larger because it is an explicit call to re-form, or to re-establish, the social contract in a manner different from how it was organized and justified by post-independence elites.

Vis populi was a soft guideline for law-making and for institution building. The assembled Arab demos enacted alternative democratic

---

[31] See min. 1:55 of www.youtube.com/watch?v=yEfCzz43lrc.
[32] On the spaces of protection offered by the UGTT, see Yousfi (2015: 33–34) and Omri (2016: 23, 31).

practices. These sustained the social life of citizenship, and proposed ideas for legal and constitutional changes. *Vis populi* was a series of informal agreements for future action that came from different groups coming and acting together. "The People" never exercised authority. The informality and constant re-articulation and re-negotiation between the various constituencies of the "many," the "multitude," the "people" guaranteed against the risk of a populist usurpation, with a group claiming to speak for the entire people. The three principles of representation prevented the rigid and misleading application of the people's *violence*. *Vis populi* flashed a metaphorical representation of violence above everyone's heads precisely to avoid a return to the pre-2011 situation. It condemned demoscopic violence rather than enacting destruction. In that sense *vis populi* is an informal "guideline for action" that is in stark opposition to the revolutionary understanding of *tabula rasa*, or foundational violence and destruction.[33]

In the summer of 2011, protesters in Egypt called on the Army to withdraw from the political process and let civilians decide the future of the country. A stencil could be seen on walls in Cairo with a civilian truck towing away a tank with the text "No parking allowed, except on the borders." Citizens did not call for the abolition of the army: They simply asked that the army do their only duty of preserving the territorial integrity of the country, and that it not suppress civic protests.[34] The other image of a tank relates to the short poem by Aref Hamza cited above. Feeding breadcrumbs to tanks is unlikely to change the dire situation in Syria or Yemen, but with pigeons defecating all over them, these weapons are to be ridiculed, providing a lull, a *hudna*, in the conditions of precarious citizenship. Thus, the dialectics of lay

---

[33] I take the formulation of a "guideline for action" from Lokdam (2019: 209), who refers to a phrase of Walter Benjamin's, "*Richtsschnuur des Handelns.*" *Richtsschnuur* is a tool used by masons to control the verticality of their constructions (a mason line). The expression indicates a preference for informality.

[34] For a reproduction of the stencil, see www.foreignaffairs.com/gallery-revolution-graffiti7, or Gröndahl (2012: 19). This "soft" expulsion of tanks is tied to the architecture of cooperation with Israel, since no tanks and armed forces were actually allowed on the border with this country since the 1978 peace treaty. This stencil is part of a larger trope of *vis populi*. In November 2011, protestors in Cairo chanted "*ya Tantawi / gaish da / gaish-na !*," "Hey Tantawi [head of SCAF), this army is *our* army!," expressing a similar attitude toward state coercion. I am grateful to Nathanael Mannone for sharing this information with me.

people – civilians – trying to subvert the meaning of these gardens for tanks might constitute a new break for the future.

* * *

It has been a striking development of the last three years to see how the song *Bella Ciao* has become a rallying reference for Arab protestors. Adding their own touch in self-representation,[35] a group of young Iraqi artists made an Arabic version of *Bella Ciao* that combines metaphorical elements of both the slow- and fast-paced versions of the song. Throughout 2019 and 2020, new protests erupted in Algeria, Sudan, Iraq, and Lebanon, generating talks of a "new Arab Spring." The slogans were direct references to the famous "the People want to bring down the regime" heard ubiquitously in 2011 (Fahmi 2020). Each of these national protests drew inspiration and motives from one another.

In Algeria, on February 22, 2019, another *hirak* ("movement") emerged when 82-year-old President Bouteflika announced he would seek a fifth mandate despite his frail health. Every Friday, tens of thousands joined the protests. In a few weeks, many millions had forced President Bouteflika to stand down and other corrupt businessmen and senior politicians, including former prime ministers, to be arrested. Campaigns, unions, and associations called for the end of the authoritarian social pact and the instauration of a second republic, through the drafting of a new constitution with the involvement of non-party actors (Boumghar 2019: 35–36). Aware that the protestors were caught between a rock and a hard place, with such an all-powerful army and deeply entrenched economic and political power vested in the name of stability, protestors targeted the clique around Bouteflika and stayed away from too confrontational a stance with the army. Yet demonstrators "questioned the role of the army in political life, the Army Chief of Staff General Gaid Salah having been the major decision maker within the regime, with signs declaring their demands for a civil and not a military state" (Northey 2021: 23).

In Sudan the protests against the increasing cost of living in December 2018 (Fahmi 2020) also pivoted against the ossified rule of President Omar Al-Bashir, who had ruled the country for more than 30

---

[35] Bouattia (2019) mentions the use of this new Arabic version by Lebanese, Iraqi, Palestinian, Turkish, and Syrian protestors. The song had been made popular in Iraq by a Spanish TV series, *Money Heist*.

years. Slogans in April 2019 were "Just Fall!" (*"tusqat bas!"*) or "Freedom, Peace and Justice! Let him fall!"[36] A combination of informal and civil society-coordinated protests forced Al-Bashir to resign. Particularly active was the Sudanese Professionals' Association (SPA, *tajamu' al-mihniyyin al-sudaniyyin*), a collaboration of doctors, health workers, and lawyers.[37] The military forced a 10-member Transitional Military Council (TMC) to replace Omar Al-Bashir at the helm of the executive.

The masses, the people, invoking what has been described in these pages as *vis populi*, simply stubbornly refused the offered transition and camped in front of the army headquarters on Buri Road, in the center of the Sudanese capital. They insisted on civilian rule. The SPA organized regular marches zigzagging through the city, and encampments grew in size, with Sudanese protestors coming from various parts of the country, Darfur included (A. Jamal 2021). Mostly non-violent protests animated the capital, with a majority of protestors being women.[38] An informal cultural festival of sorts grew in May 2019, aided by Ramadan. In his comparative analysis of the Sudanese and Lebanese protest movements of 2019, Noah Salomon (2020: 336) noted that "the [2019] revolution was, both in its articulation and its practice, an outpouring of unity through the expression of the kaleidoscope of diversity that makes up Sudan." Islamists were for a moment in with the people, but later seem to have reacted against the insistence of civilian rule (Salomon 2020: 337).

Waiting for the end of the holy month of Ramadan, the Military Council decided to brutally crush the encampment on June 3, 2019.[39] The massacre in Khartoum was the work of the Sudanese police forces and the Rapid Support Forces (RSF) unleashing their joint might on unarmed civilians. At least 87 civilians were killed, on that day,[40] with later accounts listing at least 128 dead demonstrators (A. Jamal 2021). One key figure responsible for the blood bath was Hemeti, the leader of RSF, a unit created in 2013 under the authority of the Military Council

---

[36] Picture of the slogans can be found at www.bbc.com/news/world-africa-4787 3293, April 10, 2019.

[37] On the history of the SPA, see Majdoub (2019b). See also www.bbc.com/news/ world-africa-46921480, January 18, 2019.

[38] www.bbc.com/news/world-africa-47738155, April 1, 2019.

[39] See www.bbc.com/news/51489802, February 14, 2020.

[40] The disturbing video of the BBC Africa Eye team can be found at: www.bbc.com /news/av/embed/p07gp88z/51489802, July 12, 2019.

and previously involved in the heinous war crimes perpetrated by the famous Janjaweed militias in Darfur earlier in the 2000s.[41] Hemeti was also in charge of the mercenaries sent to Yemen as part of the Saudi coalition that we encountered in Chapter 6.

Rapidly, after the massacre, Sudanese citizens enacted the principles of presentism and self-representation in action, and articulated democratic demands. They demanded public inquiries to clarify the responsibility for these killings. They also insisted on accountability. President Bashir was jailed on corruption charges in December 2019. In the spring of 2020, the government had to decide whether he would be handed to the International Criminal Court for war crimes and possibly genocide in Darfur.

A year after the massacre, the SPA resumed pressure on the TMC, headed by army chief General Abdel Fattah Al-Burhan, with a complex social media campaign. Two new slogans combined distrust toward the TMC with hope for a democratic form of representation. The first one was *"lam tasqut baad!"* ("Not fallen yet," which is an adaption of "Just Fall!," and reminds the TMC that it has to go), while the second *"al-tajamuʿ yumathiluni"* ("the SPA represents me," from the root *tamthil*) expresses the hope that self-organization can help Sudan shore up a civilian transition (Majdoub 2019b). On June 20, 2020, it called for a "popular campaign for the completion of the transitional power framework and the realization of the democratic transition."[42] Throughout July 2020,[43] the SPA organized weekly marches in cities and in the countryside, visits to the wounded in hospitals, petitions, calls for civil disobedience, strikes, and days of non-violent resistance. One of the hashtags used by the SPA and that spread in Sudan was about recovering assets from the security forces (*#istirdad al-sharikat al-amniyya*) and nationalizing the large private companies controlled by the army.[44] Like in Yemen, or Egypt, the Sudanese army and security companies hold a very large portion of

---

[41] Although not personally named in investigations into those responsible for atrocities during the height of the war in Darfur; see www.bbc.com/news/514 89802, February 14, 2020.

[42] https://twitter.com/AssociationSd, June 20, 2020.

[43] Their program in July 2020 is available on the Internet Archive at https://web .archive.org/web/20200811101846/www.sudaneseprofessionals.org/en/sched ule-for-grassroots-revolutionary-action/.

[44] With *istirdād* the Arabic word for recovery, retrieval. See, e.g., https://twitter .com/AssociationSd/status/1277846627399712769, June 30, 2019. The

the national economy, some estimated 250 companies in vital areas such as gold, rubber, meat exports, flour, and sesame, and they are exempted from taxes (Al-Jazeera 2020). Sudanese citizens are thus trying to loosen the grip that the security sector has over the country.[45]

Military and security forces are likely to influence Algerian and Sudanese politics for many years. Hemeti and Abdel Fattah Al-Burhan will be hard to remove, in part because some international actors want them to stay in power.[46] Even loyalists of Omar Al-Bashir are said to have attempted a military coup in September 2021, which was thwarted by Sudanese authorities.[47] Strong presidentialism risks becoming the new norm in Tunisia, after President Saied's suspension of the Parliament, and his effort to take control of the Ministry of the Interior and some of the judiciary circuits during the summer of 2021. But popular protests and demands for power-sharing from civil society actors have continued in Sudan and Tunisia. In Algeria, in late February 2021, two years after the first marches, and after a forced break due to the COVID pandemic, Hirak resumed weekly protests, demanding accountability and social justice. In many Arab streets, calls for *madaniyya* (civil rule), accountability of the security sector, and the end of state repression have become a staple for cultural and political representations. The combination of cultural references with political demands by Arab citizens entails more than an aesthetic form of citizenship (Salime 2015b). It makes a specific demand to neutralize state repression. The *vis populi* has now clearly become a habitus that will continue to shape the course of events and collective interactions in Arab countries.

hashtag was calling for nationalization of large industries and creating commons that would service the people, not economic elites.

[45] For example, the Sudanese Prime Minister Abdallah Hamdok showed his determination to hold the military accountable when he recalled, a year later, the memory of the civilians killed in June 2019. See https://twitter.com/SudanPM Hamdok/status/1264114451676041216 (May 23, 2020), insisting on the achievement of justice for the "martyrs of the December revolution" as a top priority for the transitional period. In December 2020, Hadok criticized the head of the TMC for refusing to allow civilian control over the constellation of security companies (Al-Jazeera 2020).

[46] For example, Burhan was the only person Israeli leader Netanyahu met after the Trump-sponsored "peace deal" forced Sudan to recognize Israel. www .middleeasteye.net/fr/node/158306, February 6, 2020.

[47] See "Sudan Leaders Say They Thwarted Coup Attempt by Loyalists of Former Dictator," *New York Times*, September 21, 2021, at: www.nytimes.com/2021/ 09/21/world/africa/sudan-coup-attempt.html, September 21, 2021.

Sources and References

A Documents and Texts

Tunisian official documents:

April 2012: Report of the Bouderbala Commission, available at: www
.leaders.com.tn/uploads/FCK_files/Rapport%20Bouderbala.pdf
January 2014: Constitution of Tunisia, available at: https://legisla
tion-securite.tn/law/44137
May 2018: Law on municipalities (Loi organique n° 2018–29 sur les
collectivités locales), available at https://legislation-securite.tn/fr/
node/104277

Yemeni constitutional texts and sources:

July 2013: National Dialogue Conference, Mid-Plenary Outcomes,
available at: https://web.archive.org/web/20140726110035/www
.ndc.ye/page.aspx?show=102
Jan. 2014: Final Communique of National Dialogue Conference,
available at: https://web.archive.org/web/20210711151011/htt
p://www.ndc.ye/ndcdoc/NDC_Final_Communique.pdf
Jan. 2015: Proposed Federal Constitution for Yemen, available at:
https://web.archive.org/web/20150121145616/www.ndc.ye/co
nstitution_draft.pdf
2019: Southern Transitional Council. The Political Vision: Paper
version received during interview with STC representatives

B *Interviews*
In Tunisia:

Name	Profile	Organization	Interviewed in	Date
Riadh MASTOURI	charitable worker	Ennahda	Tunis	July 2015
Sofia SOULA & Khaled CHAABAN	donor	Rosa Luxemburg Stiftung	Tunis	July 2015
Fatma TOUMI	party activist	Ennahda	Tunis	July 2015 & May 2016
Omayya SEDDIK	advocacy	Humanitarian Dialogue	Tunis	July 2015
Achref WACHANI	charitable worker	Organisation Tunisienne pour le Développement Social	Tunis	July 2015
Amna GUELLALI	advocacy	Human Rights Watch	Tunis	July 2015
Hosni MOUHELI	donor	Open Society Foundation	Tunis	July 2015
Abdelhamid GHRIBI	association	Association Citoyenne Djerba	Djerba	Jan. & May 2016
Hassen JRIBI	association	Doustourna – Midoun Branch	Djerba	Jan. 2016
Riad BESHIR	association	Association du développement et des études stratégiques de Medenine	Medenine	Jan. 2016
Adel Naajeh JEDID	association	Dar Al-Shabab – Medenine	Medenine	Jan. 2016
Béchir SOUIDI	party activist	Masar	Medenine	Jan. 2016
Mahdi AL-GHAMD	association	Association Droits et Citoyenneté	Tataouine	Jan. 2016
Abdelhamit AL-KHATIB	association	Association pour les Enfants Autistes	Tataouine	Jan. 2016

Name	Type	Organization	Location	Date
Ali BECHIR	association	Syndicat d'Initiatives pour le Tourisme	Tataouine	Jan. 2016
Mustafa ABDELKABEER	advocacy	Arab Center for Human Rights	Medenine	Jan. 2016
Anis KHENISSI	association	Association Culturelle Zarzis	Medenine	Jan. 2016
Faycal DCHICHA	association	Association Développement Durable et Coopération Internationale	Medenine	Jan. 2016
Fathi BELHADJ	donor	Programme d'Appui à la Société Civile (Union Européenne)	Sfax	Jan. 2016
Hassen BOUKTHIR	association	Association de Maintenance et de Gestion d'Agaret	Sfax	Jan. 2016
Zied MELLOULI	campaign	Sayyeb Trottoir	Sfax	Jan. & June 2016
Besma OMEZZINE	party activist	Masar	Sfax	Jan. & June 2016
Sumaya SGHAIER	association	CinéClub Sousse	Sousse	Jan. 2016
Faten GAFSI	party activist	Masar	Sousse	Jan. 2016
Issa HAJLOUI	journalist	Zituna Radio	Sousse	Jan. 2016
Sara MLAYAH	party activist	Ligue des Tunisiens Humanistes	Sousse	Jan. 2016
Najla LA'YOUNI	party activist	Jeune Chambre Internationale	Sousse	Jan. 2016
Néjib TRABELSI	government	former civil servant	Tunis	Jan. 2016

B (*cont.*)

Name	Profile	Organization	Interviewed in	Date
Othman KHALED	association	Municipalité Efficace	Tunis	Jan. & May 2016
Moncef KARTAS	academic	Small Arms Survey	La Marsa & New York	May 2016 & Nov. 2019
Yassine ANNABI	association	Association DERB	Bizerte	May 2016
Wissem ZARROUK	campaign	Bizerte Cleaner	Bizerte	May 2016
Tareq & Ghassen BEN BARKA	charitable workers	Ahl Al-Khayr	Bizerte	May 2016
Peter SCHAEFER	donor	Rosa Luxemburg Stiftung	Tunis	May 2016
Rida BEN HAMIDA	association	Association Citoyenneté Active	Djerba	May 2016
Myriam CHEIKH	association	Association Djerba Solidarité et Développement	Djerba	May 2016
Fares SA'ID	campaign	Expression Libre Zerzis	Zerzis	May 2016
Foued GUECHAÏ	party activist	Délégation Spéciale Houmt El-Souq	Midoun	May 2016
Amira YAHYAOUI	advocacy	Al-Bawsola	Tunis	May 2016
Abdelrahman HEDHLI	association	Forum Tunisien des Droits Economiques et Sociaux	Tunis	May 2016
Michaël AYARI	academic	Security expert	Tunis	May 2016 & May 2019
Chalbia GHORBALI	association	Association Développement de la Communication	Siliana	June 2016

Name	Role	Organization	Location	Date
Lakhdar Mohammed BECHIR	association	Association Culturelle Al-Ithaf	Siliana	June 2016
Mohammed Amin SOUMRANI	association	Association Créativité Culturelle	Siliana	June 2016
Rachid KHARROUBI	associaton	Délégation Spéciale Siliana	Siliana	June 2016
Maher HAMASSI	journalist	Fondation Hirondelle	Siliana	June 2016
Akrem YAKOUBI	association	Forum Tunisien des Droits Economiques et Sociaux	Siliana	June 2016
Collective meeting	transnational solidarity	Immigration, Development and Democracy	Mahares	June 2016
Hacem KAMOUM	campaign	Fermons SIAPE	Sfax	June 2016
Khalil KLAI	journalist	Libyan Panorama Channel	Tunis	June 2016
Mohammed Fadel AL-HAMDI	advocacy	Associations & Sustainable Development International Observatory	Tunis	June 2016
Chaima BOUHLEL	advocacy	Al-Bawsola, program Marsad	Tunis	June 2016
Samia SAHLOUL	government	DG for municipal affairs, Ministry of the Interior.	Geneva	March 2019

In Yemen:

Name	Profile	Organization	Interviewed in	Date
Abdullah AL-SAIDI	government	former Yemeni Ambassador to the UN, New York	New York	Feb. 2019
Baligh AL-MIKHLAFI	association & governmental	Youth Development Foundation. Later: Information Counselor at the Cairo Embassy	Cairo (via Skype)	Sept. 2019
Zaid bin Ali ALWAZIR	intellectual	editor of the journal Al-Masar	Fairfax, VA	June 2019
Rafat AL-AKHALI	academic & governmental	Decentralization expert, later a Minister	Oxford (UK)	Sept. 2019
Nadia AL-SAKKAF	academic & governmental	NDC Presidency (women and civil society representative), later a Minister	London (via WhatsApp)	Sept. 2019
Muhammad KHALIFA	campaign & academic	Youth NGO leader. Community leader	Socotra (via WhatsApp)	Dec. 2019 & May 2020
Abdulsalam K. MUSED & Ahmed MUTHANA	government	DG Foreign Affairs, Southern Transitional Council, Washington DC Embassy	Washington DC	Jan. 2020
Abdulsalam AL-RUBAIDI	academic	Academic Forum Muhammad Ali Luqman	Sanaa (via email)	Jan. 2021
Bachir AL-MOHALLAL	association	Pulse NGO	Sanaa (via Zoom)	Feb. 2021

Sources and References

C Bibliographical References

ABDELRAHMAN Maha, 2015. "Social Movements and the Question of Organization. Egypt and Everywhere," LSE Middle East Center Paper Series, London School of Economics, No. 08.

ACHCAR Gilbert, 2013. *The People Want: A Radical Exploration of the Arab Uprising*. Los Angeles CA: University of California Press.

ADI Hakim, 2018. *Pan-Africanism: A History*. London: Bloomsbury.

AGAMBEN Giorgio, 1995. "We Refugees," *Symposium* 49(2): 114–119.

AGGESTAM Karen et al., 2009. "The Arab State and Neo-Liberal Globalization," in Laura GUAZZONE and Daniela PIOPPI (eds), *The Arab State and Neo-Liberal Globalization. The Restructuring of State Power in the Middle East*. Reading: Ithaca Press, 325–350.

AHMAD Eqbal, 2006. *The Selected Writings of Eqbal Ahmad*, ed. by Carollee Bengelsdorf, Margaret Cerullo, & Yogesh Chandrani. New York: Columbia University Press.

AKCALI Emel, ed., 2016. *Neoliberal Governmentality and the Future of the State in the Middle East*. London: Palgrave.

AL-ADHAL Husayn Sulayman, 1993. *Al-Istiqlāl al-ḍā'i': al-malaff al-mansī li-aḥdath al-yaman al-janūbiyya* [Wretched Independence: The Forgotten Dossier in the Events of Southern Yemen]. Cairo: Dar Al-'Ahd.

AL-AMMAR Fawziah, PATCHETT Hannah, & SHAMSAN Shams, 2019. *A Gendered Crisis: Understanding the Experiences of Yemen's War*. Sanaa: Sanaa Center for Strategic Studies.

AL-ERIANI Kamilia, 2020. "Secularism, Security and the Weak State: De-democratizing the 2011 Yemeni Uprising," *Interventions* 23(8): 1140–1165.

AL-JABRI Mohammed Abed, 1998. *The Formation of Arab Reason. Text, Tradition and the Construction of Modernity in the Arab World*. London: I.B. Tauris.

AL-JAZEERA, 2020. "'Unacceptable': Sudanese PM Criticizes Army's Business Interests," *Al-Jazeera Online*, December 15.

413

AL-MAQTARI Bushra, 2020. "Qu'as-tu laissé derrière toi ? Voix d'une guerre oubliée," trans. Marianne Babut, *Arabian Humanities* (13), online.

    2021. "Yemen's Socialist Party and the Fragmentation of the Yemeni Left," *Sanaa Center Analysis*, online, January 23.

AL-MOHALLAL Bachir & STADNICKI Roman, 2020. "Villages en chantier. Le retour de l'initiative locale dans les montagnes yéménites," *Moyen-Orient* 46: 38–43.

AL-MUGHNI Qays Abd, 2020. "J'ai pleuré en français," trans. Marianne Babut, *Arabian Humanities* (13), online.

AL-MUQRI Ali, 2020. "Le pays du Commandeur d'Ali al-Muqri: un dictateur s'en va, un autre s'annonce," *Arabian Humanities* (13), online.

AL-RUBAIDI Abdulsalam, 2014. "Sixtieth versus Seventieth Street. Practices and Counter-Practices during the Yemeni Spring 2011," *Jemen-Report* 45(1–2): 27–31.

    2018a. "Scepticism among Emerging Public Intellectuals in Post-Revolution Yemen," in Marie-Christine HEINZE, ed. *Yemen and the Search for Stability. Power, Politics, and Society after the Arab Spring.* London: I.B. Tauris, 27–46.

    2018b. "Imagining an Alternative Homeland. Humanism in Contemporary Yemeni Novels as a Vision for Social and Political Reform," CARPO Working Paper, Bonn, No. 6.

    2021. "Reading Between the Lines: Political Solutions in Yemeni Fiction Writing," *Yemen Policy Center*, online.

AL-SAKKAF Nadia, 2011. "The Politicization of Yemen's Youth Revolution," Sada Report, Carnegie Paper.

    2018. "Negotiating Women's Empowerment in the NDC," in Marie-Christine HEINZE, ed. *Yemen and the Search for Stability. Power, Politics, and Society after the Arab Spring.* London: I.B. Tauris, 134–159.

AL-SALHI Al-Saghir, 2017. *Al-istiʿmār al-dākhlī. Al-tanmiyya ghayr al-mutakkāfiʾah. Manẓūma ʿal-tahmīsh' fī tūnis namūdajān* [Internal Colonization and Asymmetrical Development. A Treatise on Exemplary "Marginalization" in Tunisia]. Tunis: Sotepa Graphic.

ALATAS Syed Farid, 2014. *Applying Ibn Khaldun. The Recovery of a Lost Tradition in Sociology.* London: Routledge.

ALEXANDER Anne & BASSIOUNY Mostafa, 2014. *Bread, Freedom, Social Justice: Workers and the Egyptian Revolution.* London: Zed Books.

ALIRIZA Fadil, 2020. "Trying to Fix Tunisia's Economy with 'Solidarity'," *Meshkal*, blog, online.

ALLAL Amin, 2011. "Avant on tenait le mur, maintenant on tient le quartier!," *Politique africaine* 121(1): 53–67.

2016. "Retour vers le futur. Les origines économiques de la révolution tunisienne," *Pouvoirs* 156(1): 17–29.

ALSALEH Asaad, 2015. *Voices of the Arab Spring: Personal Stories from the Arab Revolutions.* New York: Columbia University Press.

ALVISO-MARINO Anahi, 2016. "Faire d'un lieu un symbole de politique. La photographie engagée sur la Place du Changement à Sanaa," in Hélène COMBES, David GARIBAY, & Camille GOIRAND, eds. *Les lieux de la colère. Occuper l'espace pour contester, de Madrid à Sanaa.* Paris: Karthala, 35–70.

ALWAZIR Atiaf Z., 2016. "Yemen's Enduring Resistance: Youth between Politics and Informal Mobilization," *Mediterranean Politics* 21(1): 170–191.

ALWAZIR Zaid bin Ali, 1998. *Naḥwa waḥda yemniyya itihādiyya lā-markaziyya* [Toward a Federal and Decentralized Yemeni Unity], 3rd ed. Sanaa: Yemen Heritage Center.

AMAR Paul, 2013. *The Security Archipelago: Human-Security States, Sexuality Politics, and the End of Neoliberalism.* Durham NC: Duke University Press.

AMAR Paul & PRASHAD Vijay, eds. 2013. *Dispatches from the Arab Spring.* Minneapolis MN: Minnesota University Press.

AMIRA AUGUSTIN Anna-Linda, 2014. "Chanting for Southern Independence," *Middle East Report* 272 (Winter), online.

2015. "'Aden wird siegen': Der Südwiderstand," *INAMO, Informationsprojeckt Naher undr Mittlerer Osten* 83: 11–16.

2018. "Generational and Political Change in Southern Yemen," in Marie-Christine HEINZE, ed. *Yemen and the Search for Stability. Power, Politics, and Society after the Arab Spring.* London: I.B. Tauris, 93–114.

2019. "UN-vermittelte Friedensverhandlungen und die Südfrage," *INAMO, Informationsprojeckt Naher und Mittlerer Osten* 97: 33–36.

AMRI Laroussi, 2008. "The Concept of *'umran*: The Heuristic Knot in Ibn Khaldun," *Journal of North African Studies* 13(3): 351–361.

ANDERSON Georges, 2019. "Yemen's Failed Constitutional Transition," in Michael ANDERSON & Sujit CHOUDHRY, eds. *Territory and Power in Constitutional Transition.* Cambridge: Cambridge University Press, 312–329.

ANDERSON Lisa, 1986. *The State and Social Transformation in Tunisia and Libya, 1830–1980.* Princeton NJ: Princeton University Press.

ARATO Andrew, 2016. *Post Sovereign Constitution Making: Learning and Legitimacy.* Oxford: Oxford University Press.

ARENDT Hannah, 1977a. *On Violence.* New York: Harcourt Publishing.

1977b. *On Revolution.* New York: Penguin.

ARJOMAND Said A., ed. 2008. *Constitutional Politics in the Middle East.* Oxford: Bart Publishing.

ARMBRUST Walter, 2011. "The Revolution Against Neoliberalism," *Jadaliyya,* online.

2019. *Martyrs and Tricksters: An Ethnography of the Egyptian Revolution.* Princeton NJ: Princeton University Press.

ASAD Talal, 2015. "Thinking about Tradition, Religion, and Politics in Egypt Today," *Critical Inquiry* 42(1): 166–214.

AYALON Ami, 1989. "*Dimuqraatiya, Huriya, Jumhuriyaa*: The Modernization of the Arabic Political Vocabulary," *Asian and African Studies* 23: 23–42.

AYARI Michaël B. , 2011. "Des révolutions bourgeoises ou populaires?," in Vincent GEISSER & Michaël B. AYARI, eds. *Renaissances arabes. Sept questions clés sur des révolutions en marche.* Paris: Les Éditions de l'Atelier, 17–33.

2016. *Le prix de l'engagement en régime autoritaire. Gauchistes et islamistes dans la Tunisie de Bourguiba et Ben Ali (1957–2011).* Paris: Karthala.

AYEB Habib, 2011. "Social and Political Geography of the Tunisian Revolution: The Alfa Grass Revolution," *Review of African Political Economy* 38(129): 467–479.

AYUBI Nazih M., 1980. *Bureaucracy and Politics in Contemporary Egypt.* London: Ithaca Press.

1995. *Over-stating the Arab State: Politics and Society in the Middle East.* London & New York: I.B. Tauris.

AYYASH Mark M., 2018. "An Assemblage of Decoloniality?," *Studies in Social Justice* 12(1): 21–37.

2020. *A Hermeneutics of Violence: A Four-Dimensional Conception.* Toronto: Toronto University Press.

AZIMI Negar, 2016. "Revolution as Ready-Made," in Jens HANSSEN & Max WEISS, eds. *Arabic Thought against the Authoritarian Age. Towards an Intellectual History of the Present.* Cambridge: Cambridge University Press, 336–353.

BADIE Bertrand, 2000. *The Imported State: The Westernization of Political Order.* Cambridge: Cambridge University Press.

BALIBAR Etienne, 1991. "Is there a 'Neo-Racism'?," in Etienne BALIBAR & Immanuel WALLERSTEIN, *Race, Nation, Class.* London: Verso, 17–28.

2015. *Violence and Civility.* New York: Columbia University Press.

BAMYEH Mohammed A., 2012. "Anarchist Philosophy, Civic Traditions and the Culture of Arab Revolutions," *Middle East Journal of Culture and Communication* 5(1): 32–41.

2013. "Anarchist Method, Liberal Intention, Authoritarian Lesson: The Arab Spring between Three Enlightenments," *Constellations* 20(2): 188–202.

BAQAYS Abd Al-Hakim, 2020. "Le roman yéménite dans la tourmente," *Arabian Humanities* (13), online.

BARKAWI Tarak, 2017. "States, Armies, and Wars in Global Context," in Julian GO & George LAWSON, eds. *Global Historical Sociology*. Cambridge: Cambridge University Press, 58–75.

BARKER Colin, 2001. "Fear, Laughter, and Collective Power: The Making of Solidarity at the Lenin Shipyard in Gdansk, 1980," in Jeff GOODWIN, James JASPER, & Francesca POLETTA, eds. *Passionate Politics: Emotions and Social Movements*. Chicago IL: University of Chicago Press, 175–194.

BARKEY Karen, 2008. *Empire of Difference: The Ottomans in Comparative Perspective*. New York: Cambridge University Press.

BARTHAS Jérémie, 2010. "Machiavelli in Political Thought from the Age of Revolutions to the Present," in John NAJEMY, ed. *The Cambridge Companion to Machiavelli*. Cambridge: Cambridge University Press, 256–273.

BASHA Ammar, 2012a. "Revolutionary Junctures: Documenting the Yemeni Uprising on Film," *Jadaliyya*, online.

2012b. "Documenting Yemen's Injured South," *Jadaliyya*, online.

BATATU Hanna, 2004. *The Old Social Classes and the Revolutionary Movement in Iraq: A Study of Iraq's Old Landed and Commercial Classes and of its Communists, Ba'thists, and Free Officers*. London: Saqi Books.

BAYART Jean-François, 1993. *The State in Africa: The Politics of the Belly*. London & New York: Longman.

BAYAT Asef, 1997. "Un-civil Society: The Politics of 'Informal People'," *Third World Quarterly* 18(1): 53–72.

2008. *Life as Politics: How Ordinary People Change the Middle East*. Stanford CA: Stanford University Press.

2017. *Revolution without Revolutionaries. Making Sense of the Arab Spring*. Stanford CA: Stanford University Press.

BEAUD Michel, 2002. *A History of Capitalism, 1500–2000*. New York: Monthly Review Press.

BEDAU Hugo Adam, ed. 2002. *Civil Disobedience in Focus*. London & New York: Routledge.

BEININ Joel, 1990. *Was the Red Flag Flying There? Marxist Politics and the Arab-Israeli Conflict in Egypt and Israel, 1948–1965*. Berkeley CA: University of California Press.

2015. *Workers and Thieves. Labor Movements and Popular Uprisings in Tunisia and Egypt.* Stanford CA: Stanford University Press.

BÉJI Hélé, 2008. *Nous, Décolonisés.* Paris: Arléa.

BELHADJ Souhaïl, 2019. "Décentraliser dans la Tunisie post-autoritaire: l'émergence d'un pouvoir local face aux limites imposées par le consensus sécuritaire," *CCDP Working Paper*, Geneva, No. 13.

BELHEDI Amor, 2012. *La fracture territoriale. Dimension spatiale de la révolution tunisienne.* Tunis: Wassiti Editions.

BELLIN Eva & LANE Heidi, eds. 2016. *Building the Rule of Law in the Arab World.* Boulder CO: Lynne Rienner.

BEN ACHOUR Rafaa & BEN ACHOUR Sana, 2012. "La transition démocratique en Tunisie: entre légalité constitutionnelle et légitimité révolutionnaire," *Revue Française de droit constitutionnel* 92(4): 715–732.

BEN AISSA Mohammed Salah, 2016. "What Independence? Judicial Power in Tunisia," in Eva BELLIN & Heidi LANE, eds. *Building the Rule of Law in the Arab World.* Boulder CO: Lynne Rienner, 53–66.

BENATOUIL Maxime, 2020. "The Other 8th of May," *Tribune Mag*, blog, online.

BÉNOT Yves, 2005. *Massacres coloniaux 1944–1950.* Paris: La Découverte.

BERMANI Cesare 2003. *'Guerra guerra ai palazzi e alle chiese . . . '. Saggi sul canto sociale.* Rome: Odradek.

BHAMBRA Gurminder, 2014. *Connected Sociologies.* New York: Bloomsbury.

2015a. "On the Haitian Revolution and the Society of Equals," *Theory, Culture & Society*, 32(7–8): 267–274.

2015b. "Citizens and Others: The Constitution of Citizenship through Exclusion," *Alternatives: Global, Local, Political* 40(2): 102–114.

2019. "Global Social Thought via the Haitian Revolution," in Boaventura DE SOUSA SANTOS & Maria Paula MENESES, eds. *Knowledges Born in the Struggle: Constructing the Epistemologies of the Global South.* London: Routledge, 3–20.

BIGO Didier, 2001. "Internal and External Security(ies): The Möbius Ribbon," in Mathias ALBERT, David JACOBSON, & Yosef LAPID, eds. *Identities, Borders, Orders.* Minneapolis MN: Minnesota University Press, 91–116.

BIJL Paul & VAN KLINKEN Gerry, 2019. "Citizenship in Asian History," *Citizenship Studies* 23(3): 189–205.

BLANCHARD Pascal et al., 2018. *Sexe, race & colonies. La domination des corps du XVe siecle à nos jours.* Paris: La Découverte.

BLUMI Isa, 2011. *Chaos in Yemen: Societal Collapse and the New Authoritarianism.* London: Routledge.

BOBBIO Norberto & MATTEUCCI Nicola, eds. 1983. *Dizionario di Politica*. Turin: UTET.

BOETSCH Gilles et al., eds. 2019. *Sexualités, identités & corps colonisés. XVe–XXIe siècles*. Paris: Edition CNRS.

BONINE Michael E., AMANAT Abbas, & GASPER Michael Ezekiel, eds. 2012. *Is There a Middle East? The Evolution of a Geopolitical Concept*. Stanford CA: Stanford University Press.

BONNEFOY Laurent, 2011. *Salafism in Yemen: Transnationalism and Religious Identity*. New York: Columbia University Press.

2012a. "Une brève histoire de la violence dite jihadiste au Yémen," in Laurent BONNEFOY, Marine POIRIER, and Franck MERMIER, eds. *Yémen, le tournant révolutionnaire*. Paris: Karthala / CEFAS: 93–113.

2012b. "Have the *shabab al-thawra* Lost in the Face of Institutionalized Politics?," Conference paper on "From Street to Political Mobilization," Moulay Hicham Foundation, Skhirat, 1–2 September.

2013. "Yémen, un dialogue modèle?," *Orient XXI*, online.

2018. *Yemen in the World. Beyond Insecurity*. Oxford: Oxford University Press.

BONNEFOY Laurent & POIRIER Marine, 2012. "The Structuration of the Yemeni Revolution. Exploring a Process in Motion," *Revue française de science politique* 62(5–6): 131–150.

BONNEFOY Laurent, POIRIER Marine, & MERMIER Franck, eds. 2012. *Yémen, le tournant révolutionnaire*. Paris : Karthala / CEFAS.

BOTTICI Chiara, 2014. *Imaginal Politics. Images beyond Imagination and the Imaginary*. New York: Columbia University Press.

BOTTICI Chiara & CHALLAND Benoît, 2012. "Civil Society in Revolt: From the Arab Spring to Occupy Wall Street," *Jadaliyya*, online.

2019. "Europe After Eurocentrism?," *Crisis & Critique* 7(1): 56–87.

BOU NASSIF Hicham, 2015. "A Military Besieged: The Armed Forces, the Police, and the Party in Bin 'Ali's Tunisia, 1987–2011," *International Journal of Middle East Studies* 47: 65–87.

BOUATTIA Malia, 2019. "A May '68 for the Modern Era," *The New Arab*, online.

BOUMGHAR Mouloud, 2019. "Le gant constitutionnel réversible: accessoire de l'uniforme militaire. Regard critique sur la crise constitutionnelle algérienne de 2019," *L'Année du Maghreb* 21(2): 35–54.

BOURDIEU Pierre, 1977. *Outline of a Theory of Practice*. Cambridge: Cambridge University Press.

1983. *Language and Symbolic Power*. Cambridge MA: Harvard University Press.

2001. *Masculine Domination*. London: Polity Press.

BOURDIEU Pierre & SAYAD Abdelmalek, 1964. *Uprooting: The Crisis of Traditional Agriculture in Algeria.* London: Polity Press.

BOUTROS Magda, 2017. "Place and Tactical Innovation in Social Movements. The Emergence of Egypt's Anti-harassment Groups," *Theoretical Sociology* 46: 543–575.

BRANDT Marieke, 2019a. "Ein Geschichte des Misserfolge. Konflikt-Mediation mit Jemens Huthis 2004–2016," *INAMO, Informationsprojeckt Naher undr Mittlerer Osten* 97(Spring): 21–32.

2019b. "The War in Yemen, Bottom-Up: Tribal Politics in Depth and in Motion," *British-Yemeni Society Journal* 27: 11–18.

BREHONY Noel, 2011. *Yemen Divided: The Story of a Failed State in South Arabia.* London: I.B. Tauris.

BREHONY Noel, LACKNER Helen, & AL-SARHAN Saud, 2015. "Introduction," in Noel BREHONY & Saud AL-SARHAN, eds. *Rebuilding Yemen. Political, Economic and Social Challenges.* Gottingen: Gerlach Press, 1–23.

BRENNAN Timothy, 2006. *Wars of Position. The Cultural Politics of Left and Right.* New York: Columbia University Press.

BROOKS Risa, 2016. "Subjecting the Military to the Rule of Law: The Tunisian Model," in Eva BELLIN & LANE Heidi, eds. *Building the Rule of Law in the Arab World.* Boulder CO: Lynne Rienner Publishers, 109–130.

BROWER Benjamin C., 2009. *A Desert Named Peace: The Violence of France's Empire in the Algerian Sahara, 1844–1902.* New York: Columbia University Press.

BROWERS Michaelle, 2007. "Origins and Architects of Yemen's Joint Meeting Parties," *International Journal of Middle East Studies* 39(4): 565–586.

BROWN Nathan, 2012. *When Victory Is Not an Option: Islamist Movements in Arab Politics.* Ithaca NY: Cornell University Press.

BROWNE Simone, 2015. *Dark Matters: On the Surveillance of Blackness.* Durham NC: Duke University Press.

BROWNLEE Jason, MASOUD Tarek, & REYNOLDS Andrew, 2015. *The Arab Spring: Pathways of Repression and Reforms.* Oxford: Oxford University Press.

BUDEIRI Musa, 2010. *The Palestine Communist Party 1919–1948: Arab and Jew in the Struggle for Internationalism.* Chicago IL: Haymarket.

BUJRA Abdalla S., 1971. *The Politics of Stratification: A Study of Political Change in a South Arabian Town.* Oxford: Clarendon Press.

BURGAT François, 1996. *L'Islamisme en face.* Paris: La Découverte.

BUTENSCHON Nils, DAVIS Uri, & HASSASSIAN Manuel, eds. 2000. *Citizenship and the State in the Middle East. Approaches and Applications.* Syracuse NY: Syracuse University Press.

CAMAU Michel, 1984. "L'Etat Tunisien: de la tutelle au désengagement. Portée et limite d'une trajectoire," *Monde Arabe Maghreb-Machrek* 103: 8–38.

CAMPOS Michelle, 2010. *Ottoman Brothers: Muslims, Christians, and Jews in Early Twentieth-Century Palestine.* Stanford CA: Stanford University Press.

CARAPICO Sheila, 1993. "Elections and Mass Politics in Yemen," *Middle East Report* 185(Winter), online.

1998. *Civil Society in Yemen: The Political Economy of Activism in Modern Arabia.* Cambridge: Cambridge University Press.

2013a. "Yemen," in Paul AMAR and V. PRASHAD, eds. *Dispatches from the Arab Spring.* Minneapolis MN: Minnesota University Press, 101–121.

2013b. *Political Aid and Arab Activism: Democracy Promotion, Justice, and Representation.* Cambridge: Cambridge University Press.

2014. "Seven Questions for Ammar Basha," *Middle East Report Online,* online.

CARNEVALE Alessia, 2016. "Shakespeare in Médenine," *Nawaat,* online.

CAROTHERS Thomas, 2002. "The End of the Transition Paradigm," *Journal of Democracy* 13(1): 5–21.

CASALE Giancarlo, 2010. *The Ottoman Age of Exploration.* Oxford: Oxford University Press.

CASSARINO Jean-Pierre, 2012. "Reversing the Hierarchy of Priorities in EU–Mediterranean Relations," in J. PETERS, ed. *The European Union and the Arab Spring.* Lanham MD: Lexington Books, 1–15.

CASTIGLIONI Luigi, 1996. *Vocabolario della lingua latina.* Turin: Loescher Editore.

CASTORIADIS Cornelius, 1976. "The Hungarian Source," *Telos* 26: 4–22.

CATON Steven, AL-ERYANI Hazim, & ARYANI Rayman, 2014. "Poetry of Protests: Tribes in Yemen's 'Change Revolution'," in Pnina WERBNER et al., eds. *The Political Aesthetics of Global Protest: The Arab Spring and Beyond.* Edinburgh: Edinburgh University, 121–142.

CHABANE Djamel, 2003. *La théorie du 'Umran chez Ibn Khaldoun.* Algiers: Office des Publications Universitaires.

CHALCRAFT John, 2016. *Popular Politics in the Making of the Modern Middle East.* Cambridge: Cambridge University Press.

CHALLAND Benoît, 2009. *Palestinian Civil Society: Foreign Donors and the Power to Promote and Exclude.* London: Routledge.

2011. "The Counter Power of Civil Society and the Emergence of a New Political Imaginary in the Arab World," *Constellations* 18(3): 271–283.

2013. "Against the Grain: Locating the Spirit of the Arab Uprisings in Times of Counter-Revolution," *Constellations* 20(2): 169–187.

2014. "Revisiting Aid in the Arab Middle East," *Mediterranean Politics* 19 (3): 281–298.

2015. "The Invisible Alienation of Tunisian Youth," *Middle East Report* 276(Fall): 30–31.

2017. "Citizenship and Violence in the Arab Worlds. A Historical Sketch," in J. MACKERT and B.S. TURNER, eds. *The Transformation of Citizenship: Struggle, Resistance, and Violence*, vol. 3. London & New York: Routledge, 93–112.

2020. "Current Legacies of Colonial Violence and Racialization in Tunisia," *Comparative Studies of South Asia, Africa and the Middle East* 40(2): 248–255.

forthcoming. "De-Centralization in Yemen: The Case of the Federalist Draft Constitution of 2015," in Asli BALI & Omar DAJANI, eds., *Decentralization in the Middle East*. Cambridge: Cambridge University Press.

CHARRAD Mounira, 2001. *States and Women's Rights: The Making of Postcolonial Tunisia, Algeria, and Morocco*. Los Angeles CA: University of California Press.

CHATTERJEE Partha, 1993. *The Nation and its Fragments: Colonial and Postcolonial Histories*. Princeton NJ: Princeton University Press.

CHEBBI Aya, 2016. "If the Revolution Is a Crime, then Charge All of Us," *New Eastern Politics*, blog, 3 December.

CHERIF Rached, 2013. "Affaire Chokri Belaid: aveux de plusieurs suspects," *Nawaat*, online.

CHIBBER Vivek, 2013. *Postcolonial Theory and the Specter of Capital*. London: Verso.

CHOMYAK Larissa, 2014. "Architecture of Resistance in Tunisia," in Lina KHATIB & Ellen LUST, eds. *Taking to the Streets: The Transformation of Arab Activism*. Baltimore MD: Johns Hopkins, 22–50.

CHOUIKHA Larbi & GOBE Eric, 2013. "La Tunisie en 2012: heurs et malheurs d'une transition qui n'en finit pas," *L'Année du Maghreb*, (IX), online.

2015. *Histoire de la Tunisie depuis l'indépendance*. Paris: La Découverte.

CHRISTIANSEN Connie & AL-THAWR Sabria, 2019. "*Muhamesheen* Activism: Enacting Citizenship during Yemen's Transition," *Citizenship Studies* 23(2): 115–138.

CLARK Janine, 2004. *Islam, Charity, and Activism: Middle-Class Networks and Social Welfare in Egypt, Jordan, and Yemen*. Bloomington IN: Indiana University Press.

CLARK Janine & CAVATORTA Francesco, 2018. *Political Science Research in the Middle East and North Africa: Methodological and Ethical Challenges.* Oxford: Oxford University Press.

CLARKE Victoria, 2010. *Yemen: Dancing on the Heads of Snakes.* New Haven CT: Yale University Press.

CLARNO Andy, 2017. *Neoliberal Apartheid. Palestine-Israel and South Africa after 1994.* Chicago IL: Chicago University Press.

CLAUSEN Maria-Louise, 2020. "Decentralization as a Strategy of Regime Maintenance: The Case of Yemen," *Public Admininistration and Development* 40: 119–128.

CLÉMENT Anne-Marie, 2012. Fallāḥīn *on Trial in Colonial Egypt: Apprehending the Peasantry through Orality, Writing, and Performance (1884–1914).* PhD Thesis, Near and Middle Eastern Civilizations, University of Toronto.

COLE Juan, 2006. "The Ayatollahs and Democracy in Iraq," *ISIM Paper*, Leiden, No. 7.

COOPER Fred, 2005. *Colonialism in Questions. Theory, Knowledge, History.* Los Angeles CA: University of California Press.

2014. *Africa in the World: Capitalism, Empire, Nation-State.* Cambridge MA: Harvard University Press.

COOPER Frederick & STOLER Ann L., 1997. *Tensions of Empire: Colonial Cultures in a Bourgeois World.* Berkeley CA: University of California Press.

COUTINHO Carlos N., 2012. *Gramsci's Political Thought.* Leiden: Brill.

CPT, 2014. "Critical Exchange: Debating Representative Democracy," *Contemporary Political Theory* 15: 205–242.

DABASHI Hamid, 2012. *The Arab Spring. The End of Postcolonialism.* London & New York: Zed Books.

DAHLGREN Susanne, 2010. "A Snake with a Thousand Heads: The Southern Cause in Yemen," *Middle East Report* 256(Fall), online.

2014a. "A Poor People's Revolution: The Southern Movement Heads Toward Independence from Yemen," *Middle East Report* 273 (Winter), online.

2014b. "Southern Yemen after the Fall of Sanaa," *Middle East Report Online*, online.

2015. "Four Weddings and a Funeral in Yemen," *Middle East Report Online*, online.

2018. "The STC Southern Transition Council and the War in Yemen," *Middle East Report Online*, online.

2019. "The Battle for South Yemen," *Middle East Report* 292(Fall/ Winter), online.

DAHMANI Frida, 2015. "Tunisie: le Mouvement du 18 octobre 2005, 10 ans après," *Jeune Afrique*, online.

DAKHLIA Jocelyne, 2016. "Peut-on penser dans la transition?," *Nachaz-Dissonances*, online.

DAOUD Abdelkarim, 2011. "La révolution tunisienne de janvier 2011: une lecture par les déséquilibres du territoires," *ÉchoGéo*, online.

DAVIS Uri, 1997. *Citizenship and the State: A Comparative Study of Citizenship Legislation in Israel, Jordan, Palestine, Syria and Lebanon*. Reading: Ithaca.

2000. "Conceptions of Citizenship in the Middle East," in Nils BUTENSCHON, Uri DAVIS, & Manuel HASSASSIAN, eds. *Citizenship and the State in the Middle East. Approaches and Applications*. Syracuse NY: Syracuse University Press, 49–69.

DAWISHA Adeed & ZARTMAN William, eds. 1988. *Beyond Coercion: The Durability of the Arab State*. London: Croom Helm.

DAY Stephen W., 2012. *Regionalism and Rebellion in Yemen. A Troubled National Union*. Cambridge: Cambridge University Press.

2015. "The Federal Plan in Yemen: History of an Idea and its Current Development," in Noel BREHONY & Saud AL-SARHAN, eds. *Rebuilding Yemen. Political, Economic and Social Challenges*. Berlin: Gerlach Press, 24–41.

DEGAGE, 2011. *Dégage. La révolution tunisienne. Livre-Témoignages*. Tunis: Alif & Editions du Layeur.

DELLA PORTA Donatella, 2014. *Mobilizing for Democracy. Comparing 1989 and 2011*. Oxford: Oxford University Press.

DÉPELTEAU François, ed. 2018. *The Palgrave Handbook of Relational Sociology*. London: Palgrave Macmillan.

DETALLE Renaud, 1994. "Pacte d'Amman: l'espoir déçu des Yéménites," *Monde Arabe Maghreb-Machrek* 145(July): 113–122.

DOBELLE Jean-François & FAVRE Jean-Michel, 1998. "Le différend entre l'Erythrée et le Yémen," *Annuaire Français de Droit International* 44: 337–355.

DORLIAN Samy, 2011. "The Sa'ada War in Yemen: Between Politics and Sectarianism," *The Muslim World* 101(2): 182–201.

2012. "L'enjeu identitaire de la guerre de Saada: 'confesssionalisation', stigmatisation, recompositions," in Laurent BONNEFOY, Marine POIRIER, and Franck MERMIER (eds). *Yémen, Le tournant révolutionnaire*. Paris: Karthala/CEFAS, 71–91.

2015. "Les partisans d'al-Hûthi au Yémen: de plutôt opprimés à plutôt oppresseurs," in Anna BOZZO & Pierre-Jean LUIZARD, eds. *Polarisations politiques et confessionnelles. La place de l'islam dans les "transitions" arabes*. Rome: Roma Tre Press, 61–76.

DOUMANI Beshara, 1995. *Rediscovering Palestine: Merchants and Peasants in Jabal Nablus, 1700–1900*. Berkeley CA: University of California Press.

DRESCH Paul, 2000. *A History of Modern Yemen.* Cambridge: Cambridge University Press.

EL-ISSAWI Fatima, 2012. "Tunisian Media in Transition," *Carnegie Endowment for International Peace,* online.

EL-MESSIRI Sawsan, 1978. *Ibn al-Balad: A Concept of Egyptian Identity.* Leiden: Brill.

EL-RAGGAL Aly, 2019. "The Egyptian Revolution's Fatal Mistake," *Middle East Report* 291(Summer), online.

ELIAS Norbert, 1939/2000. *The Civilizing Process. Sociogenetic and Psychogenetic Investigations.* London: Blackwell.

EMIRBAYER Mustafa, 1997. "Manifesto for a Relational Sociology," *American Journal of Sociology* 103(2): 281–312.

ESMEIR Samera, 2012. *The Work of Law in the Age of Empire: Production of Humanity in Colonial Egypt.* Stanford CA: Stanford University Press.

FAHMI Georges, 2020. "A New Wave of Arab Uprisings," *Rivista Idees,* online.

FANON Frantz, 1961/2004. *The Wretched of the Earth,* trans. R. Philcox. New York: Grove Press.

FEDERICI Silvia, 2004. *Caliban and the Witch: Women, the Body and Primitive Accumulation.* New York: Autonomedia.

FILIU Jean-Pierre, 2015. *From Deep State to Islamic State: The Arab Counter-Revolution and its Jihadi Legacy.* Oxford: Oxford University Press.

FINN Tom, 2015. "Yemen's Women Revolutionaries," *Dissent,* Winter, online.

FORMENT Carlos, 2003. *Democracy in Latin America, 1760–1900.* Chicago IL: Chicago University Press.

FOUCAULT Michel, 1977. *Discipline and Punish: The Birth of the Prison.* New York: Pantheon Books.

  2008. *Society Must Be Defended: Lectures at the Collége De France, 1975–76.* London: Penguin.

FRAIHAT, Ibrahim, 2016. *Unfinished Revolutions: Yemen, Libya, and Tunisia after the Arab Spring.* New Haven CT: Yale University Press.

FRISON-ROCHE François, 2015. "Transition et négociations au Yémen. Le rôle de l'ONU," *IFRI Working Paper,* online, October.

  2016. "Ce conflit n'est favorable à aucun pays de la région," *Al-Moudjahid,* October 19: 11.

FTDES, 2013. *"Ahdāth al-rash bi-Siliāna." Taqrir al-lajna al-mustaqila lil-tahqiq fi ahdāth Siliāna* ["Buckshot Events in Siliana." Report by the Commission of Inquiry about the Siliana Events]. Report by the Forum tunisien des droits économiques et sociaux (FTDES), Tunis.

FURNESS Mark, 2020. "'Donorship' and Strategic Policy-Making: Germany's Middle Eastern and North African Aid Programme since the Arab Uprisings," *Development Policy Review* 38: 70–90.

GANA Alia, 2012. "The Rural and Agricultural Roots of the Tunisian Revolution: When Food Security Matters," *International Journal of Sociology of Agriculture and Food* 19(2): 201–213.

2020. "Les usages sociaux de la justice transitionnelle en Tunisie: à qui profite le statut de 'région victime'?," in Eric GOBE, ed. *Justice et réconciliation dans le Maghreb post-révoltes arabes*. Paris: IRMC-Karthala, 123–139.

GANA Alia & SIGILLÒ Ester, 2019. "Les mobilisations contre le rapport sur les libertés individuelles et l'égalité (COLIBE)," *L'Année du Maghreb*, online.

GANA Alia & VAN HAMME Gilles, 2016. *Élections et territoires en Tunisie: enseignement des scrutins post-révolution (2011–2014)*. Paris: Karthala.

GANIAGE Jean, 1966. "La population de la Tunisie vers 1860. Essai d'évaluation d'après les registres fiscaux," *Population* 21(5): 857–886.

GELLNER Ernest, 1981. *Muslim Society*. Cambridge: Cambridge University Press.

1994. *Conditions of Liberty. Civil Society and its Rivals*. London: Hamish Hamilton.

GELVIN James, 2011. *The Modern Middle East. A History*. 3rd ed. Oxford: Oxford University Press.

GERVASIO Gennaro & MANDUCHI Patrizia, 2020. "Introduction: Reading the Revolutionary Process in North Africa with Gramsci," *Journal of North African Studies* 26(6): 1051–1056.

GETACHEW Adom, 2019. *Worldmaking after Empire: The Rise and Fall of Self-Determination*. Princeton NJ: Princeton University Press.

GHALIOUN Burhan, 1991. *Le malaise arabe. L'état contre la nation*. Algiers: ENAG Editions.

GHAZOUL Ferial, 1986. "The Metaphors of Historiography: A Study of Ibn Khaldun's Historical Imagination," in A.H. GREEN, ed. *In Quest of an Islamic Humanism*. Cairo: American University in Cairo Press, 48–61.

GHORBAL Samy, 2012. *Orphelins de Bourguiba et héritiers du Prophète*. Tunis: Cérès.

GIACAMAN George, 1998. "In the Throes of Oslo: Palestinian Society, Civil Society and the Future," in G. GIACAMAN & D.J. LØNNING, eds. *After Oslo. New Realities, Old Problems*. London: Pluto Press.

GIUGNI Marco, McADAM Doug, & TILLY Charles, 1998. *From Contention to Democracy*. Oxford: Rowman & Littlefield.

GLOSEMEYER Iris, 2015. "Dr Muhammad Abdulmalik al-Mutawakkil, 1942–2014," *INAMO, Informationsprojeckt Naher undr Mittlerer Osten* 83(Fall): 27.

GO Julian, 2012. *Patterns of Empire: The British and American Empires, 1688 to the Present.* Cambridge: Cambridge University Press.
2016. *Postcolonial Thought and Social Theory.* Oxford: Oxford University Press.
GO Julian & LAWSON George, eds. 2017. *Global Historical Sociology.* Cambridge: Cambridge University Press.
GOBE Eric, 2010. "The Gafsa Mining Basin between Riots and a Social Movement: Meaning and Significance of a Protest Movement in Ben Ali's Tunisia," *Hal Working Paper,* HAL Open Science (Humanities and Social Sciences).
2012. "Tunisie an I: les chantiers de la transition," *L'Année du Maghreb* VIII, online.
2018. "Chronologie Tunisie 2017," *L'Année du Maghreb* 19, online.
2019. "Chronologie Tunisie 2018," *L'Année du Maghreb* 21, online.
2020. "Tunisie 2019: chronique d'une surprise électorale annoncée," *L'Année du Maghreb* 23, online.
GOBE Eric & CHOUIKHA Larbi, 2014. "La Tunisie politique en 2013: de la bipolarisation idéologique au 'consensus constitutionnel'?," *L'Année du Maghreb* 11, online.
GOBE Eric & SALAYMEH Lena, 2016. "Tunisia's 'Revolutionary' Lawyers: From Professional Autonomy to Political Mobilization," *Law & Social Inquiry* 41(2): 311–345.
GORDON Sasha, 2012. "Yemen's Parallel Revolution," *Critical Threats,* online.
GOUDSBLOM Johan, 2003. "Christian Religion and the European Civilising Process: The Views of Norbert Elias and Max Weber Compared," *Irish Journal of Sociology* 12(1): 24–38.
GRABUNDZIJA Maggy, 2015. *Yémen. Morceaux choisis d'une révolution, mars 2011–février 2012.* Paris: L'Harmattan.
GRAMSCI Antonio, 1952. *Scritti Giovannili 1914–1918.* Turin: Einaudi.
1971. *Selections form the Prison Notebooks,* ed. and trans. by Quintin Hoare and G.N. Smith. London: Lawrence & Wishart.
GRANDIN Greg, 2010. *Fordlandia: The Rise and Fall of Henry Ford's Forgotten Jungle City.* New York: Picador.
GREWAL Sharan, 2019. "Military Defection during Localized Protests: The Case of Tataouine," *International Studies Quarterly* 63(2): 259–269.
GRÖNDAHL Mia, 2012. *Revolution Graffiti: Street Art of the New Egypt.* Cairo: Arab University in Cairo Press.
GUAZZONE Laura & PIOPPI Daniela, eds. 2009. *The Arab State and Neo-Liberal Globalization: The Restructuring of State Power in the Middle East.* Reading: Ithaca Press.

GUIRGUIS Laure, ed. 2021. *The Arab Lefts: Histories and Legacies, 1950s–1970s*. Edinburgh: Edinburgh University Press.

HABIB Irfan, 2005. "Critical Notes on Edward Said," *International Socialism: A Quarterly Journal of Socialist Theory* 2: 108–130.

HAIRI Abdul-Hadi, 1976. "Why did the 'Ulama' Participate in the Persian Constitutional Revolution of 1905–1909?," *Die Welt des Islams* 17: 127–154.

HAJJAR Lisa, 2005. *Military Courts Courting Conflict. The Israeli Military Court System in the West Bank and Gaza*. Los Angeles CA: University of California Press.

HAJJI Lutfi, 2006. "The 18 October Coalition for Rights and Freedoms in Tunisia," *Arab Reform Initiative*, Brief No. 13.

HALEH DAVIS Muriam & SERRES Thomas, eds. 2018. *North Africa and the Making of Europe: Governance, Institutions and Culture*. London: Bloomsbury Academics.

HALL Bogumila, 2017. "'This Is Our Homeland': Yemen's Marginalized and the Quest for Rights and Recognition," *Arabian Humanities* 9, online.

HALL Stuart, 1980. "Cultural Studies: Two Paradigms," *Media, Culture & Society* 2(1): 57–72.

   2016. *Cultural Studies 1983. A Theoretical History*. Durham NC: Duke University Press.

HALPERIN Sandra, 2005. "The Post-Cold War Political Topography of the Middle East: Prospects for Democracy," *Third World Quarterly* 26(7): 1135–1156.

HAMZA Aref, 2018. *Du bist nicht allein*. Berlin: Secession Verlag.

HANAFI Sari, 2011. "Les quatre leçons de la révolution tunisienne pour le monde arabe," *Rue89*, online.

HANAFI Sari & TABAR Linda, 2003. "The Intifada and the Aid Industry: The Impact of the New Liberal Agenda and the Palestinian NGOs," *Comparative Studies of South Asia, Africa, and the Middle East* 23 (1&2): 205–214.

HANEY LOPEZ Ian, 2006. *White by Law: The Legal Construction of Race*. New York: New York University Press.

HANIEH Adam, 2013. *Lineages of Revolt*. London: Haymarket.

HANLON Querine, 2016. "Dismantling the Security Apparatus: Challenges of the Police Reform in Tunisia," in Eva BELLIN & Heidi LANE, eds. *Building the Rule of Law in the Arab World*. Boulder CO: Lynne Rienner, 189–214.

HANNOUM Abdelmajid, 2010. *Violent Modernity. France in Algeria*. Cambridge MA: Harvard University Press.

HANSSEN Jens, 2019. "Review of *Restating Orientalism: A Critique of Modern Knowledge*. By Wael Hallaq," *Bulletin of the School of Oriental and African Studies* 82(1): 183–185.

HANSSEN Jens & WEISS Max, eds. 2018. *Arabic Thought against the Authoritarian Age: Towards an Intellectual History of the Present*. New York: Cambridge University Press.

HARDT Michael & NEGRI Antonio, 2013. *Déclaration: ceci n'est pas un manifeste*. Paris: Raisons d'Agir.

HARIK Ilya, 2006. "Democracy, 'Arab Exceptionalism', and Social Science," *Middle East Journal* 60(4): 664–684.

HARTSHORN Ian, 2019. *Labor Politics in North Africa after the Uprisings in Egypt and Tunisia*. Cambridge: Cambridge University Press.

HEARST David & ULLAH Areeb, 2021. "Top Secret Tunisian Presidential Document Outlines Plan for 'Constitutional Dictatorship'," *Middle East Eye*, online.

HEINZE Marie-Christine, 2015. "Krieg in Jemen: Fronten, Akteure, Ausblick," *INAMO, Informationsprojeckt Naher undr Mittlerer Osten* 83(Fall): 4–10.

ed. 2018. *Yemen and the Search for Stability. Power, Politics, and Society after the Arab Spring*. London: I.B. Tauris.

HERBERT Matt, 2018. "The Insurgency in Tunisia's Western Borderlands," *Carnegie Endowment for International Peace*, online.

HERRERA Linda & BAYAT Asef, 2010. *Being Young and Muslim: New Cultural Politics in the Global South and North*. New York: Oxford University Press.

HEVER Shir, 2018. *Privatisation of Israeli Security*. London: Pluto Press.

HEYDEMANN Steven, ed. 2000. *War, Institutions and Social Change in the Middle East*. Berkeley CA: University of California Press.

2015. "Explaining the Arab Uprisings: Transformations in Comparative Perspective," *Mediterranean Politics* 21(1): 1–13.

HIBOU Béatrice, ed. 2004. *Privatizing the State*. New York: Columbia University Press.

2011. *The Force of Obedience. The Political Economy of Repression in Tunisia*. Cambridge: Polity.

2015. "La formation asymétrique de l'État en Tunisie. Les territoires de l'injustice," in Irene BONO et al., eds. *L'Etat d'injustice au Maghreb. Maroc et Tunisie*. Paris: Karthala, 99–149.

HILAL Jamil & HERMANN Katja, eds. 2014. *Mapping of the Arab Left. Contemporary Leftist Politics in the Arab East*. Ramallah: Rosa Luxemburg Stiftung.

HINDS David, 2012. "Caribbean Great, CLR James," *CaribNation*, video available at www.youtube.com/watch?v=i2N0Y-1ZWJw.

HMED Choukri, 2012. "Abeyance Networks, Contingency and Structures: History and Origins of the Tunisian Revolution," *Revue française de science politique* 62(5–6): 31–53.

2015. "Répression d'État et situation révolutionnaire en Tunisie (2010–2011)," *Vingtième Siècle* 128(4): 77–90.

2016a. "'Le peuple veut la chute du régime.' Situations et issues révolutionnaires lors des occupations de la place de la Kasbah à Tunis, 2011," *Actes de la Recherche en Sciences Sociales* 211–212: 72–91.

2016b. "Au-delà de l'exception tunisienne: les failles et les risques du processus révolutionnaire," *Pouvoirs* 156: 137–147.

HOBSBAWM Eric J., 1996. *The Age of Revolution: 1789–1848*. New York: Vintage Books.

HONVAULT Juliette, 2012. "La fin des années 2000: le tournant ottoman de l'historiographie yéménite," in Laurent BONNEFOY, Marine POIRIER, and Franck MERMIER, eds. *Yémen, Le tournant révolutionnaire*. Paris: Karthala / CEFAS, 275–278.

HORKHEIMER Max, 1937/1972. "Traditional and Critical Theory," in *Critical Theory: Selected Essays*, trans. Matthew O'Connell et al. New York: Herder and Herder, 188–243.

HUME Leslie, 2016. *The National Union of Women's Suffrage Societies 1897–1914*. Abingdon: Routledge.

HUNTINGTON Samuel P., 1968. *Political Order in Changing Societies*. New Haven CT: Yale University Press.

IA, 2018. *Voice of Kasserine*, Dir. O. Lamloum & M. Tabet, Documentary by International Alert [IA], Tunis.

IBN KHALDUN, 2005 [1402]. *The Muqqadimah. An Introduction to History*, trans. Franz Rosenthal. Princeton NJ: Princeton University Press.

ICG, 2011. *Popular Protest in North Africa and the Middle East (IV): Tunisia's Way*, International Crisis Group, Middle East/North Africa Report No. 106.

2012. *Tunisie: relever les défis économiques et sociaux*, International Crisis Group, Middle East/North Africa Report No. 124.

2013a. *Yemen's Military-Security Reform: Seeds of New Conflict?*, International Crisis Group, Middle East/North Africa Report No. 139.

2013b. *Tunisia: Violence and the Salafi Challenge*, International Crisis Group, Middle East/North Africa Report No. 137.

2015. *Reform and Security Strategy in Tunisia*, International Crisis Group, Middle East/North Africa Report No. 161.

2016. *Tunisie: justice transitionnelle et lutte contre la corruption*, International Crisis Group, Middle East/North Africa Report No. 68.

2017. *Yemen's al-Qaeda: Expanding the Base*, International Crisis Group, Middle East Report No. 174.

2019. *Décentralisation en Tunisie: consolider la démocratie sans affaiblir l'Etat*, Middle East/North Africa Report No. 198.

IKEGAMI Eiko, 2005. *Bonds of Civility: Aesthetic Networks and the Political Origins of Japanese Culture*. Cambridge: Cambridge University Press.

IL MANIFESTO, 2021. "Basta armi ai Sauditi. Centomila morti dopo l'Italia applica la legge" [Stop to arms for the Saudis. After 100,000 dead, Italy applies the law," *il manifesto*, January 30: 4–5.

ISIN Engin & NIELSEN Greg M., eds. 2008. *Acts of Citizenship*. London: Zed Books.

ISMAIL Salwa, 2006. *Political Life in Cairo's Quarters. Encountering the Everyday State*. Minneapolis MN: Minnesota University Press.

2007. "Islamism, Re-Islamization and the Fashioning of Muslim Selves: Refiguring the Public Sphere," *Muslim World Journal of Human Rights* 4(1): 1–21.

2011. "Civilities, Subjectivities and Collective Action: Preliminary Reflections in Light of the Egyptian Revolution," *Third World Quarterly* 32(5): 989–995.

JAKES Aaron, 2020. *Egypt's Occupation. Colonial Economism and the Crises of Capitalism*. Stanford CA: Stanford University Press.

JAMAL Ammar, 2021. "Thousands of Mockingbirds," *Africa Is a Country*, blog, online.

JAMAL Manal, 2019. *Promoting Democracy. The Force of Political Settlements in Uncertain Times*. New York: New York University Press.

JAMAL Sara, 2020. "Une nuit de Aïd au Yémen: ma famille est morte mais la colère m'a sauvé la vie," trans. Franck Mermier, *Arabian Humanities* (13), online.

JAMES C.L.R., 1932/2014. *The Life of Captain Cipriani*. Raleigh NC: Duke University Press Books.

1963. *Black Jacobins. Toussaint L'Ouverture and the San Domingo Revolutions*. New York: Vintage.

JEBNOUN Noureddine, 2014. "In the Shadow of Power: Civil-Military Relations and the Tunisian Popular Uprising," *The Journal of North African Studies* 19(3): 296–316.

JOAS Hans & KNÖBL Wolfgang, 2013. *War in Social Thought. Hobbes to the Present*. Princeton NJ: Princeton University Press.

JOHNSTON Hank, 1995. "A Methodology for Frame Analysis: From Discourse to Cognitive Schema," in Hank JOHNSTON & Bert KLANDERMANS, eds. *Social Movement and Culture*. Minneapolis MN: Minnesota University Press, 217–244.

JOSEPH Suad, 2000. _Gender and Citizenship in the Middle East._ Syracuse NY: Syracuse University Press.

KALYVAS Andreas, 2008. _Democracy and the Politics of the Extraordinary Max Weber, Carl Schmitt, and Hannah Arendt._ Cambridge: Cambridge University Press.

KARTAS Moncef, 2012. "The Tunisian Popular Uprising and Rising Insecurity – A Historical Perspective on the Pathologies of the Tunisian Armed and Security Forces," unpublished conference paper, ISA, San Diego, April.

2014. "Foreign Aid and Security Sector Reform in Tunisia: Resistance and Autonomy of the Security Forces," _Mediterranean Politics_ 19(3): 373–391.

2016. "The Tunisian–Libyan Border Space of the Jefara: Informality as Resistance to Post-Colonial State Formation," unpublished paper, presented at Yale, Middle East Law State and Society.

KATEB Kamel, 2001. _Européens, "indigènes" et juifs en Algérie (1830–1962)._ Paris: Presses Universitaires de France.

KEDDIE Nikki R., 1991. "Obstacles to Early Industrialization in the Middle East," in Jean BATOU, ed. _Between Development and Underdevelopment: The Precocious Attempts at Industrialization of the Periphery, 1800–1870._ Geneva: Librairie Droz, 143–156.

KENDALL Elisabeth, 2018. "The Mobiization of Yemen's Eastern Tribes: Al-Mahra's Self-Organization Model," in Marie-Christine HEINZE, ed. _Yemen and the Search for Stability. Power, Politics, and Society after the Arab Spring._ London: I.B. Tauris, 71–92.

KHALID Maryam, 2015. "The Peripheries of Gender and Sexuality in the 'Arab Spring'," _Mediterranean Politics_ 20(2): 161–177.

KHALILI Laleh, 2013. _Time in the Shadows. Confinement in Counterinsurgencies._ Stanford CA: Stanford University Press.

KHERIGI Intisar, forthcoming. "Decentralization Reforms in Post-Revolution Tunisia: The Struggle between Political and Bureaucratic Elites," in Asli BALI & Omar DAJANI, eds. _Decentralization in the Middle East._ Cambridge: Cambridge University Press.

KHIARI Sadri, 2003. _Tunisie, le délitement de la cité. Coercition, consentement, résistance._ Paris: Karthala.

2016. "Jemna, dernière lueur de la révolution?," _Nawaat_, online.

KHOSROKHAVAR Farhad, 2012. _The New Arab Revolutions that Shook the World._ Boulder CO: Paradigm Publishers.

KHURI-MAKDISI Ilham, 2010. _The Eastern Mediterranean and the Making of Global Radicalism, 1860–1914._ Berkeley & Los Angeles CA: University of California Press.

KIENLE Eberhard, 2001. _A Grand Delusion. Democracy and Economic Reform in Egypt._ London: I.B. Tauris.

KILANI Mondher, 2014. *Tunisie, carnets d'une révolution*. Paris: Editions Pétra.

KRAIS Jacob, 2021. "Internationalist Nationalism: Making Algeria at World Youth Festivals, 1947–62," in Laure GUIRGUIS, ed. *The Arab Lefts. Histories and Legacies, 1950s–1970s*. Edinburgh: Edinburgh University Press, 110–126.

KRICHEN Aziz, 2016. *La promesse du printemps*. Tunis: Script Editions.

KÜHN Thomas, 2007. "Shaping and Reshaping Colonial Ottomanism: Contesting Boundaries of Difference and Integration in Ottoman Yemen, 1872–1919," *Comparative Studies of South Asia, Africa and the Middle East* 27(2): 315–331.

2011. *Empire, Islam, and Politics of Difference: Ottoman Rule in Yemen, 1849–1919*. Leiden: Brill.

KURZMAN Charles, ed. 2002. *Modernist Islam, 1840–1940: A Source-Book*. New York: Oxford University Press.

2005. *The Unthinkable Revolution in Iran*. Cambridge MA: Harvard University Press.

KUSCHNITZKI Judit, 2018. "A Party for Salafis? The Building of *al-Rashad* in Yemen's Transition Period," in Marie-Christine HEINZE, ed. *Yemen and the Search for Stability. Power, Politics, and Society after the Arab Spring*. London: I.B. Tauris, 204–227.

LA PRESSE, 2018. "La Constitution, An IV, Tunis," Special section of the daily *La Presse*, January 27.

2021. "Justice Transitionnelle: un bilan mi-figue, mi-raisin," *La Presse*, online.

LACKNER Helen, 1985. *PDR Yemen. Outpost of Socialist Development in Arabia*. London: Ithaca Press.

2016a. "The Change Squares in Yemen. Civil Resistance in an Unlikely Context," in Adam ROBERTS et al., eds. *Civil Resistance in the Arab Spring. Triumphs and Disasters*. Oxford: Oxford University Press, 141–168.

2016b. "Yemen's 'Peaceful' Transition from Autocracy: Could it Have Succeeded?," IDEA, International Institute for Democracy and Electoral Assistance, Stockholm.

2019. *Yemen in Crisis. The Road to War*. London: Verso.

LACORE Michelle, 2013. "Corps des citoyens, corps de la cite," *Kentron. Revue Disciplinaire du Monde Antique* 19: 143–148.

LACQUANITI Luce, 2015. *I Muri di Tunisi. Segni di Rivolta*. Rome: Exorma.

LAIQ Nur, 2013. *Talking to Arab Youth: Revolution and Counterrevolution in Egypt and Tunisia*. New York: IPI Books.

LAMLOUM Olfa & BEN ZINA Mohamed, 2015. *Jeunes de Douar Hicher et d'Ettadhamen: une enquête sociologique*. Tunis: Arabesques/International Alert.

LANDINI Tatiana S. & DÉPELTEAU François, eds. 2017. *Norbert Elias and Violence*. London: Palgrave Macmillan.

LAROUI [AL-'ARAWI] Abdallah, 1981. *Mafhūm al-Dawla* [The Concept of the State]. Casablanca: Al-Markaz Al-Thaqāfī Al-Arabī.

LAROUI Abdallah, 1982. *L'histoire du Maghreb: un essai de synthèse*. Paris: La Découverte.

LAWSON George, 2016. "Within and Beyond the 'Fourth Generation' of Revolutionary Theory," *Sociological Theory* 34(2): 106–127.

LEACH Darcy K., 2005. "The Iron Law of What Again? Conceptualizing Oligarchy across Organizational Forms," *Sociological Theory* 23(3): 312–337.

2009. "An Elusive 'We'. Antidogmatism, Democratic Practice, and the Contradictory Identity of the German *Autonomen*," *American Behavioral Scientist* 52(7): 1042–1068.

2013. "Prefigurative Politics," in David A. SNOW et al., eds. *The Blackwell Encyclopedia of Social and Political Movements*. Oxford: Wiley-Blackwell Press.

LIEVENS Matthias, 2014. "Contesting Representation: Rancière on Democracy and Representative Government," *Thesis Eleven* 122(1): 3–17.

LINZ Juan J. & STEPAN Alfred, 1996. *Problems of Democratic Transition and Consolidation: Southern Europe, South America, and Post-Communist Europe*. Baltimore MD: Johns Hopkins University Press.

LLOYD David, 1999. *Ireland after History*. Cork: Cork University Press.

LOCKMAN Zachary, 1996. *Comrades and Enemies. Arab and Jewish Workers in Palestine, 1906–1948*. Berkeley CA: University of California Press.

LOKDAM Hjalte, 2019. "A Living Constituent Power and Law as a Guideline in Walter Benjamin's 'Critique of Violence'," *Constellations* 26: 208–224.

LÜTHI Barbara, FALK Francesca, & PURTSCHERT Patricia, 2016. "Colonialism without Colonies: Examining Blank Spaces in Colonial Studies," *National Identities* 18(1): 1–9.

McADAM Doug & TARROW Sydney, 2000. "Nonviolence as Contentious Interaction," *PS: Political Science and Politics* 33(2): 149–154.

MAECKELBERGH Arianne, 2011. "Doing Is Believing: Prefiguration as Strategic Practice in the Alterglobalization Movement," *Social Movement Studies* 10(1): 1–20.

MAHMOUD Ines, 2020. "A Peasant Struggle for Land in Jemna," in Fredson GUILENGUE, ed. *Action Matters. Six Success Stories of Struggles for Commons in Africa*. Berlin: Rosa Luxemburg Stiftung, 14–20.

MAJDOUB Sarra, 2019a. "Frankenstein's Monster in Khartoum," *Africa Is a Country*, blog, online.

2019b. "Ghost Battalion," *Africa Is a Country*, blog, online.

MAKDISI Ussama, 2000. *The Culture of Sectarianism: Community, History, and Violence in Nineteenth-Century Ottoman Lebanon.* Berkeley CA: University of California Press.

2009. *Artillery of Heaven: American Missionaries and the Failed Conversion of the Middle East.* Ithaca NY: Cornell University Press.

MALLAT Chibli & MORTIMER Edward, 2016. "The Background to Civil Resistance in the Middle East," in Adam ROBERTS et al. eds. *Civil Resistance in the Arab Spring. Triumphs and Disasters.* Oxford: Oxford University Press, 1–29.

MANN Michael, 1986. *The Sources of Social Power. Volume 1: A History of Power from the Beginning to AD 1760.* Cambridge: Cambridge University Press.

MARCHETTI Raffaele & TOCCI Nathalie, eds. 2011. *Conflict Society and Peacebuilding: Comparative Perspectives.* New Delhi: Routledge.

MARSHALL Thomas H., 1941/1992. "Citizenship and Social Class," in Thomas H. MARSHALL & Tom BOTTOMORE, *Citizenship and Social Class.* London: Pluto Press, 3–17.

MARX Karl & ENGELS Friedrich, 1950. *Selected Works*, Vol. I. Moscow: Foreign Languages Pub. House.

MARZOUKI Nadia, 2011a. "Tunisia's Wall Has Fallen," *Middle East Report*, online.

2011b. "The Call for Dignity, or a Particular Universalism," *Middle East Law and Governance* 3(1–2): 148–158.

2015. "Tunisia's Rotten Compromise," *Middle East Report*, online.

MASSAD Joseph, 2001. *Colonial Effects. The Making of National Identity in Jordan.* New York: Columbia University Press.

MASUD M. Khaled, 2005. "The Construction and Deconstruction of Secularism as an Ideology," *Asian Journal of Social Science* 33(3): 363–383.

MATTHIESEN Toby, 2013. *Sectarian Gulf: Bahrain, Saudi Arabia, and the Arab Spring That Wasn't.* Stanford CA: Stanford University Press.

MATTONI Alice, 2015. "The Potentials of Grounded Theory in the Study of Social Movements," in Donatella DELLA PORTA, ed. *Methodological Practices in Social Movement Research.* Oxford: Oxford University Press, 21–42.

MAWBY Spencer, 2005. *British Policy in Aden and the Protectorates 1955–67: Last Outpost of a Middle East Empire.* Abingdon: Routledge.

MBEMBE Achille, 2003. "Necropolitics," *Public Culture* 15(1): 11–40.

2006. "On the Postcolony: A Brief Response to Critics," *African Identities* 4(2): 143–178.

MEDDEB Hamza, 2015a. "Rente frontalière et injustice sociale en Tunisie," in Irene BONO et al., eds. *L'Etat d'injustice au Maghreb. Maroc et Tunisie.* Paris: Ed. Karthala, 63–98.

2015b. "Conscription Reform Will Shape Tunisia's Future Civil–Military Relations," *Carnegie Endowment for International Peace,* online.

2015c. "L'attente comme mode de gouvernement," in Irene BONO et al., eds. *L'Etat d'injustice au Maghreb. Maroc et Tunisie.* Paris: Karthala, 345–377.

2020. "Tunisia's Geography of Anger: Regional Inequalities and the Rise of Populism," *Carnegie Endowment for International Peace,* online.

MEDIEN Kathryn, 2019a. "Foucault in Tunisia: The Encounter with Intolerable Power," *The Sociological Review* 68: 1–16.

2019b. "Palestine in Deleuze," *Theory, Culture & Society,* 36(5): 49–70.

MEIJER Roel, 2014. "Political Citizenship and Social Movements in the Arab World," in H.-A. VAN DER HEIJDEN, ed. *Handbook of Political Citizenship and Social Movements.* Cheltenham: Elgar Publisher, 628–660.

MELUCCI Alberto, 1995. "The Process of Collective Identity," in Hank JOHNSTON & Bert KLANDERMANS, eds. *Social Movement and Culture.* Minneapolis MN: Minnesota University Press, 41–63.

MELVIN Neil, 2019. "The Foreign Military Presence in the Horn of Africa Region," *SIPRI Occasional Paper,* online.

MEMMI Albert, 1956. *Portrait du Colonisé.* Paris: Buchet & Chastel.

1957/1965. *The Colonizer and the Colonized.* New York: Orion Press.

MERMIER Franck, 2012. "Le mouvement sudiste," in Laurent BONNEFOY, Marine POIRIER, and Franck MERMIER, eds. *Yémen, Le tournant révolutionnaire.* Paris: Karthala / CEFAS, 41–65.

2020. "Yémen. Ecrire la guerre. Littérature yéménite contemporaine," *Arabian Humanities* 13, online.

MERONE Fabio, 2015. "Enduring Class Struggle in Tunisia: The Fight for Identity beyond Political Islam," *British Journal of Middle Eastern Studies* 42(1): 74–87.

2016. "Between Social Contention and Takfirism: The Evolution of the Salafi-Jihadi Movement in Tunisia," *Mediterranean Politics* 22(1): 1–20.

2021. "Analysing Revolutionary Islamism: Ansar al-Sharia Tunisia according to Gramsci," *Journal of North African Studies* 26(6): 1122–1143.

MERONE Fabio & CAVATORTA Francesco, 2012. "The Emergence of Salafism in Tunisia," *Jadaliyya,* online.

MERONE Fabio, SIGILLÒ Ester, & De FACCI Damiano, 2018. "Nahda and Tunisian Islamic Activism," in Dara CONDUIT & Shahram

AKBARZADEH, eds. *New Opposition in the Middle East*. Singapore: Palgrave Macmillan, 177–201.

MESSICK Brinkley, 1993. *The Calligraphic State: Textual Domination and History in a Muslim Society*. Berkeley CA: University of California Press.

MIES Maria, 1987. *Patriarchy and Accumulation on a World Scale*. London: Zed Press.

MILLS Charles W., 1997. *The Racial Contract*. Ithaca NY: Cornell University Press.

MITCHELL Timothy, 1988. *Colonizing Egypt*. Berkeley CA: University of California Press.

1999. "No Factories, No Problems: The Logic of Neo-Liberalism in Egypt," *Review of African Political Economy* 26(82): 455–468.

MOORE Barrington, 1969. *Social Origins of Dictatorship and Democracy: Lord and Peasant in the Making of the Modern World*. Harmondsworth: Penguin Books.

MOORE Jason, 2016. *Capitalism in the Web of Life: Ecology and the Accumulation of Capital*. London: Verso Books.

MOORE Pete, 2005. "QIZs, FTAs, USAID and the MEFTA: A Political Economy of Acronyms," *Middle Eastern Report* 234: 18–23.

MORREALL John, 2002. "The Justifiability of Violent Civil Disobedience," in Hugo Adam BEDAU, ed. *Civil Disobedience in Focus*. London: Routledge, 130–143.

MOUILLEAU Élisabeth, 2000. *Fonctionnaires de la République et artisans de l'empire: le cas des Contrôleurs Civils en Tunisie (1881–1956)*. Paris: Karthala.

MUKERJI Chandra, 2007. "Cultural Genealogy: Method for a Historical Sociology of Culture or Cultural Sociology of History," *Cultural Sociology* 1(1): 50–67.

MULLIN Corinna, 2018. "Securitizing Resistance in Gafsa: Stratified Vulnerability and Surplus Labor Accumulation," *CUNY Graduate Center*, blog of the Center for the Humanities Programming, online.

MURPHY Emma, 1999. *Economic and Political Change in Tunisia: From Bourguiba to Ben Ali*. London: Macmillan.

MWATANA, 2020. "'In the Darkness': Abusive Detention, Disappearance and Torture in Yemen's Unofficial Prisons," *Mwatana for Human Rights*, report, online.

NAGUIB Rim, 2020. "The Leader as Groom, the Nation as Bride. Patriarchal Nationalism under Nasser and Sisi," *META* 14: 40–55.

NANDY Ashis, 1983. *The Intimate Enemy. Loss and Recovery of Self under Colonialism*. Oxford: Oxford University Press.

NAWAAT, 2013. "Le rapport accablant de la Commission du 4 décembre contre les LPR," *Nawaat*, online.

NEWMAN Saul, 2015. _Postanarchism_. London: Polity Press.

NORTHEY Jessica, 2021. "The Algerian _hirak_. Citizenship, Non-Violence, and the New Movement for Democracy," in Jürgen MACKERT et al., eds. _The Condition of Democracy. Vol. 3: Postcolonial and Settler Colonial_. London: Routledge, 17–32.

ODONE Maisie, 2019. "Jemna's Collective Land Association Looks to New President with Hope," _Meshkal_, blog, online.

OMAR Hussein A.H., 2019. "The Arab Spring of 1919," _London Review of Books_, blog, online.

OMRI Mohamed-Salah, 2016. _Confluency (Tarafud) between Trade Unionism, Culture and Revolution in Tunisia_. Tunis: SOTEPA-GRAPHIC.

OULD MOHAMEDOU Mohammad-Mahmoud & SISK Timothy, eds. 2016. _Democratisation in the 21st Century: Reviving Transitology_. Abingdon: Routledge.

OTTAWAY David B., 2017. _The Arab World Upended. Revolution and its Aftermath in Tunisia and Egypt_. Boulder CO: Lynne Rienner.

PAPPÉ Illan, 2011. _The Forgotten Palestinians. A History of the Palestinians in Israel_. New Haven CT: Yale University Press.

PAROLIN Gianluca P., 2018. "Al-Ṭahṭāwī 'Translating' the 1814 French Charter. Crafting a New Semiotics of Law and Governance in 19th Century Egypt," unpublished paper, ONATI conference on Sociology of Law, May 24–25.

PATEMAN Carole, 1988. _The Sexual Contract_. Oxford: Polity Press.

PEDULLÀ Gabriele, 2018. _Machiavelli in Tumult: The Discourses on Livy and the Origins of Political Conflictualism_. Cambridge: Cambridge University Press.

PERKINS Kenneth, 2014. _A History of Modern Tunisia_. 2nd ed. New York: Cambridge University Press.

PESTELLI Carlo, 2016. _Bella ciao. La canzone della libertà_. Turin: ADD Editore.

PEUTZ Nathalie, 2012. "Revolution in Socotra. A Perspective from Yemen's Periphery," _Middle East Report_ 263(Summer), online.

2018. _Islands of Heritage: Conservation and Transformation in Yemen_. Stanford CA: Stanford University Press.

PFEIFER Helen, 2020. "The Gulper and the Slurper: A Lexicon of Mistakes to Avoid while Eating with Ottoman Gentlemen," _Journal of Early Modern History_ 24(1): 41–62.

PIGENET Michel & TARTAKOWSKY Danielle, eds. 2014. _Histoire des mouvements sociaux en France_. Paris: La Découverte.

PITKIN Hanna F. 1967. _The Concept of Representation_. Berkeley CA: University of California Press.

PITTS Jennifer, 2000. "Empire and Democracy: Tocqueville and the Algeria Question," *Journal of Political Philosophy* 8(3): 295–318.

PLANEL Vincent, 2012. "Le réveil des piémonts: Taez et la révolution yéménite," in Laurent BONNEFOY et al., eds. *Yémen, Le tournant revolutionnaire*. Paris: Karthala / CEFAS, 125–148.

POGGI Gianfranco, 1990. *The State: Its Nature, Development, and Prospects*. Stanford CA: Stanford University Press.

POIRIER Marine, 2020. "Les charmes du cheikh. Construire et défendre sa notabilité au Yémen (2009–2019)," *Critique Internationale* 87(2): 175–198.

POLANYI Karl, 1944/2001. *The Great Transformation. The Political and Economic Origins of Our Time*. Boston MA: Beacon Press.

POMERANZ Kenneth, 2000. *The Great Divergence. China, Europe, and the Making of the Modern World Economy*. Princeton NJ: Princeton University Press.

PORTER Ross, 2016. "Tricking Time, Overthrowing a Regime. Reining in the Future in the Yemeni Youth Revolution," *Cambridge Journal of Anthropology* 34(1): 58–71.

2017. "Freedom, Power and the Crisis of Politics in Revolutionary Yemen," *Middle East Critique* 26(3): 265–281.

2020. "Security against the State in Revolutionary Yemen," *Cultural Anthropology* 35(2): 204–210.

PORTER Hannah, 2020. "A Battle of Hearts and Minds: The Growing Media Footprint of Yemen's Houthis," *Gulf International Forum*, online.

QUIJANO Anibal, 2014. *Cuestiones y horizontes de la dependencia histórico-estructural a la colonialidad/descolonialidad del poder*. Buenos Aires: CLACSO.

RADL Sascha, 2019. "Den Krieg kontaktualisieren: Wirtschaft & Politik 1970–2000," *INAMO, Informationsprojeckt Naher und Mittlerer Osten* 97: 17–20.

RAMADAN Dina, 2013. *The Aesthetics of the Modern: Art, Education, and Taste in Egypt 1903–1952*. PhD Thesis, Middle Eastern, South Asian, and African Studies, Columbia University.

RAMSAY Gail, 2017. *Blogs & Literature & Activism: Popular Egyptian Blogs and Literature in Touch*. Wiesbaden: Harrassowitz Verlag.

RANCIÈRE Jacques, 2006. "Democracy, Representation and Representation," *Constellations* 13(3): 297–307.

2012. *Proletarian Nights. The Workers' Dream in Nineteenth-Century France*. London: Verso.

REISS Tom, 2012. *The Black Count. Glory, Revolution, Betrayal and the Real Count of Monte Cristo*. New York: Broadway Books.

RICHARDSON Michael, 1990. "Enough Said: Reflections on Orientalism," *Anthropology Today* 6(4): 16–19.

ROBERTS Adam et al., eds. 2016. *Civil Resistance in the Arab Spring. Triumphs and Disasters.* Oxford: Oxford University Press.

RODINSON Maxime, 1973. *Israel. A Colonial-Settler State?* New York: Monad Press.

　1987. *Europe and the Mystique of Islam.* Seattle WA: University of Washington Press.

ROGERS Joshua, 2019. *Violence and the (trans)formation of the state in the Yemen Arab Republic, 1962–1970.* PhD Thesis at the SOAS University of London. https://eprints.soas.ac.uk/30895/

ROSANVALLON Pierre, 2013. *The Society of Equals,* trans. Arthur Goldhammer, Cambridge MA: Harvard University Press.

ROSS Kristin, 2008. *The Emergence of Social Space: Rimbaud and the Paris Commune.* New York: Verso.

RUTHERFORD Ian, 2013. *State Pilgrims and Sacred Observers in Ancient Greece. A Study of Theōriā and Theōroi.* Cambridge: Cambridge University Press.

SAADA Emmanuelle, 2013. "Nation and Empire in French Context," in Georges STEINMETZ, ed. *Sociology and Empire: The Imperial Entanglements of a Discipline.* Durham NC: Duke University Press, 321–338.

SADIKI Larbi, 2004. *The Search for Arab Democracy.* London: Hurst and Company.

SADIQI Fatima, ed. 2016. *Women's Movements in Post-"Arab Spring" North Africa.* London: Palgrave.

SADOWSKI Yahya, 1993. "The New Orientalism and the Democracy Debate," *Middle East Report* 183: 14–21+40.

SAID Edward, 1978. *Orientalism.* New York: Vintage.

　1995. *Al-istishrāq. Al-mafāhīm al-gharbiyyah lil-sharq.* [Orientalism. Western Conceptions of the Orient], trans. Mohammed 'Anāni, Baghdad: Maktabat Baghdad.

　[s.d.], *Al-istishrāq* [Orientalism], trans. Kamāl Abu Dīb. s.l.: Maktabat Diwan Al-Arab.

SALAME Ghassan, ed. 1987. *The Foundations of the Arab State.* London: Routledge.

SALIME Zakia, 2014. "New Feminism as Personal Revolutions: Microrebellious Bodies," *Journal of Women in Culture and Society* 40 (1): 14–19.

　2015a. "Arab Revolutions: Legible, Illegible Bodies," *Comparative Studies of South Asia, Africa, and the Middle East* 35(3): 525–538.

2015b. "'I Vote I Sing': The Rise of Aesthetic Citizenship in Morocco," *International Journal of Middle East Studies* 47: 136–139.

SALISBURY Peter, 2020. "Risk Perception and Appetite in UAE Foreign and National Security Policy," *Chatham House*, Research Paper.

SALOMON Noah, 2020. "Moments in Revolutionary Time," *Middle East Law and Governance* 12: 335–356.

SALVATORE Armando, 1996. "Beyond Orientalism? Max Weber and the Displacements of 'Essentialism' in the Study of Islam," *Arabica* 43(3): 457–485.

2011. "Civility: Between Disciplined Interaction and Local/Translocal Connectedness," in *Political Civility in the Middle East*, special issue of *Third World Quarterly*, 32(5): 807–825.

2016. *Sociology of Islam: Knowledge, Power, and Civility.* Malden MA: Wiley-Blackwell.

SANAA CENTER, 2020. "'So Now that the Houthis Have Won . . .' – Q&A With Abdulghani Al-Iryani," *Sanaa Center Studies*, March.

SAWAF Zina, 2013. "Youth and the Revolution in Egypt: What Kinship Tells Us," *Contemporary Arab Affairs* 6(1): 1–16.

SAYF Nachwan, 2020. "Un fruit pour les corneilles d'Ahmad Zein: Aden, capitale des communistes arabes se transforme en une dystopie bannie," *Arabian Humanities* (13), online.

SAYIGH Yezid, 1997. "Armed Struggle and State Formation," *Journal of Palestine Studies* 26(4): 17–32.

2007. "Inducing a Failed State in Palestine," *Survival* 49(3): 7–39.

2012. "Above the State, the Officers' Republic in Egypt," *Carnegie Middle East Center*, online.

2015. "Missed Opportunity. The Politics of Police Reform in Egypt and Tunisia," *Carnegie Middle East Center*, online.

SCHLUCHTER Wolfgang, 1999. "Hindrances to Modernity: Max Weber on Islam," in T. HUFF & W. SCHUCHTER, eds. *Max Weber & Islam*. New Brunswick: Transaction Publishers, 53–123.

SCHMITZ Charles & BURROWES Robert D., 2018. *Historical Dictionary of Yemen*. 3rd ed. Lanham MD: Rowman & Littlefield.

SCHUMPETER Joseph, 1942. *Capitalism, Socialism and Democracy.* New York: Harper.

SCHWEDLER Jillian, 2006. *Faith in Moderation: Islamists Parties in Jordan and Yemen.* Cambridge: Cambridge University Press.

SCOTT James C., 1990. *Domination and the Arts of Resistance.* New Haven CT: Yale University Press.

SEGGERMAN Alex Dika, 2019. *Modernism on the Nile: Art in Egypt between the Islamic and the Contemporary.* Raleigh NC: University of North Carolina Press.

SEWELL William H., 1996. "Historical Events as Transformations of Structures: Inventing Revolution at the Bastille," *Theory and Society* 25: 841–881.

SHA'BAN Abdel-Hussein, 2012. *Al-mujtam'a al-madani. Sira wa sayrura* [*Civil Society: Conduct and Process*]. Beirut: Atlas Publishing.

SHALAKANY Amr, 2014. "The Day the Graffiti Died," *London Review of International Law* 2(2): 357–378.

SHARABI Hisham, 1988. *Neo-Patriarchy. A Theory of Distorted Change in Arab Society.* Oxford: Oxford University Press.

SHEPARD Todd, 2008. *The Invention of Decolonization: The Algerian War and the Remaking of France.* Chicago IL: Chicago University Press.

SHUJA AL-DEEN Maysaa, 2019. "Federalism in Yemen: A Catalyst for War, the Present Reality, and the Inevitable Future," *Sana'a Center*, online.

SIGILLÒ Ester, 2016. "Beyond the Myth of the Tunisian Exception: The Open-Ended Tale of a Fragile Democratization," in Loretta DELL'AGUZZO & Emidio DIODATO, eds. *The "State" of Pivot States in South-Eastern Mediterranean.* Perugia: Perugia Stranieri University Press, 95–121.

2020. "Islamism and the Rise of Islamic Charities in Post-Revolutionary Tunisia," *British Journal of Middle Eastern Studies*, online.

SIGILLÒ Ester & DE FACCI Damiano, 2018. "L'économie sociale et solidaire: une nouvelle économie morale pour la Tunisie?," *L'Année du Maghreb* 18: 51–68.

SKOCPOL Theda, 1979. *States and Social Revolutions: A Comparative Analysis of France, Russia, and China.* Cambridge: Cambridge University Press.

SKOCPOL Theda, EVANS Peter, & RUESCHEMEYER Dietrich, eds. 1985. *Bringing the State Back In.* New York: Cambridge University Press.

SOLIMAN Samer, 2011. *The Autumn of Dictatorship: Fiscal Crisis and Political Change in Egypt under Mubarak.* Stanford, CA: Stanford University Press.

SOWERS Jeannie, 2018. "The Saudi Coalition's Food War on Yemen. An Interview with Martha Mundy," *Middle East Report* 298 (Winter), online.

SPIVAK Gayatri C., 1988. "Can the Subaltern Speak?," in C. NELSON & L. GROSSBERG, eds. *Marxism and the Interpretation of Culture.* Basingstoke: Macmillan Education, 271–313.

STEPHAN Rita & CHARRAD Mounira, eds. 2020. *Women Rising. In and Beyond the Arab Spring.* New York: New York University Press.

STOLER Ann L., 1995. *Race and the Education of Desire: Foucault's History of Sexuality and the Colonial Order of Things.* Durham NC: Duke University Press.

2016. *Duress: Imperial Durabilities in Our Times.* Durham NC: Duke University Press.

STRZELECKA Ewa K., 2018. "A Political Culture of Feminist Resistance: Exploring Women's Agency and Gender Dynamics in Yemen's Uprisings 2011–2015," in Marie-Christine HEINZE, ed. *Yemen and the Search for Stability. Power, Politics, and Society after the Arab Spring.* London: I.B. Tauris, 47–70.

SUBAY Jameel, 2012. "La vie d'une révolution," in Laurent BONNEFOY et al., eds. *Yémen, Le tournant revolutionnaire*, Paris: Karthala / CEFAS: 160i–160xii.

SULEIMAN Mahmoud A., 2012. "Celebrate the 48th Anniversary of Sudan's Glorious October 1964 Revolution," *Sudan Tribune*, online.

SZAKAL Vanessa, 2015. "In Jemna, Locals Manage Oases to Reap the Fruits of their Labor," *Nawaat*, online.

TAYLOR Verta, 1989. "Social Movement Continuity: The Women's Movement in Abeyance," *American Sociological Review* 54(5): 761–775.

THIEL Tobias, 2015. "Yemen's Imposed Federal Boundaries," *Middle East Report Online*, online.

THOMAS Martin, 2012. *Violence and Colonial Order: Police, Workers and Protests in the European Colonial Empires, 1918–1940.* Cambridge: Cambridge University Press.

THOMPSON Elizabeth, 2000. *Colonial Citizens: Republican Rights, Paternal Privilege, and Gender in French Syria and Lebanon.* New York: Columbia University Press.

[2002] "Book review of Butenschon et al. *Citizenship and the State in the Middle East. Approaches and Applications*," *Middle East Policy Council*, blog, online.

2013. *Justice Interrupted: The Struggle for Constitutional Government in the Middle East.* Cambridge MA: Harvard University Press.

TILLY Charles, ed. 1975. *The Formation of National States in Western Europe.* Princeton NJ: Princeton University Press.

1978. *From Mobilization to Revolution.* London: Addison-Wesley.

1984. *Big Structures, Large Processes. Huge Comparisons.* New York: Russell Sage Foundation.

1990. *Coercion, Capital, and European States, AD 990–1990.* Cambridge: Blackwell.

1993. *European Revolutions, 1491–1992.* Cambridge: Cambridge University Press.

2003a. *Contention and Democracy in Europe, 1650–2000.* Cambridge: Cambridge University Press.

2003b. *The Politics of Collective Violence.* Cambridge: Cambridge University Press.

TLILI Béchir, 1972. "La notion de 'Umrân dans la pensée tunisienne précoloniale," *Revue de l'Occident musulman et de la Méditerranée* 12: 131–151.

TORELLI Stefano M., MERONE Fabio, & CAVATORTA Francesco, 2012. "Salafism in Tunisia: Challenges and Opportunities for Democratization," *Middle East Policy* 19(4): 140–154.

TOSCANO Marco, 2010. "È questo il canto del partigiano?! Storia e storie di 'Bella ciao'," *Blog StoriAmestre*, online.

TOURAINE Alain, 1977. *The Self-Production of Society*. Chicago IL: Chicago University Press.

TRANSFELD Mareike, 2016. "Political Bargaining and Violent Conflict: Shifting Elite Alliances as the Decisive Factor in Yemen's Transformation," *Mediterranean Politics* 21(1): 150–169.

2019. "Police, Aqil and Supervisors: Local Security Forces in Ansarallah-Held al-Hodeidah," *Yemen Policy Center*, online.

TRIPP Charles, 2001. "States, Elites and the 'Management of Change'," in Hassan HAKIMIAN & Ziba MOSHAVER, eds. *The State and Global Change: The Political Economy of Transition in the Middle East and North Africa*. London: Curzon, 211–231.

2013. *The Power and the People: Paths of Resistance in the Middle East*. Cambridge: Cambridge University Press.

2015. "Battlefields of the Republic: The Struggle for Public Space in Tunisia," *LSE Middle East Center Paper Series*, London School of Economics, No. 13.

TROUILLOT Michel-Rolph, 1995/2015. *Silencing the Past. Power and the Production of History*. Boston MA: Beacon Press.

TUBIANA Jérôme, WARIN Clotilde, & MANGARE Mahamat Saleh, 2020. "Diaspora in Despair: Darfurian Mobility at a Time of International Disengagement," *Small Arms Survey*, Report.

TUĞAL Cihan, 2017. "The Decline of the Legitimate Monopoly of Violence and the Return of Non-State Warriors," in J. MACKERT & B. S. TURNER, eds. *The Transformation of Citizenship: Struggle, Resistance, and Violence*. Vol. 3. London & New York: Routledge, 77–92.

TURNER Bryan S., 1974. *Weber and Islam. A Critical Study*, London & Boston MA: Routledge & Kegan Paul.

2000. "Islam, Civil Society and Citizenship", in Nils BUTENSCHON, Uri DAVIS, & Manuel HASSASSIAN, eds. *Citizenship and the State in the Middle East. Approaches and Applications*. Syracuse NY: Syracuse University Press, 28–48.

TYR, 2019. "The Southern Implosion," *The Yemen Review*, Sanaa Center.

URBINATI Nadia, 2014. *Democracy Disfigured: Opinion, Truth, and the People*. Cambridge MA: Harvard University Press.

VITALIS Robert, 2006. *America's Kingdom: Mythmaking on the Saudi Oil Frontier*. Stanford CA: Stanford University Press.

WACQUANT Loïc, 2010. "Crafting the Neoliberal State: Workfare, Prisonfare, and Social Insecurity," *Sociological Forum* 25(2): 198–218.

WAGNER-PACIFICI Robin, 2017. *What Is an Event?* Chicago IL: Chicago University Press.

WATSON Kim & WILDER Gary, eds. 2018. *Postcolonial. Political Imaginaries for the Global Present*. New York: Fordham University Press.

WEBER Eugen, 1976. *Peasants into Frenchmen. The Modernization of Rural France, 1870–1914*. Stanford CA: Stanford University Press.

WEBER Max, 1919/1958. *Politik als Beruf*. Munich: Duncker and Humblot.

　1920/1992. *The Protestant Ethic and the Spirit of Capitalism*. London: Routledge.

　1978. *Economy and Society. An Outline of Interpretive Sociology*, ed. G. Roth & C. Wittich. Berkeley CA: University of California Press.

WEDEEN Lisa, 1999. *Ambiguities of Domination. Politics, Rhetoric, and Symbols in Contemporary Syria*. Chicago IL: Chicago University Press.

　2008. *Peripheral Visions: Publics, Power, and Performance in Yemen*. Chicago IL: University of Chicago Press.

　2019. *Authoritarian Apprehensions: Ideology, Judgment, and Mourning in Syria*. Chicago IL: Chicago University Press.

WEHR Hans, 1976. *The Hans Wehr Dictionary of Modern Written Arabic*. 3rd ed. Ithaca NY: Spoken Language Services.

WERBNER Pnina, WEBB Martin, & SPELLMAN-POOTS Kathryn, eds. 2014. *The Political Aesthetics of Global Protest: The Arab Spring and Beyond*. Edinburgh: Edinburgh University Press.

WIACEK Benjamin, 2012. "L'émergence de nouveaux médias pour l'expression d'une troisième voix," in Laurent BONNEFOY, Marine POIRIER, and Franck MERMIER, eds. *Yémen, Le tournant révolutionnaire*. Paris: Karthala / CEFAS: 345–350.

WOLIN Sheldon, 1968. "Political Theory. Trends and Goals," in David L. SILLS, ed. *International Encyclopedia of the Social Sciences*. Vol. 12. New York: Macmillan, 319–331.

WORTH Robert F., 2011. "Yemen on the Brink of Hell," *New York Times Magazine*, online.

　2018. "How the War in Yemen Became a Bloody Stalemate – And the Worst Humanitarian Crisis in the World," *New York Times Magazine*, online.

　2019. "Yemen under Siege," *New York Review of Books*, online.

2020. "Mohammed bin Zayed's Dark Vision of the Middle East's Future," *New York Times Magazine*, online.

WYNTER Sylvia, 2003. "Unsettling the Coloniality of Being/Power/Truth/ Freedom: Towards the Human, after Man, its Overrepresentation – An Argument," *The New Centennial Review* 3(3): 257–337.

YADAV Stacey Philbrick, 2011. "Antecedents of the Revolution. Intersectoral Networks and Post-Partisanship in Yemen," *Studies in Ethnicity and Nationalism* 11(3): 550–563.

2015. "The 'Yemen Model' as a Failure of Political Imagination," *International Journal of Middle East Studies* 47(1): 144–147.

YADAV Stacey Philbrick & CARAPICO Sheila, 2014. "The Breakdown of the GCC Initiative," *Middle East Report* 273(Winter), online.

YASSIN-KASSAB Robin & AL-SHAMI Leila, 2016. *Burning Country: Syrians in Revolution and War*. London: Pluto.

YOUSFI Héla, 2015. *UGTT. Une passion tunisienne*. Paris: Karthala / IRMC.

2019. "Utopique souveraineté pour les pays arabes?," *Le Monde Diplomatique*, blog, online.

ZEMNI Sami, 2016. "From Revolution to Tunisianité: Who Is the Tunisian People? Creating Hegemony through Compromise," *Middle East Law and Governance* 8(2–3): 131–150.

ZIMMERMAN Andrew, 2012. *Alabama in Africa: Booker T. Washington, the German Empire, and the Globalization of the New South*. Princeton NJ: Princeton University Press.

ZYCK Steven A., 2014. "Mediating Transition in Yemen: Achievements and Lessons," *International Peace Institute*, Report.

Index

abeyance network, 189, 192, 383, 399
Abu Dhabi, 336, 339, 342
Abu Iyad (Tunisia Salafi leader), 267
Abyan, 128, 159, 235, 245, 246, 334
account "26.26" (Tunisia), 147
accountability, 7, 13, 15, 26, 76, 181,
    240, 244, 250, 260, 272, 277, 278,
    289, 311, 312, 324, 353, 358, 362,
    369, 385, 393, 397, 405
    lack of, 310
    police, 244
Achour, Habib, 156
active citizenship, 5, 15, 176, 183
activist fallacy, 38, 49, 299
Aden, 54, 83, 95, 128, 159, 160, 172,
    184, 220, 234, 280, 293, 312, 334
    siege of, 309, 333, 338
Aden Declaration, 338, 344
Aden Legislative Body, 96
Aden Levies, 95
aesthetics, 102, 178, 406
Africa, 60, 78, 82, 90, 259, 325, 390
agriculture, 4, 90, 151, 164, 248, 303,
    342, 390
Ahmad, Eqbal, 134, 139, 140
akhdam, 61, 165, 218, 372
Al-Ahdal, Wajdi, 320, 372
Al-Ahmar, Abdallah, 147, 149, 160,
    165, 184, 296
Al-Ahmar, Hamid, 220, 238
Al-Ahmar, Sadiq, 220, 290, 294
Al-Akhali, Rafat, 238, 291, 295, 339
Al-Bashir, Omar, 6, 341, 404, 406
Al-Bawsola, 301, 302
Al-Beidh, Ali, 159, 160, 345
Al-Burhan, Abdel Fattah, 405, 406
Al-Eriani, Kamilia, 17, 297, 347, 392
Al-Ghashmi, Ahmad, 128, 129
Al-Hamdi, Ibrahim, 55, 128, 129, 220,
    349, 372

Al-Haqq, 162, 163, 165, 337, 374
Al-Houthaifi, Noman, 286
Al-Huthi, Abdelmalik, 241, 293, 335,
    337
Al-Huthi, Husayn, 163, 337
Al-Idrisi, Muhammad, 84, 94
Al-Iryani, Abdulghani, 217, 342, 374
Al-Jazeera, 153, 191, 364, 406
Al-Kathiri, 95, 340
Al-Krim, Abd, 117, 118, 166
Al-Mahra, 286, 291, 339, 395
Al-Mansura, 246
Al-Maqtari, Bushra, 290, 318, 345,
    372
Al-Qaeda, 133, 164, 167, 224, 235,
    238, 246, 267, 310, 339, 346, 384
Al-Qaeda in the Arabian Peninsula, 172
Al-Qawsi, Abdullah, 242, 245
Al-Qu'ayti, 95, 339, 340
Al-Rubaidi, Abdulsalam, 221, 319,
    372, 373, 387, 396
Al-Sakkaf, Nadia, 160, 221, 238, 241,
    249, 286, 287, 290, 291, 295
Al-Sammad, Ali, 294, 335
Al-Zindani, Abdelmajid, 238, 384
Al-Zubaydi, Aydarus, 309, 338, 346
Alatas, Syed Farid, 31, 389
Algeria, 6, 46, 65, 73, 74, 76, 81, 86,
    91, 92, 114, 130, 323, 396, 403
Allal, Amin, 204, 205, 215
Alwazir, Zaid bin Ali, 47, 226, 283
Amira Augustin, Anna-Linda, 237,
    288, 310, 338, 345
Ammar, Rachid, 249, 259, 262
amnesty, 132, 258, 267
Amran, 246, 287
anarchism, 66, 122, 390
ANC, 171, 207, 250, 265, 278
ancien régime, 62, 98, 252
Anderson, Lisa, 81, 87, 88

447